Children's
Literature
Review

Guide to Gale Literary Criticism Series

For criticism on	Consult these Gale series
Authors now living or who died after December 31, 1959	*CONTEMPORARY LITERARY CRITICISM (CLC)*
Authors who died between 1900 and 1959	*TWENTIETH-CENTURY LITERARY CRITICISM (TCLC)*
Authors who died between 1800 and 1899	*NINETEENTH-CENTURY LITERATURE CRITICISM (NCLC)*
Authors who died between 1400 and 1799	*LITERATURE CRITICISM FROM 1400 TO 1800 (LC)* *SHAKESPEAREAN CRITICISM (SC)*
Authors who died before 1400	*CLASSICAL AND MEDIEVAL LITERATURE CRITICISM (CMLC)*
Authors of books for children and young adults	*CHILDREN'S LITERATURE REVIEW (CLR)*
Dramatists	*DRAMA CRITICISM (DC)*
Poets	*POETRY CRITICISM (PC)*
Short story writers	*SHORT STORY CRITICISM (SSC)*
Black writers of the past two hundred years	*BLACK LITERATURE CRITICISM (BLC)*
Hispanic writers of the late nineteenth and twentieth centuries	*HISPANIC LITERATURE CRITICISM (HLC)*
Native North American writers and orators of the eighteenth, nineteenth, and twentieth centuries	*NATIVE NORTH AMERICAN LITERATURE (NNAL)*
Major authors from the Renaissance to the present	*WORLD LITERATURE CRITICISM, 1500 TO THE PRESENT (WLC)*

CLR also includes entries on prominent illustrators who have contributed to the field of children's literature. These entries are designed to represent the development of the illustrator as an artist rather than as a literary stylist. The illustrator's section is organized like that of an author, with two exceptions: the introduction presents an overview of the illustrator's styles and techniques rather than outlining his or her literary background, and the commentary written by the illustrator on his or her works is called "illustrator's commentary" rather than "author's commentary." All titles of books containing illustrations by the artist being profiled are highlighted in boldface type.

Other Features: Acknowledgments, Indexes

- The **Acknowledgments** section, which immediately follows the preface, lists the sources from which material has been reprinted in the volume. It does not, however, list every book or periodical consulted for the volume.

- The **Cumulative Index to Authors** lists all of the authors who have appeared in *CLR* with cross-references to the biographical, autobiographical, and literary criticism series published by Gale Research. A full listing of the series titles appears before the first page of the indexes of this volume.

- The **Cumulative Index to Nationalities** lists authors alphabetically under their respective nationalities. Author names are followed by the volume number(s) in which they appear.

- The **Cumulative Index to Titles** lists titles covered in *CLR* followed by the volume and page number where criticism begins.

A Note to the Reader

CLR is one of several critical references sources in the Literature Criticism Series published by Gale Research. When writing papers, students who quote directly from any volume in the Literature Criticism Series may use the following general forms to footnote reprinted criticism. The first example pertains to material drawn from periodicals, the second to material reprinted from books.

[1]T. S. Eliot, "John Donne," *The Nation and the Athenaeum,* 33 (9 June 1923), 321-32; excerpted and reprinted in *Literature Criticism from 1400 to 1800,* Vol. 10, ed. James E. Person, Jr. (Detroit: Gale Research, 1989), pp. 28-9.

[1]Henry Brooke, *Leslie Brooke and Johnny Crow* (Frederick Warne, 1982); excerpted and reprinted in *Children's Literature Review,* Vol. 20, ed. Gerard J. Senick (Detroit: Gale Research, 1990), p. 47.

Suggestions Are Welcome

In response to various suggestions, several features have been added to *CLR* since the beginning of the series, including author entries on retellers of traditional literature as well as those who have been the first to record oral tales and other folklore; entries on prominent illustrators featuring commentary on their styles and techniques; entries on authors whose works are considered controversial; occasional entries devoted to criticism on a single work or a series of works; sections in author introductions that list major works by and about the author or illustrator being profiled; explanatory notes that provide information on the critic or work of criticism to enhance the usefulness of the excerpt; more extensive illustrative material, such as holographs of manuscript pages and photographs of people and places pertinent to the careers of the authors and artists; a cumulative nationality index for easy access to authors by nationality; and occasional guest essays written specifically for *CLR* by prominent critics on subjects of their choice.

Readers who wish to suggest authors to appear in future volumes, or who have other suggestions, are cordially in-vited to contact the editor. By mail: Editor, *Children's Literature Review,* Gale Research, 835 Penobscot Bldg., 645 Griswold St., Detroit, MI 48226-4094; by telephone: (800) 347-GALE; by fax: (313) 961-6599; by E-mail: CYA@Gale.com.

Acknowledgments

The editors wish to thank the copyright holders of the excerpted criticism included in this volume and the permissions managers of many book and magazine publishing companies for assisting us in securing reproduction rights. We are also grateful to the staffs of the Detroit Public Library, the Library of Congress, the University of Detroit Mercy Library, Wayne State University Purdy/Kresge Library Complex, and the University of Michigan Libraries for making their resources available to us. Following is a list of the copyright holders who have granted us permission to reproduce material in this volume of *CLR*. Every effort has been made to trace copyright, but if omissions have been made, please let us know.

COPYRIGHTED EXCERPTS IN *CLR*, VOLUME 47, WERE REPRODUCED FROM THE FOLLOWING PERIODICALS:

The ALAN Review, v. 24, Spring, 1997 for an interview with Paul Janeczko by Patricia L. Bloem and Anthony L. Manna. Reproduced by permission of *The ALAN Review* and the authors. —*Appraisal: Science Books for Young People,* v. 13, Fall, 1980; v. 20, Winter, 1987; v. 20, Summer, 1987; v. 28, Autumn, 1995. Copyright © 1980, 1987, 1995 by the Children's Science Book Review Committee. All reproduced by permission. —*Australian Book Review,* n. 152, July, 1993. Reproduced by permission. —*Best Sellers,* v. 34, December 15, 1974; v. 35, November, 1975; v. 36, May, 1976; v. 39, November, 1979. Copyright 1974, 1975, 1976, 1979, by the University of Scranton. All reproduced by permission. —*Book Window,* v. 7, Summer, 1980; v. 8, Spring, 1981. © 1980, 1981 S.C.B.A. and contributors. Both reproduced by permission. —*Bookbird,* v. VII, December 15, 1969; v. XI, March 15, 1973. Both reproduced by permission. —*Booklist,* v. 74, October 15, 1977; v. 74, November 1, 1977; v. 75, March 1, 1979; v. 76, October 1, 1979; v. 78, March 1, 1982; v. 78, April 1, 1982; v. 79, May 15, 1983; v. 79, July, 1983; v. 80, September 15, 1983; v. 80, July, 1984; v. 81, January 1, 1985; v. 81, April 1, 1985; v. 81, April 15, 1985; v. 82, May 1, 1986; v. 82, May 15, 1986; v. 82, June 15, 1986; v. 82, August, 1986; v. 83, September 1, 1986; v. 83, April 1, 1987; v. 84, September 1, 1987; v. 84, September 15, 1987; v. 84, October 15, 1987; v. 84, January 15, 1988; v. 84, March 1, 1988; v. 85, September 1, 1988; v. 85, May 1, 1989; v. 85, June 1, 1989; v. 86, September 15, 1989; v. 86, October 1, 1989; v. 86, May 15, 1990; v. 87, September 1, 1990; v. 87, October 15, 1990; v. 87, January 15, 1991; v. 87, February 1, 1991; v. 87, March 15, 1991; v. 87, April 15, 1991; v. 87, August, 1991; v. 88, May 15, 1992; v. 89, September 1, 1992; v. 89, October 15, 1992; v. 89, January 15, 1993; v. 89, March 15, 1993; v. 89, April 1, 1993; v. 90, October 1, 1993; v. 90, November 1, 1993; v. 90, November 15, 1993; v. 91, December 1, 1994; v. 91, December 15, 1994; v. 91, March 15, 1995; v. 91, April 1, 1995; v. 92, October 1, 1995; v. 92, October 15, 1995; v. 92, November 1, 1995; v. 92, April 1, 1996; v. 92, May 1, 1996; v. 93, October 15, 1996. Copyright © 1977, 1979, 1982, 1983, 1984, 1985, 1986, 1987, 1988, 1989, 1990, 1991, 1992, 1993, 1994, 1995, 1996 by the American Library Association. All reproduced by permission. —*The Booklist,* v. 64, September 1, 1967; v. 64, June 15, 1968; v. 65, June 15, 1969; v. 68, September 1, 1971. Copyright © 1967, 1968, 1969, 1971 by the American Library Association. All reproduced by permission. —*Books and Bookmen,* v. 17, August, 1972 for a review of "Longtime Passing" by Gladys Williams; v. 18, August, 1972 for "Forward into Space" by Gladys Williams; v. 22, May, 1977 for a review of "The Wildman" by Marie Peel. © copyright the respective authors 1972, 1973, 1977. —*Books for Keeps,* n. 38, May, 1986; n. 39, July, 1986; n. 46, September, 1987; n. 54, January, 1989; n. 65, November, 1990; n. 72, January, 1992; n. 74, May, 1992; n. 90, January, 1995; n. 93, July, 1995; n. 97, March, 1996. © School Bookshop Association 1986, 1987, 1989, 1990, 1992, 1995, 1996. All reproduced by permission. —*Books for Your Children,* v. 17, Autumn-Winter, 1982; v. 22, Autumn-Winter, 1987. © *Books for Your Children* 1982, 1987. Both reproduced by permission. —*Books in Canada,* v. XXIV, April, 1995 for "Taking Care of Things" by Donna Nurse. Reproduced by permission of the author. —*British Book News,* May-June, 1986. © *British Book News,* 1986. Courtesy of *British Book News.* —*British Book News Children's Books,* March, 1986. © The British Council, 1986. Reproduced by permission. —*Bulletin of the Center for Children's Books,* v. XVII, March, 1964; v. XVII, April, 1964; v. 19, May, 1966; v. 20, December, 1966; v. 20, July-August, 1967; v. 21, June, 1968; v. 22, July-August, 1969; v. 23, December, 1969; v. 25, October, 1971; v. 28, September, 1974; v. 29, January, 1976; v. 30, September, 1976; v. 33, September, 1979; v. 33, April, 1980; v. 33, June, 1980; v. 33, July-August, 1980; v. 35, March, 1982; v. 35, July-August, 1982; v. 36, June, 1983; v. 37, September, 1983; v. 37, February, 1984; v. 37, April, 1984; v. 37, June, 1984; v. 38, June, 1985; v. 39, March, 1986; v. 39, April, 1986; v. 39, May, 1986; v. 40, December, 1986; v. 40, March, 1987; v. 40, April, 1987; v. 41, September, 1987; v. 41, November, 1987; v. 41, January, 1988; v. 41, April, 1988; v. 42, September, 1988; v. 42, October, 1988; v. 42, March, 1989; v. 43, November, 1989; v. 43, May, 1990; v. 43, July-August, 1990; v. 44, February, 1991; v. 44, April, 1991; v. 44, June, 1991; v. 44, July-August, 1991; v. 45, September, 1991; v. 49, February, 1992; v. 45, March, 1992. Copyright © 1964, 1966, 1967, 1968, 1969, 1971, 1974, 1976, 1979, 1980, 1982, 1983, 1984, 1985, 1986, 1987, 1988, 1989, 1990, 1991 by The University of Chicago. All reproduced by permission./ v. 46, September, 1992; v. 46, October, 1992; v. 46, April, 1993; v. 46, June, 1993; v. 46, July-August, 1993; v. 47, September, 1993; v. 47, November, 1993; v. 48, December, 1994; v. 48, March, 1995; v. 49, October, 1995; v. 49, November, 1995; v. 49, December, 1995; v. 49, May, 1996; v. 49, June, 1996; v. 50, November, 1996. Copyright © 1992, 1993, 1994, 1995, 1996 by The Board of Trustees of the University of Illinois. All reproduced by permission. —*Canadian Book Review Annual,* 1995. Reproduced by permission. —*Canadian Children's Literature,* n. 2, Summer, 1975; n. 7, 1977; ns. 15 &

ISSN 0362-4145

volume 47

131—

Children's Literature Review

Excerpts from Reviews,
Criticism, and Commentary
on Books for Children
and Young People

Linda R. Andres
Editor

GALE

DETROIT · NEW YORK · TORONTO · LONDON

STAFF

Linda R. Andres, *Editor*
Diane Telgen, *Associate Editor*

Deron Albright, Cindy Buck, Sheryl Ciccarelli, Alan Hedblad, Melissa Hill, Motoko Fujishiro Huthwaite,
Arlene M. Johnson, Paul Loeber, Carolyn C. March, Sean McCready, Thomas F. McMahon,
Bonnie Riedinger, Crystal A. Towns, Stephen Thor Tschirhart, *Contributing Editors*
Marilyn O'Connell Allen, *Assistant Editor*

Joyce Nakamura, *Managing Editor*

Susan M. Trosky, *Permissions Manager*
Maria L. Franklin, *Permissions Specialist*
Edna Hedblad, Michele M. Lonoconus, *Permissions Associates*

Victoria B. Cariappa, *Research Manager*
Talitha Jean, *Project Coordinator*
Tamara C. Nott, Tracie A. Richardson, Norma Sawaya, Cheryl L. Warnock, Robert Whaley, *Research Associates*
Jeffrey Daniels, *Research Assistant*

Mary Beth Trimper, *Production Director*
Shanna Heilveil, *Production Assistant*

Gary Leach, *Macintosh Artist*
Randy Bassett, *Image Database Supervisor*
Robert Duncan, Michael Logusz, *Scanner Operator*
Pamela A. Reed, *Photography Coordinator*

The paper used in this publication meets the minimum requirements of American National Standard for Information Sciences—Permanence Paper for Printed Library Materials, ANSI Z39.48-1984.

Library of Congress Catalog Card Number 76-643301
ISBN 0-7876-1141-7
ISSN 0362-4145
Printed in the United States of America

10   9   8   7   6   5   4   3   2   1

Contents

Preface vii
Acknowledgments xi

Preface

L iterature for children and young adults has evolved into both a respected branch of creative writing and a successful industry. Currently, books for young readers are considered among the most popular segments of publishing. Criticism of juvenile literature is instrumental in recording the literary or artistic development of the creators of children's books as well as the trends and controversies that result from changing values or attitudes about young people and their literature. Designed to provide a permanent, accessible record of this ongoing scholarship, *Children's Literature Review (CLR)* presents parents, teachers, and librarians—those responsible for bringing children and books together—with the opportunity to make informed choices when selecting reading materials for the young. In addition, *CLR* provides researchers of children's literature with easy access to a wide variety of critical information from English-language sources in the field. Users will find balanced overviews of the careers of the authors and illustrators of the books that children and young adults are reading; these entries, which contain excerpts from published criticism in books and periodicals, assist users by sparking ideas for papers and assignments and suggesting supplementary and classroom reading. Ann L. Kalkhoff, president and editor of *Children's Book Review Service Inc.,* writes that "*CLR* has filled a gap in the field of children's books, and it is one series that will never lose its validity or importance."

Scope of the Series

Each volume of *CLR* profiles the careers of a selection of authors and illustrators of books for children and young adults from preschool through high school. Author lists in each volume reflect:

■ an international scope.

■ representation of authors of all eras.

■ the variety of genres covered by children's and/or YA literature: picture books, fiction, nonfiction, poetry, folklore, and drama.

Although the focus of the series is on authors new to *CLR*, entries will be updated as the need arises.

Organization of This Book

An entry consists of the following elements: author heading, author portrait, author introduction, excerpts of criticism (each preceded by a bibliographical citation), and illustrations, when available.

■ The **Author Heading** consists of the author's name followed by birth and death dates. The portion of the name outside the parentheses denotes the form under which the author is most frequently published. If the majority of the author's works for children were written under a pseudonym, the pseudonym will be listed in the author heading and the real name given on the first line of the author introduction. Also located at the beginning of the introduction are any other pseudonyms used by the author in writing for children and any name variations, including transliterated forms for authors whose languages use nonroman alphabets. Uncertainty as to a birth or death date is indicated by question marks.

■ An **Author Portrait** is included when available.

■ The **Author Introduction** contains information designed to introduce an author to *CLR* users by presenting an overview of the author's themes and styles, biographical facts that relate to the author's literary career or critical responses to the author's works, and information about major awards and prizes the author has received. The introduction begins by identifying the nationality of the author and by listing the genres in which s/he has written for children and young adults. Introductions also list a group of representative titles for which the author or illustrator being profiled is best known; this section, which begins with the words "major works include," follows the genre line of the introduction. For seminal figures, a listing of major works about the author follows when appropriate, highlighting important biographies about the author or illustrator that are not excerpted in the entry. The centered heading "Introduction" announces the body of the text.

- **Criticism** is located in three sections: **Author's Commentary** (when available), **General Commentary** (when available), and **Title Commentary** (commentary on specific titles).

  - The **Author's Commentary** presents background material written by the author or by an interviewer. This commentary may cover a specific work or several works. Author's commentary on more than one work appears after the author introduction, while commentary on an individual book follows the title entry heading.

  - The **General Commentary** consists of critical excerpts that consider more than one work by the author or illustrator being profiled. General commentary is preceded by the critic's name in boldface type or, in the case of unsigned criticism, by the title of the journal. *CLR* also features entries that emphasize general criticism on the oeuvre of an author or illustrator. When appropriate, a selection of reviews is included to supplement the general commentary.

  - The **Title Commentary** begins with the title entry headings, which precede the criticism on a title and cite publication information on the work being reviewed. Title headings list the title of the work as it appeared in its first English-language edition. The first English-language publication date of each work (unless otherwise noted) is listed in parentheses following the title. Differing U.S. and British titles follow the publication date within the parentheses. When a work is written by an individual other than the one being profiled, as is the case when illustrators are featured, the parenthetical material following the title cites the author of the work before listing its publication date.

    Entries in each title commentary section consist of critical excerpts on the author's individual works, arranged chronologically by publication date. The entries generally contain two to seven reviews per title, depending on the stature of the book and the amount of criticism it has generated. The editors select titles that reflect the entire scope of the author's literary contribution, covering each genre and subject. An effort is made to reprint criticism that represents the full range of each title's reception, from the year of its initial publication to current assessments. Thus, the reader is provided with a record of the author's critical history. Publication information (such as publisher names and book prices) and parenthetical numerical references (such as footnotes or page and line references to specific editions of works) have been deleted at the discretion of the editors to provide smoother reading of the text.

- Centered headings introduce each section, in which criticism is arranged chronologically; beginning with Volume 35, each excerpt is preceded by a boldface source heading for easier access by readers. Within the text, titles by authors being profiled are also highlighted in boldface type.

- Selected excerpts are preceded by **Explanatory Annotations,** which provide information on the critic or work of criticism to enhance the reader's understanding of the excerpt.

- A complete **Bibliographical Citation** designed to facilitate the location of the original book or article precedes each piece of criticism.

- Numerous **Illustrations** are featured in *CLR*. For entries on illustrators, an effort has been made to include illustrations that reflect the characteristics discussed in the criticism. Entries on authors who do not illustrate their own works may also include photographs and other illustrative material pertinent to their careers.

Special Features: Entries on Illustrators

Entries on authors who are also illustrators will occasionally feature commentary on selected works illustrated but not written by the author being profiled. These works are strongly associated with the illustrator and have received critical acclaim for their art. By including critical comment on works of this type, the editors wish to provide a more complete representation of the artist's career. Criticism on these works has been chosen to stress artistic, rather than literary, contributions. Title entry headings for works illustrated by the author being profiled are arranged chronologically within the entry by date of publication and include notes identifying the author of the illustrated work. In order to provide easier access for users, all titles illustrated by the subject of the entry are boldfaced.

PHOTOGRAPHS APPEARING IN *CLR*, VOLUME 47, WERE REPRODUCED FROM THE FOLLOWING SOURCES:

Children's
Literature
Review

H(esba) F(ay) Brinsmead

1922-

(Also writes as Pixie Hungerford) Australian author of fiction for children and young adults.

Major works include *Pastures of the Blue Crane* (1964), *Beat of the City* (1966), *Isle of the Sea Horse* (1969), *Longtime Passing* (1971), *Once There Was a Swagman* (1979).

INTRODUCTION

Brinsmead is best known for her novels for and about adolescents and teens. Her books include a variety of settings and themes, ranging from adventures in the wilds of Tasmania and autobiographical stories set in rural 1920s Australia to contemporary portrayals of racial and class prejudice and urban violence. She has described herself as a "transition novelist" who writes primarily for adolescents, although she has written some stories suitable for younger children. Critics have praised Brinsmead's memorable characters, particularly her energetic heroines, her vigorous storytelling, and her ability to create a strong sense of setting. Her nostalgic and evocative *Longtime* series, based on her childhood in the Blue Mountains in New South Wales, is both well-known and critically praised. Her early work was prompted by her recognition of a need for young adult fiction that was neither too adult nor too unsophisticated. Brinsmead says she writes to give hope—the "seed of the future"—to young people.

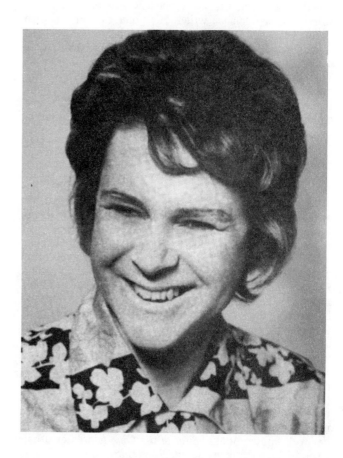

Biographical Information

Brinsmead, the youngest of five children, was born and reared in the village of Bilpin in the rural Blue Mountains of New South Wales in Australia. Her parents, May and Ken Hungerford, had been missionaries in Java, but moved to a bark hut in the rain forest of the Blue Mountains in an effort to improve the health of their eldest daughter, who was gravely ill with a tropical disease. Brinsmead's sister recovered, but the family stayed in Bilpin and eventually built a house, which was named Soekaboemi for the town in Java where Brinsmead's parents were married. Brinsmead's father was the local mailman and ran a sawmill while her mother raised and sold flowers and bulbs. As a child, Brinsmead earned spending money by helping her mother pick flowers to be shipped to florists in the city and by working in her father's sawmill. Until she was thirteen, Brinsmead was educated at home through Blackfriar's Correspondence School. Although Brinsmead says she always wanted to be a writer, she had difficulty with her lessons and suspects she may have been dyslexic. Even as an adult, she says she still finds spelling and math difficult. Despite these problems, Brinsmead's tal-

ent for writing was recognized at the small private high school outside of Sydney where she began her formal education. The headmaster of the school was so impressed with her compositions that he urged her to apply for a cadetship with the city's largest newspaper, the Sydney *Morning Herald*. Although Brinsmead lost the application papers and missed this opportunity, she later enrolled in a journalism correspondence course and has written numerous articles for periodicals. After high school, Brinsmead and her sister Sally took summer jobs in Tasmania picking raspberries. She met her future husband, Reg Brinsmead, at the berry farm. During World War II, Brinsmead briefly attended Avondale College, a teachers college, then left to become a governess in New South Wales and Tasmania. In 1943, at age twenty, she married Reginald Brinsmead, who had become a high school teacher. The couple moved to Wycheproof in the Malley Country of Victoria's Outback. Over the next few years, Brinsmead gave birth to two sons, Bernie and Ken, and held a variety of jobs, including speech therapy teacher, kindergarten assistant, and glassware painter. After the family moved to Box Hill in the Melbourne suburbs, Brinsmead joined a repertory group, the Box Hill Players. After about ten years as an amateur actress, Brinsmead was offered a job on television, but her husband, appalled by the prospect of late night work and absences from home, sent her on a holiday to Singapore in an effort to make her forget about the TV job. During the boat trip, Brinsmead began writing a book, but was not satisfied with it. On her return home, she enrolled in a journalism correspondence course and began working as a freelance writer. Her youngest son was then about twelve and Brinsmead noted that there were few books suitable for his age group. This inspired Brinsmead to write her first novel for adolescents, *Pastures of the Blue Crane*. The popular and critical success of this book has been followed by more than twenty novels for adolescents, a book for adults, *I Will Not Say the Day is Done* (1983), two children's serials, and numerous short stories and articles.

Major Works

Pastures of the Blue Crane, Brinsmead's first novel, like several of her books, explores a young person's experiences with racial issues. The main character, Amaryllis Mereweather, is typical of Brinsmead's early heroines—an outgoing girl who learns to come to terms with her mixed racial heritage. Several of Brinsmead's novels draw on her childhood experiences in the 1920s. *Longtime Passing, Longtime Dreaming* (1982), *Christmas at Longtime* (1983) and *Once There Was a Swagman* are narrated by Teddy, the youngest child of the pioneer Trulance family. In these nostalgic tales of rural Australia, Edwin and Letty Trulance and their five children live happily in a remote forest despite their lack of farming experience and money. *Once There Was a Swagman* takes place during the Great Depression and, like *Time for Tarquinia* (1982), a novel about a family in ancient Eturia, is intended for younger children. Although many of Brinsmead's books are set in remote areas of Australia, one of her well-known books, *Beat of the City,* addresses urban issues faced by teens in the Melbourne of the sixties. *Pastures of the Blue Crane* and *Beat of the City* were both made into television series by the Australian Broadcasting Commission. *Isle of the Sea Horse* is the story of five very different characters shipwrecked on an island inhabited by the last horse of a herd left on the island decades earlier. The castaways wrestle with personal problems but resolve to save the horse from people on the mainland before building a raft and returning home.

Awards

Brinsmead has won the Australian Children's Book Council Book of the Yeaar award twice. The council recognized her work in 1965 for *Pastures of the Blue Crane* and again in 1972 for *Longtime Passing*. She also won the Mary Gilmore Award in 1963 for *Pastures of the Blue Crane* and the Elizabethan Medal for *Isle of the Sea Horse*. *Beat of the City* won special mention for the Book of the Year Award and *Once There Was a Swagman* was highly commended for this award. In 1968, the German language edition of *Season of the Briar* won the Austrian State Prize and was on the Honor List for the German Children's Book Prize.

AUTHOR'S COMMENTARY

H. F. Brinsmead

SOURCE: "How and Why I Write for Young People," in *Bookbird,* Vol. VII, No. 4, December 15, 1969, pp. 24-6.

As to the "why" of any writer, it's probably more complex than we think. Sometimes when I talk to school students I tell them—"writing is a journey". I believe this to be no more than the truth—so, it seems, concerning for whom one writes, this must depend on with whom one wishes to travel! Whom one wishes to meet, in the Never Land of the imagination. And most important of all—it depends on to whom one has something to say!

I began writing books when my own boys were teenagers, as were my many nephews and nieces, complete with friends, enemies and all. In our house we read a lot. I was painfully aware that, around the book shops, and especially around the most accessible ones—the shelves of paperbacks in the corner store, the stand in the railway station—there was not a great deal of material that catered to the teenager. So—thought I—"I'll do something about this!" I pictured myself turning out books that would *not* be so unsophisticated as to insult the young ego—*not* so trivial as to insult the young (and often deep) intelligence—yet not filled with adult experience far beyond their own, which I suspect leads to a distorted view of reality. I dreamed of a Utopia where any fourteen-year-old might walk up to a bookstall—any small bookstall near home—and pluck from the shelf a slice of good literature, suited to both his tastes and his development!

Of course, such an ideal gets further away all the time! Just *look* at the bookstalls! The other day in Central Station, Sidney, I did not see one title that I would be bothered to read myself, let alone give to my children or my mother! If even there had been a Mary Steward, an Arthur Upfield, an Agatha Christie! But no, not so much as a clean who-dun-it! Nothing but wordy accounts of depression and misery, and some clinical sex! Surely a young, growing person is entitled to hope, as well as truth! To glimpses of courage and fidelity, as well as cravenness and triumphant lust! And to a brand of humour that is not sick! I don't believe in telling lies—part of my writing programme was to tell the truth at all times—but surely a young person, growing up, is entitled to be armed, with moral and spiritual weapons, before being plunged head first into the battle!

So—feeling this way—I embarked on my first book for young people. Of course, it did not start a revolution on the bookstalls—it has never shouldered aside one bit of purple pornography! But here I am—still writing for teenagers! They are welcome friends to meet in my Never Land—rewarding listeners, stimulating conversationalists. And above all, what I have to say can be said to them! Not that my characters are children. They are more like the young adults who are only a short step away from the age group of my readers. I have often noticed, with relish, how childish many adults are, and what good sense one sometimes sees in children. This dates right back to a time, many years ago, when I gave a dreadful scolding to my three-year-old son, at the same time struggling to open a tin of paint, with my bare fingers. Without doubt, it was the frustration over the paint tin that made me so bad-tempered. When I'd quite run out of breath, belabouring the poor fellow (for sins long since forgotten), and stood back to watch the effect of my verbal chastisement—he said—"I'll det you a cissel to open it wiv, Mum!"

And as to "how" do I write, for my chosen readers? Firstly, not so well as I'd like to, who does? The first essential, as I see it, is to discuss something that concerns them. I may be quite wrong, but (until recently, at least) I've felt that in this country they are interested in the present and the future, not the past. For this reason my books are set in the present; the writing of historical works I leave to others. Though my built-in barometer tells me that this may be changing. But even now, I have a feeling that it is perhaps only girls, in their wisdom, who like to escape into the past. I would like it if my books could be enjoyed by both boys and girls. I try to give them a "hard core". Now, in this day and age (as in any other) the most important problem facing adolescents is simply growing up. Now that I think of it, this seems to always be my theme.

Then again, a writer must always write to please himself. His second, and very important duty indeed, is to please his editor; not only is he the man whose money is to change hands (which gives him certain rights, undeniably!), but he is also the man with much experience of words, the stand-in for the reading public. This duty to one's editor is almost sacred! The only one more so, is one's duty to oneself. I read once in a writer's magazine of a fox dancing, " . . . all alone in a clearing, waving his brush in the sun." So must the creative writer be. If his dance does not please himself, it is not a dance, but a pathetic travesty. So I write of things, people and places which please me, hoping that, as I am a microcosm of mankind, they will please others. And as I write, I play a sort of game with myself—a dance just for myself, that, if others see it, may please them, too; but if they don't, well never mind. This is a game of analogy. I propound to myself a theorem. In *Season of the Briar* it went something like this—"Life is like a mountain ahead of us all. There are people who are compulsive climbers; and other people who keep to a made pathway that finds a safe route over or around the mountain; and others who elect to live in a sheltered valley, at the foot of it." And so on.

More recently, there was the idea behind *Sapphire for September*.

It went somehow this-wise—"Life is a precious thing, it is a precious stone. Each of us has this gift. We can cut and polish it and make it into a jewel. We can buy things with it, or sell it or give it away; we can lose it and find it again—most likely in the ashes of past experience, perhaps changed, but indestructible. We might not know its true nature, but perhaps this does not matter; what matters is that, having been given the moonstone gift of life, we can go on to find the star stone of self-fulfilment; this

way we may have a gem to lend and a gem to spend—finding ourselves, phoenix-like, when the dreams of childhood are nothing but ashes."

I think that this was the riddle that I set myself, behind the story of Binny Flambeau and her crazy friends, who could "only give her the morning". Of course, one can only write about people when one knows them very well. Because of this, I have to live with my people; their world has to be just as real to me as this other world, where I cook and shop and have my being. During the writing of the first draft of the book, one is still only making the acquaintance of one's characters. I write gropingly, mainly because at this time I can't be sure of their reactions. I have to feel my way. I could fall into the pit of setting the wrong tasks for the wrong people, so that they would be forced into doing things which they would not do, if left to themselves. The second time through, writing is easy, for, having worked out the correct circumstances, the characters will now take care of the rest.

When I set about writing *Sapphire,* my first step was to join a lapidary club. Then, the next time I visited my mother in the Blue Mountains, I took the car from Melbourne and spent a week or more, pokering about in obscure gullies and streams, churning through the dust along the roads to Sofala and Wattle Flat and Hill End—gossiping with a gold miner in a lonely hut, washing gravel (quite fruitlessly!) in Tomah Creek . . . of course, this part of a writer's job is sheer delight! All this time the characters were growing more and more clearcut, more irrepressible. But Binny Flambeau herself—I could not get close to her at first. "If only I could see her!" I thought. I took to watching out for her, among faces in crowds. One day I saw her. She was in a school uniform, hurrying to a train at peak hour, with another girl. The fleeting glimpse was enough. From the face of the unknown girl, Binny became tangible. From then on, she was as real to me as my own daughter would be, if I had one!

Now she's left home, of course, and gone out into the book shops. (Though not, unfortunately, to those railway station stalls!) But there are endless teenagers, fictitious amalgams of factual flesh and blood, with stories to be told—growing up has endless facets and connotations! No need to put the cover on the typewriter!

GENERAL COMMENTARY

John Rowe Townsend

SOURCE: "H. F. Brinsmead," in *A Sense of Story: Essays on Contemporary Writers for Children,* J. B. Lippincott Company, 1971, pp. 39-44.

Adolescents have always been around; teenagers only arrived a few years ago. The etymology indicates the difference between the two states. An adolescent is growing up; he is in transit between childhood and adult life. In my own boyhood, just before World War II, the conventional wisdom was that adolescence was a rather miserable time to be got through as painlessly as possible. It was assumed that the adolescent's chief aim in life was to become an adult. The teenager is a post-war phenomenon; he is not *becoming* something, he *is* something; and he may be as contemptuous of adult life as he is of childhood. Syd and Sabie, the teenage boys in H. F. Brinsmead's novel *Beat of the City,* comfort themselves at times when the grownups are being tiresome by recalling The Slogan: 'We are the only generation to be born superior to our parents.'

Mrs Brinsmead's novels are for teenagers and are mostly *about* teenagers. No pre-adolescent child has a significant part to play in any of them. The teenagers come and go, as teenagers will, in a crowd; they are always on the move. The books themselves are full of warmth and energy and tend to have large casts, plenty of incident, and unusual richness of background. Not only do things happen; people change and develop. All Mrs Brinsmead's books are concerned with what she herself calls 'the problem of how to cope with life'. They are also concerned with the stage which comes before coping: namely finding out who and what you are.

She is particularly good at drawing the teenager *as* teenager. Adolescent characters in novels by other contemporary writers (for instance Gwyn, Roger and Alison in Alan Garner's *The Owl Service;* Christina, Mark and Will in K. M. Peyton's *Flambards*) are shown as the people they essentially are and always will be. It is not difficult to imagine them at the ages of 25, 35 or 45. But Mrs Brinsmead's Syd and Sabie in *Beat of the City,* and Binny in *A Sapphire for September,* are specifically sixteen-year-olds, and their age is part of their character. Last year they were not as they are now; next year they will be different again; their self-discovery is still going on, and in discovering themselves they are still changing. (The difference here between Mrs Brinsmead and the other writers mentioned is not a matter of superiority or inferiority on either side; it lies partly in style of characterization, partly in the kind of person created.) And Mrs Brinsmead has an interesting way of moving into and out of her characters' minds, of seeing them now from inside, now from outside, in a way that gives perspective to her portraits. Sometimes she manages, curiously, to be both inside and outside at once. This is Sabie, preserving a tactical silence while being ticked off by his father:

> In theory one does not quarrel with one's ever-loving parents. If they insist on admonishing and advising, one fills one's mind with a kind of inner, metallic music; this is a soporific and a panacea; it shuts out the world; it shuts out the future . . .
>
> A transistor with an earplug is good. It makes the perfect anaesthetic. But even without the transistor one can keep the confused metallic theme in one's mind. If one stands and stares with one's mouth hanging open and a certain blank expression on one's face—vacant, yet studied—listening as it were to the beat

jazz-time of one's own pulse—and occasionally, with a quiet, maddening rhythm, clicking one's fingers at one's sides—why then, from the parent, or parents, one gets a reaction.

> Right now his father was saying, 'But don't you have any ambition, boy? Don't you want to succeed?'
>
> Well, not saying. Yelling, to put it bluntly.

Here the reader 'is' Sabie, but at the same time is seeing him from the viewpoint of an irritated parent. If a generation gap exists—and in Mrs Brinsmead's books it exists in individual cases such as this, not as a general phenomenon—the author is on both sides of it.

A combination of sympathy and detachment in her treatment of teenagers is indeed one of Mrs Brinsmead's strengths. It is already apparent in her first book, *Pastures of the Blue Crane,* which was published in 1964. This is the story of Ryl, a poor little fairly-rich girl who cares for nobody but whose cramped character unwinds when she finds herself joint owner of a rundown farm with her proletarian grandfather Dusty. Self-centred, stoical, snobby Ryl is one of those rare, infuriating heroines whom one doesn't much like but finds oneself caring about—presumably because the author, while seeing her clearly for the rather unlovable person she is, can also feel with her and perceive what she might become.

The four-dimensional character study of Ryl, over a period in which she changes greatly yet remains recognizably the same girl, is as fine in its way as anything Mrs Brinsmead has done. She has not again penetrated any individual to the same depth. Many of her young people are appealing, especially the girls: Gisela, the small person with the big voice and big boots in *Season of the Briar;* the cheerful urchin Binny in *A Sapphire for September;* sensitive Emma in *Isle of the Sea Horse.* But they are more lightly sketched than Ryl, and the reader does not become involved with them in the same way. This is probably because of a tendency to put a group, rather than a single individual, at the centre of a story. Gisela, Binny and Emma can be considered as the heroines of the books in which they appear, but they do not dominate the scene.

Beat of the City, Mrs Brinsmead's 'biggest' book so far, has four young people at its heart: two boys and two girls. But this is not only a book about what happens to certain individuals; it is also a portrayal of a city and a composite study of the life of young people in it; it is an exploration, too, of certain values and relationships. It is a bold and forceful novel and, taken as a whole, is Mrs Brinsmead's most impressive book up to the time of writing. Where many authors have found it easier to concentrate on the enduring realities of human nature if they avoid those immediate surface details which are so hard to get right and so sure to fall out of date, *Beat of the City* is uncompromisingly contemporary. 'In Melbourne in 1965 the way-outs were in', it begins; and the

Melbourne of 1965—no other time, no other place—is the setting of this story. And, paradoxically but deservedly, the sense of immediacy has so far proved lasting, for although it is no longer 1965 the feeling that everything is happening here and now remains fresh and strong.

The plot of *Beat of the City* is worked out in intricate detail; the characters are carefully balanced. Sabie's parents are well-to-do upper-middle-class; Syd's are plebeian. Mary lives with her uncle, a pastor. Raylene is a motherless urchin, drawn to the bright lights as moth to candle. The four lives come together, interact, tangle with danger and delinquency; and after some alarming incidents, including a near-rape, they disentangle, with Sabie and Raylene, the more mixed-up of the kids, well on the way to unmixing themselves.

Each character in turn moves into and out of the spotlight; but in spite of the lack of a continuous focus the story does not fall apart. What holds it together is the most impressive element of all, the city of Melbourne itself. Melbourne is alive on every page, beginning with the first:

> On the West Bank there is the jam-packed, claptrap, shindig-filled old inner suburb of Abbotsford, running into Fitzroy and Carlton so that nobody knows where one ends and the other begins, a hugger-mugger of factories, tenements, migrant hostels and almost brand-new slums bursting with folk coming in all colours, shapes and sizes. Half submerged by it on the one side but with the quiet of the river at its shoulders is the ivory tower, the stone-turreted Convent where the soft-spoken Sisters live, and wait upon the poor. The city batters and rattles at their gates, but behind them are their incongruous water meadows, and the river. The gardener, Manuel, and rosy Sister Martha of the Beatitudes are picking sweetcorn from the vegetable garden. Two hundred yards from the swish of traffic over the Big Bridge the Sisters' cows come sedately over the bridle-path on their way home to be milked.

The theme of the novel is the pursuit of happiness, as carried out by various people in various ways through the streets, homes and haunts of the city. Sabie's mother, expressing what it is safe to assume are the author's own views, contrasts true happiness—something to be built from your own inner resources—with an instant, ready-mixed substitute symbolized by the Tootle Bird, a mythical creature that 'probably nests in a box of empty Coke bottles' and has a call like the whirring noise of a fruit machine. This direct expression of view comes in a natural way at an appropriate moment, and does no harm to the story; but it is a pointer, I think, to the book's major flaw. One has a persistent sense that the characters and action have been designed to illustrate this very message.

The clash of values is direct and simple. Sabie and Raylene both look for 'kicks', and both come close to disaster. Mary and, increasingly, Syd create their own pleasures and are sensible and constructive. The good girl

Mary, whose approach to life is the opposite of that summed up in the quest for the Tootle Bird, seems to me to be altogether too good to be true. Pains are taken to indicate that her activities, such as folk-singing, dancing and playing the clarinet, are livelier and more with-it than canned amusements; yet the result is only to make her less convincing, less likeable. Like all excessively good fictional characters, she becomes a shade tiresome.

Emergence of the author's values is not in itself objectionable. In a story with a contemporary setting where the subject-matter, broadly, is what life is about, suppression would be difficult and in any case not praiseworthy. The point at which damage starts is when character or action is distorted, or the impression given that the story is only a vehicle for carrying a message. In *Beat of the City* the action, even if contrived, is strong, and the characters, except perhaps Mary, come alive as people. The damage is slight and the book can stand it. And it is possible that the author's strength of feeling about true and false happiness has provided the book's motive force, and is responsible for its power as well as its weakness.

Of Mrs Brinsmead's first five novels, the remaining three are slighter than *Beat of the City* or *Pastures of the Blue Crane*. Her second book, *Season of the Briar*, is an episodic story about four young men who form a weed-spraying unit in Tasmania; about their encounters with a party of trampers and with a tiny remote community, during which they make some discoveries about themselves and each other. In *A Sapphire for September* Binny, slightly common but full of fizz and goodwill, joins a club of gem-seekers with her eye on handsome but elusive student Adam; she doesn't get him, but at the end can pick herself up and dust herself down, a bit older, a bit wiser. Emma, in *Isle of the Sea Horse*, is cast away on a pleasant-enough desert island with a group of people who, like herself, are in no hurry to go back to mainland life; but they have to face it in the end. These books are still concerned with 'the problem of how to cope with life', but they are less closely at grips and their situations are more specialized.

Mrs Brinsmead is a writer with several faults. The structure of her stories can be unsatisfactory: notably in *Pastures of the Blue Crane*, which falls away in the second half, and *Season of the Briar*, which lacks any clear focal point and never really pulls itself together at all. Her male characters are rarely memorable. She is apt to scatter minor figures around without taking enough pains to make them live for the reader, although it is plain that they live for *her*, and she even has an endearing habit in her novels of throwing parties for them. What is so attractive about her is her writing personality. There is a sense of the author's presence, of her sympathy with the people she is writing for and about. Her settings have ranged widely and are strongly realized. Her vitality compensates for a great many failings. The last thing one would wish on her, the negation of her true gift, would be a cool perfection.

TITLE COMMENTARY

📖 *PASTURES OF THE BLUE CRANE* (1964)

The Junior Bookshelf

SOURCE: A review of *Pastures of the Blue Crane,* in *The Junior Bookshelf,* Vol. 28, No. 5, November, 1964, p. 327.

Ten years ago, almost all we knew of children's books in the Antipodes was *The Magic Pudding.* Every year now we are shown something more of the growing vitality of this literary field. H. F. Brinsmead—internal evidence suggests a woman writer—like Nan Chauncy and Patricia Wrightson, writes within the narrow context of an Australian scene but with an awareness of human values which is universal.

Pastures of the Blue Crane is a most appealing story of a young girl's growth into womanhood. The theme is common enough, though rarely carried out well; what gives an original slant to this story is the honest treatment of an unfamiliar situation. Ryl, at sixteen, has just ended an unhappy childhood. Neglected by her father, she has grown up among strangers, with material comfort but without love. She finds at one go a grandfather and a home, but likes neither at first sight. She grows, beautifully and convincingly, before our eyes from a cold, priggish snob into a delightfully alive, unpredictable human being. It is a lovely study. The setting too is vividly evoked.

There remains a doubt whether this is a book for children. It is beyond question a sensitive and true picture of adolescence. Many of the young people who are interested in reading about themselves and their contemporaries may well be put off by the "children's book" format. (Let it be said that the book is most beautifully designed, with drawings in Annette Macarthur-Onslow's finest manner.) It is in fact a book for the odd child, and after all we have plenty of books for the ordinary child.

Virginia Kirkus' Service

SOURCE: A review of *Pastures of the Blue Crane,* in *Virginia Kirkus' Service,* Vol. XXXIV, No. 1, January 1, 1966, p. 13.

The book faces up to the problem of personal acceptance of an interracial community. The context is distinctively Australian; nevertheless the basics of the conflict are universal. In a way, it is unfortunate that the story is so pointed towards its issue; the way the characters sometimes frankly question, other times casually overlook, the blending of colors is handled with a particular adroitness which might have been more effective without that extra pressure. Sixteen year old Ryl had been abandoned (with a very handsome annuity) by her father when she was three; she had no knowledge of her mother or of any other relatives. Her life had been spent exclusively at the

best boarding schools; the polish was burnished to the fullest sheen; she could outsnub anybody. The death of her father coincided with the end of her schooling; she and her long-lost grandfather decided to share one of the inheritances—an antiquated farmhouse in a rural, coastal village. Out on the farm she learned to develop the proper feelings towards friends and relatives, and eventually made the discovery that her good friend Perry Davis—a half-caste—was actually her brother. One might object that the author has been evasive by placing the bi-racial romance into the impersonal past (it looked at the outset as it Perry and Ryl would turn out to be more than pals) but that is really a niggling fault. The ramifications of the problem are presented through the conversations of the teenagers (also Ryl's grandfather and his cronies) which are a convincing mixture of banter and conscientious probing. The well described scenery is an extra plus for this story which girls will enjoy reading and perhaps find though-provoking. Better than most teenage friction fiction.

Zena Sutherland

SOURCE: A review of *Pastures of the Blue Crane,* in *Bulletin of the Center for Children's Books,* Vol. 19, No. 9, May, 1966, pp. 143-44.

A long junior novel, naive in one sense, sophisticated in another—and very good reading. A book set in Australia, with a plot both romantic and provocatively different. Amaryllis Merewether has lived in boarding schools since she was three, never seeing her father; her mother is dead. At the age of sixteen, she is told by a lawyer that she has inherited half her father's fortune; the other half belongs to a man sitting across the room. This impoverished pensioner is her grandfather. The two go off to an inherited property and find the joys of family life, belonging, creative work, friendly neighbors, the beauty of nature, et cetera. The exotic quality of the topography and flora frequently described save the exposition from dullness, and the important message and theme woven through all this Utopia is race prejudice. Ryl's kindest friend is Perry, who is a quartercaste; Ryl is incensed at the occasional barbed remarks directed at Perry, but he takes such remarks very calmly. (In fact, he's almost too good to be true.) It becomes increasingly clear to the reader that everybody but Ryl knows that she has some colored ancestry, and that this has some connection with her father's unfatherly behavior. By the time Ryl does find this out, she has been strengthened by Perry's calm dignity and can feel that she is no less a person. The fact that Perry turns out to be Ryl's brother seems slightly contrived; the fact that Ryl is hardly shaken by her discovery seems a reaction unbelievably mature in a girl so young. However, the familial relationships, the peer group camaraderie, the high moral tone, and the message of the intrinsic worth of man all give the book strength.

Margo Alexandre Long

SOURCE: "The Interracial Family in Children's Literature," in *Interracial Books for Children Bulletin,* Vol. 15, No. 6, 1984, pp. 13-15.

Pastures of the Blue Crane . . . treats the relationships in an interracial family as a subplot. Ryl, the daughter of a wealthy Australian, has never seen her mother (who is dead) and sees her father rarely. When her father dies, Ryl and her paternal grandfather, Dusty, inherit a sizeable amount of money and a tumbledown farm on the North Coast of Australia. It is here that Ryl's father was raised, and it is here that she and Dusty set about making a life together.

In a surprise ending, the last 25 pages are devoted to Ryl's discovery of her family background. She learns that her mother was Black and died shortly after her birth. Because Ryl "looked completely white," her father took her away to Brisbane, leaving her brother—who had had a darker complexion—to be raised by his maternal grandfather.

Several issues are suggested by the content of this story. First is the sense of shame apparently felt by Ryl's father. Why didn't he share Ryl's background with her? Why did he abandon her? Why would a father leave behind a darker child? There is also the question of extended family relations in interracial families. Why did Dusty take no interest in his grandchildren until he was an old man? And last, what does this book say about societal values? Why were so many people afraid of telling Ryl the truth?

Ryl's adjustment to her racial background is sensitively developed, although perhaps a bit too naively and quickly. Before Ryl finds out about her own background, she briefly discusses "people of mixed parentage" with a friend, saying, "Well, I suppose they can be the best of two worlds—or they can be the worst. It's just what they make of themselves." This same unquestioning adjustment appears in Ryl's acceptance of her boarding-school existence. How realistic are these easy adjustments? Still, this is an intriguing novel that would certainly be of interest to many teenage readers.

📖 SEASON OF THE BRIAR (1965)

The Times Literary Supplement

SOURCE: "A Wider World," in *The Times Literary Supplement,* No. 3328, December 9, 1965, p. 1138.

Here is a double story, converging in the end to make one: of a party of youngsters spending a summer with a weed-spraying unit, and another party who are bush-walking. The beginning has a tone of rather chummy facetiousness, but once the two parties arrive in a lost valley in Tasmania, populated by a tiny family group sprung from nineteenth-century European refugees, a fine sharpness sets in: beautiful natural descriptions, a great relish for oddity of character and for the irritations that arise among young people: and a final drama of truly breath-

taking quality, when a girl bush-walker is lost in frightful weather on a mountain near by. One of the virtues of this very distinguished story lies in the way it glances at the limitations of conventional heroism.

Margery Fisher

SOURCE: A review of *Season of the Briar,* in *Growing Point,* Vol. 4, No. 8, March, 1966, p. 668.

A long lead into the story introduces four young Australians, carefully individualised, who go weed-spraying in Tasmania as a holiday job; on a parallel route a group of young people go bush-walking, and about halfway through the book their paths converge in dramatic fashion. The boys have reached a hidden valley on one side of the unexplored mountain Groot Klaus, where they have a job to do for a community of German-born settlers living by long past tradition. On the far side of Groot Klaus, Gisela, who is sixteen, wilful and determined, is lost, and found again. The theme of growing up and into sense is followed out in the relations of the characters as well as in their doings. The setting is matchlessly described; the book is exciting enough for any child over twelve and mature enough for many up to fifteen; while the thoughtful contrast of old and new ways is more than enough to satisfy the adults who come by the book.

Kirkus Service

SOURCE: A review of *Season of the Briar,* in *Kirkus Service,* Vol. XXXV, No. 5, March 1, 1967, pp. 277-78.

H. F. Brinsmead takes her considerable talent for calling up the look of the landscape, the mood of the moment, from western Australia to Tasmania in a story of four boys; thrown together and tested against an alien environment. Two (Matt and Doug) are university students, one (Clancy) is a farmer's son, one (Fred) is a "funny bloke" who is hard of hearing; they're working temporarily as a weed-spraying crew to earn extra money. Early on, they encounter a group of bushwalkers (hikers), and three of the boys, each in his own way, are attracted by Gisela, a gallant, bossy little sixteen-year-old. Their misadventures with Grumpy Gertie and Cranky Connie, the two blitz buggies (weed-spraying behemoths) make amusing reading, but the story settles down seriously after the boys reach Lynnore, an isolated settlement, and learn that Gisela is lost on a near-by mountain. The predictable search develops quite unpredictably: the boys' loyalties are strained and then split, Matt endangers himself and the settlers by insisting on joining the rescue party, Gisela is finally found by Fred but she will never recover completely from her injuries. There are no heroes here and the only lesson is the danger of self-absorption, the difficulty of mutual involvement. It works beautifully on the level of description, effectively on the level of adventure, remains cloudy on characterization, scores sometimes on subtle sympathies and antipathies—comes out uneven but generally compelling.

📖 *BEAT OF THE CITY* (1966)

Geoffrey Trease

SOURCE: "Golden Age," in *The New Statesman,* Vol. 72, No. 1861, November 11, 1966, p. 708.

It's nice to be living in the golden age of something, even if it's only juvenile literature. And we certainly are. Twenty years ago, reviewing children's books was easy. Anybody could go off with a typical armful—school stories, pony books and hilarious holiday adventures—and turn in an urbane amusing piece. Now it's not so funny. Standards have soared. And jostling the home product come the European translations, the Transatlantic award-winners and the fruits of a quite extraordinary flowering in Australia. In *Beat of the City* we have an outstanding illustration not only of the Australian efflorescence but of the revolution in themes, attitudes and vocabulary that has transformed children's fiction as a whole in the last decade or two. The particular city is Melbourne, but in a sense it could be any modern city. Here is the universal teenage world of puzzled parents and their sulky, sultry offspring—a world of transistors and motor-bikes, deception and delinquency, flick-knives and jazz groups and the juvenile courts, a world with an understandable fascination for countless boys and girls who never experience its seamier excitements for themselves.

I can hear the snorts of shocked grandfathers leafing through this book on Christmas afternoon. The way these four young characters talk—this appalling, mysterious, vivid Antipodean slang! (Isn't American bad enough?) And their truculent slogan: 'We are the only generation to be born superior to our parents!' And the things they *do,* and the things that (nearly) get done to them! Why, here on page 177 it's obvious that Raylene is about to be raped by Blade O'Reilley and his Death Riders—of course the author doesn't *say* so, or use any offensive expressions, but a child is sure to wonder why the boy hero told her, so urgently: 'Get out, fast!' In the very next paragraph he gets someone's knee in the groin. That could never have happened to one of Henty's lads. Grandfathers may wince at the publishers' assessment (10 to 14 age-group) but I know one impeccably brought-up 11-year-old girl who is already devouring the book.

Spectator

SOURCE: A review of *Beat of the City,* in *Spectator,* No. 7220, November 11, 1966, p. 624.

The underworld Down Under is the setting for E. F. Brinsmead's *Beat of the City*. If you don't talk Strine, if you think 'chicken' is something you 'shop,' and if you can feel no compassion for the young who live by The Slogan—'Our generation is the only one to be born superior to its parents'—then *Beat of the City* is not for you. Mrs Brinsmead has enormous range: the four young people, the threads of whose lives are briefly intertwined in her story, are a banker's son (whose dream is to be a rocker),

a young bricklayer (who wants to educate himself out of his background), a welfare-conscious girl clarinettist (who brings home any stray, animal or human, so long as her aunt will take over the responsibility after the first heady forty-eight hours) and a rootless girl waif looking for kicks—and getting them. This book is as tough as it is sensitive; it is a view of youth for youth, a probe into the true meaning of freedom and the too-high price that must be paid for it in human terms: it is a book about real values in an instant-mix, press-button, with-it teenage world. Not everyone's 'cuppa cappuccino,' perhaps, but for me Mrs Brinsmead is, as her characters would put it, 'the most, but the most.'

The Junior Bookshelf

SOURCE: A review of *Beat of the City,* in *The Junior Bookshelf,* Vol. 31, No. 1, February, 1967, p. 65.

The scene is Melbourne. Raylene, running away from her slum home, and Sabie, rebelling against his affluent one, become involved with a group of Rockers, and are saved from total disaster largely by the intervention of understanding adults. Sabie's friend, Syd, learns through Mary that wholesome pleasure can be found in creative activities and humane contact with people of all ages. This is a mature book, surprisingly recommended for people as young as ten. The author expounds the attitudes of the "beat generation" with sympathetic insight, at the same time showing she thinks them wrong-headed. The city of Melbourne is portrayed with the same critical affection. The principal characters are so alive that the reader develops a real concern for them. Though William Papas' drawings are enjoyable for their own sake, they seem out of sympathy with the text.

Sidney Offit

SOURCE: A review of *Beat of the City,* in *The New York Times Book Review,* March 31, 1968, p. 30.

Introducing her tale of youngsters in search of identity in an Australian metropolis, H. F. Brinsmead observes, "In Melbourne that year the way-outs were in." For Melbourne read New York or San Francisco and this teen-age shibboleth seems no less appropriate. High on the list of outs are parents. Raylene Slater runs away because she can't communicate with her fisherman father. Sabie Korkoran cannot abide his mother's platitudes and his father's advice. When Sydney Green was an infant, his mother worked 12 hours a day so her son might have the biggest teddy bear and reddest tricycle, but as the intellectual of the Blue Beat Club he finds his parents unworthy of him.

And what would this trio of malcontents swap for the mess at home? Raylene is determined to have a fling with Blade O'Reilley, who wears a black leather jacket with a silver death's head and silver talons across the shoulders. Sabie wants Blade's motorbike, a stolen Bonneville. (When begging and borrowing don't work, he steals to get it.)

Syd is bucking for status momentarily epitomized by Sabie's striped shirt.

The winner of several Australian awards, the author describes her native land vividly and often lyrically. But the more reflective reader will find Mrs. Brinsmead's swiftly moving narrative rarely pauses to give a penetrating look into either teenagers themselves or the symbols of their aspirations.

A SAPPHIRE FOR SEPTEMBER (1967)

Margery Fisher

SOURCE: A review of *A Sapphire for September,* in *Growing Point,* Vol. 6, No. 4, October, 1967, p. 976.

In *A Sapphire for September* one character (the prospector Charlie Light) and one Blue Mountain township (the Old Vale) remind us of the past. In the ghost town one house is inhabited—the Huntsmans' home, built by an ancestor; the family stands for continuity, a factor dominant, though they hardly realise it, in the lives of the youths and girls whose talk is all of the present. They are on an expedition, these young people, to find uncut gemstones, when they envelop the Huntsmans in their friendliness and, hearing the old house is threatened by speculators, work out a wild but surprisingly successful plot to rout them. In the crowd, each boy, girl, man or woman stands out clear, recognisable: in the centre the two dreamers—half-French Binnie, sixteen, ardent, changeable as an opal, dreaming of riches but finding good friends, and Adam, with a profession before him but with his eyes on distant hills and enterprises. These two gather the action round them but the author manages her narrative so skilfully that there is never a feeling of unbalance. She has already taken us into several odd pockets of Australian life. In this book the details of gem-hunting are enough to attract a reader but it is the way the various characters *see* sapphires and opals which will keep those readers till the last page.

The Times Literary Supplement

SOURCE: "Overture, Beginners . . . " in *The Times Literary Supplement,* No. 3431, November 30, 1967, p. 1155.

At least half the anguish of adolescence is ecstatic clutching at the treasures of an opening world. Growing pains may come largely from indigestion, from too big and greedily gulped a helping of life.

So it is with H. F. *Brinsmead's* Binny Bijou (in *A Sapphire for September*). Mrs. Brinsmead, who has already demonstrated her knowledge and understanding of the Beat generation, here turns to another and more agreeable aspect of the Australian city scene. Her Rockbusters are way-out enough, but their energies go not into breaking up the town but into hunting and working precious stones. They are not above lending a hand in more altruistic

ventures. Into this wild and exuberant company erupts Binny, daughter of a French sailor (deceased) and a caterer in a very small way of business. Binny is "everybody's buddy, but nobody's fast friend", at least until she meets Adam, the student geologist. The author draws an irresistible picture of her absurd, adorable heroine in the pangs of first love. "She sat with her mouth a little open and eyes apparently sightless, looking like a zombie, sad to tell." Binny's affair is doomed from the start—Adam is clearly not of her world—but at least he takes her into his for a spell. After the absorbing always convincing adventures, dramatic and comic, which form the action of the book, Binny has enjoyed—or suffered—many experiences; has visited worlds outside the crowded streets of Sydney and is on the threshold of another discovery, of her self.

A *Sapphire for September* is one of those books into which the reader dips again and again and each time pulls out a different kind of gem: evocative descriptions of city and desert not grafted on to the narrative but growing out of it; portraits of colourful people, all individual, sometimes a shade larger than life but never exaggerated, all—even the nasty ones—drawn with an affectionate understanding; as much as anything a passionate concern for the beauty of stone and the technique of handling it.

Is it a quality of young countries to find serious things funny? Mrs. Brinsmead has in the richest measure this quality, which is to be found in so much of the vigorous literature of Australia.

The Junior Bookshelf

SOURCE: A review of *A Sapphire for September,* in *The Junior Bookshelf,* Vol. 31, No. 6, December, 1967, pp. 385-86.

The best Brinsmead yet—it will be interesting a few decades hence to know how many New Australians were inspired by reading her books in the '60s and '70s, though her main message is not "Come to Australia" but "Come to life". Her Binny Flambeau is lively enough, though somewhat rootless and aimless until dreamer and student Adam sweeps her into a group of rock-hounds in Sydney. She cannot understand Adam but adores him with a puppy-love whose waxing and waning is neatly conveyed as the group, a wildly assorted bunch, converges on a deserted township inhabited only by the pleasant Huntsmans. Finding the area may be "developed" into a phoney sort of "ghost town" the enthusiasm of the group really runs amok and a most ingenious plan is put into motion, rousing half the University. Full of young people and their talk, but with a memorable ballast of older people, like old Charley Light the gem-specker who sees that Binny might find gems but will never keep them and tells her to remember the mountain agate: "It's got a strong kind of beauty. Not much fire, but strong. And it's everywhere". Mrs. Brinsmead makes the reader feel people like that are everywhere, too.

ISLE OF THE SEA HORSE (1969)

Margery Fisher

SOURCE: A review of *Isle of the Sea Horse*, in *Growing Point*, Vol. 8, No. 5, November, 1969, p. 1426.

This very ambitious Robinsonnade does not entirely come off—partly perhaps because the author sets herself a task impossible to achieve even in an unusually long junior novel. Her castaways are as disparate as her groups of characters usually are. Emma, aged seventeen, wants to be a scientist, George the 'crew' of the Pandora is brash and sly, the Egyptian cook has resources of intellect; there is Mrs. Mulvaney, who is wise with her years and tiny Raquel whose pride in her mixed Eastern European race has sustained her through a hard life. Wrecked in a hurricane on an uninhabited island in the Great Barrier Reef, the group makes its shifting alignments while managing to sustain life and, more, to discover evidence of previous castaways, some very surprising. And there is the sea horse itself, symbol of freedom—symbol to the author, perhaps, of nature untamed by pushing civilisation. The book needs a harder, stiffer form to contain its many threads of feeling, of plot, of moral; but it is enlivened by the constant surprises—quirks of personal idiom, snatches of local colour—with which this author always delights her readers.

Robert Bell

SOURCE: A review of *Isle of the Sea Horse*, in *The School Librarian*, Vol. 17, No. 4, December, 1969, p. 396.

The ship in which Emma Conway is travelling to meet her scientist father, who is with a company prospecting for oil off the Australian Great Barrier Reef, is holed by coral, and she and four other people are marooned on an uncharted island. This, they find, provides everything needed for a lotos-eating existence, and, as each has a reason for not wanting to return to the mainland, they find themselves becoming increasingly reluctant to attempt to leave. They help each other to come to terms with their individual problems, but it is the conviction that they must keep the island secret and unexploited which leads them to leave behind the delights it offers and risk their lives once more in departing on the raft which took them there.

Of all the outstanding books Mrs Brinsmead has written, none has been more welcome than this. Her characters are brilliantly portrayed, her prose is a delight and her story is wonderfully well told. It will provide rich rewards for young readers and cannot be too highly recommended.

The Junior Bookshelf

SOURCE: A review of *Isle of the Sea Horse*, in *The Junior Bookshelf*, Vol. 34, No. 1, February, 1970, p. 29.

Five very different people are shipwrecked on an uncharted island on the Great Coral Reef off the Australian mainland. The one thing that they have in common is that they are all running away from themselves in one way or another. Emma, the main character, feels that she cannot face the world without her mother for whose death she feels in a strange way responsible. When she finds a rare horse on the island, the last of a herd left there some fifty years ago, she becomes emotionally involved with it and is obsessed by the feeling that she must preserve it from unscrupulous men on the mainland, therefore she does not want to be rescued. Twice the little horse saves her life and this strengthens her determination. None of her companions wishes, for varying reasons, to be discovered so they do not make any great effort to return to civilisation. Eventually each comes to realise that he cannot run away for ever and they build a raft to take them to safety, first of all promising to allow the island to retain its secrets. The plot is strong and the characters unusual and interesting. Mrs. Brinsmead draws a vivid picture of the remote island.

LISTEN TO THE WIND (1970)

Margery Fisher

SOURCE: A review of *Listen to the Wind*, in *Growing Point*, Vol. 9, No. 3, September, 1970, pp. 1580-81.

Listen to the wind is set on the north east coast of Australia on an estuary from which trawlers sail out after prawns. . . . [There] is a unique problem of class and colour. This is a fishing community where white people, rich and poor, live alongside aboriginals, and Islanders of mixed Australian and Polynesian blood; the groups are interdependent but consciously separate. H. F. Brinsmead explores the racial situation with understanding in the story of a white girl of eighteen and a coloured boy two years older who go into partnership in the restoring of a trawler. Through all their tribulations runs the theme of colour and it is in the determination to over-ride these difficulties that the tension lies. I am a little puzzled by the emotional content of the book. The actual given age of the two young people does not seem entirely borne out by their reaction to events nor by their attitude to each other, whether mildly romantic or comradely. Possibly this has something to do with the fact that the book seems to be written for readers of fourteen or so. There is scope here for stronger and franker writing but it seems characteristic of this author that while she draws her backgrounds with a very mature force, her books leave the final impression of being rather longer versions of the good old "holiday adventure".

The Junior Bookshelf

SOURCE: A review of *Listen to the Wind*, in *The Junior Bookshelf*, Vol. 34, No. 6, December, 1970, pp. 363-64.

Mrs. Brinsmead demonstrates once more her mastery of the social scene and her profound understanding of what makes humans tick. Her demonstration is enlivened with wit and high humour; few writers today, whether they profess to write for children or for adults, have so keen and relevant a sense of fun.

The scene is O'Brian's Point. Places matter a great deal to this writer, and here she paints a beautiful picture of a broken-down settlement of blackfellers and poor whites. Here lives Bella Greenrush, grey, strong, utterly reliable, everybody's dream mum. One of her family is Tam who, alone of the Greenrushes, has ambition. He has, too, a white friend, the lovely teenage Loveday Smith. There are serious social problems implicit in the theme, and Mrs. Brinsmead shirks none of them; she explores them, however, with an understanding at once tender and realistic. The story, potentially tragic, is a comedy, occasionally—when Uncle Zac enters—even a farce.

Out of Australia, with its clash of contradictory cultures, comes yet another joyous, shrewd, devastatingly honest picture of ordinary folk tackling man-sized everyday problems. The setting is infinitely remote from our own and the problems very different; it is difficult to believe, nevertheless, that English children will fail to recognise the truth and beauty of a fine story.

Alex McLeod

SOURCE: A review of *Listen to the Wind*, in *The School Librarian*, Vol. 18, No. 4, December, 1970, pp. 450-51.

Tam Greenrush is a twenty-two-year-old 'Islander'—that is, an Australian of largely New Hebridean descent—and Loveday Smith is a beautiful nineteen-year-old white girl, half Norwegian, whose parents are dead. They live in a coastal fishing and holiday town in Queensland, where 'Islanders', along with aboriginals, are held in contempt. *Listen to the Wind* is the story of their partnership in the purchase and fitting out of a small prawning trawler, a relationship which provokes insults and resentment on all sides, and initially isolates them from both white and black communities; but their persistence, and eventually their success win over the town, and symbolically at least increase the respect the two groups have for each other.

The township, its setting and its people are skilfully realized; there is a hilarious episode in which a half-built fruit packing shed is stolen in the night and re-erected before dawn as a church, and a brief but wholly convincing account of a night's work on a prawning trawler.

In a book which has so much to commend it, it matters less that the behaviour of Tam and Loveday towards each other is just not credible; their friendship is, until the final chapter, strictly a business partnership, and even at the last when they declare their feelings, he won't even kiss her—'Rather than risk losing what he's got, he'll let time pass.' Readers who will otherwise enjoy the book may think this puritanism a rather bad joke.

WHO CALLS FROM AFAR? (1971)

Robert Bell

SOURCE: A review of *Who Calls from Afar?*, in *The School Librarian*, Vol. 19, No. 1, March, 1971, p. 353.

Lyn Honeyfield finds life in Moree, a small New South Wales town among vast open spaces and wheatfields, very different from that of Sydney, but soon finds that she is much less lonely in the outback with her cousin Serena and family than in her city bed-sitter. She joins the staff of Moree Earth Station, a link in the Overseas Telecommunications Commission network. The station has a part to play in tracking Apollo 11's flight to the moon, and when Lyn and some of her colleagues and friends are showing a visiting American professor something of the outback they are caught up in a succession of adventures and near-disasters which work up to a very exciting climax. They return to safety just in time to see on television the even more thrilling descent to the moon's surface of Armstrong and Aldrin in Eagle. Ian Ribbons's excellent drawings deserve a special word of praise.

Judith Aldridge

SOURCE: A review of *Who Calls from Afar?*, in *Children's Book Review*, Vol. I, No. 5, October, 1971, pp. 159-60.

In comparison with much of the author's work, this book is disappointing, lacking for much of its length the usual fluency and conviction. The first half of the book, describing Lyn's arrival in New South Wales, and work at the Moree Earth Station seems unnecessarily drawn-out; discussions of the social groupings within the township somewhat heavy-handed. The latter part of the book is much more successful, full of incident, lively descriptions of the outback, its landscape, trees and weather and its inhabitants and travellers, who provide a splendid gallery of characters. Yet here, too, there is over-stressed comparison between the problems of getting an American professor to a tracking station and the ease with which the Apollo 11 crew reach the Moon.

Margery Fisher

SOURCE: A review of *Who Calls from Afar?*, in *Growing Point*, Vol. 10, No. 5, November, 1971, p. 1823.

Who calls from afar? is built round a sturdy statement that we are all responsible for the future; is man capable of keeping the resolution recorded on the moon that he 'comes in peace'? The moral is well integrated in the story of a girl in her middle 'teens who leaves the urban rat race for back-of-beyond New South Wales and takes a job as secretary at an earth-station relaying messages via satellite to the United States. The flight of Apollo 11 provides the centrepiece for a story involving, as all H. F. Brinsmead's books do, a host of major and minor characters with their attendant prejudices and preoccupations. This could have been a first rate story but for two things—its excessive length and (both reason and result of this) its lack of consistency. In one sense this is a story with a message; from this point of view, the over-long preamble about Lyn Honeyfield and her new friend physicist Henry is in theory justified. In another sense it is the story of a journey—a hilarious, super-paced, brilliantly told saga of the attempt of Lyn and her friends and a bewildered American professor to get from little Moree to Parkes, where Apollo 11 is to be tracked. Small plane, cattle lorry, opal digger's van, safari bus, even feet—the means of transport are variously hazardous and bring out the best and the worst in the people concerned. Cut by a third, tightened up, this could have made a comic picaresque of a kind only too rare these days; as it is, it is a bit of a white elephant.

E. Colwell

SOURCE: A review of *Who Calls from Afar?*, in *The Junior Bookshelf,* Vol. 35, No. 6, December, 1971, p. 393.

The background of this story is Australian and the plot is chiefly concerned with Lyn, the naive heroine, her daily life as a secretary at the Earth Station and her social contacts out of office hours. Action comes only with the arrival of an American professor who, because he has spoken to Lyn on the telephone, "stops off" to see her and the leopard wood tree about which she has told him. This quixotic action results in his missing the plane which would have taken him to Parkes Observatory to observe Apollo II's flight to the moon. The remainder of the book describes the incredible delays and difficulties, often entertaining, which prevent him from reaching his destination until the last page.

There is much that is interesting in the story, as, for instance, the description of the Earth Station with its complex instruments for telecommunication via "Fred" the satellite. There is humour and perhaps a message for young people too, for, as the Professor says, too many of our actions and thoughts are determined by "remote control", as are those of the cosmonauts, and it is essential that the pattern should be broken at times.

The author has a deep concern for young people and understands them, as is evident in this book as in her others, but the story is more superficial and not as absorbing as usual and the central characters are not as real as the four young people in *Beat of the City,* for instance, or Binny in *A Sapphire for September*.

Incidentally a glossary for non-Australians would be helpful.

📖 *LONGTIME PASSING* (1971)

Dennis Hamley

SOURCE: A review of *Longtime Passing,* in *The School Librarian,* Vol. 20, No. 1, March, 1972, pp. 251-52.

The Truelance family moves out to Longtime, in the Blue Mountains of Australia. Here they live, from their first pioneering settlement to the coming of the motor-road and the end of an old way of life.

To say that this book is an example of a fairly common and by now fairly hackneyed type—the family saga—is in no way to devalue it. The story is partly autobiographical; the material is obviously very close to the author—and this comes out in the affectionate quality of the writing. There is a sensitive delineation of place and the effective, memorable drawing of character. However, probably because its plan is strictly chronological, the book lacks subtlety. This would make it more suitable for younger children.

Nevertheless, the understanding shown in the chronicling of the unequal struggle between the old and the new, the sense of the passage of time and the relationships between the generations made me think—and the linking is not, I am sure, outlandish—of writers such as Hardy, Chinua Achebe and Raymond Williams. This book will probably appeal to girls rather than boys; however, any child between ten and fifteen will find the reading of it a rewarding experience—as will many adults.

Gladys Williams

SOURCE: A review of *Longtime Passing,* in *Books and Bookmen,* Vol. 17, No. 11, August, 1972, p. 93.

Longtime Passing is by an Australian writer, Hesba Brinsmead, based in part on her own childhood memories. This authenticity is important, for the story is about a young couple who become first settlers in a primitive bushland area in the Blue Mountains in South Wales. Homemaking is a theme that has a perennial pull on children's hearts, especially when it is accomplished in the face of peril and grim obstacles. And here is a good deal of first-rate fare of just this kind—the family's journey through pouring tropical rain, their weary arrival at the lonely shack suddenly transformed to a very citadel of home as the log fire leaps to life in the giant fireplace and the shadows dance over the blanketed bunks; the boy Mark sternly washing his row of small sisters; the magnificent birthday surprise staged by the weather-bound circus party.

J. Murphy

SOURCE: A review of *Longtime Passing,* in *The Junior Bookshelf,* Vol. 36, No. 4, August, 1972, p. 239.

"Thus shines a good deed in a naughty world" says Portia, if my memory serves me right, and thus shines a good book in a world of complications and implications. *Longtime Passing* is a sincere and simple account of one family's experience in the Australian Outback. Edwin and Letty Truelance are missionaries in Java when they are told that unless they move to a different climate their eldest daughter will not live. Edwin is impulsive, and he decides to go up country from Sydney into the Blue Gum country and make a selection. The narrative that follows is vivid and exciting and honest. Letty is a city girl at heart, she has never cooked or sewed before, but she supports her husband loyally. Their four children, of whom the author is the youngest, grow up in this wild, mysterious, majestic country and watch with secret horror "progress" take over their land.

There is little more for me to say. It is a very good book by any standards and will be enjoyed by readers of all ages, especially girls over the age of thirteen. I say this rather older group because I feel the reader should have some experience of life to appreciate the heights and depths of the writing.

Margot Potts

SOURCE: A review of *Longtime Passing,* in *Children's Book Review,* Vol. II, No. 4, September, 1972, p. 112.

In any art form there is a place by the fireside for the miniaturists. We bow before Michaelangelo, Beethoven and Dostoevsky, and smile with affection as we handle a beautifully carved jade earring, listen to a piece of chamber music, or read *Sense and Sensibility.* Hesba Brinsmead has pulled up her easy chair amongst us in ***Longtime Passing***—a story based on her own Australian childhood. Although the canvas is a small one, the many details are clearly defined, presenting us with a picture which is full of life and vitality, though what it depicts is now only a memory.

The story begins with a brief prologue, describing how the road over the mountains to Longtime was opened up several generations ago, and how the settlers came, and made the newly discovered blue-gum forest country their home.

Teddy Truelance, the narrator, is the youngest of five children born to an ex-missionary and his wife who return to Australia from Java to suit the health of their delicate second child. Edwin Truelance is one of a large family all of whom decide, for different reasons, to settle at Longtime. Edwin's children grow up, therefore, surrounded by loving relatives, each one indulged by the rest in his or her eccentricities, whilst the bullock team is replaced by the motor lorry, the circus comes to town, schoolwork by correspondence course is done at the kitchen table, and the *new* road begins inexorably to wind its way through the land—to Longtime's passing.

A delightfully nostalgic piece of writing, full of domestic laughter and tears, set against a Blue Mountain backcloth, which would engage boys and girls of ten up.

Bookbird

SOURCE: A review of *Longtime Passing,* in *Bookbird,* Vol. XI, No. 1, March 15, 1973, pp. 41-2.

Longtime Passing is a warm-hearted novel for teenage girls. It is notable for its evocation of people and place and for its expression of the author's joy in living.

Mrs. Brinsmead's story was inspired by her family's reminiscences and her personal recollections of life in the Candlebark Country in the Blue Mountains. It is presented as fiction but it has the ring of authenticity and the author has invested her characters with a sharply defined reality. There is a strong sympathy for these people, as pioneers and as members of a close family unit, and their everyday life is shown with compassion and quiet humour.

In a variety of anecdotes, some serious, others amusing, Teddy, the youngest child, tells of the Truelance family's life at Longtime. Teddy gives an account of her father's and mother's early life and their decision to come to Longtime. She describes the clearing of the land, the building of a house and the gradual changes in the family and the settlement over the years.

Although there is no strong plot, the episodic structure is loosely brought together by the interweaving of legend and symbolism with descriptions of events and scenes. Longtime is both home and place of refuge for the Truelances and its mystique pervades the story and gives it unity.

The portrayal of the family and its relationships reveals not only the author's mature insight into people but also her ability to show the interaction of personalities. This is noticeable for example in the scenes between Mark and his father: "There was always a strange jealousy and misunderstanding between the boy and his father. Yet, in his heart, Father must have known that the knights of his story must once have looked very much like Mark. Such a fair little boy, so well set-up, and unafraid."

ECHO IN THE WILDERNESS (1972)

The Times Literary Supplement

SOURCE: "Tanks and Planes," in *The Times Literary Supplement,* No. 3692, December 8, 1972, p. 1496.

Echo in the Wilderness is a lament; it is written as a tribute to Nan Chauncy, who died in 1970: the Chauncys lived in Tasmania (it was the setting for all her books) and converted their home into a wild-life sanctuary. But the real heroes of the book are the light aircraft that provide the only links between the scattered habitations and the city—a Tiger Moth, a Cessna 172, and Clippie's inheritance: a Cirrus Moth. Mrs Brinsmead enjoys every moment of Clippie's love-affair with the old plane, and the book will strike a chord in the hearts of those hapless girl-friends who, like Bev, spend half their time swinging a propeller.

J. Murphy

SOURCE: A review of *Echo in the Wilderness,* in *The Junior Bookshelf,* Vol. 37, No. 2, April, 1973, p. 125.

Clippie Nancarrow flew into Tasmania like the black swans flying south. He was going to collect a legacy left him by his uncle which turned out to be an old broken down Moth aeroplane. Clippie is delighted, he is a mechanic, and plans to rebuild the plane and use it to move people and freight around. His girl friend Bev follows him from Australia and gets a job in a travel agency in Hobart. They become involved in an effort, firstly to save an area from being flooded to build a dam, and when this fight fails, together with a professor and other conservationists, they get an area designated for a national park. Clippie rebuilds the old plane and fits it with floats so that he can ferry wild life from islands in the manmade lake in the park. He and Bev become unofficially engaged, but eventually he realises that, while she really wants an ordered existence, he is a wanderer migrating like the swans.

The age group is ten to fourteen. I think ten to twelve-year-old girls and older boys, especially those interested in the preservation of the environment as well as flying, will enjoy it.

Gladys Williams

SOURCE: "Forward into Space," in *Books and Bookmen,* Vol. 18, No. 8, May, 1973, pp. xiii-xvi.

Echo in the Wilderness is a practical, factual story about a young Australian pilot with a dream to build his own plane. The chief attraction of the Brinsmead story lies in its Tasmanian background, and the vivid portrayal of life there, especially in the unspoiled wild. Clippie, the young pilot who has inherited plans for the plane and a good deal of the materials from a deceased uncle, and Bev, his girl friend, have to witness a big mining venture flood an inland lake and the surrounding land, and the plane is used to ferry some of the rare animals and plants—under the direction of a skilled biologist—to a small island where there is some chance of their survival.

THE BALLAD OF BENNY PERHAPS (1978)

Margery Fisher

SOURCE: A review of *The Ballad of Benny Perhaps,* in *Growing Point,* Vol. 17, No. 2, July, 1978, p. 3364.

Sandy Creek, a derelict mining settlement in Queensland, is the setting, harsh and compelling, for *The Ballad of Benny Perhaps*. Benny has dropped out of university and headed back to the shacks and shafts of his boyhood, where he is confronted with an old antagonist, Rozzer Bizley, just out of prison and looking for revenge for Benny's intervention in his trickery. The few members of this remote colony—like Henk Peterson with his aboriginal wife and daughter Blue—have always settled their differences well enough until Mary and her husband and their friend Dave appear. Regarding the locals as stupid and gullible, the middle class group, with their fancy tents and bright plastic gear, try to conceal a find of opal which

they have made by tunnelling illegally into the Bizley claim. The consequences are distressing for Blue, who has wistfully admired their sophisticated ways, and for Benny whose attempt to protect her and preserve the solidarity of his own folk lands him finally in gaol. Raucous humour, rough sincerity and sentiment, characterise the noisy idiom and violent scenes of the book; worlds away from the deployment of young people in *Beat of the City,* this story has a harsh note in it that matches the setting.

Naomi Lewis

SOURCE: "Money and Murder," in *The Listener,* Vol. 100, No. 2585, November 9, 1978, p. 623.

I'm glad to see a Hesba Brinsmead novel in the lists again: *The Ballad of Benny Perhaps*. Sunday Creek is a small, remote polyglot, opal-mining community: Bret Harte brought up-to-date (I mean this agreeably) and backed with a mining expertise that will always hold a reader. Blue, 15 or so, Norwegian father, Aboriginal mother, and visibly child of both, is the characteristic Brinsmead innocent, who dreams of being a typist (she can scarcely spell) in the glamorous city. Benny Perhaps is the city student turned miner who tries to take her education in hand. A group of expensive speculators arrive at the creek, try to outwit the regulars, and go in a hurry. But they leave the air disturbed. Blue (whose parents are also innocents) gets her chance to try the city. It's an increasing disaster, though with a splendidly comic climax.

ONCE THERE WAS A SWAGMAN (1979)

G. Bott

SOURCE: A review of *Once There Was a Swagman,* in *The Junior Bookshelf,* Vol. 44, No. 2, April, 1980, p. 66.

Based in part on the author's own childhood experiences, this vignette of life in the Blue Mountains of Australia during the Great Depression of the 1930s is centred on nine-year-old Edwina Elizabeth (Teddy) Truelance. During her father's absence, Rhony, the family cow, is her special care; when the beast strays off into the Devil's Wilderness, Teddy follows and falls into a pothole. Her rescuer is Mungo Brodie, the swagman of the title, who is enjoying temporary hospitality with the Truelances in return for helping on the farm.

Two principal features add stature to this simple tale. One is the unsensational, realistic picture of a small family facing the problems of penury with dignity and commonsense. The other is the convincing portrayal of the three main characters: Teddy, a little sorry for herself but accepting the constrictions of poverty with a maturing awareness of responsibility; Mungo, cheerful, considerate and enterprising; Mrs. Truelance, practical, kind and uncomplaining, a rock on which the family stability is maintained. Noela Young's illustrations in muted browns and greys catch the spirit and atmosphere of this quiet, satisfying family story.

Margaret Walker

SOURCE: A review of *Once There Was a Swagman,* in *Book Window,* Vol. 7, No. 3, Summer, 1980, p. 21.

Any book by H. F. Brinsmead means an interesting and well written story and this one is no exception. Set in the Blue Mountains of Australia it tells of the arrival of Mungo Brodie, the Swagman, and his dog and how young Teddy has cause to be grateful to him. The illustrations are very effective and the book does much to conjure up the feeling of the wide open spaces of Australia. It is an evocative and haunting story which will appeal to its readers.

CHRISTMAS AT LONGTIME (1984; U.S. edition as *Christmas at Home,* 1986)

M. Crouch

SOURCE: A review of *Christmas at Longtime,* in *The Junior Bookshelf,* Vol. 49, No. 1, February, 1985, p. 20.

The novels that Oxford published in the 'Sixties established H. F. Brinsmead as one of the outstanding children's writers in Australia. Since then she has turned to more autobiographical themes, and she continues in this vein in **Christmas at Longtime,** which is something between a picture-book and a full-scale novel and which to some extent suffers from this half-way position.

The story is in the third person, but Teddy Truelance is perhaps something like the young Hesba. She lives at Longtime which is in the remote hill country of New South Wales. The rest of the family are away at school and college in Sydney, but Teddy does her lessons by correspondence. With her we watch the slow approach to Christmas, the passing of the winter (no more stockings!) the coming of daffodils and peach blossom, and the making of Christmas pudding. Then the children come home for the holiday, presents are bought—no easy matter when the General Store has limited resources; the set of encyclopaedias that Teddy plans to give brother Mark becomes a magazine called the Home Carpenter! But, as mother says, 'It's the thought that counts.' Christmas Day itself is celebrated with a picnic in the park at Mount Victoria after a long and perilous journey in father's ancient truck. There could be no greater contrast to an English Christmas, and reading this description in all its loving detail is a joy. The book is written with nostalgia and also with hope. Mrs. Brinsmead concludes: 'We look forward'.

SOMEPLACE BEAUTIFUL (1986)

E. Colwell

SOURCE: A review of *Someplace Beautiful,* in *The Junior Bookshelf,* Vol. 51, No. 1, February, 1987, pp. 25-6.

The distinguished Australian author who has produced so many excellent books for young people, writes here for a younger audience.

Berea, a Vietnamese 'Boat Boy', and his family, have come to Australia to find 'someplace beautiful' where they can be at peace. For Berea and his friends from many countries, the bookshop, *The Flying Trunk,* is the place where they have found friendship and happiness. The local Council plans to demolish the bookshop and put a betting shop in its place.

Berea and his friends go into action to prevent this. They draw up a petition signed by over 3000 children (thumb marks from the youngest).

There is an hilarious climax when the deputation carries the petition to the town hall. There are children everywhere, the worst traffic jam ever and, in the midst of the confusion, the children's friend, an old man, dives off the bridge and is rescued by a gallant policeman.

A delightful story of good will and kindness and fun. The bookshop is indeed 'someplace beautiful' for these exiles—as bookshops and libraries everywhere could be for children.

THE SAND FOREST (1986)

Beverley Mathias

SOURCE: A review of *The Sand Forest,* in *British Book News Children's Books,* March, 1986, pp. 31-2.

It is only after the reader is well into this book that the necessity for the long and careful stage-setting becomes obvious, and the story can be enjoyed. The sand forest itself is unusual—a sandy waste filled with petrified trees through which Sky and her uncles journey to reach the coast. Bound up in the story are the intricacies of family relationships, the obsession of the uncles with early coastal exploration, and Sky's ambivalence toward her own future. The coincidence of Clippie actually force-landing in the same area as Sky is marooned in, is not all that far-fetched. Australia is a large country, but settlements on the western coast are spaced out and a small plane could easily come down in such an area as is described. The end of the story, with the near death of one uncle, survival of the other, and the ceremonial burial of a supposed Roman oarsman, is a little too neat and contrived. However, the story is readable and will be enjoyed by those in their mid-teens.

E. Colwell

SOURCE: A review of *The Sand Forest,* in *The Junior Bookshelf,* Vol. 50, No. 2, April, 1986, pp. 74-5.

A story for young people by the author of **Pasture of the Blue Crane, A Sapphire for September** and many other books with an Australian background.

Sky Herriot has grown up in a city. Now, at the age of nineteen, she is still vague as to what she would like to do with her life. She pays a long-promised visit to her elderly uncles who live in the far West. There she becomes involved in their discovery of the site of a wrecked sixteenth century Dutch boat in the Sand Forest, a petrified forest in a desert of sand. In this spot Sky endures a nightmare happening, for one of her uncles falls ill and becomes dangerously delirious and they are without food or water. However, out of the sky crashes a helicopter piloted by a young man Sky has met in the train. Added to this, Sky has been instrumental in discovering (by dowsing) a Greek Trireme in the Sand Forest.

The story begins slowly and is rather overloaded with historical information from the two old uncles, but then it becomes exciting and sensational. The reader's credulity is rather strained by the apt arrival of the helicopter on such an extended shore line. Sky has not found her vocation but she is at least determined to train for something, if only to spite the Flying Doctor who, called to her uncle, has adopted a dictatorial attitude towards her.

Remembering the former books from this distinguished author, this one is a little disappointing, although it may well appeal to girls for its story interest.

Naomi Lewis

SOURCE: "Unreluctant Feet," in *The Observer,* No. 10150, April 20, 1986, p. 25.

In *The Sand Forest,* city-bred Sky Herriott (17), uncertain what to do next, decides to visit her legendary uncles, grape growers north of Perth. Two old men, 'dry, brown and gnarled as roots,' tell her of their secret find—a sunken vessel that sailed from Holland in 1603. But when they set out to show her the place, one brother becomes sick and deranged, possessed by ghosts of ancient seamen. That hard-wood lump that she burns for rescue—could it be the bones of a galley slave? The young helicopter pilot does catch the May Day call but don't expect the obvious even here.

Margery Fisher

SOURCE: A review of *The Sand Forest,* in *Growing Point,* Vol. 25, No. 1, May, 1986, p. 4624.

Setting is vital in *The Sand Forest,* another stretch of coast in Western Australia where Sky Herriot, who is seventeen, has gone with her two elderly uncles on a camping trip. Enthusiastic local historians, George and Hamish have found relics of a Dutch ship on the barren shore on an earlier visit and are hoping to establish the facts of the wreck of the *Duyfkin* three centuries before. The careful planning for the expedition goes for nothing when George falls ill and Hamish, driving inland for help, is beset by accidents; Sky has to cope with a sick man whose delirium mysteriously revives a far more ancient

shipwreck. In some danger from his feverish violence, as well as from the effects of heat and thirst, Sky has almost given up hope of rescue when a helicopter pilot, off his course and in difficulties, lands on the beach. The intensity of this story depends on the way the girl's thoughts and feelings are described, properly integrated with a strong historical element and with the atmosphere of an isolated and desolate shore where the past has left surprising traces.

THE SILVER TRAIN TO MIDNIGHT (1993)

Stephen Matthews

SOURCE: "From the Word Go," in *Australian Book Review,* No. 152, July, 1993, pp. 69-70.

The Silver Train to Midnight is unabashed in its adherence to the virtues of tradition and nostalgia. Linked by the presence of Emily and her spirited grandmother, the book's eight stories use subtle good humour and gentle irony in their delicately wrought depiction of episodes in the life of a close-knot family which chooses to maintain an affectionate respect for its history. Rich in language and deep in regard for the craft and artifice of efficient storytelling, Brinsmead's stories describe floods and encounters with ghosts, comically conspiratorial inter-generational disputes and small chaotic mishaps. All are seen through the eyes of Emily, a dreamer who nevertheless cannot withstand the intrusion of reality into the fancy of the title story.

Russ Merrin

SOURCE: A review of *The Silver Train to Midnight,* in *Magpies,* Vol. 8, No. 5, November, 1993, p. 30.

When she was younger, Emily, the focal character in each of these eight stories, had always believed that the Silver Train which sped through the countryside, departed from the wonderful dream city of Daybreak and travelled on and on to its final destination—the equally beautiful Midnight.

"Daybreak" (the city of Sydney) collapses into gritty reality for Emily when she catches the train from Central Railway Station to travel to her grandmother at Rangecrest. The same soft interaction of reality and fey dreaming weave through several of these tales. As with Hesba Brinsmead's earlier "Longtime" novels, there is the same sense of nostalgia for another time, another place . . .

With several stories also, there is a touch of the supernatural and contact with ghosts of the longtime dead, e.g. *The Old Corroboree Ground* and *The Man from Nowhere.* This is countered by the humour of *When Bill Got His Head Stuck* and *The Hijacked Bathtub.*

Sandra Laroche's black and white illustrations capture exactly the gentle mayhem that seems to accompany Emily's family's affairs.

These are not fast-paced stories which have unexpected twists at the endings. Rather they are enjoyable tales of normal family life—vignettes almost—set in country New South Wales. The stories display warmth and charm and the minor adventures and family crises described here will strike a response with most older readers.

Additional coverage of Brinsmead's life and career is contained in the following sources published by Gale Research: *Contemporary Authors New Revision Series,* Vol. 10; *Contemporary Literary Criticism,* Vol. 21; *Major Authors and Illustrators for Children and Young Adults; Something about the Author,* Vol. 78; and *Something about the Author Autobiography Series,* Vol. 5.

Kevin Crossley-Holland

1941-

British translator, editor, and author of fiction, poetry, history, nonfiction, radio and television scripts, and libretti for children and adults.

Major works include *The Green Children* (1966), *The Dead Moon and Other Tales from East Anglia and the Fen Country* (1982), *Axe-Age, Wolf-Age: A Selection from the Norse Myths* (1985), *Storm* (1985), *Wulf* (1988).

INTRODUCTION

Well known for his translations and retellings of traditional Norse myths and Anglo-Saxon prose, poetry, and riddles for children and adults, Crossley-Holland also is an established poet who has published nearly twenty books of original poetry for adults. His books for children range from picture books for very young children to riddles and tales suitable for middle graders. A number of the more challenging and emotionally intense books are recommended for a young adult audience. Crossley-Holland has been praised for his devotion to the preservation of traditional legends, myths, and folktales, as well as his ability to bring life to these stories with a strong narrative skill that appeals to modern readers. In a *Twentieth Century Children's Writers* review, Charles Causley set Crossley-Holland apart as an author who "has few rivals as an exponent of the traditional narrative re-told." His ghost story *Storm* was awarded the Carnegie Medal in 1985.

Biographical Information

Born February 7, 1941, in Mursley, Buckinghamshire, England, Kevin John William Crossley-Holland traces much of his interest in the folktales and history of England to the influence of his father, Peter Charles Crossley-Holland, a professor and composer. His mother, the former Joan Mary Cowper, who had been a potter and Doulton designer before her marriage, later conducted social surveys for the Central Office of Information. Although Crossley-Holland's mother encouraged his abiding interest in sports, his father's enthusiasm for folktales and archaeology now permeates Crossley-Holland's writing. Crossley-Holland and his sister Zara (Sally) spent their early childhood in a small cottage called Crosskeys in the Chiltern Hills. The author recalls his father playing his Welsh harp and entertaining the family with bedtime tales of changelings, banshees, pookas and fairies—the same fantastic folk that inhabit Crossley-Holland's stories. With his father, Crossley-Holland explored archaeological sites and gathered artifacts that he displayed in a "museum" in the Crosskeys garden shed. This early interest in Anglo-Saxon history and life set the stage for numerous books on this period. After attending local schools, Crossley-Holland was sent to boarding school at age nine-and-a-half. His Latin master instilled a love of language in him, but Crossley-Holland left preparatory school with little interest in reading. The only book he recalls with great interest is *Our Island Story*, a book about early British history. This book so inspired Crossley-Holland, that, at age eleven, he decided to write his own book: a *History of the World*. He worked on the book during holidays, eventually changing the name and scope of the book to a *History of Britain*. Several chapters were completed before he abandoned the project. After preparatory school, Crossley-Holland studied English language and literature at Oxford and received his degree with honors in 1962. In his early twenties, he began to write poetry and says his father was the first to see the drafts of his early poems. His first major prose effort, also written in his twenties, was an autobiographical and unpublished novel he called *Debendranath*. He wrote about fifty pages of a second novel, then read a poem, "Havelock the Dane," a medieval romance. He thought it was a compelling story that would be better told in prose and set about retelling the tale. *Havelock the Dane*, his first book for children, was published in 1964 when he was twenty-three. He continues to write poetry and prose, translate and edit volumes of poetry and folktales. From 1962-1977 he also worked in publishing at Macmillan and at Gollancz. He was Gregory Fellow in Poetry at the University of Leeds from 1969-1971. He now lectures at universities and has served as poet in residence at several. He has translated the majority of Old English poems, including an untraditional translation of *Beowulf* in 1968. His first wife was Caroline Fendall Thompson with whom he has two sons, Kieran and Dominic. His second wife was Ruth Marris. He and Gillian Cook married in 1982 and have two daughters, Oenone and Eleanor.

Major Works

The Green Children retells a twelfth-century English story of the discovery of two lost children whose skin is green. The sister gradually learns to adapt to England, but the brother dies of homesickness. This story was Crossley-Holland's third book for children. It received the Arts Council of Great Britain award for best children's book published in 1966-68 and has been praised for its evocation of medieval life. *The Dead Moon and Other Tales from East Anglia and the Fen Country* is a collection of eleven retellings, several of which—including *The Callow Pit Coffer* (1969), *The Green Children*, and *The Pedlar of Swaffham* (1972)—Crossley-Holland had published as separate books. Critics cited the lively prose and attention to detail in the stories and recommended the tales for reading aloud to more sophisticated children who would not be daunted by the often chilling plots. Ghosts, witches, boggarts, will-o'-the-wykes and other supernatural creatures haunt these traditional tales. *Axe-Age, Wolf-Age: A Selection from the Norse Myths* is a collection of twenty-two of the thirty-two episodes Crossley-Holland recounted in his book for adults *The Norse Myths* (1980). For the children's version of the myths, Crossley-Holland has written a different glossary and introduction and eliminated the notes. The stories begin with the creation myth, recount the exploits of gods, men, giants, and other mythical beings and culminate with Ragnarok, the Norse day of judgment. *Storm* was the 1986 winner of the British Library Association's Carnegie Medal. This very short original ghost story for seven- to nine-year-olds tells the adventures of Annie, a child who lives in an isolated area of marshland. When her elder sister goes into labor, Annie fetches the doctor with the help of a ghostly horseman. The story is notable for its strong female character, sense of place and drama, and concise narrative. *Wulf* is a revision of the trilogy *The Sea Stranger* (1974), *The Fire-Brother* (1975), and *The Earth Father* (1976), which told the story of a seventh-century boy named Wulf. At age ten, Wulf meets Cedd, a missionary, and adopts Christianity, despite hostility from his family and neighbors. He helps build a church, lives through the plague, and eventually becomes a monk. Praised for its blend of history and drama, *Wulf* illustrates many of Crossley-Holland's strengths as a storyteller and historian. *The Wildman* (1976) is one of Crossley-Holland's most disturbing books. Also a retelling of an East Anglian story, the Wildman is a merman who tells of his capture, imprisonment, and abuse during the reign of Henry II. In the end, the Wildman is alienated from life

in the sea as well as on land. Although praised for its affecting first-person account, the story may not be suitable for sensitive children. Crossley-Holland has collaborated on several children's books, including *Wordhoard: Anglo-Saxon Stories* (1969) with Jill Paton Walsh and *Tales from the Mabinogion* (1991) with Gwyn Thomas. *Tales from the Mabinogion* is a collection of Welsh folktale retellings commissioned by the Welsh Arts Council. Although inherently mysterious and complex, the tales are praised for their lively presentation and lack of bowdlerization.

Awards

Crossley-Holland's *The Green Children* was selected by the Arts Council of Great Britain as the best book for children published in 1966-68. He received the Francis Williams award in 1977 for *The Wildman* and, in 1986, the British Library Association's Carnegie Medal for an outstanding book for children for his ghost story *Storm* (1985). Several of his books of poetry for adults also have been honored.

AUTHOR'S COMMENTARY

Kevin Crossley-Holland

SOURCE: "Kings and Heroes, Horsedealers and Numbskulls," in *Books for Your Children*, Vol. 22, No. 3, Autumn-Winter, 1987, pp. 10-11.

I can see a small square bedroom. It is at the back of a cottage, on the ground floor, and an elder tree taps at its window. In one corner there is a bunk-bed. On the bottom lies a small girl with blue eyes and on the top, her wide-eyed brother. Beside the bunk sits a man, plucking a Welsh harp and telling a tale. The tale of the Cornish midwife who rubbed one eyelid with magic ointment and was able to see the fairies; or the tale of the Irish hump-back who so pleased the little people that they took away his hump; or the tale of the Welsh lady of the lake, or the Manx farmer. . . . How fortunate we were! I wish for my own small daughters, Oenone and Eleanor, the same regular magical grounding, because folk-tales so perfectly satisfy a child's requirements: they have casts of strongly delineated characters and strong and rapid story-lines; they move unselfconsciously between the actual and the fantastic; and they distil experience of the world the child is growing into.

What with kings and heroes, horsedealers and numbskulls, fairies and changelings and imps and boggarts, ghosts and giants, dragons and black dogs, devils and witches, there are well over 5000 different British folk tales—the stories that were passed by word or mouth from generation to generation, and no-one thought to write down until the 19th century.

Some of these tales describe events people believed to have happened, while others are entirely fictional. Dick Whittington, say, as opposed to Jack and the Beanstalk. Some tales, likewise, are not at all old, while others are so ancient and such strange amalgams that it's quite impossible to establish where and when and in what form they were first told. The tale of "The Green Children" for instance, who were found weeping at Woolpit only six miles from my home in Suffolk, was written down by a Cistercian Abbot in the 12th century; but this version, recording an event said to have happened during the author's lifetime, also contains traces of a very much earlier pagan vegetation myth.

But factual and fantastic, old and young, every folk-tale's existence was endangered by the erosion of settled rural communities during the Industrial Revolution, and by the advance of literacy, which naturally worked against the oral tradition of story-telling.

In 1866, the Dublin bookseller and folklorist Patrick Kennedy wrote:

> Taking into consideration the diminishing of our population by want and emigration, and the general diffusion of book learning, such as it is, and the growing taste for rubbishy tales of penny and halfpenny journals we have . . . been haunted with the horrid thought that the memory of tales heard in boyhood would be irrecoverably lost.

This was the threat, and it was countered by the efforts of a succession of highly enterprising men and women. Following the example of the Grimm brothers, and egged on by Sir Walter Scott, they began to make their way into villages and hamlets and isolated farms, hunted out the best story-tellers, won their confidence and wrote down their stories. Indeed, the history of how the 19th century folklorists went about their work, and preserved so fabulous a word-hoard makes a fascinating tale in itself.

In reading, selecting and introducing material for *Folk Tales of the British Isles*, I wanted to illustrate the astounding range and quality of tales collected in the field, to exemplify the work of individual storytellers and collectors, and to show the literary reteller at work: in short as I said in my introduction 'to offer as representative an anthology of the folk-tales of the British Isles as seems possible'.

I worked on the anthology in the British Library, the London Library and at home, and looking now at my long lists in my crabbed writing, see that I set aside between thirty and forty tales for each tale chosen. The notes simply try to answer the questions that occurred to me, and might occur to any reasonably curious mind, as I prepared the volume: who told this story? and when and where? and what do we know about the man/woman who collected it? what are this story's motifs? and where else do they turn up?

To have edited *Folk Tales of the British Isles* satisfied the scholarmanque in me, that part which is fascinated by research, documentation and argument. But beginning with my retelling of *The Green Children,* followed by other single tales and by *The Dead Moon: Tales from East Anglia and the Fen Country* I've also long been absorbed by the question of how the modern writer can approach and retell a traditional tale—and noted how very few writers have managed versions that compare at all favourably with their originals.

Is it proper, for instance, to stick as close as possible to the originals? Or to immerse oneself in an original, then set it aside and write a tale based on it? Or strip the original down and reclothe it? Or step inside a tale and speak out of the mind and mouth of one of its characters? Those and a hundred related questions have been seething in my mind since the day in 1982 when my editor and friend Judith Elliott (who, incidentally, commissioned me to write *Storm*) dared me to write on my own *British Folk Tales.* I knew at once that this was exactly what I wanted to do. For two years I selected material and circled around it, uncertain and wary; and then for two years, I wrote . . .

But it would be misleading for me to represent my *British Folk Tales* as a four year assignment. In truth, it is the book I have been working towards all my life.

And what I hope is that these tales will be shared by generations in a family—that they can be a fruitful point of contact between great-grandparent, grandparent, parent, child. There is a beautiful anonymous Welsh quatrain which says:

> Yr hên wr lwyd o'r cornel
> Gan ei dad a glywodd chwedel,
> A chan ei dad fe glywodd yntau
> Ac ar ei ôl mi gofiais innau.
>
> The grey old man in the corner
> Of his father heard a story
> Which from his father he had heard,
> And after them I have remembered.

Kevin Crossley-Holland

SOURCE: "Restraints and Possibilities," in *Books for Keeps,* No. 65, November, 1990, pp. 18-19.

From time to time, I copy out a brief quotation or aphorism and post it on the wall. Festina lente! (Hurry slowly). In the beginning was the word. Possunt quia possunt videntur (They can because they believe they can). Greening is growing. Solvitur ambulando (Solve it by walking).

I don't know why so many of these sayings are in Latin. Perhaps the very nature of that language gives them a certain resonance and gravitas! Then, there's also another, larger sheet on the wall, headed 'Folk-tale':

> Who was/is the teller?
> Who were/are the audience?
> Who did/does the tale belong to?
> Whose were/are the words?
> What did/does the audience expect of the tale?
> What is the form of folk-tale?

This small article does not directly answer these simple, though far-reaching questions. But while formulating strategies for retelling tales, they have been my constant reminders that I'm working within a tradition, however much that tradition may have changed with the advent of literacy. They remind me that an understanding of how folk-tale works, no matter to what uses one wishes to put it, will always be the best bedrock for the stream of the imagination.

Let me begin with the most unobtrusive roles available to the writer working in the folk-tale tradition: editor and translator (in my case, from English into English). One sometimes comes across an earlier version of a story so plot-perfect and word-perfect that one's instinct is largely to leave well alone. I responded in this way to much of the poet Robert Southey's beautifully-cadenced version of 'The Three Bears' (*The Doctor*, 1837), stepping in only to convert Southey's 'little old Woman' with an 'ugly, dirty head' into Goldilocks and to remove some of his moral asides. Nowadays, we expect our storytellers not to state but reveal truths!

Some of the most haunting of all English folk-tales ('The Dead Moon', 'The Green Mist', 'The Strangers', 'Share' and 'Yallery Brown') were first written down in almost impenetrable Lincoln-shire dialect: Ah! 'n ahl coom o' to'nin' fro' th' au'd wa'ays—that sort of thing! Although these tales, like the splendid gypsy Cinderella-story, 'Mossycoat', were collected from oral tradition, they seem surprisingly at home on the page. This is, I think, because they have all the immediacy, but little of the rough-edged or discursive quality of direct speech, and so with them I have seen the writer's task as one of direct translation from dialect into Standard English.

Now for something much more radical! It's perfectly possible to maintain the traditional swiftness of a tale, which moves from A to Z without digression or so much as a glance at its own navel, while at the same time stepping into it and telling it, as it were, from the inside out.

I've found this a particularly useful device in the case of 'outsider' stories (and there are many in the canon of British folk-tales) where one wants to draw attention to a protagonist's isolation, and allow him to tug at the heartstrings by telling his/her own sad story. Thus a wildman—a relative of the woodwose and merman, unforgettably portrayed by Charles Keeping (*The Wildman*, 1976) —tells us the heartbreaking story of how he is 'only free away from those who are like me, with those who are not like me'. And in 'The Field of Fine Flax', a woman describes her young mother's ostracism from her Orkney village:

She was sixteen when I was born. 'Bonnie,' she murmured, as I fed at her breast. 'Bonnie. Brave.' She was brave and bonnie.

The Northern Lights shook their curtains on the night I was born. Clean and cold and burning.

'And the father,' they said. 'Who is the father? Where is the father?'

She said, 'I cannot tell . . . '

Wind sang in the shell; sun danced in the scarlet cup; dew softened the ear.

Days and questions, questions and days. Her mother, her father, her friends, the minister, the elders.

'I know nothing you do not know,' she said. 'Why do you ask me if you don't believe me?'

'Out,' they said. 'Away. Out of our sight. You and your issue.'

We lived in a bothy by the ocean. One room with no window: it smelt of pine and tar and salt.

In recent months, I have been thinking further about the use of monologue and the possibilities of giving inanimate objects the power of speech. In retelling the story of how the church tower at Dunwich in Suffolk fell into the sea, and the church bell continues to ring under the water (a motif found in several places around the British coast), I've hit on a method of retelling I can best describe as radial. Each constituent of the story (the bell, the bellwoman, the sea-god, the sailor, the cliff, the dead, and so on) has its own brief monologue, or 'spoke', and in aggregate these spokes add up to the full wheel of the story:

I am the night storm. I AM THE STORM.

Down with the bell and down with the belfry. Down on the white head of the bellwoman. Down with the whole church and the tilting graveyard. Down with the cliff itself, cracking and opening and sliding and collapsing. Down with them all into the foam-and-snarl of the sea.

I'm the night-storm and there will be no morning.

I am the morning. I am good morning.

My hands are white as white doves, and healing. Let me lay them on this purple fever. Let them settle on the boat. Nothing lasts for ever. Let me give you back your eyes, fisherman.

What this approach lacks is driving narrative. The effect is as if one were viewing not continuous film, but a slide-show. What is won is atmosphere and, maybe, a sense of the relationship of all created things.

For some reason, I have seldom retold a tale in verse (an exception is the ghost story of 'Old Echo' in my **British Folk Tales**), but of course metrical and rhyming verse is very much part of the folk-tale tradition, and there remains important work to be done in quarrying and translating verse-tales from such anthologies as Sir Walter Scott's *Minstrely of the Scottish Border* (1802-3), which includes the ballad of 'Tam Lin', and F J Child's wondrous *The English and Scottish Popular Ballads* (1882-98) and Sabine Baring-Gould's and H F Sheppard's *Songs and Ballads of the West* (1889-91).

A surprising number of contemporary poets have, however, taken a folk-tale or a motif as a point of departure.

Walter de la Mare, Robert Graves, Anne Sexton, Randall Jarrell, Denise Levertov, Sylvia Plath and many another have turned their attention to Hansel and Gretel, Cinderella, Rapunzel . . . one of my favourites is Stevie Smith's 'The Frog Prince':

> I have been a frog now
> For a hundred years
> And in all this time
> I have not shed many tears,
>
> I am happy, I like the life . . .
>
> But always when I think these thoughts,
> As I sit in my well
> Another thought comes to me and says:
> It is part of the spell
> To be happy
> To work up contentment
> To make much of being a frog
> To fear disenchantment . . .

Most folk-tales are set in a timeless time, but some—usually known as 'historical tales'—take place at a specific moment and in a specific locality. I'm thinking of stories such as 'Dick Whittington' and 'The Pedlar of Swaffham' in which a piece of verifiable historical grit is clothed in fantastic pearl. We know, after all, that there was an historical character called Richard Whittington. He came from Gloucestershire, and was three times Lord Mayor of London, but how on earth did he get mixed up with a wealth-giving cat?

Stories like these seem to call out for full period costume, and that is what I have sometimes given them: an historical setting with much more attention to the details of day-to-day life than one finds in stories collected from the oral tradition. In retelling tales in this quite leisurely (up to 5000 or 6000 words) way, I am recognising that while I write my tales with keen awareness of how they will sound, and in the hope that they will be shared by parent or grandparent and child, they are firstly literary compositions.

At the beginning of the nineteenth century, eighty per cent of the population of Britain lived in villages, hamlets and isolated farms. Now, eighty per cent live in cities and towns. Is there a danger that today's urban children may find the experience of folk-tale somewhat remote because their contexts are so regularly rural? And if so, what is the writer to do about it?

In telling the Beauty-and-the-Beast tale known as **The Small-Tooth Dog,** I decided to transplant the story into the backstreets of some city, and begin with an attempted mugging. The intended victim, Mr Markham, is saved by the intervention of a big brindled dog:

> 'You've saved me a packet,' said Mr Markham, clasping a hand over the inner pocket of his jacket. 'I've got the week's takings in here. More than a thousands pounds.'
>
> 'I know,' said the dog.

Mr Markham offers the dog his 'most precious possession', but the dog declines various fabulous gifts in favour of Mr Markham's daughter!

> 'Me?' cried Corinna. 'Not likely!'
>
> 'He's not an ordinary dog,' said Mr Markham.
>
> 'You're daft as a brush,' said Corinna.
>
> 'You'll see,' said her father. 'He's waiting outside the door.'
>
> 'Crazy!' said Corinna.

I greatly enjoyed updating this tale; I think there is a good argument for doing so; and I think it likely that I shall attempt to do the same with other folk-tales.

I wish I could write about many other opportunities offered by folk-tale: I'm fascinated by unconsidered trifles—little tales no more than a few sentences long—and like to work them up into short, short stories; I'm interested by the tale-within-a-tale (a device I used in 'Sea-Woman' in **British Folk Tales**) in which one can implicitly comment on the form one is using; I'm concerned by sexual stereotypes, and the legitimacy of changing a tale's characters or plot; and this year, I've turned the tale of 'The Green Children' into the libretto of an opera for children by Nicola LeFanu . . .

But let me end, rather, by suggesting a successful retelling depends not so much on the form—for it is apparent that retellings in many forms can be successful—as on the writer's depth of understanding and use of language. The writer working with folk-tale has access to an inherited word-bank, and needs to take account of the fact that he is working within a great tradition, but, for all that, his story must be told in language that is keen, quick, shining, resonant and his own. Et nova et vetera! Both new and old. The writer asks himself: what does this story mean? And how am I to recast it? And in the end, the quality of his perceptions and narratives is defined by the very words that express them.

TITLE COMMENTARY

📖 *HAVELOK THE DANE* (1964)

The Junior Bookshelf

SOURCE: A review of *Havelock the Dane,* in *The Junior Bookshelf,* Vol. 28, No. 5, November, 1964, pp. 307-08.

Like *The Winter's Tale* many of the Viking legends have a symmetry and balance which are the whole basis of a well-told tale. Havelock, rightful King of Denmark, has to flee his country to escape his villainous regent, Lord Godard. Goldborough, rightfully Queen of England, is misused by her regent, Lord Godric. Havelock, having by accident made himself useful in Godric's household, is fortuitously married to Goldborough as a last indignity from Godric. Inevitably, Havelock returns to Denmark, finds friends, and deposes Godard. In time he leads an expedition against Godric and reinstates Goldborough. They live alternate years in England and Denmark and have fifteen children. For good measure Havelock founds Grimsby in commemoration of his early benefactor. What more can a reader ask, except the accurate and lively, colourful, dramatic transcription of the thirteenth century narrative romance by a youthful scholar—and, of course, Brian Wildsmith's drawings.

Kirkus Reviews

SOURCE: A review of *Havelok the Dane*, in *Kirkus Reviews*, Vol. XXXIII, No. 13, July 1, 1965, p. 628.

The story is based on a legend that started in Lincolnshire and was first written down in the 13th century. Havelok, the child ruler of Denmark, was imprisoned and almost murdered by his steward, but escaped to England where he lived for 19 years and married Goldborough, who, similarly, had been removed from the English throne by her Regent. She accompanied Havelok to Denmark, where he regained his kingship in a bloodless battle, and the two then returned to England where Goldborough also won her due. The retelling has been told with great attention to detail about medieval mores, and offers a varied collection of the minor characters and customs that must have typified the period. This approach has its weaknesses though, especially since there has been no attempt to inject humor into the story: the speech sometimes seems too casual; mystic events may appear to be illogical and out of place; battle descriptions in this familiar casing become grim and repulsive instead of heroic. It is, however, a scholarly recreation and offers both adventure and romance. Decorations by Brian Wildsmith.

Ethna Sheehan

SOURCE: A review of *Havelok the Dane*, in *The New York Times Book Review*, November 14, 1965, pp. 66-7.

The legend of **Havelok the Dane** is taken from a medieval English verse romance. Here again we have a robust adventure story, with magical overtones. A dual plot intertwines the fates of Havelok and Princess Goldborough of England, both of whom have been deprived of their kingdoms by treacherous regents. How the young people fall in love and set about regaining their respective thrones has been retold with drama, horror and fun. The author has carefully developed Havelok's likable personality and Goldborough's spirited nature. The atmosphere has been indifferently evoked, yet there are amusing echoes of the slapstick humor reminiscent of certain types of medieval plays. Sometimes old saws and rhymes are also worked into the narrative with pleasing effect. Taken as a whole, **Havelok the Dane** is a rousing book, introducing a hero all too unfamiliar today.

Ethel L. Heins

SOURCE: A review of *Havelock the Dane*, in *The Horn Book Magazine*, Vol. XLII, No. 1, February, 1966, p. 51.

The story of Havelok the Dane, based on legendary material from the Viking period and put into metrical form in the thirteenth century, is famous in English literary history. More like a folk story than one of the great medieval romances, it is dominated by the spirit of adventure rather than by the conventions of courtly love; and its bluff realism gave it a wide popular appeal. Before the King of Denmark died he designated Lord Godard to be steward until his son, Prince Havelok, should come of age. But treacherous Godard tried to kill the boy, who, helped by Grim the fisherman and his faithful family, escaped over the North Sea to England. There, working as a kitchen servant, Havelok met the beautiful Princess Goldborough, who, coincidentally, had been mistreated by her dead father's cruel regent. Havelok, with Goldborough, journeyed to Denmark; at the head of a rejoicing army he liberated the Danes and finally, returning to England, vanquished the traitor and ended another rule of terror. This is a tale of ambition, bloody murder, loyalty, love, and the triumph of freedom over tyranny; the author has retold the original, rather long-winded narrative in a colorful, vigorous manner. Marion Garthwaite used the same legend as the basis for *The Locked Crowns*.

KING HORN (1965)

The Junior Bookshelf

SOURCE: A review of *King Horn*, in *The Junior Bookshelf*, Vol. 29, No. 6, December, 1965, p. 357.

King Horn is the dramatic retelling of a Medieval "lay" by an author who is an expert on the life and times of the Kingdoms of this land at the time of the Middle Ages. This is a thrilling adventure of a young prince's escape from the barbarous Saracens and his subsequent fight to recapture his kingdom from their grasp.

There have been many other such tales of devotion and courage, of battles fought for the love of a fair King's daughter; but few have been retold with such depth and feeling, such quiet dignity and colourful background as this fascinating tale.

It is a book to be appreciated by older children for its delicate traces of the development of the Prince Horn from a frightened boy to a mighty King returning to take possession of a land that is rightly his. I particularly liked the author's use of the italic to express the thoughts of the various characters. This gave the book a maturity of feeling not usually found in tales for young people.

A book to be firmly recommended to all older children, as a gripping historical romance; a book beautifully written and delightfully illustrated by Charles Keeping, and one that any reader will not be able to leave until it is finished.

Margery Fisher

SOURCE: A review of *King Horn,* in *Growing Point,* Vol. 4, No. 7, January, 1966, p. 636.

The medieval poem **King Horn** [offers] magic and knightly conduct together, a mixture of Saracens and magic rings, an England to be found in the history book and another which belongs to Fairyland. Kevin Crossley-Holland uses racy, colloquial modern prose, which somehow by its very tone solves the problem of making the young prince and his comrades believable without robbing them of their vaguely medieval glamour. It is a style well suited also to the active elements of the story—the Saracen invasion of the kingdom of Suddenesse, the descriptions of hawking, Horn's fight with the Goliath.

> As the army continued its drive inland, Horn and Athulf were appalled by what they saw: ploughshares wantonly destroyed, rusting in the fields; the fields themselves scorched and barren; and houses which were no more than craggy mounds of stone. Not a single church or monastery remained intact; they had been gutted by fire, reduced to ruins.

The story of Horn is one of the liveliest and most exciting of medieval poems, and I think the way the writer has chosen to render it has given it a very immediate quality—something less than bardic but still belonging to the hall and the listening crowd. Its setting could be anywhere on the map but its world is very obviously that of an idealised Middle Ages, and Keeping's strong, direct drawings bear this out.

Michael G. deRuvo

SOURCE: A review of *King Horn,* in *Library Journal,* Vol. 91, No. 18, October 15, 1966, p. 5248.

This is a retelling of a folk poem of 13th-century Britain. Young Prince Horn, his father slain, his country desecrated and conquered by the Saracens, escapes with two friends to the kingdom of Westernesse (Ireland). His sojourn there, his romantic entanglement, banishment, and eventual return to his princess and his homeland are interestingly narrated to capture the flavor of the era. Fine drawings complement this fast-paced, easy-reading story which will be especially satisfying to boys wanting books about daring knights in armor and heroes in battle and in love.

Zena Sutherland

SOURCE: A review of *King Horn,* in *Bulletin of the Center for Children's Books,* Vol. 20, No. 4, December, 1966, p. 56.

A story set in England and Ireland in the thirteenth century, and based on a folk-poem. Fifteen-year-old Prince Horn and two friends escape when invading Saracens kill the king. The boys take refuge in a neighboring kingdom, keeping their identity secret. Several years later, Horn is knighted, but his host, King Aylmer, sends the young man away when his love for the princess is discovered. After a series of adventures, Horn slays the man who had killed his father, reveals his status, and weds the princess. The story is full of action and of vivid details of the medieval background. It is weakened by the dialogue, which often has a staccato quality or an obtrusively modern quality.

THE GREEN CHILDREN (1966)

Margery Fisher

SOURCE: A review of *The Green Children,* in *Growing Point,* Vol. 5, No. 5, November, 1966, p. 791.

The Green Children is in length and format a picture book for young children . . . , but the unique character of text and illustrations put the book into a far wider sphere than that of reading aloud to the very young (though they will certainly enjoy the experience too). This is a legend, written down in early Norman times but current long before, of a boy and girl found in a chalk pit whose bodies and faces were green and who were obviously not of this world. The author sets his version of the story in Stephen's England, with churls working in the field and a red-faced, jovial Lord of the Manor who helps the children to become acclimatised. Though there is nothing solemn about the book, it is intensely moving. The author's unerring choice of words suggests antiquity, and Margaret Gordon has followed his lead with pictures so rich and astonishing in colour and form that they help belief by their very strangeness.

Kirkus Reviews

SOURCE: A review of *The Green Children,* in *Kirkus Reviews,* Vol. XXXVI, No. 9, May 1, 1968, p. 507.

Two green children coming from within the earth—an old story developed with appreciable dignity and cultivation of distant time and place, concluded with open-end alternatives. The reader first shares their unexplained appearance with the English villagers, then learns with them the green children's version as the boy and girl learn English. The boy dies of homesickness; the girl survives, turns fairer gradually, even marries, but never stops looking for the lost entrance to her other world. Some jaunty illustrations characterize the villagers but the children just look sickly in phosphorescent skin tones—an unfortunate detraction from an otherwise delicate rendering.

Alice Low

SOURCE: A review of *The Green Children,* in *The New York Times Book Review,* May 5, 1968, p. 47.

Though **The Green Children** is adapted from a 12th century English tale and peppered with unfamiliar words, modern children who give it a chance should take to it. The two lost green strangers found huddled in Sir Richard de Caine's wolfpit behave like visitors from another planet. They don't speak English, won't eat Sir Richard's food, and are blinded by the sunlight. Since nobody knows where they came from, they stay on at the manor house. The green boy dies of homesickness but the green girl adapts—outwardly. She learns English (relating how she strayed from her subterranean homeland), eats earth food, loses her greenish tinge, and eventually marries. Yet she never gives up searching for home. A fine tale, told with authority and feeling. It is a pity that the illustrations lack the grace and authenticity of the text.

Zena Sutherland

SOURCE: A review of *The Green Children*, in *Saturday Review*, Vol. LI, No. 19, May 11, 1968, p. 38.

First written down 700 years ago, this folk legend is about the little people who lived below the earth. "It is the twelfth century, time of eclipses and miracles . . . " and a small company of reapers find two children in a pit, strange children who cannot understand the language of England, and who are green from head to toe. Taken in by the lord of the manor, the children are comforted. Although the boy languishes and dies, the girl grows up and weds a mortal. The picture book format affords a splendid opportunity for the riotously vernal illustrations, but it is less fitting for the age group that can understand the vocabulary.

Elinor Cullen

SOURCE: A review of *The Green Children*, in *Library Journal*, Vol. 93, No. 13, July, 1968, p. 2727.

The idea of two emerald green little children suddenly popping out of the ground and refusing to eat anything but green vegetables should be instantly appealing to the young. Beyond that, this adaptation of a medieval English tale is a little too mystifying; it offers only a casual explanation of the children's strange origin and an inconclusive ending. The narration carries a strong sense of the period, however, and the real and fantastic are very well integrated. The illustrations are bright, flat, posterish, but neither they nor the text tell a satisfyingly complete story.

📖 *THE CALLOW PIT COFFER* (1968)

V. A. Bradshaw

SOURCE: A review of *The Callow Pit Coffer*, in *Children's Book News*, London, Vol. 3, No. 6, November-December, 1968, p. 317.

An East Anglian folk legend in which two sons who set out to recover a chest of gold from a deep pond, the feared Callow Pit, are defeated by supernatural forces. The great beauty of the story is in the style and language. The coffer links the villagers in desire and fear and awe, and this link is represented in the skilful interlocking of comments that bring together the thoughts of different people. The illustrations capture perfectly the varied settings and moods in sketches that are sometimes black and uncompromising, sometimes delicate. (It is a pity that the opacity of the paper is so poor; shadows of the pictures show through the page, making it difficult to read the text, which is printed in sepia.) Some of the vocabulary is outside the range of the youngest reader, and the brief, unhelpful glossary does nothing to alleviate the situation. Nevertheless, it is a book from which some children will derive much pleasure.

The Junior Bookshelf

SOURCE: A review of *The Callow Pit Coffer*, in *The Junior Bookshelf*, Vol. 33, No. 2, April, 1969, pp. 105-06.

This is splendidly spine-chilling twelfth-century East Anglican folklore, most imaginatively told. Poetry is never far away in the alliteration, the echoes and the repetition, creating so well the sense of a small frightened village community to which the story returns at each crisis, the newly-weds, the mysterious idiot and the two brave young men who dare to challenge the sinister Callow Pit's secret. The pit wins back its treasure coffer, and they are fortunate to return with their lives and the massive ring of the coffer, still visible on the church door to witness to the truth of the legend. Seldom have illustrations been a closer part of a story: the black elipse of the Callow Pit dominates the pages, surrounded by stark solid tree-skeletons which contrast so well with the delicate tangle of brambles in the foreground.

Paul Heins

SOURCE: A review of *The Callow Pit Coffer*, in *The Horn Book Magazine*, Vol. XLV, No. 3, June, 1969, p. 302.

According to the author's note, the story "was written down by John Glyde in the *Norfolk Garland* (1872). . . . But this tale is age old. . . ." Set—in the present version—in the reign of King Stephen, it tells of a low-lying black pool located at a crossroad and said to be haunted. Despite the warning of Thor, an old peasant, one night Jakke and Keto, two of his sons, borrowed a ladder from the nearby manor, bridged the pool, probed its waters with an iron-hooked staff, and brought to the surface "a dripping, crusted, iron" chest. When Keto "shouted gaily: We've got it, we've got it; the devil himself can't get it from us now," "a hideous black hand" and "a huge black arm" yanked the chest back. All that was left to the brothers for their pains was a "massive iron ring." The story is simply and vividly told, and suggests the eerie horror of some of the episodes in *Beowulf*. There are spots of humor, and the tale ends quietly but ironically. The brown-

and-white drawings present effectively the naïve emotions of the villagers and dramatize the stark and forbidding environment of the callow pool. Excellent for reading aloud.

Zena Sutherland

SOURCE: A review of *The Callow Pit Coffer,* in *Bulletin of the Center for Children's Books,* Vol. 23, No. 4, December, 1969, p. 58.

First published in England, a retelling of an old folk tale of feudal times. The three sons of the old cottar, Thor, have been told to keep away from a dark, brooding pool in the gloomy hollow. Mysterious and haunted, people said, and concealing in its dangerous depths a coffer filled with treasure. The two older brothers bravely go to the pit and bring up the coffer, but a huge hand rises up from the water and pulls it down, leaving in their possession only the huge iron ring with which they had hooked the chest. Nailed to the church door, the ring becomes an attraction that brings visitors and wealth to the town, so the courage of the brothers has not been wasted. Notes on the origin of the tale and on its historical background are given in a brief epilogue; an eight-entry glossary is appended. The illustrations are spare and stylized; the story is told with considerable artistry, with a storyteller's flow and cadence and a restrained blending of natural and supernatural.

WORDHOARD: ANGLO-SAXON STORIES (with Jill Paton Walsh, 1969)

The Junior Bookshelf

SOURCE: A review of *Wordhoard,* in *The Junior Bookshelf,* Vol. 33, No. 5, October, 1969, p. 321.

Both authors have already contributed to the increasing number of stories for children re-written from Anglo-Saxon sources too long left untapped (at least directly) except for more mature students. The eight stories here included consist of The Woodwose, Caedmon. Asser's Book, Leof's Leavetaking, The Horseman, The Childmaster, Thurkell the Tall, and The Eye of the Hurricane, a group as varied as they are intriguing. Some savagery is inevitable from savage times, but the influences of civilisation and religion are always present both as regards content and origin. The style is clear and the pace rapid, and there is always enough dialogue to maintain interest and attention. It is hardly necessary to add that the book is printed in a style befitting the care taken over its contents.

Paul Heins

SOURCE: A review of *Wordhoard: Anglo-Saxon Stories,* in *The Horn Book Magazine,* Vol. XLV, No. 6, December, 1969, p. 680.

Deeply absorbed in Anglo-Saxon history and literature, the authors have each written four stories. Some are focused on actual people—Bede and Caedmon, Alfred and Asser, Harold and William the Conqueror. Others are suggested by the poetry and prose of the era. Each one deals with a typical but crucial situation. *The Horseman* tells of a warrior who deserted his leader, Byrhtnoth, at the battle of Maldon instead of dying with him. "Thurkell the Tall" tells of a Viking who was converted to Christianity by the heroic, but passive, resistance and martyrdom of Alfig, Archbishop of Canterbury. In *Leof's Leavetaking* are interwoven situations and quotations from Anglo-Saxon poetry: from the elegies and from "The Phoenix." And in "The Childmaster," a young boy-singer learns Latin from Ælfric from a text—"Colloquy"—that is still extant. The stories, skillfully told and subtle in construction, form a unified historical sequence, and bring to life the rigorous splendors of the Old English period. The occasional Anglo-Saxon expressions add zest to, rather than impede, the flow of the prose.

Bruce L. MacDuffie

SOURCE: A review of *Wordhoard: Anglo-Saxon Stories,* in *School Library Journal,* Vol. 16, No. 6, February, 1970, pp. 91-2.

The first successful attempt to present a sensitive vision of Anglo-Saxon life to teens. Each of the eight stories (four by Walsh, four by Crossley-Holland) is poignant, and has a literary value not dependent on its genre; for that reason, the stories present an effective picture of "the way it was" in England a thousand years ago. Miss Walsh's stories include: an account of the early days after Anglo-Saxon victory when Latin-Celts were still to be found in the nearby hills; another of an Anglo-Saxon monastery as seen through the eyes of a young boy struggling with the difficult regimen of the novitiate; and, in "Thurkell the Tall," a beautiful depiction of the Viking terrors as seen by a captured Anglo-Saxon bishop who, by his exemplary courage, converted the Viking chief. Mr. Crossley-Holland's most striking story is "The Eye of the Hurricane," about the death of Harold Hardrada, last king of the Saxons, whose entire life is beautifully fleshed out in a few pages by the skillful use of flashback. Teachers and librarians now have the means to bring the Anglo-Saxon experience alive for today's youth through stories worth having simply for themselves.

STORM AND OTHER OLD ENGLISH RIDDLES (translated by Crossley-Holland, 1970)

Kirkus Reviews

SOURCE: A review of *Storm and Other Old English Riddles,* in *Kirkus Reviews,* Vol. XXXVIII, No. 17, September 1, 1970, p. 968.

"On the way a miracle: water become bone." This is one of 36 riddles translated by Kevin Crossley-Holland from the 10th century Exeter Book. Genuinely puzzling, they characterize everyday things (fire, bread, river) as well as less familiar objects (chalice, bellows) and Christian concerns (the Bible, body and soul). Cross-hatched illustrations with enigmatic clues accompany almost all of them; possible answers and explanations where needed are in the back. We guessed fourteen (the one above is "ice"), and might have deciphered twelve more with time, but ten require an uncommon familiarity with Old English life and one of these is virtually impossible—the author posits "a one-eyed seller of onions" but we're still unconvinced. This is as competent as his earlier works (**The Green Children, The Callow Pit Coffer, Wordhoard,** et al.) but not as likely to find an audience. Only the most ambitious can weather this Storm.

Paul Heins

SOURCE: A review of *Storm and Other Old English Riddles,* in *The Horn Book Magazine,* Vol. XLVI, No. 5, October, 1970, pp. 484-85.

Thirty-six of the ninety-six riddles found in the Exeter Book, one of the few extant Anglo-Saxon manuscripts, have been transformed into modern poems. The subjects of the riddles were drawn from nature and from social life, and the riddles themselves often embody either a pagan or a Christian attitude towards life. In many of the poems "the object itself speaks, describing itself, and then asks the listener, or reader, to guess its name." For example: "My head was hammered into shape . . . " begins the riddle of the key, and "My abode's by no means silent, / but I am not loud-mouthed . . . " reveals the fish in the river. Mead and swan, iceberg and Bible, oyster and plough are among the things hidden in the elaborated kennings of the Old English poetry. The collection closes with "Storm," who not only shakes "halls / and houses . . . " and drives "the flint-grey rollers / to the shore . . . " but is at the same time a servant of the Lord of creation. The introduction contains an excellent discussion of the universality of riddling, and skillfully, but simply, sets the poems in their context of Anglo-Saxon history and culture. Solutions and Comments complete the volume, which is elegant in format. Significant and pleasing black-and-white line drawings accompany most of the poems.

Elizabeth Maslen

SOURCE: "Riddles," in *Encounter,* Vol. 37, No. 3, September, 1971, pp. 81-2.

The old english verse riddles present more than the usual problems of translation—on the one hand the original text is often obscure, if not downright corrupt; on the other, the solutions are not given in the Exeter book and scholars have exercised considerable ingenuity in finding possible answers, which now have an aura of authority about them. Take this one:

*A creature came shuffling where there sat
many wise men in the meeting-place.
He had two ears and only one eye,
he had two feet and twelve hundred heads,
a back, two hands, and a belly,
two shoulders and sides, a neck,
and two arms. Now tell me his name*

The usual solution is inspired, if desperate—a one-eyed seller of onions.

To cut through such tangles, retain a hint of the Old English alliterative line, and show the variety and appeal of subject matter and mood is quite a feat. The riddles range from heroic to homely; from poems where the solution concerns the poet less than the delights of description, to simple joke or trick verses; from sensitive accounts of suffering and triumph to cheeky sexuality. Kevin Crossley-Holland has been very successful with a wide selection of these poems. He uses alliteration imaginatively, varies pace—it would be impossible to follow the Old English slavishly in this, so much has the character of the language changed—and brings out the vitality and variety. His own enjoyment is clear, and echoes the enjoyment of Anglo-Saxon writer and compiler alike. It is, after all, rather remarkable that a body of poetry that is not specifically Christian should have been included in a predominantly religious collection; Anglo-Saxon church censorship, it seems, was not entirely fun-killing, and the riddles certainly dispel the popular notion of stern Germanic peoples drinking, raping, burning and worshipping in a relentlessly serious-minded fashion.

The translation of the "Storm" riddle is particularly satisfying, capturing the drama and violent action. One passage runs:

*Then the ship is filled
With the yells of sailors; the cliffs quietly
Abide the ocean's froth and fury
Lashing waves, racing rollers
That smash against stone*

I like the recurrent *I,* subtly reminding one of the original alliterative line. A comparison with Paull F. Baum's version (*Anglo-Saxon Riddles of the Exeter Book,* Duke University Press) of the last lines—"high the violence Crowds on the headlands"—shows the poet scoring over the conscientious translator in conveying the tone of the original.

There are one or two less happy moments: for instance, in "Swallows or Midges" the Anglo-Saxon writer managed, by skilful phrasing, an uncharacteristic sequence of open syllables, to give an airy lightness to the subect (Old English is usually a slow-moving deliberate language), and it seems to me that the translation misses this. One regrets, too, not having an interpretation of the longer "Horn" riddle with its haunting and ambiguous mixture of exultation and bitterness. But on the whole this selection gives us the poetry, the teasing charm and above all the pleasure of the riddles—which is no small achievement.

Alexander Taylor

SOURCE: A review of *Storm,* in *Children's Literature,* Vol. 3, 1974, pp. 199-200.

Kevin Crossley-Holland has translated thirty-six Anglo-Saxon riddles from the *Exeter Book* for his fine collection *Storm*. These are excellent translations. Mr. Crossley-Holland keeps the flavor of the four stress alliterative Anglo-Saxon line, but does not become a slave to it. Thus the poems read as poems, rather than translations.

> I saw a strange creature,
> a bright ship of the air beautifully adorned,
> bearing away plunder between her horns,
> fetching it home from a foray.
> She was minded to build a bower in her stronghold,
> and construct it with cunning if she could do so.
> But then a mighty creature appeared over the
>   mountain
> whose face is familiar to all dwellers on earth;
> he seized on his treasure and sent home the
>   wanderer
> much against her will; she went westward
> harbouring hostility, hastening forth.
> Dust lifted to heaven; dew fell on the earth,
> night fled hence; and no man knew
> thereafter, where that strange creature went.

The delight in riddles is ageless. Mr. Crossley-Holland's introduction to the book is lucid and interesting and provides teen-age readers just enough background for understanding and enjoying the form and content of Anglo-Saxon poetry. A "Solutions and Comments" section at the end of the book is a fine example of intelligent literary and historical scholarship which should be made more available in texts for young people. The excellent illustrations by Miles Thistlethwaite give clues to the riddles—aids but not answers. One might say that they themselves are pictorial riddles, and as such they are a fitting complement to the text.

THE PEDLAR OF SWAFFHAM (1971)

Paul Heins

SOURCE: A review of *The Pedlar of Swaffham,* in *The Horn Book Magazine,* Vol. XLVII, No. 6, December, 1971, p. 607.

Based on Norfolk, or East Anglian, legendry, the story is more extensive than the simple narrative found in Joseph Jacobs' *More English Fairy Stories*. The terse narrative about the pedlar who in a dream was advised to journey from Swaffham to London Bridge where "he should hear joyful news" has been happily expanded. The pedlar is given a name—John Chapman—as are the members of his family: Cateryne, his wife; Margaret, Hue, and Dominic, his children; and when he leaves for London, he is accompanied by his mastiff, who "thumped the ground with his tail" while "'Come back,' called little Dominic." The retelling has the rich earthiness and the wholesome humor of

a story by Chaucer; and the pure white pages of the handsome volume form a perfect background for the text as well as for the illustrations, which are found on most of the pages. Although the line drawings are filled with all the colors of the spectrum—rich blue, muted red, mustard yellow, and medium green predominate. Perspective and proportion are sacrificed for medieval picturesqueness while farmyard and marketplace, birds and cattle and men, and Gothic arches and machicolations are joyously depicted to go along with a joyous story.

Nash K. Burger

SOURCE: A review of *The Pedlar of Swaffham,* in *The New York Times Book Review,* December 19, 1971, p. 8.

Like most folk tales (indeed, like history itself) *The Pedlar of Swaffham* exists in several versions. Kevin Crossley-Holland has retold one of the longer, more interesting ones: more characters, more incidents, more details of medieval English life.

It seems that a worthy, hardworking pedlar at Swaffham in Norfolk, some 100 miles northeast of London, had a dream in which he was told to go down to London, to London Bridge, where something good would happen to him. After the dream was repeated and the pedlar conferred with his wife and the village priest, he set out with his dog for London. The trip itself was quite an adventure; London was a kaleidoscope of strange sights and sounds and folk very different from those at Swaffham. And, sure enough, something good happened (a pot of gold in William Stobbs's version, *two* pots of gold in the Crossley-Holland).

There is enough texture in the Crossley-Holland narrative (and enough life in Margaret Gordon's cheerful, colorful, medieval-type drawings) to make the pedlar, his wife and family, the village priest and other characters come alive. In a phrase, a bit of dialogue, the workaday activities, beliefs and recreations of rural and city folk are amusingly revealed.

It is a teeming, picturesque world that recalls the somewhat earlier one of Geoffrey Chaucer; Swaffham's pedlar, indeed, would have been quite at home with Chaucer's pilgrims, who set out from London for Becket's shrine at Canterbury. In fact, there is mention in Crossley-Holland's story of that other English shrine not far from Swaffham and second only to Canterbury as a place of pilgrimage, the shrine of Our Lady at Walsingham. There is suspense in this well-told version of an old legend, especially in the matter of the second pot of gold; but the reader is not surprised that the good-hearted pedlar shares his fortune with fellow villagers and makes possible the rebuilding of the Swaffham church.

Edward Hudson

SOURCE: A review of *The Pedlar of Swaffham,* in *Children's Book Review,* Vol. II, No. 2, April, 1972, p. 46.

All too rarely one comes across a book which one would like to be assured would always be available for future generations of children to read. Down the ages from *Divine Songs* to *Figgie Hobbin* each era has produced its writers and its handful of titles for posterity and so a heritage of literature is built up. But here is part of our historical heritage in this re-told folk tale from the fifteenth century which could perhaps be described as a Canterbury Tale in reverse.

From the village of Swaffham in East Anglia comes the pedlar John Chapman on a pilgrimage to London Bridge, guided only by instructions in a recurring dream that 'good will come of it'. Surviving what was in those days a long and perilous journey, he finally reaches his goal only to find that nothing wonderful happens. Nothing, that is, until a shopkeeper relates how he had dreamed about a pedlar in Swaffham having a pot of gold buried in his garden. The pedlar returns home immediately not only finding one but two pots of gold buried there. Much of this is given to the village priest to enable the church to be rebuilt. There are relics still in existence in the church to vouch for the authenticity of the story.

A great deal is owed to Kevin Crossley-Holland, whose knowledge of Anglo Saxon and the Chaucerian age in particular, have enabled him to present in this story such a vivid picture of life as it must have been in those times. Margaret Gordon, who collaborated with him in the illustrations for another outstanding book—*The Green Children*—has, with her paintings based on illustrations of the period, helped to portray visually the story and the period.

Patricia Jean Cianciolo

SOURCE: "The Imaginative World: The Pedlar of Swaffham," in *Picture Books for Children,* second edition, American Library Association, 1981, pp. 161-62.

Because of a persistent recurring dream, John Chapman, a pedlar from Swaffham, went to London Bridge where he waited for three days from dawn to dusk, hoping to meet someone who would lead him to a fortune. When Chapman told a shopkeeper why he was waiting at the bridge, the shopkeeper's response was that only fools follow their dreams. He told the pedlar that the night before he dreamed there was a pot of gold buried by a hawthorn tree in a garden which belonged to a pedlar in a place called Swaffham. Chapman returned home and found the treasure buried where the shopkeeper dreamed it was. Keeping only enough money to care for his family's needs and to buy a strip of land, Chapman gave the rest of the gold to the parish priest to build a new church so that everyone in Swaffham could share in the treasure. Portions of that church can be seen in Swaffham today; fragments of John Chapman's chair and the old stained-glass window portraying the pedlar, his wife, and three children also remain. The atmosphere of fifteenth-century England is vividly reflected in the book's full-color illustrations. Could be compared with *The Treasure* by Uri Shulevitz.

THE RAIN-GIVER (1972)

Alan Brownjohn

SOURCE: "Wastes," in *New Statesman,* Vol. 84, No. 2167, September 29, 1972, pp. 440-41.

Some of the poems in Kevin Crossley-Holland's first volume, ('Our Love's', 'The Wall', 'Suggestions') recall the Anglo-Saxon riddles he translated scrupulously and vividly in *Storm*. This kind of translator's attentiveness and honesty has come over effectively into both the personal and the landscape poems in *The Rain-Giver:* a craftsman's concern to get it right, emotionally as well as descriptively. The action of places on people is treated even more quietly here than in Crichton Smith's Scotland and Thomas's Wales, occasionally in too received a style. But the clear and careful organisation of these poems makes for a final technical sureness that lifts them into something better. . . .

The personal poems (including 'My Son', 'Sober as a Judge') are lucid and honest. One wishes, though, for more of the scope, boldness and imaginative projection that comes out when an original method of treatment, or simply an interesting external subject, has really absorbed him.

Marcus Crouch

SOURCE: A review of *The Rain-Giver,* in *The School Librarian,* Vol. 21, No. 1, March, 1973, p. 52.

Kevin Crossley-Holland's formidable reputation depends largely on his sensitive and relevant versions of Anglo-Saxon poetry and a little less on a few disturbing texts for picture-books. All the indications are of a writer who looks backwards into the remote past. His first book of original verse corrects this partial impression. Here is a poet whose technique is much influenced by the patterns and alliterations of pre-Conquest English, but whose interests and sympathies are engaged with contemporary concerns. Whether writing of intimate personal problems, painting miniature East Coast landscapes, or commenting sardonically on current follies, he is always sensitive and crystal clear. This is not a book for the young, except in the sense that all good verse springs from a candid vision, but it may well commend itself to older children who can identify with his strong harsh vision.

PIECES OF LAND: JOURNEYS TO EIGHT ISLANDS (1972)

Angus Calder

SOURCE: "Dreams of Islands," in *New Statesman,* Vol. 84, No. 2169, October 13, 1972, pp. 516-17.

It is one of Kevin Crossley-Holland's several strengths as a writer that he is not afraid of seeming corny. This well-illustrated and absorbing book gives vivid impressions of eight of the small islands round Britain's coasts. It explores their histories with scholarly care; it shows, without flattery, what sorts of people live in them; and, with sensible concern, it thinks about their futures. But why worry? Why go there, anyway? Mr Crossley-Holland is not abashed to admit to feeling the same 'need to escape' which Yeats projected towards Innisfree, and which all our bother about pollution has now made rather more excusable. He appears to be entirely honest, and his attitudes, well expressed, have representative status.

He has this dream of 'a simple life, a practical life, a community life, a life of writing words that would have some use'. But he knows perfectly well that it wouldn't work for him, and before long he is chiding the Orkney poet George Mackay Brown—a man rooted in his own quiet place, where its people greatly esteem him—for his refusal to travel south of Berwick. Islands don't in fact solve any problems for us; they just pose them for their own inhabitants.

However, on his chosen resorts, Mr Crossley-Holland has achieved what he calls 'communion with nature' (it doesn't sound affected, just rather commonplace) and has been able to experience and express—in words, perhaps, not sufficiently far from Eliot's own—that intersection of time with the timeless which was set up for us in *Four Quartets*. In short, he offers for our inspection one typical product of our own confused habitat of mind and feeling—that cautious, dry sort of mysticism which suits a culture like ours, so worldly-wise, so clever, so frightened by the present.

We're not too far, however, from the classic Japanese love of old things and of places haunted by a violent past. Since Mr Crossley-Holland fits in poems, I found myself reminded of that great pedestrian Basho, organising his travelogue to make a setting for his *haiku*. Mr Crossley-Holland's poetry doesn't work so well, perhaps because a highly-concentrated, formal sort like *haiku* is in much less danger than is free verse of seeming pallid beside good prose. And the prose of *Pieces of Land* is good. It rises easily to clear, cool, set-piece descriptions of high seas and rugged places, and reveals an excellent ear for dialect.

The little island cultures which he catches in the act of perishing seem to echo the death of confidence within the wider British culture to which they relate. If Glasgow lures away the Irish islanders of Tory—a people marked, in Mr Crossley-Holland's memorably unappealing description, by 'claustrophobia, suspicion, violence . . . inbreeding, feuding, fear, laziness, disappointment and isolation'—then the metropolitan glitter of America has us all hooked. But while in mainland Britain it is overcrowding which fosters pessimism, on the little islands it is crofts abandoned; it is industries (lime, granite, kelp, even the flower-farming of the Scillies) already sunk or sinking; it is folklore phuttering out and young people running away.

Hoy, in the Orkneys, which had 1551 people in 1851, and now has only 438, sounds, even so, a spankingly cheerful place compared to Eigg, with 40 or 50, half of them pen-

sioners, split into feuding Protestant and Catholic factions. Alderney seems bucolic enough, and the handsome and dignified Aran Islanders, still winning their incredible fields by laying sand and seaweed on bare rock, move Mr Crossley-Holland as they once did Synge. But elsewhere tourism seems the main hope for people whose ways of life will be finished off by tourism. Silence, in the age of noise, destroys itself. And, after all, there is nothing so traditional as change.

The histories of these places offer little scope for nostalgia. On Lindisfarne, in spite of the rancour of the present inhabitants, Mr Crossley-Holland is able to feel the spirit of St Cuthbert and of those monks who made such fine manuscripts. But in St Agnes churchgoers used to cry:

> We pray Thee, O Lord, not that wrecks should happen, but that if any wrecks should happen, Thou wilt guide them into the Scilly Isles for the benefit of the poor inhabitants.

Eigg has had three striking moments; two wholesale massacres and one Highland Clearance. 'Not since the 19th century has anyone lived all his life on Lundy.' On the credit side, only Orkney and Aran have produced good poems and stories to weigh against the centuries of nasty Norse barbarities or superstitious stultification.

Mr Crossley-Holland cherishes still, it would seem, his dream of an island, which brings him 'a renewed willingness to go on living in the wilderness without losing hope'. He thinks, perhaps rightly, that 'most of us' share it. But there is another dream, Jerusalem, the ideal city, which might better repay devotion. To those who want hope, it should seem that, with the motor car banished and the hoardings torn down, even London could, in months, be made to come palpably closer to the dream. The main job of quiet spots (as I think Mr Crossley-Holland might admit) is to provide food so that mankind can get on with its proper business in centres where the present is inescapable.

Norman Culpan

SOURCE: A review of *Pieces of Land*, in *The School Librarian*, Vol. 21, No. 2, June, 1973, p. 123.

In *Pieces of Land* Kevin Crossley-Holland describes his impressions of eight islands lying off the coast of Great Britain: Hoy, St Agnes, Lindisfarne, Tory, Alderney, Eigg, Lundy, Inishmore. For the first few pages I thought the book was over-written, but as I read on I became more and more absorbed. To begin with the book is a unity: each island takes shape and identity by contrast with the others. The present is brought alive by description, dialogue and narrative, by discussion of resources, problems and possible future. The past is made equally alive by the author's considerable knowledge of the visits, in peace and war, of Irish missionaries, Viking marauders, by Hitler's troops. Quotations are numerous and range through Anglo-Saxon poetry (usually in his own translation) guidebooks old and new, and poetry of the Orcadian poet,

George Mackay Brown. There are some very good plates, and the maps are excellent: an end-map of the British Isles shows clearly the situation of each island, while each chapter is prefaced by a full-page map of the relevant island giving exactly the right amount of information clearly and pleasantly. Many sixth-formers will want to visit islands after reading this book, and those who do so will make their approach with a wide-ranging attitude of inquiry and sympathy which cannot be too highly commended.

📖 *THE SEA STRANGER* (1973)

A. R. Williams

SOURCE: A review of *The Sea Stranger,* in *The Junior Bookshelf,* Vol. 38, No. 2, April, 1974, p. 110.

The stranger is Cedd, a Northumbrian missionary of the year 653, to whom King Æthelwald granted land at Bradwell-on-Sea to build a monastery, much of which remains. Mr. Crossley-Holland introduces Cedd through contact with the boy Wulf, dreamy and hopeful in his poverty; the monastery is to be built at Wulf's special "place"; eventually, Wulf himself receives the consent and encouragement of his family to join the monks. Along the line, one gets an impression of fresh if astringent winds of change blowing through the East of England; some insight into the attitudes of contemporary rulers and their subjects to the largely welcome ideas of Christianity; a picture of family rural life and court organisation, possibly too simplified for the profound historian but adequate for the age-group for whom the work is designed. Miss Troughton's pictures in line and colour help to confirm *The Sea Stranger* as a real children's book.

Kirkus Reviews

SOURCE: A review of *The Sea Stranger,* in *Kirkus Reviews,* Vol. XLII, No. 8, April 15, 1974, pp. 423-24.

Based on the recorded career of Cedd, a Christian missionary among the East Saxons in the seventh century, and incorporating findings from the Sutton Hoo ship burial discovered in 1939, this is really the story of a boy named Wulf, an outsider type who develops a strong and sudden attachment to a stranger who comes by ship and spends a night with Wulf's family, introducing them to Christian beliefs and promising to return in spring. When Cedd does return it is to build a cathedral and Wulf, overjoyed on seeing him again, decides to join the monastery that will be attached. The slight but seriously told story has the air of a pious legend although Wulf does not exist even in legend and his conversion has little to do with piety as it is clearly the presence and personality of Cedd that motivates the fatherless boy.

Paul Heins

SOURCE: A review of *The Sea Stranger,* in *The Horn Book Magazine,* Vol. L, No. 3, June, 1974, pp. 280-81.

By one of the co-authors of *Wordhoard,* another story of the Anglo-Saxon period. Eleven-year-old Wulf, an East Saxon boy more interested in wood-carving and bone-carving than in battles and vengeance, felt that the ruins of the old Roman fortress near Ythancestir—where he lived—were "'My place, made by giants.'" But something new came into his life the day Cedd, a Northumbrian monk on his way to convert the East Saxon king Æthelhere, was driven off his course and debarked at the seaside entrance to the fortress. Wulf learned about Christianity from Cedd and was won over to the message of hope; and when the Northumbrian returned the next year with permission to build a cathedral on the site of the fort, Wulf was baptized and allowed by his mother to join the monks "'to pray, to help in t'monastery, to carve bone and stone.'" Wulf, the other members of his family, and Cedd are well-drawn, and the simple narrative is rich with historical, literary, and archaeological details. To explain the significance of human life, Cedd quotes a story told in the Venerable Bede's *Ecclesiastical History;* and Wulf and his brother Oswald journey to be present at the filling of a ship with treasures to be buried in the king's memory (the Sutton Hoo ship burial). The stylized black-and-white line drawings and the three full-page colored illustrations suggest an ill-advised compromise between the art of Charles Keeping and that of Pauline Baynes, but they serve honorably as a decorative adjunct to the book.

Zena Sutherland

SOURCE: A review of *The Sea Stranger,* in *Bulletin of the Center for Children's Books,* Vol. 28, No. 1, September, 1974, pp. 4-5.

A story set in Britain in the mid-seventh century, first published in England, is illustrated with strong-lined drawings that suit the subject and period although they are rather busily detailed. Wulf is a dreamy, placid child whose heart is won by Cedd, a missionary who comes from the north of England to the Essex coast to preach Christianity. He promises to return, and by the time he does so the boy has decided he wants to become a Christian. Cedd has returned to build a cathedral, and Wulf joyfully agrees to become his student and to become a monk when he is older. The story is based on some historical facts, but it is possible that ignorance of these—and the Northumbrian dialect used by Cedd—may prove a hindrance to American readers. Period details are convincing, but the story line is static; the book may be useful in religious education programs.

📖 *THE FIRE-BROTHER* (1974)

Kirkus Reviews

SOURCE: A review of *The Fire-Brother,* in *Kirkus Reviews,* Vol. XLIII, No. 13, July 1, 1975, pp. 710-11.

A year after the 7th century missionary Cedd built his monastery and young Wulf, a convert, moved in, the harvest is bad, and people blame the monks for persuading them not to sacrifice to Freya. Then Wulf's resentful brother sets the monastery on fire and flees. Although the huts all burn and only the great stone church is left, Cedd sends Wulf after his fleeing brother with a message of forgiveness and a plea to return. This has more action than its predecessor but the same pious tone; mostly its specialized interest lies in the glimpse of the routines and rituals of early monks.

Publishers Weekly

SOURCE: A review of *The Fire-Brother*, in *Publishers Weekly*, Vol. 208, No. 4, July 28, 1975, p. 123.

A sequel to *The Sea Stranger*, in which the Saxon boy, Wulf, was converted to Christianity, this continues his story through a dreadful summer in the year of our Lord 657. Cedd and his missionary brothers have built a monastery on land granted to them by King Aethelwald. The Christian ascetics are hated and feared by the villagers, especially when their crops fail. Wulf's brother, Oswald, claims that their goddess, Freya, is displeased because of obeisance rendered to the "new" Christ. Finally, Oswald vents his rage by setting fire to the monastery, and the outcome of this devastating act is not vengeance and tragedy but rather the triumph of faith and love. The story is simply, fervently told and the illustrations are faithful, handsome evocations of rural 7th century life.

Donald K. Fry

SOURCE: A review of *The Fire-Brother*, in *School Library Journal*, Vol. 22, No. 2, October, 1975, p. 97.

This sequel to Crossley-Holland's *The Sea Stranger* continues the story of Wulf, an East Saxon boy living in the monastery at Ythancestir in 657. Bad weather and poor harvests turn the villagers against the monks and Wulf's brother Oswald sets the monastery on fire. Wulf coaxes Oswald out of exile with love and forgiveness. Like the previous title, the style is simple, interlaced with touches of Anglo-Saxon poetry, and the plot is thin and a trifle tedious. Troughton's illustrations are attractive but lack the excitement of those in *The Sea Stranger*.

Paul Heins

SOURCE: A review of *The Fire-Brother*, in *The Horn Book Magazine*, Vol. LI, No. 6, December, 1975, p. 591.

In the sequel to *The Sea Stranger*, Wulf, the seventh-century East Saxon boy who had been converted to Christianity by Bishop Cedd and gone to live at the monastery at Ythancestir, learned how difficult it was to be a Christian in a pagan world. First, Wulf's brother Oswald and the villagers blamed the monks for the poor harvest: "'If we'd sacrificed to Freya, as we used to do, instead of praying to Christ.'" Then Oswald set fire to the monastery

and fled into the forest. But Wulf, out of love for his brother and in obedience to the precepts of Cedd, sought Oswald and entreated him to return home, assuring him that there would be no feud. A nice balance is kept between the presentation of the purposeful, hopeful activities of monastic life and worship and the labors and tribulations of primitive land-cultivators, while the story revolves around the relationship between Wulf's love for his family and his devotion to the teachings of the bishop. The black-and-white illustrations are supplemented by four full-color pictures that depict the orderly activities of monastery and church and embody the terrors of fire and forest.

GREEN BLADES RISING: THE ANGLO-SAXONS (1975)

Kate Pretty

SOURCE: "Picking up the Fragmented Pieces," in *The Times Literary Supplement*, No. 3847, December 5, 1975, p. 1458.

The second volume in "The Mirror of Britain" series is *Green Blades Rising*, a study of the Anglo-Saxons by Kevin Crossley-Holland. Like Mrs Paton Walsh, he manages to avoid discussing the use of archaeology, and this is a serious omission in a book covering a period when archaeological evidence provides substantial information about the nature and scope of the Anglo-Saxon invasions. Although the author is forced to use archaeological evidence, his analysis of the material is didactic, naive and old-fashioned. One among many of his unsubstantiated statements, is that the British lived on the light soil of the hill-slopes and the Anglo-Saxons, who preferred a clay soil for their ploughs, in the valleys. Recent archaeological evidence has demonstrated the opposite and it is unfortunate that Mr Crossley-Holland has not kept up to date in his reading—a fact amply demonstrated in his bibliography. In a series which lays emphasis on artistic achievement it is also unfortunate that he cannot use the technical terms correctly, as where he links the technique of chip-carving to the engraved, nielloed Fuller Brooch. His thematic approach, with the full use of documentary evidence, is a good idea and will bring his readership into contact with a wide range of Anglo-Saxon literature, but the imbalance of archaeological and literary evidence prevents the reader from gaining a realistic view of the Anglo-Saxons. . . .

In his conclusion, Kevin Crossley-Holland writes that his book "tries to simplify the Anglo-Saxons, our ancestors. . . ." The archaeologist, the historian and the teacher might well question the validity of this approach. The past has been oversimplified for too long for the theoretical benefit of children. Most children like facts, and to know how these facts were derived. Given these facts they can then test existing general pictures or build pictures of their own. To give them pictures of the past without the underlying, up-to-date evidence is to deny them any real key to a better understanding of how our concept of the past is established.

Kirkus Reviews

SOURCE: A review of *Green Blades Rising: The Anglo-Saxons,* in *Kirkus Reviews,* Vol. XLIV, No. 3, February 1, 1976, p. 140.

The three sections of this introduction to a people are labeled War, Daily Life and Religion, and the early part of "Religion" reads much like that of "War"—which is more a history of conquests than a description of weapons and tactics. But Crossley-Holland also has an eye for the beauty of an early sword or shield, and he devotes much of "Religion" to the illuminated manuscripts and other artistic achievements of the early Christians (especially the monks of Northumbria which in 664 became the "nerve center of Christianity not only in England but in Europe as a whole"). Frequent quotes, not only from the Anglo-Saxon Chronicle but from Beowulf and other poetry, evoke or elucidate aspects of life on the farm, in town, at court or on the road. When Crossley-Holland asks, "Who were the Anglo-Saxons? What were they really like?" it is clear that the question has seized his own imagination; his answers—supported by a splendid sampling of photos and reproductions—might well fire others.

Charles Hannam

SOURCE: A review of *Green Blades Rising: The Anglo-Saxons,* in *The School Librarian,* Vol. 24, No. 1, March, 1976, p. 62.

We are taken from the earliest signs of human civilisation to the coming of the Romans. I like the explanation of the nature of civilisation: there had to be food to spare and then men could begin to think of other things. Jill Paton Walsh is not content with sticking to insular 'progress' but sees civilisation with reference to other peoples and other cultures. The book is written lucidly and difficult concepts are made plain for young people without a trace of condescension. Time is a relative thing: to a butterfly it must seem that twenty-four hours are the end of time; for human beings a hundred years are just about comprehensible. There is a very good appendix on carbon dating, a good reading list and illustrations that fit well into the text rather than existing apart. Definitely recommended for the fourth form and above, and I would not hesitate to give it to anyone as an introduction to the period.

In the fifth century the tribes migrate across Europe and England is abandoned by the Romans. The second book ends with the Norman Conquest. Careful and scholarly attention is given to the civilisation of the Anglo-Saxons. I like the way the book is written, the avoidance of the clichés of the more commonplace textbooks and the introduction of known and relevant events which helps children to enter into another world, using what they already know as signposts. At times the author includes his own translations from the Anglo-Saxon and they are very good. The last chapter left me dissatisfied: I am not at all sure

that characteristics of the Anglo-Saxons can be isolated and transferred to present-day life; even Churchill's stubbornness might have derived from different ancestors or events. The real achievement is the evocation of the quality of Anglo-Saxon literary and artistic achievement and the flavour of every-day life. Again the illustrations are good and there is a bibliography.

Both volumes are so well produced and readable that I am looking forward to additions to this 'Mirror of Britain' series.

Mary Columba

SOURCE: A review of *Green Blades Rising: The Anglo-Saxons,* in *Best Sellers,* Vol. 36, No. 2, May, 1976, p. 62.

This book describes in detail the cultural achievements and the daily life of the Anglo-Saxons. About 50% of our words are derived from Anglo-Saxon words. Our art, literature, laws, and many of our attitudes originated with the Anglo-Saxons. The author explores poetry, sculpture, architecture, jewelry, the manuscripts which were copied by the Anglo-Saxon monks and artistic productions. These monks were saintly and scholarly and their dedicated writings and art work produced books for use at home and abroad on grammar, scientific treatises on chronology, medicine, astronomy, lives of the saints, poetry, hymns, and commentaries on books of the Bible.

Later, King Alfred was a powerful promoter of education. He reestablished monasteries and monastic schools, he urged bishops to start cathedral schools, he learned Latin himself and translated five great Anglo-Saxon books. He set out to make his court a center of education. His restless endeavors prevented the decay of learning, but met with limited success. Two generations after his death there was a revival of the hunger for learning. The twelfth century saw the development of religious literature and literary and scholarly achievements.

The book gives a remarkable picture of the Anglo-Saxon life and its contributions to our own. There are excellent black-and-white illustrations and maps and the colored plates. A bibliography of source material that has been translated, fiction and non-fiction materials for grade six and up, and a "wider reading" list and an index are included in this volume.

Paul Heins

SOURCE: A review of *Green Blades Rising: The Anglo-Saxons,* in *The Horn Book Magazine,* Vol. LII, No. 4, August, 1976, pp. 413-14.

"The Anglo-Saxons loved ornament and ceremony. Their poems were highly wrought; their illuminated manuscripts are formal masterpieces; entertainment in the hall was the enactment of a time-honoured ritual." Thus the author, a translator of Old English poetry and an inventor of stories about the early periods of English history, characterizes the culture of the earliest Englishmen. Divided into three sections, the book is a comprehensive review of the history, sociology, and religion of the Anglo-Saxons. In "War," the author considers not only weaponry but the occasions of conflict between the Anglo-Saxons and the Romano-British, the invading Vikings, and the conquering Normans. In "Daily Life," he deals with social and economic distinctions as well as with the function of the royal court. The section on religion reaches out to include the development and expansion of literature and the arts until the Norman Conquest. Examples from archaeology and architecture as well as from art and literature are constantly used as evidence of the activities and ideals of the Anglo-Saxons; and many of the author's own translations from the Old English illustrate his discussions. The bibliography contains scholarly materials as well as books for young readers. Unfortunately, two of the plate identifications are faulty.

THE EARTH-FATHER (1976)

Mary Hobbs

SOURCE: A review of *The Earth-Father*, in *The Junior Bookshelf*, Vol. 40, No. 2, April, 1976, p. 87.

Though the historical theme is central in this third book about the Anglo-Saxon boy Wulf and his father-in-God Cedd, apostle to the East Saxons, it is the human situations which are conveyed most strongly, particularly the special relationship between youth and age, and the effort of remaining alive and carrying on after the death of a loved one. The plot is slight. The earlier books are neatly summarised, and the reader gets a strong feeling of the hardships of daily life at the time, the remoteness of one district from another, the plague, which killed all except Wulf of the brothers who devoutly journeyed by sea to Northumberland to pay their last respects to their dying Bishop, and the strong faith and vision of those early English Christians. The formal style of illustration, owing something to Anglo-Saxon illumination but with modern liveliness of movement and expression, is most attractive, especially in the four colour plates.

Gordon Parsons

SOURCE: A review of *The Earth-Father*, in *The School Librarian*, Vol. 24, No. 2, June, 1976, p. 134.

Kevin Crossley-Holland attempts more than the limited format can successfully contain. True, his story of Anglo-Saxon Wulf, whose burning desire to be with his friend and mentor, Bishop Cedd, in the latter's dying hours, drives him to journey far and risk the dreaded plague, is the final book of a trilogy. The author, however, in his anxiety to convey a sense of human interdependence and spiritual need, necessarily reduces the narrative presence to a shadow. . . .

THE WILDMAN (1976)

Nicholas Tucker

SOURCE: "A Picture of Ugliness," in *The Times Literary Supplement*, No. 3900, December 10, 1976, p. 1550.

A sad little story, told in clotted prose and illustrated by sombre, grey pictures—it's hard to imagine that anything in this book would appeal to most children. Charles Keeping's illustrations, in that swirling, grainy style he reserves for legend and mythology, have their usual high quality, while the story is an old and haunting one, about a merman caught at Orford during the reign of Henry II. But together the effect is dark and depressing; something that must have been intentional, since ugliness is emphasized in the pictures and underlined in the text, with the merman turning into a Suffolk Caliban, surrounded by rustic Yahoos, mouths agape and in need of urgent dental treatment. The whole thing would have been better as a limited edition aimed at connoisseurs who could appreciate the skill of Keeping's draughtsmanship and the aqueous effects he creates so vividly, although they would have to look harder to find anything in Kevin Crossley-Holland's prosey narration. For children, however, put off by the initial harshness of appearance, I fear the whole effort will be wasted.

Marcus Crouch

SOURCE: A review of *The Wildman*, in *The School Librarian*, Vol. 25, No. 1, March, 1977, p. 39.

This is the fourth of Kevin Crossley-Holland's retellings of East Anglian tales, the saddest and the most disturbing. It tells, following an authentic record, of a merman captured during the reign of Henry II, imprisoned and tortured, then lost. Mr Crossley-Holland boldly chooses to tell the story in the first person. The merman, who knows no English, is nevertheless articulate, and he describes with moving simplicity the dilemma of a creature dragged into an alien environment. The grimness of the story is underlined by Charles Keeping at his most powerful. Using only the finest of line, he claims human sympathy for a most unhuman creature. Who will read the story is not clear, although in picture-book format, it is not for the very young. Will older children, who might be receptive of its message, miss it for superficial physical reasons? If they do, they miss too a most moving experience.

Marie Peel

SOURCE: A review of *The Wildman*, in *Books and Bookmen*, Vol. 22, No. 8, May, 1977, p. 66.

Kevin Crossley-Holland is well known for his special interest in East Anglian folk tales and Norse literature generally. Yet, whatever marvels he has already found in these, it must have been a moment of extraordinary excitement for him when he came upon the seed of his new tale, *The Wildman,* in Ralph of Coggeshall's *Chronicon Anglicanum.* The details of the entry are summarised on the last page of the present book: 'A merman was caught at Orford in Suffolk during the reign of Henry II (1154-1189). He was imprisoned in the newly-built Castle, did not recognise the Cross, did not talk despite torture, returned voluntarily into captivity having eluded three rows of nets, and then disappeared never to be seen again'.

With this to work on, the author gives us the Wildman's tale in his own words, entering into his consciousness in a very moving way, first in his free life in the deep, then suddenly kicking and flailing in the strange web that has entrapped him. This hauls him up from darkness through indigo, purple, pale blue until, in bright daylight, he first sets eye on man, a creature oddly like himself but with little hair on his body and wearing animal skins and furs. Everything the Wildman sees and everything that happens to him has the sharp strangeness of first knowing, which gives the tale an immediate affinity with children's half-forgotten early experience. They will also be drawn to him because he is rejected and misunderstood. On the other hand he is convincingly monsterish in the way he loves to pounce on small creatures for his food, then suck their blood and chew them afterwards.

As the brief sad tale unfolds, the Wildman senses that in himself he belongs more with men than the fish he has left behind. Yet throughout men hit him and howl at him, especially when he does not recognise the cross they thrust at him. They also recoil particularly when, from a natural instinct to touch in order to know, he moves to embrace them.

In the end he is returned to the sea as alien and unwanted, but he twists and dives his way out from the nets set against him. Why, he wonders, is he only free away from those whom he resembles, why is he only free with those quite unlike himself in the sea? This paradox is never resolved for this time men truss him up and throw him in a dungeon and treat him so cruelly he wants to escape, and so he does, even though this means returning to the sea.

The author writes very simply and vividly throughout. His style is neither modern nor old-fashioned, but what I would call substantial, working through images and the lightness or heaviness of actual sentences. Like Ted Hughes's *The Iron Man,* which it resembles in poetic power, I think *The Wildman* will be enjoyed by children of very varying ages from about seven to eleven or twelve. Unlike Ted Hughes, Kevin Crossley-Holland does not seek to impose a message on the story, he is content to let its power come from the symbolic nature of the human behaviour involved. The Wildman cannot be explained, but the experience of his tale will certainly be remembered.

This is especially so, perhaps, because the illustrator, Charles Keeping, has been inspired by it to produce pen and ink drawings of remarkable quality, even for him.

Marcus Crouch

SOURCE: A review of *The Wildman,* in *The Junior Bookshelf,* Vol. 41, No. 5, October, 1977, pp. 285-86.

The fourth of Kevin Crossley-Holland's East Anglian tales is perhaps the saddest, the more so because it is the sufferer who tells the story. In the twelfth century fishermen caught a man in their net and brought him to Orford Castle. He was naked and covered with hair. They tried to communicate with him, by words and signs, kindly and brutally, all without success. Eventually the sea-man escaped. Seen through the confused mind of the wildman himself the strange and incomplete story is more sad, not less strange. Keeping at his most powerful preserves the enigma, even as he explores the mystery and the cruelty of the tale. A deeply disturbing book.

THE DREAM-HOUSE (1976)

Marcus Crouch

SOURCE: A review of *The Dream House,* in *The School Librarian,* Vol. 25, No. 2, June, 1977, pp. 189-90.

Kevin Crossley-Holland's sensitive, richly stored mind probes the meaning of past and present, Britain and its islands and the Mediterranean, the sadness and the fun, and spins out of these elements verses in which word and thought and form are inseparable. In a delectable makeweight at the end he poses a couple of dozen riddles, or crossword clues without the crossword, which test both the wits and the knowledge of the reader (I scored 15 and was proud of the achievement). Read the book for the poetry, and perhaps try it out of context in the classroom. **'Fortification',** for example, might give an additional dimension to a lesson on the Iron Age, or **'Restless One'** could be used as a comment on Anglo-Saxon verse technique or a critique of W. H. Auden and so on. Don't be misled by the writer's reputation in the child's picturebook: this is strong stuff.

THE FABER BOOK OF NORTHERN LEGENDS (edited by Crossley-Holland, 1977)

Ralph Lavender

SOURCE: A review of *The Faber Book of Northern Legends,* in *The School Librarian,* Vol. 26, No. 1, March, 1978, p. 38.

Those who know Kevin Crossley-Holland's stories of the Anglo-Saxons will be ready to welcome his new anthology. Between a beginning and an end of Norse myth, the one showing the gods in their glory and the other showing them in their decline and fall, there are two other sections of Germanic hero-legends and Icelandic sagas.

The ostensible purpose of the collection is 'to identify the common imaginative strain of the Teutons': but, in one sense, whether or not it does this is not important—what *does* matter is the effect that each individual story makes. I am not sure, however, that the right stories are here and rightly told. *The Lay of Thrym* by Paul Taylor and W. H. Auden, and Kevin Crossley-Holland's own version of *Beowulf* have the voice of the bard and the thrumming of the harp in the words. Penelope Farmer's telling of the story of Wayland the smith has considerable sinew, although it has nothing like the dark menace of Ursula Synge's, who herself contributes a racy account of how the walls of Asgard were built. I do not think I will be alone in finding that Thor's beefiness is rather tiresome in Annie Keary's narrative, or that several of the Icelandic sagas such as *Thorstein Staff-Struck* and Sir Walter Scott's *The Hauntings at Frodriver* are too literary. Similarly, the drift of the story about Thorfin Karlsefni is none too clear in the context of this anthology, and *The Burning of Bergthorsknoll* from the saga of Njal, in the translation by Magnus Magnusson and Hermann Palsson, loses its power by being taken out of context. It is in this Icelandic section that the anthology really loses its way, both in quality of telling and in collective purpose. Only Roger Lancelyn Green, with the final story *Ragnarok*, rescues it, suddenly lifting the narrative beyond narrative and the reader beyond reading.

📖 THE NORSE MYTHS: A RETELLING (edited by Crossley-Holland, 1980)

Kirkus Reviews

SOURCE: A review of *The Norse Myths,* in *Kirkus Reviews,* Vol. XLVIII, No. 17, September 1, 1980, p. 1201.

The Norse myths are usually left to children, to Wagner, and to William Morris; but hope and help are at hand—just in time, too, for the great Viking art show. Kevin Crossley-Holland—poet, translator of *Beowulf,* editor of related books for children—has provided a reader's guide to the myths and retold the key narratives, as parts of a single, developing story, from the Creation to Ragnarok, or (in popular parlance) the Twilight of the Gods. In the introduction, he describes the Norse world, introduces the leading gods and goddesses (noting, apropos of Odin's violence, that "a culture gets the Gods it needs"), identifies the sources of the myths (chiefly in 13th-century Iceland, where they live longest), and explains their literary structure—in effect, what to expect and what to look for. His retellings are splendid, varied in tone (to reflect variations among the sources), but generally brisk, tight, wry, beefy—very strong on verbs, and on yeoman Anglo-Saxon words overall. With their many scenes played out in short, active dialogue exchanges (not set-speeches), these have always been tales closer in form to modern fiction than a reader of classical myths might expect; but Crossley-Holland has heightened that aspect—and given the characters' words more psychological spin (Loki the Trickster, scheming, "Exactly"; and "Odin smiled"). And pragmatically, the chapters are short, the paragraphs are short, the sentences are short (or clearly subdivided)—even in the majestic "Death of Balder," where the pace slows, the rhythms lengthen out, become more deliberate, like a keening: "The gods and goddesses did not sleep; they kept vigil in Gladsheim. Ranged around Balder's body, so white that it was gleaming, each of them was prey to his own thoughts and hopes and fears. . . . "

Donald K. Fry

SOURCE: A review of *The Norse Myths,* in *Library Journal,* Vol. 105, No. 19, November 1, 1980, p. 2339.

Crossley-Holland, best known for his Old English translations and his children's books, retells the mythological stories of the Norse gods in detail, drawing mostly on Snorri Sturluson, but also on Skaldic and Eddic poetry. Despite a few small errors, he synthesizes well and captures the burlesque side of Norse humor. His introduction capsules the essence of Viking concerns and myth in general. This volume avoids the usual ponderous anthropological apparatus without falling into reductive simplification. Despite a sprinkle of Briticisms, the prose is very readable. For general and YA collections.

Gwyn Jones

SOURCE: "Odin and His Underlings," in *The Times Literary Supplement,* No. 4072, April 17, 1981, p. 441.

There have been many English retellings of the Norse myths, on many levels of authorship and audience; and the engrossing interest of the mythology itself and the stories through which it is expressed guarantees that there will be many more. . . .

Kevin Crossley-Holland's retelling of these and other brave happenings is an ambitious one, and likewise a successful and enjoyable one. He has decided to retell not just the well-remembered favourites but the entire Eddic corpus of mythological story. This means a recourse not only to Snorri Sturluson's justly famed *Prose Edda* of c 1220-30, but also to the appropriate lays of the *Poetic Edda* of c 1270 ascribed to Saemund the Learned, and the Edda-type poems that go with it. His use of skaldic verse and saga is discreet, and of Saxo chary and infrequent, which can grieve no one save Saxo. All told he has assembled thirty-two "myths", and without straying into the wide fields of heroic legend and folktale that is more or less an all-present roll-call.

A main problem is that of order. It is easy to settle where to begin: where *Voluspa's* Sybil began, and Snorri Sturluson after her, with five pieces which tell of the origin of the world and the beings that inhabit it: gods and giants, elves and dwarfs, all feathered, furred and finny tribes, monsters and men. The same early redactors similarly defined the end, the seven pieces which conduct from the seizure of Andvari's gold by way of Balder's death and Loki's punishment to the world's destruction. For the remaining twenty narratives and excursions there is no ordained or "right" order, and Mr Crossley-Holland has sought, successfully, to establish a reasonable and coherent sequence: Creation, Adjustment, the Golden Age, Corruption and Strife, Destruction. A terrible destruction it was, the Ragnarok, but at least one which permitted a new and greener earth to emerge in innocence and hope, and let a survivor or two find half-hidden in the grass the golden chess-pieces of the great ones of yore.

Between Creation and Destruction we find deployed an impressive and more than usually inclusive selection of narratives, discourses, riddling contests, displays of lore and their like. Loki's hideous brood and the binding of Fenrir; the theft of Idun's apples; Freyja and the Brisings' necklace; Thor fishing up the Midgard-snake; Utgarda-Loki, Hrungnir and Skadi; Geirrod and his squalid daughters are all handsomely present. With commendable dexterity we are offered in addition a notably successful excerpt from the *Hávamál* or "Utterance of the High One" (ie, Odin), summing up our wily All-Father's views on the guile and pillow-talk of women, reinforced with a cautionary tale of how Billing's saucy daughter led him up no fewer than three garden-paths in a single night of dashed amorous expectation. The tone is perfect, the portrait exact.

The retellings throughout are managed with a story-teller's resourcefulness. The language is lively and fresh, the narrative has pace and sinew, there is a proper regard for the originals but no subservience—which is as it should be. Like those originals, Mr Crossley-Holland's versions are not written for children, though children of all ages are welcome. Stately or bucolic, heroic or comic, romantic or gross, horrific or gentle, deeply ironic or deeply moving, the myths here retold yield up their mood and substance sometimes by keeping close to the stylistic master-strokes of the two Eddas, but often by a well-timed expansion of dialogue and a developed landscape and setting.

Retelling is not translation. It invites, even directs its practitioner to a tactful use of explicatory and forwarding devices which while not obliterating the difficulties or mysteries of an original allow the reader to keep moving forward without undue distraction. Mr Crossley-Holland is good at this, and his running glosses on things like Gjalp's river, Loki's flytings, and Thor's hammer (as prompt to bless weddings as crack skulls) are a ready help to those in need. He has further catered for his reader's understanding and enjoyment by supplying a substantial introduction of easily assimilable information about the Norse medieval world, its pre-Christian cosmology and catalogue of other than human beings. Here too he offers advice how to win from these stories and their seizable mysteries a valid, satisfying, and powerfully affecting sense of the magnificence of the Norse mythological system.

Towards the end of the book there are fifty-five pages of notes on the individual myths. They are cast in the form of brief essays intended to be very much part of the book's fare, and never more so than when they relate alternative versions and striking variants. In addition we are supplied with a glossary of proper names, a bibliography, and an efficient index. In its over-all plan, proportions, and general effect this is a very pleasant book.

Margery Fisher

SOURCE: A review of *The Norse Myths,* in *Growing Point,* Vol. 20, No. 1, May, 1981, pp. 3874-75.

It may be because we have been misled by late additions and interpretations of the great Greek tales, by the bowdlerisation of Polynesian myth and the medievalising of Celtic lore, that the myths reflecting the earliest beliefs of the Scandinavian countries seem so crucial and so primitive. Certainly we do need help in appreciating them properly and this help Kevin Crossley-Holland has given in abundance in his retelling of *The Norse Myths.* His long introduction, a model of intelligent compression, analyses the aspects of Norse character reflected in the myths, lists and defines gods, giants and other beings and explains the written sources from which he has put together this overwhelming, impressive version of the world in its beginning and its end. His admirable notes suggest many parallels with European myth and legend but it is the differences, the special nature of the Norse tales which he establishes. He varies his style to encompass the violence of war and the working of malice within the family of the gods, to suggest the gnomic riddles of certain lays, the pathos of Balder's death and the terror of the destruction of the world. His prose, often stark and laconic to match its subjects, can draw also on unexpected poetic feeling. Here is a prophecy of the descendants of Odin returning to a new earth after the devastation of the old:

> *They will sit down in the sunlight and begin to talk. Turn by turn, they will call up such memories, memories such as are known to them alone. They will talk over many things that happened in the past, and the evil of Jormungand and the wolf Fenris. And then, amongst the waving grass, they will find golden chessboards, treasures owned once by the Aesir, and gaze at them in wonder.*

The poetic force and psychological truths of one of the world's great mythologies are reflected with scholarly perception and strong personal commitment in a finely produced and magnificently stirring book.

THE FABER BOOK OF NORTHERN FOLK-TALES (edited by Crossley-Holland, 1980)

Ann Evans

SOURCE: "Rituals and Rewards," in *The Times Literary Supplement,* No. 4051, November 21, 1980, p. 1326.

This is a companion volume to *The Faber Book of Northern Legends* and contains thirty-five folk tales from a variety of sources within the countries and islands of Northern Europe. It is a work of artistic integrity and dedicated research, and perhaps because of this some of the stories may have more appeal to the scholar of folklore than to the child of seven to twelve for whom the book appears to be intended. The editor's policy of choosing the best available translation in each case is good, putting us in the hands of distinguished writers such as Walter de la Mare and Helen Waddell, but it does have the effect of disturbing the continuity of the book as a whole and it makes for restless, fragmented reading. An important publication, nonetheless—albeit for the head rather than the heart.

Eileen A. Archer

SOURCE: A review of *The Faber Book of Northern Folk-Tales,* in *Book Window,* Vol. 8, No. 2, Spring, 1981, p. 24.

This companion volume to the **Faber Book of Northern Legends** is admirable in every way. The thirty-five folk-tales are drawn from collections made by the great names. . . . the Brothers Grimm, Joseph Jacobs, Andrew Lang, Asbjornson and Moe, and there are also little jewels of stories by many others including Helen Waddell, Barbara Leonie Picard and Gwyn Jones. This last writer has retold a particularly fine story from Norway called 'True and Untrue' and Helen Waddell's contribution is the beautiful Shetland tale of 'The Woman of the Sea'. Because the stories come from many countries and ages, the variety presented proves so tempting that the reader is compelled to go on to just one more tale, be it of witches or water-sprites, goblins or ghosts.

Richard Ashford

SOURCE: A review of *The Faber Book of Northern Folk-Tales,* in *The Horn Book Magazine,* Vol. LVII, No. 3, June, 1981, p. 315.

Drawing on traditional and modern sources, the editor has produced a beautifully balanced anthology of thirty-five folk tales from northwestern Europe that can serve to represent the genre in small libraries and to supplement larger collections. Familiar stories from the British Isles and Germany are blended with more exotic fare, including six Icelandic tales full of curious encounters with ghosts, wizards, and death. The style of telling varies from the well-crafted prose of such writers as Walter de la Mare, Helen Waddell, and Barbara Picard to terse Scandinavian narratives and to the musical dialect of "Johnnie in the Cradle" and Joseph Jacobs's "Yallery Brown." While magical beings and mysterious transformations predominate, tales of ordinary foolishness like "Peter Bull" are not forgotten. The variously comic, grotesque, and awesome drawings add to the handsomely produced volume. Includes bibliography and sources.

THE RIDDLE BOOK (edited by Crossley-Holland, 1982)

Books for Your Children

SOURCE: A review of *The Riddle Book,* in *Books for Your Children,* Vol. 17, No. 3, Autumn-Winter, 1982, pp. 22-3.

A puzzle book with a strong literary flavour. Riddles date from Anglo-Saxon times and come in different kinds which will intrigue clever children of between eight and twelve and beyond. It is a book that can be dipped into like a bran tub and riddles of varying difficulty brought up and answers checked so that it will last over a wide age span. If at first it is not understood, turn over or turn to another section and there is another riddle all with entertaining illustrations, but all mind stretching, for example—'Who is that solitary one who sleeps in the grey ash, and is made from stone only?'

'This greedy one has neither father nor mother. There he will spend his life'.

E. Colwell

SOURCE: A review of *The Riddle Book,* in *The Junior Bookshelf,* Vol. 46, No. 6, December, 1982, p. 229.

Riddles are as old as civilisation—3000 years ago riddles were inscribed on Babylonian clay tablets. They are an ancient pastime and are still a favourite and challenging activity.

Kevin Crossley-Holland has made a varied selection from the wealth of material of riddles old and new. Each section from *In the beginning* to *The last word* is prefaced by an explanatory note on the origin and nature of the riddles that follow. It seems that even marauding Vikings indulged in them and in the early days of printing, Wynkyn de Worde printed a collection. An appendix gives an impressive list of sources, from learned books to modern school children.

Riddles can be of many kinds—word play, puns, catch questions, misleading descriptions—but the same ones appear again and again through the centuries. They vary in difficulty from the ancient Greek 'Speechless, you shall speak my name. / Must you speak? Why then again / In speaking you shall say the same.', or the well-known 'In marble walls as white as milk . . . ' to the kind of schoolboy riddles heard in the television programme *Play Away*.

The illustrations are amusing and apt. The collection is both interesting and entertaining and will confound friends and relations. Answers are given!

Marcus Crouch

SOURCE: A review of *The Riddle Book,* in *The School Librarian,* Vol. 31, No. 1, March, 1983, p. 42.

With such an editor you may be sure that this is not just another collection of those awful, punning, joke-riddles which crop up seasonally in the playground. Kevin Crossley-Holland is a scholar riddler who collects his material from the Sphinx, the Anglo Saxons, and the Danes, and the 'Demaundes Joyous' of Wynkyn de Worde. Being a man of widely ranging interests and bubbling humour, he spreads his net even more widely and gives us a generous selection of modern riddles, some of which illustrate the black humour of our own times. Riddles are not always funny, but often they reflect the ideas and attitudes of their own days. So, while many children will give a hearty welcome to the book for its fun (to which Bernard Handelsman's illustrations contribute substantially), teachers may find that it provides them with useful material in history, literature, and natural and social sciences.

BEOWULF (translated by Crossley-Holland, 1982)

Margery Fisher

SOURCE: A review of *Beowulf,* in *Growing Point,* Vol. 21, No. 5, January, 1983, pp. 3998-99.

The poem *Beowulf* consists of three sensational episodes, wrapped in flashbacks, allusions, set speeches of boasting, identification or statesmanship, myth-details and heroic description. Polished and complex, this pre-Christian work is far from primitive and its conventions of structure and style are not easily accommodated in modern English. Even Gavin Bone's gallant and scholarly attempt to adjust the involuted sentences and strange rhythms to the 'modern reader' (in his case, of 1945) has its puzzling moments. At the opposite end of imitating the stressed alliterative line lies the alternative of prose; here, plot and detail have to compensate for the loss of the rhythms and images of poetry. A story-version has one distinct advantage. It can cancel out the flashbacks and allusions and explain simply the national enmity of Geats and Danes which lie behind Beowulf's heroic stand against the monster Grendel and his mother. The heroic celebratory poem, whose intertwined elements of lore and history would have been understood by its listeners, becomes a tale of action, direct in motive and in atmosphere. With Rosemary Sutcliff, indeed, the legend became a romantic one, the characters being depicted almost as people in a novel—Beowulf 'fair-headed and grey-eyed . . . with strength that could out-wrestle the great Northern bear showing in the quiet muscles of his neck and shoulders', jealous Hunferth 'bitter-tongued and envious, fierce-tempered in his cups'.

Kevin Crossley-Holland's new prose version is in many ways a compromise. Modern idioms, a tidied-up story-line, a sense of personality, all help to make the poem into an approachable story for young readers, adding a less familiar legend to those of, say, Finn McCool, King Horn or Roland and Oliver. Yet the style adopted here has a sternly pictorial nature which at times recalls the compound epithets of the poem and its alliterative technique (Grendel's grasp is 'blood-stained and battle-hardened', the sea is still 'gulls-path' and 'whale-road'). Against the more mannered epithets is set a colloquialism which occasionally jars. The somewhat self-conscious opening describes Hygelac's warriors in the great hall 'picking their teeth and swilling stone-cold mead over their gums'; 'Leave him to me,' Beowulf says of Grendel, 'I'll fight him hand to hand';

the dragon of his last conflict gasps and gargles as it dies. Besides, the story is cut so short, with so many of the interpolations omitted, that the moments of high drama seem flat and conventional.

> *Now the Geat sprang to his feet. He saw a sword, massive and double-edged, made by giants, lying in one corner of the chamber. It was so huge that only he of all men could have handled it.*

> *Beowulf ran across the floor, gripped the ringed hilt and swung the ornamented sword—he struck Grendel's mother as she lumbered towards him. The blade slashed through her neck, smashed the vertebrae. The monster moaned and fell dead at his feet:*

The special qualities of mystery that belong to myth and which surely attach to the three evil beings against which Beowulf fights is touched more closely in Bone's version, where the more specific, heroic manner supplies its own aura:

> *Then, lying with other arms, a giant brand*
> *He saw, edged doughtily, the honour of a man,*
> *A master sword, bigger than any other hand*
> *Could fetch to the play when battle began:*
> *. . . Rough and grim he drew it in angry passion,*
> *And, past hope of life, he struck*
> *That the thing gripped hard at her neck*
> *And broke the rings of time; utterly it speeds*
> *Through the flesh - case of the doomed: She*
>   *dropped in her track.*
> *Bloody was the sword: the man rejoiced in the*
>   *deed:*

while there is more warmth and colour in Rosemary Sutcliff's somewhat ornate version of 1961 in *Dragon Slayer.* The choice is open.

The version reviewed here is given a picture-book format, and Charles Keeping, who had contributed forceful drawings to *Dragon Slayer* more than twenty years ago, has returned to the subject with a starker and more fluid line. . . . All in all, a remarkable new presentation of a hero-tale basic to our culture.

G. Bott

SOURCE: A review of *Beowulf,* in *The Junior Bookshelf,* Vol. 47, No. 2, April, 1983, pp. 73-4.

Beowulf, the Geat, travels to Denmark to destroy Grendel, the evil monster, in a hand-to-hand fight. Grendel's mother avenges her son's death; Beowulf wrestles with the old sea-wolf deep in her watery lair and carries her dripping head in triumph back to Hrothgar, king of the Danes. Beowulf returns home to rule over the Geats for fifty years, "a strong land-guardian, a wise king", until a dragon burns down his stronghold. His final victory brings his own death; his warriors cremate him on Whaleness and build a barrow to their leader—"of all kings on earth, he was the kindest, the most gentle, the most just to his people, the most eager for fame."

Kevin Crossley-Holland's vigorous prose narrative, a skilful and sensitive compression of over 3,000 lines of verse in the original, retains much of the unvarnished directness of the earlier version. Individual words echo the poet's facility with picturesque compounds and kennings: gold-harvest, whale-road, gift-throne, ale-thane. Phrases catch the alliteration of the Anglo-Saxon poem: the fen and the fastness, they springheeled over the shingle, bloodstained and battle hardened, whipped waves reared up and reached for the sky. There is no shying away from gory details; bold actions fuel the pace of the story; the folklore of monsters and superhuman achievements is tempered by ideas and ideals of man's struggle against the evil powers of darkness. Kevin Crossley-Holland's decisive narrative, economical and concentrated, moves from the celebration of youthful exuberance and heroic confrontations to the quiet climax of an elegy for a dead king.

Zena Sutherland

SOURCE: A review of *Beowulf*, in *Bulletin of the Center for Children's Books*, Vol. 37, No. 8, April, 1984, pp. 144-45.

Shorter and more simply retold than Rosemary Sutcliff's version of the classic tale, this uses more dialogue, and is therefore easier to read than Sutcliff's sonorous style, but what it gains in comprehensibility it loses in grandeur. It has accessibility but little style. In oversize format, the book looks like a picture book version for older readers, and certainly the illustrations are, in their dramatic sophistication, most likely to be appreciated by older viewers. This is the Keeping his fans knew before he focused on picture books: brooding contrasts of light and dark, tortured figures, often nude but half-masked, gruesome details, the heavy use of parallel lines in black and white illustrations, often full-page, dominate the book. An edition of the epic that is converted to adequate prose has stunning, if stark, pictures.

Paul Heins

SOURCE: A review of *Beowulf*, in *The Horn Book Magazine*, Vol. LX, No. 3, June, 1984, pp. 347-48.

About ten years ago, the reteller produced a complete translation of the Anglo-Saxon epic of the exemplary hero who slew monsters and fought with a dragon. The text of the retelling has been considerably condensed but remains faithful to the spirit as well as to the content of the original. As in Rosemary Sutcliff's version, the story is introduced by a narrator in a great banquet hall, and the three sections of the poem follow in order: Beowulf's contest with Grendel, the slaying of Grendel's mother, and Beowulf's battle with the dragon. Occasionally filling out the narrative by judiciously developing suggestions in the text, the teller has at the same time retained the essence

of the original even to such details as the allusion to Sigemund and the name of Unferth's sword—Hrunting. The long epic speeches have been transformed into staccato dialogue; and the diction is tactile and terse—intended to appeal to the ear as well as to the eye. And, as in the original epic, horror and destruction are balanced by nobility and courage. Like the reteller, the artist, who illustrated the Sutcliff version more than twenty years ago with strong line drawings, has caught the primitive force of the original narrative. In black and white, ranging through shades of gray, he has depicted bleak landscapes and nightmarish monsters without neglecting scenes of human dignity and human solidarity. Author and artist have seen the Old English work eye to eye and transmuted its power for contemporary readers and viewers.

Bonnie Saunders

SOURCE: A review of *Beowulf*, in *School Library Journal*, Vol. 31, No. 8, April, 1985, pp. 84-5.

When he hears of the havoc being wrought upon the Danes by Grendel, Beowulf volunteers to travel to Denmark to rid his father's friends of this enemy. Although the monster has defeated all others, Beowulf slays both him and his mother and returns to his homeland a gift-laden hero. The story of his death over 50 years later while slaying yet another dragon is told in the final chapter. This retelling of the classic epic maintains much of the ancient storytelling tradition in its richly tapestried prose. It is told in a high, formal style worthy of an epic, yet the picture book format makes it accessible to today's youth. Keeping's harsh, stark etchings enhance the somber majesty of the tale and show greater depth of feeling than his illustrations for Rosemary Sutcliff's version of the Beowulf legend. This is an excellent introduction to Beowulf for students with some background in the classic myths and legends of epic heroes.

THE DEAD MOON AND OTHER TALES FROM EAST ANGLIA AND THE FEN COUNTRY (1982)

M. Hobbs

SOURCE: A review of *The Dead Moon*, in *The Junior Bookshelf*, Vol. 47, No. 1, February, 1983, p. 38.

Several of these eleven East-Anglian stories have already appeared separately, with other illustrators. They are brought together here in a collection which gives a powerful impression of the closeness of the sinister marshes, particularly at night, and the isolated world of the Fens and East Anglia, with their sturdy, independent country folk keeping their own counsel. These are sophisticated retellings of traditional stories, in vivid, vigorous style, making the most, by their language, of suspense and drama for the maximum spinechilling effect. Some of the tales account for features of buildings still surviving, like the least sinister story, 'The Peddlar of Swaffham'. Others, like the title story, are myths. There is ghoulish humour in 'The Dauntless Girl' and true tragic pathos in 'The Green Mist'. It is a world where the supernatural, ghosts and bogles, will-o'-the-wykes and witches, waiting to pounce on fearful humans, are very real. This fine collection is enhanced by Shirley Felts' unearthly black-and-white illustrations. Nevertheless, the tales are so powerful that they had perhaps more impact singly than together.

Margery Fisher

SOURCE: A review of *The Dead Moon*, in *Growing Point*, Vol. 21, No. 6, March, 1983, pp. 4038-39.

Kevin Crossley-Holland has retold eleven tales in which the mists and mysteries of fenland are brilliantly suggested. The lively, colloquial prose, the easy alternation of dialogue and narration, the pertinent details, all commend the book for reading aloud, when the full flavour of idioms and rhythms may be felt. Here is that grim treasure-tale 'The Callow Pit Coffer' and the touching legend of 'The Green Children'. Here is the immediacy of the Tudor tale of 'The Pedlar of Swaffham' and the manacing apparition of 'Yallery Brown'. Each story offers a particular pattern of weather and landscape, a distillation in fantasy form of a land and its people, of marsh and pool, of cottage and farmhouse, of kind neighbours and evil companions. However swift the story-telling, there is room allowed for the kind of writing that stirs the imagination—for example, in this description of a marsh spirit:

> *Tiddy Mun lived in the deep and dark green water-holes that never moved from dawn to dusk. But when the evening mist dipped and lifted and dipped over the marsh, Tiddy Mun rose to the surface and hoisted himself on to some marsh path. He went creeping through the darkness, limpetly lobelty, like a dear little old grandfather with long white hair and a long white beard, all matted and tangled; he hobbled along, limpetly lobelty, wearing a grey gown so that people could scarcely make him out from the mist. His movement was the sound of running water and the sough of the wind, and his laugh was like the screech of a peewit.*

Ralph Lavender

SOURCE: A review of *The Dead Moon and Other Tales from East Anglia and the Fen Country*, in *The School Librarian*, Vol. 31, No. 3, September, 1983, pp. 243-44.

Kevin Crossley-Holland's eleven stories from East Anglia and the Fens are not all new: 'The green children', 'The callow pit coffer', and 'The pedlar of Swaffham' have already been published before, though this isn't made clear, not even in the notes on sources. His writing is always powerful, every story is imbued with the spirit of the marshes acting like a miasma, and the imagery possesses the hard brilliance of the poet's eye and ear. For example, in 'The dauntless girl', the blacksmith's 'last inch of whisky glowed like molten honey in the flickering firelight', and the pale faces of the congregation in the story

about the black dog of Bungay 'shone like anemones'. The imagery can be sharp enough to resemble repartee. In 'Tiddy Mun', the marshes are being drained by the Dutchmen until the water-holes become 'as dry as two-year-old Mothering Cakes'. Through the understanding of what makes a narrative, many stories end with an ambiguity: the fate of the green girl is not stated, no one knows where Tiddy Mun ended up, and the secret gold of the callow pit coffer remains buried after all. At the end of the best stories there always stands a question mark. But there is no question mark about this book as the best of the three [reviewed].

Betsy Hearne

SOURCE: A review of *The Dead Moon and Other Tales from East Anglia and the Fen Country*, in *Bulletin of the Center for Children's Books*, Vol. 44, No. 10, June, 1991, p. 235.

Eleven chilling folktales have been elegantly—and carefully, from cited sources—adapted for the benefit of sophisticated young readers and adult storytellers. The pen-and-ink drawings will insult neither, for they maintain the atmospheric integrity of these marsh tales involving boggarts, will-o'-the-wykes, witches, dead hands, green children, and a marvelous character called Tiddy Mun, who mourns the passing of the swamp to modern drainage systems . . . and demands retribution. Feminists will delight in "The Dauntless Girl," who agrees to rid a farm of unnatural visitors with these words: "I'm not afraid of ghosts. But you ought to take account of that in my wages." Later she says to the haunt, "I've no cause to be afraid of you, for you are dead and I'm alive." Bravo Mary, and bravo, once again, Kevin Crossley-Holland, whose **British Folk Tales** was a landmark collection.

📖 *TALES FROM THE MABINOGION* (with Gwyn Thomas, 1984)

Marcus Crouch

SOURCE: A review of *Tales from the Mabinogion*, in *The School Librarian*, Vol. 32, No. 4, December, 1984, p. 359.

The Mabinogion is not the easiest of the great national collections of tales to present to young readers. For one thing it is not a homogeneous book but a random collection of stories from different periods brought together in the Middle Ages and given their most familiar form in early Victorian times by a lady with scholarly and romantic inclinations. The best of the stories—the four branches of the Mabinogi—spring from traditions far older than their earliest surviving text and reflect a society and a code infinitely more alien to our own times than that of, say, *Beowulf*. Having read these four stories through many times in recent years I was prepared to pronounce them inaccessible to present-day children. That was before reading Gwyn Thomas's new version, commissioned by the Welsh Arts Council and translated and adapted for English-reading children by Kevin Crossley-Holland. The two names are evidence of authenticity: the one an outstanding Welsh scholar, the other our leading interpreter of the Dark Ages and an eloquent writer too. **Tales from the Mabinogion** is a most notable achievement, one which does the seemingly impossible. Wisely the two writers have stuck to the first four stories, so giving their book a degree of unity. They cannot iron out the fundamental inconsequence of some of the narratives, but by emphasising the movement, the inevitability and the occasional wry humour of the original, and without, as Lady Charlotte Guest did, shirking its frankness and brutality, they succeed in making their book highly readable. Much of the mystery remains, and perhaps it is right that it should. If you could explain *The Mabinogion* you might explain it away. The book is handsomely produced, and Margaret Jones's illustrations, if they are not particularly likeable, are certainly most impressive.

Karen Stang Hanley

SOURCE: A review of *Tales from the Mabinogion,* in *Booklist,* Vol. 81, No. 15, April 1, 1985, p. 1123.

Crossley-Holland, whose potent retelling of **Beowulf** was reviewed in *Booklist* 80:1396 Je 1 84, here collaborates with a Welsh scholar in an ambitious translation of the four traditional parts, or branches, of the Mabinogion, the Welsh cycle of hero tales that Lloyd Alexander, Susan Cooper, and Alan Garner, among others, have drawn on in their fantasy novels. The tales are set forth in resonant, fluid language, and dialogue framed in colloquial patterns enhances their readability. Illustrations, consisting of line drawings in addition to 17 full-color scenes, are stiffly composed and manneristic, but attentive to the story's imagery and details. One painting contains a frontal nude of Blodeuwedd, the maiden created for Lleu to wed. Like Beowulf and Norse myths, these tales espouse a moral code rather different from our own, which may prompt discussion among readers. An extremely useful glossary of Welsh names, including pronunciations, is appended.

Zena Sutherland

SOURCE: A review of *Tales from the Mabinogian,* in *Bulletin of the Center for Children's Books,* Vol. 38, No. 10, June, 1985, p. 190.

A distinguished interpreter of folklore, Crossley-Holland worked with Gwyn Thomas, professor of Welsh, to produce this new version of the four major parts, called "Branches," of the larger (eleven) tales that constitute the Mabinogion, a collection of medieval fantasy tales. The illustrations, romantic and conventional, are—although not imitative—reminiscent of the grave solidity of Pyle and the gnarled line of Rackham. One picture shows a nude woman; generally, they are primly decorous. The four branches (the core of the Mabinogion) are linked; the translation is fluent, the dialogue nicely balanced between language easily comprehensible to today's readers, and

the mood of ancient magic that pervades the tales. Fans of such fantasy writers as Lloyd Alexander and Alan Garner will be prepared for the many Welsh names; for others, a glossary is provided.

AXE-AGE, WOLF-AGE: A SELECTION FROM THE NORSE MYTHS (1985)

Marcus Crouch

SOURCE: A review of *Axe-Age, Wolf-Age,* in *The Junior Bookshelf,* Vol. 49, No. 4, August, 1985, p. 184.

For this handsome and lucid selection from the myths of the Vikings Kevin Crossley-Holland has drawn on his own **The Norse Myths,** which is available from Penguin. This new edition is selective and in format is aimed towards a youthful audience.

The Norse myths are notoriously difficult. All those strange names, not to mention the topography of Asgard and Midgard and Niflheim. Then there is the alien morality, with men and gods following, as did the Vikings, a code of honour very different from that of Christendom. And yet, as Mr. Crossley-Holland says, memorably, in his introduction: 'The myths are not imprisoned in their own time and place; they tell us of their makers but they also tell us a lot about ourselves—our own deep longings and fears.'

So it is worth the effort of grappling with the formidable difficulties of *Axe-age, Wolf-age,* and to follow Mr. Crossley-Holland in the long trek from the creation of the world to its disintegration in Ragnarok. On the way we meet many familiar figures and read some stories that have their parallels in other and homelier cultures, some that are unique to this strange world. We are helped over the many hurdles by the writer's language which is blunt and direct, releasing all the latent strength in the sagas. And he relates the stories to their own time and place and to the passage of the seasons, for these are stories not only of gods and super-humans but also of people living in the world and meeting the demands of the elements.

For this edition Hannah Firmin has provided a large number of illustrations which reinforce the unique mixture of strangeness and homeliness, of brutal action, tragedy and farce, which are the essence of the myths.

Ralph Lavender

SOURCE: A review of *Axe-Age, Wolf-Age: A Selection from the Norse Myths,* in *The School Librarian,* Vol. 34, No. 1, March, 1986, pp. 44-5.

Myth is a 'different way of seeing', Kevin Crossley-Holland points out, and he helps us to do so in his new book. The title of the new selection from his own **The Norse Myths** is taken from the beginning of his account of Ragnarok, the Norse day of judgement. What we have here is twenty-two of the thirty-two episodes given in the earlier book, together with a different introduction and the glossary, but minus the notes. Some of the stories have been renamed and a few textual changes made; and a few important elements in the naming, which is so important in the recitations of myth—for example, the eleven rivers of Elivagar—are omitted. The psychological unity of the original has been disturbed inevitably, even though all the important episodes, from creation and the building of Asgard's walls through Thor's picaresque adventures to the death of Balder are present. Indeed, the latter is the high point of the cycle and stirring in the telling here. In *The Norse myths* it was set out like a symphony, in movements; unaccountably, one of the changes of movement has been lost in the new setting. Children may find this volume more welcoming, less scholarly, since it is lighter to handle, and the woodcuts add a fresh dimension. I would have it only if I couldn't have its begetter.

Kirkus Reviews

SOURCE: A review of *Axe-Age, Wolf-Age: A Selection from the Norse Myths,* in *Kirkus Reviews,* Vol. LIV, No. 21, November 1, 1986, p. 1648.

In these retellings of the Norse myths, based on Icelandic Eddas of the 13th century, Icelandic scholar Crossley-Holland has given a flavor of the original while making the language comfortable for modern children.

Beginning with the Creation and ending with Ragnarok, the death of the gods, these are brief adventures or tales of gods, giants, dwarves and men trying to outdo or outtrick each other. Many of the stories center on brave Thor, God of the Sky, or Loki, the trickster; they have a majestic grandeur and a coarse, earthy humor, giving us an interesting glimpse of Viking culture. The woodcut illustrations have a crude strength and humor to match the tone of the retellings.

Good for reading aloud or for telling, following the oral tradition of their origins, these retellings are less refined in style than Roger Green's *Myths of the Norsemen,* sounding more like folk tales than epic poetry.

This fine version of the Norse myths belongs in any good folklore collection.

Denise A. Anton

SOURCE: A review of *Axe-Age, Wolf-Age: A Selection from the Norse Myths,* in *School Library Journal,* Vol. 33, No. 6, February, 1987, p. 88.

Certainly one of the most authoritative collections of Norse mythology written for adults is Crossley-Holland's *The Norse Myths*. These 32 tales cover the wide variety of Norse lore and are the result of impeccable research. Here he has repackaged 22 of them into a collection intended for juvenile audiences. Most of the tales have been re-

printed verbatim from the original, and they will be inaccessible to all but the most sophisticated and motivated YA readers. Small woodcuts complement the roughness of the myths, yet they seem fragmented overall. Save your money and send those YA patrons with a pronounced interest in Norse mythology to the adult department for *The Norse Myths*.

Zena Sutherland

SOURCE: A review of *Axe-Age, Wolf-Age: A Selection from the Norse Myths,* in *Bulletin of the Center for Children's Books,* Vol. 40, No. 7, March, 1987, p. 124.

In a retelling of the cycle of Norse mythology first published in his *The Norse Myths,* Crossley-Holland relied, he states in a prefatory note, on two 12th-century sources, the *Elder Edda* and the *Prose Edda* of Snorri Sturluson. The storytelling quality is notable, giving humor and narrative flow to the granite characters and forceful drama of the Nordic legends. A glossary (chiefly names of people and places) is provided; the rigid naivete of the woodcut illustrations is appropriate for the text but not always in agreement with it—a reference to the first human beings emerging out of the primeval ooze under Ymir's left armpit is contradicted by the picture that shows this happening under the right armpit, for example.

STORM (1985)

A. R. Williams

SOURCE: A review of *Storm,* in *The Junior Bookshelf,* Vol. 49, No. 5, October, 1985, p. 215.

Annie's home is in an isolated house in an extensive marsh. The emergency which leads to the story's climax is therefore naturally exploited. In between the author points confidently and economically Anne's environment and family background, from 'the sucking sound of draining mud' to the wind which 'whistled between its salt lips and gnashed its sharp teeth', all of which fits in easily enough with the ghost of the farmer who paid with his life for defying two highwaymen and reappears, it would seem, to carry Annie to the doctor needed to assist at her older sister's confinement. A great deal of convincing drama is packed into so few pages without limiting character to cardboard cut-outs. From another point of view the text may tend to 'stretch' readers of the 7 to 9 year-old group. This is not strip-cartoon stuff. Alan Marks' illustrations strike an appropriately eerie note.

Gill Johnson

SOURCE: "How the Medal Was Won," in *Books for Keeps,* No. 39, July, 1986, p. 8.

Turning to *Storm* the [Carnegie Medal] panel was faced with a very short book of only some 3000 words in the

Banana Books Series aimed at young readers of approximately 7-9 years. The panel judged this to be an excellent book for its intended purpose. Perhaps because of the author's poetry experience it was thought that every word counted in his outstanding use of language. The description conveyed a strong sense of place and atmosphere; drama and suspense. In Annie there was a strong, female character who is naturally apprehensive about the task in front of her which only she can perform, but who overcomes her fears when it is needed. The book is part of a series which is recognised to be outstanding value for money with hardback covers, colour illustration and sewn binding. At first consideration doubts were expressed about whether the book was sufficiently memorable and some thought the surprise element might be lacking, but questioning young readers some of the panel members found that this was not the case. Children, it was true, did predict the ending but this did not distract from their enjoyment of the book, rather it gave them a feeling of confidence and superiority that they guessed, and guessed correctly, what was going to happen. Neither did it seem to detract from the drama of the story and children who had since read many other books could still remember the ghostly shiver down the spine on reading the last page.

So a decision was made to award the Medal to a book which was considered to be an outstanding piece of miniature writing, comparable to a miniature painting in its attention to fine detail and lasting impressions.

THE FOX AND THE CAT: ANIMAL TALES FROM GRIMM (with Susan Varley, 1985)

Marcus Crouch

SOURCE: A review of *The Fox and the Cat,* in *The Junior Bookshelf,* Vol. 50, No. 1, February, 1986, p. 21.

These new versions of some of the Grimm Brothers' animal stories, done with the assistance of Susanne Lugert, are adequate if not particularly exciting. The same cannot be said for Susan Varley's illustrations. These, in well reproduced colour throughout, are most admirable. They identify the humour, the drama, and the occasional satire in the incomparable tales and render them with strength and vivacity. Only once, and then perhaps for a sound reason, does Miss Varley put her animals into human clothes. Mostly they appear, as surely the Grimms' peasants saw them, as neighbours, friendly or hostile, concerned with their own affairs which may sometimes echo or comment upon human activities. The pictures are set into the text with considerable skill so that their commentary is made discreetly and with no undue fuss. A notable piece of book-making.

Carolyn Phelan

SOURCE: A review of *The Fox and the Cat,* in *Booklist,* Vol. 82, No. 18, May 15, 1986, p. 1396.

Crossley-Holland provides a collection of eleven entertaining animal tales from the Brothers Grimm, including the familiar ("The Wolf and the Seven Young Kids" and "The Bremen Town Musicians") and the more obscure ("The Fox and the Horse"). His lively choice of words and direct style are well suited to folklore, as are Varley's attractive illustrations. In a style somewhat reminiscent of Shepard and Ardizzone, Varley works a traditional English vein of thoughtful composition, crosshatched line, and watercolor washes in gentle, harmonious hues. With only one or two illustrations per story, this will not be the first choice to read aloud to young children, though most of the stories are unavailable in picture-book editions. Still, children old enough to read them and motivated by assignment or inclination to read folktales will find this a well-designed volume: the stories are only a few pages long, the layout avoids double spreads of type, and the print is comfortably large without appearing babyish.

Mary M. Burns

SOURCE: A review of *The Fox and the Cat: Animal Tales from Grimm,* in *The Horn Book Magazine,* Vol. LXII, No. 4, July-August, 1986, pp. 460-61.

Although several complete collections of Grimm's folk tales are available, a sharply focused compilation has its place as well, particularly one as attractively produced and intelligently translated as this one. Familiar tales such as "The Bremen Town Musicians," "The Wolf and the Seven Young Kids," and "The Cat and the Mouse in Partnership" are among the eleven selections—and rightly so, for they are not only good stories but also typify the outlook of the peasants who first told them. Although similar in tone, the other eight tales—"The Fox and the Cat," "Old Sultan," "The Hedge-King," "The Fox and the Geese," "The Fox and the Horse," "The Hare and the Hedgehog," "The Wolf and the Fox," and "The Hedge-King and the Bear"—are less frequently anthologized; consequently, it is a welcome treat to rediscover them in so lively a setting. Varied in length and paced exactly right for oral interpretation, the stories are well suited to the talents of beginning storytellers, for reading aloud, or for independent perusal. The beautifully composed, full-color illustrations complement the mood and the subject. Pleasantly nostalgic without looking simply old-fashioned, lively without becoming frenetic, they are remarkable for the use of fine pen-and-ink lines, which both define shape and detail while adding texture and dimension. Like the text, they reinterpret the past for a contemporary audience while remaining faithful to the spirit of the original sources.

Ralph Lavender

SOURCE: A review of *The Fox and the Cat: Animal Tales from Grimm,* in *The School Librarian,* Vol. 34, No. 3, September, 1986, pp. 246, 249.

These animal tales taken down by the Grimm Brothers

make an interesting collection about a theme. Although the eleven stories are ostensibly about animal families, animal partnerships and animals unwanted in old age, they are actually all about human foibles and follies. Compared to the translations by Brian Alderson, they are a little more literary, perhaps slightly less colloquial. For example, in the case of 'The wolf and the seven little kids', the opening is quite different. Kevin Crossley-Holland has the nanny-goat explaining to her children that the wolf will disguise himself, but 'you will recognise him at once by his gruff voice and by his black feet'. Brian Alderson omits this detail, and the wolf's disguises are only revealed by the unfolding of the tale. In this way, some of the carefully composed narrative is broken and its patterning lost. Again, the drama and the emotion of the nanny-goat's return home, finding the kids all eaten but one, is missing in Brian Alderson. Compared to the translations by Peter Carter, Kevin Crossley-Holland is sharp and concise, and more than once there is a presentiment of Hans Andersen's wit in the dialogue. This fresh selection does read aloud well, nevertheless, only storytellers have less to do for themselves. The book's failing is its illustrations, which have none of the power of Michael Foreman's, nor, for that matter, of Kay Nielsen's.

WATERSLAIN AND OTHER POEMS (1986)

Raymond Tong

SOURCE: A review of *Waterslain, and Other Poems,* in *British Book News,* May-June, 1986, p. 429.

Although this is Kevin Crossley-Holland's fourth volume of poems, he is more widely known as a writer for children and as a translator of Anglo-Saxon poetry, especially perhaps for his outstanding translation of *Beowulf.* However, his reputation as a poet has continued to grow and certainly the present collection well merits its recommendation by the Poetry Book Society. The title is taken from the cycle of twenty-five poems that makes up the first part of the book. These poems are concerned with the inhabitants of Waterslain, a remote village on the north Norfolk coast, which the poet remembers from many childhood visits there in the 1950s. Returning to this 'indeterminate and empty quarter', with its creeks and saltmarshes, he vividly recalls a number of colourful characters, such as a wildfowler, a beachcomber, a fisherman, a great painter, an old lag and a woman with webbed feet, all of whom make a memorable contribution to the village's identity.

Similar voices in the wind are present in the second part, but here the background has been widened to include, for example, the grave of a Viking girl, a Stone Age village and a church in Suffolk. While this adds variety to the collection, Kevin Crossley-Holland is clearly at his best when he is deftly sketching his village notables, and through them conveying the beauty of a stark, watery landscape, with the sea 'grinding her spears' and with 'little but memory for company'.

Simon Rae

SOURCE: "Meaning from the Land," in *The Times Literary Supplement,* No. 4368, December 19, 1986, p. 1423.

Kevin Crossley-Holland's new book of poems is divided into two parts. The first consists of the cycle which gives its name to the collection as a whole, describing the life of a village on the north Norfolk coast. The second, "Coming Home", is devoted to domestic concerns, childhood memories and historical re-creations.

Crossley-Holland's imagination has consistently shown itself to be rooted in the distant past and the Viking north, drawing on the grim fatalism of Old English poems such as "The Wanderer". Norfolk, too, has attracted his attention as a poet before. In 1970 he published a pamphlet, *Norfolk Poems* (with photographs by John Hedgecoe), later incorporated into his first full collection, *The Rain-Giver.* These poems were sparsely populated, and generally took the form of a reflective eye / "I" surveying a given landscape. The new poems in *Waterslain* are very different. Although description is given its place—the first poem, **"Lifeline"**, opens: "Between skywide fields / shadow-ribbed, / crammed with wurzel and beet, / and the salt-quarterings' shine and shift, / this lifelong earthwork stands"—the main focus of the poems is the personalities of those living in and around the village: Mrs Riches Diz, Billy, Bodge, Shuck, Beachcomber, Mason, Vic, Miss Queen, Old Lag. Snippets of gossip, oracular sayings and elliptical monologues make up a compelling community of disparate voices, given an underlying structure by the thread of personal memory (Crossley-Holland spent much of his boyhood in the place). . . .

"Coming Home" contains some fine, quiet celebrations of married life; **"Preparatory School"** reaches back to a boyhood of headmasterly "backhanders", bullying, and (a clinching detail) humiliation on the cricket field—"the scoreboard showing the whole team / out for 13". **"Orkney Girls"** adds to Crossley-Holland's already impressive tally of historical resurrections, and other poems continue the poet's attempt to wrest a personal meaning from places visited or returned to, from the processes of the land, and from language itself.

BRITISH FOLK TALES: NEW VERSIONS (1987)

Jennifer Westwood

SOURCE: "Tales within Tales," in *The Times Literary Supplement,* No. 4415, November 13-19, 1987, p. 1261.

Always exact in his scholarship, Kevin Crossley-Holland calls his tales "new versions". So, indeed, some of them are: he has set **"The Small-Tooth Dog"**—a "Beauty and the Beast" variant collection by S. O. Addy in Derbyshire in the nineteenth century—in present-day London, and under the title "Sea-Woman" made a tale-within-a-tale of Thomas Keightley's "The Mermaid Wife".

His changes from his sources, meticulously recorded in his notes, are those of a fine story-teller with a poet's ear: where he finds an already grand tale, he lets it pretty well alone. As in his earlier collection *The Dead Moon* (1982), he scarcely intervenes between the reader and Mrs Balfour's tales from the Lincolnshire carrs, of which the title story and *Yallery Brown* in that collection, and *Samuel's Ghost* in this, are among the eeriest things in British tradition. He doesn't indulge in eye-boggling semi-phonetic spelling—the bane of many regional retellings—but reproduces the cadence of a dialectal tale largely through its grammar. In *Tom Tit Tot*, the Suffolk "Rumpelstiltskin", for example, he preserves the characteristic East Anglian "that" for "it".

The publisher's blurb describes the book as "the first comprehensive retelling of the great body of British Folk Tales for very many years"—a large claim, as the "body" of British folktales is greater than the publisher allows and, thanks largely to the School of Scottish Studies, is still growing. None the less this selection of fifty-five stories is the most representative by a modern reteller. It includes examples of most of the main types of British folk-tale, and reproduces them in both prose and ballad form, traditional or otherwise—the Border ballad of "Tam Lin" is included, so is the riddle-contest "The False Knight on the Road", and the West Country song "Sir John Barleycorn", with its mysterious undertones of primitive sacrifice. Unlike most retellers, Crossley-Holland is no more afraid of the inconsequential snippet than he is of the fully developed narrative that gives scope for larger effects. What he makes of very slight tales such as "Dathera Dad" is often a revelation.

Considered simply as storytelling, *The Small-Tooth Dog*, fast-paced to begin with, has never been better done nor, under different titles, have "A Legend of Knockgrafton" and "The Brownie of Copinsay". The latter, retitled *Hughbo* (which is the Brownie's name), is retold from a shortish paraphrase in Ernest Marwick's *Folklore of Orkney and Shetland* and is a fine example of sensitive handling. Art, insight and wide reading have gone into its making: it becomes a little tragedy, the more intimate note sounded by its ending prepared for from the first by that apparently small thing, a change of title.

If the collection has a fault, it is that responsiveness to words sometimes carries the author too far. The emphasis in traditional storytelling is on narrative and narrative devices such as repetition, not on freshness and originality of vocabulary. The "gritty chuckle of the quernstones" is fair enough—very few of us have heard a quern in action—but I'm not at all sure about "silver-roan forests" or an "oyster-and-pearl afternoon". This kind of highly wrought language seems inappropriate in a folk-tale context, as, too, are a few of the stories. *The Wildman* is a highly original retelling (from the Wildman's point of view) of Ralph of Coggeshall's account of the capture of a merman off Orford in the twelfth century—but its tone is far removed from that of folk-tale. *The Green Children*, from the same source, sits uneasily among stories with the timeless quality of traditional folk and fairy tale because

of too much contextualizing medieval detail. This occasionally swamps even *The Pedlar of Swaffham*, an otherwise first-class version which introduces as a character a marvellous pedlar's dog not mentioned in the original story.

But this is little enough to complain about. Just as the same author's *Folk-Tales of the British Isles* was an excellent introduction to the subject for adults, so is this for children. The book is generously produced, and its stories enhanced with atmospheric and frequently sinister woodcuts by Peter Melnyczuk—see, for example, those for *The Dark Horseman* and the *King of the Cats*.

Betsy Hearne

SOURCE: A review of *British Folk Tales: New Versions,* in *Bulletin of the Center for Children's Books,* Vol. 41, No. 5, January, 1988, pp. 86-7.

In both range and depth, this is a rich collection of 55 British folktales adapted from widely varied sources which the author has cited in careful, if idiosyncratic, end notes. While some of the titles sound familiar, the versions here may not seem so. The satisfyingly rhythmic *Frog Prince* is distinctly different from Grimm #1. *King of the Cats* appears in monologue form, and *The Small-Tooth Dog*, a variant of "Beauty and the Beast," has acquired a modern setting. The author is intimate with this lore, and some of his innovations render the tales more immediate. A few, however, seem slightly disconcerting. Casting *The Sea-Woman* (about a Selkie) as a tale within a tale, for instance, distracts more than it adds. Yet Crossley-Holland has a strong sense of selection and consistent respect for motif. His most vivid writing adheres closely to the basic shape of the tales. In many cases, as he himself says, "the best thing a reteller can do is 'translate' the dialect into modern English and keep well out of the way." The bookmaking is worthy of the text: handsome print on fine, creamy paper with discretely miniature, skillful scratchboard drawings opening each chapter (the illustrator remains mysteriously unidentified). In its revealing and revitalizing of the traditional, this makes a long-lasting contribution to readers and storytellers alike.

Constance A. Mellon

SOURCE: A review of *British Folk Tales: New Versions,* in *School Library Journal,* Vol. 34, No. 5, January, 1988, p. 72.

This "comprehensive retelling of the great body of British folktales" includes 55 stories and ballads chosen to represent all of the major types of folk tales. Ghost stories, hero tales, tales of trials and conflict, brave princes, tricksters, fairies, and goblins—the many characters and plots of folk literature have their place in this volume. Familiar old favorites such as "Jack and the Beanstalk" and "The Three Bears" rub elbows with lesser known versions of old favorites such as "Mossycoat," a version of Cinderella, and "Hughbo," a version of "The Shoemaker and the Elves." Less familiar tales, such as "Yellow Lily," "Three Heads of the Well," and "Tam Lin" will delight both readers and listeners. Crossley-Holland combines traditional telling with modern or unusual reframing of stories to provide a valuable new resource for storytellers, folk tale lovers, and listeners, young and old. In "Sea-Woman," for example, the seal-woman's story is told to a young girl on "an empty, oyster-and-pearl afternoon," by a curious shell which she holds to her ear. The use of language is marvelous—for example, describing the Picts as having "feet so broad that when it rained they could put them up over their heads and use them as umbrellas." A pronunciation guide (although it is not comprehensive) and an appendix giving scholarly sources and author's comments adds to the value of this highly recommended collection.

Carolyn Phelan

SOURCE: A review of *British Folk Tales: New Versions,* in *Booklist,* Vol. 84, No. 10, January 15, 1988, p. 860.

Some may recoil at the subtitle "New Versions," but retelling traditional tales is a tradition in itself. Crossley-Holland's devices for re-creating old folktales include combining several older tellings, providing introductory frameworks, shifting points of view from third to first person, and changing form from prose to poetry. Given the author's gifts as a writer and his respect for his material, it is not surprising to find many wonderful stories among the 55 collected here, some familiar and others relatively unknown. "The Frog Prince," "Tom Tit Tot," "Goldilocks and the Three Bears," "Dick Whittington," and "Sea Women" (a selkie story) are among the well-known tales included. Occasionally a modern touch or tone seems a little incongruous, yet on the whole the offerings ring true. An appendix contains fascinating discussions of the source material and treatment of each tale. Storytellers take note, here is a handsome, scholarly, creative collection.

📖 *WULF* (1988)

D. A. Young

SOURCE: A review of *Wulf,* in *The Junior Bookshelf,* Vol. 52, No. 6, December, 1988, pp. 288-89.

Ten year old Wulf lives in the Kingdom of Essex and in 655 AD welcomes a lone sailor from across the sea. His name is Cedd, a servant of God, seeking permission from the King to build a cathedral and bring the news of Christ to his people.

Wulf joins Cedd and his monks. Through Wulf's eyes we see the funeral rites of King Aethelhere's burial. He tells us how quarrels broke out between the locals and the servants of God. He watches the plague sweep through the land taking Cedd to his death.

The author's deep knowledge and love of this period enable him to bring alive the life and landscape of a dark and distant time. His prose has a poetic strain and he captures in a seemingly effortless way the atmosphere of hope and wonder of that time. The neat and simple black and white illustrations support the text most successfully.

Juliet Townsend

SOURCE: A review of *Wulf,* in *The Spectator,* Vol. 261, No. 8370 December 10, 1988, pp. 37-8.

Kevin Crossley-Holland's *Wulf* . . . catches brilliantly the flavour of Anglo-Saxon imagery, expressed in simple modern English. The subject is the bringing of Christianity to the East Saxons in the seventh century by the down-to-earth missionary Cedd. Wulf the Saxon boy is his first convert, and, as one of his monks, experiences the conflict between the new religion and the old, the hostility of the villagers and his own family and finally the dreadful outbreak of plague which swept through Cedd's northern monastery at Lastingham. The story is based on Bede's account and captures admirably the facts and feeling of this remote age.

Heather O'Donoghue

SOURCE: "Actually Anglo-Saxon," in *The Times Literary Supplement,* No. 4472, December 16-22, 1988, p. 1406.

Wulf is the story of a seventh-century East Anglian child and, as one has come to expect from Kevin Crossley-Holland, there is a wonderfully evocative and accurate sense of time and place about the book. Wulf meets by chance the Northumbrian missionary Cedd (a real Anglo-Saxon one can read about in Bede's *Ecclesiastical History*) and becomes a Christian. When Cedd sets up a monastery in Wulf's home village, Wulf is one of his first recruits, and learns to suffer the hostility of his family and of the rest of the villagers. Finally, while Cedd is visiting his own original foundation at Lastingham, the plague breaks out there. Of a large company of monks loyally making the arduous journey to North Yorkshire to be with Cedd, only Wulf survives a stay in the plague-ridden monastery to return to East Anglia (the *Ecclesiastical History* makes mention of this catastrophe also).

The novel is full of the conventional good things of children's literature: Wulf's fetching baby sister, who comically mispronounces her words; a dramatic contrast between Wulf, dreamy and creative, and his brother Oswald, aggressive and unsympathetic; Wulf's own "special place", a ruined Roman fort by the seashore, where he first meets Cedd and where he goes to be alone and sort out things in his mind. The text also has an agreeable sprinkling of familiar actual Anglo-Saxonisms: the comparison of the pagan's life to the sparrow's brief, dazzled flight through the mead hall between the two great outer darknesses; the riddles Wulf mutters idly to himself while he carves bone combs at home or reliquaries in the monastery. There is excitement when the monastery is dramatically set on fire, and sadness in the serious, moving death-scene.

Despite all this, *Wulf* is not a total success. According to the dust-jacket, it is a "completely revised version" of a trilogy—*The Sea-Stranger, The Fire-Brother* and *The Earth-Father*—published during the 1970s. In fact, re-reading those three short works will show that there are few differences beyond some minor stylistic revisions. Thus *Wulf* falls starkly into three major episodes, and the links between them are rather crudely and perfunctorily effected. For example, at the end of *The Fire-Brother* (now the second section of *Wulf*), Oswald, Wulf's brother, who has burned down Cedd's monastery and then run away, is confronted by Wulf, who argues that though Oswald, as a pagan, is afraid to return because he believes the monks will want revenge, in fact Christians live according to different principles, and Oswald may expect forgiveness. It is a good exchange, and *The Fire-Brother* ends there, not with Oswald's return, but simply with Wulf's sudden intuitive, almost mystical conviction that he has persuaded Oswald. However, in *Wulf,* this turns to anticlimax as the next chapter (originally the opening of *The Earth-Father*) opens with a "two years have now passed" prologue explaining that differences have been buried.

Finally, Cedd's speech is unconvincing. The East Anglians speak standard English; Cedd the Northumbrian peppers every utterance with "happen" and "anyroad" and substitutes "t" for every definite article. It's hard to read (especially for children), linguistic nonsense and infuriating.

Margery Fisher

SOURCE: A review of *Wulf,* in *Growing Point,* Vol. 27, No. 6, March, 1989, p. 5116.

Wulf consists of three linked stories, revised from earlier separate publications, which follow the life of the monk and saint Cedd, his conversion of the East Saxons and his building of a church at Ytancester (the present Bradwell on Sea in Essex). Wulf is another dreamer like prehistoric Tao, a lad who expresses his ideas in stone-carving and who is patronised by his older brother Oswald, a hard-working, practical farmer. Captivated by Cedd's personality and inspired by his ideas, Wulf joins in the building of the church and supports Cedd when he is attacked by the local people, who blame his new religion for the disastrous harvest. When plague hits the Northumbrian monastery where Cedd has retired, Wulf, now a monk himself, goes to nurse the dying saint and returns to take his place at Ytancester. The dignified, simple narrative, decorated with small drawings perfectly in keeping with it, evokes the feeling of change and of a dedication to Christianity that takes practical and spiritual forms in the achievements of a young man whose life has been given a new direction by the incomer Cedd. The mixture of history and imagination is an entirely successful one.

UNDER THE SUN AND OVER THE MOON (1989)

Kirkus Reviews

SOURCE: A review of *Under the Sun and Over the Moon,* in *Kirkus Reviews,* Vol. LVII, No. 15, August 15, 1989, p. 1242.

An intricate counting book that displays dozens of objects in a series of ten formal gardens, all shown together on the grounds of a great house on the first double spread. The neatly composed verse combines a sense of mystery with a certain number of clues; summary pages describe, verbally and visually, the items collected by the boy who appears in each picture, along with the many others that didn't fit in his sack (much flora and fauna plus a few other garden items). In this first book, Penney reveals a gift for organization of meticulous detail into formal, decorative patterns. A sophisticated puzzle for the patient, aesthetically inclined child.

Susan Perren

SOURCE: A review of *Under the Sun and Over the Moon,* in *Quill & Quire,* Vol. 55, No. 9, September, 1989, pp. 25-6.

The picture book *Under the Sun and Over the Moon* is a fine example of the fruitful partnership of artist and poet, in this case Ian Penney and Kevin Crossley-Holland. This counting book in verse uses magical gardens to explore the possibilities of each number from one to 10.

With the opening lines "Under the sun and over the moon / Ten secret gardens, a long afternoon," the reader is taken into the first garden, where there is one of everything: one sundial, one folded wing, one unicorn—and one door where "we'll find out how one leads to more." In the second garden pairs of magpies lead to threesomes in the third: "two threecans—three toucans, I mean!" And so on, until the 10th garden, which is a culmination of all that has gone before, full of magpies, sheep, butterflies, feathers, opals, and apples.

Crossley-Holland's verse is witty and teasing: "What has six faces and twenty-one eyes?" and "What has a tongue and never lies?" Penney's brush and pen produce exotic gardens full of surprises, mystery, and half-hidden things.

Denise Wilms

SOURCE: A review of *Under the Sun and Over the Moon,* in *Booklist,* Vol. 86, No. 2, September 15, 1989, p. 175.

Ten secret gardens and a long afternoon: "Will you come through these gardens with me, / And look, and count whatever we see?" Crossley-Holland's invitation beckons children to scrutinize a series of formal, mannered pictures filled with a variety of items to tally. Each of the gardens has its own delights, and each is decorated with assorted numerical groupings for plenty of counting practice. Some of the objects are subtly placed, giving this the look of a challenging puzzle. An exercise for children equipped with sharp visual discrimination skills, i.e. older rather than younger picture-book readers. A key at the finish shows all the objects that appear throughout the 10 gardens.

Phyllis G. Sidorsky

SOURCE: A review of *Under the Sun and Over the Moon*, in *School Library Journal*, Vol. 35, No. 14, October, 1989, p. 103.

A diverting set of rhymed couplets invites children to participate in a counting puzzle. Progressing through a series of gardens, viewers are challenged to discover all of the objects of a given type. The first garden contains one of each; the number of objects increases by one in each succeeding garden until ten must be found. Not content to have readers look for just one set of hidden items, the artist expands the search by cunningly concealing additional animate and inanimate objects within each garden. The precisely drawn illustrations are stylized depictions of colorful, exotic gardens full of absorbing detail. Some are reminiscent of medieval gardens with wattle fences, topiary trees, and crenelated towers; others have a distinct Eastern atmosphere. The book is a stimulating exercise in observational skills, ideal for primary-grade children or for adults to share with younger children. The satisfaction gained with each new discovery is well worth the effort—and, while difficult, it's fun.

Margery Fisher

SOURCE: A review of *Under the Sun and Over the Moon*, in *Growing Point*, Vol. 28, No. 5, January, 1990, pp. 5277-78.

In ten secret gardens, objects numbered one to ten are placed in scenes stunning in colour and design, placed so that the children turning the pages must find and group the objects as they are cunningly hidden in a wealth of detail; two pages at the end summarise all the delights there to be noticed while the child picks out one unicorn, four bees, six ewes, ten ripe apples and so on. Neat rhymes and incidental snatches of arithmetic (adding, grouping, multiplying) support beautiful, intriguing and enormously inventive scenes in gardens autumnal, exotic, formal, flowery or topiarised, in a book which stands out in the intricate glories of its artwork and its nudge towards accurate thought and observation.

LONG TOM AND THE DEAD HAND (1992)

Ralph Lavender

SOURCE: A review of *Long Tom and the Dead Hand*, in *The School Librarian*, Vol. 40, No. 3, August, 1992, p. 100.

The crux of Kevin Crossley-Holland's collection of East Anglian tales is, perhaps, 'The spectre of Wandlebury', in which Sir Osbert Fitzhugh rides with his squire down the spine of England to Cambridge Castle and the Gogmagog Hills in search of wonders. This tale is told by 'blood-bright words' and with dialogue of extreme terseness, both of which imply a hinterland of meanings to be guessed at. All these tales are steeped in 'the boggarts and bogles, and dead hands in the fen, woodwoses and phantoms', not to mention witches; and Brent Pelham, Cambridge, Watton, Coggeshall—the famously wise 'jobs'—and Suffolk are gazetted. There is a useful sequel to 'Tom Tit Tot', which shows how the king's wife avoids spinning flax the year after she guesses the impet's name. Two stories—'Sea tongue' and 'The wildman' (the latter deprived of Charles Keeping's tormented illustrations from an earlier version) are told by the historic present in what the author calls 'fractured narrative', something new for him. There are also tales which are short and pithy with wit in this most savoury collection of fifteen tales with notes.

D. A. Young

SOURCE: A review of *Long Tom and the Dead Hand*, in *The Junior Bookshelf*, Vol. 56, No. 5, October, 1992, p. 206.

There is an insatiable market for folk tales, ghost stories and spine-chilling accounts of strange happenings which take place in the lonely dark. Fifteen examples in this genre make up a collection of more tales from East Anglia. The first anthology. **The Dead Moon** is also available in this series as *A Children's Classic*.

We have straight-forward horror in the title story; tales with a moral in *That's None of Your Business* and *A Pitcher of Brains Tom Tit Tot* is a Suffolk version of *Rumpelstilzchen* and a neat sequel, *The Gipsy Woman*.

Children will enjoy these stories deep-rooted in the past. Adults and literary buffs will appreciate the Sources and Notes at the end of the book and the style in which the author has presented the legend of the village swamped by the sea and the church bells that can be heard ringing beneath the water. This tale from Dunwich he has cast as a play for several voices crying out for choral presentation after the manner of *Under Milkwood*.

Kevin Crossley-Holland writes for children but he always seems aware of an adult audience in the background.

THE LABOURS OF HERAKLES (1993)

R. Baines

SOURCE: A review of *The Labours of Herakles*, in *The Junior Bookshelf*, Vol. 57, No. 6, December, 1993, p. 225.

Kevin Crossley-Holland tells this well known story in a stylish, lively and readily accessible way. Short, well structured sentences describe how Herakles was conceived when Zeus deceived the most beautiful woman in Greece into believing that he was her husband; how the infant saved himself and his brother by strangling menacing snakes, and how the young man, made mad by the jealous goddess Hera, killed his own family.

Throughout his twelve labours this Herakles adopts a splendidly practical approach, and the lively stories, most of which are dealt with on a double page, maintain a brisk momentum.

In Peter Utton's marvellously lively water colour illustrations Herakles bears some resemblance to Ian Botham and is shown setting about his terrifying opponents with the utmost vigour and sufficient common sense to place a clothes peg on his nose before cleaning the Augean stables.

Mary Medlicott

SOURCE: A review of *The Labours of Herakles,* in *The School Librarian,* Vol. 42, No. 1, February, 1994, pp. 18, 20.

Like all Greek myths, the stories of Herakles are fraught with complexities of purpose and nomenclature. In this telling, Kevin Crossley-Holland creates a strong, forthright narrative which is economical with language but not mean on humour. Zeus begets Herakles on Alcmene because the time will eventually come when the giants will attack the gods. At that time, only the child of a god and a mortal woman will be able to defeat them. Herakles's birth, however, gives reason for revenge to Zeus's wife, Hera. First she tries to drive him mad by making him kill his wife and children and it is to work out penance for this crime that Herakles is obliged by the Delphic oracle to submit for twelve years to the mouse-like King Eurystheus. The tasks he is given would be impossible for anyone but a hero and they culminate in his bringing Eurystheus the three-headed Cerberus, watchdog of Hell. Herakles's reward for his labours is endless life.

A TV tie-in, the book is humorously illustrated by Peter Utton. I particularly appreciated having a map at the end indicating where each of Herakles's twelve tasks were performed.

Jessica Hygs

SOURCE: A review of *The Labors of Herakles,* in *Emergency Librarian,* Vol. 22, No. 1, September-October, 1994, p. 47.

There is action, excitement and tragedy in this retelling of Herakles' labors. Tricked into murdering his family, Herakles must go into the service of King Eurystheus for 12 years in order to pay for his crime. His tasks are monumental, but ultimately Herakles obtains forgiveness and immortality. The text is easily read and flowing, and the plentiful watercolor illustrations express Herakles' experiences with liveliness and emotion.

Additional coverage of Crossley-Holland's life and career is contained in the following sources published by Gale Research: *Contemporary Authors New Revision Series,* Vol. 47; *Dictionary of Literary Biography,* Vol. 40, 161; *Major Authors and Illustrators for Children and Young Adults, Something about the Author Autobiography Series,* Vol. 20; *Something about the Author,* Vols. 5, 74.

Dennis Hamley

1935-

English author of children's fiction.

Major works include *Very Far from Here* (1976), *The Fourth Plane at the Flypast* (1985), *Hare's Choice* (1987), *The War and Freddy* (1991), *Hawk's Vision* (1993).

INTRODUCTION

Lauded for authenticity and a simple style that appeals to young readers without condescending to them, Hamley is known for two perennial elements in his work: the supernatural and war. Many of his tales center on uncovering the truth or revealing hidden stories. Hamley uses period detail and sensitive characterizations to bring history and people alive. His books, with their ghosts, soldiers, and football players, have often been cited for keeping children reading, whatever their reading level. In him they find an author who has the thrilling ability to scare them (but not too much) and to make noncontemporary settings and characters seem real. Moreover, Hamley is a devoted advocate of children's right to expression, whether in telling their own stories, as in the "Hare's Choice" trilogy, or in having the larger story told from their perspective (*The War and Freddy*). Most recently, Hamley has added crime fiction to his repertoire, to the delight of his young adult audience and despite skepticism from the critics who disavow "Point Crime." His overwhelming success in the genre, in which he considers himself following in the steps of Dorothy L. Sayers, P. D. James, Ruth Rendell, and Colin Dexter, has furthered his goal to help create a new generation of dedicated, discriminating readers.

Biographical Information

Born in 1935 in Kent, England, Hamley and his working-class family lived in southern England throughout World War II, which, in retrospect, was "a sort of childhood fantasy" to the author. Higher education had not been available to anyone in his family before, and he credits the understanding and sacrifice of his parents in sending him to grammar school and Cambridge University, from which he earned both a bachelor's degree and a master's; eventually he would earn a Ph.D. from the University of Leicester. Hamley describes himself as a part-time writer and full-time educator. He began the latter career as an English teacher at grammar and secondary schools and also taught at Milton Keynes College of Education in the sixties and seventies and at Open University through much of the seventies. His work in education has included counseling and tutoring, and since 1978 he has been county advisor for English and drama for the Hertfordshire Local Education Authority.

After mulling over an idea for a children's novel for about a year, he began writing in 1971. Three years later the book was published as *Pageants of Despair*. He subsequently judged it to be a "good idea badly presented" and set out to improve his writing skills. His next two books, *Very Far from Here* and *Landings* (1979), were based on less original ideas, he thought, but "better done." Much of the improvement, he felt, could be traced to having subjected himself to the "self-imposed discipline" of writing short stories. Indeed, Hamley set himself the challenge of writing an entire collection of short stories. Working with the scraps of a failed novel, he managed to write two successful stories; thereafter he found that the other stories in what would be the 1984 collection *The Shirt off a Hanged Man's Back* were much easier to write. While recovering from major heart surgery, he lengthened one story that was too long for that collection and published it as *The Fourth Plane at the Flypast* in 1985.

Hamley's own interests are well represented in his books, including a detailed passion for football (*Haunted United*, 1986; *Dangleboots*, 1987; *Death Penalty*, 1994), a great understanding of and affection for cats (*Tigger and Friends*, 1989), and knowledge of the history of railways (*Very Far from Here, The Railway Phantoms*, 1995) and of drama (*Pageants of Despair*). His one trilogy ("Hare's Choice") came about because he could not stop thinking about the questions raised by *Hare's Choice,* the first title in the trilogy. *Badger's Fate* (1992) was the dark sequel to that novel, and *Hawk's Vision* the "joyful (partly!)" last book of the trilogy. The writing of children figures prominently in the trilogy, and Hamley is dedicated to fostering children's expression through writing, which he considers "everybody's right and entitlement." His own writing was inhibited at first by the popular notion that a writer should outline a plan for an entire piece before setting out to write. Experience taught him, however, that it is impossible to know what one has to say before writing it down. By letting the story unfold by itself, he learned that "the end of a story is implicit in its beginning. . . . This to me is now a simple fact which only writing as a sort of act of faith taught me."

Hamley married his Irish wife in 1965 and has two grown children, Peter and Mary, whom he describes as "helpful and assiduous critics" whose "advice I ignore at my peril." He is a member of the Society of Authors.

Major Works

In Hamley's first novel, *Pageants of Despair,* twelve-year-old Peter travels back in time five hundred years to take part in one of the popular miracle plays that had great influence over the people of that time. The mysterious Gilbert has retrieved Peter from the twentieth century to help defeat a demonic plot to send the world into a downward spin morally. Some critics found the work ponderous and overly complex. Hamley's next work, *Very Far from Here,* is a forceful portrayal of mass hysteria and xenophobia before and during World War I. The protagonist, Eddy, and his friend Jim are persuaded that their hometown on the south coast of England may be harboring German spies, and they set out on a crusade to find them. The book was praised for skillful characterization, authenticity, intuitiveness, and humor. In *Landings,* his third novel, Hamley tells the story of two brothers, Philip and Reg, whose grandfather, both as a ghost and through his World War I diary, helps each to deal with his own military experience. Noted for its realism, the book received mixed reviews on the success of its fantastical elements.

Hamley's supernatural tales in *The Shirt off a Hanged Man's Back,* on the other hand, were uniformly praised for craft, cleverness, and depth. Ghosts figure prominently in these stories about mysterious links between the past and the present; indeed, Hamley has declared ghosts to be "useful devices for an author," since they "are good short-circuits for revealing the past." On a somewhat larger scale, ghosts appear also in *The Fourth Plane at the Flypast,* which critics found to be another deft handling of supernatural themes. Sixteen-year-old Sue and her younger brother John are the only ones who see a shattered Wellington bomber plane at an airshow for rebuilt World War II planes. Their search for an explanation for the ghost plane takes them on a journey into their mother's tragic past, which also reveals to them the reason for

the current crisis in their parents' marriage. Hamley was praised once again for his deft handling of the supernatural. *Haunted United* combines Hamley's interest in the supernatural with his detailed knowledge of football. In 1939, the luck of the renowned Bowland Football Club was abruptly reversed by a curse laid on it by a player who was cut from the team; mysterious accidents have befallen some of the team's best players ever since. It takes a psychic girl and an enigmatic old man to unravel the curse.

What turned out to be the "Hare's Choice" trilogy begins with the book of the same name. When Harry and Sarah find a dead hare by the side of the road, they want to honor her life in some way before the day is over. They fix on telling stories about the hare, a project their classmates enthusiastically take up as well. Each child's story reflects his or her preoccupations and interests and contributes to the larger narrative they eventually weave together, one that presents the hare with a choice: to stay with the multitude of deceased animals in an anonymous afterlife or to become one of the animals immortalized in fiction. This intriguing tale was praised for its ingenuity and complexity, and the author felt that a sequel would be a good way to explore the questions it raises. The format of *Badger's Fate* is similar to that of *Hare's Choice*: a class of schoolchildren compose a story about a badger family destroyed by baiters. Hamley was lauded once again for successfully merging a simple prose style with a fairly intricate structure. He used that structure once again in the final book in the trilogy, *Hawk's Vision,* which was even more warmly received than its predecessors. A country school is threatened with closure, and the schoolchildren write a story in which only the hawk that soars over their village can save the whole valley from destruction at the hands of Wizard Worsening. Both their own story and the one they tell are compelling and poignant.

In a vastly different vein, *Tigger and Friends* is an illustrated book for younger readers about a cat modeled on the author's own feline companion. Tigger resents Thomas, the new tabby kitten in the house, but is concerned when the younger cat has an accident. After Thomas dies, Tigger bristles when the Siamese Claudia is introduced but accepts her after he "remembers" his friendship with Thomas. *Coded Signals* (1990) is another collection of supernatural tales, featuring ghosts past and present. Not for the first time, Hamley was cited for employing a clear, simple style that never condescends to his young readers. That style stands him in good stead in *The War and Freddy.* The title character, like the author himself, is three when World War II begins and nine when it ends. Freddy brings a range of qualities and emotions—humor, bewilderment, growing understanding—to this pivotal experience of his childhood, during which his own father goes off to fight, a friend's father is killed, and prisoners of war appear in the fields.

More recently, Hamley has turned to writing crime stories. *Death Penalty* centers, once again, on football, and *Deadly Music* (1995) follows the adventures of two musicians, Katie and Dave, as they study a well-known composer's theme-and-variations composition to figure out the identities of prospective murder victims, whose initials are embedded in the musical work.

AUTHOR'S COMMENTARY

Dennis Hamley

SOURCE: "On Writing Point Crime," in *Books for Keeps,* No. 93, July, 1995, pp. 4-5.

When I said I was attempting a 'Point Crime', some asked, 'Why are you doing this, Dennis?' I understand their problem. Series books are seen as formula fiction, cliché-ridden, slackly written, full of venal wish-fulfilment fantasy, actually inimical to the development of good reading habits: they are published for profit and exploitation of the market; bad money drives out good and children will drown in pap—or worse. 'So have I heard and do in part believe it.' Or *did*. Now I'm not so sure.

I'm not talking about changes in the sociology of children's books or new rules of engagement in the battle for their survival. Though I could, at length. But when my long-standing publisher Andre Deutsch sold the children's division to Scholastic I was suddenly in the Point camp: the UK 'Point Crime' list was being set up together with the existing US 'Point Horror' list, with Fantasy, Romance and Sci-Fi. And the intriguing proposition was put to me: 'Ruth Rendell or Colin Dexter for kids'.

Well, I regard Rendell and Dexter as among today's finest writers—in fiction generally as well as their own sub-genre. And what a sub-genre! All new writing is within a tradition: that's my central tenet. If you aren't in a tradition there's nothing to follow: nothing to rebel against. An invitation to join—in however small a way—the tradition of Poe, Wilkie Collins, Dickens himself, Conan Doyle, Dorothy L Sayers, Raymond Chandler and P D James was something to take very seriously. To check, I read previous 'Point Crime' titles by writers I admire—Jill Bennett, Anne Cassidy, Peter Beere, David Belbin, Malcolm Rose. These books, I thought, were no soft options. They bore the hallmarks which make crime fiction an important branch of the novel—and also important texts for young people to grapple with and interrogate.

All narrative starts with a problematic situation which, through action and formal construction, is resolved. Both author and reader have tasks in this resolution. The author plays fair, setting a track which, though concealed, can be followed. The reader attends to the text, asks it questions and reserves the right to find the answers unsatisfactory. Crime fiction, with its built-in puzzles, shows these features clearly. The ideal close for crime fiction, when the villain is unmasked, is for the reader to say two things at once: 'That was absolutely inevitable: that was a complete surprise.' That's a double seldom won, always aimed for. The two reactions together mean the great satisfaction for the reader. And, of course, it is so with *all* narrative.

I know this satisfaction. When I was 'Point Crime' age myself, I read detective stories, many by names I've long forgotten. Oddly, though, Agatha Christie was not among them. Dorothy L Sayers was—and I still think *The Nine Tailors* is one of the great twentieth-century novels. Like many of my generation I found radio a huge influence—if our parents could afford television sets, what was shown was choiceless, grey patronising rubbish. But Francis Durbridge's *Paul Temple* radio plays in particular held us agog—eight half-hour episodes, a murder an episode, the criminal unmasked at the end and *always* committing suicide before the police (*never* the cops or the Old Bill) came puffing up. We made bets on the school bus on the murderer's identity, discussed plot leads, character, relationships, motive. Unconsciously, we were learning to discriminate and talk critically. This is what Charles Sarland in his *Signal* articles on Teenage Horrors notes children doing with their shared 'Point Horror' books—which Steve Rosson (I believe fatally for his case) does not.

For me, the form dropped away as I moved to other literature. But I knew detective and crime fiction had helped me become a critical reader and I still found peculiar pleasure when I read a Freeling, a Rendell, or a P D James.

Then the suggestion came. I said at once, 'Yes, I *will*.' Here was a chance to attempt a significant form to the best of my ability. I was *not* writing *The Hardy Boys* or *Nancy Drew* (but what right have I to knock them?), nor was I indulging 'a morbid taste for bones'. (Let us, by the way, dispose of the canard that by writing murder stories we descend into the gutter. Deaths in these books are plotted, not gloried in for their own sakes, are punished by an in-built and rigorous system of justice. I have no patience with those who think we are writing video-nasty equivalents. And they should be careful as well—we are *supposed* to be on the same side.)

So I was committed. The feeling which comes after promising to deliver, by an ominously close date, a 40,000-word work of original fiction when there's not a thought in your head is an odd mix of recklessness and despair—doubly so because this was a form I was not sure, despite writer's bravery in the face of the editor, I could tackle adequately.

However, I started from first principles. In all fiction, the background is important: in detective fiction the need is to introduce a tight cast of characters which includes the villain because you can't tack your solution on at the end. My first decision was quickly made. I would return to football, a lifelong passion and already the setting for novels and stories of mine. Straight away I had a potential cast-list of victims and suspects—the personnel of a football club. I had a structure—the rhythm of the football season: a match and a murder every week. The climax was obvious—it *had* to be at Wembley. What would happen there? As a football purist I don't like cups and leagues decided by penalties but as a spectator I find penalty shoot-outs incredibly exciting. Was there a way, I wondered, to make a whole plot balance on the tip of the final penalty which would decide everything? That was a good challenge because it properly defined the task and gave me a title—***Death Penalty***.

When I reviewed progress I realised I'd done nothing different from what I always do in setting up stories. Many writers see characters first, others pose questions to answer. I recognise what C S Lewis said in *On Three Ways of Writing for Children* about seeing pictures and from them deducing an appropriate form. But, so far, there were no individual characters, no motive. How would I find them?

There's only one way. Look back into what you *know*. My football club needed a name. I wanted it to play real clubs although it was fictional. Into my mind swam 'Radwick Rangers', the club at the centre of a wonderful football story in *The Hotspur* in the early 50s: 'The Team That Died'. This uncannily forecast the 1958 Manchester United Munich disaster. Then came memories of a huge football bribes scandal in the 60s (that ***Death Penalty*** coincided with a new one was coincidence, not prescience), and with it the mainsprings for a revenge theme, a murderer and a motive. Good—but where was the dauntingly intricate construction of Dexter or James?

I used to think there were two sorts of writer. The first planned everything before writing: the second just wrote. I tried to be the first, failed, decided I was the second. Now, I see no difference. My first draft, bashed through quickly to see where it goes, *is* my plan. Only in the act of writing can I pick up the hints, make the necessary connections, experience the delight of 'Of course!' as the relationships and causes appear. I read my first chapter to Year 7 in a Middle School, asking them how they thought the story might progress. I was pleased: they picked up one big hint that I wanted them to but didn't spot what I feared was a real giveaway (and no one has since, which is amazing!). Then came a little miracle. I told them the finale would be at Wembley but I needed to know more details about the place. Whereupon one boy gave me exact details of the layout of the Twin Towers while another produced a ticket for a Wembley Tour. Wonderful! So was the tour: I recommend it. And Corry and Graham found the book dedicated to them.

I sent the manuscript to Scholastic three months and five drafts later knowing this would not be the end of things. Julia Moffatt, the Point Editor, is a close and critical reader, homing in unerringly on slips, illogicalities, non-sequiturs. For these books, that's essential. One miscalculation can make the whole edifice collapse. Julia gave me a daunting agenda of revisions, all of which tightened and improved the book, accounting for a complete extra draft.

Some odd things happened on the way. My first wish was for my murderer's justice-cheating leap to be from Wembley's famous Twin Towers. A telephone conversation with the Wembley press officer put paid to that! Hunting for an alternative high place I settled on a road bridge visible from our front bedroom windows. The spot now has an eerie significance for me. In reading the first manuscript, Julia showed why it's sometimes hard for males to write football books for female editors: 'I don't know much about football and I'm always intrigued to find out new things, so is it some sort of initiation rite that young players are "lid-gonged"?' I found the reference and corrected the typing slip in my first mention of Stu and his mates living in a 'club *lodging* house.' Another piece of editing showed how closeness to a story can make its writer sometimes peculiarly blind. I don't want to give too much away, but Mrs. Grundy and her dead Radwick-supporting husband are not all they seem. I sent the manuscript in, quite sure there was no need to explain this. Julia conclusively demonstrated otherwise. Abashed at my myopia I stitched in a passage I now regard as one of the best, most chilling things in the book.

So there it was: my 'Point Crime' in the can. I wanted to repeat this invigorating experience, and resolved to make every autumn 'Crime Time' for as long as I can hold a pen. ***Deadly Music*** appears in November with the background of a youth orchestra on tour, playing a specially written piece. Elgar dedicated his Enigma variations to particular people. What if my composer did the same but every time the variations are played, a dedicatee is murdered? That's a nice 'What if?'—I made a story out of it. Next will be a horse-racing mystery (Dick Francis, eat your heart out . . .) and after that I hope to fulfil a long ambition and write a medieval mystery.

That's the beauty of writing for young people. I can write Crimes *as well as* other books, not *instead of*. I don't want to sound teacherish, but there's a real way in which books for young people enable them to tackle more complex and demanding texts later. When I wrote ***Hare's Choice, Badger's Fate*** and ***Hawk's Vision,*** part of me said, 'These readers one day may want to tackle Italo Calvino.' Anyone who reads my forthcoming ***Spirit of the Place*** may be drawn to Antonia Byatt and Peter Ackroyd. So if a reader comes to ***Death Penalty*** because of the football and leaves with the start of a taste for Ruth Rendell and Colin Dexter I'll be well pleased. And if the adult Rendell-addict finds ***Death Penalty*** worth reading I'll be equally pleased. After all, 'in my father's house are many mansions' and there are just as many routes to the ideal goal of a society of discriminating and critical readers. Critics of the whole Point concept carp at their peril. Evidence from the readers is overwhelming: the testimony of its writers, not just me, should be as significant.

TITLE COMMENTARY

PAGEANTS OF DESPAIR (1974)

G. Bott

SOURCE: A review of *Pageants of Despair*, in *The Junior Bookshelf*, Vol. 38, No. 4, August, 1974, p. 229.

The ancient tussle between God and the Devil seems to

lie at the heart of this tale of sinister skulduggery in the Middle Ages. The central character finds himself whisked back six centuries from a north-bound train to the Towneley Cycle of Mystery Plays at Wakefield. Twelve-year-old Peter is enrolled as an actor, an unwilling participant in a feud that bursts into violence. A good deal of background information on Mystery Plays and extracts from some of the performances crystallise the setting; the atmosphere of religious superstition and its hold over simple folk are captured with a grim reality and a sense of lurking foreboding. Some young readers may well be confused but those who persist and allow the tensions of time and mystery to work will share a strange experience in an unfamiliar world.

Kirkus Reviews

SOURCE: A review of *Pageants of Despair,* in *Kirkus Reviews,* Vol. XLII, No. 19, October 1, 1974, pp. 1065-66.

On the train to Dunfield, twelve-year-old Peter falls into conversation with Gilbert, author of the Dunfield mystery cycle (actually the Wakefield plays) and volunteers to go back with him five hundred years to battle the forces of darkness. According to Gilbert the Evil One plans to infiltrate the pageants and twist their endings into a triumph for the devil. Under these circumstances, it's hard to understand why Peter, who seems an intelligent boy, agrees to accept the role of Isaac, and the vagueness of his scheme to foil the devil by sheer acting prowess is unsettling. Actually the other villagers, who have suspected what is going on, prove far more clever than Peter at beating the devil at his own game, and their strategems are both funny and in tune with the spirit of the plays. Hamley does create a lively picture of how the audiences and actors must have responded to the powerful messages of the miracle plays, but time-traveling Peter is merely a device—more successful as a historical voyeur than as an instigator of action.

Mrs. John Gray

SOURCE: A review of *Pageants of Despair,* in *Best Sellers,* Vol. 34, No. 18, December 15, 1974, p. 422.

The struggle between good and evil, a constant continuing down through time, will, ultimately, end in victory for one—which one? Traveling back through time, young Peter must play a part in the popular Miracle Plays. The mysterious Gilbert, who came to the twentieth-century to get Peter, explains that simple peasants lead good or bad lives depending on such simple influences as the yearly plays that demonstrate the triumph of good. He fears a demonic plot to twist the audience to cheer for Cain, to shout for Abraham to slay Isaac, and, eventually, to start the world on a downward spiraling morality.

Things work out—depending on what condition you think the world is in today—and the history is fascinating. An interesting solution employs ridicule and scorn as the

weapons best suited to put down evil—perhaps Hamley has hit on the right road back to such lace-edged, antique virtues as honesty, gentleness, vision, and love. Regretfully, the writing has all the depth and darkness of a Middle-Ages tapestry—much there but work to ferret out. Bypassing the school children for which it was designed, *Pageants* should find ready users in adults who look for light, historical reading with a satanic tone.

VERY FAR FROM HERE (1976)

Margery Fisher

SOURCE: A review of *Very Far from Here,* in *Growing Point,* Vol. 15, No. 2, July, 1976, pp. 2904-05.

If jingoism has not been entirely eradicated from stories currently offered to the young (and some of the popular anthologies of war stories are certainly keeping it alive), the books under review here are based on attitudes very far from a blind, unthinking nationalistic justification. In *Very Far from Here* the First World War provides a succinct illustration of the need for change in reality and in fiction. The story opens briskly and vigorously when Eddy and Jim, twelve years old, watch the Harold's Bay Wanderers line up for an official photograph after a victory over another South-East coast team in April 1914. Nobody takes the possibility of war seriously—nobody, that is, but the local toff, Mr. Foskett, a retired public school master who is writing a minatory book on the probability that the Germans will invade at this very spot and who has offered his scale-model of Harold's Bay and its rail system to the Government as a base for defence plans. Impulsively Eddy asks if he may see Mr. Foskett's model railway and from that point events proliferate, for the old man, whose obsession grows from loneliness, convinces the lad that there are spies already in the place who must be identified and imprisoned. Who more likely, in the opinion of Eddy and his boon companion Jim, than the polite, probably foreign Mr. Brown at the cycle shop; and, lurking and eavesdropping in the manner of boys, egged on by Eddy's Uncle Bill, whose overbearing manner hides a basic stupidity, the boys come to believe they have enough evidence to rouse public opinion against a man who has in fact fled from oppression in his native Bohemia. The author drives his story towards its harrowing climax, achieving tension by showing clearly how misapprehension is fed—by the departure of George (Eddy's prospective brother-in-law) for the Front, by the appearance of a stout gentleman from Eastbourne with a German car, even by the sensible cautions of Eddy's father which make the boy still more anxious to fulfil what he has come to see as an urgent personal crusade. The story has an actuality that comes from period details naturally used and from the skillful development of character through action, dialogue and description, with a particularly intuitive interpretation of the motives of a schoolboy of sixty years ago. This is a book that should fit present-day taste, with its irony and throwaway humour and its unemotional condemnation of prejudice and mass hysteria.

Brian Baumfield

SOURCE: "Spy-Hunt," in *The Times Literary Supplement,* No. 3879, July 16, 1976, p. 884.

As a straightforward adventure story for children of eleven or over this is successful enough, but it is a far cry from the author's first story *Pageants of Despair*—lacking both its inventiveness and dramatic intensity.

Very Far From Here is set in England, immediately before and during the First World War, and tells the story of Eddy and his search for a German spy in a little Sussex coastal village. Mysterious strangers, and a dread secret weapon being prepared for a German invasion, add to the plot. The pace is slow, and only quickens in the last few chapters when the hunt begins. Young readers might well feel cheated by being presented with a long spy-hunt, and no real baddy at the end of it.

The book is well written, lucid, and there is no suggestion of writing down to children, but the atmosphere of the period does not often come over and characterization is patchy. Eddy does not really come alive, although some of the other characters do—Mr Foskett, the chauvinistic Englishman, George the football star who gets wounded in battle, and Uncle Bill, the slightly seedy lodger.

The documentation is accurate, and there's some splendid stuff about railways—both model and real. It is a pity everything couldn't have moved just a little faster, and had a bit more bite.

Benny Green

SOURCE: "Man and Boy," in *The Spectator,* Vol. 237, No. 7725, July 17, 1976, p. 24.

[W]hen I was ten or eleven, I came across several books dealing with adventurous young lads of around ten or eleven who did things like searching for German spies at respectable watering places, or joining the Boy Scouts and finding plans for the invasion of Britain. Well, Dennis Hamley's *Very Far From Here* is in the same category. Now that the Great War is two crises ago instead of one, and has acquired the patina of antiquity, I'm not sure that schoolboys will thrill as my own generation did to this sort of stuff. I can only report that I thrilled to it greatly. The text assumes a fairly sophisticated grasp of the world as it then was. For instance, we get mention of 'HMS Pinafore', Woolwich Arsenal Football Club, and the London, Brighton and South Coast Railway, all of which ought to stir junior curiosities about the way the world around us has changed and why. I found the book one of the firmest bridges for months along which the schoolchild's sensibility can stride towards mature fiction.

Gordon Parsons

SOURCE: A review of *Very Far from Here,* in *The School Librarian,* Vol. 24, No. 3, September, 1976, p. 243.

First and foremost Dennis Hamley has written a truly exciting story concerning the suspicions of Eddy and Jim that their south-coast home town may be harbouring dangerous German spies only waiting for the critical moment to destroy the nation from within during the First World War.

There is, pleasingly, much more. Without a trace of fashionable nostalgia, he has recreated a vivid sense of small town life in days when children found themselves much more detached from the adult world than they do today. Hamley's novel is informed with a nice sense of the realities of class consciousness, and of the sadness of people caught up in either the political currents of history or in their own personal obsessions—both cruelly destructive. The principal achievement is the writer's ability to deal with such relatively sophisticated themes and ideas without once making one doubt that he has written a book that the young reader will enjoy to the full.

LANDINGS (1979)

A. R. Williams

SOURCE: A review of *Landings,* in *The Junior Bookshelf,* Vol. 43, No. 5, October, 1979, p. 278.

Dennis Hamley has combined his own experience of gliding and National Service pleasantly with memories of the past to present a story full of suspense and human interest. Philip Eastham allows himself to be sent on a gliding course although he is under the permitted age and has to suffer the indignities of failure and the contempt of less friendly cadets. At the same time his brother Reg works himself into deserting from the army as the threat of action in Suez looms over the national serviceman of 1956. Their grandfather's diary of World War I makes Reg even less inclined to undergo the misery of war but the ghost of the grandfather which appears at crucial moments in one way or another helps both boys to 'come up to scratch'. The extracts from the diary should form a salutary experience for younger readers who know war only through films and strip cartoons. There is not a great deal of character drawing but Philip's friend, Debby, emerges as an interesting young lady with sound ideas of loyalty and initiative.

Barbara Elleman

SOURCE: A review of *Landings,* in *Booklist,* Vol. 76, No. 3, October 1, 1979, p. 276.

Set during the Suez crisis in mid-1950s England, this novel perceptively explores the fears of two teenage boys. After their grandmother's death, 14-year-old Philip and his soldier brother Reg inherit their grandfather's diary, kept while he fought (and died) in World War I. Graphic descriptions of his experiences haunt Reg, who faces the prospect of being sent to the Middle East with his tank corps; and when the specter of the dead man arises, Reg, interpreting this to mean his own approaching death, deserts. Philip, whose own fears center on his failure to land a glider plane successfully, also sees the ghost but realizes the reason for its appearance—a message from grandfather about facing life's fears or losing one's self-esteem—and sets out to find his brother. Hamley's fantastical elements are smoothly integrated and the emotional turmoil comes across well in strong characterizations. A thought-provoking theme that crosses boundaries of place and time.

Stanley Swanson

SOURCE: A review of *Landings,* in *Best Sellers,* Vol. 39, No. 8, November, 1979, p. 290.

Philip Eastham, a young British lad, is having trouble making landings in gliders during his Air Training Corps course. Part of his trouble is a worry that his age will be discovered. He is fourteen and should be sixteen. His older brother, Reg, has his problems too. It is 1956 and Reg fears he will have to go to Egypt during the crisis there over the nationalization of the Suez Canal. Their grandmother dies and leaves them a diary kept by their grandfather during the First World War. Reg reads the diary and begins to see his grandfather's ghost, and becomes convinced that he will be killed; he is sure his grandfather is trying to warn him. Eventually Reg deserts his Army Camp.

Philip, the young brother, is sure he can find Reg and sets out on a long train trip to search. The grandfather is now appearing to Philip and encouraging him. Philip finds Reg, persuades him to give himself up, and later, back at his own training camp, manages to learn to land gliders without smashing them.

The book is interesting enough; one does keep reading; but the fantasy of the grandfather's ghost, benevolent as he may be, is too unbelievable. Philip, at fourteen, is playing at something out of the Hardy Boys—he and his grandfather's ghost can do more than adults. Also, the British scene and terms may be too much to interest American adolescents. And then there is the ghost appearing before Reg and Philip, talking to them and even showing Philip how he died in France. Not recommended.

Susan Rosenkoetter

SOURCE: A review of *Landings,* in *School Library Journal,* Vol. 26, No. 6, February, 1980, p. 66.

It's 1956 and the Suez Crisis is boiling. Philip, 14, is attending glider school although (unknown to the instructors) he's too young. He does well except when it comes to landing, but each failure coupled with the growing antagonism of the other boys ruins his self-confidence. His brash older brother Reg enjoys the comraderie of his fellow servicemen. However, the brothers inherit the diary of their grandfather, killed in World War I, and read about the grim realities of war and the hopelessness of the soldiers involved. Seeing his grandfather's ghost as an

omen that he too will die, Reg goes AWOL. Philip, fearing Reg will be shot as a deserter, travels to the army camp in futile hopes of talking to the C.O. Spending the night in a bus shelter, he sees his grandfather's ghost and learns that he died saving two men—one English, one German. The ghost continues to drive the runaway Reg toward Philip while he's attempting a final make-or-break landing. All ends well with Philip learning to fly and Reg returning to his regiment to face only a mark on his service record and some loss of pay. The morals (be true to one's self, it's o.k. to be afraid) are obvious; the plot ending, and characterization are predictable, pat, and uninvolving. The best parts are the diary excerpts which give a fairly good picture of trench warfare.

THE SHIRT OFF A HANGED MAN'S BACK (1984)

Margery Fisher

SOURCE: A review of *The Shirt off a Hanged Man's Back,* in *Growing Point,* Vol. 23, No. 4, November, 1984, p. 4343.

Dennis Hamley's stories of the supernatural are long, substantial and formidably argued. Many of them link past with present when young people are able to set tormented spirits at rest. The title story invokes a bare-fist fight in the past, as a young couple walking home at night from a disco see a shirt fluttering on a tree and in dreams and visions learn the truth about a boxer who as a supposed suicide had been buried at a crossroads. Retribution comes for murder in **'Fraternal Greetings'** and expiation in **'His last Lesson',** as a schoolmaster makes a confession to his bewildered class—but was he alive when he was speaking? Each of these elaborate, reflective tales winds slowly towards a dénouement which surprises the reader even after the preparation provided within the narrative. This is of course a matter of technique. The interaction of past and present in short paragraphs in **'Hear my Voice'** conveys a real sense of horror through verbal rhythms and particularised details; music is the link between a medieval monk and a modern schoolboy, each in his way a genius, each encountering evil as a way towards a deeper understanding of his craft. The purpose of these stories is not to shrivel the blood but to use the supernatural and the supernormal as a way of imaging some of the deepest and most enigmatic processes of the human heart and will.

A. R. Williams

SOURCE: A review of *The Shirt off a Hanged Man's Back,* in *The Junior Bookshelf,* Vol. 49, No. 1, February, 1985, p. 39.

The supernatural elements of Dennis Hamley's nine stories are largely benign and need not lead to nightmares or fear of the dark. If there is a faintly horrific tinge to **'The Last Lesson'** and **'The Shirt off a Hanged Man's Back'** it is balanced by the sheer cleverness of **'Hear My Voice'** and **'The Substitute.'** **'Fraternal Greeting'** has an aura and an ending worthy of Dickens. This is not to say the stories are fun; they all have their moments of dread and tension which arise from confrontations with circumstances which do not yield to reason, and the basic craftsmanship is always sound. Very enjoyable.

David Bennett

SOURCE: A review of *The Shirt off a Hanged Man's Back,* in *Books for Keeps,* No. 38, May, 1986, pp. 22-3.

Dennis Hamley's collection of nine longer stories are less about the strange in ordinary things and more about the past visiting a powerful influence on the present—barefist pugilist Lanahan of the title story seeks the forgiveness of a young ancestor of the man he killed in a fight and to be buried in sacred ground; Brother Leofric seeks to remove the fiend of his medieval making from musically gifted Colin Chiltern in **'Hear My Voice'**, whilst Alfie in **'Study Skulls'** is drawn into a chilling flashback, which sets the record straight between two brothers, one dead and the other hell-bent to wreak vengeance.

📖 THE FOURTH PLANE AT THE FLYPAST (1985)

Margery Fisher

SOURCE: A review of *The Fourth Plane at the Flypast,* in *Growing Point,* Vol. 24, No. 4, November, 1985, pp. 4510-11.

Fate and freewill are in opposition in this story of three generations. Fate in the shape of terrible coincidence lies behind the crisis in Josie Grace's marriage, precipitated not so much by the move from familiar Manchester as by the mysterious familiarity of the new home in an East Anglian village. Freewill is the answer Josie's sixteen-year-old daughter Sue tries to set against the past, when the long forgotten tragedy in her mother's past is finally teased out the girl makes a passionate protest against the helplessness of men, and more especially of women, against the pressures of war and society.

In *The Fourth Plane at the Flypast,* as in earlier novels by Dennis Hamley, the mystery and the substance lie in the interaction of past and present, an interaction that could be generally called supernatural. Italicised passages, not to be fully understood until the end of the book, indicate that a 'plane from the past is being flown by a ghostly crew for some purpose which bears most strongly on Sue and her younger brother John. Perhaps this is partly just because of their youth but it seems also that they are especially receptive because of the unease, even hostility between their parents. At any rate, from the moment when the two children, watching an air-display by three rebuilt World War II planes, see (as nobody else does) a limping, shattered Wellington bomber flying along behind, images of the plane haunt them. John finds an unopened model-kit of a Wellington on the rubbish dump when he has failed to find one in the local shops; the lad who seems in an offhand way to covet Sue's friendship has a better model, wood rather than plastic; the ghostly plane appears more than once before in an alarming moment Sue and John are snatched separately into the past of forty years before, to realise what is hidden in their mother's unhappy, uneasy mind and how events have, as it seems, disturbed and dislocated their lives.

Dennis Hamley confidently integrates a supernatural element into his story, building on the intuitions of adolescence a mysterious force at once outside and part of the two young people. In a note at the end he explains that a tragic accident such as he describes in his story had certainly happened to his knowledge in a town similar to the Lowshall of his setting. But it is not really provenance that makes this such a compelling and believable tale. It is, rather, the very direct prose he uses to carry his characters through events, the entirely unsensational way he adds one detail after another to his fiction, the historical accuracy and pertinence of these details, and most of all the easy, unfussy way he implies mystery in something ordinary:

> It was a fine spring evening. Dusk was falling and the air grew still. Light from the house windows lit up the back garden where John and Sue sat together on a wooden bench talking in low voices. Between them stood the two model Wellingtons, side by side. As John had said, if you bent down and squinted along them at the level of the bench seat, you really did get the impression of two real planes standing massively together in perspective, poised and expectant as if ready to break into throbbing life.

Here is one more novel of unmistakeable quality to add to Deutsch's Ad Lib paperbacks, which offer at a reasonable price books that, added to Secondary School libraries, should help to retain as readers the impatient or lethargic young whose earlier impulses towards speculative and provocative fiction so often dwindle into indifference.

Terry Downie

SOURCE: A review of *The Fourth Plane at the Flypast,* in *The School Librarian,* Vol. 34, No. 1, March, 1986, pp. 72-3.

Boys' title and cover; girls' (mostly) third-person narrative with internal monologue. So who's going to read it? Quite a few, I hope, if ways can be found to break the stereotype barriers—and to cope with the demands of shifting times and viewpoints. An interesting book, it presents a series of italicised fragments within a story which gropes, like its main character, towards challenging the fact that 'We're all at the mercy of things we don't understand.' A family moves and nearly breaks apart as the mother becomes strangely withdrawn. The children are haunted by a Wellington, the fourth plane, which only they appear to see. An agonising flashback or timeslip reveals how their grandparents died when the pilot crashed on his own house in

1943. Their mother has buried this horror in her mind and a way must be found to help her to face it. The daughter, sixteen, perceives other patterns in her family's life and her own future which are potentially just as destructive. She is outraged at how women, and also men, are trained to let things happen to them. 'Life might doom her to failure but she'd do her best to be in charge of her own fate.' In italics, the book ends with the shadowy crew having completed their mission. Or begun it: 'We can do no more. It is up to them. The girl especially.'

Bill Boyle

SOURCE: A review of *The Fourth Plane at the Flypast,* in *Books for Keeps,* No. 46, September, 1987, p. 21.

They are common enough, World War II commemorative flypasts, although dwindling in numbers as the venerable Lancasters and Spitfires gradually give up their ghosts. Sue and John are watching such an air display, when they, and only they it seems, notice an extra plane in the sky: The Wellington, with the black fuselage and the hole in the side, and one engine not working. They couldn't have been mistaken. Or could they? There was no sign of it landing anywhere. Spooky! The apparition won't go away. Why is it happening? Is it hallucinations? Well-constructed plot keeps the suspense as Sue and John get personally involved in the mission of the mysterious Wellington.

HAUNTED UNITED (1986)

Margery Fisher

SOURCE: A review of *Haunted United,* in *Growing Point,* Vol. 25, No. 4, November, 1986, p. 4717.

The North Country town of Bowland enhanced its reputation when in 1879 a patriotic local millowner became Chairman of the newly formed Football Club, which moved quickly up the competitive ladder for more than half a century. But in 1939 the luck changed. A rough, uneducated but talented player was sacked for disruptive behaviour; in revenge he cursed the Club and a series of inexplicable accidents removed over the years several of the best players. A girl with a family association with the Club, and her boyfriend who plays for Bowland United, determine to find the reason for her nightmares and for the curse. Someone else is concerned in the Club's history as well, an old business man who has lost all memory of his life up to 1939, when he enlisted under an assumed name. Football and personal history move slowly forward together in a story filled with action on and off the football field; underneath this action runs a pattern of motive whose tangles are gradually smoothed out. Told in many styles, from antiquated journalese to boardroom formality, from intimate talk to tight description, this fine book reflects the problems of a whole community; it is the kind of multi-faceted novel which the mid-'teens should be able to find more often.

D. A. Young

SOURCE: A review of *Haunted United,* in *The Junior Bookshelf,* Vol. 51, No. 1, February, 1987, pp. 40-1.

This is a football story with considerable complications. Bowland United has slipped to the Fourth Division. Its players are mysteriously assaulted. A young girl's dreams give warning of disaster. An old man turns the pages of his scrap book which informs the reader of the club's activities in 1939 when they won the F.A. Cup and Dan MacCavity, the centre-half, was dropped from the team. MacCavity did not take kindly to his dismissal. He cursed the club and vowed to destroy the players who would replace him.

The resolution of this tangled skein of a plot will strain the credibility of all but the most naive reader. If he is prepared to worry it as a dog worries a bone he may get to the marrow of the matter and enjoy some satisfaction but persevere he must. An interest in football and jigsaw puzzles are probably essential.

Dorothy Nimmo

SOURCE: A review of *Haunted United,* in *The School Librarian,* Vol. 35, No. 1, February, 1987, p. 62.

You would have to be really keen on football to find this compelling; for one who is not it is pretty hard going. Bowland United has been struggling for years. Any promising young player is mysteriously nobbled by a ghost. Who is the benefactor who comes forward to rescue the club? Why does he keep the football reports from the Bowland Bugle of 1939? He has lost his memory, even he does not know that he is MacCavity, turned off unjustly after Bowland's triumph in that year. His *alter ego* haunts the grounds making sure Bowland will never win again. In spite of awkward plotting and interminable extracts from the sports reports, you do get a chilling picture of demoralised players, derelict stands and the end of a great tradition.

David Bennett

SOURCE: A review of *Haunted United,* in *Books for Keeps,* No. 54, January, 1989, p. 21.

'I'll stalk the place. As long as I have breath I'll be at Bowland's heels. I'll lay them low.' Dan MacAvity's revengeful curse against Bowland's Football Club, who have just fired him, fulfils all its tragic potential in the havoc it wreaks on succeeding generations of club officials, players and supporters. It takes a mysterious, ailing old man and a young psychic girl to right past wrongs and make the two facets of Dan MacAvity one.

Dennis Hamley has managed to combine the two popular themes of sport and horror into one successful tale full of thrills, suspense and variety. It's a bit melodramatic at times but most young readers ought to stick with it to the last page.

DANGLEBOOTS (1987)

D. A. Young

SOURCE: A review of *Dangleboots,* in *The Junior Bookshelf,* Vol. 52, No. 1, February, 1988, p. 47.

When Andy Matthews, known to his mates as Dangleboots owing to his uselessness on the football field, spied the miniature pair of boots which might go well on a keyring he felt he just had to buy them. The stall-holder spun him a yarn about the luck they would bring him but Andy was not impressed. Still at 80p they were quite a bargain and he needed all the luck in the world if he was going to get anywhere in the school football team.

The tiny pair of football boots started to make the kind of things happen that Andy wanted but never in quite the way that he intended. He does get into the team but boots the ball into the face of his Dad who has just decided to return home. Dad needs work and he gets it when Andy's well-intentioned efforts at getting back the football stuck in a tree cause the demolition of the school changing rooms.

The stories are exciting and the world of twelve year old school kids is vividly depicted. The illustrations are untidy in keeping with the small boy ethos and match the zany lifestyle of Andy and his friends.

Rodie Sudbery

SOURCE: A review of *Dangleboots,* in *The School Librarian,* Vol. 36, No. 1, February, 1988, p. 20.

This is a story about wishes coming true. The magic isn't taken for granted (though in accordance with the convention for fantasies of this kind, both Andy and Karen respond with coolness to phenomena which ought to have them frightened out of their wits—as they themselves admit). The implications are considered, and Andy reaches a more sober appraisal of himself and his father through realising that his talents alone were not enough to put him into the football team or to achieve the defeat of his school enemy, and that it is hard for his father to avoid or endure family friction, and to find work.

Just at the moment when Andy decides he is living a lie and should get rid of the dangleboots, he gets caught up in a situation where he does need help and immediately loses the boots (I like this). Found by Karen, they do give limited assistance; but when things get crucial, they tell Andy he is on his own—and he triumphs. A little magic help has built him up into a character strong enough to manage by himself. This sounds pat, but is acceptable within the framework of a story which has some very good moments. Although the villains are rather too luridly bizarre for my taste, the downfall of the lesser nasties (the

overbearing Johnny and a supercilious education official) is nicely contrived. There is also a curious and thought-provoking twist at the end of the book.

HARE'S CHOICE (first novel in the "Hare's Choice" trilogy, 1987)

Margery Fisher

SOURCE: A review of *Hare's Choice,* in *Growing Point,* Vol. 27, No. 6, March, 1989, pp. 5109-10.

A hare racing against a car in the road, a man and woman captivated by the beauty of the animal's free movement and then—a swerve under the car, and movement ceases. From the direct, lucid account of an incident hardly unusual on country roads a narrative unwinds in the prescribed limits of a few hours in a particular place. When Harry and Sarah, children of a downland farm, find the dead hare by the roadside and take it to school, they both feel that before the day is up and the animal has to be buried some way must be found to celebrate its life. Divided into two groups to discuss possible stories about it—Harry's at first concerned with space-fiction, Sarah's with witches and their familiars—the children quickly expand their original stereotyped ideas into something more expressive of their preoccupations and of the embryonic understanding of human nature which they are able to work out most readily through some form of fantasy. They begin to construct a story in which both groups join in giving free rein to their feelings of responsibility towards nature and the world they live in.

There is nothing didactic in this move in the story. It emerges naturally from classroom disputation and finds a place in the linked episodes in which each child in turn reads a piece to the Infants and the two teachers. As the tale of 'the Great Queen of the Hares' and of 'Dame Isabel, the Wise Woman' builds up, something of the individuality of the contributors is glimpsed; the episodes reflect the way the imagination of the pupils has been enriched by listening to myths and folk tales and by the continuous interpretation of past and present in terms of their own experiences. Derek is sulky at first because he wanted to bring football in somewhere but he manages to introduce space ships and rockets with an ingenious twist; Freddy is determined to be biologically accurate and when he has finished he is satisfied that Hare 'may have done a lot of unharelike things but she has done them in a very harelike way'; serious Jenny uses shape-changing intelligently and podgy Arthur takes the chance for Hare, in Dame Isabel's shape, to play tricks on a futurist city; skinny Liz and pretty Emma develop the animal's skill and cunning still further in the anthropomorphic terms natural to them but it is Kirsty who describes the blackened waste where Hare hopes men can be persuaded to build their space-port, leaving more fertile country for the animals. So the story winds to the end, its purpose becoming clearer as each child adds to it, until Harry finds an inevitable, simple end-in-a-beginning. But there is yet another immortality for the hare beside the one devised by the children and rising from it. Hare can move on to an idealised Paradise from the limbo in which the author imagines her to be held or she can join another group of animals, those given renewable life in fiction. And so Hare makes her choice and the children, happy with the book made from their stories, are confirmed in their relations to the country they can wander in and explore. Harry and Susan, walking home, look back on the road:

> Far over to the right, on the other side of the road, they could see their own farmhouse, and all its familiar surrounding out-buildings. Beyond that the patchwork landscape stretched into the distance. Far away was the straight gash of the motorway; even at this distance they could hear a faint roar from its traffic.

And a hare appears, white and golden-brown like the Queen they had celebrated. The essential simplicity of the writing and the clear forward movement of the plot carries a message easily and agreeably. The book has a warm and enlivening tone in its picture of a village school with its flexible teaching methods and responsive pupils. It is a stylish tale accessible to readers as young as nine and, like the best fiction always, it pricks one into awareness of insights and ideas beyond its straightforward course.

Kirkus Reviews

SOURCE: A review of *Hare's Choice,* in *Kirkus Reviews,* Vol. LVIII, No. 6, March 15, 1990, p. 424.

Two children find a beautiful female hare dead at the roadside, where she has just had a fatal encounter with the car she was joyously racing. The children take her to school, where she becomes the heroine of a story composed by their entire class.

At first, each child has an independent idea based on a favorite genre; but as they listen to each other, they begin to recognize the value of all these threads and decide to weave them into a single narrative. Negotiations and writing complete, they share their creation—which is at once an entertaining story, a reflection of its contributors, and believable as the invention of imaginative children. And, as Hare herself discovers in the final scenes, it is more: by giving her life in the story, the children have also given her a special immortality that requires her to make a choice. There are two places for animals in the afterlife: one for the anonymous, memoryless multitudes who died unsung; the other for such immortal literary creations as Peter Rabbit, Rat and Mole, Charlotte, and Hazel, empowered by language and imagination. Will Hare join them, or her own kind?

Hamley builds skillfully toward this intriguing, multileveled question; then, wisely, he leaves it open. An appealing, elegantly wrought story that lingers in the mind and is sure to provoke lively discussion. The lovely, delicately suggestive b&w illustrations, reminiscent of Japanese animal paintings, are perfectly in tune with the text.

Roger Sutton

SOURCE: A review of *Hare's Choice,* in *Bulletin of the Center for Children's Books,* Vol. 43, No. 9, May, 1990, p. 214.

A dead hare is immortalized when a group of schoolchildren make up a story about her; having been brought to consciousness by literature, the hare has the choice of two heavens: the ordinary animal heaven, or the literary heaven, populated by Peter Rabbit, Fiver, Wilbur, etc. For a fiercely genuine animal fantasy see William Mayne's *Antar and the Eagles;* Hamley's book is a theme-laden, gimmicky fable best used, perhaps, as discussion material in creative writing class. The schoolchildren's story (which comprises the bulk of the book) is a tepid ecological fable-within-the-fable; its theme of respect for animals seems contradicted by the theme of the book as a whole, which inadvertently implies that animals have no reason for living until a writer assigns them one.

Michael Cart

SOURCE: A review of *Hare's Choice,* in *School Library Journal,* Vol. 36, No. 5, May, 1990, p. 106.

A hare is not a rabbit—a distinction worth noting, for bunnies have become the bad guys of children's books, symbolizing the genre at its saccharine, sentimental, and *cuddly* worst. Happily, this very British import is about a rabbit's larger—and decidedly uncuddly—cousin. When a brother and sister, "both about ten," discover a dead doe hare by the side of a road, they find it too beautiful to bury without a "proper funeral." At school, they—and 13 classmates—spontaneously decide to create a story about the hare so that it will stay alive for them even after the burial. Their invention creates a cosmic choice for the hare, who—although dead—is yet alive in a different state of being. Should she choose to go to an eternally peaceful Valley where she will be the Queen of the Hares, or should she go to a place where dwell animals whose purchase on eternity is guaranteed by the fact that they are characters in children's stories? The hare's choice is deliberately left ambiguous so that readers will have to make their own decision about which is better. If the book has a fault, it is that the differences between the choices are too subtle, neither of them requiring any ennobling sacrifice on the hare's part. Otherwise, **Hare's Choice** is a gratifyingly unsentimental celebration of the life-affirming and life-enriching power of story and offers readers—in the hare— a character who will, indeed, live in their imaginations and memories.

TIGGER AND FRIENDS (1989)

Margery Fisher

SOURCE: A review of *Tigger and Friends,* in *Growing Point,* Vol 28, No. 1, May, 1989, p. 5164.

When a tabby kitten is introduced into the house which Tigger, a Burmese, has regarded as his exclusive property, he exhibits hostile behaviour but eventually accepts the kitten and shows obvious concern when Thomas loses a leg in an accident. The death of his companion does not prevent Tigger from bristling when Siamese Claudia is added to the household, until he 'remembers' Thomas and makes friends. The touch of humanised feeling makes it clear that this may be read as a fable of human relationships but the illustrations [by Meg Rutherford], in a rich range of brown and white shades, extend the brief text by defining cat postures and movements with unerring accuracy.

M. Hobbs

SOURCE: A review of *Tigger and Friends,* in *The Junior Bookshelf,* Vol. 53, No. 3, June, 1989, p. 113.

Dennis Hamley's brown Burmese Tigger, so lovingly portrayed, must be based on a real cat. We follow his move by basket to a family, his jealousy when a grey-striped kitten is introduced into the home, his subsequent close friendship with Thomas and difficulty in understanding his death, his sense of outrage when a new Siamese kitten arrives and his gradual acceptance of Claudia—with Thomas' help. This is a book for cat-lovers rather than children-lovers. Meg Rutherford's delicate paintings show beautifully observed large and fluffy cats, at rest or in action, with vivid blue or grey eyes, well set-off against economic backgrounds.

Phillis Wilson

SOURCE: A review of *Tigger and Friends,* in *Booklist,* Vol. 85, No. 19, June 1, 1989, p. 1723.

The dust jacket notes that the author "observed the events recorded" and Tigger, a coffee-with-cream-colored Burmese cat, is alive and well, a member of Hamley's household. Tigger is boss cat, but his place is usurped by a tiny ball of gray fur named Thomas. Over time there's an affectionate truce, and after Tigger loses a front leg in an accident, Thomas helps him adapt. Then Thomas dies. Once again Tigger must deal with an intruder (a feisty Siamese), but the memory of his gentle companion softens Tigger's reaction and helps him bond with Miss Claudia. The China-blue borders framing each page offer handsome counterpoint to the tan, gray, and cream-colored cats, and the muted, hazy backgrounds harmonize with the fluffy softness of the feline bodies. A sense of realism and honest struggle—akin to sibling adjustment—pervades this tale, making it a fine vehicle for discussion.

BLOOD LINE (1989)

Margery Fisher

SOURCE: A review of *Blood Line,* in *Growing Point,* Vol. 28, No. 5, January, 1990, p. 5267.

The title *Blood Line* refers to a family tree and reveals relationships in the course of an intricate tale in which a television set and a computer provide the medium through which past and present dramatically fuse. The central characters have their own reasons for being receptive to emanations from the century before. Rory, who is fifteen, lives with a mother who brings men home and leaves him to cope with an unexplained situation: the new girl at school, blonde Janine, seems preoccupied with problems of her own. When Rory puts the television on at home one evening he finds every channel is running a family saga, 'The Wolseys of Winderby', set in North Country moorland in 1892, where a local squire needing agriculture and land for iron-works has evicted Adam Barnwell, a shepherd, from his tied cottage. When Adam shoots Luke Wolsey he triggers off a feud which night after night is developed on the screen to the enthralled and alarmed Rory; to his amazement he realises that the new girl Janine, with whom he is building a tentative friendship, is identical with the actress portraying Luke's daughter, and the connection is clinched when a final act is played out in his own house by 'ghosts' whose dangerous influences are deflected by Rory and Janine only just in time. The painful move towards maturity in the young is spelled out in this ghost-story, which in its perception and emotional logic is in fact a great deal more than that.

Dorothy Atkinson

SOURCE: A review of *Blood Line,* in *The School Librarian,* Vol. 38, No. 1, February, 1990, p. 28.

Modern realism seems to be the keynote at first: Rory is a teenage boy with a grey life at school. At home his mother, who is a prostitute, provides him with an electronic nest to exclude her own world next door. The boy escapes into television which is where the fantasy begins. A five-part mini-series, conveniently spanning a week, draws him into its events and Rory finds the programme on all channels while other viewers are watching football. As the episodes reach modern times and he begins to recognise familiar faces, Rory, watching the screen, identifies a personal drama in which his mother is involved. By saving her, he breaks the long run of violence and leaves his own future open before him. Time and the generations, conveyed in terms of TV technique—cuts, close-ups, mood-music—make the business of sorting out a long chain of events a demanding task. It is an ingenious plot and, I think, interested the author more than the matter of expression, which is sometimes rather self-indulgent.

Alice Cronin

SOURCE: A review of *Blood Line,* in *School Library Journal,* Vol. 36, No. 9, September, 1990, p. 250.

Rory, a high-school loner, is scorned by his classmates because his mother is a prostitute. Captivated by a television saga of the rich Wolseys and their many-generations struggle against the impoverished Barnwell family, he notices that it is the only show on every channel. No sports, no news, nothing else. **Blood Line's** fascinating plot will draw in teenage fantasy fans and hold them until the very end, for the final chapter of the Wolseys and Barnwells comes to life in Rory's home, explaining why Rory and his mother are what they are.

Nancy Cleckner

SOURCE: A review of *Blood Line,* in *Booklist,* Vol. 87, No. 1, September 1, 1990, p. 46.

Television is Rory's obsession and the emotional center of his entire world. One evening, a disturbing program about two families appears on every channel. Rory soon finds out that no one else at school has seen the drama. When a new girl who resembles one of the show's main characters appears in his class, he realizes he must be dreaming, and his world suddenly becomes full of haunting questions: What is Mum's given name? What happened to his father? Why is his family background never discussed? Why does Janine, his beautiful, distant classmate want to see him? By the time Rory discovers how the television drama relates to his own middle-class British life, the final episode of the series is evolving in his own apartment.

CODED SIGNALS (1990)

Margery Fisher

SOURCE: A review of *Coded Signals,* in *Growing Point,* Vol. 29, No. 4, November, 1990, p. 5430.

The vagaries of mind and heart in these stories edge from ordinary to unordinary, first in uncertainty as a group of young people hold a seance which evokes more power than they are ready to understand and then into more alarming encounters. A bicycle tragedy is re-enacted in **'Time Trial'** and an imaginary monster exercises a malign power over adolescents in another chilling piece. These tales are more than 'ghost stories', for they perceptibly sway the feelings and attitudes of the young and in doing so they are likely to stretch the imagination of readers who should be ready to respond to strange and unpredictable events.

Margaret Campbell

SOURCE: A review of *Coded Signals,* in *The School Librarian,* Vol. 38, No. 4, November, 1990, p. 158.

A selection of ghosts—one a modern cyclist, one a boy who died in hospital, and a starving family from the Irish famine of 1840—appear in this selection of short stories, along with a monster who comes out of the TV screen and a group of strange creatures seen by only one girl at a seance. The encounters are too brief to worry the reader unduly but all are curious enough to interest anyone over

about ten. It is a book to dip into rather than read straight through since one story needs to settle before you go on to the next one.

The Junior Bookshelf

SOURCE: A review of *Coded Signals,* in *The Junior Bookshelf,* Vol. 55, No. 1, February, 1991, p. 39.

The prolific Dennis Hamley has gathered together eight short stories under the Adlib paperbacks imprint (Deutsch). A number of the stories have appeared in previous anthologies and are now revised for this new book. 'Eight tales to ponder on' is the book's sub-title and it accurately reflects the use of mystery and the supernatural. The title story, **'Coded Signals,'** directs the reader's attention to a seance, not towards scarifying aspects but more humorous events. Hamley's tone is rich and he in no way writes down to a youthful audience. The teenage market should persevere with these stories for there is much to be gained by way of quality and literary value. Hamley's characters stand out clearly, and his descriptiveness while not being poetic is always fully and colourfully painted. The variety of subject matter, the diversity of character and the overall sense of the unknown and its mysteries makes for a solid and entirely enjoyable collection of stories.

THE WAR AND FREDDY (1991)

George Hunt

SOURCE: A review of *The War and Freddy,* in *Books for Keeps,* No. 72, January, 1992, p. 9.

Freddy is three when the war begins, and nine when it ends. In the intervening time he observes the world, goes to school, struggles into reading and endures the delights and disappointments attendant upon friendship and family. At the end of the book, Freddy is glad the war is over, but an awareness of atrocity and holocaust have changed his world forever.

The story is vividly told with a great deal of warmth and humour, and no sentimentality. Its social history value is enhanced by excellent illustrations. A book to provide thought-provoking shared reading for groups of older children.

Margery Fisher

SOURCE: A review of *The War and Freddy,* in *Growing Point,* Vol. 30, No. 5, January, 1992, p. 5638.

From the age of three to the age of nine Freddy experienced the war as a series of incidents unordered and seldom understood. By arranging facts chronologically from a single point of view the author makes matters of rationing, air raids, the dislocations and tragedies of war, seem fresh and personal. At first the emotional reactions of a small child seem a little contrived ('Wars, thought Freddy, must be everywhere' . . . but why should crossness 'lead to sad, tired men coming to their town in long, slow trains') but the oblique view of World War II settles down into close, convincing narrative as Freddy is affected by the 'Big boy' Michael who leads the local, informal 'South Road Army,' by his first sight of German and Italian prisoners, by the Meccano set so desperately desired and so hard to sort out, by the farewell to Dad and his happy return. His experiences are related to national events in a sharp, moving and vigorously expressed sequence of recent history.

Marcus Crouch

SOURCE: A review of *The War and Freddy,* in *The Junior Bookshelf,* Vol. 56, No. 1, February, 1992, pp. 30-1.

This is history as seen through the eyes of Freddy, who is three when the Second World War begins, nine when it ends. The author never cheats. Here are bewildering events, and the little hero has to work out their meaning for himself. This leads inevitably to confusion and much hearty, but never unkind, comedy.

The adult world that Freddy inhabits is a puzzle. Why don't grownups say what they mean? Colloquialisms and irony alike are lost on Freddy. Grandad Bassett 'did his bit' in 1914. To Freddy, who is expected to do his bit in the lavatory every day, this is a mystery. Then Uncle Jim, who is in a reserved occupation (and what can this be?) 'should be out there doing his bit'. Freddy decides that this must be a family complaint. 'He's no son of mine', thunders Grandad. In that case, reasons Freddy, he must be a spy. Confronted with official propaganda and the simplistic philosophies of his family, Freddy struggles towards understanding. He also has trouble at school, deciding, after a brief acquaintance with a 'reading scheme', that 'reading definitely wasn't worth the effort'. He and Mummy solve that problem by following Daddy's progress across North Africa in the newspaper. It isn't all fun. The reality of War intrudes. Daddy is taken prisoner, Stella's daddy is killed. Prisoners-of-war appear in the fields, and Freddy learns from a big warm-hearted Italian that the wornout conventions of Grandad and Mr. Binstead-next-door are not a key to reality. At nine, Freddy begins another lesson, about peace. 'Another life was starting and he was ready for it.'

Funny, wise, wonderfully readable, this book, with its admirable illustrations by George Buchanan, should find a wide readership, among war veterans as well as the nine-year-olds for whom it is probably intended. The latter should not be put off by the extreme youth of Freddy at the outset. The way he grows, develops and forms his own conclusions is the essence of the story. This is by no means kid's stuff, although it is great stuff for kids.

Sue Rogers

SOURCE: A review of *The War and Freddy,* in *The School Librarian,* Vol. 40, No. 1, February, 1992, p. 20.

The Second World War can seem like a long ago historical event to young people, but stories like this have the effect of capturing the essence of the everyday lives and problems of ordinary people during the war years and of bringing history alive in a far more effective way than any textbook history. The book starts in 1939 when Freddy is three. To him, gas masks, men in uniform, low-flying Spitfires are the norm, and playing soldiers with his gang a wonderful game. Reality strikes home when his father is called up into the army and has to leave home. Eight chapters later, it is 1945 and Freddy is nine. Six years have gone by without his father and Freddy has grown in many ways. He has seen how people have suffered and had to make do, and he now understands more about war and why the adults are glad it is all over.

Dennis Hamley will captivate his readers with this wonderful, thought-provoking and, above all, humorous collection of stories. George Buchanan's line drawings complement the text superbly and the overall production is excellent. A must for every library, it will be enjoyed by both older junior and secondary pupils.

📖 *BADGER'S FATE* (second novel in the "Hare's Choice" trilogy, 1992)

A. R. Williams

SOURCE: A review of *Badger's Fate,* in *The Junior Bookshelf,* Vol. 56, No. 4, August, 1992, p. 154.

It seems readers will have to adjust to or reconcile themselves to a steady recurrence of stories in which animals fight bloody wars in defence of themselves or their environment, assisted by humans on the side of Right. Following on a resumé of his earlier *Hare's Choice* Mr. Hamley embarks upon an indirect crusade on behalf of local badgers already exploited by a blood-sport gang, their sett destroyed. In the pattern of *Hare's Choice,* the local primary school children compose a badger story to illustrate the possible fortunes of a badger in the wild. This device offers interesting opportunities for class discussion, entertaining dialogue about story-telling and some conflict over badger mentality, all woven among everyday details: the mechanics of the school day; home life and personal relationships among the children and adults. Working in pairs they put together their allocated sequences prior to reading them before the whole school. (Was a word processor really necessary for this exercise, one wonders.) Their badger reluctantly undertakes to be king of the creatures that include mice, voles, shrews and rabbits supported by the birds against the weasels and stoats. The latter are bested but the badger king calls a meeting of *all* the creatures to plan coexistence in peace. The book is rather more intricately conceived than a summary can suggest with flashbacks and cross-cutting which demand the reader's whole attention. The author's—and children's—style is simple but not woodenly so, and, although adult characters are less rounded than the younger, good use is made of them to preserve a sense of usualness amid the euphoria of story-making. Natural backgrounds are drawn with care but not obtrusively. Meg Rutherford's illustrations bear out her personal interest in the book, acknowledged in the author's Note, which includes a brief reading list.

Marcus Crouch

SOURCE: A review of *Badger's Fate,* in *The School Librarian,* Vol. 40, No. 4, November, 1992, p. 146.

Like the author's *Hare's choice,* this clever story treats in parallel a nature theme (a badger family destroyed by baiters) and an exercise in communal creative writing in a village school. Comparisons with the earlier book are inevitable, and are in effect invited by the writer. Nothing in *Badger's fate* quite rises to the heights of the description of the hare's delight in the joys of speed, but in other respects this is the more successful book. The scenes in the school, where children discuss the story they are to write about the dead badger and iron out their differences (or agree to differ) are admirably done, although I fancy that most primary teachers will envy Mr. Bray his highly articulate pupils. Each child's contribution reflects an individual personality, even if they all subordinate their will to the general theme. I am less happy about the chapters which follow Badger on his posthumous quest through the animal limbo. The book would be equally powerful and more convincing without these mystical elements. Dennis Hamley has strong support from Meg Rutherford, whose accurate and evocative studies of animals lift the story on to a higher artistic plane.

HAWK'S VISION (third novel in the "Hare's Choice" trilogy, 1993)

Geoffrey Hammond

SOURCE: A review of *Hawk's Vision,* in *The School Librarian,* Vol. 42, No. 1, February, 1994, p. 20.

A village school is about to close. A hawk is aloft close by. The fates of the two are intertwined in this compelling tale, for in the doomed school are children who are storytellers and it is their wish that the last story they will create will centre on the hawk. They create a character called Wizard Worsening, whose aim is to destroy the valley and thus the homes of all who live there. Only the hawk can prevent this destruction, but can the children realistically allow this to happen while their own school tips towards closure? As before, in *Hare's Choice* and *Badger's Fate,* Dennis Hamley has written a book which compels on two levels: not only presenting the children's struggle to tell a tale well, but also creating a story by them which is exciting in its own right. It will probably be most enjoyed as the culminating triumph of the trilogy, a fine read for those around 10.

The Junior Bookshelf

SOURCE: A review of *Hawk's Vision,* in *The Junior Bookshelf,* Vol. 58, No. 2, April, 1994, p. 67.

Dennis Hamley's third book in his trilogy (*Hare's Choice* and *Badger's Fate* being the two earlier books) is a most seductive mixture of realism and the fantastical. The quiet tone and gentle handling of the narrative give *Hawk's Vision* a sense of timelessness and profound peace although there is great sadness in the telling. The story of how children in a tiny (and threatened) village school relate their own story to the Infants, is moving and memorable. The reader will find him/herself sucked into a vortex of captivating fiction in which the struggle for life goes on against stacked odds. *Hawk's Vision* is not a long book— less than 100 pages—but what is there has been pared to the bone. This is story-telling of importance as the author communicates the very nature of compassion. Dennis Hamley knows children (he worked for years in education) and his writing lifts young readers to higher levels of understanding. It all seems a world away from contemporary writing devoted to the street-wise and trendy. Meg Rutherford's fine drawings of kestrels add to an altogether elegant book. *Hawk's Vision* should without doubt feature on any short list for book awards.

DEATH PENALTY (1994)

Adrian Jackson

SOURCE: A review of *Death Penalty,* in *Books for Keeps,* No. 90, January, 1995, p. 10.

Not only does this come as part of a very popular series, from a popular writer, it's also cheap, it's exciting, it centres on football and has a marvellous climactic scene at Wembley when the whodunnit is solved in the most surprising way. Add to this the fact that it's about the fixing of football matches and you have a further reason to buy copies knowing it will be read to death.

THE RAILWAY PHANTOMS (1995)

Peter Hollindale

SOURCE: A review of *The Railway Phantoms,* in *The School Librarian,* Vol. 43, No. 3, August, 1995, p. 117.

The fictitious preserved railway in Dennis Hamley's novel is fairly clearly based on the Keighley and Worth Valley line in Yorkshire, which runs through Haworth. Something of the atmosphere of *Wuthering Heights* reaches into this book, with its bleak grey village, desolate moors, and tyrannous, passionate, hate-filled stationmaster, a Heathcliff of the tracks. He belongs to a nineteenth-century world, where a terrible railway accident has caused death and tragedy. This accident is the source of a recurrent dream for Rachel in the present day, and when she reluctantly accompanies her divorced father for a week's holiday on his beloved preserved railway in Yorkshire, she recognises the line as the location of her nightmare. By dreams and ghostly presences she is summoned to unlock the mystery of a century-old disaster, to correct an old injustice and lay troubled ghosts to rest. Helped by new friends in the railway village, she gradually discovers that her own ancestors are the victimised people of her dreams. In releasing them, she also releases her father and herself from nightmare.

This is a powerful, atmospheric story, full of the sights, sounds and smells of steam railways, which provide an authentic backdrop to the ghostly happenings. The dreadful truth about the crash is revealed through a shameless narrative contrivance, but the haunting of Rachel, rather than the mystery of the accident, is the true subject of this compelling story.

SPIRIT OF THE PLACE (1995)

Gill King

SOURCE: A review of *Spirit of the Place,* in *The School Librarian,* Vol. 44, No. 1, February, 1996, p. 30.

There couldn't be a link between Lindsey Lovelock, a university student, her boyfriend, Rod Grainger and an 18th-century poet and scientist called Nicholas Fowler—or could there? Nicholas Fowler builds an underground grotto on his Coswold estate, writes poetry and is convinced that man's role is to perfect what nature was unable to make perfect herself. Lindsey chooses Fowler and his poetry for her long study. Rod, also a student, is becoming increasingly interested in genetic research and Coswold, Fowler's old estate, is now a genetic research unit next to the university. Throughout the twists, turns and sudden shocks of the plot weaves the sinuous body of the cat, as enigmatic as the sphinx one moment, helpless and vulnerable the next.

From the first page to the last one—which had me wiping a tear from my eye—I couldn't put the book down. The story is superb and very poignant, and suitable for age 14 to adult. Just out of interest, Mr. Hamley, how many cats do you have in your family?

Steve Rosson

SOURCE: A review of *Spirit of the Place,* in *Books for Keeps,* No. 97, March, 1996, p. 13.

Shades of Peter Ackroyd in this time slip novel. Eighteenth-century poet and scientist, Nicholas Fowler, believes that Man's destiny is to perfect Nature. He commissions large scale landscaping, builds a grotto and experiments with electricity at his country estate, Coswold. Modern-day Literature undergrad, Lindsey Lovelock, chooses Fowler as the subject of her major study while boyfriend, Rod, is more interested in the genetic research that's taking place there. The historical scenes as Fowler incurs the fear and loathing of servants and neighbours are inter-cut with modern times—Lindsey, in a hospital bed suffering from amnesia, and Rod being questioned by the police about a break *out* from Coswold. Slowly the story is pieced together and, yes, Fowler, Lindsey and Rod *did* make contact across the centuries. It's all very cleverly done and with references to Pope, to a number of Fowler's Philosophical Odes (courtesy of the author), and much debate and discussion, this is one for potential A* Literature candidates I think.

DEADLY MUSIC (1995)

Sheila Allen

SOURCE: A review of *Deadly Music,* in *The School Librarian,* Vol. 44, No. 2, May, 1996, p. 72.

Katie, a cellist, and Dave, a trombonist, play in a county youth orchestra which is giving a series of concerts. Their conductor persuaded Hugo Malvern, a well-known composer with whom he was at college, to write a new work for them. Hugo produced a piece in four movements, a theme and variations composition with place names and initials as titles of the movements. Katie and Dave live near the first of these places. After the first performance conducted by Hugo, Katie and Dave learn that a murder occurred at the site mentioned while they were playing and that the victim's initials were those of the following movement. Other murders follow, obviously connected with the music. Katie and Dave become friendly with the solo pianist and together they begin to learn of events which took place when the conductor, the composer and the leader of the orchestra's mother were all at college together. Katie gets herself into a dangerous situation before the villain is unmasked.

This is a complicated story and the book begins with an incomprehensible prologue which fortunately is only a few pages long but must be read first in order to understand the plot as it is revealed. However, by the end of chapter one, the reader is hooked.

Additional coverage of Hamley's life and career is contained in the following sources published by Gale Research: *Contemporary Authors New Revision Series,* Vol. 26; *Something about the Author,* Vols. 39, 69; *Something about the Author Autobiography Series,* Vol. 22.

Christie (Lucy) Irwin Harris
1907-

Canadian author of fiction and reteller of folktales for young people.

Major works include *Once Upon a Totem* (1963), *You Have to Draw the Line Somewhere* (1964), *Raven's Cry* (1966), *Secret in the Stlalakum Wild* (1972), *Mouse Woman and the Vanished Princesses* (1976).

INTRODUCTION

With over twenty books to her credit, as well as numerous short stories and radio plays, Christie Harris is best known for her fiction for young people that is based on the history and mythology of the Canadian Northwest Indians. In addition to her retellings of Indian legends, Harris has also written books in other genres—including historical fiction, such as *Forbidden Frontier* (1968), and fictionalized biography, in which a young protagonist, in each case based on one of Harris's own children, comes to terms with his or her familial role and experiences the rewards and setbacks of a challenging career. Yet Harris has received the most critical acclaim for her works on Indians of the Pacific Northwest. Following extensive research that is anthropological in its attention to the details of lost Indian cultures, Harris has brought these cultures to life in such works as *Raven's Cry*, her "Mouse Woman" series, and *The Trouble with Princesses* (1980), offering an authentic depiction of Indian life that gives younger readers a sense of how these tribes once functioned and flourished. She has been praised not only for placing the stories in a historical and cultural framework that serves as a kind of road map for the reader, but for retaining the original flavor of the legends while recasting them in her own lyrical writing style. Most notably, however, Harris has been commended for her compassion and insight into these Indian cultures; she neither romanticizes nor patronizes her subject matter, reporting about Indian life and lore with a clear eye and sympathetic heart. Her goal has been to capture the interest of and enlighten middle-grade and high-school readers regarding Indian culture, while remaining true to the integrity of those cultures. Harris derives the deepest personal satisfaction from her reputation among Indian people. "[All the] native approval of what I do makes my heart sing," she told Cory Davies of *Canadian Children's Literature,* "so I just keep on writing."

Biographical Information

Born in Newark, New Jersey, in 1907, Harris moved with her family when she was an infant to a farm in western Canada. Having inherited her Irish-born father's gift of storytelling and growing up before the age of radio and

television, Harris, whose one-room schoolhouse education gave her access to only a smattering of books, often told stories or recited poetry to make her farm chores seem less tedious. In high school she wrote the district news for her town's newspaper but did not aspire then to become a writer, enrolling after graduation in a teacher's college. It was while teaching in a primary school in Vancouver that Harris's interest in and talent for telling stories resurfaced; reading and making up tales for elementary-age children became her passion, and after selling several stories to the *Vancouver Daily Province,* she became a regular contributor to its children's page. In 1932, after a long engagement, she married Thomas Harris, a member of the Royal Canadian Mounted Police, and was forced to leave her job because married women at that time were not permitted on school staffs. Harris divided her time during this period between raising her five young children and bolstering her writing career: she wrote several short radio programs for children and was asked by the Canadian Broadcasting Corporation (CBC) to create a longer juvenile production for King George VI's Coronation Day in May of 1937. This led to many other projects for the CBC over the next twenty-five years, including plays and sketches for adults, school broadcasts, women's talks, and a children's adventure serial. Harris published her first children's book, *Cariboo Trail*—which told the story of the 1860s gold rush in British Columbia—in 1957, after she was asked by the publisher Longmans, Green, of Toronto to write a historical novel. Soon after, the CBC invited her to write a series on the declining Indian cultures of the area, and Harris spent three years doing intensive research in museums, among archives, and amidst Indians before retelling legends traditionally associated with totem poles in *Once Upon a Totem*. Her growing fascination with Indian cultures evolved into a long and remarkable writing career, and over the next three decades she produced a sequel book retelling Indian legends about totems; a work featuring supernatural creatures inhabiting the Lower Fraser Valley; a series about the Mouse Woman figure of Indian lore; and *The Trouble with Princesses*, recounting the dangerous and romantic adventures of Northwest Coast Indian princesses. She has also written several books in collaboration with her own children, who became models for the main characters in *You Have to Draw the Line Somewhere*, *Confessions of a Toe-Hanger* (1967), and *Let X Be Excitement* (1969). Harris has received numerous awards for her books, and in 1981 was invested in the Order of Canada.

Major Works

Harris's first work about Northwest Pacific Indian culture is *Once Upon a Totem*, a collection of five tales based on the adventures of Indian ancestors and tales of mythical tribal heroes, which were represented on the intricately carved and beautifully painted totem poles of this era. Each of her retellings is prefaced with a brief description of the legend and its historical context, and the stories have a lyrical quality that captures the creativity and intelligence of these Indians and the conflicts they encounter between good and evil. In *You Have to Draw the Line Somewhere*, Harris shifts her focus to her own family, basing this work on the aspirations to become a fashion artist of her eldest daughter—and the book's collaborator and illustrator—Moira Johnston. As much biography as it is fiction, favoring episodic accounts over linear plot, this book follows Linsey Ross-Allen from her dreams at age nine to her success as a fashion artist, including the difficulties she experiences as a young woman in trying to balance a career with marriage and children. Using humor and a light touch, Harris nevertheless de-glamorizes the world of fashion art and emphasizes the hard work it takes to succeed in this field. *Raven's Cry* signaled Harris's return to the study of Indian culture. This historical novel traces the lives of three great Haida Eagle chiefs, beginning in 1791 when the Haida nation—with its dynamic system of trade, ancient tribal traditions, and collective sense of dignity—was a powerful force, to three generations later, when the tribe was scattered, depleted, and nearly stripped of its riches. In her treatment of how English and New England seamen carried away by ship the treasures of the Haida people, Harris manages not only to evoke a deep sympathy for the Haida perspective but to reproduce and resurrect—through accurate detail and strong illustrations—the former greatness of this now dead culture. The dramatic tension in *Secret in the Stla-*

lakum Wild is built around the presence of "stlalakums"—unnatural spirits in a natural world, according to Indian folklore—and their influence on a sensitive teenager called Morann, who feels that she will never measure up to her more accomplished, older siblings. Combining elements of family drama and fantasy, Harris uses this book as a bid for the conservation of the wilds of British Columbia, her message coming through Morann, whose alliance with the "stlalakums" earns her the self-esteem and respect from others that she seeks. In her "Mouse Woman" series, including the titles *Mouse Woman and the Vanished Princesses*, *Mouse Woman and the Mischief-Makers* (1977), and *Mouse Woman and the Muddleheads* (1979), Harris recounts the adventures of a supernatural, shape-changing being, who can appear as a mouse or as a tiny and prim grandmotherly figure. With a penchant for raveling bits of wool into mouse nests, the title character in *Mouse Woman and the Vanished Princesses* is saddled with the task of giving advice to princesses who have been lured away from their tribes by "narnauks," and assisting them in returning to their homes. In each tale, Mouse Woman acts as intermediary between the supernatural world and Earth, where she is regarded by the Indians as a helpful, if meddling, spirit.

Awards

Harris earned the Canadian Association of Children's Librarians Book of the Year for Children in 1967 for *Raven's Cry* and in 1977 for *Mouse Woman and the Vanished Princesses*. *Secret in the Stlalakum Wild* won British Columbia's International Book of the Year Award for Juvenile Literature, in 1972. *Mouse Woman and the Vanished Princesses* received an International Board on Books for Young People (IBBY) honor list citation, 1978. *The Trouble with Princesses* earned the Governor General Award and Canada Council Children's Literature Prize in 1980 as well as Canadian Library Association runner-up honors and the Amelia Frances Howard-Gibbon Award in 1981. For her body of work, Harris earned the Vicky Metcalf Award in 1973 and was named a member of the Order of Canada in 1981.

AUTHOR'S COMMENTARY

Christie Harris with Cory Da

SOURCE: in an interview in *Canadian Children's Literature*, No. 51, 1988, pp. 6-24.

[*The following excerpt is from an interview by Cory Davies.*]

Davies: I would like to begin by asking you just how you began writing.

Harris: When I was a young teacher in Vancouver—I was teaching grade one, actually—I was always telling stories to the children, and reading stories. I really don't know how it happened. Just one day, out of the blue—I must have been about twenty—out of the blue it hit me. I could write my own stories. I got so excited I couldn't teach; I mean, I could teach, but I couldn't wait for recess and noon and after school; and by the end of two weeks I had nine little stories for children. Little kind of nothing stories.

I didn't know what to do with them, but I was all excited. I took them down to the *Vancouver Daily Province,* where they had a children's page. I just went in and handed them in—all written out in longhand—I didn't even have a typewriter—then I went back to teaching. Then I began to wait, and I was just going crazy waiting to hear if anything had happened. One day when I couldn't stand it any longer, I took a street car and went down to the *Province,* walked in and told them my name. Somebody jumped up from a desk and said, "You left stories here and you didn't leave a telephone number or an address. We're buying them all, and we've already got two of them set up in print." That was the very first time I'd ever tried to write a story, and I'd sold the nine, like that. So I was hooked for life.

Davies: You must consider that there's an incredible power that the storyteller uses and then transmits. You speak with such excitement about storytelling.

Harris: It's just, I grew up with this. My father, an Irishman, was a farmer, and he told stories. His stories were always very funny, extremely entertaining. Everybody came to our farm just to hear him tell his stories. I guess I grew up thinking stories were an important part of life; a storyteller was a natural part of life.

Davies: You speak of entertainment as being so much a part of the storytelling.

Harris: Very much. I mean, if it isn't entertaining; if you don't want to listen to it; if you're not just delighted with it, forget it!

Davies: What else?

Harris: I would never tell a story to teach anything. It's the story that matters. To me, it's the story.

Davies: And yet you have a commitment to writing that also includes a sharing of other worldviews. I'm thinking particularly of your commitment to—

Harris: The Indian view?

Davies: The Indian view partly; to the Indian legends; to Haida Art.

Harris: Yes, yes, but you don't think of it that way. It's just like my children say, "Mother, you're so disciplined." I don't feel disciplined. I start work every morning at eight, just because it's wonderful to start work. I'm happy to start work at eight. I don't sense a commitment to anything. I just like stories, and they've got to be right. I suppose I unconsciously feel they have to say something.

Davies: For whom do you write them, then? As much for yourself?

Harris: I write the story for the story, I think.

Davies: And the story will take the shape that it needs to take?

Harris: I think so.

Davies: You don't consciously write for a certain market?

Harris: No; I don't consciously write for children. I have it in mind. I even have the American market in mind in that that's where I'm published first. I have to write "labour" "labor" but that's about all the attention I pay to it, just my spelling. And I don't keep thinking—my husband says "You don't write for children; you write for the family." I write the story the way I want to write that story. My editor, Jean Karl, says that children's writers are like that. They write what they want to write, the way they want to write it, and it just happens to be right for children.

Davies: C. S. Lewis says the same thing; that if you're writing the proper kind of story for children, you're writing the story; it takes the form it does because that's the best form in which to say what you want to say.

Harris: That's it. And you're not thinking, "This is for the children."

Davies: Can you talk about your relationship with publishers for a minute? I know you're published by Atheneum, first. What link is there between Atheneum and your Canadian publisher?

Harris: Actually, everything is done in New York, as far as I'm concerned. Jean Karl is a wonderful editor, and I've had her now for practically all my books.

Davies: Could we talk about that relationship? Does she ever make suggestions to you? Could you think of one book in which she's made suggestions that have perhaps changed the shape of a character or an incident?

Harris: Well, more—she's very astute. She will say, "Somehow this isn't right yet. It isn't involving the reader enough yet." But she'll never make a suggestion—she'll never say how. She says, "It isn't scary enough," or "It isn't involving enough." I think it over and she's nearly always right, but she assumes that I'll know how to do it.

Davies: Which was the first book you worked on with her?

Harris: Oh, *Once upon a totem*.

Davies: In 1963.

Harris: You see, I had sold my first book, ***Cariboo trail,*** to a Toronto publisher, and my contract said I had to send them the next one. I sent them the manuscript of ***Once upon a totem,*** and they just returned it without any comment at all. They just rejected it. Moira, my daughter, was in New York, and she said, "Mother, I'll give it to an agent." She gave it to an agent who gave it to Jean Karl, who was just starting this brand new children's department at Atheneum. And—now this shows how astute Jean is—she read it, and she wrote back and said, "These are magnificent stories, but they seem to have been written for the ear instead of the eye."

I thought, "I have been writing steadily for radio for twenty-five years. Of course I write for the ear. I write fragmentary sentences. I don't write formal children's literature." Then Jean Karl said, "but if the writer would be willing to do some work on this, I would like to see these stories made publishable." She told me which book of style to read. She told me I had to read a lot of good children's books, just so I could observe that children's literature was not like radio. I rewrote *Once upon a totem* three times. But you see, in Toronto, they didn't tell me. They just sent it back, but they didn't tell me what was wrong.

Davies: Which books did she suggest that you look at, as children's books? Do you remember?

Harris: Oh, dear. It seems to me, *The white stag*. Was that out then?

Davies: Yes. . . . Can we go back to your past? Do you remember children's books that you especially liked in your childhood?

Harris: Not particularly. You see, I lived away out on a farm where we didn't have libraries, and I went to a one-room school where we practically didn't have books. Really, the first time I got into stories they were school readers. You know, "The Lady of the Lake," and things like that which just enthralled me. At home I wasn't getting books, but I was getting my father's stories. As my youngest son says, "Mother, you were lucky you were brought up in the oral tradition. You've got the real feeling for a story." And the Sunday School papers. I mean, they may have been appalling stories, but I waited for them, because those were stories.

Davies: I was wondering, too, if perhaps when you worked first on *Once upon a totem,* you were influenced by the oral tradition in the North West Coast Indian tales, and if some of that might have been carried over—

Harris: Well, perhaps so, but there's an awful lot of work behind that. I'd been working for radio, and I'd done lots of plays, but I had also done over 350 school broadcasts. I had reached the point where I couldn't broadcast because it was too much teaching. I said to my children, "If I ever say 'yes' again to a series of school broadcasts, shoot me."

I went down to the C.B.C. and I said, "My husband's been posted to Prince Rupert. I'm moving north, and I can't possibly do any more school broadcasts. I am finished." And they said, "You're going up north? We've always

wanted to do a series on those wonderful old Indian cultures. Of course, you're the one to do it."

When I got to Prince Rupert I didn't know anybody and had nothing to do. I dived into research for the school broadcasts. I discovered the totem pole; I discovered the Indian villages; I discovered that whole world up there. And there was something—I don't know what it was—but there was something; that North West Coast just clicked for me. A hypnotist said I probably lived there in my past life. But you know, I just had that feeling about it.

I discovered the old museum collections. I couldn't really understand the stories. They didn't always make sense. But then I realized it was because I didn't know the culture; I didn't know the motives of the people. Those stories were told for people who knew the background, who knew the animals, who knew the fears, who knew the culture. And I found that it was just endless. The more I learned, the more I seemed to have to learn about what was behind them all.

I had a very good friend up there, Ken Harris, who's a chief. He was the highest ranking Killer Whale on the Skeena. He was a lab technician, and he was an officer in the militia, and very white-oriented—I said to him one day, "Do you still tell these stories to your own children?" He said, "Yes. Don't children still need to learn about courage and beauty and truth?"

Then I began talking to him about a story, just what did it mean? I had to talk to Ken a lot, and other Indians. I had a wonderful weekend with almost no white people among a lot of Indians. It took me the whole four years I was living at Prince Rupert to really somehow suddenly get the key to these things. Mostly, I got it from studying, studying, studying; talking to the oldtimers, the people of the old missionary families; you know—but I didn't always go by them. I read everything; but mostly, I talked to Indians. It's funny, all of a sudden everything went together, and I seemed to understand them. Now the stories don't look obtuse to me at all. . . .

Davies: Could I talk about your source material for some of your other books? Could we discuss the historical fiction, and then the books you've done about your family?

Harris: Right, okay. The first one, I guess, was *Cariboo trail*. In that I was interested in the Overlanders. I have the complete Overlanders book and that intrigued me, but of course I couldn't use a pregnant woman with little tiny children. They're no fun. So I had to use the setting, but make some teenagers. I've done a lot with the Overlanders, including one thing and another. Of course I'd done a radio play. Then, the next one I did was *Forbidden—no—*

Davies: *West with the white chiefs*.

Harris: When I was living out at Huntington when my children were quite young, there was an old man there who had a little mining museum and somewhere he had picked up Dr. Cheadle's journal. I thought it was fabulous. The more I read it, over the years, I kept thinking the most interesting part was about coming over the mountains. Somehow that boy haunted me. Why had a boy wanted to shoot Lord Milton in the middle of the Rockies? They didn't give you any reason. He was always a good boy with the horses, you know. But all of a sudden, he grabbed the rifle and was going to shoot Lord Milton. Why? So I studied a lot about the Assiniboines to find out what they believed, and what they believed was that these mountains were really wild places, pretty scary to them. Then there was O'Byrne—he was an authentic character. He might have been very funny to the Englishmen, but it must have been pretty awful for the Indian boy. I just kept looking, kept thinking, in the back of mind for years, why did that boy do that? And when it finally came to me why he had done it—why I thought he had done it—I stuck to their diary, but I made it into this boy's story. Why they went, how anxious he was; and of course, I put his whole mind on his father's keeping this job, and that is why everything meant so much.

Davies: Was the murder true? That the Assiniboine had killed the half-breed?

Harris: Oh, yes, that was absolutely true. Yes, I really do stick to—

Davies: How about the trip to Victoria at the end?

Harris: That was all true. Yes, I thought that was all wonderful. And you know, I had a lot of letters from American children about it. That story looks pretty glamourous to them. My husband, Tommy, helped me a lot with that book because he's much better with horses than I am. He said he'd get my horses over the rockies, because if you tell him what a horse is doing, he'll tell you what its ears are doing, and its tail, and everything.

Davies: When I read the journal, and one of the horses fell down—I don't know what horse you named him in the story . . .

Harris: Bucephalus.

Davies: That's right. He fell down and he straddled the logs. . . .

Harris: Yes, that was all true, except the feeling behind it, which made it a novel. That was what I had to imagine.

Davies: I liked that book a lot. It had one plot, and it seemed to have incredible momentum.

Harris: Well, there's a professor of English over at Simon Fraser, who had me come over to see his students and I said, "What do you want me to talk about?" He said, "Anything, as long as it's *West with the white chiefs,*" and he said, "*That* book should have had the medal." That's his strong opinion.

Davies: The next book that is still history is *Forbidden frontier*.

Harris: Now that's interesting. You see being from British Columbia, I'm interested in the MacLean Boys. Have you ever heard about the MacLean Boys?

Davies: No, I haven't.

Harris: Well, if you read about the bad men of Canada, the MacLean Boys come in it. They were halfbreed boys who—do you know about the camels on the Cariboo Road?

Davies: Yes—only from your stories.

Harris: The camels were turned loose, and in truth, these MacLean Boys took these camels and used them to stampede cattle, and actually, at 14, one of the MacLean Boys was the youngest person ever hanged in the British Empire for murder. I was intrigued by this, because I'd read an old furtrader's journal in which he said, about the MacLean Boys, that they were such great kids; he'd known them as kids. They were wonderful, they were bright, and then the Gold Rush came, and their father, who was a furtrader, abandoned them, and they and their Indian mother went back to the Reserve. Of course, they were humiliated and outraged, and wanted to get rid of these people who'd spoiled their world. They grabbed the camels and they did all these things.

I didn't want to write about the MacLean Boys. But those outraged young halfbreeds who'd been in this very good position with a furtrader, a chief trader, and a high ranking Indian mother, for them to be humiliated and outraged, it seemed to me that was such a good situation; and so, I decided to invent the characters. And because I wanted to set it at Fort Kamloops where it had happened, I got into the old journals of the Hudson Bay fort, and that was wonderful. I found, for that year that I wrote about, every day when they'd plant the potatoes, when the brigade was coming, and when the brigade didn't come. And the whole thing behind it, how many horses were in the brigade, and who knew it was coming, and all the background is utterly authentic. The people are fictional. . . .

Davies: Can we talk about the way you worked with material your own family has provided for you?

Harris: Oh, yes. This has been great. The first one was *You have to draw the line somewhere*.

Davies: Yes, I've read that.

Harris: When Tommy retired, he and I spent a year in Europe, and on the way home, we stopped at Moira's house. She was then working for Bergdorff-Goodman, and she was sketching children's fashions. She had little children coming in from a little private school, and she'd put this Bergdorff stuff on them. They always said, "Oh! you draw so pretty. How do you get to be the artist?" I said to Moira, "A lot of kids would like to know, how do you get to be the artist?" She said so many funny things had happened to her in getting to be the artist, she'd always wanted to write a kind of "our hearts were young and gay" story, but she'd never had time—so I said, "Why don't we do it?" When we had it ready, we took it to the agent who'd already placed my Indian books, and she said, "Oh, no. This is a whole wrong idea. This is a career book. You can't do a career book that way."

Davies: I was going to say, were you trying to do a career book?

Harris: No, we were just trying to do Moira's story. But she said, "In a career book you take the girl for a year and a half and have 'X' this and 'X' that."

Davies: Like formula career books.

Harris: And we said, "But that's not what we want. We wanted to show what it's really like; you know, the awful truth." She thought we were pretty stubborn, so she phoned up about six publishing houses and said, "I have a client here with an idea," and every one of them said, "If your client will write to our formula, fine," and we said, "No way; the awful truth, or nothing!" So she said, "The only person who would conceivably buy such an off-beat career story is Jean Karl, who bought that off-beat Indian legend." She thought those were off-beat. So we went to Jean Karl, and she just began to read it and she began to laugh. She said, "This is wonderful! Go ahead."

Davies: Did she get to the green carpet? I thought dyeing the green carpet was just so hilarious!

Harris: Well, it's all absolutely true. And the way we worked it, Moira and I—you know, you can't have a lot of funny incidents and put them in and call it a story. You have to think where you're going and what the theme is, and so on. We talked about all that and decided where we were going. Then I made lists and lists and lists of every little thing, every little incident I wanted to hear about. And Moira was so busy! But whenever she had time she went into her bedroom and she'd tape an incident. Then when I had time, I'd go into another room and I'd listen to the incident. Then I would write it up. And of course, an awful lot of this—I took notes on my own kids when they were young, and I had lots of stuff myself. . . . Moira had shelves and shelves of art books. I just started burying myself in art. We stayed for a year. Moira was fixing a big brownstone house so they had scads of room, and I read all her art books. She took me down to *Women's Wear Daily* and introduced me to various young fashion artists so I would know how a young fashion artist in New York felt. I followed them around 7th Avenue. I listened to the way they spoke. Moira got all her—we lived in Greenwich Village—she got all her art friends to invite Mother to their parties. I just soaked in, for that whole year I was there . . . So much so that when I was doing that first scene of her going to the Metropolitan Museum of Art and Moira had to go away for a week and just couldn't help me with that scene, I went ahead. Moira had told me the five things that interested her, and by that time

I had gotten so much—I felt like a medium somehow. I went though the Metropolitan Museum and I thought, "I'm this young artist, and I would look at that." I just wrote it all up. When Moira got back, she said, "Mother, that's just astonishing! That's just the way I felt about those things." It begins to be just a little eerie. Anyway, we worked it through, and, you know, it was the runner up for the Spring Festival Award from the *New York Herald Tribune*.

Well, when I finished that book, people kept saying, "I liked the sister, Feeny. What happened to Feeny?" So Sheilagh, my other daughter, was living in Prince Edward Island with her children, and I went there, and I said, "You know, Sheilagh, people keep asking, and I'd better ask you about *you*." She said, "Mother, you never knew what it was like when I was growing up." I'd never worried about her because she was very pretty, very popular, she had boyfriends coming out of the woodwork, she was very athletic. She was always a bit rebellious, but she was just great. She said I hadn't realized she'd always been losing her self-confidence because her sister could draw, and paint, and sing, and play the piano, and get straight "A's". She thought the only thing she could do was terrify the sister by the way she could hang by her toes from that exercise bar, which was a very narrow little bar. I said, "It's just as valid to write about a girl who's losing her self-confidence." So, Tommy and I took a house on Prince Edward Island for a year and—

Davies: Did the same?

Harris: And did the same thing all over again. It was fabulous. We called it, *Confessions of a toe hanger*.

Davies: One reviewer—I was going over some of the old reviews—said that it was a "fascinating insight into Canadian family life."

Harris: Well, it is family life. Then I wanted to do Michael, my oldest son, because he's had so many adventures, and such an interesting life, but boys don't want to help you; they don't want to tell Mother a lot of things. So it was that, when I'd gone to Ottawa to get my medal for *Raven's cry*, I met Michael at Expo, and he was going to drive me to his home. He was then a test pilot and aeronautical research engineer at Cornell and he said, "Well, I'll help you if you don't get too personal." He meant, you know, no romances. Anyway, I said, "If you'll help me, great."

I picked up a whole batch of notebooks, at a drugstore, and for the ten hour trip I interviewed Michael, and wrote notes all the way. And so, when I got there, I just stayed there. I stayed at his place for a month. They had a new baby, and I was helping with the baby. Anyway, I had put it down into 14 pages of headings of things I wanted to know, and Michael started doing this on tape for me.

He did take me down to Cornell and introduce me to a cockpit; he gave me lessons in aerial navigation; he put me into the scene. When I wrote that book I wrote each chapter and sent it to Michael, and he edited it with a tape, and sent it back to me. He took complete responsibility for that book [*Let X be excitement*] because he wasn't going to have his pilot friends and his scientist friends reading it, and finding it wrong. . . .

Davies: The one book that we haven't talked much about is *Mule Lib,* Could you say a few words about it?

Harris: Well, this is the smallest book in the world. Actually, Tommy—he's quite a storyteller—and all the years we've been married, he's been telling stories, funny stories about this mule; so many funny stories that one day I just nailed him to the chair while I got this out of him.

[voice of Tommy, in background, indistinct, at several points in the following paragraph]

Harris: He was at one of those English Boys' Schools when the First World War broke out. Thought all the excitement in the world was going to be over. So he managed to join up at 16, pretending he was 18. He went through the Army School of Equitation, but when he got to France he drew this mule, which was the worst—biggest and worst—mule in the British Army. It's the story of the encounters of this 16-year-old soldier and his mule. It's very funny. . . .

GENERAL COMMENTARY

Kenneth Radu

SOURCE: "Canadian Fantasy," in *Canadian Children's Literature,* No. 2, Summer, 1975, pp. 73-9.

Christie Harris, a prolific writer of books for young readers, has produced a novel which illustrates some of the problems of our fantasy fiction. The recent reprint of *Secret in the Stlalakum Wild,* originally published by McClelland & Stewart in 1972, gives us an opportunity to enjoy what is good about the novel itself, and to discover why it is a less than satisfactory fantasy.

Mrs. Harris's career as a writer has been varied and not undistinguished. The general competency of *Secret in the Stlalakum Wild* is surely the result of years of tending to the craft of writing for young readers. The hallmark of her style is a good-humored briskness which carries the story along in an uncomplicated, well-paced narrative. There is insufficient space here to examine all of Mrs. Harris's work in detail; but a measure of her achievement is perhaps suggested by the fact that she has written radio plays, domestic comedies for juvenile readers, notably *You Have to Draw the Line Somewhere* and *Confessions of a Toe-Hanger,* true-life adventure stories, especially *Let X Be For Excitement,* based upon the life of her own son, and historical fiction, particularly her impressive work, *Raven's Cry*. She has also successfully re-told West Coast Indian legends in *Once Upon a Totem.*

Indeed, Indian folk-lore and mythology have quite clearly made their imprint upon Mrs. Harris's imagination. Her finest work is directly concerned with the Indian life and legends of the Northwest. *Raven's Cry,* a winner of the Canadian Association of Children's Librarians Book of the Year Medal, remains a singularly moving paean to the now extinct Haida civilization of the Queen Charlotte Islands. Fully and accurately researched, *Raven's Cry* portrays the complexities and uniqueness of the Haida culture with insight, wonder, and compassion. Mrs. Harris's view is neither sentimental, romantic, nor patronizing. She reports Haida life as it was lived on the islands with the clear eye and honesty of the sympathetic chronicler. Mrs. Harris returns to the Haida again in her later novel, *Forbidden Frontier*. In the character of Djaada, the Haida wife of a Hudson's Bay Company official, Mrs. Harris created a figure of dignity and pride, a woman who could ignore the white man's insults and stupidity but who could not ignore the loss of Haida self-respect. Again, one trusts the historical accuracy of the writing.

When it comes to fantasy, however, historical accuracy and sympathetic chronicling are of secondary importance. Fantasy is an art form in its own right and as such must be granted special attention. A writer should therefore be more concerned with creating a "secondary world," to use Tolkien's famous phrase, than with reporting the conditions of reality, past or present. Fantasy gives insight into reality, illumines imperishable truths of human life; but it does not depend upon the real world for its conception or its logic. When a writer attaches a moral or spiritual view onto the fantasy like a piece of bunting, he is, in effect, depending upon the idiom of the real world for thematic support. Such a dependence leads to uninspired writing and an essentially unconvincing fantasy. All significant fantasy, however, is autonomous to the degree that it does not at all draw upon the patented formulae of reality in order to express "the inexpressible."

One thinks of the way E. B. White handles the complicated issue of life and death, for example, in *Charlotte's Web,* or how George MacDonald introduces the concept of evil in *At the Back of the North Wind*. In both instances, the morality is an intrinsic part of the prose and situation, growing out of the story like perennial flowers from a rich soil. Canadian writers, on the other hand, generally tend to record their stories, imagine various suitable, fantastical characters and incidents, and then frame it all with an unsubtle moral lesson. Anne Wilkinson's *Swann & Daphne* suffers from this kind of moral imposition as does Pierre Berton's fantasy with its intrusive social satire. Catherine Anthony Clark often fails to integrate fully the moral situation of her young heroes into the actual fantasy so that one is often confronted with a double framework: the fantasy itself, and the child's moral and/or emotional development.

The morality of *Secret in the Stlalakum Wild* also shows signs of this tendency in Canadian fantasy literature. Morann, the heroine of the story, is introduced as a somewhat dissatisfied young girl who feels particularly ignored by her family. This is demonstrated by the way everyone rushes out of the car at an airport where the family drove to meet a visiting cousin, Sarah, a university student planning a preliminary anthropological investigation into Indian life of the region.

> Somehow, everyone got out ahead of Morann. Somehow, everyone got in front of her, blocking her off after they spotted Sarah. She knew she wouldn't even be noticed, as usual.

Morann's feelings of neglect are very real and stem from her own sense of worthlessness. Unable to believe in herself and her special qualities, she is prone to saying and doing tiresome and foolish things, in a vain attempt to be noticed.

> Why did she always blurt out something stupid when she desperately wanted to say something nice? Somehow, what she said never came out cute or smart, it just seemed to come out loud. Keeping up a bold front, Morann cringed inwardly. She had panicked as usual. But what were you going to do if you hadn't been born with something that just naturally made you noticeable.

The ultimate point of Mrs. Harris's fantasy, it would seem, is to teach Morann that she has unique value and individual worth. To this end, Morann's self-education process becomes involved with her quest for treasure which, an Indian spirit informs her, has been built up over millions of years, a fact that provides some indication of its fabulous value.

She first meets the spirits, the Band of Invisibles, after initially hearing their voices when she gets separated from the others on an expedition up a mountain to Stlalakum lake. Stlalakum itself, the book informs us, means "Anything uncanny. The place. The thing. Stlalakums are unnatural beings living in the natural world."

There is marvellous opportunity here for the creation of a convincing, secondary world, even if the world is represented by a single agent. More importantly, such a meeting is a chance for the suggestive qualities of an evocative, subtle prose to play upon the reader's imagination. The author disappoints us.

> A shimmer of pearl flashed up onto a hummock of grass. It was a little person. Yet it wasn't a little person.
>
> A UFO has landed, Morann thought. A flying saucer. It's a little being from Outer Space.
>
> It was a little person. Yet it wasn't a little person.

Morann's response, as Mrs. Harris portrays it, is anticlimactic. The odour of cliché hovers about such terms as "flying saucer," and "UFO." The description of the spirit immediately after this is not without its fine touches; but unfortunately the book stylistically remains one of occasional effects. The writing is more consistently functional than inspired.

The limited quality of the prose seems to be the natural consequence of Mrs. Harris's uncertain grasp of the nature of fantasy. She is not primarily a writer of fantasy literature, and the prose of *Raven's Cry,* significantly enough, is considerably more interesting than that of *Stlalakum*. Because of her inexperience in the genre, the author persistently undercuts the fantasy elements of the novel. Instead of creating a logic which arises from and supports the fantasy, Mrs. Harris relies upon the empirical data of the real world to give scientific respectability to the central fantastical conception, the Indian view that all nature is richly endowed with communicating spirits or stlalakums who are sensitive to the presence of humanity. This is unfortunate because it wastes so much time at the beginning of the book where Mrs. Harris, for example, quotes directly from an article in an issue of *Wildlife* magazine concerning experiments about the psychogalvanic reflex of plant cells to prove that they do indeed "react emotionally to every threat to their well being."

The point of this information has its thematic relevance later when Morann discovers what constitutes the real treasure she takes such great pains to seek. Hence, one is aware of the basic contrivance of the fantasy; but, to her credit, Mrs. Harris does show the creative good sense to translate the jargon of the article into comic terms.

Morann is fascinated by the concept.

> She asked Neil a few more questions when she took the magazine back. And standing there, trying to follow his answers, she absent-mindedly pulled a leaf off a rosebush and began tearing it apart. "Oh! Excuse me!" she gasped to the rosebush. And she meant it. She could just *feel* the other leaves' horror at what she had done.

If she is ever to discover the treasure and be noticed, however, Morann has first to prove her moral worth to the Stlalakum spirits, represented by one Siem, handsomely dressed in robes "like spun mother-of-pearl." Siem is the most important fantastical character in the novel; but the difficulty with his characterization is that one cannot really believe in him as either an Indian or a spirit. He sounds too much like Henry Higgins. In response to Morann's exclamation, "Leaping leppercorns!" Siem says: "Do not conjure up those grasping immortals!" Later he adds: "I distinctly heard you summoning leprechauns, though your pronunciation leaves something to be desired." Too often as well, he is a mouthpiece for castigating the white man's stupidity about the wilds.

> You are all the same. Distrustful. It must be from the tales you hear. Tales that make the Wild a dreadful place full of dripping red claws and bared fangs. Tales that turn our friendly wolves into fearsome, bloodthirsty villains. 'The Big Bad Wolfe!' they tell you. 'The Wicked Dragon! The Sly Fox! The Satanic Serpent!'

As a character, Siem illustrates what is wrong with *Secret in the Stlalakum Wild* specifically, and what is wrong with Canadian fantasy generally: the absence of memorable characters who are unmistakably a part of a richly imagined fantasy and who never sound a false note therein. When an author concentrates upon getting the story told and making the moral point clear, however, character is evidently sacrificed. That aside, Morann proves her moral worth to the Band of Invisibles and to herself by spending a night alone on Devil's Mountain next to Stlalakum lake, no mean feat when one considers that Sexqui, the two-headed serpent, inhabits the waters. But it is important enough to Morann that she do so.

> Sooner or later, Sarah and the girls would have to decide whether Morann was a sulky, snivelling freak or a courageous adventurer. If she had anything to do with it, she intended to be a courageous adventurer.

Those chapters describing Morann's ordeal of being alone, stuck in her sleeping bag, in forbidding surroundings are among the best in the book. Mrs. Harris is quite capable of creating a very tense mood, of depicting an environment which could, seemingly, come alive to destroy an intruder. At moments like these, her style deepens in quality to convey some rather fine effects.

> Deeper in the woods, the ferns took over. They spouted up from the earth in vigorous fountains, luminous green where the sun filtered through to them, brooding and dark where the trees' shadows fell across them. She could smell the ferns. Or perhaps it was the moist earth she could smell, and the dark slugs hiding there, watching her. She could sense the worms crawling along through the loose forest floor, turning everything back into wilderness. She could feel the woods' rejection of her. If she fell and couldn't get up, everything there would work to silently cover her over until they silently turned her, too, into quiet green growth.

Because she survives this experience, Morann goes on her way to find the treasure. Earlier references to the white man's stupidity about nature, especially oil spills, are explained. The natural world is threatened with extinction. Hence, the stlalakum spirits or the psychogalvanic reflexes of the plants are alarmed. Morann's moral education whereby she becomes an individual of real worth now depends upon her recognition that the fabulous treasure of the Stlalakum wild is really the awesome beauty and mystery of nature herself.

Having actually discovered a nugget of gold, Morann has a moral decision to make: whether or not to reveal to the world that she did indeed find gold and begin the process of the rape of the wild. By remaining silent, she respects the integrity and inviolability of the natural world. As Siem says: "Everything and everybody has a potential for good or for harm, Morann. You must make you own decision."

Morann's choice is indicated by the following passage.

> Morann slipped the gold nugget swiftly into her pocket and zippered it up tight. She was not going to be rich. Not going to be important. She was going to be something better. She was going to be worthy of the beauty the world had built up.

Secret in the Stlalakum Wild works hard to be a "relevant" book for young readers. Hence, the moral vision, if one can call it that, sounds a bit thin, a kind of truism which it is now fashionable to introduce into a book of this kind. Because Mrs. Harris's fantasy is not provided with its own controlling logic and is by and large undeveloped as a fantasy, because it is not conveyed in a prose of "poetic overtones," because no single character emerges strongly and memorably, *Secret in the Stlalakum Wild* is not a success as an example of significant fantasy fiction.

That should not, however, blind us to the novel's real merits. It is a book that asks us to respect the natural world. It is a book that describes some of the beauty of that world with love and precision. It is a book of good humour and good companionship. The illustrations by Douglas Tait more than enhance the text. They are sensitive drawings of the wild, touched with mystery and dignity. Highly readable, *Secret in the Stlalakum Wild* deserves a wide audience and, hopefully, that audience will now avail themselves of the reprint.

Gwyneth Evans

SOURCE: "Nothing Odd Ever Happens Here: Landscape in Canadian Fantasy," in *Canadian Children's Literature*, Nos. 15 & 16, 1980, pp. 15-30.

The fantasies of Christie Harris . . . have a didactic edge, although in structure they are novels rather than fables. One difficulty in discussing Harris as a fantasist is that her books postulate the validity of para-normal phenomena—the fantasy, she insists, is not really fantasy. Real or unreal, the spirit-life with which Harris' characters come into contact is always intimately associated with the natural life of a specific environment, as it is in the Indian legends which she has studied and adapted elsewhere. *Sky Man on the Totem Pole?* and *Mystery at the Edge of Two Worlds* are not full-fledged fantasies but do both contain fictional episodes where modern children have mystical experiences of communication with supernatural beings who inhabit the natural world. The spirit of the mythical Indian princess Skawah in *Sky Man* appears to one of her modern descendants, encouraging him to value the old belief in the inter-relatedness of man and nature, and the immanence of the spiritual world within the natural. But because the didactic and theoretical concerns of this book are so prominent, and because the locale and characters change so frequently, the reader is not left with a vivid impression of that Nature which the book is intent on respecting. [W. T. Cutt's] *A Message from Arkmae* makes a similar point more effectively by depicting the beauty and fragility of a single landscape. Harris' recent novel, *Mystery at the Edge of Two Worlds,* has a clearer focus in its Prince Rupert and Lucy Island settings, and effectively evokes the unusual terrain and atmosphere of the latter. The island is seen first in a painting which has a mysterious, visionary quality; her reactions to the painting and then to the island itself eventually impel the protagonist of the story to accept and use her own psychic gifts.

Secret in the Stlalakum Wild, Harris' only true fantasy, also concerns a young girl's attitude towards the natural environment. Again set on the Northwest coast, it stresses the wildness and mystery of the area, where stlalakum or uncanny presences abound. "The timid gasp and edge away from the silent forest, away from the lonely waters. For there *is* something strange about the northwest wilderness." The stlalakum spirits, it emerges, are concerned with the threat of civilization encroaching on these their "last hiding places," and so take a rather gormless young girl on several out-of-the-body tours in a cloud to persuade her to help preserve the wilderness. Harris' descriptions of the plant life on the mountain trails are exact and vivid, as are the heroine's timid reactions to the wilderness.

> Fallen timber lay crumbling, rotting away, with flabby fungi that seemed like big ears listening for something. You'd need big ears to hear anything, she thought. It was gruesomely quiet.

An uncertainty of tone unfortunately mars all of Harris' ventures into fantasy. Sincere as her beliefs in the "stlalakum" world may be, she never succeeds in making it convincing to the reader. Her efforts to assert its scientific validity only tend to destroy its imaginative validity within the novels. Attempts to rationalize fantasy are almost invariably destructive, and all the quotations from *Wildlife* magazine about experiments done with psycho-galvanic reactors don't help at all to make us believe in Morann's experiences with the stlalakum sprites. At the end of the novel, after having laboured to create a sense of the mystical beauty of a mountain valley, Harris has Morann's father—very impressed with the sight—exclaim, "Straight out of Disneyland!" The comparison is unfortunate, and typical of Harris' inability to blend slangy realism with a spiritual perception of power and grandeur in nature.

TITLE COMMENTARY

📖 *ONCE UPON A TOTEM* (1963)

Virginia Kirkus' Service

SOURCE: A review of *Once Upon a Totem,* in *Virginia Kirkus' Service,* Vol. XXXI, No. 3, February 1, 1963, p. 113.

This is a set of five story/legends inspired by the "People of the Potlatch" whose totem poles held the stories of families and tribes in the Pacific Northwest. The author lived and worked with the descendants of the Indians of this area and there is the ghostly ring of authenticity in the phrases of her retellings. The story/legends are about the origins of things, tribes and heroes. These Indians had a system of aristocracy and held slaves. Their customs are unfolded with the unfolding of the stories. The woodcut illustrations by John Frazier Mills are well suited to the totem subject matter in mood and form. Not all five stories

are uniformly well-constructed and although the Indian names and spellings are occasionally impossible, it is an interesting addition to any collection of North American legends and folktales.

Ruth Hill Viguers

SOURCE: A review of *Once Upon a Totem,* in *The Horn Book Magazine,* Vol. 39, No. 2, April, 1963, p. 173.

Five exceptionally well-told legends of the Indians of the North Pacific Coast from Alaska to Oregon. These were a proud people, living in permanent cedar lodges where food from the sea and forests was abundant, who had time to decorate their lodges and to carve their poles with symbols of their past. The stories have the complexity, variety of human beings and supernatural creatures, and conflicts between good and evil that characterize all great hero stories and reflect mythology, history, and intricate social systems. Mrs. Harris's interest in these Indians, first aroused when her husband was Officer in Charge of Canadian Immigration in British Columbia, was heightened as she came to know them, visited their villages, and listened to their tales. The brief introductions, one for each story, throw light on unusual customs or traditions and give the book additional value. For older boys and girls interested in backgrounds for understanding other peoples as well as for those who just want colorful heroic tales.

Zena Sutherland

SOURCE: A review of *Once Upon a Totem,* in *Bulletin of the Center for Children's Books,* Vol. XVII, No. 7, March, 1964, p. 110.

Five stories based on legends of the Indian tribes of the north Pacific coast, with appropriately primitive woodcut designs in black and white. The tales are dramatic, elaborate in structure and rich in cultural detail. The writing style is very good on the whole, although an occasional phrase or sentence is noticeably contemporary, not in vocabulary but in construction.

Ethel L. Heins

SOURCE: A review of *Once Upon a Totem,* in *The Horn Book Magazine,* Vol. LXI, No. 4, July-August, 1985, p. 468.

Thoroughly familiar with the proud, energetic, artistic Indians of the North Pacific coastal region and mindful of their complex beliefs and their splendid legendary history, a fine writer tells five heroic tales of human courage, supernatural creatures, and the timeless tension between good and evil. The black-and-white woodcuts are strong in symbolism and the primitivism suggestive of modern art.

YOU HAVE TO DRAW THE LINE SOME-WHERE (illustrated by daughter Moira Johnston, 1964)

Zena Sutherland

SOURCE: A review of *You Have to Draw the Line Somewhere,* in *Bulletin of the Center for Children's Books,* Vol. XVII, No. 8, April, 1964, p. 124.

Written in the form of autobiographical reminiscence, a fictional career story based on fact; the author's daughter is a fashion artist, as is Linsey, the protagonist of the book. Superior by far to most career-and-love junior novels, the story gives a delightful picture of Linsey's unusual family and of her childhood as well as of the hazards and delights of art schools and the world of commercial art and fashion. The writing is easy and informal, humorous in the egg-and-I vein, and more realistic about preparation for a job and finding the right job than are many career stories.

Helen M. Kovar

SOURCE: A review of *You Have to Draw the Line Somewhere,* in *School Library Journal,* Vol. 10, No. 8, April, 1964, p. 72.

An enjoyable blend of fiction and biography, this is the story of a young Canadian girl who aspires to become a *Vogue* fashion artist. The British Columbia setting is refreshing, and the style humorous. Although the emphasis is on the heroine's pursuit of her career, there is enough of family life and boy-dates-girl to interest a wide variety of readers. It is a frank picture of the non-glamorous side of fashion art and modeling and the amount of work necessary to become first-rate in either profession. With a light touch the story offers depth and mature values, and one is not surprised to find that the author is a mother writing the story of her daughter. This has much more to offer than most girls' fiction.

Pearl Strachan Hurd

SOURCE: "Of Ponies and Princes," in *The Christian Science Monitor,* May 7, 1964, p. B5.

Young art students, especially those approaching womanhood and facing the challenge of combining marriage with artistic development, will enjoy this entertaining novel by Christle Harris, whose own life as a writer, wife, and mother has provided her with useful experience. Her daughter, Moira Johnston, whose success as a fashion illustrator no doubt contributed background material, is the artist responsible for the delightful drawings in the book.

The story moves in an interesting and amusing vein from the day when Linsey Ross Allen, at the age of nine, posing for an aunt, an amateur artist, discovers it is far more important to her to become an artist than a model, even at ten cents an hour.

The author vividly conveys the life of the art student in the highly competitive field of fashion illustration, which is Linsey's choice. After winning and losing a number of lesser suitors Linsey finally meets the one right man, sympathetic to art and ready to cooperate with a wife already a success in the New York world of fashion. After several breaks with commercial art, in order to preserve domestic harmony, the full-rounded dream comes true. Linsey can free-lance at home and give plenty of attention to the domestic side of her happy life.

Ruth Hill Viguers

SOURCE: A review of *You Have to Draw the Line Somewhere,* in *The Horn Book Magazine,* Vol. XL, No. 3, June, 1964, pp. 290-91.

Linsey Ross-Allen tells the story of the long road—from her dreams at the age of nine—to her successful career as a fashion artist. The book is episodic, without real plot, reading like lively autobiography, which it comes close to being. It is based on the experiences, and written with the close co-operation, of the author's own daughter, who also illustrates the book. Because this is first of all the story of a career, no great effort is made to develop the characters; but, even so, the parents particularly emerge very clearly. Especially interesting to girls who look forward to art careers are the detailed accounts of art school in British Columbia and California, and jobs in Vancouver and New York. The book gives a special bonus by continuing after Linsey's marriage to show how she meets the challenge of being simultaneously successful in home and career. Written with verve and humor, it is often very funny and should find a wide audience among teen-age girls and their mothers.

Joan Cook

SOURCE: A review of *You Have to Draw the Line Somewhere,* in *The New York Times Book Review,* August 16, 1964, p. 18.

The 3,000 miles between the Western Canadian border and New York City measure the dream of Linsey Ross-Allen. From age 9, when she first sketched her sister, Linsey was determined to be a fashion artist.

In telling how Linsey achieved her ambition, Christie Harris, whose own daughter is the real-life counterpart of Linsey, also relates the high and low points of a girl's growing up, sometimes with joyous laughter, other times through tears.

Surrounded by a loving, unconventional family, with little money, Linsey makes her way through the perilous shoals of adolescence. After graduation from high school her job on the local paper provides the necessary funds for art school in Vancouver. From there, she moves to California and has a variety of amusing adventures which culminate in marriage and final success in New York.

Mrs. Harris has traced the development of a fashion artist with wit and humor and, at the same time, shown how Linsey, through sacrifice, discipline and work, learned to draw the line in life as well as art.

WEST WITH THE WHITE CHIEFS (1965)

Virginia Kirkus' Service

SOURCE: A review of *West with the White Chiefs,* in *Virginia Kirkus' Service,* Vol. XXXIII, No. 5, March 1, 1965, p. 242.

Louis Battenote had killed a man. As a noted hunter he had also killed many buffalo. The white men and their priests boycotted him, even though he had only killed in self defense. His tribe, with equal unfairness blamed him because the buffalo herds were depleted. The year was 1863 and the Assiniboine Indian saw the chance to redeem himself and regain respect by guiding two young Englishmen over seldom travelled terrain to the Canadian gold fields from Fort Pitt. It was a difficult party for a short tempered man to handle: Lord Milton got peevish when he got tired; Dr. Cheadle was in the habit of supporting Lord Milton; and Felix O'Byrne, who had attached himself to the group, was swinishly lazy and only the horses were as stupid and easily frightened as he was. The story is based on actual journals kept by Milton and Cheadle. The dangers and discomforts of the trip are vividly caught. Louis Battenote conquered the route and himself and his young sons first and frightening confrontation with white civilization is very well handled.

RAVEN'S CRY (1966)

Virginia Kirkus' Service

SOURCE: A review of *Raven's Cry,* in *Virginia Kirkus' Service,* Vol. XXXIV, No. 18, September 15, 1966, pp. 979-80.

This is outstandingly well written narrative history. It follows the last 100 years of the Haidas, a prosperous, highly cultured tribe which once dominated the western shores of Canada. Mrs. Harris starts their story in the late eighteenth century, showing enough of their matriarchal family structure, their legends, their livelihood and their devotion to excellence in the arts to make the reader suspect that North America had a tribe to compete with the Aztec and Mayan. At this point, the first fur trading schooner finds them with brutally dramatic results. The intrusion of Western civilization brought firewater, tuberculosis, and the loss of a rigidly structured courtesy. No children's book has ever conveyed so well without rationalizing what the fundamentalist missionary can do when tribal myth and rite are withdrawn and a narrow Christianity offered in its place. By following one family of chiefs through the

generations to the 1870's, the author shows the decimation of their numbers and the destruction of their pride.

Priscilla L. Moulton

SOURCE: A review of *Raven's Cry,* in *The Horn Book Magazine,* Vol. XLII, No. 5, October, 1966, pp. 574-75.

In the eighteenth century, English and New England sea captains found that trinkets, cloth, and chisels would buy otter and seal pelts from Indians inhabiting the coastal regions north of Vancouver. Later, the white men's ships carried away as well carved canoes, beautiful blankets, slate sculpture known as curios to European collectors, and even some gold. Left behind with the Indians were muskets, liquor, diseases, missionaries, and rulers both unfamiliar and unsympathetic with the "primitive" and "heathen." To varying degrees the Indian chieftains realized the implications of the white men's influence. More than any other, Chief of the Haidas resisted the new invader, but the only methods of defense that he used were those worthy of a great Haida chief. In the end, the teachings and principles that had made the Haidas masters of the sea and an unconquerable people were not enough. By the time anthropology and primitive art were subjects for scholars, the Haida culture was nearly dead. The nineteenth-century scholars found only superficial evidence of the greatness that had been. Now, in our own day, the storyteller and the artist have rediscovered and reproduced a dignified and inspiring picture of that culture in a work of epic proportions. Painstaking research and intense absorption in anthropological details have enabled the author to write with rare commitment and involvement from the Haida point of view. She sings the saga of the three chieftains, of their larger-than-life deeds, of the people they led, of the gods they honored. Her account is richly adorned with details of custom, ceremony, and costume. Dealing as it does in a highly artistic and complicated manner with the whole range of human emotion and character, it makes demands of the reader but rewards him with new understanding of the forces that shape civilizations. Strong illustrations by a descendant of the Haidas give a glimpse of the way in which his ancestors expressed themselves. This distinguished work, probably classified as fiction, will occupy a respected position in historical, anthropological, and story collections. Through its faithful and almost reverent reconstruction, the Haida culture can be reborn in the hearts and minds of readers.

Ann Currah

SOURCE: A review of *Raven's Cry,* in *The New York Times Book Review,* November 20, 1966, p. 55.

The tragic destruction of a unique culture is shown in this occasionally plodding but distinctive account of the Haida Indians. This unusually art-conscious people flourished in the Queen Charlotte Islands off the Canadian Pacific coast until they were discovered in the late 1700's by traders eager for otter pelts. Within 150 years the powerful Haidas were destroyed—massacres, greed, disease, firewater, well-intentioned missionaries and Government officials contributed to their extinction.

The Indian point of view, re-created through the lives of their last great chiefs, is sympathetically drawn. However, weak characterization, awkward dialogue and a reserved writing style make the book unlikely to captivate any but the most avid readers. Handsome, symbolic pictures, executed by a Haida descendant, grace a book that's excellent as history but much less as fiction.

The Christian Science Monitor

SOURCE: A review of *Raven's Cry,* in *The Christian Science Monitor,* December 8, 1966, p. 19.

The folklore and folk art of the North American Indian have gained a secure place in our culture, offering superb examples of the creative imagination which impels a man to set down, as best he can, the thoughts which come to him as he looks out on the world. Particularly art-oriented were the aristocratic Haidas of the islands off the coast of Alaska. The present book, although describing their tragic history after the coming of the white man, also pays repeated tribute to their unique contributions in art and legend.

Norman Newton

SOURCE: "How Not To Do It," in *Canadian Literature,* Vol. 36, Spring, 1968, pp. 93-4.

There would seem to be little justification in reviewing this book in *Canadian Literature.* That is the tragedy of it.

Mrs. Harris' book is the story of the Edenshaw family, one of the noble families of the Queen Charlotte Islands, from the time of the white discovery of the islands in the 18th century to the present day. It includes the story of Charles Edenshaw (Tahayghen), who lived between 1835 and 1920, and was arguably one of Canada's greatest sculptors. It ends with a few perceptive remarks on Haida art by Bill Reid, who is related to the Edenshaw family.

I am sorry that I can only praise Mrs. Harris' intentions, not her performance. While much of her material on the Edenshaws is not new, she has thoroughly researched Haida culture, she has visited the Queen Charlottes, and she has a proper respect for the pre-Christian cultures of our province. But while the facts are right on the whole, the tone is hopelessly wrong. Her book is a virtual anthology of the faults which mar most Canadian books about Indians, and its chief value is as a horrid example.

What exciting material she had to work with, after all! There is enough beauty and horror in the bare facts of the extirpation of Haida culture: they shine and glower through the dullest prose of anthropologists, sea-captains, missionaries and government men. She needed only to have put her story together with intelligence, taste and professional competence, and the colour would have burst forth of itself. Instead, we find ourselves in the same mythological Disneyland in which all Canada's pre-Christian history seems to be set. The Indians emerge as marvellous clean-thewed children, who tell the most super stories, and whose art is simply fab. (*Raven's Cry* is pre-fab.) We are continually being told how really wise and kind and cultured they were, but since they tend to act like Wolf Cubs on an outing, we have to accept this on faith. Mrs. Harris' style, straight out of the latest pop-up fairy-tale book, turns everything into papier-mâché. Perhaps this, rather than gold, or some other archaic standard of value, is the appropriate material for Canada's hundredth anniversary. . . .

In short, *Raven's Cry* is a waste—a waste by Mrs. Harris of a valuable story and much useful research, and a waste, presumably by the publishers, of the talents of a fine artist.

Kathleen Krahnke

SOURCE: A review of *Raven's Cry,* in *Voice of Youth Advocates,* Vol. 16, No. 3, August, 1993, p. 152.

Raven's Cry, a reissue from 1966, is a book whose message is as poignant today as it was almost thirty years ago. To quote the prologue, it "is a story of three great and greatly gifted Haida Eagle chiefs caught in the tragedy of culture contact along our northwest coast. It is a true story, as a storyteller sees the truth, through the eyes and passions of her characters . . . " It begins in 1791 when the Haida nation was a strong and powerful force with a complex system to trade, traditions that worked, slaves to do the work, and most important dignity. It ends with the tribe scattered and depleted in numbers and almost purged of its rich native culture. It was amazing to read how the white culture imposed its religion, its whiskey, its firearms, its greed and its diseases on a culture and almost exterminated the tribe in the name of civilization. It is wonderful to have this book reissued, to give these people a voice from which we can all learn. It is well written and insightful. It will move the reader to tears of compassion and understanding. The only unfortunate change in the book is the omission of the map which was included in the 1966 edition. Check your shelves, if you don't own it, you should and then talk it up.

CONFESSIONS OF A TOE-HANGER (illustrated by daughter Moira Johnston, 1967)

Ruth Hill Viguers

SOURCE: A review of *Confessions of a Toe-Hanger,* in *The Horn Book Magazine,* Vol. XLIII, No. 2, April, 1967, p. 213.

Girls who enjoyed *You Have to Draw the Line Somewhere* will be delighted to learn of a companion book that recounts sister Feeny's story with the same humorous touch. Feeny (a nickname for Fiona) differs from Linsey of the earlier book, however, in having no absorbing ambition. In her own eyes she is the problem child, the one who has opportunities but who always just misses success either because of bad luck, which she is sure could happen only to her, or her own bungling. As the middle child, she struggles for attention and is primarily concerned with how she looks to others. The background of family is just as strong here as in the other book, and the Ross-Allens are a warm and engaging family to have behind a growing girl, even through her worst periods of feeling inferior. Boy friends are very important—the ones Feeny does not take home as well as those of whom the family approves. The pattern of her life is very familiar, from her childhood escapades to her sudden marriage to a new acquaintance—not the boy she is engaged to—and life in a trailer with three tiny children and her student husband. The book should give both fun and reassurance to the reader who is also trying to discover the answer to a problem Feeny takes twenty years to solve. The author's second daughter collaborated on this lively piece of true-to-life reporting just as her older one (whose illustrations embellish both books) did on *You Have to Draw the Line Somewhere*.

Elinor Cullen

SOURCE: A review of *Confessions of a Toe-Hanger,* in *School Library Journal,* Vol. 13, No. 8, April, 1967, p. 86.

Feeny Ross-Allen's story starts when at six she gets caught climbing a forbidden tree. And being up a tree turns out to be her habitual condition throughout this book, which sees her through her mid-twenties. Loosely draped around Feeny's problem, her self-conscious attempts to impress others which invariably end in disgrace, this is a very genuine, endearing portrayal of a Canadian girl until she becomes a young wife and mother of the present. Feeny is the sister of Linsey of *You Have to Draw the Line Somewhere*. Feeny's descriptions of her childhood scrapes, her boyfriends, the pleasures and frustrations of her early married years are refreshingly natural and remarkably free of moralizing.

Marilyn Gardner

SOURCE: "Girls and Growing Up," in *The Christian Science Monitor,* May 4, 1967, p. B10.

From its off-beat title to its equally off-beat conclusion, the book is a marvel—one of those rare portraits of family life that combines warmth, humor, and meaningful detail without becoming sticky or trite.

Mrs. Harris lets Feeny Ross-Allen tell her own story—a young Canadian's lively recollection of childhood, adolescence, marriage, and motherhood. Growing up can be difficult at times. Feeny finds, especially when your "only accomplishment" is the ability to hang by your toes from

an exercise bar. She is no whiz in school, doesn't like the "right" boys, and finds that things never turn out quite right for her. What she lacks in ability, however, she makes up for in humor and enthusiasm—a spirited resolve that eventually gives her the freedom, courage, and confidence she has so long been seeking. Mrs. Harris's dialogue is superbly freeflowing and natural; expressions like "scared spitless" give vitality to both conversations and characters.

Zena Sutherland

SOURCE: A review of *Confessions of a Toe-Hanger,* in *Bulletin of the Center for Children's Books,* Vol. 20, No. 11, July-August, 1967, p. 170.

A companion volume to *You Have to Draw the Line Somewhere* in which the story of a fashion artist's career was based on the experiences of the author's daughter. Here the younger sister of that artist tells the story of her childhood and youth, her marriage, and her experiences as a young wife and mother. Having felt always eclipsed by her brother and sister, Feeny discovers comparatively late in life she need make no comparisons, need imitate no patterns—that she has a freedom of choice about her hobbies and her work. This is an excellent story of a Canadian family, a good story of a girl's growing up, and an amusing book in general, written with humor and with good dialogue in an easy, colloquial style.

Sally C. Estes

SOURCE: A review of *Confessions of a Toe-Hanger,* in *The Booklist,* Vol. 64, No. 1, September 1, 1967, p. 54.

Feeny, younger sister of Linsey Ross-Allen of Harris' *You have to draw the line somewhere,* is the likable protagonist-narrator of this realistic, humorous story which follows Feeny's life and adventures from age six through the first years of her marriage. Lacking self-confidence Feeny tries too hard to impress others and invariably ends up in sticky situations. Believable characterizations and depiction of family life add to the delightful narrative which will appeal to teen-age girls who enjoyed the author's earlier book.

FORBIDDEN FRONTIER (1968)

Kirkus Service

SOURCE: A review of *Forbidden Frontier,* in *Kirkus Service,* Vol. XXXVI, No. 4, February 15, 1968, p. 190.

Acknowledging [Albert] Camus' *The Rebel,* the *Forbidden Frontier* in the 1860's lies not between Hudson's Bay Company and the rest of North America but between white men and their "halfbreed" offspring who, deploring what whiskey has done to their Indian relatives, nevertheless find themselves declasse among the whites. Alison

Stewart upholds her mother's argument that *Haida* children belong to the maternal family but she dislikes being considered inferior by Scots neighbors, even wonders about her father's opinion until he sends her to a frilly white boarding school. Childhood friend Ross, an early activist, champions the Indians' cause as, burning for recognition, he is met by insults like "halfbreed bastard" and "savage," the latter from his deserting father. Into the melting pot leaps Megan Scully whose Irish immigrant aspirations will welcome anything except potato farming, preferably the good life from one Connell who looks like a sound investment. In between lines from "Lady of the Lake" and "Young Lochinvar" (they *all* read Scott), Megan mistakes Ross' agitation for murder, informs on him, then recants and, with an assist from truant Alison, captures the real villain. The old Frontier is relevant, especially with the romantic ambience to delineate the rebel rousers, but some hasty knotting at the end lessens the impact.

Ruth Hill Viguers

SOURCE: A review of *Forbidden Frontier*, in *The Horn Book Magazine*, Vol. XLIV, No. 2, April, 1968, pp. 181-2.

Alison was a rebel. After she had been to her mother's Haida village and seen what the white man had done to the Indians, she no longer took pride in the Scottish heritage from her father, the Chief Trader at the Fort. Megan, too, was a rebel, chiefly against the dull idea of homesteading when there was gold to be found, and she knew too much about the massacre of whole villages of peaceful settlers to think kindly of any Indians. Longing for the companionship of a white girl, she was bitterly disappointed when the Chief Trader's daughter turned out to be Indian. The two girls maintained their bitter antagonism until a common cause brought them together and gave Megan a chance to broaden her outlook and show her courage. The author's ability to create convincingly alive characters is as evident here as in her other books, but Mrs. Harris has such a lot to say about the times, the people, and the problems that she has crammed too much into one story. Events move fast enough to hold readers, however, and girls who read the book for the story of Alison and Megan will learn a great deal about the settlement of the Far West.

Zena Sutherland

SOURCE: A review of *Forbidden Frontier*, in *Bulletin of the Center for Children's Books*, Vol. 21, No. 10, June, 1968, p. 159.

A story set in British Columbia in 1962. Alison Stewart was proud of her father, an official of the Hudson's Bay Company—and just as proud of her mother's Haida heritage. She expected the white girl, Megan, who had just come to the frontier post, to sneer at her—and she met Megan with hostility. When both girls became involved in trying to help a common friend, they slowly became aware of the false basis of their prejudices. The story has a great deal of action, a vivid portrayal of the frontier atmosphere, and a lively sense of immediacy; its only weakness is a shifting of viewpoint.

Ruth P. Bull

SOURCE: A review of *Forbidden Frontier*, in *The Booklist*, Vol. 64, No. 20, June 15, 1968, p. 1185.

The author of **Raven's cry** and **West with the White Chiefs** again uses the cultural conflicts between white man and Indian as the underlying theme of a story about the Canadian Northwest Frontier. Attention focuses on Ross MacNeil and Alison Stewart, whose Scottish fathers are officials of the Hudson's Bay Company and whose mothers are Indian, and on Megan Scully, an Irish immigrant girl whose family have come west in search of land and gold. The adventures of the three spirited young people brought together by their common concern over unjust discrimination against the Indians is told against a background of fur trading and gold rushes in the 1860's.

Kathryn C. James

SOURCE: A review of *Forbidden Frontier*, in *In Review*, Vol. 2, No. 3, Summer, 1968, p. 15.

The arrival of farmers and gold seekers to the Canadian West brought change and upheaval. To the Indian it meant adjustment to a new way of life often with disastrous results. To the fur trader it meant the loss of livelihod. To Alison Stewart, daughter of a chief trader and an Indian princess it brought grief and bitterness. To Ross MacNeil, the son of a chief trader and a Shuswap Indian it brought ignomy and revolt. To Megan Scully, newly come to the West and with the memory of an Indian massacre fresh in her mind, it meant fear and a chance for wealth. Through their eyes, the conflict of Indian and white settlers is portrayed with honesty and fairness.

In spite of real and vivid characters, the story often lacks cohesion and often becomes a mere recital of case histories. But because it does describe with a fair amount of success a time of trial and turmoil in the settlement of the West, not yet resolved, I would recommend this book.

📖 *LET X BE EXCITEMENT* (1969)

Kirkus Reviews

SOURCE: A review of *Let X Be Excitement*, in *Kirkus Reviews*, Vol. XXXVII, No. 4, February 15, 1969, p. 185.

Those Ross-Allens are some family. Even after Feeny (**Confessions of a Toe-Hanger**) and Linsey (**You Have to Draw the Line Somewhere**), there's enough energy, imagination and humor in brother Roger to satisfy the least sedentary. Roger starts as an active teenager who prefers manual labor but reluctantly agrees to study engineering at the University of British Columbia. Almost losing a finger, mountain climbing through a snowstorm, working for a rowing championship, learning aeronautics *and* test pilot flying—his dry comic descriptions take him through his twenties as he works through college, marries (practically between flights), fathers two children, and finally finds something that he wants to do, that satisfies his dual need for adventure and intellectual stimulation—the Cornell Aeronautical Research Laboratory. He's exceptionally bright (even if he equates Penn State with the University of Pennsylvania), amazingly rugged, and an unusually amusing narrator, whether recalling crew contests at Henley or explaining his own theory of magnetohydrodynamic energy. No formula story here: X = top-flight reading.

Anne S. Echols

SOURCE: A review of *Let X Be Excitement,* in *The Booklist,* Vol. 65, No. 20, June 15, 1969, p. 1170.

Based on the experiences of the author's eldest son this first-person story follows the adventurous life of Ralph Ross-Allen, older brother to Feeny of *Confessions of a toe-hanger* and Linsey of *You have to draw the line somewhere.* Driven by the need for physical excitement and the compulsion to understand how things work Ralph acquires two engineering degrees, meanwhile keeping fit by working for a logging outfit and a mining company, mountain climbing, and rowing on the school team. Suddenly deciding to become a test pilot he joins the Royal Canadian Air Force and eventually finds the job that satisfies both his mechanical interests and need for action. A well-written book which reads like a wryly humorous reminiscence, this will appeal to boys and to girls who want to keep up with the doings of the Ross-Allen family.

Jean Williams

SOURCE: A review of *Let X Be Excitement,* in *In Review,* Vol. 3, No. 3, Summer, 1969, p. 13.

As she has done twice before, Mrs. Harris has given us a borderline book; who would enjoy it more, youngsters in the children's library or their older brothers in the teenage section? For those lucky few whose library collections are integrated there is no problem. But for most of us, with grade eights and perhaps grade sevens too, using the adult collection, it is a question of whether our younger readers would find the book interesting.

Told in the first person it is based on the struggle Mrs. Harris' son had to find his own niche in life. In the story, which moves rapidly to university level, Ralph with his mechanical leanings sees no reason to continue his education. Finally convinced he should take an engineering course at UBC he becomes involved in the rowing team, skiing and mountain climbing. Unable to decide which branch of engineering to enter, Ralph finally becomes interested in aerodynamics. He manages to juggle a scholarship in England with a career in the RCAF in order to

learn to fly jets. All this takes place in the mid fifties. One wonders if it would be possible today to cut red tape quite so easily.

There are many exciting incidents in the book—the rowing races, the skiing, Ralph's problems in learning to fly. I should imagine older boys would recognize their own feelings of indecision in Ralph's struggle to find the right career. But I feel I must recommend it with reservations as far as the children's library is concerned, however there would doubtlessly be many older boys to whom this book would be of interest.

Zena Sutherland

SOURCE: A review of *Let X Be Excitement,* in *Bulletin of the Center for Children's Books,* Vol. 22, No. 11, July-August, 1969, p. 176.

In *You Have to Draw the Line Somewhere* and *Confessions of a Toe-hanger,* Mrs. Harris described, in lively narrative style and in first person, her daughters' careers. Here the vivacity and the light, amusing style are again evident; the first-person is used again (remarkably convincing, too) and the book tells the story of the author's son. His search for a career is interspersed with stories of hikes, college sports, courses of study, and part-time jobs; his choice of a career makes for excitement indeed, since Ralph becomes a test pilot.

FIGLEAFING THROUGH HISTORY: THE DYNAMICS OF DRESS (with daughter Moira Johnston, 1971)

Sally C. Estes

SOURCE: A review of *Figleafing through History: The Dynamics of Dress,* in *The Booklist,* Vol. 68, No. 1, September 1, 1971, p. 53.

A chatty, occasionally verbose, but informative history of styles in dress from prehistoric times to the present looks at clothes as a visible expression of identity and status as well as a reflection of the times. The account discusses in their historical and social context the prevailing fashions throughout human history around the world. The many simple, pertinent drawings are not text-keyed but are placed in the margins of the appropriate page; two sections of photographs also complement the text. The bibliography is intended to guide the reader to further information.

Penelope M. Mitchell

SOURCE: A review of *Figleafing through History: The Dynamics of Dress,* in *School Library Journal,* Vol. 96, No. 16, September 15, 1971, p. 127.

More than a who-wore-what version of the history of dress, this account attempts to show that clothing has never been merely utilitarian, that it is a reflection of mores, rank, and philosophies. As a result, what is had here is a brief history of civilization—Eastern and Western—as seen through man's bodily adornment. Simplification has not distorted the overview, and the necessary postulation of changes in attitude during pre- and early history does not seem out of line. The author's personal bias does occasionally emerge, especially in the final (approving) chapter on current Western trends in dress. Simple black-and-white drawings in the ample margins of each page accompany the text, but the lack of identifying captions at times causes confusion. And, the illustrations are not as intricate and detailed as those in such standard costume histories as Gorsline's *What People Wore*. Nevertheless, this book overall offers a refreshing new look at a popular subject.

Zena Sutherland

SOURCE: A review of *Figleafing through History: The Dynamics of Dress,* in *Bulletin of the Center for Children's Books,* Vol. 25, No. 2, October, 1971, p. 26.

Long, detailed, profusely illustrated, a history of clothing and styles of dress is given against a background of world history from prehistoric times to the present day: the protest against furs, the African styles worn by Afro-Americans, the revolt against the suit, the new dress rules of the nuns of the Roman Catholic Church. The material is interesting and the treatment full, but the breezy writing style that makes stories by Christie Harris so delightful seems here inappropriate, and there are just enough uses of "probably" in the first part of the book to rob it of an air of authority. A good divided bibliography and an index are appended; there is no table of contents.

Ina Govan

SOURCE: A review of *Figleafing through History: The Dynamics of Dress,* in *In Review,* Vol. 6, No. 1, Winter, 1972, pp. 30-1.

Written in literate, lively style and intricate detail, this absorbing book provides enlightening entertainment as the reader travels down the pathways of world history, via the vehicle of fashion, from earliest times to the present day, with intriguing side excursions along the route. Men (and women, as far as the dominance of men has permitted them through the centuries) have found in their garments not only a functional use in adapting themselves to the exigencies of climate and occupation, but also an expression of magical protection, closeness to nature, tribal pride, love of colour and beauty, status and individuality. Today the role of the western businessman's suit, symbolic of the ethic of hard work and scientific progress at the expense of human values as expressed in the realization of man's basic kinship with nature is being questioned. Scientists are wondering whether, after all, animal "dress" such as "the grandeur of a stag's antlers" and "the glory of a peacock's train" do serve merely a functional purpose, or are they not saying, in effect, "Look! This is what I am!" Hippies, American negroes, priests, nuns

and many other men and women are using clothes as an expression of today's social revolution. Must this mean the "death" of the suit? Not necessarily. The authors conclude that . . . "if the suit and the headband joined forces, we might go into one of the great ages of dress. For the tools of science could do fantastic things to open up the senses and serve individual expression."

The drawings with their free-flowing simplicity, clarity and dignity of line capture in detail the many modes of dress and ornament. In addition, there are several black-and-white photographs of modern dress and reproductions of paintings, a lengthy selected bibliography and a detailed index. Highly recommended.

SECRET IN THE STLALAKUM WILD (1972)

Kirkus Reviews

SOURCE: A review of *Secret in the Stlalakum Wild,* in *Kirkus Reviews,* Vol. XL, No. 8, April 15, 1972, p. 478.

"Anything uncanny is stlalakum," and practically everything uncanny—sasquatches, sprites, lie detector evidence of plants' emotions, and a very unlikely British Columbian faery named Siem—plays a role in convincing hard-headed Morann that the real treasure of the Stlalakum Wild is not gold but natural beauty. It's a little disappointing that more isn't made of these fantasy elements after they've been introduced: the sasquatch is dismissed as "a pitiful buffoon. . . . Big as a grizzly, yet timid as a rabbit"; the wonderful Ogress Squirrel plays only a minor role; and the encounter with the two-headed Seexqui is inconclusive—it's supposed to be a test of courage, but Morann *would* have run away if she could have gotten her sleeping bag unzipped. Perhaps if we knew earlier that the Wild was being threatened by miners, Morann's quest would seem more purposeful. As it is, the mix of Indian legends, scientific speculation and traditional make-believe is powerfully suggestive, even though it never really coalesces; readers might be inspired to hunt for sasquatches themselves, or listen for the voices of sprites when they're out in the woods, or even invent some of the adventures Morann should have had, but didn't.

Doreen Livingstone

SOURCE: A review of *Secret in the Stlalakum Wild,* in *In Review,* Vol. 6, No. 3, Summer, 1972, p. 25.

This is Mrs. Harris's bid for conservation of the wilds of British Columbia and she does it in a unique way. Using her knowledge of the beliefs of the West Coast Indians, she involves the forest spirits in really quite a satisfactory fantasy.

Her protagonist, Morann, is an introspective, imaginative and sensitive teeny-bopper who would love the chance to win respect and self respect. Her opportunity comes when she is involved in unearthly experiences with the stlalakums;

these experiences help her to grow up a little and provide a plausible ending to the tale.

Girls of the senior elementary level will enjoy Morann, her family, the witty dialogue and the story line. However, they will be impatient with the first chapter of description and explanation, short as it is. This chapter simply wasn't necessary and upsets the balance of the book. Also, there are moments throughout the story when the worlds of reality and fantasy don't always blend naturally or convincingly.

British Columbia has provided the setting for the fantasies of Catherine Clark, Ruth Nichols and now, Christie Harris; the natural environment coupled with the fascinating body of Indian legends make it a natural spawning ground for fantasy. Quite possibly our first really fine Canadian fantasy will appear from the West Coast: this latest novel by Mrs. Harris isn't it, but it *is* a worthy attempt!

📖 *ONCE MORE UPON A TOTEM* (1973)

Dorothy J. Beesley

SOURCE: A review of *Once More Upon a Totem*, in *In Review*, Vol. 7, No. 3, Summer, 1973, p. 31.

This second collection of stories, like those in the author's *Once Upon a Totem* has as its basic source, "Tsimshian Mythology" by Franz Boas, a collection printed in the *Thirty-first annual report of the Bureau of American Ethnology* to the secretary of the Smithsonian Institution 1909-1910.

The book contains three stories; interspersed with them are chapters which give the reader the setting for the stories, an explanation of the illustrations which are derived from the highly developed, elegant Northwest Coast art forms, background information about the people who listened to and told the stories, and lastly, those who saved the stories for us.

This is a handsome book with large clear print, ample margins and a colourful, eye-catching cover. Douglas Tait has achieved a remarkable success in his black and white illustrations which are based solidly and boldly upon the native idiom. No doubt many other readers will be conscious of a desire to see the originals.

These are absorbing narratives, lightened by humour, written in a smooth, flowing prose which is a delight to read. As an integral part of the story, the author gives the reader valuable insights into the spiritual beliefs of the Indians as reflected in their customs.

A welcome addition to Canadian books for children!

📖 *SKY MAN ON THE TOTEM POLE?* (1975)

Shirley M. Wilton

SOURCE: A review of *Sky Man on the Totem Pole?*, in *School Library Journal*, Vol. 21, No. 9, May, 1975, p. 55.

Von Daniken's theories about beings from outer space and the ideas described in Tompkins and Bird's *Secret Life of Plants* are strangely interwoven here with Indian legends from the Pacific Northwest. Traveling from the planet Tlu to their earth colony, space ships appear to the ancient Indians to be sky-beings, or spirit visions. The Indians, who sense the mystic kinship between man and all other forms of life, are envied by the men from Tlu who live in a barren technological society. One day, a spaceman carries off an Indian bride, thereby fathering sons and daughters of a new totem, the sky man, or Thunderbird. While the idea of psi phenomena in history may appeal to some young readers, the episodic story is awkwardly told and disappointing. The narrative jumps erratically through time and space and fails to build a convincing case for man's higher consciousness. At least one of the incidents, the legend of the mountain goats on Stek-yaw-den, is taken word for word from an earlier book by Harris, *Once Upon A Totem*.

Virginia Haviland

SOURCE: A review of *Sky Man on the Totem Pole?*, in *The Horn Book Magazine*, Vol. LI, No. 4, August, 1975, pp. 380-81.

Sources cited in the bibliography indicate the genesis of the ideas in this complex blend of West Coast Indian legend and space-age science. The book combines mythological beliefs with the possibility of men coming from outer space and with modern theories about bio-plasmic energy in an attempt to explain what might have happened in Temlaham, the Indian's Promised Land. The story's structure is confusingly episodic, weaving back and forth with changes of scene and points of view. An Indian community sees a falling star or comet; it turns out to be the spaceship *Colonizer*, directed to the planet Tlu's colony on Earth. After the Indians migrate to Temlaham, the narrative returns to the spaceship. It is aiming to save its doomed planet when data banks show the extermination of growing things to be imminent and Doomsday only 102 years away. Finally, after the spaceship's landing, the men from Tlu lead the Indians to regard scientific phenomena as manifestations of the spirit world. The conglomeration of ideas could provide material for fresh and interesting science fiction, but the story lacks suspense and clarity, and the sum of its parts does not make a successful whole.

📖 *MOUSE WOMAN AND THE VANISHED PRINCESSES* (1976)

Marilyn Richards

SOURCE: A review of *Mouse Woman and the Vanished Princesses*, in *School Library Journal*, Vol. 22, No. 8, April, 1976, pp. 86, 89.

From Haida and Tsimshian Indian folklore come six well-written stories about Mouse Woman, a supernatural being. Sometimes a mouse, sometimes a tiny woman, always sympathetic, enterprising, and very proper, she is especially interested in young people in trouble. In each story a different princess is lured from her village by other supernatural beings and helped to return to her family by Mouse Woman who is rewarded with her favorite gift of long woolen ear tassels. Black-and-white drawings help set the mood; action is quickly developed and well sustained; and, factual material is very deftly woven in. The original purpose—to teach young people good manners and respect for animals—comes through in a subtle way, never dampening the enjoyment of these stories.

Beryl Robinson

SOURCE: A review of *Mouse Woman and the Vanished Princesses,* in *The Horn Book Magazine,* Vol. LII, No. 3, June, 1976, p. 286.

The Indians of the Pacific Northwest told many tales about a frightening race of supernatural creatures known as *narnauks* who came in many sizes and shapes. The smallest narnauk was a tiny woman with mouselike characteristics. With her magical powers and bright eyes she was quick to observe all that happened, and with her grandmotherly ways she often intervened on behalf of people, particularly young people and princesses who had been threatened by other narnauks. The six lively and dramatic stories in this collection tell of princesses who had been kidnapped and who were rescued by the intervention of Mouse Woman. Based on scholarly records of the Bureau of American Ethnology, the tales reveal not only the culture and beliefs of these early Americans, but also their elaborate art forms and their dependence on the natural world.

S. Yvonne MacDonald

SOURCE: A review of *Mouse Woman and the Vanished Princesses,* in *In Review,* Vol. 10, No. 4, Autumn, 1976, pp. 41-2.

This collection of legends from the mythology of the Northwest Coast Indians of Canada is uniquely linked through the character of Mousewoman, a Narnauk or Supernatural Being. This tiny being, with her "big, busy mouse eyes," and her fetish for bits of wool, appears in all the tales as a guardian spirit for young people in trouble. She's a "very, very proper little being" with a love of justice and a wish to see all things somehow become equal (a quality that should appeal to young readers of this collection). The stories are clearly and lyrically told, with perhaps the most distinctive quality being the characterizations of the Narnauks. Harris manages to evoke the magical and essentially alien World of the Supernaturals and also its familiarity to the Indians, for these spirits were a daily part of their lives. Mousewoman's role in these legends is that of intermediary between the World of the Supernaturals, where she is affectionately regarded

as a busybody, and the Earth, where the Indians regard her as a grandmotherly helping spirit. Her reward in each case? The opportunity to give advice, and obtain pieces of wool that she could rend with her "ravelly little fingers" into a "lovely loose nesty pile of mountain sheep wool."

There is a surprising amount of variety in this collection, given the confines of the theme, vanishing princesses. Some of the tales are poignant, others almost grisly in their outcome. All of the retellings reveal the author's detailed knowledge of Northwest Indian culture and customs, in addition to the actual legends. Douglas Tait's black and white illustrations seem appropriate, many of them supplementing the eerie tone or traditional nature of the legends.

Mouse Woman and the Vanished Princesses follows other books of Indian mythology by Christie Harris such as *Once Upon a Totem* and *Once More Upon a Totem.* By comparison, they have a more scholarly approach to Indian mythology, because of the introductory essay preceding each tale, perhaps. In these essays, Harris formally discusses Northwest Coast Indian life, potlatches, marriage customs, the relationship between myth and reality for the Indian, and the daily need to appease the spirit world to avoid disaster. They could easily be used by an adult studying cultural anthropology, although as a selection of legends, it is suitable for use by older children as well. *Mouse Woman* seems to have a more integrated approach to Indian mythology, and more likely to be pleasurable reading for children. In these books, the author shows considerable skill as a storyteller.

Frances M. Frazer

SOURCE: "Indian Folklore and Fantasy," in *Canadian Children's Literature,* No. 7, 1977, pp. 28-31.

Like Mrs. Harris's *Once upon a Totem, Raven's Cry, Once More upon a Totem,* and *Sky Man on the Totem Pole, Mouse Woman and the Vanished Princesses* concerns the Indians of the Pacific Northwest who, in their wealth and pride, developed a culture sophisticated enough to give their stories a socially complex background comparable to the court-and-castle settings of European fairytales. The young heroines of *Mouse Woman* are not sweet and simple variations on Pretty Redwing, but accomplished, haughty young ladies who guard their dignity even more strenuously than they do their personal safety. And although the narnauks of these stories, like the supernatural beings of other Indian cultures, can change their physical forms, they confine themselves to two guises, one animal, the other human. Consequently, the ground-rules of the fantasy are kept reasonably clear, and the stories seem less arbitrary than most others of the *genre.*

Mrs. Harris also has a winning card in Mouse Woman, the little narnauk she first caught sight of in *Tsimshian Mythology* by Franz Boas and later traced in texts recorded early in this century for the Smithsonian Institution. Beyond her ability to shift her own shape, and on one occasion in this book to lend mouse guise to a human being, Mouse Woman is not a miracle-worker. But she is benevolent and wise, within the confines of her Grundy-like concern for proprieties. Her only moral weakness is a lust for wool to ravel with her 'ravelly little fingers', a lust that makes her demanding and sometimes pushes her to the brink of larceny. Otherwise she is a stauch defender of good sense and good etiquette among narnauks as well as people. She is also a champion of justice, although she occasionally exhibits alarming powers of rationalization, discovering ingenious reasons for believing that things have been 'made equal' even when her well-meant interferences are not entirely successful. Her quirks, her civilized intelligence, and her very limitations, which accommodate suspense, make her an interesting and effective intermediary between the real and the supernatural worlds.

Of the six stories in the book, the first, "The Princess and the Feathers", is by far the strongest. It has a clean-lined, exciting plot, and, apart from one lapse (of princesses who vanish permanently, we are told, "Again and again they vanished."), it is lucidly as well as briskly written. Wy-en-eeks the Eagle Princess is a spirited, resourceful heroine who keeps her head in horrifying circumstances, and Mouse Woman, appearing briefly as a white mouse to help the princess save herself, does only what any mouse might do by happenstance. Magic is present, but it does not detract from the achievement of the human heroine. The story also, unemphatically but clearly, introduces the remorseless justice that the Indians of old evidently approved, as Wy-en-eeks calls down terrible but just retribution upon her murderous enemy. This tale is a good introduction to the social and natural milieu of the book and also a gripping, pleasing story for readers of all ages.

In contrast, "The Princess and the Bears" is a strange mixture of pathos and mordant humour about a bizarre case of miscegenation which seems likely to evoke awkward questions from young readers despite the narration's careful avoidance of suggestive details. Braving Mouse Woman's prim displeasure, a bear narnauk adopts his handsome human form to abduct a beautiful, petulant Indian princess—partly for her beauty and partly to give pause to her bear-slaughtering brothers. In due course the princess is conducted to a bear's den where

> The child was born. Twins.
>
> Twins! Twin balls of dark fur!
>
> They were BEAR CUBS.
>
> "My children?" Rh-pi-sunt cried out, horrified.
>
> "And mine," their father said, holding the cubs close. He touched their little black noses fondly. He scratched their tiny bellies.

The story's rather melancholy conclusion, melancholy for the disgraced princess at any rate, will do little to distract youthful questioners. The short emphatic sentences and half-sentences and the relatively undemanding diction are well suited to child readers; the tale itself is not, though it has a ruefully whimsical appeal.

The remaining four stories fall between these two stools; they are somewhat less interesting and satisfying than the first, but free from the sadness and perversity of the second. Supernatural wonders tend to accumulate in them, with proportional losses in human endeavour and hence in human interest. In "The Princess and the Magic Plume", the titular heroine does little but ignore Mouse Woman's frantic squeaks of warning and thus assists the narnauk Raven, Prince of Tricksters, in his grotesquely funny punishment of raucous, uncontrolled children and their permissive parents. Mouse Woman needs her ingenuity to reconcile herself to this outcome, but she manages:

> . . . suddenly, her big, busy, mouse eyes narrowed. And her nose twitched. Raven had won. But perhaps she had won, too. For, by doing such an outrageous thing, Raven had shown his arrogant disregard for human beings. So, in the future, no powwow of Supernatural Beings would challenge HER right to handle troublesome young people. By losing, she had won. By winning, Raven had lost. And that was strangely satisfying.

Mouse Woman has more obvious reasons to be complacent in the other stories, but once she has to invoke the aid of her best supernatural friend, a 'dazzling lady' named Great-Charmer, to help her with an appalling opponent, Great-Whirlpool-Maker, who renders his captive princess quiescent by 'thinking grease into her mind'. And once her supernatural antagonists, gigantic snail narnauks, are so stupid that only their stupendous, ingenuous vanity keeps the story entertaining.

But when the fault-finding comparisons have been made, it must be stressed that all of these stories are entertaining—and fascinatingly different from the myths of eastern tribes that have dominated the field, numerically at least, to date.

And for the most part, Mrs. Harris does them justice with her pleasant tone and economical style. She does have some irritating habits. In or out of season, whether the subject matter is tense or active or neither, she habitually uses short snappy sentences (all too many beginning with "for") and sentence fragments that carry a story forward at a rapid clip but also produce a staccato, hiccoughing effect. Her typographical emphases are obtrusively frequent. Ritualistic repetitions that probably echo the verbal formulas of oral storytellers become monotonous and suggestive of laziness, at least to adult eyes and ears. A penchant for word-play and verbal whimsy sometimes misleads her into near-coyness or even downright obscurity, as in "At the other end of awesomeness, there was Mouse Woman. . . . " Nevertheless, her descriptions are concisely evocative, and she places her bits of information and her provocative hints with a sure hand. Mouse Woman has found an appreciative biographer and an efficient teller of tales. . . .

In short, as she is presented in this book, Mouse Woman was well worth resurrecting, and so were the characters who live again to receive her benign busybody attentions.

MOUSE WOMAN AND THE MISCHIEF-MAKERS (1977)

Jane Abramson

SOURCE: A review of *Mouse Woman and the Mischief-Makers,* in *School Library Journal,* Vol. 23, No. 8, April, 1977, p. 67.

Busiest of busybodies, Mouse Woman once again pokes her twitching little nose into the problems of the Northwest Coast people; and whether it is a greedy hunter who is killing off too many porcupines, a young chieftain whose grief for his dead wife turns self-destructive, or a giant witch with a fondness for gobbling down children, the tiny narnauk always finds a just solution. As in *Mouse Woman and the Vanished Princesses* these seven cautionary folk legends, told with spare strength and humor, are exceptional for revealing the bedrock uponwhich the Northwest Indian culture stood. Harris recreates a world where balance and harmony among living creatures are valued above all and where even supernatural narnauks (including proper little Mouse Woman herself) can occasionally become "mischief-makers." Although [Douglas] Tait's somberly bizarre drawings seem inappropriate, the outcomes of these magical and wise stories will be as satisfying to readers as they are to Mouse Woman herself.

Paul Heins

SOURCE: A review of *Mouse Woman and the Mischief-Makers,* in *The Horn Book Magazine,* Vol. LIII, No. 4, August, 1977, p. 436.

The author, who has already retold many stories based on Indian lore of the Pacific Northwest, states in her introduction, "Mouse Woman liked everyone and everything to be proper. To her, anyone who was disturbing the proper order of the world was a mischief-maker." A tiny narnauk, or spirit that roamed the Northwest coast, she spent her time frustrating mischief-makers and helping young people who were kind to her. Among other things, she prevented Porcupine Hunter's wife from killing too many porcupines, helped a young prince destroy a monster—part wolf and part whale—who had swallowed his brothers, and even saved an annoying child from the Snee-nee-iq, who ate children. The well-told tales, rich in dialogue and effectively using the devices and transitions of good oral storytelling, are compounded of horror and humor, in which man, nature, and spirit each plays its part.

J. Kieran Kealy

SOURCE: "Narnauk & Badger," in *Canadian Literature,* No. 78, Autumn, 1978, pp. 76, 78.

Readers familiar with the work of Christie Harris are well aware of her interest in the lore of the Northwest Coast Indians and, in particular, her affection for Mouse Woman, a supernatural being whom she first discovered in Boaz' collection of Tsimshian myths and who has become the central figure of her last two books, *Mouse Woman and the Vanished Princesses* and *Mouse Woman and the Mischief-Makers*.

This second collection of tales, chronicling Mouse Woman's encounters with a series of both human and supernatural mischief-makers, is not as successful as the first, perhaps because only four of the seven tales appear to be derived from sources which do, in fact, include this attractive little narnauk. Ms. Harris seems to have exhausted the potential of the character in the first collection, and thus is forced to invent shrewish wives and magical talking blankets to fill out the tales. This is nowhere more obvious than in the last tale, which purports to relate Mouse Woman's own childhood. In the original text, the Mouse Woman, no relation to the kindly grandmother figure of the Boaz texts, is not forgiven for her transgressions, and dies. Thus Ms. Harris not only distorts the substance and meaning of the original legends, but more importantly in terms of examination of the text as an independent entity, she is forced by the nature of the collection to include a central figure who often does very little to enhance the narrative flow of individual stories. Thus the Mouse Woman, so enchanting and attractive in the first collection, becomes a bit of a burden to the storyteller in this text.

Margery Fisher

SOURCE: A review of *Mouse Woman and the Mischief-Makers,* in *Growing Point,* Vol. 17, No. 5, January, 1979, p. 3459.

Six of these tales, adapted from North American anthropological collections, follow the tricks and changes of a certain nanauk, a supernatural being revered by the Indians of North West America, a being who can be a grannie or a mouse, a being with a passion for order and balance and also for woollen tassels and textiles as nest-material. The dual roles make for humour and mystery alike. Mouse Woman is equal to dealing with the ecological greed of a porcupine-hunter, the malice of a kidnapping demon and the sorrow of a chieftain for his dead wife, and in a seventh tale she is seen as a small child stealing pine-nut cakes and betrayed by a broken tooth. In a leisurely, reflective style the [Canadian] re-teller has built up the character of a spirit whose power resides as much in inspired common sense as in shape-changing. These are fascinating tales with primitive overtones that add to their solid human ground-bass.

D. A. Young

SOURCE: A review of *Mouse Woman and the Mischief-Makers,* in *The Junior Bookshelf,* Vol. 43, No. 1, February, 1979, p. 31.

It was in the time of very long ago, when things were different and the people in the totem pole villages told stories. Mouse Woman was a spirit being with a marked dislike of any disturbance in the proper order of the world and a love of woollen things which her ravelly little fingers would tear into lovely, loose, nesty piles of wool. There are seven stories of the Mouse Woman at work and all have the essential ingredients of the classic folk-fairy tale. The foolish are taught sense; the compassionate are rewarded and the strong are worsted by the weak. Like all good stories they possess the repetitious phrases and sentences which so delight young children. Drawn from the North American Anthropological Archives, they have been nicely turned into contemporary English by the author and made the transition with excellent grace.

MYSTERY AT THE EDGE OF TWO WORLDS (1978)

Janice Bick

SOURCE: A review of *Mystery at the Edge of Two Worlds,* in *In Review,* Vol. 13, No. 1, February, 1979, p. 49.

An imaginative, well-told story of two teenagers, Lark and brother Joe who take a trip to visit their Gran and learn the art of sailing from Gran's neighbour Skipper Peery. Lark had been told by her mother that it was time she got out and did things, not just sit and think and read. But Lark had her problems: being tall wouldn't have been so bad if only she could get it all together—the long arms, the long feet. She describes her perplexing situation: "even when I slouched down, I was still gangling, the dictionary word for 'awkwardly long'." However, the unravelling of the mystery of Lucy Island and the meeting with red-haired Andy Fergus did much to change Lark's summer. Both Lark and Andy begin to investigate the mysterious appearance of a strange man, and question the possibility of someone stealing valuable argillite Indian artifacts.

With all the magic potions needed to make a successful mystery, Christie Harris draws undivided attention from her reader. Characters are well-drawn, the plot moves at a swift pace and enough chills and excitement complete the story. Although carefully researched, facts do not overburden the novel's impact, yet add to the quality of the tale. The novel will surely invite readers from the fourth grade and up.

MOUSE WOMAN AND THE MUDDLEHEADS (1979)

Childrens Book News

SOURCE: A review of *Mouse Woman and the Muddleheads,* in *Children's Book News,* Toronto, Vol. 2, No. 2, September, 1979, p. 2.

Mouse Woman is back—this time to rescue young muddleheads (young people who persist in doing the wrong thing) from the snares of supernatural beings. The mischief and

magic of these fast-paced Indian tales are intertwined with valuable messages urging compassion and respect for living things. Children who have come to love Mouse Woman in earlier books will enjoy the adventures and misadventures that Christie Harris creates for her here.

Marjorie Lewis

SOURCE: A review of *Mouse Woman and the Muddleheads,* in *School Library Journal,* Vol. 26, No. 1, September, 1979, p. 139.

Seven more legends from the heritage of the Northwest Coast Indians about tiny *Mouse Woman* . . . whose sharp little eyes and shrewdness turn the tide for a variety of narnucks (supernatural beings) and humans. The tales are clever enough—particularly the one about Slow Mink who wants to marry a human princess but whose muddleheadedness leaves him nailed to a log while she runs home to her own true love. The trouble with the collection is not in the stories but in the telling of them. The prose is clumsy, dull, and awkward; typographical tricks such as words in UPPER CASE to indicate drama, italics for emphasis, and elipses for pauses seem to take the place of verbal acuity. Sentence structure is peculiar and somewhere, somehow, all the excitement and humor is lost. The pictures [by Douglas Tait] are exquisite pen and inks but are far too brooding for their subject matter.

Virginia Haviland

SOURCE: A review of *Mouse Woman and the Muddleheads,* in *The Horn Book Magazine,* Vol. LV, No. 5, October, 1979, pp. 542-43.

A third collection of tales about the *narnauks*—tiny supernatural creatures of the Northwest wilderness. Mouse Woman, the "busiest little busybody in the Place of Supernatural Beings," appears in seven stories, saving both narnauks and human beings from the catastrophic results of their foolish behavior. Among the fantastic characters are Slow Mink, who was stupid enough to want to marry a human princess; Copper Canoeman, who took the human princess Summer Stream to his private island; and Big-Raven, a "none-too-bright narnauk" tricked by the little Mouse Children. The narratives are rich in descriptions of folkways—taboos, charms, and superstitions. The artist uses black line and stippling for strong, handsome effects contrasting light and dark. Authenticating the tales is a list of five source collections published between 1899 and 1953.

Elizabeth E. Watson

SOURCE: A review of *Mouse Woman and the Muddleheads,* in *In Review,* Vol. 13, No. 5, October, 1979, pp. 43-4.

The latest collection of stories about the little grandmotherly narnauk or spirit, Mouse Woman, involves her with humans and supernatural beings who upset the proper natural order of life. Some of these "muddleheads" are foolish or stupid, others are proud and thoughtless, and one young chief is raised to be tragically willful by foolishly indulgent parents. As before, Mouse Woman is always ready to help young people who have been tricked into trouble, but something must be given in return for her help or advice. A most mischievous story is one in which Mouse Woman, as a young mother in a time long before the other tales take place, is actively involved in tricking Big-Raven who had tricked her children out of a supply of seal meat.

These tales are interesting in their portrayal of the easy interaction of the natural and supernatural worlds in the traditional stories of the Northwest Coast Indians. This familiarity with spirits leads only to trouble, however, when marriage is involved, for no good comes of interfering with proper procedures and tradition in such an important area, and the marriage of human and supernatural beings is not proper. The author has such a sure grasp of the culture which is the source of these stories that revealing details can be used casually and unobtrusively where appropriate. The importance of princesses to the continuation of royal bloodlines in their Clan; the value of proper procedures and ritual in the important occasions of life; respect for all creatures; respect for another's dignity and position are cultural values revealed by action and plot.

The oral tradition from which these stories descend is lovingly preserved in the flow of language and phrase. They deserve to be told, or at least read aloud. Then, also, the little descriptive tags used to identify recurring themes or characters, such as Mouse Woman herself, become unifying devices rather than annoyingly repetitive phrases.

THE TROUBLE WITH PRINCESSES (1980)

Children's Book News

SOURCE: A review of *The Trouble with Princesses,* in *Children's Book News,* Toronto, Vol. 2, No. 4, April, 1980, p. 2.

Christie Harris provides readers with a new perspective on the Northwest Coast Indian legends she has chosen for this volume by prefacing each legend with a quick summary of princess legends from around the world. But while the links between European fairy tales and Canadian Indian legends may be thought-provoking, older readers will enjoy the stories of Eagle, Raven and Bear for the sheer entertainment they offer. The legends are exquisitely illustrated with eerie black and white drawings by Douglas Tait.

Adele Ashby

SOURCE: A review of *The Trouble with Princesses,* in *Quill & Quire,* Vol. 46, No. 5, May, 1980, p. 31.

The trouble with princesses is that they spell trouble for everyone around them, including themselves. They defy parents in the important matter of marriage, they are very hard on adventurous young men, and they often have wicked spells cast on them. And it does not seem to matter if they come dressed in silk and satin slippers from the old world or cloaked in marten fur from the new.

Christie Harris makes these points very clearly in her new collection of seven stories taken from the legends of the Indians of the northwest coast. Each begins with a preamble that makes connections between the two worlds, and each is illustrated with an outstanding drawing by Doug-las Tait who has collaborated successfully with Harris in the past.

As for the princesses. Maada takes off in search of the dreaded Mountain Dweller, Princess Djoon breaks the spell cast over her people, and the Eagle Princess again and again rescues her foolhardy suitor from the consequences of his folly. But my favourite character is the reluctant hero of Little Fester who finds himself caught up in that bothersome business of rescuing captive ladies.

These stories will appeal to everyone. Fans of Mouse Woman (the subject of three of Harris's previous books) will be pleased to find her included. Folklorists in search of archetypes and universal themes and adults looking for positive female images for their children will be gratified. And storytellers will gain a new batch of delightful choices.

Zena Sutherland

SOURCE: A review of *The Trouble with Princesses,* in *Bulletin of the Center for Children's Books,* Vol. 33, No. 11, July-August, 1980, p. 213.

Each of the seven stories about the New World princesses of the northwest coast is prefaced by an introduction that draws a parallel between the heroic Native American princess and her counterparts in the fairytale literature of the Old World. Each introduction begins, "The trouble with princesses was that . . . " and the theme is introduced. The familiar figures of Mouse Woman and Raven appear in the stories, which are long magical tales with doughty heroines, retold with polished zest. Notes on the sources (Kwakiutl, Haida, Tlingit, and others) are appended.

Christine McDonnell

SOURCE: A review of *The Trouble with Princesses,* in *The Horn Book Magazine,* Vol. LVI, No. 4, August, 1980, pp. 419-20.

In a collection of seven Pacific Northwest Indian tales the author draws comparisons between princesses of the Old World—fairy tale and folk tale princesses from European traditions—and Indian princesses of the New World. Each of the seven tales is introduced by a brief preface that mentions old-world versions with similar characters. The unifying theme of the book is that princesses are always getting into trouble, taking matters into their own hands, rejecting chosen suitors, marrying unsuitable husbands, needing to be rescued, and even vanishing; as a group, the Indian princesses are proud and headstrong. The tales are filled with magic, totems, ghosts, and witches. Similar in format and style to the author's other books of Northwest Indian tales, the collection of fairly long stories is clearly written, smooth, and detailed. Sources for the legends are included, and each tale is illustrated with a full-page black-and-white drawing that helps to convey the mystery and the power of a rich culture.

Sriani Fernando

SOURCE: A review of *The Trouble with Princesses,* in *In Review,* Vol. 14, No. 4, August, 1980, p. 50.

'The trouble with princesses was that . . . '. So begins a collection of stories in this latest production by Christie Harris.

The book contains seven tales about princesses in the New World. As mentioned in the introduction, Harris's objective is to recreate the New World counterparts of the princesses that frequent the traditional fairy tales of the Old World. Though princesses were important and integral to the culture of the 'Totem Pole Coast', the setting and the accoutrements were different. So the author creates a world where the grandeur has a distinct west coast flavour—satins and jewels of the Old World princesses are replaced by fur robes and abalone-pearl ornaments. Splendidly carved and painted cedar houses and not castles are the dwelling places of these New World princesses. They moved in magnificent totem-crested cedar canoes and not in golden coaches. In place of giants and dragons there are fearful dangers set against the awesome backdrop of mountains, rivers and Spirit Beings.

Within each story, the characters are distinctive and adequately developed. The difference in impetus—depending on whether the protagonists resort to wit, cunning or magic to achieve their ends—lends variety to the stories which counteracts the repetitive format.

Also included is a list of sources for the Indian legends and the fairy tales used in the 'preambles' to each tale.

This is an impressive book, meticulously produced and appropriately illustrated. The stories are interesting and eminently readable.

📖 THE TROUBLE WITH ADVENTURERS (1982)

Adele Ashby

SOURCE: A review of *The Trouble with Adventurers,* in *Quill & Quire,* Vol. 48, No. 6, June, 1982, p. 36.

The unpredictable seas, steep mountains and dense forest, all seething with spirits, made the northwest coast of Canada a perfect setting for adventure. And so the legends of its native peoples abound with heroes such as those who leap off the pages of Christie Harris's latest collection of six tales. They include princes: Asdiwal, a joyous young man whose birth was heralded by the whistle of the Bird of Good Luck and whose prowess as a hunter roused so much envy that he was driven from one exploit to another; the young Wolf Prince who was caught up in a clan war that began because members of one clan were early risers; and a playful Eagle Prince who set out on a quest to find a guardian spirit to help his people when they ventured out on perilous seas and who became what he set out to find. They also include Raven, the glutton whose antics make people wonder whether good ends justify bad means, and Porcupine and Beaver, who discovered that Nature had reasons for making them different.

Harris's ordering of the stories is masterly: lighthearted humour follows gripping adventure, and the last story, told from the point of view of a young white man, raises the question of who is a savage and who is civilized. And her language ensures that the power of the story will cast its spell on the reader. Once again Harris's tales are dramatically illuminated by superb black-and-white drawings by Douglas Tait. An outstanding collection for all lovers of story from children to adults.

Mary M. Burns

SOURCE: A review of *The Trouble with Adventurers,* in *The Horn Book Magazine,* Vol. LVIII, No. 4, August, 1982, p. 420.

"The Northwest Coast of America was never without its adventures. . . . [whose] tales long set the drums throbbing in enormous feasthouses." Recalling these throbbing drums, six tales—five drawn from native American lore and one from the embellished experiences of a young Englishman—have been retold in flowing, cadenced prose. Each one is introduced by an italicized prologue, setting the mood and tone of the narrative which follows. The use of the book title as the initial phrase of each prologue provides a connecting link among the individual stories and emphasizes the unifying theme. Familiar folkloric elements—magic objects, tasks and trials, trickery, transformation—are perceived in the context of the culture, lending color and authenticity to plots which range from the heroic to the humorous. Thus, stories of somber mood, such as "The Bird of Good Luck" or "Revenge of the Wolf Prince," depicting sacrifices made by a brave hunter or warrior, are counter-balanced by such tales as the one in which gluttonous Raven outwits the chief who monopolized the world's supply of *oolikan*—tiny silver fish eaten by many a family at the "hungry end of every winter." A map indicates the geographic location of the stories, and finely executed pen-and-ink drawings reminiscent of nineteenth-century engravings provide an appropriate accompaniment through the juxtaposition of representational detail with expressionistic design. With the author's list of her basic story sources.

Gale Eaton

SOURCE: A review of *The Trouble with Adventurers*, in *School Library Journal*, Vol. 28, No. 10, August, 1982, p. 116.

As in **The Trouble with Princesses**, Harris has linked half a dozen tales with brief, strained introductions, pointing out that the trouble with adventurers was that "sometimes they became famous, and their fame aroused envy," or that "they did not always survive to enjoy the happily-ever-after." The heroes themselves are widely varied, from Asdiwal, the supernaturally gifted son of the Bird of Good Luck, to Raven, whose trickery is for good ends, to Porcupine, whose friend Beaver decides to teach him how to swim. All the narratives are energetic, readable and reflective of Pacific Northwest culture. Especially illuminating is the historic account of Chief Maquinna, whose wounded pride led him to massacre the crew of the American brig *Boston,* and John Jewitt, a young ironworker who survived to endure several seasons of uneasy friendship and cultural conflict with Maquinna's tribe before his eventual rescue. Flippancy of tone is a minor flaw in this solid, well-designed book.

SOMETHING WEIRD IS GOING ON (1994)

Linda Granfield

SOURCE: A review of *Something Weird Is Going On*, in *Quill & Quire*, December, 1994, p. 33.

Few Canadian writers for children can say they've spent 60 years writing for young people, or that they have received the prestigious Order of Canada. At 87, B.C. writer Christie Harris can, and she updates her list of publications with **Something Weird is Going On**.

In this unsettling novel, young Xandra Warwick moves to Vancouver at the start of the summer. Dad, an actor, and Mum, a hard-working single parent, have split up, and little brother Hughie is too small to offer comfort, and there's a nice girl, Hilary, who works on her father's boat off Granville Island and might be the answer to Xandra's loneliness, and what's a poltergeist, anyway? Added to the story of mysterious attacks aimed at Hilary are Flora Lee, the imaginary friend of Xandra's childhood, and a much-described pendant. For all the rushing back and forth between the city and Granville Island, the capsizing in English Bay, all the red herrings, and all the thumping, bumping, and guesswork, however, the story drags. Repeated discussions of ghosts slow the action and there are too many bits that take the reader away from the basic mystery, which could be solved all too quickly by even mildly observant readers. The sub-plots of marriage break-up, single parenthood, and boy troubles are unsatisfying sidebars.

One does wish, however, for more of Xandra's grandmother, the novel's most attractive character. Clad in purple stockings and constantly at work on her latest children's book, Gran provides wonderful moments of elan and a charming eccentricity. Enough of Xandra: bring on more Gran. She moves things better than any poltergeist.

Elizabeth St. Jacques

SOURCE: A review of *Something Weird Is Going On,* in *Canadian Book Review Annual,* 1995, p. 485.

Xandra has a ghost of a problem. It's all because of a pendant she found in the garden of her new home in Ontario when she was 4 years old. Lonely at the time, she pretended it belonged to Flora Lee, her little imaginary friend with a fiery temper—a friend her mother disapproved of. But that was long ago. Now, Xandra, her little brother, and her mother have just moved to Vancouver; the pendant is with her too, and she carries it everywhere, looking for a suitable chain for it.

But strange things are happening. Windchimes sing when there's no wind, and her brother is mysteriously pushed into the lagoon, as is Hilary, whom Xandra wants very much to befriend. As more spooky events unfold, Xandra is haunted by the memory of Flora Lee. Could Flora Lee be a genuine ghost who has followed her to Vancouver? Or is a poltergeist causing these problems? Whoever or whatever is responsible is making Xandra's life miserable . . . and dangerous.

Christie Harris knows how to spin a spine-tingling story that glues the reader solidly to the page. Opening with a hair-raiser, the story builds suspense at a steady pace and with smooth transitions, an interesting plot, and humorous moments keeps the reader eagerly turning pages. Planted along the way is fascinating information about Vancouver, sailing safety, and even acting. And believable dialogue and likable characters sparkle here (e.g., Xandra's grandmother writes books for kids, wears purple, and believes in psychic phenomena and past lives).

This well-written, eerie story—which also delivers messages about human values—is highly recommended for young-adult readers.

Donna Nurse

SOURCE: "Taking Care of Things," in *Books in Canada,* Vol. XXIV, No. 3, April, 1995, pp. 57-8.

An adolescent girl . . . figures in **Something Weird Is Going On**. When Xandra Warwick meets Hilary Olsen it looks like her lonely summer days are over, but someone, or something, seems determined to keep the two girls apart. The celebrated author Christie Harris sets in motion a confrontation between the earthly and the supernatural. Yet it's hard to know whether Xandra's active imagination is working overtime or if something weird really *is* going on. Suspense intensifies with each chapter and even after the mystery is revealed, the story retains an element of intrigue. In the Warwicks Harris creates an extended family of characters who are typically joyful, difficult, and idiosyncratic; they teach Xandra the importance of being a true friend, especially to herself.

Additional coverage of Harris's life and career is contained in the following sources published by Gale Research: *Contemporary Authors New Revision Series,* Vol. 6; *Contemporary Literary Criticism,* Vol. 12; *Dictionary of Literary Biography,* Vol. 88; *Junior DISCovering Authors; Major Authors and Illustrators for Children and Young Adults; Something about the Author,* Vols. 6, 74; *Something about the Author Autobiography Series,* Vol. 10.

Paul B. Janeczko

1945-

American author, compiler, and editor of poetry and prose.

Major works include *Don't Forget to Fly: A Cycle of Modern Poems* (1981), *Poetspeak: In Their Work, About Their Work* (1983), *Bridges to Cross* (1986), *Brickyard Summer* (1989), *Poetry from A to Z: A Guide for Young Writers* (1994).

INTRODUCTION

Janeczko is best known as the compiler and editor of contemporary poetry anthologies for middle graders and young adults. Praised for their lively and engaging introductions to reading and writing poetry, his collections are especially noted for their authenticity of voice and mood, diversity in theme and style, and high level of unity. Typically grouped around a general theme—family life, growing up, small-town experience, emerging voices of adulthood—the anthologies are subdivided into more closely related groups such as poems on AIDS, friendship, death, love, sports, unemployment, and sexuality. Maintaining that exciting students about poetry is a matter of finding the right material, Janeczko has attained a reputation as a leading advocate and educator of contemporary poetry. Critic Myra Cohn Livingston writes, "It is difficult to imagine where, in the late 1970s, 1980s, and the beginning of the 1990s, young adults might have found exciting collections of contemporary poetry were it not for Paul Janeczko."

Biographical Information

Janeczko was born in Passaic, New Jersey, the son of Frank John and Verna Janeczko. His childhood was spent in the company of his brothers Jay and John, and later with younger siblings Mark and Mary. His early passion was baseball, an activity his mother forestalled by forcing him to read a Hardy Boys mystery fifteen minutes each day. Soon, he was reading voraciously, interested mainly in books about crime, but remained a mediocre student. He worked throughout his school years, first delivering newspapers, then in a supermarket. In 1963 he left home to attend St. Francis College in Biddleford, Maine, where he first began writing poetry and received an A.B. in English. He continued his education at John Carroll University, and received his Master's Degree in 1970. After his first year of graduate school, Janeczko began teaching high school full time, and, finding the existing anthologies to be weighty and dated, began collecting contemporary poetry as a way to introduce the subject to his high school students. Janeczko continued teaching his collections after moving to Massachusetts in 1972. Initially, he had no

intention of publication, but following a chance meeting with an editor at a teacher's convention, arrangements were made to publish *The Crystal Image* (1977), the first of over a dozen anthologies which were to follow. Janeczko returned to Maine in 1977, continued teaching high school, and, in 1980, met Nadine Edris, a social worker, whom he married in 1985. After twenty-two years of teaching, Janeczko retired in 1990 to concentrate on his own writing as well as to have more time to speak at schools. He also became a father with the birth of his daughter, Emma, that same year.

Major Works

To date, Janeczko has produced fifteen anthologies of poetry, representing the bulk of his published work. The initial success of *The Crystal Image* was followed by *Postcard Poems* (1979) and the award-winning *Don't Forget to Fly*. Although criticized for its often somber mood, the collection was praised for its wide range of topic and style and the quality of the poems by over seventy writers. In his next book *Poetspeak: In Their Work, About Their Work*, Janeczko juxtaposed the selected poems with thoughts, comments, and anecdotes from the poets themselves. Strengthened by the commentary of the various writers, the collection was praised by Karen Jameyson in *The Horn Book Magazine* as having a "powerful feeling of unity," and *The English Journal*'s Dick Abrahamson called it, "a real find for teachers of poetry." Janeczko revisited this form again in *The Place My Words Are Looking For* (1990) and in *Poetry from A to Z: A Guide for Young Writers*. Janeczko's own work comprises both poetry and prose. The children's book *Loads of Codes and Secret Ciphers* (1984) followed his childhood fantasy of being an FBI agent, while his first novel, *Bridges to Cross*, tells of a teen-age boy struggling to come of age in the restrictive atmosphere of a Catholic high school. The first collection of his own poems, *Brickyard Summer*, celebrates summer life in a small mill town and was praised for its authenticity of mood and atmosphere. *Kirkus Reviews* lauded the work for having a "sometimes charming, always believable adolescent voice." Janeczko returned to the theme of boyhood in small-town America once again in his second collection of original poems, *Stardust otel* (1993).

Awards

Janeczko has received numerous awards for his anthologies including the American Library Association's Best Young Adult Book of the Year for *Don't Forget to Fly* (1981), *Poetspeak: In Their Work, About Their Work* (1983), *Strings: A Gathering of Family Poems* (1984) *Pocket Poems: Selected for a Journey* (1985), *Going Over to Your Place* (1987), and *The Music of What Happens: Poems That Tell Stories* (1988). A collection of his own poetry, *Brickyard Summer* garnered the Lupine Award for children's literature in 1990.

AUTHOR'S COMMENTARY

Paul B. Janeczko

SOURCE: "Confession of a Collector," in *Children's Literature Association Quarterly,* Vol. 12, No. 2, Summer, 1987, pp. 98, 110.

James Dickey said it best: "What you have to realize . . . is that poetry is just naturally the greatest goddamn thing that ever was in the whole universe. If you love it, there's no substitute for it." I love it. It's important. Vital. It must be a part of the lives of young people. They need to hear the music of language. That's why I put together my first poetry anthology ten years ago, why I've put together five anthologies since then. And that's why I'm still collecting poems and working on a new anthology right now. Poetry is vital.

My first collection, **The Crystal Image,** was published a decade ago, but I had been working on it ever since I began teaching, when I realized that the poetry in the nine-pound anthology that I was required to use was not exciting my students about poetry. Already a poetry junkie, I turned into a thief of sorts, robbing from books and journals rich in poetry, and sharing it with my students, young people who believed that poetry a) always rhymes; b) is generally about flowers, clouds, and courage; and c) is read only by sissies.

Since the day I took a deep breath and handed out my first mimeographed poem, my files of poems have grown. So have small piles of poems that sprout up around the house from time to time like clumps of dandelions on the lawn. In many ways, for me the easiest part of creating an anthology is finding poems to put into files and piles, because I read poetry the way some people watch soap operas, eat junk food, or follow the Red Sox: irrationally, compulsively, endlessly. I read poems nearly every day, whenever I find myself with a few unfilled minutes: at the airport waiting for a visitor, in the yard waiting for the lawn mower to start by itself, and even at faculty meetings waiting for them to get relevant.

The poems I read come from books and magazines that I buy or borrow from friends and libraries. When it comes to libraries, I'm a gambler, frequently taking a book of poems with no knowledge of its author. Such gambles have paid off with some of my best friends. A new source of poems is the poets themselves. Since I worked on **Poetspeak: In Their Work, About Their Work,** I've stayed in touch with a number of poets who are eager to send me new poems and books of their work. These men and women have recommended other poets to whom I've written, often delighted with what is sent to me. This has been a good source of poems—despite the protests of my quickly aging mail carrier—and has allowed me to include in my books the work of poets whose poems deserve wider exposure.

I look for poems that strike me. These are the ones I save, copying and filing them in subject/topic folders where they wait to be rediscovered like so many promising rookies. After the poems sit in folders for a time, I read through them again. Not all of them at one sitting, of course, but perhaps a folder at a time. This reading refreshes my memory about the poems I saved. It also helps me to make connections, to see similarities and differences in the poems that may help me place them with other poems. But it does more than that. Some of these poems stick in my subconscious where they rest for weeks, even months, until reading other poems may recall them.

In addition to the files of poems that are candidates for a book, I have other files, my private stock, my fantasy files. Those contain poems that will never see their way into a book because the subject, while perhaps interesting as a section of an anthology, is not commercial enough to interest a publisher. Baseball is a good example. Countless people, myself among them, number baseball as one of their passions. But, most publishers will tell you that there aren't enough baseball lovers who will shell out twelve dollars for a poetry book. Pity. It doesn't matter, though, because I have some absolutely great baseball poems.

And who knows, maybe when Billy Martin or Tommy Lasorda becomes an administrator for the National Endowment for the Arts, things will be different. While I won't hold my breath, I will hold onto my baseball file, as well as my other fantasy files.

Files of poems do not an anthology make. Poems must connect with other poems. Some associations are obvious, but I look for the connections that aren't apparent at first reading. I want my readers to think about why poems are where they are. I want to bring order to the poems, an order that will bring out the order in the poems themselves, and an order that will give the timid inexperienced reader of poetry a gentle nudge in a helpful direction. I discovered while working on **Don't Forget To Fly** that groups of two to six poems work better for me than larger groups. Small groupings, however, make the anthology more difficult to organize because I must not only connect the poems in each section, but I must also connect the sections. My latest collection, **Pocket Poems,** contains thirty-four sections arranged to show three major movements: being someplace, going away, coming back. Within those three major movements are smaller, more subtle movements.

An important part of creating an anthology is trying to forget about it. I try to do that after I have made my initial decisions about poems, sections, and order in the book. Because I have lived with the poems for some time when I get to this point, putting the book away isn't easy. Forgetting it is impossible. I think about it, fret about it, fight the urge to tinker with it. When it has rested for a while, then I tinker, fine tuning the book by cutting out some poems, changing the order, perhaps adding a poem or two to make the book flow more effortlessly. Making cuts isn't easy for me, and I tend to think, at this point in the process of making an anthology, of the good poems I have cut from the book instead of about the good poems I've included in the book. Encouraging words from my editor at Bradbury Press, however, help me focus on the book rather than on what went back into my files.

As anthologist, I go through a process of discovery when I read poems, when I look for order in disorder. I discover the possibilities of poetry, and I want to share those possibilities with my readers—possibilities in form, language, images, structure, rhythm, voice, sound, feeling. I want my readers to see that poems are expressions of human experience, that poems are as different as people. Further, I want them to understand that the feelings they have are shared by many people. The possibilities of subjects poets choose to write about seem endless. I've offered young readers poems about teeth, suicide, lasagna, movies, swimming, insomnia, gluttons, dentists, war victims, crows, cars, cats, and gnats, to name a few. Young readers need to recognize that poems can do many things. Poems can comfort, advise, recall, implore, describe, narrate, mourn, warn, laugh.

Although the possibilities of poetry are endless, I want my readers to see that all poems have a purpose, described well by Jonathan Holden: "to give shape, in a concise and memorable way, to what our lives feel like . . . Poems help us to notice the world more and better, and they enable us to share with others." And today, with civilization minutes or a misunderstanding away from being destroyed, we need to share. That's what poets do. That's what I try to do with my books. I want my readers to feel that each of my collections and every poem in them is a sharing. My hope is that my readers will carry on that sharing.

Paul Janeczko with Patricia L. Bloem and Anthony L. Manna

SOURCE: in an interview in *The ALAN Review,* Vol. 24, No. 3, Spring, 1997, pp. 12-16.

In Paul Janeczko's anthology **The Place My Words Are Looking For,** poet Naomi Shihab Nye writes:

> Maybe if we reinvent whatever our lives give us we find poems . . . (p. 145)

Finding poems comes naturally to Janeczko, who has created numerous poetry anthologies, written several volumes of his own poetry, and, for the past six years, run poetry workshops for schools throughout the country. Although Janeczko expects to publish his twenty-second book this year, each anthology is a distinctive invention—or re-invention. In each book Janeczko has broken ground, carefully crafting thematic units, finding new poems that speak to adolescents' ears, or inspiring students to read and write.

To explore his award-winning work, several of our classes at Kent State University spoke by phone with Janeczko in April and May of 1995. We also talked with him after his presentation at the 1995 Virginia Hamilton Conference, an annual forum on multicultural literature at Kent State University.

The following conversation is a compilation and composite of these several interviews.

Interviewer: We'd like to begin with a question that came up when we read the piece you wrote for the Nilsen and Donelson text. You say that an anthologist needs to "break new ground." What do you mean by that?

Janeczko: Soon after I published my first anthology, I realized that my job as an anthologist demanded more from me than gathering together some well-known poems. I set out to widen my circle of reading and began looking for contemporary poets—women poets, poets of color, and poets who weren't in the mainstream journals. But I knew I wouldn't find these people easily because new poetry is reviewed so sparingly. I came up with a system for finding poems. When I have a theme for an anthology, I send out postcards to about a hundred poets inviting them to submit a few poems. I always ask them if they know of other poets I should learn about, poets whose work deserves a wider audience. As this database has grown, I've been able to break new ground by bringing together truly diverse groups of contemporary poets in my books, many of whom are new poets. If my anthologies sometimes feature nontraditional or unconventional forms of poetry, it's because younger writers in particular tend to be experimental, not only in how they go about making poems, but in the issues they write about.

I: Do you think that your "teaching books" are breaking ground? I'm thinking here about books like *Poetspeak, Poetry from A to Z,* and *The Place My Words Are Looking For,* books that encourage us to read and write poetry in a more focused way.

J: I think that in some ways they do break ground. For instance, in *The Place My Words Are Looking For,* I combined poetry and comments by the poets about their poems. *Poetry From A to Z* is even more ground breaking in that it includes an anthology, comments from the poets about the poems and suggestions on how to write poetry, and my suggestions for writing activities. To combine those elements in a trade book is unusual. The tone of this book isn't like a textbook's, though, because the activities are open-ended. I tried to give kids credit for their sense of creativity and their willingness to experiment.

I: When you sit down to shape an anthology, are you influenced by the fact that the book will be marketed for young adults?

J: Well, yes and no. The first rule for me is that I need to like the poems myself. But I also need to keep in mind that these are kids I'm appealing to, from early to late adolescence. Kids, after all, are exploring, and I want to give them poems that will help them do that, that are going to widen the avenues that they explore. So I do have them in mind, but it's not from a manipulative standpoint. What I set out to do is to give them a book that recognizes where they are in life and that will, at the same time, push them, a book that will help them reach out and go beyond themselves.

I: How can an anthology do this?

J: An anthology to me is like a deli counter. You know, you go to a deli counter and you order a half a pound of provolone, some pastrami, a little cheese maybe; and, when you get home and make sandwiches, you say you like this or that and you're ready to go back and buy more. That is what an anthology is. You read an anthology, you like Marge Piercy, so you pursue her poetry. You like Ted Kooser, so you pursue him. I've been blessed with an editor who understands this. I'm not so sure another editor would have taken so readily to Marge Piercy's "Rape Poem," which found its way into *Poetspeak*.

I: When did you begin to realize that an anthology could work this way?

J: My first anthology grew out of the poems I'd been using when I was teaching in a high school in Cleveland in the late '60s. When I discovered that my students weren't excited by the poems in the required nine-pound

literature anthology, I started bringing them copies of poems I thought they'd like. At around this time, I happened to meet Jerry Weiss, who was responsible for the Laurel Leaf imprint for Dell, a company that was a leader in young adult and paperback publishing. Weiss said he would take a look at whatever poetry I had collected. I augmented the selections I'd been using with my students, organized them, and sent them off. That manuscript became *The Crystal Image.* When the book came out, I sent a copy to Stephen Dunning because I had so much respect for *Reflections on a Gift of Watermelon Pickle—* talk about a ground-breaking poetry book—and for his books on teaching literature. When he wrote back, he wasn't able to give me a glowing report on *The Crystal Image.* His point was—and I will never forget these words—that an anthology should break ground. He told me it wasn't enough just to put together a lot of poems that had appeared in other books.

Dunning was right, and I've tried to follow his advice ever since by taking risks. For one thing, I've experimented more and more with the overall format and structure of an anthology. My early anthologies were traditional in the sense that I organized many poems around one subject such as death or nature. It's much more difficult to do what I do now, which is to form brief sections of three or four poems on a particular topic. Not only do the poems need to connect in subtle ways, but so do the different sections of the anthology. I've also come to realize that the first and last poems are perhaps the most important: they're the anchors. Once I have those, I'm much more relaxed. I can get a little crazy until I've settled on that first and last poem.

I: Is this the format you follow for all your anthologies?

J: What I feel more comfortable doing now is to allow smaller groups of poems to create their own powerful connections and then to make sure that each section of the book grows out of all that precedes and follows it. I carried that to the extreme in the anthology of narrative poems, *The Music of What Happens,* where there are no divisions at all. I wanted it to read like one long poem, like a long story. I've learned that there always must be some kind of plan, some good reason for where poems are placed in an anthology. This plan is what transforms a gathering of different poems into a memorable movement or evolution.

If you look at the table of contents in *Pocket Poems,* for example, you see that the poems are divided basically into three major sections. The first section is about childhood experiences. That section ends with poems about leaving and going away. What follows is a small group of seasonal poems, a spinoff, which I placed in the middle of the book as a kind of interlude to demonstrate the passing of time. The last half of the book contains poems with more adult concerns, and this leads, naturally I hope, to the final few poems about returning, about coming back home after gaining much experience. The very first poem in this anthology is Ted Kooser's "Pocket Poem," and you don't have to be a Rhodes Scholar to understand why that one gets the entire thing moving. The last is David Allen Evans' "Sunset," which, of course, connotes a closing. So, for me, *Pocket Poems* is a book that is fairly typical of what I'm after as an anthologist. There just has to be a sturdy structure, something that holds the entire thing together.

In *This Delicious Day,* a book for younger readers, the poems move you through the course of a day. It opens with a Richard Snyder poem about taking full advantage of the day and ends with Adoff's "Past," which talks about savoring the present day and anticipating the possibilities of the future. I know that very few people will pick up an anthology and read it from cover to cover as they would a novel. But were they to do that and be mindful of what they're reading, they would more than likely figure out the arrangement of the poems and perhaps increase their enjoyment of them.

I: In many of your anthologies the arrangement seems to be a progression from innocence to experience. Yet, things always seem to end on an upbeat note. Is that why you ended *Going Over to Your Place* with Kooser's "At Midnight"?

J: That raises an interesting point. I'm very careful about the tone of an anthology. You know, adolescents can be terminally existential. That kind of gloom doesn't seem to bother many of them; in fact, they revel in it. But I don't want a dark tone to dominate a book of poems. I want an anthology to have some kind of balance—different points of view, different moods. In *Going Over to Your Place,* there's a chronological progression to the way poems are laid out and a balance in the ways people think about life. Striking that kind of balance is something I have to work on consciously when I'm shaping an anthology. This was the challenge I faced when I did *Looking for Your Name.* When I started working on it, I had in mind the idea of battles—that was even the working title—because it was to be a book about conflict, not only in a physical or militaristic sense, but in a psychological and spiritual sense as well. But even though *Looking for Your Name* evolved into something quite different from what I had intended. I still had to be careful about not making it too dark. Even though it's the most somber of my books, I tried not to let the dark poems take over.

I: Let's go back to the issue of breaking ground. How do you think it applies to what you're working on now?

J: The most groundbreaking anthology I'm working on now is a collection for young adult readers, that I'm doing with Naomi Shihab Nye. It's called *I Feel a Little Jumpy Around You.* It's a YA book that deals with gender issues. On the left-hand side of each page you find a poem written by a woman, and on the right, a poem written by a man. The two poems are somehow related—they may have the same theme, same topic, or whatever. So readers will be able to open the book and find two poets of different sexes talking about basically the same thing. The book will also include translated poems, which is one of the things Naomi brought to the book. There are going to

be some unusual graphics, and then Naomi and I have a running commentary about the book.

I: The two of you are commenting on the poems?

J: No, we're conversing about the process we used to put the book together. The point was to introduce a little by-play between us that would echo the by-play between the two poets on those pages. And Naomi has her introduction where she talks about growing up female, and I have mine about growing up in a house of mostly boys. We also talk about how we decided to do the book.

I: What else is in the works?

J: Another project I'm working on, an anthology again, is a collection of cowboy poems for elementary students. There is no book of cowboy poems out for kids. I think it might have more appeal for boys, which is one reason why I was interested in doing it, because boys, so they say, are not interested in poetry. Another book that's on the way is called *Friends . . . Or Not,* a book for kids that will explore the whole notion of the ups and downs of friendship. Friendship is so powerful and is such an important part of our lives, or could be, that it's a topic I wanted to devote an entire book to. I also sold a collection of my own poems—baseball poems. Its working title is *That Sweet Diamond,* and again it's for middle grade readers. So, those are some of the projects I've been working on when I'm not in the schools.

I: We understand that you spend a lot of time in schools throughout the country leading poetry workshops. What do you do to interest students in poetry?

J: First of all, I want teachers and kids to know that there is little correlation between academic and artistic achievement, particularly where writing is concerned. I don't want them to think that poetry is only for the gifted and talented. Teachers always seem surprised when students who usually don't do very well academically, come up with good poems. But this doesn't surprise me at all, because often it's the disenfranchised students who latch onto poetry. I'm not completely sure why this happens, but it's probably because poetry gives these kids a chance to speak about things from the heart. Poetry is the perfect vehicle for that. Also, many disenfranchised kids are rebellious to one degree or another. I think they see poetry as a form of rebellion because it has its own set of rules. They relate to this thing called "poetic license" and go with it.

When I'm out in the schools, I also tell them the truth about how I got started writing. I know they probably expect to hear some heartwarming story about how I wrote my first poem on the kitchen wall when I was three, and how my parents were so pleased that they cut out that piece of sheetrock and saved it in our attic in New Jersey.

Well, the truth is that when I started writing in fifth or sixth grade, I didn't write poetry or stories. I started by sending away for all the free stuff that was advertised in magazines I found around the house. I think it was that sense of an audience that intrigued me. To know that there was somebody out there, somebody I could write to and for, besides myself, sparked my interest in writing. What did I need a free sample of tarnish remover for? What I needed was to get that package back with my name and address on it. I think that was the first time I felt the narcotic of seeing my name in print. A lot of kids take heart in this story. I mean, here is this guy who didn't do particularly well in school but still managed to wind up being a writer. There's hope for them in my story.

I: How do you motivate students to write poetry?

J: Kids like to write poetry, because they like to play with language. I simply try to take advantage of this interest when I visit a classroom.

I: Have you found that it's easier to involve younger students in writing, given their attraction to language play, than it is to involve older students?

J: When I do get a chance to work with high school students, I find there is always a group of them that writes poetry. For a lot of high school kids, poetry writing is simply a great way to give voice to their emotions. I believe that one of the biggest failings in high schools is the lack of attention given to kids' emotional lives. Consequently, they turn to violence or graffiti or other destructive ways of dealing with their emotions. If they had opportunities to give voice to their emotions in more constructive ways and in a supportive environment, it would make a big difference. Poetry is one way—there are other ways, of course—but poetry is one productive way for adolescents to express what they're experiencing inside. So, I'm never surprised that high school students are writing poetry because I know what poetry can do.

I: How do you get kids started reading and writing poetry?

J: One of the things that has always worked for me is using humor in the classroom. Approaching poetry with a certain degree of levity always helps. When you first plunge into poetry with kids, start with humorous or nonsensical verse with lots of rhyming. After you've established a relationship with the kids and see that they are taking to the process and that it can be fun, it's time to move on to more serious subjects and more demanding forms like free verse. I used this approach when I was still teaching full-time, and I use it now when I go into the schools. Kids tend to complain about having to come up with rhymes, but they generally prefer to write poems that rhyme because they can easily tell where the line is supposed to end. Rhyming sets a limit to the form, and for them, this is comforting. I might start with one of the forms I included in *Poetry from A to Z,* such as the clerihew or the "opposite."

Many teachers start by reading a lot of poetry and then move into writing. I have always come at it the other way around. I feel that, as kids write poetry, they not only begin to understand what goes into making a poem, but

also they begin to read poetry with a different kind of attention. You know, an important part of the writing process as it's taught now is publication. It's important for kids to see their work in print. For many kids, that's pretty heady stuff. When they publish their poems in a small class book or put them on the walls for everyone to read, they're taking ownership of their work. Once they do that, you've really got them hooked.

I: You've said a lot about encouraging students to write poetry, but what suggestions do you have for getting them to read poetry with the same kind of excitement?

J: If we want kids to be readers of poetry, we have to be readers of poetry ourselves. Most of the teachers I meet are not. Every single time I do a workshop for teachers, many tell me afterwards that poetry is their worst area. They tell me they want to include poetry in their programs, but they just don't know what to do with it. Well, let's face it, poetry does demand more. It demands that we read differently, but that shouldn't scare us away. When I work with teachers, I especially like to use "A History of the Pets" by David Huddle, which I included in *Pocket Poems*. After I read the poem, I say, "What does this poem mean?" Naturally, my audience becomes a little uneasy. Then I tell them that the poem doesn't mean anything; it simply is.

I: But if we don't explain the poem, what *do* we do? We're thinking especially about teaching learning disabled kids. Although many teachers have gotten away from the diagnostic, prescriptive approach that LD teachers were trained to follow, the challenge still persists.

J: It would be a great start if we just let kids read poems and enjoy them. Now, once they are enjoying poetry, then you could get them to look more closely at particular poems by asking them how poets do what they do. What I'd like to see changed is the mind set that says we have to explicate a poem to death. I applaud a teacher who gets up in front of a class and reads a poem with no strings attached as though saying, "Here's a poem I came across; I liked it, and I wanted to share it with you." Maybe it's a poem about apples in the fall, or snow, or sports, or peace. Poems don't need to mean something; poems are something. And a good poem is bound to make you react. Maybe it makes you laugh, maybe it makes you angry, or disgusts you, or makes you cry. Poetry shouldn't be put on a pedestal because poetry is everyday stuff. It's about things of the heart, about things that have an impact on us. That's why I think poetry needs to be part of everyday life in a classroom.

I don't think it's necessary to prepare a special lesson or unit on poetry every time you bring it into the classroom. After you read a novel with ninth graders, for instance, you can make poetry writing one of the options for their response. When my students and I used to read *A Day No Pigs Would Die,* one of the assignments was to write acrostic poems about the characters. While an acrostic poem may seem artificial, it's a form that got my students thinking about the relationships in the novel, and it also encouraged them to see the importance of finding the right words to communicate their ideas. Of course, another effective extension to reading a novel is to bring in poems that relate to the novel's themes and concerns. If you do this, kids will see that poems can express many of the same feelings they found in the novel. I think we need to do all that we can to demystify poetry for our students, and that's why I recommend that we begin with having them experience poetry on a daily basis instead of building anticipation and anxiety for it by reserving it only for special occasions like poetry week.

I: Don't you think we can also decrease anxiety about poetry by offering students poems they can relate to?

J: Absolutely. If you find the right poems, kids will respond the same way they do to a piece of fiction that strikes the right chord in them. That's what an anthology can do. Here's how this poet did it, and here's another. Let's compare and contrast to see who did a better job. There are poems that are going to be better than others, and there are poems that you're going to understand better than others, that you feel more about than others. A poem can touch a reader in many different ways. I mean, you read a poem by J. Patrick Lewis and you have a good laugh over it, or you read one by X. J. Kennedy and you see how mischievous he is with his characters. Kids need to know that response to poetry runs the gamut, just as it does with all literature. Sometimes we should expect nothing more from reading poetry than being satisfied with the emotions a poem evokes.

I: Why do you think is it so important to read poetry?

J: Anatole Broyard, who used to write for *The New York Times,* said that, if we don't read poetry, we won't have our hearts broken by language, which to his way of saying that thinking is one of the prerequisites of a civilized world. You know, a good poem can put you in touch with strong emotions. Philip Booth once said that poetry brings us closer to what it means to be alive. There's also James Dickey's famous assessment of poetry, that poetry is "just naturally the greatest goddamn thing that ever was in the whole universe." A good poem is like a booster shot of humanness. We need more of that. I think that's the "so what" of poetry.

TITLE COMMENTARY

📖 ***POSTCARD POEMS: A COLLECTION OF POETRY FOR SHARING* (edited by Janeczko, 1979)**

Ethel L. Heins

SOURCE: A review of *Postcard Poems: A Collection of Poetry for Sharing,* in *The Horn Book Magazine,* Vol. LVI, No. 1, February, 1980, pp. 69-70.

The link between the book's title and its contents is somewhat tenuous, and the editor's introduction far more unsophisticated than much of the fine, unhackneyed poetry in his anthology. "The poems in this collection are gifts from the poets, meant to be shared. . . . Each of the 104 poems here is brief enough for jotting, hence the title. . . . Share these poems with a friend who needs to know he's not alone. Or with someone who needs to smile." Readers who would be snared by such statements might well find many of the poems fairly demanding. The few poets of the last century—such as Whitman, Emerson, Shelley, and James Russell Lowell—are in good company; for Marianne Moore, William Carlos Williams, Eve Merriam, Howard Nemerov, Robert Graves, Karl Shapiro, and Langston Hughes are but some of the notable modern poets represented. Although the selections vary in complexity, they are gathered into untitled groups dealing with subjects like the city, nature, youth, old age, love, and death; and the only abiding unity in the book comes from the brevity of the poems. The size and shape of the volume suggest a photograph album; it is possible that the tempting format may attract readers normally reluctant to dip into poetry.

Paula Nespeca Deal

SOURCE: A review of *Postcard Poems,* in *Voice of Youth Advocates,* Vol. 2, No. 6, February, 1980, p. 46.

This volume of short poems is shaped like a large postcard and filled with verses to be savored, jotted down and sent to a friend because as editor Janeczko states, "The poems in this collection are gifts from the poets, meant to be shared." The very brief poems by mostly 20th century authors contain common themes of the cycles of life and the gamut of human emotions. Because of the appealing format and simple brevity of the poetry, teens will let the book do as Judith Hemschemeyer's opening poem suggests. "Let me wrap a poem around you." This YASD Best Book nominee is for all school and public library YA poetry collections.

Zena Sutherland

SOURCE: A review of *Postcard Poems: A Collection of Poety for Sharing,* in *Bulletin of the Center for Children's Books,* Vol. 33, No. 8, April, 1980, p. 154.

A very pleasant, very personal choice of poems short enough to be used on a postcard, this; the compiler, a high school English teacher, takes as his theme the lines from the first selection, Judith Hemschemeyer's "Gift," "Let me wrap a poem around you . . . a poor shawl for your perfect throat." The introduction suggests that the poems be shared by passing them on, that "Good poetry is an endangered species. It needs to be protected from extinction." Most of Janeczko's choices are the work of contemporary writers: Shapiro, Nemerov, Swenson, Brautigan, Hughes, Sandburg, Giovanni, Graves . . . a knowledgeable skimming of brief delights.

Marjorie Lewis

SOURCE: A review of *Postcard Poems: A Collection of Poetry for Sharing,* in *School Library Journal,* Vol. 26, No. 9, May, 1980, p. 76.

A slim anthology of 104 poems of exemplary brevity and sensibility just right for sharing on a note, a post card, or as a gift from one friend to another. Twelve lines and under, they avoid the triviality that often characterizes the short poem and are variously witty, wise, tender, sad, or thoughtful. A wide range of poets from Shelley (Percy) to Shapiro (Karl) with Emerson, Yeats, Nemerov, Giovanni, Graves, Ignatow in between are represented by work rarely anthologized except in those thick "Complete Works of . . ." books. The emotional overtones expressed with skillful exactitude testify to the fine taste of the anthologist, matched by the liberal use of white space and large clear type on the oblong pages. One only wishes that the cover, three typical scenic post cards, were more of an invitation to poetry than a travel come-on.

DON'T FORGET TO FLY: A CYCLE OF MODERN POEMS (edited by Janeczko, 1981)

Publishers Weekly

SOURCE: A review of *Don't Forget to Fly,* in *Publishers Weekly,* Vol. 220, No. 16, October 16, 1981, p. 78.

The Crystal Image and *Postcard Poems,* Janeczko's previous anthologies, have been praised by critics and embraced by young poetry lovers. It's not certain that this collection of 70 creations will fare so well, although they attest to the greatness of the contributors, like Siegfried Sassoon, Walt Whitman, Marge Piercy, Maxine Kumin and others, some not instantly recognizable but all exceptionally gifted. The general tenor is depressing, with bitterness or sorrow described over the hurt suffered by a homely girl, the death of a classmate no one liked, the feel of graveyards, laments for suicides, lost friends, etc. Even the astringent wit in several works by Ogden Nash fails to lighten the gloom.

Lillian L. Shapiro

SOURCE: A review of *Don't Forget to Fly,* in *School Library Journal,* Vol. 28, No. 4, December, 1981, p. 71.

When Richard Peck's *Pictures That Storm Inside My Head* was published, it demonstrated that an audience for poetry exists among teenagers. Janeczko's collection of poems from the works of 70 modern writers is a similar book and deserves attention. Included are such well-known names as Marge Piercy, May Swenson, Richard Eberhart, Denise Levertov, Karl Shapiro and William Carlos Williams. The examples offered from less well-known writers may serve as a springboard for further reading among their works. The poems are arranged in a pattern that brings similar subjects together: relationships between parent and child, night-

time, Sundays, houses and cemeteries. Other poems celebrate cats, crows and cars (Dodge, Buick and Packard cars are highlighted). There are poems that amuse (Ogden Nash) and poems that cause pain (Richard Shelton's "Letter to a Dead Father"). The love poems, both sad and joyful, will touch the hearts of young and old.

Sally Estes

SOURCE: A review of *Don't Forget to Fly: A Cycle of Modern Poems,* in *Booklist,* Vol. 78, No. 13, March 1, 1982, p. 853.

The compiler of *Postcard Poems* has put together a wonderfully teen-enticing anthology of 130 modern poems by more than 70 poets, among them Richard Eberhart, Langston Hughes, Denise Levertov, Eve Merriam, Ogden Nash, Joyce Carol Oates, Theodore Roethke, May Swenson, and David Wagoner. Thematically clustered in groups of two, three, or four, the mostly short poems run a broad gamut of styles and moods and treat subjects as diverse as morning, night, suicide, friendship, love, parents, marriage, Sundays, insomnia, cats, crows, cars, war, movies, and poetry. Recommended for young adult as well as junior high and high school collections.

Nancy Sheridan

SOURCE: A review of *Don't Forget to Fly: A Cycle of Modern Poems,* in *The Horn Book Magazine,* Vol. LVIII, No. 3, June, 1982, pp. 303-04.

Over seventy modern poets are represented in an anthology of poetry encompassing such diverse topics as cars, death, dentists, insomnia, and love. Poems on similar subjects are grouped together, but there are no headings to break up the feeling of unity that runs through the book. Although some of the selections are humorous, like Ogden Nash's "The Perfect Husband"—"He tells you when you've got on too much lipstick, / And helps you with your girdle when your hips stick"—many are evocative and haunting, stressing the ephemeral quality of life. "Suicide's Note" by Langston Hughes lingers long after the first reading: "The calm, / Cool face of the river / Asked me for a kiss." Lucille Clifton, X. J. Kennedy, Denise Levertov, Theodore Roethke, and John Updike are just a few of the talented poets whose work is combined to create—from start to finish—a beautiful volume. Index of poets.

English Journal

SOURCE: A review of *Don't Forget to Fly,* in *English Journal,* Vol. 71, No. 5, September, 1982, pp. 87-8.

Many *EJ* readers are familiar with Janeczko's previous collections of poetry: *The Crystal Image* and *Postcard Poems.* This third collection is his best. It deserves its place on the ALA Best Books for Young Adults List for 1981.

Seventy modern writers of poetry are included. Poems by Donald Justice, Richard Eberhart, Langston Hughes, and Karl Shapiro are interspersed with offerings by equally good but less familiar poets. Janeczko expands our knowledge and introduces us to new poets worth reading.

The book's organization is one of its greatest strengths. The poems are arranged like a symphony with similar subject matter grouped together. Key poems act as transitions to move from poems about parents into poems about nighttime into poems about children and so forth until the symphony ends.

Well balanced for laughter and tears, this is the best collection of modern poetry with teen appeal to be published in the last five years.

POETSPEAK: IN THEIR WORK, ABOUT THEIR WORK (edited by Janeczko, 1983)

Zena Sutherland

SOURCE: A review of *Poetspeak: In Their Work, About Their Work,* in *Bulletin of the Center for Children's Books,* Vol. 36, No. 10, June, 1983, p. 191.

In an anthology that includes the work of sixty contemporary poets, Janeczko includes comments by the poets about themselves, their writing, and at times about the particular poem that precedes the comment. The contributors include such well-known writers as William Dickey, Nikki Giovanni, X. J. Kennedy, Howard Nemerov, Joyce Carol Oates, and John Updike, as well as others, and many poets who are less well-known. The book has variety in mood, style, theme, and subject, and the poems reflect many of the interests of adolescents, although they will probably be of equal interest to adult readers. The inclusion of the poets' discussion of their work should make the book especially appealing to young writers.

Sally Estes

SOURCE: A review of *Poetspeak: In Their Work, About Their Work,* in *Booklist,* Vol. 79, No. 21, July, 1983, p. 1396.

An inveterate reader and hoarder of poems, Janeczko, whose most recent anthology was *Don't Forget to Fly,* has gathered a rich and inviting salmagundi of almost 150 poems by 62 poets, who share some of their thoughts about their own work. Eschewing arrangement by poet or chronology, the editor has chosen a random grouping—several poems loosely linked by theme, mood, and/or subject lead gracefully into a next batch of two to four similarly companionable selections, which, in turn, give way to the next group. Therefore, the collection never becomes "ho hum"; indeed, it tends to stimulate through not only the well-selected poems but also the constant change of pace and sometimes surprising juxtaposition, as well as through the added personal comments by the poets. Though death themes seem to be the most prevalent, the subject matter ranges widely—parents, sports, dreams, adolescence, Vietnam, nature, love, etc. Contributors include William Dickey, Marge Piercy, Peter Meinke, X. J. Kennedy, Stanley Kunitz, William Stafford, Maxine Kumin, Joyce Carol Oates, and Gregory Corso. Recommended for pleasure or collateral reading. To have a portfolio of poets and an index of poems.

Daisy Kouzel

SOURCE: A review of *Poetspeak: In Their Work, About Their Work,* in *School Library Journal,* Vol. 30, No. 1, September, 1983, p. 135.

This copious collection offers poems by 62 contemporary North American authors, some famous (Joyce Carol Oates, John Updike), some not so famous (Phil Hey, Don Welch), who in many instances have appended their own explanations and comments on a given piece. This device will aid young readers who might not otherwise understand the genesis or grasp the full significance of poems like "First Practice" by Gary Gildner or the haunting "Requiem for Sonora" by Richard Shelton. Moreover, the overall tone of modesty in these welcome prose addenda is bound to establish a sympathetic bond between authors and readers. The anthologist's choice of poems is inclined toward particularly touching real life incidents, memories of an especially poignant character, daydreams circling about everyday concerns, *et similia*. With few exceptions, the poems are in modern idiom—unrhymed and with prose-like rhythms. All told, a book which is likely to hook a goodly number of teenagers, and hopefully spur them on to explore even grander poetic vistas.

Dick Abrahamson

SOURCE: A review of *Poetspeak: In Their Work, About Their Work,* in *English Journal,* Vol. 73, No. 1, January, 1984, p. 89.

Here's a real find for teachers of poetry. Janeczko, who put together the highly praised collection of modern poetry *Don't Forget to Fly,* is back with a new collection with a special addition. Once again, the compiler has brought to this collection his gift for selecting poems and placing them in sequences that seem to flow from one grouping to another. His special addition is that intermixed with these 148 poems by living North American writers are their comments on specific poems Janeczko has selected and the craft of poetry writing in general. These poet comments provide insight into the genesis of the poems, the poet's intent, and/or his method of writing and revision. It's like Cormier's collection of short stories *8 plus 1.* Cormier provides the reader with a look over the writer's shoulder as he tells the story of how each short story developed. In *Poetspeak,* we have the same over the shoulder look, but we see the process from many individual viewpoints and it's poetry oriented as opposed to prose.

As usual, the compiler has done a good job of weaving well-known poets like Wilbur, Eberhart, Dickey, and Giovanni in with lesser-known but good contemporary artists. Will adolescents like it? One high school junior returned it to me and said it was the only poetry book he had ever read straight through from page one to the end. Janeczko has created another book that ought to be selected as a Best Book for Young Adults (and for teachers of English as well).

Patricia Berry

SOURCE: A review of *Poetspeak: In Their Work, About Their Work,* in *Voice of Youth Advocates,* Vol. 6, No. 6, February, 1984, p. 348.

Janeczko has done an excellent job compiling this anthology of 148 poems written by 62 working North American poets. He organizes these carefully selected poems into a connected, thematic, poetic progression. Many of the poems are followed by the poet's anecdotal or biographical comments. These personal remarks help to deepen the reader's appreciation of what the artist is communicating through the poem.

Poems on such subjects as nature, feelings, sports, families, and school by such well-known poets as David Ignatow, Marge Piercy, Karl Shapiro, Nikki Giovanni, and Joyce Carol Oates will appeal to many. A special feature of four pages of black and white mini-portraits of the poets make this volume a super anthology of poems that will attract young readers. An Index of poets is included. The cover art is inviting.

STRINGS: A GATHERING OF FAMILY POEMS (edited by Janeczko, 1984)

Zena Sutherland

SOURCE: A review of *Strings: A Gathering of Family Poems,* in *Bulletin of the Center for Children's Books,* Vol. 37, No. 10, June, 1984, p. 187.

Drawing from small presses and magazines as well as from mainstream collections, Janeczko has gathered another outstanding contemporary anthology. The 125 poems of parents and children, brothers and sisters, and also of the extended family, are often positive; but they do not dodge the anger that may be mixed with love, the guilt between brothers, the strain in intense relationships. Rosemary Joseph remembers a warm kitchen in "Baking Day;" Jeannine Dobbs remembers rejection ("My mother's kitchen. Where my hands / betrayed me: too big, too slow/ . . . Get out.") The poetry leaps out of ordinary words and the familiar rhythms of conversation: "She wore her lore and old age home," George Ella Lyon grieves for a cousin; Norma Richman revitalizes the whining cliche of her childhood, "and there was nothing on earth to do," as she applies it literally to her dying father. Young people will find these poems accessible and relevant: library and class discussions could explore their rich, multiple implications.

Stephanie Zvirin

SOURCE: A review of *Strings: A Gathering of Family Poems,* in *Booklist,* Vol. 80, No. 21, July, 1984, p. 1543.

Dedicated presumably to his own family—his three brothers, his sister, and his parents—editor Janeczko's newest collection of poetry resonates with vitality. One hundred and twenty-seven selections, chosen from the work of more than 70 modern poets (including familiar names such as John Updike, Anne Sexton, Mary Oliver, and Richard Eberhart) celebrate, investigate, and appraise familial bonds—"strings" as Janeczko calls them—between parents and children, husbands and wives, brothers, sisters, nephews, nieces . . . They're poems about relationships torn apart, put back together, or just rolling along; poems filled with disappointment, pride, anger, aspirations, nostalgia, love, and laughter. Some are earthy and plainspoken, some irreverent, and some as fragile as the emotions they attempt to capture on paper; and they represent as many styles as they do moods, situations, and feelings. It's a rich, rewarding anthology, with much that's memorable and much that's meaningful for the poetry student as well as the poetry enthusiast. Index of poets appended.

Kate M. Flanagan

SOURCE: A review of *Strings: A Gathering of Family Poems,* in *The Horn Book Magazine,* Vol. LX, No. 4, August, 1984, pp. 482-83.

More than one hundred and twenty poems by contemporary American poets explore the mysteries of family life. Whether it mulls over the poignant memories of a father's death or celebrates the eccentricities of a great aunt, each poem—like each family—is unique yet somehow universal. The introductory poem, "The String of My Ancestors" by Nina Nyhart, sets the tone of the volume and ends with the lines: "I tie bows on my children's fingers. / They must not forget their ancestors. / When you cut string / it crawls off / in two directions." The poems are divided into sections; there are "strings" from wives and husbands, parents, children, brothers and sisters, cousins, nieces and nephews, and grandchildren. Some of the selections glow with love, joy, laughter—remembrances of shared moments. Others recall bitter memories—deaths, quarrels, disappointments. John Updike, Stephen Spender, Richard Wilbur, Anne Sexton, X. J. Kennedy, and others less well known are among the eighty-four poets represented in a stirring collection that flows smoothly from beginning to end. With an index of poets.

Daisy Kouzel

SOURCE: A review of *Strings: A Gathering of Family Poems,* in *School Library Journal,* Vol. 31, No. 1, September, 1984, p. 129.

This collection of contemporary poems from a few well-known and many not-so-well-known authors revolves around the subject of family ties, or *Strings*. The book reads easily and seems to have a lot to say about the nature of the family today, nuclear and other. Each poem is a fragmentary story tugging at some heartstring—a pang of regret, a feeling of nostalgia, a surge of tenderness, a wistful reminiscence; all intimately enmeshed with one's family relationships. John Updike is represented by his witty "Commencement, Pingree School," in which a certain aloofness vis-à-vis sentimentality constitutes a refreshing note. On the other hand, Gerald Locklin's vulgar and mindless "Poop" adds nothing. There's much subtlety of perception abounding in this anthology, although not all of the entries break through into a completely satisfying poetic evocation beyond the mundane. Still and all, young adults will find some food to nourish their sensibilities, and will no doubt enjoy carving out their favorites among the 128 pieces offered.

LOADS OF CODES AND SECRET CIPHERS (1984)

Susan Kurz

SOURCE: A review of *Loads of Codes and Secrets Ciphers,* in *School Library Journal,* Vol. 31, No. 5, January, 1985, p. 86.

In the introduction to this book, Janeczko invites readers to write to him about their own ways of sending secret messages and promises to answer every letter. This sets the tone for a treatment of codes and ciphers that is almost conversational, but still informative and thorough. There are codes from history and literature, as well as exercises for students to decipher. Since many of the standard works on the subject are geared toward a younger audience, this new profusely illustrated title is a good choice for older beginners as well as enthusiasts who would like more depth and a greater challenge.

Barbara Elleman

SOURCE: A review of *Loads of Codes and Secret Ciphers,* in *Booklist,* Vol. 81, No. 9, January 1, 1985, p. 641.

Would-be international spies and detective aficionados will find this array of codes and ciphers fun to practice on. The text is easy to comprehend and the multiplicity of figures and diagrams is a helpful aspect. Information on breaking codes as well as on building simple coding devices to transmit secret messages is interspersed with historical background notes on the ciphers used, for instance, by the 1920s hobos, cowboys of the Old West, and U.S. naval navigators. Practice codes are given with handy answers for beginners to check out their expertise.

Kevin Kenny

SOURCE: A review of *Loads of Codes and Secret Ciphers,* in *Voice of Youth Advocates,* Vol. 8, No. 2, June, 1985, p. 146.

For those who have complained that the trouble with 20th century life is that it lacks complication and simply plods on, mired in the obvious, Janeczko has just the paregoric. *Loads of Codes and Secret Ciphers* is a warm and readable introduction to the less than sinister world of codes and ciphers. The text assumes no prior knowledge in the area, and leads the reader through a series of historical anecdotes, examples, and sample exercises beginning with the very basics of code books and concealed messages and progressing on to more difficult transposition ciphers and cryptanalysis. An appendix which includes instructions for the use of invisible inks and the construction of a working telegraph key is included for those with C.I.A. aspirations.

Janeczko's infectious love of the subject, patient presentation, and exceedingly simple style should make this book accessible to all but the most severely reading disabled YA.

POCKET POEMS: SELECTED FOR A JOURNEY (edited by Janeczko, 1985)

Hazel Rochman

SOURCE: A review of *Pocket Poems: Selected for a Journey,* in *Booklist,* Vol. 81, No. 16, April 15, 1985, p. 1176.

In a pocket-size anthology of 120 short modern poems, Janeczko once again draws young adults to the pleasure and power of poetry rooted in the familiar. The subjects from a daily, contemporary world include food, flowers, cars, travel, pets, love, friendship, family, and the threat of war. The 80 poets include the famous, such as Angelou, Stafford, and Zimmer, as well as some new voices. There's broad humor, as in Blount's "Song against Broccoli" ("The local groceries are all out of broccoli, / Loccoli") and in Stetler's "Arf, Said Sandy" about a backward-trained dog. There's also the anguish of Nemerov's "Elegy" for his fierce cat ("If Death should stroke thee, Thompson, scratch Him for me") and Hemschemeyer's mourning of a suicide, "That Summer." Always there is closely observed physical detail, as in the fragility of Scheele's "Poppies" ("When the breeze moves across them they totter") and Ondaatje's tender "Bearhug" of his toddler son ("all his small bones and his warm neck against me"). As in Janeczko's *Postcard Poems,* brevity makes the poetry inviting to browsers, grabbing them with the lilt or wit of a line, the surprise of an image, the intensity of felt experience.

Nancy C. Hammond

SOURCE: A review of *Pocket Poems,* in *The Horn Book Magazine,* Vol. LXI, No. 3, May-June, 1985, p. 322.

A keen scout in the field of modern poetry, the anthologist has gathered an enticing selection of short American poems in an inexpensive, pocket-sized volume that has its own appeal yet could also serve as an effective introduction to his other fine collections. The one hundred twenty poems range in length and style from David McCord's witty, succinct "Epitaph on a Waiter" ("By and by / God caught his eye") to the litany of juxtaposed images in the sixteen lines of Jonathan Holden's "Night: Landing at Newark." Grouped loosely by subject matter, many entries reflect the preoccupations of our modern time: telephones, airports, suicide, and war. The expressed feelings and tone extend from Paul Zimmer's ebullient, effusive love in his autobiographical "Suzie's Enzyme Poem" to the sarcastic, detached anger of Robert Francis in "Light Casualties": "Did the guns whisper when they spoke / That day? Did death tiptoe his business? / And afterwards in another world / Did mourners put on light mourning, / Casual as rain, as snow, as leaves? / Did a few tears fall?" Among the eighty poets represented are Linda Pastan, Seamus Heaney, Coleman Barks, and humorist Roy Blount, Jr., with his "Song against Broccoli" ("The local groceries are all out of broccoli, / Loccoli"). Index of poets.

Dawna Lisa Buchanan-Berrigan

SOURCE: A review of *Pocket Poems: Selected for a Journey,* in *School Library Journal,* Vol. 31, No. 10, August, 1985, pp. 76-7.

Janeczko has created a trim little book in this offering of 120 brief but powerful poems about love, longing and humanity observed unguarded. The small format is appealing for presenting thoughts sometimes packed into only one line, but the type is rather cramped. The collection holds some evocative pieces, such as Bruce Guernsey's "June Twenty-First" in which a young person laments, "At fourteen, I'm too old / to run naked with my brother, / too young to laugh with my father." Thoughtful images probing at death and the disappointment and struggles of loving and living are nicely counterpointed by celebrations of love, the seasons and humor, such as in David McCord's delightful "Epitaph on a Waiter": "By and by / God caught his eye." This pocketful of poems will enjoy the same popularity as *Reflections on a Gift of Watermelon Pickle,* compiled by [Stephen] Dunning and others. *Pocket Poems* introduces writers both known and new, is accessible even to those who think they do not enjoy poetry and offers a strong current of joy along with the dark side of life. A collection that will be of interest to all those who are growing up and trying to fit into an adult world—no matter how old they are.

BRIDGES TO CROSS (1986)

Zena Sutherland

SOURCE: A review of *Bridges to Cross,* in *Bulletin of the Center for Children's Books,* Vol. 39, No. 9, May, 1986, p. 168.

Fourteen-year-old James has an incredibly restrictive mother who insists he follow the letter of the law as defined by the Catholic Church. To reinforce her home supervision, she has selected a rigid high school, Our Lady, Queen of Angels, where James runs up against an autocratic, even sadistic principal. His father is sympathetic but not strong, his best friend not always supportive; it is a wandering artist who ultimately shows James that he must choose to live his own life, regardless of others' opinions. The first-person narrative has a quality of forthright vulnerability that saves it from some technical flaws: several one-dimensional characters, a bridge-crossing incident that's climactic but not well-integrated with the rest of the book, and some flat writing. At the same time, the conflicts between institutional and personal codes of ethics are well and specifically addressed, as in James' questioning his own dishonesty in light of his rage at hypocritical behavior on the part of one of the brothers. His interest in baseball is a constant theme that never seems to develop any depth, but his discomfort with compromise is sharply drawn and resolved with a rather graceful ambiguity at the end.

Publishers Weekly

SOURCE: A review of *Bridges to Cross,* in *Publishers Weekly,* Vol. 229, No. 26, June 27, 1986, p. 92.

Set in the early '60s, this novel of stumbling into selfhood will be easy for readers to identify with. Freshman James Marchuk must reconcile hypocrisy with everything he's been told about honesty and following rules. What should he make of his Catholic high school, where strident teachers—Christian Brothers—slap the boys and visit pornography stores? At home, he wants to break away from being "Helen's boy," but his perfectionist mother won't listen, so he begins to lie. Through believable dialogue and a logical, fast-paced buildup of incidents, James comes to view the intrigues of the adult world in more complex ways. In a satisfying conclusion, James dares to cross the shaky town bridge of the title, gets hurt, and comes out able to stop spiting his mother. He confronts her, calls a halt to the web of deceit, and begins to pick and choose among rules to find his own ethical direction.

Denise M. Wilms

SOURCE: A review of *Bridges to Cross,* in *Booklist,* Vol. 82, No. 22, August, 1986, p. 1689.

James Marchuk's first year at Our Lady Queen of Angels High School is a year of growing up the hard way. Rules at home and at school suddenly seem unbearably oppressive, and James is champing at the bit for a measure of independence. At home, it's his mother who is the problem. An active churchwoman, she is also unbending in her expectations and narrow in her views. She is the one who insists he attend Our Lady; James would rather go to public high school. At school it is the strict atmosphere that offends. Boys are slapped, and many of the rules are petty, even destructive. James deals with all of this by lying to his mother whenever he wants to do something he knows she will not like. His activities aren't delinquent ones by any means, but they do reflect a disrespect for some of his mother's views and values. How much obedience is required of a son? James' lying bothers him a lot, and he finally stops. But standing up to his mother escalates tension, and there is a major blowup when she refuses to believe his innocence after school officials unjustly accuse him of hitting a teacher. James is expelled and bitterly judged by his mother, but he refuses to give up his newfound integrity, even if it means displeasing her. The story is an ambitious one and raises some important questions about ethics and honesty. But it is undermined by a lack of finesse. Key characters lack subtlety, and the story's mechanics are a little too visible. Still, its earnestness exerts a degree of power, and there is sure to be discussion over the merits of James' behavior.

Dorcas Hand

SOURCE: A review of *Bridges to Cross,* in *School Library Journal,* Vol. 32, No. 10, August, 1986, pp. 100-01.

The story of an adolescent's coming to terms with himself, his parents and his Catholic surroundings. James Marchuk and his friend Will are headed to Our Lady Queen of Angels Catholic High School. Will just views it as "four more years of boredom," but James sees it as prison-like. Neither a leader nor a prankster, James nevertheless keeps running astray of the Brothers' rules. The principal is portrayed as especially unbalanced in his enforcement of the many rules. Meanwhile, Will and James visit the forbidden joke emporium where they recognize a Brother leaving the back room, in which X-rated books are sold. James, disturbed by the Brother's hypocrisy, is more upset with his mother's attitude: she does not believe James and refuses to accept that a Brother could do anything wrong. Throughout the story, James continues to visit his new friend Shoe, an itinerant hippie artist who talks of being himself. The conclusion of the book shows James returning home determined to be himself, to not bow to his mother and apologize and therefore to leave OLQA for Regional. The message here is mixed. The exaggerated Catholic school stereotypes show a bitterness on the part of the author, which results in the adolescent coming-of-age motif being lost in the negatives. Some might identify with the situations, but in general, characterization is minimal and the plot dull and predictable. Janeczko has compiled some excellent poetry anthologies; this book is not in the same class.

Tony Manna

SOURCE: A review of *Bridges to Cross,* in *Voice of Youth Advocates,* Vol. 9, Nos. 3 & 4, August-October, 1986, pp. 144-45.

James Marchuk is living through the worst year of his life. As a freshman at Our Lady Queen of Angels High School, the school his parents have forced him to attend, he must submit to the insensitive tactics of suspicious and infamously harsh teachers who are armed with an endless supply of inflexible rules. At home, he must try to appease his over-bearing and over-protective mother who, obsessed with raising a perfect Catholic son, equates goodness with his ability "to get straight A's, read just classic books, not like baseball, not mess up my room." And in the small-town world that borders school and home, he is expected to be "Helen's (his mother's) little gentleman." But will it be possible for James to develop his identity and to evolve into his own person in the midst of so much pressure to live up to the various images that others would have him fit?

With remarkable insight into the psychology of personal change and the basic human need to discover and assert one's identity, Janeczko places his main character in a number of dramatic situations and provides him a series of relationships that effect little moments of personal revelation about what he must do to fashion and live his own life. As the title implies, each insight is like a bridge leading inexorably and often painfully to a simple yet profound truth: for James to be happy and fulfilled, he must stop trying to live his life through and for other people. It is not an understanding that is gained easily, for the lies he tells to cover up his visit to a local joke and porno shop and the fact that he has developed a relationship with a vagabond painter haunt and confuse his already fragile sense of morality until he accepts his painter friend's advice: "That was what *I* had to do. Put aside what I thought other people wanted from me and paint my own picture."

Believable, frequently humorous dialogue and incidents, a deft sense of how to pace a scene, and a genuine concern for his character's survival make this a memorable finely crafted first novel.

GOING OVER TO YOUR PLACE: POEMS FOR EACH OTHER (edited by Janeczko, 1987)

Betsy Hearne

SOURCE: A review of *Going Over to Your Place: Poems for Each Other,* in *Bulletin of the Center for Children's Books,* Vol. 40, No. 8, April, 1987, p. 148.

An ample and varied collection of contemporary poetry explores human relationships in their diversity of mood and involvement. Some, like Richard Shelton's "My Love," treat of intimacy; others, like Henry Treece's "Conquerors," of the connection among strangers—in this case, soldiers finding the body of a child. The many poets represented include Nikki Giovanni, Ted Kooser, Jim Wayne Miller, Mark Strand, and Elizabeth Jennings. The 132 poems are well balanced, with notes of the humor as well as the tragedy that commonly touch everyday life. Janeczko has the energy and resources to find poems that are not frequently anthologized, and he clusters them so that transitions are smooth between selections. There is an accessible tone consistent with Janeczko's other books, although on the whole this one seems less intense, more wide-ranging, and sometimes more adult in focus.

Hazel Rochman

SOURCE: A review of *Going Over to Your Place: Poems for Each Other,* in *Booklist,* Vol. 83, No. 15, April 1, 1987, p. 1194.

"You're a strange new story every time," Jim Wayne Miller says of his love in "Rechargeable Dry Cell Poem." That excitement in the ordinary is the focus of Janeczko's fine new anthology of modern poetry. Some poems are directly about writing poetry; all demonstrate the power of the imagination to discover what Nancy Price calls "fields you'd spent the years of your life among / and never seen before." This fresh perception of the familiar may be funny, as in David Jauss' self-obsessed "On Certain Mornings Everything Is Sensual" ("Even the alarm clock / Had its hands all over me") or desperate, as in Mary Oliver's empathy for a suicide ("somewhere, for someone, life / is becoming moment by moment / unbearable"). Drawn from the small magazines as well as from collected works of the famous, these are mainly contemporary American poems, pastoral and domestic, and often about the complex bonds and strains of friendship, family, and love. More urban settings and more regional and cultural diversity would have been welcome, and some poems seem too adult for teens, but most reach out to universal experience. The range in form and tone is wide: from the cozy togetherness of Alden Nowlan's three friends eating cinnamon toast "silly with sleepiness" at 4 a.m., to Adrienne Rich's bleak "the wind will rise / We can only close the shutters" and David Huddle's long, carefully structured poem about his inability to cope with his dying father ("we say our word for love. Goodbye"). There are unsentimental poems about teachers, about the aftermath of war, and about the old, including Paul Ruffin's fiercely characterized Grandma who doesn't want to be buried beside her husband ("life was too hard for him / he's soured the soil"); and there's a startling poem by Jonathan Holden in which a first kiss begins in conventional awkward comedy and ends "quietly, trembling." The language is direct, casual, often colloquial, concentrated in imagery and sound that reveal the daily world with precision and mystery. Poets and readers will dip into this again and again, for one poem, or several, or for a few lines apt and echoing.

Ethel R. Twichell

SOURCE: A review of *Going Over to Your Place: Poems for Each Other,* in *The Horn Book Magazine,* Vol. LXIII, No. 4, July-August, 1987, pp. 479-80.

Drawing from a broad field of poetic endeavor and using consummate skill in selection, the editor brings to the reader an opportunity not merely, as the title implies, to exchange a few ideas with a neighbor but to explore his inmost thoughts or perhaps read a stranger's diary. The poetry, as a whole, is thoughtful, introspective, and tinged with melancholy. Only a few poems are playful. Most express the regrets of a child with unexpressed love for a parent, describe the alienation of parent and child, mourn loves lost or friends

forgotten. Although arranged by similar subjects, the poems move from topic to topic with an easy juxtaposition which keeps the reader eager to continue. The spectrum of the poetry is impressive, ranging from some which is presently less well known to the work of Stanley Kunitz, Henry Treece, and John Updike. Each reader should find one or two poems that over-whelmingly stab the heart with the recognition of a shared experience or an unspoken thought. All have been selected for the sharp memories they evoke, for their gift for saying much with an economy of words, and for the way they weave the minutia and greater moments of decision and confrontation into the fabric of our lives.

Becki George

SOURCE: A review of *Going Over to Your Place: Poems for Each Other,* in *Voice of Youth Advocates,* Vol. 10, No. 4, October, 1987, p. 186.

Janeczko has created another poetry anthology masterpiece which, for readers of his poetry collections, has a similar familiarity to *Strings: A Gathering of Family Poems.* With the 132 poems, readers will find familiar experiences of spring thunderstorms, first loves, friendship and other fond remembrances. Janeczko has included a collection of poets, among them John Updike, Nikki Giovanni, John Ciardi, Elizabeth Bishop and other lesser-known writers.

This is an anthology which will have great appeal to high school readers. It's possible to read through the entire collection (though there aren't many high schoolers who will) or to pick-and-choose by browsing through the pages or titles. His collection of poems of the familiar will allow every reader to find a poem and remember and relate to the experience it reveals. The poems are both long and short, some serious while others are light. Janeczko has maintained the quality of his other anthologies—*Strings, Don't Forget to Fly, Pocket Poems,* and *Postcard Poems*—with this newest collection. This anthology will be an excellent addition to any poetry collection

Elizabeth A. Belden and Judith M. Beckman

SOURCE: "Poems, Short Stories, and a Play," in *English Journal,* Vol. 78, No. 2, February, 1989, pp. 84-85.

With his usual gift Paul Janeczko has done just what his first poem, "The Heart's Location," suggests. He has discovered "poem(s) full of ordinary words about simple things in the inconsolable rhythms of the heart."

Those of us who held hands in hot movie theaters in the fifties may vividly relive movie dates and smile softly at Jonathan Holden's "First Kiss." While our students may look askance at such a response, together, as a community of writers, we can share Larry Levis's "The Poem You Asked For." All of us bear battle scars gained through hand-to-hand warfare with words, waged while trying to breathe life into inert ideas—armed with only sincere intent, a blank sheet of paper, and a pitifully small eraser.

Reading Janeczko's collection is only part of the pleasure. Frank Steele's "The Departure" explains the better part. When the book is finished, the melodies of these poems become " . . . curtains blowing at the window speaking to me."

📖 *THIS DELICIOUS DAY: 65 POEMS* (edited by Janeczko, 1987)

Betsy Hearne

SOURCE: A review of *This Delicious Day: 65 Poems*, in *Bulletin of the Center for Children's Books*, Vol. 41, No. 1, September, 1987, pp. 10-11.

"Meals for the eye . . . meals for the ear . . . meals for the tongue . . . meals for the mind—any and all of the 65 poems presented here—and, yes, of course you may come back for seconds!" An inviting anthology, from the jacket copy quoted above to the last poem by Arnold Adoff, called "Past," a fresh mixture of imagery centering on time and food: "But I know that tomorrow / morning / I'll wake up / empty, and hungry for that / next / bite / of my new / day." For younger readers than Janeczko's previous books have targeted, this brings together a lively assortment of brief poems by Richard Snyder, ("O I have Dined on This Delicious Day"), X. J. Kennedy ("The Cat Who Aspired to Higher Things"), Dennis Lee ("Alligator Pie"), William Stafford ("Rover"), and many others. Once again, Janeczko has shown characteristic sensitivity to mixing the known and the unknown, to coordinating styles and subjects into a smooth flow. The general tone is light and lively, varying from the abruptly humorous (Jim Daniels' "Blubber Lips") to the softly descriptive (Gary Soto's "Stars"). Children who enjoy dipping their fingers into poetry will find here a tasty buffet of structured and free verse.

Carolyn Phelan

SOURCE: A review of *This Delicious Day: 65 Poems*, in *Booklist,* Vol. 84, No. 2, September 15, 1987, pp. 153-54.

Anthologist Janeczko has assembled a fine collection of 65 short poems, all fresh and diverse, yet all resonating with the spirit of the title selection. Written by Richard Snyder (to whose memory the volume is dedicated), it begins, "Oh I have dined on this delicious day, / on green-salad treetops wet with beaded / water, tossed by the fork tines of the wind . . . " Images of eating recur throughout the book, as in Lilian Moore's "Sunset," "There's dazzle in the western sky, / colors spill and / run. The pond mouth / lies open / greedy / for the last drop / of / melting / sun." Yet it is not this theme, but the intertwined threads of exuberance, wit, and sharp imagery that bind the collection of poems together and make the anthology more than the sum of its parts. Combining artistic integrity with child appeal, here's an excellent poetry collection to give, to recommend, or best of all, to share with children.

Mary M. Burns

SOURCE: A review of *This Delicious Day: 65 Poems,* in *The Horn Book Magazine,* Vol. LXIII, No. 6, November-December, 1987, pp. 752-53.

True to the tone and theme set by the initial selection—Richard Snyder's "O I Have Dined on This Delicious Day"—Janeczko, one of today's foremost anthologists for young readers, has provided a feast for mind, heart, and senses. His interpretation of the world *delicious* covers a broad spectrum of experiences, from Siv Cedering Fox's assertion that dawn comes when "a little bird / that has no name / flies westward / pulling away / the dark blanket of the night" to Arnold Adoff's confession that "tomorrow / morning / I'll wake up / empty, and hungry for that / next / bite / of my new / day." Sixty-five poems by fifty-five poets are represented, including N. M. Bodecker, Russell Hoban, X. J. Kennedy, Karla Kuskin, David McCord, Theodore Roethke, Carl Sandburg, Judith Thurman, William Carlos Williams, and Valerie Worth; Dennis Lee's hard-to-find "Alligator Pie" is also included. Nor are the selections tired from constant recycling: Carl Sandburg, for example, is represented by "Bubbles" rather than the more obvious—and food related—"Arithmetic." "Two bubbles found they had rainbows on their curves. / They flickered out saying: / 'It was worth being a bubble just to have held that rainbow thirty seconds.'" This collection is like that rainbow: it makes the day—and the effort of reading—worthwhile. Index by poet.

Tony Manna

SOURCE: A review of *This Delicious Day,* in *Voice of Youth Advocates,* Vol. 10, No. 5, December, 1987, p. 254.

In his latest anthology Janeczko has laid out a hardy feast of 65 short—mostly contemporary—poems which provide ample nourishment for the heart, mind, and senses. Janeczko opens with "O I Have Dined on This Delicious Day," Richard Snyder's exuberant celebration of nature's many wonders which offers a foretaste of the treats that lie ahead. With Snyder establishing the upbeat mood that characterizes the entire anthology, the poets guide us through the course of an ordinary day, capturing along the way a remarkable assortment of everyday happenings "Shadows" by Patricia Hubbell, "The Schoolbus Comes Before the Sun" by Robert Currie "Zimmer's Street" by Paul Zimmer), familiar objects ("Stone" by Donald Justice, "Bubbles" by Carl Sandburg, "The Chair" by Theodore Roethke), and the little miracles that unfold so abundantly in nature ("Sunset" by Lilian Moore, "Evening Tide" by X. J. Kennedy, "The Crow" by Russell Hoban). This rich and varied smorgasbord of images and impressions is seasoned with humor ("Mixed-Up School" by X. J. Kennedy, "Alligator Pie" by Dennis Lee, "Celery" by Ogden Nash), with delightful language play ("The Gnat" by Eugene Rudzewicz, "I Wouldn't" by John Ciardi, "Feline Fine" by J. Patrick Lewis), and with genuine affection and love ("Real Talent" by Sheryl L. Nelms, "Kate and I" by Susan Navarre Tarrant, "Lullaby" by

Steve Kowit). There's certainly enough here to satisfy even the most voracious appetite or to entice the pickiest of readers.

Janet Hickman

SOURCE: A review of *This Delicious Day: 65 Poems,* in *Language Arts,* Vol. 65, No. 4, April, 1988, p. 417.

Two possible misconceptions about this volume are that, like Janeczko's other collections, its best audience would be young adults; and that, given the title and the table setting pictured on the cover, it's a selection of poems about food. Wrong on both counts. Younger students will discover many poems with immediate appeal, like Dennis Lee's rhythmical "Alligator Pie," X. J. Kennedy's nonsensical "Mixed-Up School," or the familiar content of Elizabeth Coatsworth's "The Two Cats" and other poems about animals. There are also more demanding poems that invite children to enjoy metaphor, as in Joan La Bombard's "Marbles" ("They are his planets, / his suns and milky spheres, his red Mars"), or to consider the stories between the lines of "Zimmer's Street" by Paul Zimmer ("All things have come down / This street: Thanksgiving, / Christmas, victory, marriage"). While there are several poems about food included, the "delicious" of the book's title comes from the opening piece by Richard Snyder, "O I Have Dined on This Delicious Day," and refers to savoring all sorts of experiences—sights and sounds and thoughts as well as tastes. This is an unusually fine collection for classrooms where there is a serious interest in poetry, not just because of the consistently high quality of the selections, but because so few of them are available in other anthologies for children.

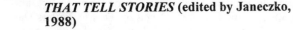

THE MUSIC OF WHAT HAPPENS: POEMS THAT TELL STORIES (edited by Janeczko, 1988)

Kirkus Reviews

SOURCE: A review of *The Music of What Happens: Poems That Tell Stories,* in *Kirkus Reviews,* Vol. LVI, No. 13, July 1, 1988, p. 975.

Taking as theme the title (derived from one of James Stephens' Irish fairy tales), a noted poet/anthologist has selected 75 poems by contemporary, lesser-known poets, each compressing a narrative into a carefully honed moment, with the effect of a series of finely tuned short stories. Each depicts an incident—or series of incidents—leading the reader to an epiphany related to its subject. Ranging from adolescent and family concerns to historical themes, they are organized so that ideas flow smoothly from one poem to the next.

The selections are of consistently high quality and interest; sophisticated in both theme and interpretation, they do require some knowledge of the world and its foibles for

best appreciation. For the older reader who can accept this challenge, then, a moving, revealing introduction to the poet as storyteller.

Barbara Chatton

SOURCE: A review of *The Music of What Happens: Poems That Tell Stories,* in *School Library Journal,* Vol. 34, No. 11, August, 1988, p. 109.

As with all of Janeczko's anthologies, this collection of 75 narrative poems reaches beyond its projected young adult audience to all readers who admire contemporary poetry. The mood of these poems is often haunting and melancholy, beginning with Jared Carter's "The Purpose of Poetry" and moving through stories of death, heartache, discoveries about sex, and despair. Some of the poems provide insightful looks into the lives of people who played small parts in history. Erika Mumford's lengthy poem, "The White Rose: Sophie Scholl, 1921-1943," for example, would add a powerfully different perspective to studies of the Third Reich. "The Ghost Dance: August, 1976" by David Jauss, an apology to Sitting Bull, would fuel discussions of Native American history and events. The anguish and pain of coming to terms with life which is reflected in many of these poems is softened by the ironic insights of poems such as "Progress" by George Ella Lyon and the zany images of "When Angels Came to Zimmer" by Paul Zimmer. Teachers and librarians will find many selections to read aloud or share with young adults in this sober collection. Serious young readers of poetry will find much to ponder here as well.

Betsy Hearne

SOURCE: A review of *The Music of What Happens: Poems That Tell Stories,* in *Bulletin of the Center for Children's Books,* Vol. 42, No. 1, September, 1988, p. 11.

A book that demonstrates the rich potential for originality in anthologizing, this features 75 untraditional narrative poems deeply reflective of the events they relate. Most are long contemporary selections in free verse reverberating with internal rhythms and rhyme. Subjects are sustained through intertwined imagery and language patterns that underscore taut or richly surprising endings. "The White Rose: Sophie Scholl 1921-1943" by Erika Mumford—as compressed a biographical comment on victims of World War II as any—is deeply moving, as is the next selection, "Tending the Garden" by Eric Pankey. Together they chronicle the experience of a doomed German resistance fighter, a French prisoner of war, and a Jewish girl gassed by the Nazis. Balancing the tragic stories are lighter moments of buoyant humor and incidents of everyday familiarity caught unawares, as in Michael Pettit's piquant "Driving Lesson." Janeczko has played these poems like a piano, combining themes, tones, and even sounds for a true composition that will take young readers beyond the usual dose of Henry Wadsworth Longfellow or Rudyard Kipling.

Ethel R. Twichell

SOURCE: A review of *The Music of What Happens: Poems That Tell Stories,* in *The Horn Book Magazine,* Vol. LXIV, No. 5, September-October, 1988, p. 640.

Progressing smoothly from subject to subject, a profoundly moving collection of poetry leaves vivid pictures in the mind and piercing reverberations in the emotions. While not arranged in well-defined categories, the poems are linked in mood and idea as they move from the awkward dreams of adolescent love through the nostalgic and bittersweet memories of parents and childhood and on to the joys and anguish of later life experience. While many poems seem touched by sadness and regret, humor, often wry, bursts through in both image and in language. No one poem can be singled out for special praise as inevitably some selections will sing with a clearer note for the individual reader. The selector has again proven his ability to discover, choose, and arrange a broad span of fine poems, each telling its own tale and clothed in the spare economy or rich vision of the poet's imagination.

Tony Manna

SOURCE: A review of *The Music of What Happens,* in *Voice of Youth Advocates,* Vol. 11, No. 4, October, 1988, p. 204.

You can't rush through an anthology compiled by Janeczko; you need to pore over it in order to savor moments distilled by poets who penetrate the inner life of large and small experiences as though they were seeing through a high-powered microscope. A Janeczko anthology is much more than a potpourri of good poems, however, for Janeczko's gift is an ability not only to unearth enticing poems that ponder universals, but also to order the poems into a subtle and revealing symmetry, a pattern of insight created by a seasoned sense of how the pieces interrelate. *The Music of What Happens* is no exception. It contains 75 narrative poems that explicate what matters in life from a variety of voices, perspectives, moods, and styles, many of which are connected by topic, temperament, and imagery.

Janeczko begins with reminiscences of childhood that tell, for example, of tragedy averted ("The Flood") by Ann Stanford), of memorable first encounters and achievements ("Driving Lesson" by Michael Pettit), of lasting impressions ("Outhouse Blues" by Sheryl Nelms and "Constipation" by Ronald Wallace), and of the first stirrings of love ("The Kiss" by George Bogin and "Early Love" by Herbert Scott). He ends with a surreal dream ("When Angels Came to Zimmer" by Paul Zimmer) which moves into the outer reaches of human consciousness. Along the way, Janeczko clusters poems around topics which should attract even the most reluctant reader of poetry. Some carry implicit morals about death and dying ("Still Life" by Mike Angelotti, "Something Left to Say" by Katherine Soniat, and "The Dog Poisoner" by Keith Wilson), while others dramatize incidents in history ("The Huts at Esquimaux" by Norman Dubie, "Postcards of the Hanging: 1869" by

Andrew Hudgins, and "The White Rose: Sophie Scholl 1921-1943," Erika Mumford's deeply moving account of the Nazi purge of the Jews). There is also a series of poems that tells of incidents—many of them humorous—in the lives of ordinary people whose experiences reveal human foibles and predicaments ("Progress" by George Ella Lyon and "The New Lady Barber at Ralph's Barber Shop" by Leo Dangel). And among the lot there is a tall tale about the ghost of a rooster that haunts Nebraskans ("The Chicken Poem" by Don Welch), a well known legend about a country bridegroom who is killed by snakes on his wedding night as his bride looks on ("Mountain Bride" by Robert Morgan), and a letter from a father to his daughter which reveals her mother's suicide ("Secrets" by Robert Pack). This is the kind of anthology you return to again and again to catch glimpses of life held still.

BRICKYARD SUMMER (1989)

Hazel Rochman

SOURCE: A review of *Brickyard Summer,* in *Booklist,* Vol. 86, No. 2, September 15, 1989, p. 160.

Poems of a small-town boyhood celebrate family warmth, community, and friendship. Janeczko—whose splendid YA anthologies of modern poetry have often had a small-town focus—looks back with affection, but not with false nostalgia, to the summer between eighth grade and high school. Funny without being arch, he remains true to the viewpoint of an innocent Catholic boy. There is sorrow and loss, but menace is distant. Shoplifting is mischief (the boys take combs and thumbtacks "since taking / something we wanted / would be too much like stealing"); the public library provides shelter from the local hoods; he feels shock when his father hurts himself and says "The Word" ("He looked at me. / I looked away / as if his pants had fallen down"). The style is direct and accessible for reading aloud, especially the poems about his friendship with Raymond. Best of all are the tender lines that reveal surprise in intimate moments, as in **"The Kiss,"** where dancing with his classmate Molly, "spelling champ and crossing guard," he suddenly loses his awkwardness in a moment of gentle beauty.

Kirkus Reviews

SOURCE: A review of *Brickyard Summer,* in *Kirkus Reviews,* Vol. LVII, No. 19, October 1, 1989, p. 1475.

From a much praised anthologist for this age group, an approachable group of 30 of his own poems concerning the summer after eighth grade as experienced by the narrator and his best friend.

From the last-day-of-school **"Bonfire"** of memorabilia ("the report on flax I delivered / the day of the hurricane, / when a wedge of the ceiling collapsed / on the Blessed Virgin") to **"The Kiss"** that "started when I danced / with Molly Burke, / spelling champ / and crossing guard, / when I could feel / that bumpy bone in the middle of her back," these are a little prosaic, yet strongly evocative of that time of life when boy and man uneasily share one changing body. The dark side frequently surfaces here: the mischievously pursued cat ends up dead, as does one of the boys on the forbidden railway trestle; and though "The gargoyle/owner of Gold's Fix-It Shop" can mend most things, "his history / tattooed on one wrist" is a grim reminder that "Some things remain forever broken."

Glints of humor and a good measure of compassion lighten this sometimes charming, always believable adolescent voice, while [Ken] Rush's somber b&w paintings emphasize the poems' serious side.

Zena Sutherland

SOURCE: A review of *Brickyard Summer,* in *Bulletin of the Center for Children's Books,* Vol. 43, No. 3, November, 1989, p. 62.

Paul Janeczko is known to poetry readers primarily as an excellent anthologist; this is his first book-length collection, earlier poems having been published in magazines or anthologies. The voice is that of a boy who, just graduated from eighth grade, is experiencing the delights of summer and looking forward to the more heady delights (as listed by Sister Mary Ellen, when she "hoisted a storm warning") of high school; the last poem is a description of the first kiss. Most of the selections, however, are descriptions of the people of the town, a depressed mill-town in New England, and they are incisive and insightful, free verse that has parameters and focus and sharp images. Accompanying the poems are seven thickly textured oil paintings reflective of Janeczko's setting and reproduced in black and white.

Barbara Chatton

SOURCE: A review of *Brickyard Summer,* in *School Library Journal,* Vol. 35, No. 16, December, 1989, p. 126.

In 29 poems, Janeczko, best known for his anthologies of poems for young adults, captures the people and events of the small mill town in which he grew up. The poems are written as fragmented thoughts in the free verse appropriate to memories, and they vividly reflect the triumphs, fears, and friendships of adolescent boys. A number of the poems directly evoke characters from novels, including old Lester Darby of **"Stories,"** who seems to have stepped from Kinsella's *Shoeless Joe* and Marty Morgan of **"The Bridge,"** who meets a fate explored in Burns' *Cold Sassy Tree.* These connections are a testament to the universality of small town life and experiences, and to Janeczko's ability to portray it in simple language. The seven black-and-white paintings and the strong cover highlight the qualities of both exuberance and darkness which are developed in the poems.

Nancy Vasilakis

SOURCE: A review of *Brickyard Summer,* in *The Horn Book Magazine,* Vol. LXVI, No. 2, March-April, 1990, p. 215.

Irreverent yet innocent, these verses by an editor of several popular anthologies of poetry for young adults evoke a small-town, Catholic ambiance. His themes are friendship and love, loss of innocence and of life, and the small victories that give life its savor. "Bad," in which the young narrator is warned by a nun in junior high school—"'It will be easier to be bad / in high school,' / she told us / and then explained how"—concludes, "I moved on quickly, / anxious for the storm." The poet's spare New England voice harks back on occasion to that essential Yankee, Robert Frost. In another poem, when the town prophet pronounces that the youthful narrator's strength is friendship, the boy's best friend mutters darkly, 'Should be against the law / to take money / for telling something / as plain as bark on a tree.'" The best poems, however, are those to which Janeczko brings his own unique sensibilities. There is a poignant irony in **"Roscoe,"** where two friends, after causing the accidental death of a pet cat, make up a story about its disappearance and offer its owner a new cat. "Mrs. Carlucci thanked us, / offered us a dollar each / for our lie. / 'Take it,' / she said, / 'for what you did.'" Whether Janeczko is pointing out the contrast between Dad's awkwardness on the dance floor and his grace on the ball field, describing an eighth grader's exhilarating sense of freedom on the last day of school, or offering a soft-focus glimpse of a first kiss, he keeps his own sharp focus on the fears, dreams, and hopes of the teenagers who are his true and loyal fans.

📖 *THE PLACE MY WORDS ARE LOOKING FOR: WHAT POETS SAY ABOUT AND THROUGH THEIR WORK* **(edited by Janeczko, 1990)**

Kirkus Reviews

SOURCE: A review of *The Place My Words Are Looking For: What Poets Say About and Through Their Work,* in *Kirkus Reviews,* Vol. LVIII, No. 8, April 15, 1990, p. 579.

Thirty-nine contemporary poets are represented by 63 poems in this fine collection from a noted anthologist, himself a poet; each poet also contributes a brief essay on personal sources of inspiration. The poems, many of them culled from recent poetry magazines or small-press books, are fresh and of high quality, as well as being accessible and of interest to children. The essays are wonderfully provocative: "I write poetry [because] the sound of words, their taste on my tongue, is irresistible," says Bobbi Katz. Jim Daniels, who had a speech defect as a child, liked "the paper that didn't make fun of what I said or how I said it." In seventh grade, Ronald Wallace was bowled over by discovering Dickinson's "terror and joy and exhilaration and surprise and whimsy [so that] when the bell rings I don't hear it." Paul Zimmer wrote "Yellow Sonnet" in memory of his mother—"a love gift," like dandelions from a child. Poems are arranged so that the ideas grow; photo portraits of the poets picture them as friendly and approachable. An inspiration and a delight.

Renee Steinberg

SOURCE: A review of *The Place My Words Are Looking For: What Poets Say About and Through Their Work,* in *School Library Journal,* Vol. 36, No. 5, May, 1990, p. 118.

Sensitivity, wonder, anger, joy, humor, and more fill the pages of Janeczko's newest collection. The variety of the poetry alone renders this book valuable, but combined with the juxtaposed comments by the poets about their attitudes toward writing and poetry itself raises this offering to an even higher level. Poetry is sometimes considered the province of the special few, but the views of many of these contributors suggest that there is the potential for it within us all; it's just a matter of seeing and hearing beyond the surface. Youngsters will not find patterns to follow or syllable counts here, but rather a common feeling of passion for poetry as a way of putting one in touch with feelings and the often unobserved or unappreciated details of the everyday world. Selections dealing with myriad and diverse matters including mosquitos, horses, loneliness, a carousel, new love, the pain of abandonment, the end of summer, skateboards, and poetry can be found. Among the contributors are Eve Merriam, Paul Fleischman, Cynthia Rylant, Nancy Willard, Bobbi Katz, and Paul Janeczko. The book's format rivets readers' attention. Similar to Janeczko's *Poetspeak,* this new collection is more suited to a younger audience. It could easily excite young readers, as Joanne Ryder suggests, to be able to see the amazing in the ordinary that surrounds them.

Nancy Vasilakis

SOURCE: A review of *The Place My Words Are Looking For: What Poets Say About and through Their Work,* in *The Horn Book Magazine,* Vol. LXVI, No. 3, May-June, 1990, pp. 343-44.

In his latest poetry anthology Paul Janeczko returns to the format he employed so successfully in *Poetspeak,* published for adolescents. Both books include comments by the poets themselves, who reveal their sources of inspiration for a particular work or discuss the transcendental joy of the experience itself. This present volume is intended for a middle-grade audience and is destined to become an indispensable part of any poetry collection for children. More than forty contemporary poets are included: Eve Merriam, X. J. Kennedy, Felice Holman, Gary Soto, Mark Vinz, Karla Kuskin, and John Updike, among others. Their contributions vary widely in theme and mood and style, though the preponderance of the pieces are written in modern idiom and unrhymed meter. The accompanying comments frequently are as insightful and eloquent as the poems themselves. "A poem is portable," Maxine Kumin, who toils year round on her farm, tells us. "You can carry

it around with you in your head for days while you work on it in secret." An amusing anecdote by Ronald Wallace concerning some seventh-grade shenanigans in English class ends with the revelation that the introduction he got that day to the poems of Emily Dickinson left him feeling he was in the presence of "the rare and the strange." His poem "A Hot Property" shows the influence of the poetess on his work. Siv Cedering describes a snowy day; from his keen observations of that experience come the simple, majestic lines: "When it is snowing / the blue jay is / the only piece of / sky / in my / backyard." There is much to digest in this superb collection; much to entice. Young readers will not find it intimidating and may even be tempted to write some poems of their own. Certainly, they are encouraged to do so. "When you see a poem," suggests Cedering, "read it as carefully as you would open a surprise package. And someday when it is snowing, or some night when everyone is asleep, try writing a little poem." Who could resist such a beguiling invitation?

Roger Sutton

SOURCE: A review of *The Place My Words Are Looking For: What Poets Say About and Through Their Work,* in *Bulletin of the Center for Children's Books,* Vol. 43, No. 11, July-August, 1990, p. 268.

Like the compiler's *Poetspeak,* this is a diverse assortment of contemporary poems accompanied by comments from the poets on the particular poem, or on poetry in general. Intended for younger readers than was *Poetspeak,* this collection of sixty-odd poems includes some lightweight verse ("Yuk! How I hate Nancy Feder! / I can't think why the world would need her") that may be seen as patronizing by readers capable of the more sophisticated selections: "If you were exchanged in the cradle and / your real mother died / without ever telling the story / then no one knows your name . . ." (William Stafford). In general, the humorous verse included here is both less successful and for younger readers than are the darker or more meditative selections. The poets' comments are sometimes self-important ("I notice things other people don't"—Cynthia Rylant), generally genial ("It's not too hard, and it's fun"—John Updike), and probably not of great interest to most young readers ("If I could have the work of just one poet on a desert island I think it might be Rilke"—Russell Hoban). The poems themselves speak most distinctly, as in Hoban's own verses: "The thing about a sea gull is its eye—/ Eye of the wind, the ocean's eye, not pretty." Junior high readers are too often marooned between children's poetry and YA collections; here's an anthology that, at its best, takes itself and its audience seriously.

Miriam Martinez and Marcia F. Nash

SOURCE: A review of *The Place My Words Are Looking For,* in *Language Arts,* Vol. 67, No. 5, September, 1990, pp. 510-11.

This is a wonderful collection of poetry—funny poems;

poignant poems; moving poems; and poems about friendship, loneliness, skateboarding, and mosquitoes that tell lies. Best of all, many of the poets—Michael Patrick Hearn, Jack Prelutsky, Myra Cohn Livington, Nancy Willard, and Gwendolyn Brooks to name a few—speak directly to the readers, sharing their inspirations, memories, thoughts, and personal anecdotes. Naomi Shihab Nye tells us, "For me poetry has always been a way of paying attention to the world. We hear so many voices every day, swirling around us, and a poem makes us slow down and listen carefully to a few things we have really heard, deep inside." We learn from Lillian Morrison that "writing poems can be a way of pinning down a dream (almost); capturing a moment, a memory, a happening; and, at the same time, it's a way of sorting out your thoughts and feelings. Sometimes the words tell you what you didn't know you knew." By introducing the reader to the ideas of these poets and to some of their works, Janeczko has helped to make poetry accessible to all.

PREPOSTEROUS: POEMS OF YOUTH (edited by Janeczko, 1991)

Ellen D. Warwick

SOURCE: A review of *Preposterous: Poems of Youth,* in *School Library Journal,* Vol. 37, No. 3, March, 1991, p. 223.

A collection of more than 100 short poems by contemporary authors such as Leo Dangle, David Allan Evans, Gary Soto, and Charles Harper Webb that center on the bittersweet experience of growing up. Those who have enjoyed Janeczko's *Pocket Poems, Going Over to Your Place,* and *Don't Forget to Fly* will recognize the appeal of this one—a wide range of poems that describe basic human experiences in deceptively simple language. Some of the epiphanies are lighthearted, but the overall tone is wryly serious. The narrator in Eric Trethewey's "Rescue" ponders over his brother: "how to keep him out of jail is what I want / to know, and keep his fists in his pockets / through one more year of school." The girl in Linda Schandelmeier's "Secrets" doesn't let her mother know she's begun menstruating, hating the thought she's now "like her." Zeroing in on issues that concern most adolescents—alienation, belonging, friendship, movies, sex, school, truancy, family, and death—these poems will grab readers and not let them go. The anthology concludes with William Stafford's lines, "It's hard being a person. / We all know that." Janeczko makes the notion that poetry is boring seem totally preposterous.

Hazel Rochman

SOURCE: A review of *Preposterous: Poems of Youth,* in *Booklist,* Vol. 87, No. 14, March 15, 1991, p. 1503.

Absurd, uncertain, dreaming, wild: Janeczko's anthology shows that he knows poetry and the YA audience. He once again extends our reading pleasure by gathering from

quality small presses and magazines, as well as from collected works, some of the best contemporary poetry that speaks to young adults. As usual, his primary focus is on his own American mainstream small-town, rural tradition of growing up male, but he also includes some exciting female, minority, and urban voices. His choices are immediate without being condescending, rooted in colloquial language and precise experience—family rows and bonds, school, friendship, secrets, sexual fumbling, adventure, the "glitter" of danger and risk. There are quiet, intense lines to mull over alone and drama and comedy for sharing aloud.

Gary Soto captures the grinning bravado of two friends and their sudden glimpse of mortality. In the few casual lines of Robert Penn Warren's "Orphanage Boy," there's a whole novel with fully realized character, plot, place, and enduring sadness; read it aloud to YAs. Or read Jim Hall's touching farce about a teenage drug dealer imagining his glorious funeral ("Cadillacs from here / to Miami, gridlocked in grief"). *Preposterous* is the word for this stunning collection.

Kirkus Reviews

SOURCE: A review of *Preposterous: Poems of Youth,* in *Kirkus Reviews,* Vol. LIX, No. 8, April 15, 1991, p. 536.

By more than 80 authors, including Robert Penn Warren, Anne Sexton, Langston Hughes, and Herbert Scott, an anthology of recent (70's and 80's) poems plus a few nostalgic looks at long-gone youth, with references to WW II and earlier. Many relate sharply poignant stories or epiphanies, succinctly and powerfully recalled; Janeczko's familiar themes (e.g., small-town life, Catholic *angst*) frequently recur. The voices are almost overwhelmingly male (an imbalance echoed in the handsome jacket painting of a small, worried girl peering from behind a much larger, confident man), but the quality is so high, the appeal so immediate, and the selection so personal that it's a forgivable happenstance; teen-agers will easily identify with the problems expressed, often reflecting adolescence as a time of deep self-absorption and loss of faith in childhood beliefs. An excellent collection for any library, especially those with activities involving poetry.

Deborah Stevenson

SOURCE: A review of *Preposterous: Poems of Youth,* in *Bulletin of the Center for Children's Books,* Vol. 44, No. 10, June, 1991, pp. 240-41.

This anthology of mostly male poets and mostly male voices may be seeking to woo poetry-resistant teenage boys. Among the poets are the nationally known (Robert Penn Warren's stunning "Orphanage Boy" and Gwendolyn Brooks' famous "Gang Girls" are included) as well as people more familiar from other contexts, such as Jim Wayne Miller and Ron Koertge. Some formal variation (nearly all the poems are free verse) would have enhanced the collection, but it is nonetheless full of varied and vivid insights. Janeczko has a particularly strong selection of dead-on "boy's-eye-view" vignettes with added perspective, such as David Allan Evans' "Bus Depot Reunion" and Herbert Scott's "That Summer," which seem likely to lure any audience into reading further. An index and source notes are included.

Ellen Fader

SOURCE: A review of *Preposterous: Poems of Youth,* in *The Horn Book Magazine,* Vol. LXVII, No. 4, July-August, 1991, p. 471.

Janeczko's collection of short contemporary poems—many reprinted from small presses and probably unknown to young adults—addresses the pain and pleasure of growing up. Twenty-two unlabeled but thematically arranged sections offer insightful selections which deal with themes that preoccupy teenagers: school, family, sex, death, and the danger and attraction of running with the pack. Although wry humor informs some of the poems, the majority of Janeczko's choices are serious and thoughtful, often demanding repeated readings; yet most speak so directly to adolescent concerns that readers will feel that these poets know what is in their hearts. More than half of the over one hundred poems reflect a male point of view, perhaps indicating special appeal to older boys who often feel that poetry has little to offer them. Whether exploring two boys' rivalry in Leo Dangel's "No Question"—"There was no question, / I had to fight Arnold Gertz / behind the high school that Friday. / All fall he kept throwing pool balls / at me in the rec room"—or the bravado of skipping school in Sheryl L. Nelm's "Anne Frank," this anthology is firmly focused on its audience. Readers will agree: this collection offers a preposterously enjoyable reading experience.

📖 *LOOKING FOR YOUR NAME: A COLLECTION OF CONTEMPORARY POEMS* (edited by Janeczko, 1993)

Hazel Rochman

SOURCE: A review of *Looking for Your Name: A Collection of Contemporary Poems,* in *Booklist,* Vol. 89, No. 10, January 15, 1993, p. 899.

The Vietnam Veterans Memorial is one place where you find "your name" in this collection that confronts dark facts and images of the American popular imagination. Janeczko has moved far from the strongly male, pastoral kind of poetry that dominated his early fine collections. This time the conflict is in the city, and in soldiers' clinging memories of children burned by napalm, and in girls on the firing line of family violence. There are lots of strong women's voices—Christine Hemp, Sheryl L. Nelms, Grace Paley, and others—and a few poems about gay and lesbian relationships. There's boisterous sports poetry, such as Jonathon Holden's "Ice Hockey," with its wild, skimming movement, and Ann Townsend's "Play," with its

celebration of tough, hard tennis and a girl's wanting to win. There's wry love poetry, including a piece about Frankenstein's wife, who writes to Ann Landers. Many of these poems are grim—"America, it's hard to get your attention politely," says David Baker—but though they deal with harsh daily reality, both political and domestic (layoffs, AIDS, suicide, etc.), there are no shouting slogans. The best poetry shows its power to control fists and grief in intensely personal moments of enduring fragility.

Sharon Korbeck

SOURCE: A review of *Looking for Your Name: A Collection of Contemporary Poems,* in *School Library Journal,* Vol. 39, No. 4, April, 1993, p. 147.

Janeczko's latest collection paints a potent landscape of American life in the 1990s, while harkening a universal time and place. Over 100 poems, some by such renowned poets as Ronald Wallace and Paul Zimmer, cover topics as timely and dynamic as AIDS, war, gun control, and unemployment. The writers pull no punches and spare no taboos when it comes to presenting the conflicts of contemporary life. Unrecyclable Styrofoam pellets, a family coping with suicide, and animals tortured to make cosmetics energize lines that beg responses, whether emotional or active. The pure energy of the selections evokes anger, distrust, remembrance, and a host of other true emotions. Similar in layout and scope to Janeczko's *Going Over to Your Place,* this book's main strength is its ability to offer strong, concise perspectives for young adults and adults as well. A silent reading of the poems will provoke thought; reading them aloud amplifies their power. Janeczko's ever-sharp ear for poetry is more than obvious here; his ability to integrate the sum is outstanding. Our time, our place, and our fears are all recorded here in stellar form.

Donna L. Scanlon

SOURCE: A review of *Looking for Your Name,* in *Voice of Youth Advocates,* Vol. 16, No. 2, June, 1993, pp. 117-18.

The poems in Janeczko's new anthology evoke images and emotions rooted in the stresses of contemporary society. The scope of the collection spans such universal themes as death, war, love, the environment, and relationships, yet each poem is a personal statement, reflecting a powerful and singular feeling.

The poems are at once poignant and disturbing. A father reflects on his son's suicide, asking "What do you do when the past is / no longer yours?" A mother is haunted by the threat of AIDS until the needle jabbed in her son's hand by a playmate is identified as harmless, saying "it helps, it always helps when you know / what things are." Some of the poems express the hopelessness of both the unemployed and those employed in dead end or deadly jobs, while others explore aspects of the family.

Janeczko arranges the poems by subject, but the transition from subject to subject is virtually seamless, effectively drawing the reader from poem to poem. Many of the transitional poems incorporate elements of both themes, such as "Tom Lonehill (1940-1956)," which connects poems about games and sports with poems about death, or "Why I'm in Favor of a Nuclear Freeze" which connects poems about the violence of modern society with poems about war.

As in his other poetry collections such as *The Music of What Happens* and *The Place My Words Are Looking For,* Janeczko demonstrates a remarkable talent for selection. The quality of *Looking For Your Name* makes it a more than worthwhile purchase for both school and public libraries.

Betsy Hearne

SOURCE: A review of *Looking for Your Name: A Collection of Contemporary Poems,* in *Bulletin of the Center for Children's Books,* Vol. 46, No. 11, July-August, 1993, p. 347.

What seems a rather sprawling thematic motif of "conflict" assumes a tight focus as Janeczko assembles hardhitting poems by some relatively unknown, as well as relatively famous, contemporary poets. As a group, the poems are almost overwhelmingly intense—occasionally shocking in moments of bitter epiphany, as when Sheryl Nelms' "the hard way" describes the frying of a Cambodian prisoner in a copper pit, or Herbert Scott laments a victim of abuse in "The Burnt Child," or Elliot Fried in "For a Sister Not Yet Dead" assures his sibling that her suicide attempts will eventually prove successful. There's a tonal range of reflective to sad to tragic, though humor occasionally glints through, as in James Nolan's "Modern Times" or Ron Koertge's "The Black Thumb." While some of the poems are by young adult authors, many show an adult perspective on past experience (Christopher Hewitt's "The Enticing Lane," for instance) but will nevertheless be accessible to teenage readers. AIDS, war, environmental pollution, child abuse, cruelty to animals, and other bleak subjects get far from bleak treatment. These are rich poems that will fascinate readers even as they exert stress on them: "how losses and disasters first attract, but then repel us, all our carefree cells / shouting out at recess, *Not me! Not me!*" (from Ronald Wallace's "Flames"). The 112 poems, mostly anthologized here for the first time, are indexed by first lines, authors, and titles.

Nancy Vasilakis

SOURCE: A review of *Looking for Your Name: A Collection of Contemporary Poems,* in *The Horn Book Magazine,* Vol. LXIX, No. 4, July-August, 1993, p. 474.

This pre-eminent anthologist continues to produce works that speak provocatively and unsparingly to young adults about life in contemporary America. The collection contains 112 poems, most of them relatively brief, by celebrated and little-known contemporary poets. With conflict as the central focus, the poems stir strong emotions, covering a variety of bedeviling issues that characterize modern life—pollution, AIDS, family relations, homosexual love, gun control, alcoholism, and joblessness. Peter Meinke's "Bones in an African Cave" finds glory in the violent nature of young men, a trait that fossil records trace back to prehistoric times. In "The Penance," Leonard Nathan describes a horrific recurring dream that has hounded him since his days in Vietnam. In six exquisite lines Phil Hey contemplates the undefinable origins of love. "Where is there school / to learn how suddenly and slightly / the history of love begins?" The volume is loosely organized along the lines of a developing life, with the first poem summoning up the uncontained enthusiasm of a first-grader raising his hand to answer a question that he is never called upon to answer, and the last poem marveling at the unbelievable swiftness of life's passing. Once again, Janeczko makes a valuable contribution by calling attention to so many new voices. His thoughtful, inspired choices will be taken to heart by all lovers of good poetry.

📖 *STARDUST OTEL* (1993)

Barbara Chatton

SOURCE: A review of *Stardust otel,* in *School Library Journal,* Vol. 39, No. 11, November, 1993, p. 134.

Bittersweet lyrics that ring true to the voice of a sensitive teenager awakening to the complexities of life. These 30 poems are written from the point of view of the son of now-grown flower children who own the Stardust Hotel (the "H" came off when his father swung on it on the day of Leary's birth 14 years earlier). The verses describe the tenants of the hotel, as well as the boy's parents, friends, and neighbors, forming a mixture of ordinary people and extraordinary characters. Leary comes to know the undertaker who loves to go out dancing; the lady barber who fixes her '57 Chevy as a hobby; and "The Prince of the Dump" who salvages treasures. Also, Leary describes playing ball, the restitution of a bully, taking a dare to kiss an angel headstone, and other more typically youthful activities. As in the author's *Brickyard Summer,* this volume provides brief, careful portraits of individuals in a small community. Like Cynthia Rylant and Mel Glenn's poems for YAs, Janeczko's pieces invite young writers to try their hands at describing people they know.

Jim Morgan

SOURCE: A review of *Stardust otel,* in *Voice of Youth Advocates,* Vol. 16, No. 5, December, 1993, p. 321.

Leary, the speaker throughout this collection of poems, was born to a pair of flower children who named their first home *Stardust Hotel* after powdering their faces with stardust in a psychedelic vision. "The H fell nearly 15 years ago: / the day I was born / Nick swung on it in joy / until it snapped off in his hands. / He never replaced it, / saying he liked to be reminded / of how he felt that day."

Thus begins this curious collection by prolific YA poet Janeczko, thirty poems narrated by a teenager growing up in a rural town where the shadow of the sixties lingers on. An eccentric assortment of characters unfolds: Alice Singer, a romance novel addict who enjoys an erotic thrill when Leary reads one of her books aloud; Tommy, whose ambitions are to become a Red Sox announcer, disc jockey, stuntman and *Playboy* photographer; Wanda, the black woman who sang with a piano player at the Boxcar. One of the most effective poems is **"Evil Eye,"** in which Leary and a few friends visit a fortune teller who prophesizes that "One of you will go to college / One of you will marry young but happily / One of you will travel far / One of you will make a great discovery / And one of you will be lost." To determine which fate belongs to whom, they must return one at a time. The boys laugh at the woman's foolish mystic profession while departing but never return.

The quality of the poetry is uneven: Janeczko often presents themes with all the subtlety of a *Sanford and Son* episode. Regardless, these poems will connect with many adolescents through their vivid and unpretentious descriptions of old folks, abandoned drive-in theatres, girls, cars, sports, summer nights, and other things that make small-town life in America worth living.

John H. Bushman and Kay Parks Bushman

SOURCE: A review of *Stardust otel,* in *English Journal,* Vol. 83, No. 2, February, 1994, p. 81.

Unlike most of his books, **Stardust otel** offers poems written by Janeczko himself. He presents a series of poems in which Leary, a fourteen-year-old boy, describes life with his flower-children parents, his friends, and neighbors, all of whom either live at or visit frequently the Stardust otel. We read about Nick, Leary's young father, who swung from the hotel sign when Leary was born and tore the H from the sign. He never replaced it. He wanted to always remember how he felt that day when Leary came into his life. We read of Alice Singer, who has a room down the hall, and her attempt to get Leary to her room; Becky, Charlie Hooper, Jackie Slattery, and many others bring a variety of stories to this short but delightful collection of original poetry.

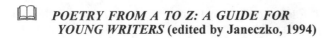 *POETRY FROM A TO Z: A GUIDE FOR YOUNG WRITERS* (edited by Janeczko, 1994)

Hazel Rochman

SOURCE: A review of *Poetry from A to Z: A Guide for Young Writers,* in *Booklist,* Vol. 91, No. 8, December 15, 1994, p. 748.

"You need to find the right words and use them in the best order." Janeczko brings Coleridge's famous dictum right into the world of today's middle-graders and encourages youngsters to give poetry a try. As in his *Poetspeak* for older readers, Janeczko selects poems and has the poets talk about writing; but this time, it's his own commentary—warm, sunny, informal, enthusiastic, encouraging, rooted in ordinary things—that carries the narrative. "Try this" is a repeated subhead, and he applies it to everything from haiku to list poems, letter poems, and memory poems. The examples he chooses make up a fine anthology, with contributions by several children's poets as well as adult writers, nearly all of whom tell young poets to read and read as a way to find their own voices. Janeczko's suggestions clearly grow from his own teaching success, and the book will be a natural for creative-writing classes. It will show that although poetry isn't easy, it can be a lot of fun to write about what you imagine.

Betsy Hearne

SOURCE: A review of *Poetry from A to Z: A Guide for Young Writers,* in *Bulletin of the Center for Children's Books,* Vol. 48, No. 7, March, 1995, p. 240.

A more likely subtitle might be "Fun for Young Writers," because there's a jigsaw puzzle aspect to this book despite its organizational scheme. The alphabetical arrangement makes for pretty haphazard thematic juxtapositions, which is evidently the author's intent, "to help you see that you can write poems about nearly any subject." Thus *A* is introduced by a poem called "Autumn Beat," followed by instructions for writing an acrostic poem, along with two examples of acrostic poems ("Autumn Beat" is not one). Some of the themes are explicit, others less obvious: *D* for dreams in "I Picked a Dream Out of My Head," for instance, as opposed to "The Animals Are Leaving" for *E* (extinction) and "Harvey" for *F* (friendship). Janeczko's sixty-one examples are accessible (from Gwendolyn Brooks to John Ciardi and William Jay Smith), his direct address to the reader is easy and informal (even sometimes glib), and his enthusiasm is catching; modest but lively line drawings dot the text. If the format's a little jumpy, juvenile TV addicts will probably get all the more out of it.

Nancy Vasilakis

SOURCE: A review of *Poetry from A to Z: A Guide for Young Writers,* in *The Horn Book Magazine,* Vol. LXXI, No. 2, March-April, 1995, p. 211.

The sixty-one selections in this collection are intended by Janeczko to be used as models for students in creating their own poetry. As was true in two of his earlier volumes, *Poetspeak* and *The Place My Words Are Looking For,* the poets offer scattered comments on their own work throughout the book. Their remarks occupy a modest place in this latest anthology, however; Janeczko's own suggestions about how to go about experiencing the "outrageous joy of reading and writing poems" are the main focus. He includes several poetry-writing exercises, talks about a writer's tools—from the concrete (thesaurus, notebook) to the abstract (feelings, ideas)—and stresses the importance of experimentation. Janeczko uses the alphabetical format to organize the poems by title, subject, or type, so that under the letter *H,* for example, he includes Virginia Driving Hawk Sneve's "My Horse, Fly Like a Bird" and the haiku "Which" by William Stafford, as well as some suggestions for writing haiku and "how-to" poems. The contributors—Patricia Hubbell, Marilyn Singer, Lillian Morrison, Naomi Shihab Nye, and Bobbi Katz, to name a few—will, for the most part, be recognized by readers of children's poetry. The poems are varied and brief in length. They are well-suited to the audience, dealing as they do with subjects of general interest and containing just enough of a challenge to make the reach accessible with modest effort. An excellent bibliography, organized by theme, is appended. The book offers evidence of Janeczko's skills as a teacher and furthers his reputation as a poet and, above all, a poetry lover.

Deborah L. Dubois

SOURCE: A review of *Poetry from A to Z: A Guide for Young Writers,* in *Voice of Youth Advocates,* Vol. 18, No. 2, June, 1995, pp. 120-21.

In his guide, Janeczko gives many examples and ideas to get young writers started writing poetry. The book is organized alphabetically with seventy-two poems on almost any topic you could imagine. In addition, fourteen exercises labeled "Try This" explain how to write different types of poems and help a young writer get started. These exercises are possible to do without outside help. Twenty-three poets represented in the book give advice on how to become a better poet. The advice is frank and encouraging.

The style is conversational and the reader feels that Janeczko is right there explaining the poetry, making the book very readable. As in his previous work *Poetspeak,* Janeczko helps the reader understand poetry in all its forms, but this book is much more a working guide for students who want to write poetry.

Poetry from A to Z is an attractive book illustrated with line drawings throughout and the letter represented in each poem in a running line across the top of each page. The quotes from the poets are set off with a line above and below, and they are positioned near one of that person's poems. The main purpose of this book is to encourage young writers to try writing poetry and to give them instructions to get them started. Janeczko fulfills his purpose admirably without making poetry seem too difficult for a young writer to be successful. I recommend this for all teachers of poetry and for libraries serving young adults of all ages.

Anthony Manna

SOURCE: "Should We Read (More) Poetry (More Often)?" in *Voice of Youth Advocates,* Vol. 18, No. 4, October, 1995, pp. 201-03.

[*Poetry from A to Z*] is a call to action, an invitation cordially extended to young writers to have a go at shaping all sorts of experience into the stuff of poetry. This is an up-beat, user-friendly learner's primer, and Paul Janeczko, the quintessential mentor, eases his students into the writing process by collaborating with them as they face the pleasurable work at hand.

Janeczko has set a comprehensive course for his young cohorts, and the entire enterprise is shrewdly organized so as to build the writers' confidence over time through their involvement in brief, incremental spurts of activity. In each of his brief chapters, Janeczko first introduces his students to the works of professional poets and then invites them to act on their ideas and impulses by experimenting with some of the techniques and forms discovered in the models. He has grouped the poems and the accompanying writing exercises alphabetically by subject or theme, thereby suggesting that the matter of poetry is all life, all experience. In the chapter devoted to the letter "m," for instance, John Ciardi's "A Lesson in Manners," which cleverly counters the moralism implied in the title with a bit of playful advice, and Leo Dangel's "Corn-Growing Music," a quirky meditation on human values, pave the way to an exercise centered around the challenge of writing a memory poem, the motivation provided by Janeczko's helpful suggestions and Ellen Gilchrist's recollection of "The Best Meal I Ever Had Anywhere." As a way of offering further encouragement, Janeczko peppers the text with brief commentaries on process and product from twenty-three of the poets whose work appears in the guide. And so it goes in its steady pace through the alphabet: "A" is for acrostic poem and Kulling's "Autumn Beat;" "L" is for letter and list poem and Moore's "Letter to a Friend;" "S" is for shape poem, Vina's "Line Storm," and LaBombard's "Sparklers;" and "Z," of course, is for Katz's "Zebra." This energetic hands-on manual puts into reassuring practice the age-old belief that we learn best by doing. It's the next best thing to participating in a poetry writing workshop.

WHEREVER HOME BEGINS: 100 CONTEMPORARY POEMS (edited by Janeczko, 1995)

Kirkus Reviews

SOURCE: A review of *Wherever Home Begins: 100 Contemporary Poems,* in *Kirkus Reviews,* Vol. LXIII, No. 18, September 15, 1995, p. 1352.

The latest collection from Janeczko is an exploration of *place* as the arena for human lives. True to his usual practice, the poet and anthologist brackets the collection with single works that open and close the curtain on groups of poems evoking towns, farms, cities, landscapes, homes, and workplaces, and how lives and memories are rooted in them. The places may be as confined as "The Closet," by Brooke Horvath, or as expansive as the unnamed foreign country at the "End of the Line," by John Taylor. Stylistically, they vary from the formal rigor of the Elizabethan sonnet in Jim Wayne Miller's "Closing the House" to the free-floating, unpunctuated strut of Holly Scalera's "Riverside Park." With the exception of Gary Soto and X. J. Kennedy, few of the 79 poets are well known, but most have been represented in Janeczko's previous anthologies. First-rate, mature poetry for serious readers.

Hazel Rochman

SOURCE: A review of *Wherever Home Begins: 100 Contemporary Poems,* in *Booklist,* Vol. 92, No. 3, October 1, 1995, p. 303.

There's always a strong sense of place in Janeczko's fine anthologies that introduce YAs to contemporary poetry. Here, home is the explicit theme, and once again, Janeczko brings us powerful poems of smalltown America: casual, immediate, precise images of lonely cafés and empty streets at dusk and drifters from disappearing small farms. Several voices are of older people looking back to a more innocent time ("It was really quiet at night"). Home is also the city, of course, often a littered "lost river of hell," but sometimes a dancing, magical center ("hot city, hot blooming"). The poems are loosely organized into small units about farms, mines, hills, beaches, workplaces, etc.; a few are set outside the U.S., and one moving poem is about a border café in Arizona. "On the Back Porch" evokes a warm and rooted place ("Inside my house are those who love me"), but mostly we glimpse a solitary road with people far from home.

Sharon Korbeck

SOURCE: A review of *Wherever Home Begins: 100 Contemporary Poems,* in *School Library Journal,* Vol. 41, No. 11, November, 1995, p. 129.

Everything from strewn litter to last season's maple leaves can remind one of "home," wherever that may be. But even the title of Janeczko's latest anthology is telling— through these poems readers learn not where home *is,* but where it *begins.* That sense of home is at the heart of these tightly rendered, carefully selected, and thoughtfully arranged selections. Some reminiscences are pleasant, warm, and joyful. Others express the cynicism, dismay, or discomfort of remembering the past. All are well crafted and quite mature in viewpoint. The material things that make a home—porches, closets, and country roads—are well visited, as are the faces and memories. Here is a dirty service station, a graveyard, disappearing farms, and even a Polish post office. These diverse locales fit the universal theme of the book and, as he usually does, Janeczko skillfully organizes the volume to reap the most impact from each poem. Once again, he has collected gems from around the world, representing the best of contemporary poetry. His experience and trained eye and ear deliver nothing less than unqualified realism. Both the painful and joyous memories and definitions of home offer this volume its power.

Deborah Stevenson

SOURCE: A review of *Wherever Home Begins: 100 Contemporary Poems,* in *Bulletin of the Center for Children's Books,* Vol. 49, No. 3, November, 1995, pp. 94-5.

Despite the titular emphasis on home, much of the poetry is about motion: moving in, moving past, moving around, and moving on. Janeczko's predilection is for small-town and rural scenes (although cities do get a small section) and for free-verse poetry, so, as with most of his collections, there is a definite sense of a guiding sensibility behind the anthology. Poets of different degrees of celebrity appear, some of whom (Jim Wayne Miller, David Alan Evans, Naomi Shihab Nye, and Gary Soto, for instance) will be familiar to experienced readers of poetry in general and of Janeczko's collections in particular. Despite some similarities there's an intriguing variety of textures in the poems here: Jim Wayne Miller's pokerfaced but rueful "Small Farms Disappearing in Tennessee" rubs shoulders with Richard Snyder's intricately detached "A Grammar of the Sea," Jack Anderson's singable "blues on the ranch," and Katherine Soniat's sensual evocation of place in "Forecast: New Orleans." While the poems vary in difficulty, the language, concepts, and events keep them teen-accessible without being condescending.

Mary Ann Capan

SOURCE: A review of *Wherever Home Begins: 100 Contemporary Poems,* in *Voice of Youth Advocates,* Vol. 18, No. 5, December, 1995, p. 334.

This collection of thoughtful unrhymed poems reflects the myriad places people call home from the sleepy, rural towns to the noisy, city streets. Reading the poems in order takes you on a trip to: Alabama, North Carolina, Detroit, Berkeley, New Orleans, Texas, Utah, and Washington, DC, then, abroad to Poland, France, Nicaragua, and Amsterdam. The images drawn by the figurative language reflect places we don't think about consciously but which are always there: the filling station, subway, closet, garden, back porch, school, hospital, park, and public library. The volume contains poems by familiar writers including Gary Soto, George Ella Lyon, Ronald Koertge, X. J. Kennedy, and Naomi Shihab Nye. Readers will also recognize poets from Janeczko's other collections including Jonathan Holden, Paul Zimmer, and Keith Wilson. The nostalgic element of many poems will make the collection appealing to adults as well as teenagers.

I FEEL A LITTLE JUMPY AROUND YOU: A BOOK OF HER POEMS AND HIS POEMS COLLECTED IN PAIRS (edited by Naomi Shihab Nye and Janeczko, 1996)

Hazel Rochman

SOURCE: A review of *I Feel a Little Jumpy Around You:*

A Book of Her Poems and His Poems Collected in Pairs, in *Booklist,* Vol. 92, No. 15, April 1, 1996, p. 1351.

An anthology needs a unifying theme, and this collection focuses on the experience of gender—how men and women see things differently and the same. Two fine YA anthologists have collaborated in gathering nearly 200 rich, subtle poems about "the multitudes of hes and shes" among children, parents, siblings, friends, lovers, spouses, outsiders. The politics is great fun as a framework. Janeczko and Nye each contribute a lively introduction in which they open up issues of gender and of anthology making. The brief excerpts from their faxes to each other are argumentative, irritable, profound, and teasing ("Is this a boy thing?" Nye asks him). Notes at the back by the contributing poets are earnest, comic, sometimes lyrical; one famous poet is furious at being asked to think about gender in relation to his poetry. The pairing arrangement seems a bit tight: always a poem by a man and a poem by a woman set off together. Instead of enjoying each poem for itself, you feel pushed to read the companion piece and work out why they're together. (Is my problem a "girl" thing?) Best of all, of course, are the individual poems; you dip into this great collection anywhere and discover something astonishing to read, one poem at a time.

Kirkus Reviews

SOURCE: A review of *I Feel a Little Jumpy Around You: A Book of Her Poems and His Poems Collected in Pairs,* in *Kirkus Reviews,* Vol. LXIV, No. 7, April 1, 1996, p. 534.

A remarkable anthology, though not for its gender gimmick—his and her poems collected in tandem by his and her anthologists with separate introductions and even separate indexes to male and female poets. Often the pairings seem subjective even while the poems themselves shine with universality; and the sheer variety—only a fraction by poets who are even relatively familiar—is extraordinary. There are powerful and fascinating poems about crushes, kisses (his, visceral; hers, romantic), roots, guilt, memory and the influence of the past ("the heart remembers home and will make you walk water to find it"), and grief. There are stunning selections about daughters and mothers ("something is moving / in the water. / she is the hook. / i am the line"); fathers; brothers and sisters; boys "having moved on naturally from zapping / ants with a magnifying glass, to disfiguring / toy soldiers with a woodburning kit" and girls "bearing supper, / our heads on fire." With moments of fierce humor ("Emily Dickinson's To-Do List") and true communion ("I will / try to wait for you, / on your side of things"), this is a wonder, whatever it has to say (or doesn't) about men and women.

Deborah Stevenson

SOURCE: A review of *I Feel a Little Jumpy Around You: A Book of Her Poems and His Poems Collected in Pairs,* in *Bulletin of the Center for Children's Books,* Vol. 49, No. 9, May, 1996, pp. 311-12.

Nye and Janeczko have each independently produced worthy poetry anthologies; here they join forces for a collection with a twist. The poems come in pairs, the male-authored entry always leading and the female-authored one always getting the last word. The coupled poems sometimes share a subject, sometimes a setting, sometimes a theme or an image (Agha Shahid Ali's "Snowman" and Robin Boody Galguera's "Alloy" both address questions of culture, E. Ethelbert Miller's "Dressed Up" and Naomi Stroud Simmons' "With Reservation" offer quirky takes on fancy dress) that directs readers to a specific way into each poem. The poems themselves, almost all contemporary free verse and from poets ranging from famous (Rita Dove, W. S. Merwin) to less known, are of a high standard. Though the gender counterpoint really plays little part in the juxtaposition, the pairings are piquant and provide a manageable way to start talking about a very large collection of poetry. An engaging marginal dialogue, taken from Nye's and Janeczko's collaborative fax correspondence, appears alongside the appendix and permits a revealing peek behind the scenes. Highly readable notes from contributors are included, as is an index of poems and a gender-segregated index of poets.

Kathleen Whalin

SOURCE: A review of *I Feel a Little Jumpy Around You: A Book of Her Poems and His Poems Collected in Pairs,* in *School Library Journal,* Vol. 42, No. 5, May, 1996, p. 143.

Nye and Janeczko, distinguished anthologists, have fittingly combined their talents to create this collection of 190 modern poems celebrating women and men's varying points of view. The selections are on a variety of subjects (love, parents, everyday objects); each is paired with one written by a poet of the opposite gender. Gunnar Ekelof's view of marriage in "For Night Comes" (". . . when happiness and unhappiness / rest in peace with each other") meets Joan Logghe's "Marriage" ("Marriage, the sweet watered down"); George Bogin's memories in "Nineteen" ("I could have taken her by the hand and walked the whole 60 blocks / to the piers right onto a steamer to France or somewhere, / but I said nothing and after a while got up / and walked out into middle age") is contrasted with Miriam Kessler's thoughts on boys from her past ("All Their Names Were Vincent"). The book concludes with an appendix of musings by the poets on growing up male and female. Indexes of titles and male and female poets are included. Teachers or older adolescents wanting a rich source for thought and discussion need look no further.

Anthony Manna

SOURCE: A review of *I Feel a Little Jumpy Around You: A Book of Her Poems and His Poems Presented in Pairs,* in *Voice of Youth Advocates,* Vol. 19, No. 3, August, 1996, p. 178.

The 194 poems in this fascinating anthology go a long way in revealing the extraordinary range of perspectives and sensibilities that females and males bring to bear on whatever piece of human experience they happen to be pondering at the moment. By arranging these mostly free verse poems into 97 provocative he/she pairs wherein a male and female fathom the same or a thematically related phenomenon, Nye and Janeczko reveal the role gender plays in the ways this culturally diverse community of contemporary poets makes sense of the world. Included among the phenomena these poets reach into with characteristically spare, sharp-edged wonder are the forces that shape one's identity, the power of memory, family ties, friendship, estrangement, loss, death, and, of course, the complex ways in which men and women perceive each other. What ultimately makes this gathering so intriguing, thanks to the careful lay out, is the degree to which the voices blend and gender boundaries give way to quests, quirks, and needs which signal the ties that bind us. Augmenting the all-of-a-piece feel of the entire volume are amusing, often emotionally charged excerpts from the compilers' correspondence about the anthology, which illuminate both the selection process and their own sense of equity, and the contributors' responses to Nye's and Janeczko's query about gender. What an eye- and heart-opening experience!

📖 *HOME ON THE RANGE: COWBOY POETRY*
   (edited by Janeczko, 1997)

Kirkus Reviews

SOURCE: A review of *Home on the Range: Cowboy Poetry,* in *Kirkus Reviews,* Vol. LXV, No. 17, September 1, 1997, p. 1390.

A timeless portrait of cowboy (and cowgirl) life emerges from 20 illustrated poems. Some of the selections are humorous, some respectful, some impassioned, but most have the echo of truth that comes from those who know their subject. The poems deal with friendship, hardship, weather, hay, and hungry cows; all speak to a love and respect for the land, animals, open skies, and freedom. Janeczko includes examples of the sentimental doggerel that has become, unfortunately, the hallmark of the genre, but children will find them funny and involving—a way into the more serious pieces. Following a reading of "The Trail of an Old Timer's Memory," there won't be a dry eye in the house. On colored backgrounds, [Bernie] Fuchs has created from oil and pencil striking scenes in which the subjects are on the verge of vanishing, specter-like, into the haze. A good collection, with an unfeigned, cumulative effect that leaves readers with a real sense of a disappearing way of life.

Additional coverage of Janeczko's life and career is contained in the following sources published by Gale Research: *Authors and Artists for Young Adults,* Vol. 9; *Contemporary Authors,* Vol. 104; *Contemporary Authors New Revision Series,* Vol. 49; *Something about the Author,* Vol. 53; and *Something about the Author Autobiography Series,* Vol. 18.

E. L. Konigsburg

1930-

American author and illustrator of fiction.

Major recent works include *The Second Mrs. Giaconda* (1975), *Father's Arcane Daughter* (1976), *Throwing Shadows* (1979), *Journey to an 800 Number* (1982), *The View from Saturday* (1996).

For information on Konigsburg's career prior to 1973, see *CLR,* Vol. 1.

INTRODUCTION

The inimitable author of humorous, highly innovative, thought-provoking stories and novels for elementary and junior high-school children, Konigsburg is best known for her two Newbery Medal winners: *From the Mixed-Up Files of Mrs. Basil E. Frankweiler* (1967) and *The View from Saturday.* Her intriguing book titles attest to her lively imagination and are indicative of the diversity of her material, which encompasses historical fiction, fantasy, contemporary realism, and picture books for preschoolers. Although her settings vary widely, from Leonardo da Vinci's Renaissance Italy to suburban America and downtown New York City, her down-to-earth, well-developed, articulate protagonists and her keen wit, unique plots, and ear for dialogue make for absorbing reading. An artist as well as an author, Konigsburg has illustrated several of her own books, using her own children and now her grandchildren for models and as sources of new ideas. She has also published one book for adults, *TalkTalk: A Children's Book Author Speaks to Grown-Ups* (1995), a collection of her lectures and speeches stressing the importance and evolution of children's literature over the last three decades. Despite the fact that Konigsburg's books deal with middle-class neighborhoods and children with above-average IQs, her works address the universal theme of "Who am I?" that besets all young people, regardless of race, class, or creed.

Biographical Information

Born in New York City and raised in small Pennsylvania towns, Konigsburg was a voracious reader as a child, an excellent student in school, and the first member of her family to seek a college education. She majored in chemistry with hopes of immediate gainful employment after school, and she graduated with honors from Carnegie Mellon University. She then married David Konigsburg, an industrial psychologist. When her husband's work took him to Florida, Konigsburg accompanied him and found a job teaching chemistry at a private girls' school. There she found she really was not interested in chemistry as much as she was with her young students themselves.

Konigsburg left teaching to raise a family, two boys and a girl, and moved with her husband and children to New York, where she began to write after her youngest started school. Her first two books made children's literature history when *From the Mixed-Up Files of Mrs. Basil E. Frankweiler* won the Newbery Medal and *Jennifer, Hecate, Macbeth, William McKinley, and Me, Elizabeth* was named a Newbery Honor Book, both in the same year. With the books that followed, which generally took her a year to a year and a half each to write, more when extensive research was necessary, she continued to garner awards, culminating in her second Newbery Medal-winner, *The View from Saturday,* in 1997. In 1968 she moved to Jacksonville, Florida. Her children are now grown up and her picture books are written for and with her grandchildren. Besides her writing, she continues to enjoy art and gardening.

Major Works

The Second Mrs. Giaconda, Konigsburg's second historical novel, is based on true events in the life of Leonardo da Vinci and his apprentice, Salai, whom Leonardo called a liar and a thief in his notebooks, but whom Konigsburg credited with playing an essential part in humanizing the brilliant genius. In *Father's Arcane Daughter,* Konigsburg returns to the present with two over-protected children, Winston and his handicapped sister. Together, with the help of the older woman who pretends to be their once kidnapped sister, they manage to overcome the barriers that imprison them emotionally as well as physically. Konigsburg wrote a collection of short stories on a similar theme, children coping with growing up problems, in *Throwing Shadows,* which was nominated for an American Book Award. *Journey to an 800 Number* is about a snobbish boy from a fancy private school who is sent to live with his hippie father while his mother takes off on a honeymoon with her new stepfather. Through meeting a series of unconventional characters and making friends with Lily, an anonymous operator at an 800 number, and her sensible daughter, Max comes to see below the surface and appreciate people for themselves, including his father. Konigsburg's second Newbery-Medal winner, *The View from Saturday,* focuses on four sixth-graders chosen by their paraplegic teacher, Mrs. Olinski, to be the Academic Bowl team for their school. Told from the different points of view of each member of the team, the novel combines their unusual background stories with the incredible success of the team as they triumph over the other sixth-grade teams, the seventh-grade team, the eighth-grade team, and make it to the state finals. Typical of Konigsburg, the story combines humor, brilliant characterization, positive relationships, and young people discovering strengths they never knew they had.

Awards

Earning a Newbery Medal for *From the Mixed-Up Files of Mrs. Basil E. Frankweiler* and a Newbery Honor citation for *Jennifer, Hecate, Macbeth, William Mc-Kinley, and Me, Elizabeth,* both in 1967, Konigsburg also won the William Allen White Award, the Carnegie Mellon Merit Award, and was nominated for the National Book Award and American Book Award among other honors prior to 1973. Both *The Second Mrs. Giaconda* and *Father's Arcane Daughter* were selected as American Library Association Best Book for Young Adults; *Throwing Shadows* was named an American Library Association notable children's book and nominated for the American Book Award; *Journey to an 800 Number* was chosen by the Child Study Association of America as Children's Book of the Year; and *The View from Saturday* won the coveted Newbery Medal in 1997.

AUTHOR'S COMMENTARY

E. L. Konigsburg

SOURCE: "Ruthie Britten and Because I Can," in *Celebrating Children's Books: Essays on Children's Litera-* *ture in Honor of Zena Sutherland,* Lothrop, Lee & Shepard Books, 1981, pp. 62-72.

If I had gone to a school where Ruthie Britten wasn't, I would never have started writing children's books. Ruthie Britten could tap-dance and sing on key and was an only child, so she got private singing and private tap-dancing lessons and the lead in the sixth-grade play, and I didn't even get a speaking part. In all the world there was only one Ruthie Britten, and I got her. If I had gone to a school where she wasn't, I was certain I would have gotten the lead in the sixth-grade play, and I was certain I would have gone on to become a Broadway star. If I had gone to a school where Ruthie Britten wasn't, I would have been so busy being a famous star on Broadway, I would not have had time to write children's books.

Ruthie Britten is one reason why I write children's books. She is the only reason that has a proper name. The other reason why I write children's books is *because I can*.

I know some of the reasons why I can, and since a writer—except for authors of textbooks, diet books, and Hollywood biography or autobiography—is supposed to write about what he or she knows, and since I don't know what happened to Ruthie Britten, I shall write about why I can write for children.

When I was nine years old, my family moved from the small town of Phoenixville, Pennsylvania, to Youngstown, Ohio. Youngstown, Ohio, was a big city, big enough to be given boldface type and three complete sentences in our fourth-grade geography book.

In Phoenixville, I had just begun learning Hebrew; to me, Hebrew was God's language. The Jewish people have always relied heavily upon the word. Synagogues are solemnly free of mosaics, frescos, and other visual aids. I, like all my other classmates who were beginning to study Hebrew, made the sounds of the bold, black letters even when we didn't understand them. It wasn't necessary to understand what we were saying; God did. I memorized the important prayers in Hebrew as well as the Ten Commandments in translation. The Ten Commandments were the core of everything. They were firm and positive and absolutely without shadows, just like the big uppercase Hebrew letters. I was very pious. I was in a religious fever.

I didn't trust big cities.

Add to this black-and-white small-town world the blue laws of Pennsylvania, and you can see why I easily found sin in Youngstown, Ohio.

In Youngstown, Ohio, beer and wine were sold right in the grocery store within easy reach of pet food or cornflakes. In Pennsylvania a person had to go to a state liquor store to buy alcoholic beverages, and that was obviously more decent because Pennsylvanians kept liquor out of the hands of dog and breakfast lovers.

Also.

In Youngstown, Ohio, the movies were open on Sunday. They didn't obey the Sabbath, the Fourth Commandment: *Remember the Sabbath, to keep it holy*. They should have observed it even if they did it on the wrong day of the week.

Also.

In Youngstown, Ohio, they had a burlesque theater right on a side street of downtown.

I waited for sin to come into the classroom. I knew that it would. And I knew that Miss Mayer would bring it. I knew that, sooner or later, it would be she. Miss Mayer wore strange clothes, ones that didn't stop moving until long after she did. Furthermore, Miss Mayer had not come from Europe, she had *toured* Europe. Twice. She came to our classroom at irregular intervals to show us art. There were photographs of statues of Venus (no arms, no bra) and Apollo and other gods. There, in black and white, we could see how the pagans of Greece and Rome had made graven images. The Second Commandment clearly states: *Thou shalt have no other gods before Me. Thou shalt not make unto thee a graven image.* But, of course, long before I had moved to Youngstown, I knew that pagans not only ate too much but also didn't know enough to capitalize the word *god*.

At Christmas time, Miss Mayer came into our class and unfolded an accordion pleat of photos. When laid out flat, it showed the whole of a ceiling, the work of an Italian named Michelangelo.

I gasped.

There, in full color was Adam, absolutely stark naked with his you-know-what showing, his hand reaching out to receive the touch of life from none other than God. I knew it was God—not god, god, but God, God. The beard, the grandfather look, intense and worried. It was not a pagan god, but my very own dear God. A *graven image* of Him. There were more graven images. God creating the sun and the moon. God separating light from darkness. He was doing creation in full color just as my black-and-white word pictures had said he would.

"Where are these pictures?" I called out without raising my hand.

"In Rome. In the Vatican," Miss Mayer explained. "The Pope asked Michelangelo to paint the ceiling of this chapel called the Sistine."

"What's a chapel?"

"A place of worship, a small place, sometimes a private one."

"Is the Pope excused from the Ten Commandments?"

"Of course not," she answered. "No Christian is."

Miss Mayer then told us some facts about the artist's life. I remembered all the important ones: Michelangelo had been raised in a small town called Florence, and the Pope had called him to the big city, Rome. His early works, his small-town jobs, were statues, white marble photographed against a black ground: a David, the Virgin Mary holding her son. Only after he moved to Rome did Michelangelo dare to draw God. Only in Rome did he add color to his work.

I have now twice been to the Sistine Chapel. I have lain on my back and looked up into the face of God, high, high on the ceiling above. And even though there is no artist that I love more than Michelangelo, even though there are decades that separate that first view of the accordion-pleated reproduction from the crowds of the summertime Sistine, even though, even though—I still see the contradiction: a graven image in a house of God.

And it is because I can look up at that active, colored ceiling and still see a black-and-white contradiction, that I can write for children. And it is because I am aware, the grown-up part of me is aware, that no child growing up today can gauge the lack of color in my own growing up, that my stuff is readable.

When my daughter, Laurie, was four years old, she was dancing around our living room, a process that involved spinning and whirling and turning, holding her arms out and ultimately stubbing her finger against the wall. The finger grew swollen and discolored, and since I was temporarily without the *off* knob on my panic button (my husband was out of town), I took her to Baptist Memorial Hospital, the hospital on our side of town, the one where she had been born.

We arrived at the X-ray room, where a young technician, Clearasil still wet on his face, adjusted the machine for us. He moved the machine this way and that, and had her move her hand this way and that. As she pointed her finger downward and upward, following his instructions, she looked up at him and said: "You probably don't remember me, but I was born here."

I am still charmed when I think of her face, the quick sucking in of her breath before reminding him of her importance, wanting him to be certain that her birth had once been the focus of hospital life.

In 1968 when I won the Newbery Award, I flew to New York a day in advance of the announcement party, and I and my two suitcases and one cosmetic case and one dress on a hanger got into the taxi that would take me from the airport to the hotel. In the way of clothing, I was prepared for anything from warm weather (it was the end of February) to Truman Capote's black-and-white masked ball or a pot party for the Panthers at Lenny Bernstein's, in case he should ask.

"Where ya from?" the driver asked.

I told him not only where I was coming from, but also (eagerly) why. Furthermore, I told him that if he read *The New York Times* the next day, he would be able to read all about me. I, of course, had visions of his telling his wife and children that he had transported this very talented lady from Newark Airport to a midtown hotel, and the kids' asking him what was I really like.

The following day, *The New York Times,* the newspaper of record, for reasons entirely within its control, chose not to print news of the Newbery and Caldecott awards that year. Between my annoyance was my embarrassment that that taxi driver would think I had lied to him.

Believing that the taxi driver would give me longer thought than it took to transport me from Newark to a midtown hotel is similar, is it not, to my daughter's belief that her birth was long remembered and well noted at Baptist Memorial Hospital?

But because I retain this ability to see myself as the center of the universe, I can write for children. And because the adult part of me can see how absolutely ridiculous I am when I am doing it, my writings are readable.

Earlier this year I was visiting a woman whose son was an art student in New York. He was home for a short vacation and had with him two sketchbooks that his mother wanted me to see. She thought that he might find a career as a children's book illustrator. His were the only truly pornographic sketchbooks that I have ever seen. He told me that most of the pictures in them came from his head, but I'm convinced that some of them were done with mirrors. I thought that they had humor and technique, but I didn't think that the children's book world was quite ready for them. Because the pictures were difficult to comment upon, I asked him what he was going to do over the summer, that is, what he was going to do *besides* the activities recorded in the sketchbook. He said he was going to be a camp counselor, and I asked him if he was looking forward to it.

"Yes," he said, "I love children."

"I don't," I said.

His mother said that she was shocked at me, Elaine, and I don't blame her. I surprised myself when I first discovered it.

"Well!" I asked her, "You don't like all housewives, do you?"

And she said no, and I said aha! and I left.

I could, of course, have asked her if she liked all adults, but I didn't. And I could have asked her if she liked all old people, but I didn't. People who profess to love all children generally think that they love all old people, too. It seems to me that people who profess to *love children* really love *childhood* and, what's more, I think, they really love only one childhood—their own—and only one aspect of it, called *innocence*.

I had asked her if she liked all housewives, people engaged with various modifications, specifications, and success in essentially the same activities. I regard childhood as a stage of life, as housewifery is. Some parts are pleasant. Some are unpleasant. Some parts are learned and stay with you all the rest of your life and, like housewifery, a lot of it is just to be got through.

I have never liked all parts of housewivery, and I've never liked all housewives. I have never liked all parts of childhood, and I've never liked all children. And I have certainly never regarded housewifery as something precious or any practitioners of its arts as beatified.

Some people make better housewives than others. Some people make better children, and it is because I don't like all children that I can write for them. But it is because the adult layer of me enables me to understand (and even sometimes have compassion for) those that I don't like, that my stuff is readable.

Several years ago I was invited to a neighbor's house for a showing of slides of a trip they had made from New Jersey to Jacksonville via various historical landmarks. (I was certain that I had been invited out of revenge. We had recently returned from a trip to Africa with 740 slides, mostly of urinating rhinos and copulating lions; we always try for action shots.)

There they were—momma and two daughters in front of the White House gate.

Click. Momma and two daughters in front of the Washington Monument. *Click.* In front of the Lincoln Memorial. *Click.* Now we were at Valley Forge. *Click.* Momma and two daughters in front of Washington's headquarters. The entire presentation was done without comment except for Momma occasionally asking the girls, "Do you remember that?" "Nuh uh." "Nuh uh." Finally, *click.* There they were at the door of Washington's headquarters at Valley Forge, and the younger of the two girls spoke up. "Oh!" she said. "Yes?" Mother responded eagerly. "Oh," the girl continued, "I remember that dress."

I thought that was a pretty dumb thing to remember after her parents had gone to all the trouble and expense to come south anti-interstates. How awful of that little girl to remember something so trivial, something as incidental as a dress.

Why, I remembered Valley Forge. It was near Phoenixville, Pennsylvania, and my parents took me there a couple of times. I remember going to Washington's headquarters and I couldn't possibly remember what I wore. What I remember is seeing the quill pen General Washington had used. *The feathered pen,* I had called it. And now, years later, I can still recall my delight in that feathered pen. I don't remember much about those trips, but I do remember George Washington's feathered pen.

The nine-year-old in me who remembers a quill pen parallels the nine-year-old who remembers only a dress. And because I still see the incidental and delight in it, I can write for children. But because I am grown and I can see the greatness of Washington as well as his feathered pen, my stuff is readable.

Not very long ago I was having a dinner party and I wanted to serve veal parmesan. I went to the supermarket and rang the buzzer that said that that was what you should do if you want special service, and I waited for the butcher to come out. When he did, I asked him if I could please have some veal cutlet, sliced thin, and he said that he didn't have any veal, but that he was expecting some tomorrow, and that I should call up to see if the veal did arrive and order then. So the following day I dialed the number of the Winn Dixie, and I got a central operator who asked me my name and my phone number and said that she would deliver my message to the butcher and call me back and tell me what he said, and that *no,* I could not talk directly to the butcher, that it was against company policy, but that she would find out about the veal and tell me, and would I please wait by my phone? I said that this was a fine state of affairs. I said, (a) I have long known that the housewife's time is less precious than that of dentists or pediatricians, and (b) I know that because I have spent some of the best years of my life waiting in those offices, but (c) I thought our country had come to a sad state, a very sad state indeed, when (d) a housewife's time is less precious than a butcher's. (You see, I don't like all housewives, but I do believe in their civil liberties.)

I served chicken to my dinner guests.

When my son Ross was eleven, we went to Montgomery Ward to purchase a gear cable for his bike. It was our second trip there; the previous trip had been fruitless. They were out of the part, but they had assured us that they would have it by the week's end. It was now three days past that, and they still did not have it in. After asking the clerk a few questions, Ross discovered that a certain model of Sears bike was the same as his Montgomery Ward one. We went to Sears. He couldn't find the part on the shelves, so he found a clerk. *She* couldn't find the part on the shelves either. She said to wait a minute, and we did, and she brought us a different clerk, who also could not find the part. The different clerk told us to go to the third floor and order it. We went to the third floor and waited in line. When our turn came, the lady asked us if this was a catalogue order, and we said we didn't know, and she asked us what we wanted and we told her, and she said that she didn't know how to do that kind of order and that she would call someone who did, and the someone-who-did came and the first thing that she asked Ross was what was the model number of his bike, and Ross said that he didn't know and that it had come from Montgomery Ward anyway, and she said that he should come back when he had the number and that they would have to do a cross-reference and that she couldn't even take his order until he had the number to tell her.

Ross turned on his heels, threw up his arms, yelled, "Dum-my girl," and marched out of the store. I marched with him, proud to do so.

What I experienced at the meat counter and what my eleven-year-old son experienced at the catalogue counter was the same thing: an outsized sense of outrage. Because I have not lost my sense of outrage, because I am still furious at Ruthie Britten, I can write for children. And because I cannot yell "DUMMY GIRL," I do.

E. L. Konigsburg

SOURCE: *Forty Percent More than Everything You Want to Know About E. L. Konigsburg,* Simon & Schuster Children's Publishing Division, 1995.

Hello Mrs. Konigsburg.
Hello.

I thought that I might ask you some questions about your work and your life.
That's perfectly all right with me. I'll tell you everything except my age and weight.

Where do you live?
On the beach in North Florida. It's all right, isn't it, if I don't answer in complete sentences?

You're the writer, Mrs. Konigsburg. Let it be on your conscience. Do you have any children?
I have three. Their names are Paul, Laurie, and Ross. They have posed for the illustrations in my books. Laurie was Claudia and Ross was Jamie in *From the Mixed-up Files of Mrs. Basil E. Frankweiler.* Paul was Benjamin Dickinson Carr in *(George).*

Do they still pose for you?
No. Do you want to know why?

Because they are all grown up now, and they have children of their own who can pose for you.
Right you are! Samuel Todd, my oldest grandchild, is the star of *Samuel Todd's Book of Great Colors* as well as *Samuel Todd's Book of Great Inventions,* and Amy Elizabeth Konigsburg, my oldest granddaughter, is the star of . . .

I think I can guess. She is the star of *Amy Elizabeth Explores Bloomingdale's.* Are they your only grandchildren?
No. I also have Anna, Sarah, and Meg. But Sam and Amy are the only two who have their own books so far. Aren't you going to ask if I have a husband?

That was my next question. I wish you'd be more patient, Mrs. Konigsburg. Do you have a husband?
Yes, I do, thank you. My husband's name is David, and he is a psychologist. . . .

Did you always want to be a writer?
No. When I was in college at Carnegie Mellon Universi-

ty, I wanted to be a chemist, so I became one. I worked in a laboratory and went to graduate school at the University of Pittsburgh; then I taught science at a private girls' school. I had three children and waited until all three were in school before I started writing.

Where do you get the ideas for your books?
From people I know and what happens to them. From places I've been and what happens to me. From things I read. . . .

How did winning the Newbery for [*From the Mixed-Up Files of Mrs. Basil E. Frankweiler*] make you feel?
Proud and courageous.

Courageous? The Newbery Medal is an award for an outstanding contribution to children's literature. It is not given for courage. Are you getting your medals as mixed up as your files?
Not at all. I'm not saying that I won the Newbery Medal for *having* courage; I'm saying that winning the Newbery Medal gave me courage. Let me explain. After I won the Newbery Medal, children all over the world let me know that they liked books that take them to unusual places where they meet unusual people. That gave me the courage to write about Eleanor of Aquitaine in *A Proud Taste for Scarlet and Miniver* and about Leonardo da Vinci in *The Second Mrs. Giaconda.* Readers let me know that they like books that have more to them than meets the eye. Had they not let me know that, I never would have written *The View from Saturday.*

I'm glad you brought up the subject of *The View from Saturday.* Why did you write that book the way that you did—having four short stories right inside the novel?
It was the most natural thing in the world. I had started writing a story about a young man named Ethan Potter who boards a school bus the first day of sixth grade. The bus takes an unexpected turn, and a strangely dressed young man boards and sits down next to Ethan. He introduces himself as Julian and explains that his father is about to open a bed and breakfast inn—*a B and B.* At that point, I left my desk and took a walk along the beach.

When I write a book, I more or less start a movie in my head, and there I was walking along the beach, doing a re-run of what I had written. When I got to where Julian was telling Ethan about the B and B, I remembered that I had a story in my files—my mixed-up files—about a young man named Noah whose mother insists that he write his grandparents a bread and butter letter, a B and B letter. Fact: That made me remember another short story I had about a dog named Ginger that plays the part of Sandy in the play *Annie.* And that led me to another story about an Academic Bowl team.

Fact: Before I had finished my walk, I realized that all those short stories were united by a single theme. Taken together, they reinforced one another, and the whole became more than the sum of the parts.

I knew that kids would love meeting one character and then two and three, and I also knew—because I had learned it from them—that they would think that fitting all the stories together was part of the adventure.

So how did you feel when you found out that you had won a Newbery Medal for *The View from Saturday?*
Filled with joy. And that's a fact. I knew I had been right about the spirit of adventure shared by good readers. . . .

Do you have any hobbies?
I love to draw and paint. I love to read and walk along the beach. I also love movies.

What makes you feel bad?
Eating too much chocolate, reading trash, and letting dust balls gather under the sofa.

What makes you feel good?
Eating too much chocolate, reading trash, and letting dust balls gather under the sofa.

Really, Mrs. Konigsburg, will you try to be serious?
I am very serious about chocolate.

Let's get back to your books.
I am very serious about those, too.

People tell me that your books don't always appear to be serious.
I consider that a compliment. Thank you. . . .

I guess that's about all I had to ask. I don't know how to end this interview.
Try saying "Thank you."

Thank you, Mrs. Konigsburg.
You're welcome Mrs. Konigsburg.

GENERAL COMMENTARY

Joan B. Friedberg

SOURCE: "E. L. Konigsburg: A Sense of Self," in *Children's Literature Association Quarterly,* Vol. 4, No. 4, Winter, 1980, pp. 32-4.

The LC cataloging summary for E. L. Konigsburg's most recent book, *Throwing Shadows,* reads "Five short stories in which young people gain a sense of Self." Western culture has become increasingly concerned with the search for a sense of self, a search made possible in part by the relative comfort and leisure of middle class life and made conscious in part by the investigations of psychology. We encourage our children to take pride in the uniqueness of their selfhood and yet we expect them to temper the demands of the ego; we want them to maintain the integrity of the self while at the same time learning to live in harmony with a mixed group of other selves equally devoted to wholeness and integrity. So we present our children with a complex challenge. It is a challenge that will occupy them all their lives, until death quiets what Melville has called one's "own inexorable self."

That phrase of the cataloguer, "gain a sense of self," can be applied not only to Konigsburg's latest publication but to all the books preceding it. To gain a sense of self implies thoughtful response and growth, qualities which are significantly lacking in the experience of some characters in both adult and children's literature. Nancy Drew, for example, doesn't have to *gain* anything except a solution to her current mystery. Heaven forbid that she change or grow in understanding of self or in anything else—indeed, part of her charm for young yeaders is in the undemanding predictability that precludes growth and change.

Konigsburg's first two published children's books came out in 1967. The second and probably the best-known of all her novels, *From the Mixed-Up Files of Mrs. Basil E. Frankweiler,* won the Newbery Medal in 1968. Since then she has published eight more books. This is an extraordinary accomplishment in terms of output alone, but in addition the books represent an accomplishment in range. Konigsburg is a writer who is continually trying new subjects and new techniques. She has written historical fiction (*A Proud Taste for Scarlet and Miniver* and *The Second Mrs. Giaconda*), a suspense story (*Father's Arcane Daughter*) a novel which examines the alter ego [(*George*)], a story with a black co-heroine (*Jennifer, Hecate, Macbeth, William McKinley, and Me, Elizabeth*), and one with a Jewish hero (*About the B'nai Bagels*). She has used both first- and third-person narrative. In *A Proud Taste for Scarlet and Miniver* she develops a framing device and tells the story through four narrators who sit in heaven and look back at their experience. In *From the Mixed-Up Files of Mrs. Basil E. Frankweiler,* a frame is provided by Mrs. Frankweiler's narrative addressed to her lawyer. She likes suspense as provided by withheld information—for example, in *Father's Arcane Daughter* and *From the Mixed-Up Files*.

Konigsburg is an experimenter, then, not afraid to try different techniques and unusual subject matter, but through this diversity of approach and material run certain constant themes. She is looking at honesty, both towards oneself and towards others; at the meaning and challenge of responsibility; at the question of identity; at relationships with parents, with siblings, with friends and peers. Like George Eliot, she sees that our actions have consequences and that we are responsible for the effects of what we choose to do. Konigsburg is a moral writer—not because she presents exempla of behavior with the hope of instructing her readers but because the worlds of her books, however diverse, include a moral dimension.

For example, Ben in (*George*) has to wrestle with very real and urgent questions about honesty and responsibility. George, the little man who lives inside Ben and who has helped him through much of his growing up so far, has deserted him. What should he do when he suspects that the boy who has been his friend and hero is making dope in the school lab? He has to take action on his own, and once he does, George returns to him and helps him make other choices. Eventually, Konigsburg suggests, George will merge more completely with Ben; their voices will become indistinguishable but Ben will always be aware of this part of his self which sees clearly, comments acidly, and helps him act independently without reference to unworthy considerations. Similarly, in *About the B'nai Bagels,* when Mark realizes that his Little League team has won an important game through deception, he has to decide whether to expose the cheating or keep quiet. He chooses to speak out—not an easy decision. At the end of the book, he is looking back at his Bar Mitzvah which has just taken place and thinking about its significance:

> According to Hebrew Law, now I am a man. That is, I can participate fully in all the religious services. But I figure that you don't become a man overnight. Because it is a becoming; becoming more yourself, your own kind of tone-deaf, center-fielder, son, brother, friend, Bagel. And only some of it happens on official time plus family time. A lot of it happens being alone. And it doesn't happen overnight. Sometimes it takes a guy a whole Little League season.

Father's Arcane Daughter treats a different kind of dishonesty from that figuring in *(George)* and *About the B'nai Bagels.* Here the parents, especially the mother, fail to be honest in the way they see Heidi. Unable to face the reality of their daughter's physical limitations and problems, they pretend that everything is normal and allow Heidi to wrap herself up in babyishness and self-indulgence; her lack of progress and skill in certain areas can then safely be seen as immaturity rather than impairment. It takes an outsider to cut through the web of deception, a web in which the narrator, Heidi's older brother Winston, is also entangled. Konigsburg here provides a complex irony because Heidi is saved from the kind of life to which the self-deception of her parents would have condemned her by a different kind of deception. The outsider who forces the family to re-evaluate Heidi is Martha posing as the long-lost daughter Caroline. Martha/Caroline is a different kind of duality from Ben/George because she is an imposter, but just as with Ben/George, duality makes possible eventual integration and healthy growth—of Heidi, of Winston, of Ben.

Yet honesty alone doesn't always make happy relationships happen. When the boy in the short story "The Night of the Leonids" does some self-absorbed arithmetic and announces that he'll be middle-aged before such a shower of stars again, his grandmother is offended and slaps him. He has to recognize the stark implications of what he has just said—honest arithmetic isn't called for at this moment—before they can be amiable friends again. And Salai in *The Second Mrs. Giaconda* is seen as a charming, dishonest rascal who prospers through deception and never gets his comeuppance. Konigsburg is herself too honest to pretend that truth is always easy, that it is the same for everyone, or that those who don't practice it will invariably be punished.

Characters who struggle with questions of right action, as Konigsburg's do, will be confronting also the question of how one assumes responsibility. It is Ben's feeling of responsibility about the secret activity in the school lab that precipitates his moral crisis in *(George)*. Winston in *Father's Arcane Daughter* resents having to spend Thursday afternoons amusing his thumbsucking, uncoordinated, spoiled little sister, but beneath the irritation is a sense of obligation; he refuses to pretend her handicaps away as their parents do. The moral dilemma of *About the B'nai Bagels* involves the responsibility of the individual to the team and to telling the truth even when doing so seems to hurt the team.

Interacting in relationships with parents, with other adults, with siblings, with friends and peers, the most successfully drawn Konigsburg characters grow and change—and that growth makes possible the sense of competence and triumph so satisfying to the child reader. In *From the Mixed-Up Files of Mrs. Basil E. Frankweiler,* for example, Konigsburg combines the familiar themes of the runaway and the Robinson Crusoe adventure, putting the story in an unexpected setting (how many run-aways before Claudia have headed for an art museum?) The author shows a relationship between sister and brother which grows during the course of the adventure: having chosen Jamie because he was quiet, good for a laugh, and rich, Claudia comes to value him as a collaborator. Konigsburg also shows how Claudia, who ran away from home to make a statement about injustice and to escape monotony, goes back with a certain sense of having come to terms with herself and with her world. Jennifer and Elizabeth, in Konigsburg's first book, spend months in the elaborate make-believe world that Jennifer has created—a world analogous to the Robinson-Crusoe-like island of the Metropolitan Museum in that it is secret and self-contained, cut off from other human beings. When Elizabeth fails the flying ointment test, her misery forces her to recognize things about Jennifer that she hasn't seen before. Both of the girls can leave the witch world that Jennifer has created for them and, in becoming themselves, can also become friends.

Konigsburg is not for me a uniformly successful writer. For example, I find the mother in *About the B'nai Bagels* a caricature—a flaw shared by almost all the characters in *The Dragon in the Ghetto Caper*. She sometimes uses repetition in a way that makes language act as caricature: Edie in *The Dragon* repeats "Harry—he's my husband—" like a verbal tic. *Altogether, One at a Time* is interesting in that not many such collections of short stories are published for children (one wonders why not; it would seem an ideal form for young readers) but for me it is marred by a sameness of voice and narrative technique from one story to the next and by a poor arrangement: it would have been better to alternate male and female storytellers. *A Taste for Scarlet and Miniver* does a good job of making history accessible to young readers but Konigsburg's other historical fiction, *The Second Mrs.*

Giaconda, might have offered more background information in a preface or afterword. But even when she falters, Kongisburg remains an intriguing writer both for what she is attempting stylistically and for content. Thus in *Altogether, One at a Time,* she explores moral issues: prejudice and pride in **"Momma at the Pearly Gates,"** cruelty in **"Inviting Jason,"** thoughtlessness and the responsibility that love demands in **"The Night of the Leonids."** Konigsburg does her readers the honor of taking them seriously.

Throwing Shadows is, like *Altogether, One at a Time,* a collection of short first-person narratives. The collection as a whole works better than the earlier book. The characters are more fully explored and defined, the voices more sharply differentiated. As in most of Konigsburg's writing, there is often a note of wry self-mockery, there is sharp observation, there is humor, there is well-paced narrative that keeps the reader with the story. While the setting and characters differ widely, there is thematic coherence. Each story, whatever its plot, is also about giving and learning. In **"On Shark's Tooth Beach,"** Ned gives pompous President Bob a shark's jawbone that his mother has called the Nobel Prize of trophies because in watching the older man's face he's been made to think about his own. "If his face was a movie called *Jealousy and Greed,* I didn't like the words I could put to mine." By giving up this coveted treasure, Ned becomes more fully himself, a person of perception and understanding. In **"At the Home,"** Phillip finds himself almost accidentally making an oral history tape at an old age home. As he tapes reminiscences, he learns something about aging, something about stereotyping, something about boredom, and a lot about giving. Avery in **"The Catchee"** hasn't often been on the giving end. As a catchee, he's had things done to him, usually unpleasant things that land him in the principal's office or with a department store security guard. His older brother, congenitally a catcher rather than a catchee, is able at the end to give Avery something infinitely valuable—a picture of himself as a person made honest and brave by his position as a catchee. And thus Avery gets a new sense of self.

Young readers of Konigsburg's fiction will find stories with suspense and humor, often told by child narrators who give the child's eye view of other people and events. They will also get something they may not be conscious of. Konigsburg's readers will typically be on the verge of adolescence, that turbulent period of conflict and doubt. In creating characters with a capacity for self-knowledge and growth, Konigsburg sets before her readers the possibility that they too can find out who they are, can develop strength and selfhood, and can make moral choices with which they are pleased to live.

D. Thomas Hanks, Jr.

SOURCE: "The Wit of E. L. Konigsburg: 'To One Dog Squatting' from the Metropolitan Museum of Art," in *Studies in American Humor,* Vol. 5, No. 4, Winter, 1986-87, pp. 243-54.

Wednesday, January 4th, 1989. I was sitting in the waiting area at American Airlines Gate 17 at the Dallas-Fort Worth Airport. I had an hour to wait, and was reading to pass the hour. I suddenly burst into laughter—into guffaws, in fact. Red-faced, and smothering my continuing laughter, I stood up and hastened down the corridor to the snack bar, retreating from the wondering gazes of my neighbors in the waiting area. I had been reading one of E. L. Konigsburg's latest books, *Journey to an 800 Number.*

The passage that caused my undignified outburst was the narrator's, Bo's, account of receiving his name. Bo writes that his father, Woody, had promised Bo's mother to "name me according to an old Indian custom"—that is, to name him for "[t]he first thing he saw" outside the hospital of Bo's birth. Led outside, "[t]he first thing my father saw was a rainbow. . . . My real name is Rainbow Maximilian Stubbs." Bo adds, "Both my parents always regarded it as a good omen that the first thing that Father saw after I was born was a rainbow. So do I. After all, there was a chance that I could have been called One Dog Squatting."

The joining of the celestial image of the rainbow, of the semi-Indian (and therefore semi-dignified) form of the final phrase, and of the earthy image of the squatting dog, typifies Konigsburg's wit. She continually, and successfully, joins "seemingly . . . disparate things," in an "ingeniously humorous manner," an operation at the heart of wit (*The American Heritage Dictionary,* "wit"). She has been displaying this wit since her earliest publications.

Konigsburg won both the Newbery Honor Award (the Newbery "second prize") and the Newbery Award itself in 1968 for her first two books, both published in 1967. They were *Jennifer, Hecate, Macbeth, William McKinley, and Me, Elizabeth* (Honor Award), and *From the Mixed-up Files of Mrs. Basil E. Frankweiler* (Newbery Award). The plots of both books, though very different from one another, depend upon witty joinings of incongruous elements. In the first, *Jennifer,* the plot seems to involve witchcraft; the title itself shows the disparate elements yoked together in the book (moreover, the two main characters are a black girl and a white girl). In the second book, *Files,* the two main characters—Claudia and her brother Jamie—do not so much run away *from* home as they run away *to* The Metropolitan Museum of Art in New York, where they take up residence for a time.

In short, her first books showed the pattern Konigsburg has thus far followed in all her books: a witty conjunction of incongruous elements, elements ranging from the basic plots of her books through character interactions and right up to a remarkable level of word-consciousness. A survey of her works demonstrates that wittiness, and suggests that Konigsburg expects a great deal from her audience.

Wit at the Plot-Character Level

Konigsburg's plots in her non-historical books always center upon a situation at least partially witty—witty, again, in the sense of juxtaposing incongruous or disparate elements. I have already noted that witty conjunction in the plot elements of her first two books.

Equally incongruous are the elements of the plots of her other non-historical books: *About the B'Nai Bagels* centers upon a Jewish mother managing a Little League baseball team; *(George)* concerns the yoking of the protagonist, Ben, with a little man who lives inside him; *The Dragon in the Ghetto Caper* involves, as you might imagine, dragons and not one but two ghettos, one black and the other a wealthy suburb; *Father's Arcane Daughter* concerns, it seems, an attempt to establish the identity of a daughter kidnapped years ago—but, as eventually appears, the daughter the establishment of whose identity is central to the book was not kidnapped; *Journey* combines a camel and a camel-driver father with its determinedly preppie protagonist; and *Up from Jericho Tel* involves a boy and girl interacting with the ghost of Tallulah Bankhead (and with the ghosts of her Dalmatians).

Konigsburg's plots, in short, exemplify wit. Inside those plots, moreover, one finds a multitude of wittily-described character interactions.

In *Files,* one interaction recurs frequently: Claudia tries to correct her brother Jamie's English, and Jamie resists. A representative passage, and one which clearly shows Claudia as fussbudget and Jamie as triumphant individualist, appears early in the story. Jamie tells Claudia he needs the compass he brought to find their way "'[o]ut of the woods.'"

"What woods?" Claudia asked.

"The woods we'll be hiding out in," Jamie answered.

"Hiding *out in?* What kind of language is that?"

"English language. That's what kind."

"Who ever told you that we were going to hide out in the woods?" Claudia demanded.

"There! You said it. You said it!" Jamie shrieked.

"Said what? I never said we're going to hide out in the woods." Now Claudia was yelling, too.

"No! you said '*hide out in.*'"

"I did not!"

Jamie exploded. "You did, too. You said, 'Who ever told you that we're going to *hide out in* the woods?' You said that."

"O.K. O.K." Claudia replied. She was trying hard to remain calm, for she knew that a group leader must never lose control of herself, even if the group she leads consists of only herself and one brother brat. "O.K.," she repeated. "I *may* have said *hide out in,* but I didn't say the *woods.*"

"Yes sir. You said, 'Who ever told you that . . . '"

Claudia didn't give him a chance to finish. "I know. I know. Now let's begin by my saying that we are going to hide out in the Metropolitan Museum of Art in New York City."

Jamie said, "See! See! you said it again."

"I did not! I said, 'The Metropolitan Museum of Art.'"

"You said *hide out in* again."

"All right. Let's forget the English language lessons. We are going to the Metropolitan Museum of Art in Manhattan."

Jennifer likewise contains wit. For example, at one point Elizabeth has just taken part in a "magical" ritual with Jennifer outdoors in the snow-covered park. She has had to take off shoes, socks, and boots and go barefoot in the snow for the ritual; afterwards, she has dried her feet with her socks and put on her shoes and boots over her bare feet. Having forgotten her mittens, she has put her socks on her hands. Then she goes home, where she tracks water and snow into her mother's kitchen. Her mother, seeing the puddle, says "'Take off those boots,'" which Elizabeth does. Wearing her socks as mittens, she has forgotten her feet are bare of socks.

> My mother noticed. When I had removed only the left shoe, she didn't quite believe that I had actually put on shoes and boots without socks. She waited until I took off the right shoe, too, to make sure. Then she said . . . "Have you ever thought that most people wear their socks on their feet, not on their hands?"
>
> I shook my head, "Yes."
>
> She said, "Will you repeat after me: socks are for feet; mittens are for hands."
>
> I said, "Socks are for feet; mittens are for hands."
>
> She said, "Say it again."
>
> I said, "Socks are for feet; mittens are for hands."
>
> She said, "Now please tell me, where are your mittens?"
>
> I said, "In my sock drawer."

A later book, *About the B'Nai Bagels,* is Konigsburg's one book of suburban Jewish humor. The central humorous element of the book is the situation brought about by the protagonist's mother, Bessie, becoming the manager of his Little League baseball team. The humor of this unlikely conjunction is evident, but Konigsburg underscores it in a central scene: Bessie's players want to know why they have to have a woman manager instead of the man all the other teams have. She immediately replies:

> "The reason why you have a lady manager is because chlorophyll is a catalyst that enables a plant to use the energy of the sun to convert carbon dioxide and water into sugar and oxygen."
>
> Long, long pause. . . .

Finally, Hersch said, "But, Mrs. Setzer, that about chlorophyll is just a fact of life."

Mother didn't give his sentence a chance to cool off before she pressed in hers, "And so is your having a lady manager! It's just a fact of life, and you have to face it. You have to face facts." . . . She shrugged her shoulders and smiled at the boys. "Now that we have that over with, can we play ball?"

Her stratagem works—the boys burst into laughter and accept her as their coach.

Bessie Setzer's devotional life in *Bagels* is also funny as it yokes together normally disparate elements. In fact, her religious devotion at first appears solely comical, owing primarily to her praying habits. Bessie spends much of her time in the kitchen and does much of her praying there. Whenever moved to pray she looks upward and addresses the Deity. For young Mark, the protagonist, this produces some confusion: "Up until the time I began Sunday School, I thought that [God] lived in the light fixture on our kitchen ceiling." (Later events, I should note, show that Bessie's devotion is as sincere as its practice is comical; Konigsburg does not mock Bessie's religious practices.)

Another example of Konigsburg's wittily-described situations occurs after Mark has gone to Barry Jacobs's home for dinner. Mark observed the Jacobs family's practice of discussing a stimulating topic—often a current event—during dinner. Mark decides to initiate the practice in his own home:

> The next night at our supper at home I said, "What do you think will happen if the Russians get to the moon first?" My fork fell onto the floor.
>
> Dad answered, "Please pass the herring."
>
> I started to pass the dish when it slipped. Only two pieces slid to the floor, and I put them in the garbage and immediately wiped the spot with a sponge as I had always been taught to do.
>
> "Well," I repeated, "What do you think will happen if the Russians get to the moon first?"
>
> Mother said, "Save some of the potatoes for Spencer; he said that he'd be late home."
>
> I helped myself to potatoes; they were buttered and parsleyed and only one slipped off the dish. I put it on my plate after I picked it up. I reached for a roll and knocked over my milk. "Now about the moon," I persisted as I was cupping my hands to catch the dripping and as Mother was running for some paper towels.
>
> Dad looked up and said, "Mark, why don't you try eating on the floor and see if you can drop things up to the table?"

In a later book, *The Dragon in the Ghetto Caper,* a recurring situation involves the fractured syntax of Edie Yakots, an eccentric young housewife in the protagonist's wealthy suburban addition, "Foxmeadow." As the narrator, Andy, reports at one point, "Edie always talked in confetti" to strangers. Andy's first exposure to her syntax happens as he visits her home in the process of selling a painting of a dragon. He has just said he likes her house:

> "We thank you very much," she said. "My husband is out of town. That's where I want to hang him. His name is Harry," she said, pointing to a spot over the sofa. "How much would it take?"

In her uncommon syntax, Edie has thanked Andy for his compliment, told him her husband's name and that he is out of town, asked Andy how much he wants for the painting, and told him where she wants to hang it. Edie is not always easy to follow. As Andy tells her later, "'Half the time you talk as if you were born without conjunctions.'"

Dialogue is one of Konigsburg's favorite devices for displaying her characters' wit, as has perhaps appeared above. Dialogue becomes trialogue in *(George)*. Benjamin Dickinson Carr and Howard Carr, the two brothers of the story, often provide diverting dialogue. George, however—the "little man" inside Ben—does much of the wit. For example, when the two (three) walk home together after school early in the book, Howard asks:

> "How are you today, George?"
>
> George answered [in a deep voice coming from Ben's mouth], "Exhausted."
>
> Howard asked, "How do you think Ben feels, lugging a heavy bookcase on the outside and you on the inside?"
>
> "I am no harder for Ben to carry around than a slight case of indigestion," George replied.
>
> "Speaking of indigestion," Howard said, "what's for supper tonight?"
>
> "Tonight," George answered, "our Busy Little Homemaker, known to one and all as Mother, will provide us with frozen pot pies, instant mashed potatoes, and canned peaches. The last, she calls *dessert*."
>
> "Tell me," Howard urged, "do you eat when Ben does? Ben sure eats a lot."
>
> "Don't get personal," George answered.
>
> Howard appealed to Ben, "I noticed that you sure eat a lot, Ben. You eat a whole heck of a lot. Is that because you're eating for George, too? You sure eat a lot. Do you know when George eats?"
>
> Ben moaned, "Aw, c'mon Howard. I don't pry into what goes on inside of you."

More witty dialogue takes place in *Up from Jericho Tel* in an exchange between Jeanmarie Troxel and Malcolm Soo, the two main characters. Jeanmarie and Malcolm have just found—they think—a dead Dalmatian. They set out to bury it. Jeanmarie suggests he ought not be buried "'naked,'" to which Malcolm responds,

> "I'll start digging while you go home and get a plastic garbage bag."
>
> "A garbage bag! You can't treat a dead Dalmatian like garbage!"
>
> "Okay. I'll start digging while you go home and get a plastic burial shroud."

Similarly humorous plots, incidents, and dialogue appear in all Konigsburg's books. In each work, her wit is the chief characteristic of the action.

Wit and Words

Another of the chief manifestations of Konigsburg's wit appears in her use of words, as when in *Jennifer* Elizabeth characterizes herself as a "fussy eater", saying about her not eating eggs, "Even when I was a little baby before I knew better, I knew better."

Another example comes from *Files:* When Mrs. Frankweiler first meets the two children, who think themselves anonymous to her, she asks, "'Are you the children who have been missing from Greenwich for a week?' . . . They both looked as if their hearts had been pushed through funnels."

Konigsburg enjoys metaphors, as appears above. In *(George)* she describes the end-of-vacation attitude of students as inertia—"the tendency of a student body at rest . . . to stay at rest." Another example is the narrator's comparison between Charlotte Carr's kitchen habits and those of Marilyn Carr, Ben and Howie's mother:

> Mrs. [Charlotte] Carr knew about germs, but she did not believe in them the way that Marilyn, the second Mrs. Carr, did. Marilyn was a home economics major and regularly waged anti-germ warfare. In Marilyn's house the milk cartons were put away so promptly that they never sweated, and the mayonnaise was treated like some hopelessly insane relative that was never allowed out. Ben was certain that Marilyn Carr would call the riot squad if she ever looked inside Charlotte Carr's refrigerator. Nothing was covered, and only things that made puddles were laid level.

As the preceding passage shows, Konigsburg also likes puns and other forms of word play. They appear throughout her work; an example of her puns appears in *(George)* when George comments on Charlotte Carr's homemaking abilities:

> [Concerning Thanksgiving dinner:] "Please tell the Queen of the Maytag that the oven will not roast the turkey unless it happens to be turned on. . . . I swear that if that lady, our mother, had a General Electric oven, it would get broken to corporal."

The cleverest of her puns appears in *Father's Arcane Daughter*. Heidi, the handicapped daughter of the Carmichael household, has just called her mother "'Mummy.'" Winston asks, "'Why don't you call our mother. *Mother*'? A mummy is something all stiff and wrapped in bandages.'" Three pages later their mother returns home wearing a yellow scarf tied tightly under her chin. Heidi climbs into her lap and works at untying the stubborn knot of the scarf:

Heidi's finger tugged and pulled. Mother sat there, wearing a smile like a cosmetic, as Heidi unwrapped her Mummy.

The pun on "Mummy" presages the stiffness, even the deadness, which will characterize Mrs. Carmichael throughout the book.

Other puns appear throughout all Konigsburg's works; one final example from *Up from Jericho Tel* must suffice: Tallulah says about a man who proposed to her, suggesting that he was in love with the part she played in a movie, not with her: "'I told him that I, Tallulah, was much more than the sum of my parts. . . .'"

Wordplay of another sort appears in **"On Shark's Tooth Beach,"** one of the short stories from *Throwing Shadows*. Late in the story, when Ned has found a "trophy" consisting of several sharks' teeth still attached to part of its jaw bone, he thinks of his tooth-finding rivalry with "President Bob" and reflects,

I had never seen such a trophy. I felt that the spirit of the Lord had come mightily upon me, like Samson. Except that I had the jawbone of a shark and not the jawbone of an ass. And I wanted to smite only one president, not a thousand Philistines.

Wordplay likewise appears in the historical novels. In *A Proud Taste for Scarlet and Miniver,* for instance, appears a description of William by his granddaughter, Matilda:

"Before he invaded England in the year 1066, my grandfather was called William the Bastard because he was. After the year 1066, he was called William the Conqueror because he was."

Following logically from her fondness for puns and other wordplay is Konigsburg's ability to say something freshly—to use words in ways one has not seen before. An example comes from another of the short stories from *Shadows,* **"The Catchee,"** which involves a young boy, Avery. Fresh wording first appears when Avery is caught illegally directing traffic with a school-patrol flag. He says he is sharply addressed by "'a voice that wore a uniform.'"

Another example follows from Avery's being black, a fact that barely figures in his characterization—one does not even learn he is black until more than halfway through the story. At that point, while Avery is looking for colorful panties for his mother's Christmas present, he says of himself in the ladies'-wear department, "'I had not counted on how pastel it would be. In my black skin, blue jeans, and maroon sweater, I felt like a walking exclamation point in a sea of whispers.'"

More such fresh wording appears in *Daughter,* in Winston's comment on an ineffectual test of his putative half-sister, Caroline, by his mother: "'Mother's last testing of Caroline resembled . . . a frontal attack with cuticle scissors.'" Still more freshness appears regularly in *Up from Jericho Tel,* where from the second chapter on the narrator begins each chapter with an epigraph composed of one of Tallulah's witticisms. An example:

"The difference between going to school and getting an education is the difference between picking an apple and eating it."

Similar wit appears when Tallulah interrupts Malcolm as he continues a lengthy explanation of chlorophyll and energy cycles:

"Now, now, Malcolm, let's not get carried away. Good explanations are like bathing suits, darling; they are meant to reveal everything by covering only what is necessary."

A major subset of Konigsburg's wit appears in a strain of earthy wit running throughout her later books. In *(George),* for example, one reads in the first sentence that George, the little man who lives inside Ben, "used foul language." George does use what young people often see as foul language: he says "damn" several times, he calls Marilyn a "jackass," and when Howard must be persuaded to attend a private kindergarten called "The Wee House in the Woods," George provides effective persuasion by doubling "just one word in the school's name," which makes it sound ridiculous enough that Howard is willing to try the school out. Nor is George the only earthy one: when kindergarten-aged Ben discusses with Charlotte Carr a starfish's anatomy, "he said something for tentacles that made Mrs. Carr laugh out loud."

More bathroom humor like "The Wee House in the Woods" appears in *The Second Mrs. Giaconda,* where one of the two major characters, Salai, comforts the other major character—Leonardo da Vinci—by saying of the academics whose bookishness Leonardo envies,

"Why, those guys . . . would rather read about a horse than go look at one. . . . Why, those guys could get peed on by a horse, and they wouldn't know how they got wet if they couldn't look it up in a book."

Konigsburg also puts earthiness into *Daughter,* where when asked, "'What did you learn in school today?'" Winston retorts, "'In school today . . . I learned that flatulence is a polite word for fart.'" He adds that he also learned that "'you can get a monstrous hickey from a Kirby vacuum cleaner. Freddie Houser has one on his neck; he claims it came from a passionate maid.'"

Another piece of sexual wit appears early in *Tel*. Jeanmarie tells Malcolm she wants to have theaters named after her. She then asks Malcolm what he wants to have named after him. His response: "'A planet, an atomic particle, and ten bastard sons.'"

The crowning example of this sexual strain of earthy wit appears in *800 Number,* when Bo and his father Woody go to Las Vegas. The star of a show there is an old friend of Woody's and has engaged his camel, Ahmed, for all her performances. The star—Trina Rose—greets Woody, then asks, "'How's that short-haired, long-legged beast of yours? I'm referring to Ahmed, of course. Nothing private intended.'"

In short, Konigsburg incorporates remarkably witty wording—witty wording ranging from wordplay through originality in metaphor to sexual innuendo—into virtually all her books.

Conclusion

The foregoing survey of wit in Konigsburg's books shows her continual joining of disparate/incongruous elements in all her writing, from the level of plot to the level of diction. The examples I have cited—which are only representative, and far from exhaustive—should also show that Konigsburg has a high opinion of her audience.

She has said that her audience is the "middle-aged child"—that is, children aged six to twelve ("The Middle-Aged Child is Not an Oxymoron"). Her plots usually involve one or two children within that age range, so her audience can, I suppose, "identify" with the characters, and thus with the plots. The level of language, though, would be considered by many far above what six- to twelve-year-olds could comprehend.

Konigsburg would argue that such a slighting evaluation of "middle-aged children" errs dangerously. She has argued that language not only expresses our culture to our children, but that it also expands the perimeters of their culture. In her books, she has said,

> I . . . make an effort to expand the perimeter of [children's] language, to set a wider limit to it, to give them a vocabulary for alternatives, perhaps. Because language not only tells you the shape of a culture; it helps shape it. [We] are at the mercy of the particular language which has become the medium of expression for our society.

Konigsburg, clearly, has decided to expand the cultures of her young readers. Her joining together of incongruous elements will expand their minds, as her witty use of words will expand their language. I am not sure Konigsburg's books are written for all six- to twelve-year-olds; I am sure they are written for children who can appreciate wit—and grow from it.

One final example, from *Up From Jericho Tel* (her latest book), demonstrates her use of wit to expand the cultural sensitivity of her readers. Tallulah reports a dialogue between Nicolai, a ventriloquist, and his "Russian" puppet, Anna Karenina, and quotes the puppet's response to the idea that members of the United Nations are discussing "'the business of the nations'":

"How can be business? Everybody say how poor he is. Just like big house party. Everybody dress up, everybody arrive in limousine, everybody kiss and shake hands in front and say terrible things in back, everybody talk, and nobody listen. Is house party, I tell you. Is house party."

A moment later the puppet learns that in Russia "'everyone serves the party.'" She asks, "'Who are guests if everybody serve?'"

> Nicolai: "Your whole country is now part of the Communist Party. No one is a guest, and no one is a host."

> Anna: "Is no fun at such party."

TITLE COMMENTARY

THE DRAGON IN THE GHETTO CAPER (1974)

Publishers Weekly

SOURCE: A review of *The Dragon in the Ghetto Caper,* in *Publishers Weekly,* Vol. 206, No. 10, September 2, 1974, p. 70.

When Andy draws pictures, they always turn out to be dragons, no matter what they started as. When Mrs. Edie Yakots buys one of his drawings, she becomes his patron, then, to Andy's disconcerted surprise, his sidekick. Young Mrs. Yakots has a much older husband who usually isn't around, and also a weekly charity, driving Sister Henderson around the ghetto every Thursday to collect her "donations." Andy goes along, too, and neither of them has the least idea what they're *really* doing (despite Andy's ambitions to become a detective) till they get caught. This author has a solid record so far (*From the Mixed-Up Files of Mrs. Basil E. Frankweiler* became a Newbery winner and a movie) and this novel, with its charm, sly wit and insights about dragons and their place in life, shouldn't hurt it a bit.

Ethel L. Heins

SOURCE: A review of *The Dragon in the Ghetto Caper,* in *The Horn Book Magazine,* Vol. L, No. 6, December, 1974, pp. 692-93.

The author's abundant talent is fruitlessly expended in her latest book. Andrew Chronister lives in a swank, sheltered, suburban community with his parents and his older sister, who is about to be married "and making a very big fuss about it." In or out of art class, Andy compulsively paints or sketches dragons; but he insists that his only real ambition is to be a "cool, tough, famous detective" with a sidekick to help. He strikes up an offbeat friendship with Edie Yakots—a lonely, deceptively slow and simple young married woman. Edie takes him in her car on mysterious weekly missions into the black ghetto, where, unwittingly or not (it is never made clear), she is involved with an illegal numbers lottery. Ultimately, the boy innocently participates in a crime instead of solving one. Andy, an intelligent eleven-year-old, makes statements and asks questions about ghetto life that are incredibly naïve, if not downright insulting; and the inhabitants speak not black English, but an outmoded, stereotyped dialect. The author's wittiness becomes a bit too clever, and the reiteration of her theme—that dragons are merely difficulties to be overcome—turns into a tiresome homily. Questions are implied but never properly answered, and the book leaves a dubious, disagreeable aftertaste.

Margery Fisher

SOURCE: A review of *The Dragon in the Ghetto Caper,* in *Growing Point,* Vol. 18, No. 2, July, 1979, p. 3541.

Andrew Chronister, almost twelve, hero of **The Dragon in the Ghetto Caper**, has the bounce and confidence of an only child in a well-to-do literate family and a manner, cocky and at times insolent, which supports his determinations to become a famous detective. This manner conceals the respect and admiration with which he views Mrs. Edie Yakots, a highly individual young woman whom he adopts as his Watson but who is continually stepping out of line. In fact, although he does not like to admit it, Edie does a great deal to correct prejudices which life in a carefully screened suburb have encouraged. When Andrew joins her in driving Sister Henderson to her weekly meeting with her colleagues in the local church he regards their passenger as an inhabitant of a black ghetto with a separate "ghetto culture" and is affronted when Edie assures him that his homeground, Foxmeadow, is just as much of a ghetto. The shock of finding that Sister Henderson is helping in an illegal lottery hurts his pride as an aspiring detective but leaves him with a healthy resolve to look rather more carefully at his obsession about dragons. The author's elliptical humour and the stiletto effect of her character-drawing require intelligent and attentive readers, so that although her book concerns a boy of rising twelve it is only the rare child of this age who will follow its close, elusive argument; I would more readily offer it to someone in the mid-'teens who is prepared to make some effort in order to discover the pleasure in the novels of this stylish and original writer.

THE SECOND MRS. GIACONDA (1975)

E. L. Konigsburg

SOURCE: "Sprezzatura: A Kind of Excellence," in *The Horn Book Magazine,* Vol. LII, No. 3, June, 1976, pp. 253-61.

[*The following excerpt is from a speech Konigsburg gave at the Fourth Annual Festival of Children's Books on April 12, 1975, in Fresno, California.*]

When people ask me why I write for children, I usually give them the answers they most want to hear. For example, when the ladies who wear flowered hats and who go to afternoon teas ask me, I tell them that I write for children because it's so damn much fun. That's what they thought all along, anyway. I always add the "damn" because writers are supposed to be profane; writers for children are allowed to be only slightly profane so that's why I say "damn" instead of "goddam." When my in-laws—who still refer to me as "whats-er-name"—ask, I tell them that I write for children because I have a very limited vocabulary. And they like that because it is what they believed all along, anyway. To a chance dinner partner, the gentleman on my left, the executive making polite dinner conversation with Dr. Konigsburg's wife, I say that I write for children because my husband won't allow me to write hard-core pornography. He likes to hear that; it means that, working woman though I am, the man of the family is still boss.

But now I would like to give the smartest possible answer. Smartest because it is the real one, and I would like to tell you why I write for children by tracing very specifically the roots of my last book, **The Second Mrs. Giaconda**.

The whispered beginnings of that book go back to George Washington's Birthday in 1963. In that year you could ask any schoolchild in the northeastern part of the United States, where we lived then, "When was George Washington born?" And the child would tell you, "February 22, 1732." Nowadays, he would answer that George Washington was born on the third Monday of every February, and so was Abraham Lincoln. Back in 1963, George's birthday was a school holiday that fell during the period when the *Mona Lisa* was on loan from the Louvre to the Metropolitan Museum of Art in New York. The grand lady was receiving, and I and my entire family were in the reception line behind a police barricade in the cold 25° weather, stamping our feet to keep them warm because we certainly weren't moving very much. It took us forty-five minutes to climb the steps to get a glimpse of the lady. And we got just that—a glimpse. We were herded in and out, just a little more slowly—a little, mind you—than in and out of the doors of the subway. Because of the cold weather and the brief reception, my family vocalized on the way home about how Madonna Lisa wasn't worth our trip from New Jersey, let alone hers from France. It had been my idea to go to see her, so I came to my own defense as much as to Lisa's, and I said finally, "Well, it was free," and my husband reminded me of the parking fees, the bridge tolls, the five giant pretzels and the six bags of roasted chestnuts that we managed to consume during that forty-five-minute climb up the stairs. I was quiet and resentful for the rest of the way home. And for years to come. I don't carry a grudge well, but I carry it forever—or almost.

On October 26, 1965, the *New York Times* announced that the Metropolitan Museum of Art had acquired a wonderful bargain. It had obtained at an auction a statue for $225, and the statue was possibly the work of Leonardo da Vinci or of his teacher, Andrea del Verrocchio. When I used that piece of information as well as the experience of waiting in line to see a famous work of art in my book *From the Mixed-Up Files of Mrs. Basil E. Frankweiler* I changed the possible sculptor of the mystery statue from Leonardo to Michelangelo. Because I liked Michelangelo better, I didn't resent him at all.

In 1967, the National Gallery of Art in Washington, D. C., probably paid between five and six million dollars for a portrait of Ginevra de' Benci, the only painting by Leonardo in the United States. I read with relish John Canaday's assessment of the deal. He questioned whether Ginevra was worth it, and I did, too. I continued to ask that question until a few years ago when I went to Washington and saw her.

Now we're up to 1969, and my husband and I made our maiden trip to Italy. The trip was a Michelangelo pilgrimage, really, but there in the Uffizi, I came within arm's length of two of Leonardo's paintings. They were early works, and one of them, *The Annunciation,* held me spellbound—grudgingly spellbound. There is a quality in that painting that one experiences after a summer rain in a temperate climate, a feeling of freshness, of newness, that suits the mood of an annunciation with a kinship that borders on the eerie. When we went to Milan, we visited the refectory of Santa Maria delle Grazie. As I gazed at that wall, it happened again. In the presence of the magnificent ruin of *The Last Supper,* I once again felt touched by some magic—some magic that not only superseded my pigheadedness but also overcame all the triteness that comes from the myriad copies and the roadside interpretations done on black velvet.

What quality does Leonardo have that comes through in the original work and not in the reproductions? Something shrinks—something besides size—when his work is reproduced. Something organic is lost. I stood there before that great work and wanted to bite my tongue for a joke I had made at a friend's house where I had seen a reproduction on her wall and had given it the subtitle, "Separate checks, please."

So I returned from that trip to Italy with respect but not yet love for Leonardo. New love comes slowly in middle age. But love came at—of all places—an estate sale. A friend of mine who is an antique dealer was given the contents of an estate to dispose of. The sale had to be private and by appointment because the property belonged to the wife of a man whose name is notorious; his brother had committed murder fifty years ago in a case so famous that the details of it and the names associated with it will not die. I found my way into the study of the house, and there, all alone, I pored over the books. All the lovely coffee-table books were being sold by size. The largest were four dollars each, and I bought several, one of which was called *The Horizon Book of the Renaissance.* It contained an essay that led me first to a love of Leonardo and then to writing a book about him.

The essay was written by the scientist Jacob Bronowski,

who speculates that Leonardo, at the age of thirty-one, left Florence and went to Milan because he was uneasy in the rarefied, super-snobbish, intellectual atmosphere that prevailed in the Florence of the Medici. Leonardo was not a bookish man; he was not a Neoplatonist believing in ideas instead of in observation. In his notebooks one finds heated defense of his beliefs, which is all right, but there is also an almost adolescent scorn for the very bookish. Leonardo calls men fools who will not trust their own senses. Leonardo needed approval; he needed admiration. And he was not emotionally equipped to fight it out in Florence. So he chose to go to Milan where he had less competition, where he was indisputedly the Master.

Bronowski's article made Leonardo into something much more than a genius; it made him a human genius. Every great love requires some imperfection in the love object, and Leonardo's pride was a weakness that I found endearing.

I began to study Leonardo's life and work, and that study took me, ultimately, to the question with which I begin *The Second Mrs. Giaconda*.

The book begins:

> Why, people ask, why did Leonardo da Vinci choose to paint the portrait of the second wife of an unimportant Florentine merchant when dukes and duchesses all over Italy and the King of France as well, were all begging for a portrait by his hand? Why, they ask, why?
>
> The answer to that lies with Salai.

Yes, Salai. Let me set the stage.

The year was 1492 in Milan. I picked the year 1492 because it was a very good year. If you remember your history, Columbus discovered America on the second Monday of every October of that year.

First, meet the Duke of Milan. His name was Ludovico Sforza, and he was forty years old. He was also called *Il Moro* because his complexion was dark, and he resembled a Moor. Like Othello, he was an excellent lover and soldier. He rose to his position not through a direct line of descent but through an L-shaped move and maybe a few judicious murders. But remember this was the age of Machiavelli, and Il Moro was a product of his times. His court, the Court of Milan, was rich, richer than Florence; it was *nouveau riche,* a bit too lavish in its display and a bit too loud in its self-celebration. The Court of Milan was to the city of Florence as Los Angeles is to the city of New York: more spread out, flashier, more experimental, and just a little defensive about being so.

But Il Moro had an eye for quality; he was a fine patron of the arts. Not only had he good taste and vast powers of organization, but he was also capable of minute attention to detail. Milan, under his rule, was proclaimed the new Athens. He gave free rein to talent; he had an openness to new ideas. It is no wonder that Leonardo stayed with him for seventeen years. In 1492, Il Moro was in love with a beautiful lady named Cecilia Gallerani; he had Leonardo paint a portrait of her. Not only was she beautiful, but she was also intelligent and accomplished.

About a year before, Il Moro had married a young lady who was just seventeen—the daughter of the Duke and Duchess of Ferrara. Her maiden name was Beatrice d'Este; she was small, dark, and plain. Her older sister was Isabella d'Este, beautiful, talented, and precocious. Il Moro had wanted Isabella, not Beatrice. He had asked for her hand in marriage, as was the custom, when she was only a child. His request was ill-timed: It was two weeks too late. Isabella had just been promised to Gonzaga, the Duke of Mantua, a much younger man. So Il Moro, anxious to cement political ties with the House of Ferrara, consented to marry Beatrice, his second choice.

Poor, pitiful Beatrice, married to a man twenty-three years her senior, who was in love with another woman. No sooner had their wedding ceremony been performed than her husband left his bride at the church and rushed back to Milan. He had to arrange for her reception, he said; but Cecilia was in Milan.

Now meet Isabella d'Este. She has been called The First Lady of the Renaissance, but I think she paid someone to call her that; she was forever commissioning poets. She was acquisitive and spoiled; she was an accumulator rather than a collector. Leonardo did a drawing of her in charcoal, but she could never get him to commit it to oils. She nagged and nagged through letters and messengers; she was an inveterate letter writer.

There was Beatrice, overshadowed by her husband's beautiful mistress as she had been overshadowed by her sister at home. But then something happened—something strange and wonderful and terribly romantic. Sometime after he married her, Il Moro fell in love with his wife. It is recorded fact. Letters tell how attentive he became to her, how he spoke endearments and kissed her in public. But why? What made him appreciate her? What made him send Cecilia packing?

Leonardo was in Milan when the duke fell in love with his own wife. Knowing the influence of Leonardo on the tastes, manners, and style of those who dealt with him, I couldn't dismiss his presence in the court of Milan as being entirely passive. Leonardo was there and so was Gian Giacomo de' Caprotti—called Salai. He was a young thief whom Leonardo took on as an apprentice in the year 1490. In his notebooks Leonardo complains of Salai; he calls him *glutton, thief, mulehead, liar.* He lists items that Salai stole and the dates on which he stole them. Yet, Leonardo kept this young man with him for more than twenty years. He helped pay his sister's dowry, and he remembered him in his will. Why did Leonardo do that? There is a simple explanation; Leonardo da Vinci was a homosexual. His relationship with Salai, as Kenneth Clark so delicately puts it, "was of the kind honoured in classical times, and partly tolerated in the Renaissance, in spite of the censure of the Church."

> **Just as Salai lacked reverence toward important works, so do young readers. They provide me with a wild element, and that is why they are a challenge to write for. And because they are that challenge, I like to write for them.**

But you see, I am glad that I write for children. For that explanation of his use of a young boy will never do. It is simply not enough; it is not deep enough. It does not tell the whole truth. If I were writing for adults at this moment in American literary history, I would concoct a sordid, best-selling tale of this relationship, but, you see, I know that children need a deeper truth. You cannot explain a twenty- or a twenty-five-year relationship on the basis of sex alone. Anyone who has been married for even half that length of time knows that. Long relationships that withstand annoyances and independent bad habits and that stand up to time are based on mutual need. What could Salai supply to Leonardo's life—Leonardo, the complete, the total, the Renaissance man? But was Leonardo complete? I don't think so.

Study his scientific work, and I venture that you will come away more impressed by its breadth than its depth. He was, I believe, a supreme gadgeteer. He was such an empiricist, so much the anti-Platonist, that he would never generalize. For example, he came close but did not discover the circulation of the blood. He came close but did not discover the wave theory of light. He came close, but he did not discover the laws of gravity. Leonardo lacked the ability to make a giant leap; he was too inhibited. He was too much the experimenter and too little the thinker. He could look at something in a totally accurate way, for I believe he was the world's greatest observer, but he could not synthesize his observations. In science Leonardo was not a genius; geniuses always make quantum leaps.

Leonardo sometimes made that leap in art. Not always, but often. Why did some of his works of art have the quality of genius and others not? What is it that is lacking, for example, in his last painting, a study of St. John the Baptist? An inhibited, self-conscious, androgynous St. John. He had written a book of rules, his famous *Treatise on Painting,* and he was conscientiously following these rules.

Even in his great commission for Il Moro—the giant statue of a horse—he ultimately produced a work that was stupendous in size but was not great art. And in the recently rediscovered notebook in Madrid, there is a drawing which shows Leonardo's design for the casting of the horse in bronze, a drawing which shows again his weakness for and love of gadgetry.

I think I know what is lacking in these works of art. They are missing a wild element; everything in them is tight and controlled. Nothing swings. Every great work of art, every work of genius, has a wild element. Some artists carry that wild element within them. Michelangelo did; Rembrandt did; Beethoven did; but Leonardo did not.

Leonardo, the bastard son, the uneducated, defensive, self-conscious, inhibited genius, needed Salai to supply that irreverence, that wild element, that all-important something awful that great works of art have. Salai gave Leonardo a necessary sense of unimportance. We all need a child to do that; Salai in many ways was a perpetual child.

In the court of Milan, Leonardo was employed by Il Moro on many projects. He was Il Moro's resident wizard. Design a war machine, Maestro Leonardo; design costumes for a pageant, Maestro. Paint the ceilings in my new rooms; paint the wall of the refectory; paint the portrait of my good friend, the lovely Madonna Cecilia Gallerani. Leonardo did those things. And after Ludovico and Beatrice had been married a few years, and Beatrice was pregnant with their third child, Il Moro called Leonardo to him and requested that he paint another portrait—a portrait of one Lucrezia Crivelli, Il Moro's new mistress. Leonardo painted Lucrezia. He painted the ceiling, and he painted the wall of the refectory; he painted Il Moro's mistresses. He did a sketch of Isabella, but he never, never painted Beatrice. Why? Why did he never paint Beatrice? Her early death was not the reason. Beatrice died at the age of twenty-two, but there had been time enough before she died for him to have painted her. Shortly after Beatrice died, Milan was invaded by the French, and Ludovico was exiled. Leonardo went to Florence, stopping en route in Mantua to visit Isabella. It was then that he did the charcoal drawing of her.

When he returned to Florence after having been away for seventeen years, his reputation, partly as a result of the success of *The Last Supper,* was at its peak. He was bombarded with requests for paintings. Kings, bishops, princes, and duchesses—most especially the Duchess Isabella—were begging for a portrait from his hand. He promised them all, and he delivered to none.

And yet, during these years back in Florence, he spent three years painting the second wife of an unimportant Florentine merchant. And he did the work entirely by himself; he allowed no apprentice to touch it.

This is the point at which I begin my book, **The Second Mrs. Giaconda**. Look at Madonna Lisa Giaconda. Can you look at her without awe? Can you look at her without feeling bored by the countless reproductions of her face? Can you look at her without resenting having had to wait in line outside the Metropolitan Museum of Art on a cold February day? Well, if you write for children, you have a chance for a fresh look. You have a chance to introduce some unjaded, but awe-free, young readers to the mysteries of this lady.

What a joy to write for people who are not sick of seeing the *Mona Lisa,* people who can see her as a woman who knows that she is not pretty and who has learned to live with that knowledge. This is a woman whose acceptance of herself has made her beautiful in a deep and hidden

way, a woman whose look tells you that you are being sized by an invisible measuring rod in her head, a measuring rod on which she alone has etched the units. A woman who knows how to give pleasure and how to give pain; a woman who knows how to endure, whose very unimportance allowed Leonardo to swing loose and free with the composition. Is she possibly what Beatrice would have become had she lived? Is this possibly the portrait of Beatrice that Leonardo never did, a surrogate Beatrice without the royal clothes and the regal jewelry?

Young readers give me what Salai gave Leonardo: a highly developed sense of unimportance. We match up quite well. Just as Salai lacked reverence toward important works, so do young readers. They provide me with a wild element, and that is why they are a challenge to write for. And because they are that challenge, I like to write for them. Should you ask why I write for children, I would tell you that writing for them makes me research history and human emotions. Writing for children makes me research deeply, beyond and beneath the slick, sexy explanations you first come across.

And writing for children demands a certain kind of excellence: the quality that Salai helped to give to Leonardo, the quality that young readers demand, as Renaissance viewers demanded it—that works of art must have weight and knowing beneath them, that works of art must have all the techniques and all the skills; they must never be sloppy but must never show the gears. Make it nonchalant, easy, light. The men of the Renaissance called that kind of excellence *sprezzatura.*

And because Salai appreciated this quality, Leonardo kept him with him. And because children demand it subliminally and appreciate it loudly, and because I do, too, I write for children.

Shirley M. Wilton

SOURCE: A review of *The Second Mrs. Giaconda,* in *School Library Journal,* Vol. 22, No. 1, September, 1975, p. 121.

The riddle of the Mona Lisa is solved in a most ingenious reconstruction of the middle years of Leonardo da Vinci's life. Under Konigsburg's deft hand the bare bones of history are fleshed out with some remarkable characters, especially the street urchin, Salai, who becomes servant and companion to Leonardo, and the Duchess Beatrice of Milan, the young wife of Leonardo's patron. The interaction of these personalities and their influence on the master are the focus of the novel and finally explain why, in later years, Leonardo refused commissions to paint Duchesses and great ladies and chose, instead, to grant immortality to an unknown merchant's wife, **The Second Mrs. Giaconda**. Based upon the known facts of Leonardo's life and times, Konigsburg uses this information, not just as a framework for the retelling of history, but as living clay from which a thoroughly entertaining and believable story is molded. The result is a unique bit of creative historical interpretation, and a slice of Renaissance life artfully and authentically illumined.

Ethel L. Heins

SOURCE: A review of *The Second Mrs. Giaconda,* in *The Horn Book Magazine,* Vol. LI, No. 5, October, 1975, pp. 470-71.

Reflecting on the known facts of Leonardo da Vinci's life, the author—from whom one has learned to expect the unexpected—posed to herself an irresistible question and answered it in a logical, wonderfully inventive work of fiction. "[W]hy did Leonardo da Vinci choose to paint the portrait of the second wife of an unimportant Florentine merchant when dukes and duchesses all over Italy . . . were all begging for a portrait by his hand?" At the end of the fifteenth century, the master was living in Milan, working at painting, sculpture, and engineering for his patron, Il Moro, the Duke. Leonardo was aloof and brilliant, always observing, always probing, often failing to complete his projects. Salai, his youngest apprentice, was a beautiful street urchin; he was also a mischievous, unconscionable liar and thief. For political reasons, the powerful Duke had married the plain, unglamorous Beatrice d'Este. It was fun-loving Salai who first learned to appreciate the keen, sensitive girl, and it was she who perceived that the rude, irreverent boy was filling a void in Leonardo's character. "'He needs a wild element. . . . All great art needs it: something that leaps and flickers. . . . He is too self-conscious. When he has an important commission. . . . [h]e strives, not to let himself go, but to be perfect.'" Ultimately Salai, after Beatrice's early death, realized that Madonna Lisa Giaconda, the merchant's wife, would be the ideal subject for Leonardo—"the one importantly unserious element, the one wild thing" necessary to ignite his genius. With a quiet style, punctuated by occasional bursts of energy and passion, the story is subtle, witty, and penetrating. Deceptively simple and ageless in appeal, its fate with young people may well depend on the persuasiveness of a perceptive adult.

Margery Murphy

SOURCE: A review of *The Second Mrs. Giaconda,* in *Best Sellers,* Vol. 35, No. 8, November, 1975, p. 259.

Leonardo da Vinci is the subject of this remarkable story. The author has written a book of fiction, using true events to answer the question of why Leonardo chose to paint the portrait of the second wife of an unimportant Florentine merchant, when dukes and duchesses, even the King of France, were all begging for a portrait by his hand. The answer lies with Salai, a young boy who was taken as an apprentice into Leonardo's studio in Milan. In his notebooks Leonardo calls Salai "liar, thief, glutton, mulehead." Yet Leonardo was devoted to him, remembers him in his will. Salai becomes an important influence in the life of the plain, young Beatrice d'Este, married to the powerful Duke of Milan. The development of the characters of Salai

and Beatrice and their influence upon the genius Leonardo make this novel not only a good, fascinating story but a remarkable philosophical and psychological study of what contemporary writers refer to as "person-hood." The author had been a chemist. One can be grateful that she left the science laboratory for the less predictable laboratory of the human psyche. She has given some brilliant flashes of insight into the art of living and painting. Her descriptions of life in an Italian city such as Milan in the fourteenth century are convincing. Participation at the festivals, the court-life, the studio becomes a real experience. Her gift is the understatement, the vitality she extracts from the most common place. This is a book for adults, but one would hope it would have a special fascination for the intelligent teen-ager. Several good reproductions of Leonardo's paintings that pertain to the story are included.

Zena Sutherland

SOURCE: A review of *The Second Mrs. Giaconda,* in *Bulletin of the Center for Children's Books,* Vol. 29, No. 5, January, 1976, pp. 80-1.

An interesting fictional treatment of Leonardo da Vinci focuses on his pert young apprentice Salai, often amusing but—alas—not always truthful. Much of the story has to do with the familial jealousies and bickerings of Beatrice d'Este and her mother and sister; Salai was devoted to Beatrice and was a great stimulus to Da Vinci. He supported his master in his firm resistance to painting the portrait of Beatrice's beautiful and importunate sister Isabella. The theory is advanced here that Salai will persuade the artist (for the story ends before the painting is done) to paint the wife of the humble merchant Giaconda because the woman reminds him of the dead Beatrice, whom he, Salai, adored. However highly fictionalized, this is a warm and intimate picture of Leonardo, of the court circles in which he moved, and of the role of an artist in those circles in Milan and Florence. Reproductions of some of the artist's work are included.

M. Hobbs

SOURCE: A review of *The Second Mrs. Giaconda,* in *The Junior Bookshelf,* Vol. 41, No. 1, February, 1977, p. 39.

The lively iconoclastic guttersnipe Salai, who became servant to Leonardo da Vinci, is the angle character of this pleasant attempt by Mrs. Konigsburg to suggest the master's motive for painting the new wife of a Florentine merchant, in preference to such important sitters as Isabella d'Este, the haughty villainess of the book. Her unhappy sister Beatrice, neglected by her Sforza husband for his mistresses, is sympathetically drawn, and so is Salai's devotion to her, his calculating mind and his gradual but never complete social education by Leonardo. His slangy Americanisms jar, however, because out of keeping with the reverential tone of the body of the book. The background is well created: the business transacted in a fifteenth-century artist's studio, and the social structure of an Italian dukedom. Inevitably, 'The Last Supper' gets painted during the book, and the text is followed by black-and-white reproductions of some of the works mentioned.

FATHER'S ARCANE DAUGHTER (1976)

Publishers Weekly

SOURCE: A review of *Father's Arcane Daughter,* in *Publishers Weekly,* Vol. 210, No. 3, July 19, 1976, p. 132.

The author has won many awards for her extraordinary novels; here, she's at her best in a brilliantly sustained mystery. In the early 1950s, the home of a Pittsburgh tycoon (Charles Carmichael) is disrupted. A woman of 35 arrives and claims to be Carmichael's daughter Caroline, kidnapped 17 years earlier. Winston, young son of the second Mrs. Carmichael (Grace), describes the polite hostility of his mother toward the newcomer and the life led by him and his small sister, Heide. Her real name is Hilary; she's uncoordinated, hard of hearing and Winston's charge. Both children are virtual prisoners, Grace's excuse being that she's protecting them from kidnappers. Her real reason, and the effects Caroline has on the lives of all, are the bedrock of a haunting, marvelously developed plot.

Zena Sutherland

SOURCE: A review of *Father's Arcane Daughter,* in *Bulletin of the Center for Children's Books,* Vol. 30, No. 1, September, 1976, p. 12.

Beginning this unusual story, and alternating with the longer sections of the narrative, are passages of dialogue in italics. The speakers are not identified until the very end of the book, providing an element of surprise that adds to its suspense. They are speaking in the present, referring always to the unfolding tale told by Winston, son by a second marriage of a very wealthy man, and older brother to Heidi, an awkward, often uncouth, and apparently retarded child. Winston is torn between his protective love for Heidi and his resentment at the demands she makes of him and that their mother makes on Heidi's behalf. Then comes father's other daughter, Caroline, who has been missing for seventeen years. Kidnapped, she had disappeared. *Is* the woman who claims to be Caroline genuine—or is she an imposter who knows that a large fortune is at stake? Winston's mother is dubious and jealous, but Caroline passes every test and is accepted by their delighted father. The children love her, but her stepmother, irritated by Caroline's efforts to have Heidi tested and helped, decides that the child should no longer visit her stepsister. The conclusion is strong and dramatic, the characterizations and relationships drawn with depth and perception, and the story line original and beautifully crafted.

Ann A. Flowers

SOURCE: A review of *Father's Arcane Daughter,* in *The Horn Book Magazine,* Vol. 52, No. 5, October, 1976, p. 504.

Winston Carmichael and his sister Heidi are the children of the second marriage of a wealthy Pittsburgh industrialist. Their every moment is supervised and guarded; the chauffeur and the maid accompany them everywhere when they are out of school because their much older half-sister Caroline had been kidnapped and presumably killed seventeen years earlier. Then a woman claiming to be Caroline appears and effects a great change in the lives of the children. Although it is not made clear at the outset of the story, Heidi is a severely handicapped child, almost totally deaf and walking only with difficulty. Her shallow, socialite mother spoils her and pretends she is normal; her reserved, aristocratic father takes little part in her upbringing. Only Caroline, who perceives that Winston is imprisoned by his unwilling responsibility for Heidi, is able to free both of the children by strongly recommending arduous training for Heidi and education suited to her high intelligence. There are some unnecessary obscurities; each chapter is preceded by a conversation many years later between Winston and his sister (*which* sister is not clear until near the end)—conversations that heighten the suspense but take away from the impact of a serious, thoughtful, and surprising story.

THROWING SHADOWS (1979)

Zena Sutherland

SOURCE: A review of *Throwing Shadows,* in *Bulletin of the Center for Children's Books,* Vol. 33, No. 1, September, 1979, p. 10.

Once again Konigsburg demonstrates that her versatility in approach and concept is equalled by her consistency in polished writing and depth of perception. Each of the five stories in this collection is told by a young person, and in each the protagonist gains insight into his or her own character, although such knowledge emerges in different ways. Each throws a shadow, and the shadows are distinct and unique. Ned, in **"On Shark's Tooth Beach,"** finds that he cannot find satisfaction in outwitting a greedy collector, a pathetic old man; in the end he gives his avid rival a prize specimen and knows for the first time his own capacity for compassion. In Avery's story, **"The Catchee,"** a natural victim of circumstance comes to a recognition of the fact that his experiences of being a shy and quiet victim have had an annealing effect. There's enough action to provide narrative flow, but the strength of the collection is in the provocative depth of the stories.

Marilyn R. Singer

SOURCE: A review of *Throwing Shadows,* in *School Library Journal,* Vol. 26, No. 1, September, 1979, p. 141.

E. L. Konigsburg displays her virtuosity in this book of short stories. She creates with equal sureness five situations so diverse, one wonders how they came from the same hand. A boy, his Thai mother and American father, and an insensitive retired college president jam together in a fishing camp on the Florida coast; a young Black boy faces his life as a "catchee" with the help of an older brother and a sense of humor; a young Equadorian tour guide and a 12-year-old Otovalo Indian come to understand and trust each other; an old people's home turns into a treasury of stories when a boy with a tape recorder meets a fiery Hungarian woman; an oppressed small-town Southern widow develops into a capable business woman with the help of necessity, her son and a pair of antique dealers whose knowledge she surpasses without letting them know. There is a wealth of information on a variety of subjects: hunting fossilized shark teeth; life in an Equadorian weaving village; Hungary during World War II and the Communist takeover; antiques; etc. The stories are equally valuable on the personal level as all the characters—young and old—struggle and grow, try to understand themselves and each other. There are no solos here, mostly duets and trios, as characters bounce off, surprise, and ultimately help one another, though the help sometimes comes in strange ways. The stories each occupy about 30 pages but have the spacious quality of a novel; characters and events have a chance to develop naturally rather than seeming pushed along. Another good one from the files of E. L. Konigsburg.

Paul Heins

SOURCE: A review of *Throwing Shadows*, in *The Horn Book Magazine*, Vol. 55, No. 5, October, 1979, p. 535.

Five short stories, each one told in the first person, relate the significant experiences of four boys and one girl with other people—chiefly adults—in diverse localities. Ampara, a tour guide in Ecuador, tells of her discovery of the talents of an enterprising Indian boy; Avery, an American Black child, reveals how it was his fate always to be doing something wrong—even when he didn't plan to. Two of the narratives are essentially flashbacks: Phillip learned in a nursing home the story of an ugly old Hungarian woman who had evaded the clutches of the Nazis and the Russians; William helped his widowed mother get the better of a pair of self-styled antique dealers. All of the accounts are written in a perceptively humorous and occasionally brash style, and four of the narratives present realistic vignettes of life in the United States. The best story, however, is the first—**"On Shark Tooth's Beach"**—in which Ned's conversation and dealings in Florida with an old retired Michigan college president ironically reveal the astuteness and the dignity of the young son of an American Vietnam veteran and a Thai mother.

Cynthia King

SOURCE: A review of *Throwing Shadows*, in *The New York Times Book Review*, December 9, 1979, pp. 34-5.

Throwing Shadows is a collection of five seemingly unrelated stories, each with a different narrator, told in the first person. They remind me of William Saroyan ("My Name Is Aram") and Langston Hughes ("Simple"), with their high humor, easy pace and sharp social comment. In each story a child encounters an adult, and both are changed. All are serious, thoughtful and extremely funny. Also they are moralistic and sprinkled with aphorisms.

Ned's mother, who knows she cannot visit her native Thailand, says, "It is more important to love where you're at than to love where you're from." Ampara, an Ecuadorian tour guide says, "It is sometimes necessary to use unnecessary words like *thank you* and *please* just to make life prettier."

In **"At the Home,"** the best and most complex of the stories, Miss Ilona, a paralyzed Hungarian refugee in the old folks' home, tells young Phillip how she turned bad into good and that being ugly saved her life. But when she says that the people in the home speak a common language, "It's called boring," Phillip tells her, "You have to overcome your prejudice about old people."

Overcoming prejudice is one of the by-products of these tales. Avery, in **"The Catchee,"** learned when he was 6 that "the world is made up of two kinds of people: the catchers and the catchees." Avery committed the "federal offense" of putting trash in the letter box instead of the litter box because he "had not yet learned the short vowel sounds." Later Avery was apprehended by the police in a department store trying to buy underpants for his mother's Christmas present. Feeling conspicuous, he says, "In my black skin, blue jeans and maroon sweater. I felt like a walking exclamation point in a sea of whispers."

E. L. Konigsburg continues to be an exceptional writer. These people are lovable and real. They speak convincingly in Spanish/English, Hungarian/English, or deep Southern English. However, there is a common voice here that will be familiar to anyone who has read Mrs. Konigsburg's other books. It is the voice of the wry observer, a skeptic who, in a side comment or a line of dialogue, can make you laugh while illuminating the poignancies, inequities and paradoxes of contemporary life.

Today's young readers are lucky. This is E. L. Konigsburg's 11th book since 1987, when *From the Mixed-Up Files of Mrs. Basil E. Frankweiler* was published, and it is as good as her best.

📖 ***JOURNEY TO AN 800 NUMBER*** (1982; published in England as *Journey by First Class Camel*, 1983)

Zena Sutherland

SOURCE: A review of *Journey to an 800 Number*, in *Bulletin of the Center for Children's Books*, Vol. 35, No. 7, March, 1982, p. 133.

Two centuries ago, this might have carried such a subtitle as "The Humanization of a Snobbish Boy, as He Meets a Variety of People on His Travels and Learns to Appreciate Them." The story is told by Maximilian, whose mother, remarried, has gone on her honeymoon and sent Max to stay with his father. Insistent on wearing the wool blazer with his private school's crest in the sweltering heat of the Southwest, Max feels superior to his father, his father's way of life (Woody travels with a camel from fair to convention to shopping centers, offering rides) and his father's trailer, to say nothing of his father's odd friends. However, prig though he is (and this is revealed by Max, who is the narrator), Max is also very bright and perceptive. By the time he's ready to go home, he's learned a lot about making allowances for other people, a lot about loving Woody, and perhaps most of all about himself. The title refers to Max's eagerness to keep in touch with a girl he's met (he's a young adolescent, she's a pre-teen, and they are an enchanting pair) whose mother works for catalog firms at a toll-free number. Konigsburg has a remarkable flair for including off-beat characters who are eccentric but believable, and the story has her usual combination of originality of conception, felicity of style, and suffusion of wit.

Kirkus Reviews

SOURCE: A review of *Journey to an 800 Number,* in *Kirkus Reviews,* Vol. L, No. 5, March 1, 1982, pp. 275-76.

The loosening up of Maximillian Stubbs, who goes off to stay with his father Woody while his mother is off honeymooning with a rich man near retirement age. Draped in the blazer of the exclusive prep school he'll be entering in the fall, Max is not enamoured with his father's itinerant mobile home, or with the camel his father takes to fairs and conventions to sell rides. His father, in contrast, is a footloose, unambitious, earthy type, well liked by other carnival regulars such as Mama Rosita and her kids at the taco stand, and affably tolerant of his snobbish son. Max has occasion to regret his own icier stance toward the taco family; but it is later, sharing a luxury suite with singing star Trina Rose, that Max comes to appreciate Woody. For insight on his own airs, Max gets some help from lovely Sabrina, about eleven, who collects clippings on freaks and keeps popping up because she spends vacations crashing conventions with her mother Lilly, who spends the rest of the year answering an 800-number telephone service. Sabrina and Lilly's masquerade is an obvious device and an unlikely hobby, but diverting anyway; and if Woody and his friends are more predictably obvious, they are all nice people, well worth Max's attention.

Amy Rolnick

SOURCE: A review of *Journey to an 800 Number,* in *School Library Journal,* Vol. 28, No. 9, May, 1982, p. 72.

When Maximillian (Bo) Stubbs' mother marries Mr. F. Hugo Malatesta the first, Max is sent to spend a summer month with his father, Woody, who leads a peripatetic life as the keeper of Ahmed, a disagreeable camel. Max is less than thrilled at the thought of this less than first-class way of life. Before joining his Father, he insists that his Mother equip him with a blazer from the prep school he will be proudly attending in the fall. Woody and Max accompany Ahmed as he gives rides at a shopping center, becomes part of a display at a travel agent's convention, works as an attraction at a State Fair and at a dude ranch and takes a role in a Las Vegas nightclub act. Along the way, Max gets to know Manuelo and his family, who run a taco stand, Ruth, a school librarian who also works on a ranch, and Trina Rose, a famous singer and old friend of his father. And he meets Lilly and Sabrina, who are and are not what they seem. In fact many things turn out to be and not be what they seem and Max, for all his smarts, takes a while to recognize this and to learn the lessons of love that come his way this summer. . . . The writing is sharp and tough, shot through with whimsical tenderness and compassion, funny and kind. Buy this book and offer it to all comers!

Michele Slung

SOURCE: A review of *Journey to an 800 Number,* in *The New York Times Book Review,* May 30, 1982, p. 14.

In Mrs. Konigsburg's **Journey to an 800 Number,** eccentricity so permeates the story from start to finish that what it means to be "eccentric" or "freakish" is several times discussed by Bo Stubbs, the narrator. The notion of being intentionally odd (or fascinated by oddity) is a hard one for Bo to accept, struggling as he is to embrace conventionality. You can imagine how hard it must be for him, stepping off the plane in his blue school blazer, when his extravagantly mustachioed father bear-hugs him and carts him off to a trailer camp. Think what suffering's involved when you have a rich, respectable stepfather and a father who makes his living by selling camel rides at shopping malls, conventions and fairs. There's just nothing romantic about the itinerant life, the lure of the open road and all that, for Bo, who's got no gypsy in his soul; it never occurs to him to revel in this chance for adventure. He just grits his teeth ostentatiously, rebuffs his father's affection with sarcastic criticism and wants to get the whole visit over with. But, not surprisingly, before he does depart for home, Bo learns that "respect" is more important than "respectable."

Ethel L. Heins

SOURCE: A review of *Journey to an 800 Number,* in *The Horn Book Magazine,* Vol. 58, No. 3, June, 1982, pp. 289-90.

With a fine display of irony yet without aiming over the heads of young readers, the author has written a splendid satire on modern American life and has peopled it with some of her most original and eccentric characters. Bo Stubbs (whose real name is Rainbow Maximilian Stubbs) is sent by his mother—about to leave on a honeymoon cruise with her wealthy new husband—to spend a month with his father Woody Stubbs, who travels about with a camel. The boy is unusually bright and knows it; smug and a bit pompous, he is openly disgusted at the prospect of living in a camper accompanied by an "undeluxe, unglamorous, unhousebroken" beast. And he fails to perceive that his calm, casual father is actually a gentle, tolerant, much-loved man. Bo joins Woody in a small Texas town; they go to Dallas, where the animal is to be a special attraction at a travel agents' convention, and later north to a state fair in Tulsa. Then come a sojourn at a Colorado dude ranch and finally a climactic stay in Las Vegas, where Woody and the camel are booked into a show and where Bo discovers that the celebrated star performer is actually his godmother and a devoted friend of Woody's. Meanwhile, during their journeying the boy has constantly crossed paths with two baffling, unidentifiable fellow travelers: a woman attended by her poised, precocious ten-year-old daughter—in whom Bo more than meets his match. At the end of the month the boy has learned a lot about people—their pretense, disguises, and vulnerability—and a good deal about the many aspects of kindness and love.

Margery Fisher

SOURCE: A review of *Journey by First Class Camel,* in *Growing Point,* Vol. 22, No. 4, November, 1983, p. 4164.

Elaine Konigsburg's quirky, impatient prose is modified a little to suit readers in the middle years in *Journey by First Class Camel,* but they still need to reach out to the bizarre plot and see behind it a cool, shrewd appraisal of a father-son relationship changed by unusual circumstances. Maximilian Stubbs, living with his divorcee mother, is too snobbish to accept the second name, Rainbow, which his father liked to use, nor is he at all happy to have a father who travels with his camel Ahmed, giving rides and shows. While his mother goes on honeymoon with the stuffy, tycoon second husband so much more acceptable to her than her first, Bo is sent off to his father in Texas and in the course of travels hilarious and varied, and with the powerful influence of elusive Sabrina and her mother, he finds an unexpectedly first-class element in his father's life and sees his preppy existence with his mother as flat and unenterprising. This sly look at social pretensions comes in a sparkling package of wit and surprise with an unexpected look at the fabulous façade of Las Vegas which seems to match the delusions of the boy about his parents.

📖   *UP FROM JERICHO TEL* (1986)

Kirkus Reviews

SOURCE: A review of *Up from Jericho Tel,* in *Kirkus Reviews,* Vol. 54, No. 3, February 1, 1986, pp. 209-10.

In Konigsburg's novel, her two talented child protagonists, Jeanmarie and Malcolm, learn the three requirements for fame in a sometimes whimsical, sometimes mysterious tale. A study in ambition—its origins and effects—the story integrates a fantasy into reality when Jeanmarie and Malcolm meet Tallulah, a once-famous, long-dead actress. From her incorporeal luxurious room below Jericho Tel, Tallulah gives the children assignments to carry out "Topside" using a magic invisibility. The assignment: find Tallulah's street-performer friends and her servants who were present at the moment of her death and discover who took her precious Regina Stone.

As the story opens, Jeanmarie and Malcolm, two lonely latchkey children, form an uneasy partnership when they create an animal cemetery, which they call Jericho Tel. Malcolm is not shy in declaring his talents of neatness and logical thinking, and his goal of becoming a famous chemist or physicist. Jeanmarie confides her ambition of being a famous actress. "You may not be pretty enough, but you sure are peculiar enough" is Malcolm's reaction, though he thinks she does have a talent for dramatizing things.

Tallulah's influence on the two is reflected in her sayings which precede each chapter. For example, "The difference between going to school and getting an education is the difference between picking an apple and eating it." Or "A happy person strikes a balance between doing good and doing well." Or "If you must complain in public, either be amusing or outrageous."

The first two essentials for stardom, the children learn, are talent and timing. The third requirement they realize when they discover the thief of the Regina Stone necklace from among the suspects: a ventriloquist, a singer, a record-shop owner, or the former butler; all were present at the moment of Tallulah's death.

Konigsburg has once again brought her readers a set of memorable characters and a unique perspective on children's hopes and ambitions. The story is told with a light touch but contains some substance as well—a good exploration of aspirations to and attainment of fame.

Zena Sutherland

SOURCE: A review of *Up from Jericho Tel,* in *Bulletin of the Center for Children's Books,* Vol. 39, No. 7, March, 1986, p. 131.

Whether she is writing a realistic or a fanciful story, Konigsburg always provides fresh ideas, tart wit and humor, and memorable characters. As for style, she is a natural and gifted storyteller. Here she gives a firmly matter-of-fact matrix for a fantasy about two children, Malcolm and Jeanmarie (each an assertive and articulate character) who find that Jericho Tel, their secret place, is a doorway to another world—and to an imposed but fascinating quest. And who is the imposer? Children may not recognize the loving spoof of Tallulah Bankhead, but they'll enjoy this salty character, drawn as a chain-smoking ghost named Tallulah who sends the children on missions that bring them into theatrical circles. This is a lively, clever, and very funny book. When reproached for smoking, Tallulah says, "When I want health advice, darling, I'll haunt the Mayo Clinic." She also says, "The difference between going to school and getting an education is the difference between picking an apple and eating it."

Publishers Weekly

SOURCE: A review of *Up from Jericho Tel,* in *Publishers Weekly,* Vol. 229, No. 17, April 25, 1986, p. 80.

Konigsburg delivers a witty, fast-paced story of two likable, headstrong children, who encounter the ghost of an old actress. Jeanmarie and Malcolm are plummeted into the magic underground world of flamboyant, red-haired, cigarette-puffing Tallulah. Tallulah sets them a series of tasks righting wrongs on earth (including exposing a phony faith healer by *exposing* him, in one of the book's funniest scenes), and making them invisible in order to perform these works. The tasks lead, in fine fairy-tale fashion, to the one big task, and then to the reward—in this case, realizing their talents and finding the courage to let them emerge. The dialogue is sharp and funny, the characters pleasing and Tallulah is a pip. And although Konigsburg is not didactic, it seems clear that with all this talk of magic, the *real* magic is the discovery of one another by two lonely children, and the loving friendship that ensues.

Ilene Cooper

SOURCE: A review of *Up from Jericho Tel,* in *Booklist,* Vol. 82, No. 17, May 1, 1986, p. 1313.

In *Up From Jericho Tel,* Tallulah (based on the actress of the same name) tells young Jeanmarie, "Really, darling, don't seek great reviews from small minds. They have neither the character nor the vocabulary for them."

Well, we try darling, really we do, and we know lots of superlatives, but sometimes works of art are so complex that they need a little extra reflection. *Up from Jericho Tel* is just such a book.

Note the plot: 11-year-old Jeanmarie, a newcomer and an outsider with theatrical aspirations, meets up with Malcolm Soo, another latchkey kid who lives in her trailer park. Their initial relationship consists of burying dead animals they find in the clearing that Jeanmarie poetically names Jericho Tel. But the friendship is forged when they meet Tallulah, who sends them on a mission—to find the necklace containing the famous Regina Stone that she was wearing when she died.

That's right, Tallulah is dead, but this in no way stops her from being the most fascinating person in the book. Not only does she have the ability to whisk Jeanmarie and Malcolm underground (to an artfully lit room featuring a satin-pillowed couch) and to make them invisible for their tasks, but she is also full of pithy sayings: "Never have long conversations with anyone who says between you and I."

The primary suspects in the thievery are some dear friends of Tallulah. In the last years of her life, she befriended three buskers, whom she was entertaining at a Twelfth Night celebration the evening she dropped dead. At the time of the party, Nicolai Ion Simonescue was a ventriloquist; he now has become a Jim Henson-like puppet mogul. P. H. Mermelstein, then an avid if incompetent magician, currently owns a flourishing music shop. Did either of these men finance their successful businesses through the sale of the stone? Or what about the sweet street singer, Emmagene Krebs? Emmagene had come to New York to find fame and fortune, bringing with her 18,000 songs to sing. Each day she would open her big notebook where the songs were listed and cross off the ones she had performed. Emmagene always said she had 18,000 songs to sing, she was counting down, and nothing could make her sing 18,001—but she did want a bigger audience. At present, Emmagene is still crooning on corners, but with only 500 tunes left. Perhaps *she* wanted the Regina Stone as insurance in case she ever sang her last note.

Jeanmarie and Malcolm are sent off in their invisible states to find the culprit, but as in all good quests, what they truly find is self-knowledge.

Konigsburg writes with flashes of brilliance, and her multilayered story is as fresh and funny as any that has come center stage in a while. This is not to say it is without its share of problems.

Some of the incidents, especially one that takes place in the ladies' room of a fancy restaurant, are oblique to the point of obscurity. The highly diverse plot elements are not always well integrated, and the rambling structure could have used tightening. Moreover, despite its irreverent humor, the book frequently lapses into didactism as Tallulah and the other characters tell instead of show.

But the most serious question here is—who is the intended reader? Middle graders will love the farce and the fun of being invisible, but it is the 13-, 14-, or 15-year-olds who will most relish the sophisticated verbal humor and appreciate the important messages here. They, however, may be deterred by the 11-year-old protagonists who look even younger on the book's cover. Some will say that even the average young teen might find the convoluted plot a bit much, and that, consequently, this is best suited for that elusive creature, the "special reader."

Oddly, though kids will probably not know who Tallulah is, this does not detract from the book. She is such a marvelously droll character that she stands alone.

By the book's conclusion, Jeanmarie, the stubborn actress-to-be who relishes the unseen world and the stalwart

Malcolm, who loves science but comes to realize that there is more to life than facts, do, indeed, find the person who has stolen the Regina Stone. It is lovely Emmagene, who has taken it for a talisman. Surely, she thinks, with the stone hidden beneath her clothes she will get the break that she needs. But Jeanmarie now knows what Emmagene never has learned—talent, even when coupled with luck, is not enough. One must be generous with talent, and Emmagene, carefully crossing off her 18,000 tunes, is not.

Konigsburg, however, is that generous. She puts her story out for the inquiring reader to find and savor and for reviewers to quibble with, the whole time getting obvious satisfaction from the exhilaration that comes with taking risks. And as Tallulah would surely agree, this is what having talent is all about.

Ethel R. Twitchell

SOURCE: A review of *Up from Jericho Tel,* in *The Horn Book Magazine,* Vol. 62, No. 3, May-June, 1986, p. 327.

Few authors could pull off the zany complexity of Jeanmarie Troxell's adventures: she and her friend, Malcolm Soo, are launched on a quest for their own self-knowledge and the whereabouts of the famous Regina Stone by the corporeal, yet undoubtably dead, Tallulah Bankhead. Preposterous? Of course! Yet their plunge down through Jericho Tel, their name for a small clearing in the woods, into Tallulah's Rehab station is but the beginning of the outrageous fantasy. The reader must suspend all logical thought and surrender instead to the appeal of characters like Emmagene Krebs, a folk singer working her way through a repertoire of eighteen thousand songs, and Edgar and Fiona Widdup, who chatter comfortably with the leafy specimens in their Smarty Plants greenhouse. As Tallulah sends Jeanmarie and Malcolm rocketing up through the Orgone, they become invisible, a boon to those carrying out a mission and a glorious opportunity for slapstick humor and some fast-talking repartee. Fortunately for all, the author keeps a toehold on reality. Food is bought and laundry folded. The two attend school, bicker and make up, and reveal, quite believably, the quirks and facets of their own personalities. The mystery surrounding the Regina Stone is unraveled, and Tallulah's soul is brought to rest, but along the way Jeanmarie and Malcolm discover a good bit about themselves and accept from Tallulah the knowledge that to be a star one must be gifted and blessed with luck and, above all, generous with one's talents.

Marian Rafal

SOURCE: A review of *Up from Jericho Tel,* in *Voice of Youth Advocates,* Vol. 9, No. 5, December, 1986, p. 219.

Jeanmarie and Malcolm are both unpopular, both bossy, both latchkey children, both live in a trailer park, and both want to be famous. Jeanmarie knows that she will be a famous actress and that Malcolm will one day be a famous scientist. These two friends embark on a series of adventures encouraged by the spirit of the long dead actress, Tallulah. Yes, presumably *the* Tallulah! Tallulah, as a ghost, has the ability to make them invisible, and in that state the kids are sent to find the missing Regina Stone. Which of Tallulah's friends stole the necklace after Tallulah's death? Was it Nicolai Ion Simonescu, Emmagene Krebs, or Patrick Henry Mermelstein the hapless magician? Jeanmarie and Malcolm uncover the culprit and in doing so gain much needed confidence in themselves. Mystery solved, Jeanmarie and Malcolm never again are spirited through the ground to do Tallulah's bidding and never again become invisible. Konigsburg's writing style will appeal to the young adult who has an extensive literary background.

SAMUEL TODD'S BOOK OF GREAT COLORS (1990)

Kirkus Review

SOURCE: A review of *Samuel Todd's Book of Great Colors,* in *Kirkus Reviews,* Vol. LVIII, No. 2, January 15, 1990, p. 105.

In her first picture book, the author of the longest-titled Newbery Award and Newbery Honor books (both 1967) puts a cheerful new spin on a tried-and-true topic. All the rainbow colors are here, plus five others, but not in the usual order. Konigsburg begins with a four-page celebration of orange, dropping ideas to intrigue young minds ("a pumpkin is all orange, but not all orange is a pumpkin") and suggesting connections (the speckles on bananas "are brown like freckles"). And there's a nicely muted message here, climaxed by a row of kids in different sizes and colors, their faces a lot more similar in hue than their bright suspenders. Konigsburg is not a great artist, but she's a grand wordsmith, and her attractive illustrations suit her text perfectly. A useful, mildly provocative concept book.

Susan Hepler

SOURCE: A review of *Samuel Todd's Book of Great Colors,* in *School Library Journal,* Vol. 36, No. 3, March, 1990, p. 208.

This color attribute (rather than identification) book has audience problems. The opening illustration, "A pumpkin is all orange" clearly shows a green stem, and literal-minded children will be quick to point this out. Accurately painted in full color, other foods such as egg yolks, pickles, spinach, and eggplant seem curious choices to demonstrate colors for an age group known for rigid food preferences. A multiracial group of children, each wearing different colored suspenders and different kinds of pants, underlines color variety and diversity: "Some things can be any great color." Paintings of Samuel Todd, Konigsburg's winsome grandson, appear in the opening and closing pages but do not lend much to the child appeal. An open-ended invitation to consider some of the best things that have no color, such as kisses, is followed by an off-putting "Wrong: Kisses are pink." Samuel Todd is shown with a big pink lipstick blot on his cheek, looking confused. Readers probably will be, too.

Zena Sutherland

SOURCE: A review of *Samuel Todd's Great Book of Colors,* in *Bulletin of the Center for Children's Books,* Vol. 43, No. 9, May, 1990, p. 216.

Konigsburg's first picture book reaffirms what most of her fans already knew: she's a good illustrator. Her text is strong in clarity and simplicity; it is useful as a new and effective book on color; and it is lightened by the kind of unexpected humor that readers have enjoyed in her writing before. Not just "a pumpkin is orange," but "A pumpkin is all orange, but all orange is not a pumpkin." "When you see a lot of gray shaped like an elephant, it is one." A concept book that amuses its young audience may very well make color concepts more memorable.

Elizabeth S. Watson

SOURCE: A review of *Samuel Todd's Book of Great Colors,* in *The Horn Book Magazine,* Vol. 66, No. 4, July-August, 1990, p. 468.

The author-illustrator engages her audience with a fresh approach to books about colors. Not intended for toddlers learning to separate and identify colors, the book effectively prods the reader to think beyond simple concepts such as "what is red." Using wit and humor—as in her juvenile novels—Konigsburg adds a sparkle and twist to an already voluminous genre: "When you see a lot of gray shaped like an elephant, it is one," or "Pink is for little girls, they say, unless they know about flamingos. Boy flamingos are just as pink as girl flamingos—and in all the same places." The illustrations are realistic paintings of some unusual items, including eggplant, pickles, and spinach. The hues are true to life; you might expect the blue jay to fly off the page. Samuel Todd looks like a child you'd like to know, and his friends shown on the page that tells us "some things can be any color" look like a nice bunch, too. The children sport different colors of suspenders—and different colors of skin. A book that could truthfully have been called "A *Great* Book of Colors."

SAMUEL TODD'S BOOK OF GREAT INVENTIONS (1991)

Kathryn LaBarbera

SOURCE: A review of *Samuel Todd's Book of Great Inventions,* in *Booklist,* Vol. 87, No. 22, August, 1991, p. 2150.

As she did in *Samuel Todd's Book of Great Colors* Konigsburg uses her wit and understanding of children to create a picture book. This time the front matter displays a series of black-and-white drawings (done to look like Polaroid snapshots) of Samuel Todd's feet approaching the toilet. The text begins with "The *second* thing I do every morning. . . . " These same "snapshots" elsewhere in the book are incorporated into Konigsburg's full-color spreads. Throughout the pages, Samuel Todd narrates why the following inventions are his favorites: mirrors, belt loops, velcro, gloves (as opposed to mittens), backpacks, thermos bottles, training wheels, step stools and ladders, boxes, candles, Halloween, cuddle blankets, and French fries. For fans of Konigsburg's fiction, this diversion is especially worth a look.

Publishers Weekly

SOURCE: A review of *Samuel Todd's Book of Great Inventions,* in *Publishers Weekly,* Vol. 238, No. 37, August 16, 1991, p. 57.

This Newbery winner's second picture book, after *Samuel Todd's Book of Great Colors,* again centers on her oldest grandchild. Here, the bespectacled Samuel muses on familiar items he considers worthwhile inventions. The genial child shares his views on the importance of mirrors, belt loops, Velcro, gloves, backpacks, training wheels, ladders, candles, boxes and Halloween. But to Samuel, the telephone and television are not particularly impressive inventions; rather, "They come with the house like mothers and windows and fathers and walls." Kids and adults alike will appreciate the humor—and the truth—in Samuel's astute observations, which are likely to open young eyes to numerous "great inventions" they've hitherto taken for granted. Konigsburg's affection for her perspicacious grandson shines through her boldly colored paintings, effectively juxtaposed with smaller drawings that simulate black-and-white photos.

Starr LaTronica

SOURCE: A review of *Samuel Todd's Book of Great Inventions,* in *School Library Journal,* Vol. 37, No. 10, October, 1991, p. 98.

In this companion volume to *Samuel Todd's Book of Great Colors* a boy offers random observations and appreciation of everyday things, from the marvel of mirrors to the ups and downs of belt loops and the advantages of Velcro. On the surface, the concept and the language are straightforward, but are presented with a sophistication that may be a bit confusing to young readers accustomed to concrete plot lines. For the most part, the musings themselves reflect a genuinely childlike perspective and are brilliant flashes of clarity that will provide fresh insight into one's surroundings. A few, however, may be slightly abstruse for the average picture-book audience: ". . . I don't think the telephone and television are great inventions. They come with the house like mothers and windows and fathers and walls." Meticulously executed full-color paintings realistically depict Samuel Todd's perceptions, while overlays of black-and-white snapshot-style pencil sketches that feature a multicultural cast of children further illustrate his commentary.

Maeve Visser Knoth

SOURCE: A review of *Samuel Todd's Book of Great Inventions,* in *The Horn Book Magazine,* Vol. 68, No. 1, January-February, 1992, pp. 59-60.

In this new book Samuel Todd tackles the subject of inventions. Mirrors, he declares, are great inventions because they allow him to "make sure that I am still Samuel Todd." He goes on to discuss belt loops, velcro, backpacks, training wheels, and Halloween, among others. Konigsburg maintains Samuel Todd's point of view flawlessly; he is the center of his world, and the great inventions are those things he enjoys and appreciates. Telephones, he maintains, are not such great inventions because "they come with the house like mothers and windows." The illustrations are double-page color paintings which most often have Samuel Todd for their focus. The art and simple narrative present a perspective on the world that invites the reader to look at his or her own world as a series of inventions. Children will delight in deciding for themselves why Halloween was invented—Samuel Todd claims it was "so that no one has to go trick-or-treating as his or her same old self." A humorous and thought-provoking look at the world from the point of view of a reflective child.

AMY ELIZABETH EXPLORES BLOOMINGDALE'S (1992)

E. L. Konigsburg

SOURCE: "Better than the Nobel Prize: The Newbery Sells Books," in *The New York Times Book Review,* May 21, 1995, pp. 26-7.

It is summer. It is L.A. It is A.M. We are doing brunch. This is the city where directors became *auteurs* and authors became content providers. This is where the phone is a prosthesis. My host is a children's book editor. She is a recent hire of a large publishing house with a West Coast presence. She asks if we can do a deal. I know she means a book. I tell her I've been thinking about a picture book in which my second grandchild will be a character. I have a title. "Amy Elizabeth Explores Bloomingdale's." She expresses enthusiasm. We part, mellowed out on champagne and promise.

I submit the manuscript. I do not receive a reply—not even an acknowledgement of receipt—for more than a month. *Uh-oh.*

Experience has taught me that when a response to a re-

> **The difference in these two criticisms points out the difference between market-driven and book-driven publishing. [A good editor] trusts her own judgment to find books that will satisfy the marketplace. She also trusts her writers.**

quested manuscript is long in coming, the manuscript is in trouble. What experience had not prepared me for was the source of the problem. In her less-than-grammatical letter (the italics are mine), the editor wrote:

"What confuses me however, is that the title is misleading, and I think the reaction of *sales reps and booksellers* will be negative rather than positive. The book is about something completely different than the title suggests and I think the reader will ultimately be disappointed. It seems to me that it could be called 'Amy Elizabeth Tries to Explore Bloomingdale's' or 'Amy Elizabeth Doesn't Explore Bloomingdale's' or perhaps more clever than the above that conveys to the reader that the book will be satisfying even if you don't get to go to Bloomingdale's. I also think that reviewers would object to the book disappointing the child."

We could not agree on a treatment for the book, and I requested that she return the manuscript to me. I then submitted it to Jean Karl, who has been my forever editor. Her letter, talking about the same book, said.

"The idea of setting out for someplace and never getting there—but seeing a good many other places along the way—is always amusing. However, somehow . . . the text . . . sits on the surface of events in a way that does not bring the reader fully into the experience."

The difference in these two criticisms points out the difference between market-driven and book-driven publishing. Jean Karl trusts her own judgment to find books that will satisfy the marketplace. She also trusts her writers. Her criticism showed that she trusted me to rework the text in a way that would bring the reader in, for that was the real problem with the book. Since its publication in 1992, not one reviewer, bookseller or librarian has objected to the title.

Publishers Weekly

SOURCE: A review of *Amy Elizabeth Explores Bloomingdale's,* in *Publishers Weekly,* Vol. 239, No. 30, July 6, 1992, p. 55.

Newbery Medalist Konigsburg, who featured her grandson, Samuel Todd, in two prior picture books, here names her heroine after her granddaughter. Youngsters may miss the irony of the title, since Amy Elizabeth—a Houston resident who is staying with her grandmother in Manhattan—never does make it to Bloomingdale's. Though they repeatedly plan to visit "the most famous store in the world," the duo gets side-tracked by some of the city's other attractions, including Chinatown, the Empire State Building, the Carnegie Deli and a Broadway musical. Amy Elizabeth's rambling, first-person narrative is chatty and entertaining, even if she doesn't always speak in credible, age-appropriate jargon—"I am a child who enjoys a good pickle." Konigsburg's large-scale, characteristically realistic color pictures, together with black-and-white panels similar to film frames, offer a vivid portrait of a distraction-filled city—and a most affectionate relationship between grandmother and granddaughter.

Roger Sutton

SOURCE: A review of *Amy Elizabeth Explores Bloomingdale's,* in *Bulletin of the Center for Children's Books,* Vol. 46, No. 1, September, 1992, p. 16.

Actually, Amy Elizabeth never does make it to Bloomie's; nevertheless, she and her Grandma have a fine time anyway, sampling the customs (getting the *Times* on Sunday), trials (poop-scooping) and delicacies (Rumplemayer's hot chocolate) of New York City. Konigsburg's story is savvy and snappy, accompanied by sophisticated—yet warm—paintings that convey a great deal of the fun a grandmother can have entertaining a visiting tourist from Houston. However, the tone of the text is annoyingly arch, with disingenuous quips ("In Houston we don't have to leave home to do the laundry. We do it one load at a time and don't watch") that young listeners might find patronizing were the humor not so obviously directed over their heads. Amy Elizabeth's remark about "grandmothers and primary caregivers" trying to get taxis is cynically amusing to adults, but when you laugh, don't be surprised if your listeners feel left out of an inside joke. The full-color, double-spread pictures (and accompanying filmclip-like sidebars) show the real story: an intrigued, sometimes exhausted little girl and patient grandma having a fine time together.

Judith Gloyer

SOURCE: A review of *Amy Elizabeth Explores Bloomingdale's,* in *School Library Journal,* Vol. 38, No. 9, September, 1992, pp. 206-07.

Sometimes one's journey is more important than one's destination. Such is the case with Konigsburg's new book. The story relates, from a young girl's perspective, her week-long visit with her grandmother in New York City. The first day, her grandmother wants to take her to "Bloomies." But that day and each succeeding day something interferes with their plans. Amy Elizabeth is clearly not comfortable in New York, and she continually makes comparisons to her home in Houston. She looks overwhelmed by the city, and her face in the illustrations portrays her relations with her grandmother as equally unsure. But little by little, the child gets to know and enjoy New York and her grandmother. Before they leave for the airport, Amy can say about the department store,

"I have had an excellent time not getting there." The book has a bold and energetic layout. The text and pictures are set off in a border of bright taxicab yellow and black-and-white checks. The paintings are colorful and realistic, but flat in tone. There is also a series of smaller gray-and-white drawings running along the side like photo negatives. They add to the feeling of being a tourist and provide details of the places visited. While this may not have instant appeal, any child who can be led to explore it will, like Amy Elizabeth, find much to enjoy.

Ilene Cooper

SOURCE: A review of *Amy Elizabeth Explores Bloomingdale's,* in *Booklist,* Vol. 89, No. 2, September 1, 1992, p. 67.

Amy Elizabeth is up from Houston, visiting her grandmother in New York City for the first time. Grandmother wants to take Amy Elizabeth to Bloomingdale's, "the most famous store in the world," but each day something interferes with the plan—a trip to Chinatown, a carriage ride, a Broadway play, even a protest march. By the time Amy Elizabeth leaves for home, she hasn't seen Bloomingdale's, but she's seen plenty. Konigsburg nicely portrays an intergenerational relationship set against an exciting New York City backdrop. But Amy Elizabeth is not just a wide-eyed visitor; she contrasts for readers the differences she observes between life at home and in New York. While most of these remarks are pertinent, sometimes Amy Elizabeth's comparisons are a bit fuzzy. For instance, after a visit to Chinatown, she says. "In my town, Chinatown would be in another country like China." Konigsburg, who is best known for her novels, continues a recent trend, illustrating her own picture books. Here, attractive color drawings share space with small black-and-white art arranged like strips of film. The page design, yellow backgrounds with a taxicab check around the borders, adds to the big city feeling. Like Amy Elizabeth, readers will enjoy the trip.

Kirkus Reviews

SOURCE: A review of *Amy Elizabeth Explores Bloomingdale's,* in *Kirkus Reviews,* Vol. LX, No. 17, September 1, 1992, p. 1131.

Amy Elizabeth is visiting Grandma in New York; each day, Grandma plans to take her to "Bloomie's," but there's always something else they should do first: walk the dog, visit Chinatown to get green tea, go to a laundromat, or share lox and bagels and the Sunday *Times.* Amy Elizabeth never complains; but her expression is often doleful, and, in her astringently clearsighted narrative, she points out just how everything in New York differs from her home in Houston. As the week wears on, there are more smiles—for hot cocoa in a snowstorm, for a live production of *Peter Pan,* or just because the two are getting more companionable; as for Bloomie's, when it's time to go home Amy Elizabeth says, "I have had an excellent time not getting there." Understated, witty, and right on target; creatively extended in the author's perceptive, warmly colorful illustrations.

T-BACKS, T-SHIRTS, COAT, AND SUIT (1993)

Nancy Menaldi-Scanlan

SOURCE: A review of *T-Backs, T-Shirts, COAT, and Suit,* in *School Library Journal,* Vol. 39, No. 10, October, 1993, pp. 124, 126.

It's summer, and Chloë, 12, is about to sign a compact with her best friends that if one girl has a "bad hair day," all three must jump in the water. If she refuses, they'll shun her; if she signs, she faces the possibility of immersion in the local pool—a much-feared consequence, since she cannot swim. Her stepfather comes to the rescue, sending her to Florida to visit his sister, and advising her to "give the unexpected a chance." Chloë begins to develop real affection for and understanding of the woman, a former flower-child activist. When a heated debate ensues over the decency of wearing revealing bathing suits to work, Bernadette is caught between COAT (Citizens Opposing All T-Backs) and the pressure of her co-workers for "solidarity." With the help of her lawyer-friend, she stands up for her own beliefs, teaching Chloë an invaluable lesson and opening up her own closed-off life to the possibility of loving another person. Konigsburg has developed unusual characters who reveal their innermost secrets as the story unfolds. Despite the initially trivial premise, the plot is carefully constructed and the humorous dialogue will engage readers. While it offers a lighter look at self-discovery than that found in the author's *Throwing Shadows, T-Backs* could serve as a possible discussion-starter on the importance of commitment and personal values.

Roger Sutton

SOURCE: A review of *T-Backs, T-Shirts, COAT and Suit,* in *Bulletin of the Center for Children's Books,* Vol. 47, No. 3, November, 1993, p. 88.

Konigsburg's penchant for weird titles is long-established; what's new here is that her always subversive tone has been amplified into full-blown farce. When watershy Chloë learns that summer with her best friends is going to involve jumping into the local pool, she knows she has to get out of town; and even if spending a few weeks with her Aunt Bernadette in Florida isn't exactly what she had in mind, her parents don't give her any choice. "Promise me that you'll help Bernadette," says Chloë's adoptive father, Bernadette's younger brother, "and that you'll give the unexpected a chance." Chloë does help Bernadette, who drives a food-service wagon to various office buildings and construction sites, and even grows to like her, although simultaneously secretive and absolutely honest

Bernadette is not someone easy to get close to. As for the unexpected, well, that erupts in the form of the great T-back war, when Bernadette finds her business threatened as other commissary drivers begin wearing sexy T-back bathing suits (called "thongs" here up north), and she refuses to go along. Bernadette becomes a virtuous heroine in the eyes of the town's more conservative residents (wickedly caricatured by the author), but she doesn't like them any more than she does her buttock-baring competition (an equally wicked portrayal). While there's a weak and implausible subplot about Chloë's convincing a boy that Bernadette is a witch, the story is carried along by the satiric bite of the commentary, and it's given heart by the growing bond between aunt and niece. Konigsburg has never been afraid to let adults be adults, and the portrait of Bernadette is one of her best. Kids will want to meet her.

Hazel Rochman

SOURCE: "The Trouble with T-Backs," in *Booklist,* Vol. 90, No. 5, November 1, 1993, p. 515.

The protagonists in YA books are getting younger: 12 seems to be the most popular age, though many seem to be 12 going on 16. In contrast, Chloë in Konigsburg's new novel is 12, and she sounds like 12. The problem here is that for much of the book Chloë seems to be an onlooker of adult wars, though the plot is contrived to drag her into the fray.

At first the setting is contemporary, the dialogue sharp and funny. Chloë is escaping from peer pressure and a negative self-image (especially frizzy hair) when she goes to spend the summer in Peco, Florida, with her 45-year-old stepaunt, Bernadette. Fiercely independent, Bernadette is an ex-hippy who works as a driver-server on a food-service van at the docks and shipyards. The relationship between aunt and niece is beautifully drawn. When Chloë first hears that they get up at five-thirty for work, she asks, "Five-thirty? A.M.?" But with "neither friend nor phone around," she begins to grope for her own independence.

Trouble erupts for Bernadette when some of the more well-endowed driver-servers wear T-backs (thong bathing suits) while doing business. The forces of respectability rally to ban such indecency. Konigsburg gets a lot of comedy out of the silliness of both sides: the dumb pinup types who think they have a constitutional right to "bare arms," as well as the righteous Christians who rail against vulgar nudity as devil's work. Bernadette won't wear a T-back, won't protest against those who do, and won't say why not. She has the freedom to remain silent, but all sides turn on her. Protest is good for business—the food service vans are booming, and the churches are full.

The conflicts about conformity and freedom of expression are of crucial interest to Chloë and many young people. But for the second half of the book, Konigsburg belabors the politics and reexamines some 1960s issues. Bernadette tells preachy "stories" (on one occasion she even apologizes, "Do you think you can stand another story, Chloë?") about how she put individual duty above the good of the group in a Vietnam draft protest, and she also tells a story about Savonarola in Renaissance Italy. An ex-hippy lawyer even tells Chloë the story of how Galileo was accused of being a heretic.

The plot is awkwardly contrived to carry these messages. Most jarring is a subplot about a boy whom Chloë tricks into believing Bernadette is a witch. He goes one better and notices that there's something wrong with Bernadette's "pap" (the word he uses throughout for breast)—therefore, she's a witch who suckles imps . . .

The truth is that Bernadette has had a mastectomy and is ashamed of how she looks. That's why Chloë has been forbidden to come into Bernadette's bedroom, and that's why Bernadette won't consider being seen in any state of undress. Although her shame may not be politically correct feminism, it does humanize the wise strong mentor, who turns out to be as vulnerable as she is nonconformist. When Chloë finally learns her aunt's secret and reaches out to hug her, their loving embrace is a physical dramatic reality that says more to all ages than the political babble.

Rachel Axelrod

SOURCE: A review of *T-Backs, T-Shirts, COAT, and Suit,* in *Voice of Youth Advocates,* Vol. 16, No. 5, December, 1993, p. 294.

When Chloë's mother marries Nick, she gains an aunt named Bernadette, who wears her hair in an unruly Afro and is thin as a stick. With summer approaching, Chloë's dislike of sleepovers and hassling with her friends over make-up and hair intensifies; to help her out, Nick suggests that she spend a few weeks with Bernadette, "to help her out." Bernadette leads a solitary life, and teaches Chloë to help her with her vending business; much to Chloë's surprise, she not only becomes an asset to Bernadette, she likes the work, and also likes Bernadette's dog Daisy. When Zack, the owner of the business, and his sidekicks Velma and Wanda, work out a scheme to make more money for themselves by wearing t-back bathing trunks, Bernadette is just about the sole hold-out for decency. Both she and Chloë suffer at hands of the righteous people in the town, and those that are angry that they will not give in to the pressure on them to conform. During this period of time, Tyler, Velma's son, spies on them and turns in evidence that Bernadette is a witch; the harassment that ensues becomes an issue that both Bernadette and Chloë must endure and overcome. Chloë learns some of Bernadette's secrets, and begins to understand that her aunt is a very special person, who adheres to her principles regardless of the pressures around her. When she eventually flies home again, she has learned some valuable lessons about being truthful, and about being herself. Some valuable lessons will be learned by the stu-

dents reading this book. I found it difficult to interrupt my reading. Konigsburg has produced another winner!

THE VIEW FROM SATURDAY (1996)

E. L. Konigsburg

SOURCE: "Newbery Medal Acceptance," in *The Horn Book Magazine,* Vol. 73, No. 4, July-August, 1997, pp. 404-14.

[The following is E. L. Konigsburg's acceptance speech for the Newbery Medal, which she delivered at the annual meeting of the American Library Association in San Francisco, June 29, 1997.]

. . . As I was saying, four days and twenty-nine years ago, thank you.

Between the banquet in Kansas City where I received what my family currently refers to as Newbery I and this evening's glorious celebration for the award we are calling Newbery *Eye Eye,* you have taken me on a journey. You invited me to many places. They were places where I could have grown-up conversations, places where I could shed the burden of my personal self and become part of the community of children's books.

And those places became my Third Place.

The Third Place is where we go that is neither work nor home. It is where we are taught to measure up in a different way from home and from work. The Third Place is the destination of people who want to meet, to mingle, and to participate both as individuals and as part of a community. It is a place where we feel accepted for ourselves and where we learn to conduct ourselves as grown-up members of a larger community. The Third Place attaches us to the human tradition.

Civilized society has always had a Third Place. It is as ancient as the agora of Greece where Socrates walked among the youth of Athens. It is as old as the forum in Rome where Marc Antony came to praise Caesar. The Middle Ages had the church; the Renaissance, the piazza. At the turn of the century, Vienna had its coffeehouses. Between the two World Wars, New York City had the Algonquin for the *New Yorker* and Paris had Shakespeare and Company for the expatriates; and after the wars, there was the Café des Deux Magots for the existentialists. Ireland has its pub. England, its club. Colonial America had its town square. Suburban America has—what?—the workout center? the sports bar? Could it be—Barnes & Noble? I don't know if suburban America even has a Third Place. But I do. I have a Third Place, and it is the one you opened for me after Newbery I and have kept open ever since.

My first Third Place was Cleveland. The Ohio Association of School Librarians was meeting there at a time when Dorothy Broderick was on the faculty at Case-Western Reserve in their School of Library Science (of blessed memory). Broderick was scheduled to be in the audience when I spoke. The Third Place demands that we test ourselves, and I knew that this audience would not have much patience with an author ramble—a talk that was not properly dressed as discourse—so I extended the thoughts of my Newbery address wherein I had spoken about my love of words, and I spoke about language and how language is God's gift to us as humans and how we must take care of it as we would any treasure, for it not only reflects our culture but also helps to shape it. Language demands being treated with dignity. It makes demands, but it also delivers rewards, for precise language helps shape precise thinking.

The Third Place also makes demands, and it also delivers. From the Third Place we give something, and we take something, and we return with our lessons transplanted and transformed. From the agora Plato took the teachings of Socrates and returned with the Academy. From the Piazza della Signoria in Florence Michelangelo took the spirit of the Renaissance and returned it in the heroic figure of David.

To my surprise and delight, I have found traces of my Third Places in *The View from Saturday*. Here is how the echo of that talk on language plays back.

It is the day before the contest with Knightsbridge for the district championship of the Middle School Academic Bowl. Mr. Connor LeDue, the principal, visits Mrs. Olinski, the Epiphany coach, and says:

> "I heard a rumor that your team is expecting to blow mine out of the water." His smile was as genuine as a Xeroxed signature. "I told our coach that she could expect to be hung if she lets your sixth grade grunges beat us out."

> "Well then," Mrs. Olinski replied, "much as I respect your coach, I recommend that you start buying rope." She . . . added, "By the way, Mr. LeDue, in our grunge neighborhood, we say *hanged,* not *hung.* Check it out."

. . . . .

The first call I ever received from a reader of my published work was from Amy Kellman, a children's librarian who lived in Rye, New York, the town neighboring Port Chester where we lived at the time. Both Amy and I had once called Pittsburgh home. In 1976 when I was invited to speak at the Fall Festival of Children's Books in Pittsburgh, Amy had returned and was at the Carnegie Library there, but I had moved to Florida. So Pittsburgh was now a Third Place for me.

The Third Place is where we go to talk about what is current but not necessarily quotidian. In our bicentennial year, the classics of children's literature were being re-reviewed for political correctness. Language that was once merely colorful was being attacked as racist or sexist or both.

The Third Place is where we learn to listen to different voices and where we learn how to agree to disagree, so in the auditorium of that great Carnegie Library on Forbes Street in Pittsburgh, I spoke about how it is important to maintain color in children's literature, that true diversity does not prescribe, proscribe, or circumscribe language, and that for the sake of accuracy as well as poetry it is best not to skew or skewer language to be current or to be politically correct.

And I found that those thoughts, too, have surfaced in *The View from Saturday*.

> Mrs. Eva Marie Olinski always gave good answers. Whenever she was asked how she had selected her team for the Academic Bowl, she chose one of several good answers. Most often she said that the four members of her team had skills that balanced one another. That was reasonable. Sometimes she said that she knew her team would practice. That was accurate. To the district superintendent of schools, she gave a bad answer, but she did that only once, only to him, and if that answer was not good, her reason for giving it was.

Mrs. Olinski's bad answer is her response to political correctness.

Part of that Fall Festival was the dedication of the Elizabeth Nesbitt Room. That's *Nesbitt* with two *t*s, named for a children's librarian, not a children's book writer. In the wonderful way that the world of children's books has of circling back on itself, The Third Place that Pittsburgh had become has once again become home, for the Elizabeth Nesbitt Room in the Library School at the University of Pittsburgh is now home to my manuscripts and illustrations.

. . . . .

Pat Scales and I met over the telephone when her students at Greenville Middle School called me for an author-interview. The degree of preparation, the quality of the questions, and the courtesy of that interview were prelude to not only another Third Place but to a friendship as well.

It was upon the recommendation of Pat Scales that I was invited to address a joint conference of the Southeastern and Southwestern Library Associations when they met in New Orleans. New Orleans is an American city that retains a downtown. As I grew up in small towns in Pennsylvania, downtown was The Third Place for town folk, but it was also home for me, for we almost always lived over the store.

I thought about the homes I had known as a child. I thought about how I had always looked for home in the books I read, and how I *still* look for home in the books I read. I talked about that and about how, now that I am grown up, I have a chance to create homes in the books I write.

All of us long for home.

Nadia's story in *The View from Saturday* is about that. Her need for finding home is there when she says that her mother moved the two of them from Florida "to upstate New York where she had grown up [because she] needed some autumn in her life." And it is there in Nadia's account of how the turtles, after decades of absence, return to their home shore to nest.

My friendship with Pat Scales that began with a telephone call is maintained by phone, and our late-night long-distance calls have come to qualify as a Third Place, for—sometimes sooner, sometimes later, but always—our conversation gets around to what is current in children's books. But we usually begin our marathon phone visits by talking about home. We discovered that we have a lot in common. We were both raised by Jewish mothers even though Pat's Jewish mother happens to be a Methodist. We are both the middle child, and we both have an older sister. During one long call, Pat told me about her sister's taking the family dog to an audition for the part of Sandy in the play *Annie*. Daisy not only got the part, she made the front page—above the fold—of the Leisure section of the Anderson, South Carolina, *Independent-Mail*. Pat sent me the clipping. I still have it in my files. It is dated September 15, 1983.

Daisy is now in Dog Heaven enjoying the company of other celebrities like Lassie, Rin Tin Tin, and Toto. But I hope those other stars realize that, unlike them, Daisy led the life of a real dog and was the inspiration for a character named Ginger. I wish Daisy a long after-life in Julian's story, "When Ginger Played Annie's Sandy."

. . . . .

Simmons College was my next Third Place. The theme of the institute that summer was "Do I Dare Disturb the Universe?" I thought about how every creative act disturbs the universe and how every creative act requires risk.

Addressing the theme, I used the example of Galileo to show that those who dare disturb the universe must first have the courage to dare disturb the neighborhood. It sometimes takes more courage to disturb the neighborhood than it takes to disturb the universe. I discovered that kind of courage in Julian Singh.

At the state finals of the Academic Bowl, the commissioner of education reads the question, "An acronym is defined as a word formed from the initial letters of a series of words . . . Can you give me two . . . examples of acronyms that have entered our language as words?" Julian answers, "Posh and Tip."

> The commissioner looked over his list of possible answers. "Posh and tip?" he asked.
>
> Julian quickly answered, "Posh means fashionable and is the acronym for Port Out, Starboard Home . . . And tip, meaning the small sum of money given for services rendered, is the acronym for To Insure Promptness."
>
> The commissioner laughed. " . . . I don't have either

of those acronyms on my list. We'll have to check with our advisory panel." He nodded to the three people sitting at a table on the far side of the room. . . . The three of them conferred briefly and passed a note to the commissioner.

> "We can allow posh, but we do not find a reference for tip."
>
> Julian said, "With all due respect, sir, I think you ought to check another source."

In *The View from Saturday* Mrs. Olinski says, "sometimes to be successful, you have to risk making mistakes . . . [and] sometimes we even have to risk making fools of ourselves."

The structure of *The View from Saturday* was a risk. The Third Place is where we learn to take risks. Newbery banquets are where we learn whether or not we have made fools of ourselves.

. . . . .

It is in the Third Place that we learn to wear a mask or risk taking one off because it is here that we learn to identify—or not identify—with people whose lives are not our own.

1989 was designated the Year of the Young Reader. The Florida Center for the Book invited me to speak at a conference on writing for young readers. I gave a talk entitled, "The Mask Beneath the Face." I believe that a writer wears a mask every time she sits down to write, and readers try on masks every time they read. I also believe that children design the masks they will wear by the time they finish sixth grade.

In that talk I asked my husband, the psychologist, Dr. David Konigsburg, "Do you think wearing a mask allows a person to be someone else, or do you think that a mask allows a person to be that which he really is?" And my husband, the psychologist, Dr. David Konigsburg, answered, "Yes."

Now listen to what Ethan Potter, a sixth-grade Soul, has to say in *The View from Saturday*.

> It was dark when I left Sillington House. Mrs. Gershom had offered to drive me home, but I wanted to walk. I wanted to walk the road between Sillington House and mine. I wanted to mark the distance slowly. Something had happened at Sillington House. Something made me pull sounds out of my silence the way that Julian pulled puzzle pieces out of Nadia's hair.
>
> Had I gained something at Sillington House? Or had I lost something there? The answer was yes.

. . . . .

Maureen Hayes, Mo, of blessed memory, recommended that even though I was going to Rochester, New York, on a different assignment, I ought to speak to an assembly of children's librarians there. Mo was an extraordinary match-maker, the Dolly Levy of author appearances. She knew that I needed to meet Julie Cummins, who was Children's Services Consultant in Rochester at the time. Following our meeting, Julie, a few other librarians, and I went to lunch. This was not the Café des Deux Magots, and this was not the Round Table at the Algonquin. This was better. Not even the chocolate dessert was as rich and savory as our conversation.

In 1992 Julie Cummins was at the New York Public, and she invited me to give the Anne Carroll Moore lecture. It was here that I chose to explore the relationship between reading and the brain. I learned that the human brain must be jump-started with experience. For example, a baby kept blindfolded may have all his equipment in perfect order but will never function as a seeing person even when the blind-fold is removed, because the pathways that allow him to interpret what he sees will not have been carved out. Experience is necessary to start function, and more experience is necessary to refine it. A child must see in order to be able to see. A child must speak in order to speak.

I also learned that there is for each of these senses a critical age by which these nerve pathways must be carved out if they are ever to be reinforced. For most developing brains, that critical age comes before adolescence. I came to believe that there is a critical age for establishing the nerve pathways that allow us to interpret the printed word. We must read in order to read.

I found those thoughts—that the human brain must be jump-started with experience as well as the thought that there is a critical age for experience to shape our brains—translated in *The View from Saturday*. But here it is an emotion that must be experienced to be expressed.

After the state championship of the Academic Bowl has been decided, Mrs. Olinski and Mr. Singh are driving home from the state capital, and Mr. Singh speaks:

> "How can you know what is missing if you've never met it? You must know of something's existence before you can notice its absence. So it was with The Souls. They found on their journeys what you found at Sillington House."

> "A cup of kindness, Mr. Singh? Is that what I found?"

> "Kindness, yes, Mrs. Olinski. Noah, Nadia, and Ethan found kindness in others and learned how to look for it in themselves. Can you know excellence if you've never seen it? Can you know good if you have only seen bad?"

A person must experience kindness to recognize it. He must recognize it in order to develop it. Being kind makes us kind. And just as there is a critical age by which we must speak in order to speak, there is a critical age by which we must experience kindness to be kind. And that critical age is before adolescence. That critical age is in the cruelest year—grade six.

· · · · ·

There are some Third Places where I have been three times. Call it an *exponential three*. Or *three to the third power*. These three-times Third Places have all been very kind to me.

I have been to Oklahoma, and I have been to Maine three times. Conversations with Donna Skvarla in the former and Mary Peverada in the latter reassured me that a writer can trust the kindness of readers. Librarians who work with children as well as books know that young readers want to connect and are willing to reach down and up and into a book that has more to it than meets the eye.

Herb Sandberg and Hughes Moir invited me to the University of Toledo three times, and each time I went I met not only with kindness at that university but also with kindness in the community, for through their efforts, the Children's Literature Institute has become a Third Place for the people of the town. Every year lay citizens support the institute by participating in the events both social and educational. In Toledo I learned to trust an informed community. Herb Sandberg knows that an informed community fears its children's not finding books more than it fears what they might find in them.

I met Ethel Ambrose in the mid-seventies when she and Esther Franklin invited me to their Stockton/Sacramento gig. Ethel left California for Little Rock, Arkansas, and where Ethel goes, a Children's Literature Festival follows. On one of those days in Little Rock, I was in Ethel's office signing books when the custodian came in to redd up—as we ex-Pennsylvanians say. Out of sheer enthusiasm Ethel picked up a copy of one of my books and began to read it out loud. She had hardly turned a page before the young man had bought the book. He had to, of course. Whether he had children or not, he had to. Ethel Ambrose's enthusiasms are not to be denied, and neither is her commitment to excellence. There is no greater kindness to readers or to writers than the commitment to excellence of an outstanding children's librarian.

· · · · ·

The Third Place is neither work nor home but would have little meaning without them. Had I not found trust and kindness at a critical time at work, would I have ever been able to recognize them in the Third Place?

Jean Karl has been my editor since she took a risk on a manuscript called *Jennifer, Hecate, Macbeth, William McKinley and Me, Elizabeth* that had come in over the transom. We have worked together on eighteen books since, and she has never been less than brilliant as an editor. Over the course of our association, through waves of political no-nos, Jean has demonstrated such intellectual integrity that never once has she asked me to shape my text to the times. That is trust. Thank you, Jean Karl.

It is Jon Lanman, as editorial director, whose understanding of the head of an author as well as the head of a publishing house has maintained the flow of thought as well as the flow of paper from manuscript to bound book.

His understanding of the bookmaking process borders on the Talmudic. If genius is an infinite capacity for taking pains, Jon is a genius. And he is kind. Thank you, Jon.

I believe that courtesy is the threshold to kindness, and I believe that courtesy begins at home—in the First Place—and I also believe that in a forty-five-year-old relationship, courtesy is no longer the threshold to kindness, but is maintenance. And in a forty-five-year-old empty-nest relationship, courtesy is mandatory. And in a forty-five-year-old empty-nest relationship where one's husband is one's agent, courtesy is a miracle. But I'm here to tell you, miracles do happen. Thank you, David, for the pretty thing our years together have been.

In the thirty years since my first books were published, the children of our children are now the same age that Paul, Laurie, and Ross were in 1968—a little in-house guarantee for a long shelf life for one's books. Thank you, kids.

. . . . .

In his 1997 State of the Union Message, President Clinton said, "As the Internet becomes our new town square, [we need] a computer in every home." The Internet may be the new town square, but it can never be my Third Place. The Third Place is community; the Internet is isolation. The Third Place is dress-up; the Internet is dress-down. The Third Place is learning to interpret a wink, a blink, a flick of the hand; the Internet is learning to keyboard. The Internet is not a Third Place.

But I discovered that Sillington House is.

In *The View from Saturday,* when Ethan Potter tells his story, he says:

> Something in Sillington House gave me permission to do things I had never done before. Never even thought of doing. Something there triggered the unfolding of those parts that had been incubating. Things that had lain inside me, curled up like the turtle hatchlings newly emerged from their eggs, taking time in the dark of their nest to unfurl themselves. I told jokes I had never told before. I asked questions I had never asked before.

In *The View from Saturday* I told a story I had never told before, for Sillington House is not only the Third Place for Ethan and the Souls and Mrs. Olinski, it is my return on the Third Place you have given me. It is my statue returned to the piazza. It is my rendering of the place you gave me to see in order to see, the place you gave me to speak in order to speak.

Ethan again:

> One Saturday afternoon . . . as we sat around the table-for-four where we had had our tea, I broke the silence by asking—I really don't know why—except that it was something I had been thinking about, "If you could live one day of your life all over again, what day would it be?" . . .

> When it was my turn to tell what day I would like to live over . . . The Souls . . . were not embarrassed to hear, and I was not embarrassed to say, "I would like to live over the day of our first tea party. And, look," I added, "every Saturday since, I get to do just that."

Now, in a paraphrase of Ethan Potter's desire, "I am not embarrassed to say, and you are not embarrassed to hear, I would like to live over the evening of my first Newbery party. And look," I can add, "after a fulfilling twenty-nine years, I get to do just that."

Thank you, John Edward Peters—I love all your names—and all the members of the 1997 committee—I love all your names, too—thank you for letting me do just that. Thank you, members of the American Library Association, for then. Thank you for now. Thank you forever.

Publishers Weekly

SOURCE: A review of *The View from Saturday,* in *Publishers Weekly,* Vol. 243, No. 30, July 22, 1996, p. 242.

Glowing with humor and dusted with magic, this contemporary novel explores the ties that bind the four members of a championship academic quiz-bowl team. Sixth-grade teacher/coach Mrs. Olinski, teaching for the first time since becoming paraplegic, proudly observes her students' victories from the confines of a wheelchair. She is not sure what propelled her to choose the members of her team, nor does she fully comprehend the secret of their success in repeatedly beating older, more sophisticated competitors. Readers will be equally mystified until the backgrounds of the foursome (who call themselves The Souls) unfold during a series of first-person narratives that reveal the links between the students' private lives. Newbery Medalist Konigsburg orchestrates a stunning quartet of harmoniously blended voices. She expresses the individual struggles of each of her characters while showing how they unite to reach a common goal. Wrought with deep compassion and a keen sense of balance, her imaginative novel affirms the existence of small miracles in everyday life.

Julie Cummins

SOURCE: A review of *The View from Saturday,* in *School Library Journal,* Vol. 42, No. 9, September, 1996, p. 204.

Take four sixth graders; combine them as the Epiphany School team for Academic Bowl; add one paraplegic teacher; toss in formal tea times, grandparents of team members getting married, and some magic and calligraphy. Stir them with Konigsburg's masterful hand and you have an ingenious story. Nadia, Noah, Julian, and Ethan are not the top honor students, but Mrs. Olinski has chosen them for other reasons, ones unclear even to her. As the team beats all odds and expectations and reaches the finals, flashbacks told by each member shape a scenario that's like a bundle of pick-up sticks, each piece touching, supporting, and overlapping with the others, and one move affects them all. Stunning interplay of Nadia's turtle watches on Florida beaches, Noah's role as best man at a senior-citizen wedding, Ethan's discovery of himself through new friends, and Julian's ethical decision involving a bully skillfully wrap their stories into one, with amazing insights. Brilliant writing melds with crystalline characterizations in this sparkling story that is a jewel in the author's crown of outstanding work.

Ilene Cooper

SOURCE: A review of *The View from Saturday,* in *Booklist,* Vol. 93, No. 4, October 15, 1996, p. 424.

Four sixth-graders are chosen by their teacher, Mrs. Olinski, to be the class representatives for the Academic Bowl team. When the team goes on to perform amazing feats of erudition, including winning the state championship, people keep asking Mrs. Olinski how she chose the participants. Although the questioners never get a real answer, the story, told from different perspectives, lets readers in on the secret. Konigsburg's latest shows flashes of her great talent and her grasp of childhood, but the book is weighted down by a Byzantine structure that houses too many characters and alternating narratives that will confuse readers. The story begins at the wedding of two senior citizens in which young Noah is the best man. Two of the other team members, Ethan and Nadia, are grandchildren of the bride and groom, and the fourth member, new boy Julian Singh, cements the group when he invites the others for tea (yes, tea). Mrs. Olinski, who is wheelchair bound, only thinks she is choosing the quartet, when it is just as true they are choosing her. Overriding themes of civility and inclusiveness add interesting elements, but this is more ambitious than it is successful.

Janice M. Del Negro

SOURCE: A review of *The View from Saturday,* in *Bulletin of the Center for Children's Books,* Vol. 50, No. 3, November, 1996, p. 103.

The assembly of a sixth-grade Academic Bowl team doesn't appear to be a likely candidate for lively fiction, but Konigsburg, through her ability to create believable characters and place them in believable (even if slightly off the wall) situations, manages to make even an academic competition intriguing, at least at first. This partial success is achieved by giving each of the four team members (collectively known as The Souls) a distinct voice: Noah tells how he was the best man at a senior citizens' wedding, Nadia relates her reconciliation with her divorced father, and Ethan tells how the three of them became friends with Julian, the new boy in town. Quiet, bright Julian quietly makes friends with Nadia, Noah, and Nathan; quietly saves a classmate's dog from a nasty practical joke; and quietly gives the winning answer in the academic competition. Mrs. Olinski, their paraplegic sixth-grade teacher, conducts her class from her wheelchair, and her story intermingles with that of the chil-

dren. Konigsburg nearly keeps her from taking over the plot, but by the end of the book, the story is no longer about the four children but about Mrs. Olinski's spiritual enlightenment, which leads to a dismally self-conscious and flat ending. This is one of those books that just should have ended on page 159, but instead goes on to page 160. A list of academic bowl questions is appended.

Beth Gutcheon

SOURCE: "Wise Guys," in *The New York Times Book Review,* November 10, 1996, p. 49.

Mrs. Olinski's sixth grade Academic Bowl team mopped up the floor with the other sixth-grade teams at Epiphany Middle School. Then it skunked the seventh grade team, a thing that had never happened in history. Then it whomped the eighth grade and steamed on through the regionals, and New York is agog as little Noah Gershom hits his buzzer for the first question in the state finals. Question: "What is the meaning of the word *calligraphy* and from what language does it derive?"

This is a cakewalk for Noah Gershom, and you are about to find out why, as you cut away from the Academic Bowl to Noah's hilarious description of his summer visit to his grandparents in Century Village, Fla., where he helped orchestrate the wedding of Izzy Diamondstein and Margaret Draper. Tillie Nachman taught Noah to address invitations beautifully, and he ended up serving as best man when the groom's son, Allen, broke his ankle.

Beautiful, upset Nadia Diamondstein has just moved to Epiphany with her mother; her parents have recently divorced (see above). She has a dog named Ginger who is a genius. She and Noah are both starting Mrs. Olinski's sixth grade this fall. You might think this is a little too much coincidence, but you are not taking into account that Margaret Draper, Nadia's new step-grandmother, was once school principal in Epiphany and as such has put many of the balls here into play.

Margaret's grandson Ethan Potter, smart, shy and painfully silent, is also in Mrs. Olinski's class, but the unexpected catalyst for the team is the Sikh newcomer Julian Singh, whose father has just opened a bed-and-breakfast in town. Julian recognizes the others, in the Emersonian sense, and institutes a tea party for them every Saturday (hence the title of the book.)

Perfect. Each of the four is brainy, funny and big-hearted, and they all know "Alice's Adventures in Wonderland" inside out. A tea party is just right. Some of us have already read every book E. L. Konigsburg ever wrote, starting with *From the Mixed-Up Files of Mrs. Basil E. Frankweiler,* which won the Newbery Medal in 1968, but others are going to begin with this book and will probably find it very hard to stop before going through the whole shelf. This constitutes nearly perfect praise. And it takes great self-control to resist telling what happens when Nadia's genius dog Ginger is cast in the role of Sandy in the holiday production of "Annie." Not to mention what happens when Julian Singh offers "posh" and "tip" as acronyms that have entered the language and the bozos running the state finals can't find "tip" on their answer list.

The structure of *The View From Saturday* might confuse some younger readers, but that isn't anything to worry much about, because it's all too delicious. If Ginger is a genius, what do you call E. L. Konigsburg?

Roger Sutton

SOURCE: A review of *The View from Saturday,* in *The Horn Book Magazine,* Vol. 73, No. 1, January-February, 1997, pp. 60-1.

Mrs. Olinski's sixth-grade Academic Bowl team, self-named "The Souls," has made it all the way to the state finals. Each of the four Souls must answer a question, and their answers blossom from their surprisingly intertwined lives and aspirations. As the Souls tell their stories we learn, for example, that Nadia's grandfather married Ethan's grandmother, and fellow soul Noah was the best man—all the way down in Florida, no less. The interlockings are clever, but they contribute to an aura of artifice that haloes the book: nothing seems and no one sounds quite real. Characters speak archly and aphoristically, and while we are given to understand that these students are "gifted" (although Konigsburg's good sense and wit would never allow her to use such a word without irony) and therefore quirky, they sound too much alike. (Mrs. Olinski, in fact, emerges as the most rounded character, and in some ways the book is about her more than it is anyone else.) Smart readers, though, may be drawn to this story of smart kids who win—on many levels.

Additional coverage of Konigsburg's life and career is contained in the following sources published by Gale Research: *Authors and Artists for Young Adults,* Vol. 3; *Contemporary Authors New Revision Series,* Vols. 17, 39; *Dictionary of Literary Biography,* Vol. 52; *Junior DISCovering Authors 2.0* CD-ROM; *Major Authors and Illustrators for Children and Young Adults; Major Twentieth-Century Writers;* and *Something About the Author,* Vols. 4, 48

Bruce McMillan

1947-

American author and photo-illustrator of children's books.

Major works include *The Remarkable Riderless Runaway Tricycle* (1978), *Counting Wildflowers* (1986), *One Sun: A Book of Terse Verse* (1990), *Eating Fractions* (1991), *Nights of the Pufflings* (1995).

INTRODUCTION

McMillan is best known as the author of children's photo-illustrated concept books. Acclaimed for his skilled, colorful photography, McMillan has created a body of work that appeals to a range of children from the very young through the primary grades. Using the backdrop of his native rural Maine, McMillan's work reflects the life and landscape of school, town, shoreline, and ocean. And while it is his photographic work that is consistently lauded, McMillan considers himself on a par as a writer. "I tell a story so that the whole is greater than the sum of its parts—the book is more than a collection of photos." Praised for the engaging, witty presentation of simple concepts such as counting, rhyming, colors, or shapes, McMillan's work is often layered with lessons in science, history, and multiculturalism. "[The concept books] are quite complex and work on many levels," writes McMillan. "I enjoy the mental challenge these books pose. I love being inside my head . . . challenging myself, playing games with myself. . . . Working on a book makes me feel happy."

Biographical Information

McMillan was born in Boston but spent most of his childhood in Maine. On his fifth birthday he received a camera from his father, Frank, and was given his first professional camera—a Rolleicord—when he was nine. He worked as a photographer for his high school newspaper, and, because he couldn't afford the cost, produced his own senior pictures, costumed as various historical figures. McMillan attended the University of Maine as a biology major, but spent a great deal of his time in a work-study position with a local television station. There he worked as a cameraman, then later as a director and producer. Following graduation he worked three more years in television before "retiring" to McGee Island, where he resided as the island's caretaker. During the last year of his stay he wrote and photographed his first book, *Finestkind O'Day: Lobstering in Maine* (1977), using his then five-year-old son, Brett. After moving ashore to Shapleigh, Maine, where he lives with his beagle, Julio, and his two cats, McMillan has continued to write and photograph a prodigious number of books for the young. Additionally, he offers children's picture book courses at both the University of Southern Maine and the University of New Hampshire.

Major Works

McMillan has published nearly forty photo-illustrated books, comprising works of documentary, fantasy, and concept. Working in the former category, McMillan takes readers on a lobstering expedition in *Finestkind O'Day*, through the manufacture of a pair of shoes in *Making Sneakers* (1980), whale-watching in *Going on a Whale Watch* (1992), and on a trip to the polar regions in *Summer Ice: Life along the Antarctic Peninsula* and *Nights of the Pufflings* (both 1995). His fantasy works include *The Remarkable Riderless Runaway Tricycle*, a work McMillan refers to as his "autobiography," which features the trials of a discarded tricycle finding its way home from the city dump by way of perseverance and humor; and *Ghost Doll* (1983), in which the apparition of a doll challenges a young girl to be brave. The majority of his works, however, can be described as concept books, such as *The Alphabet Symphony: An ABC Book* (1977), which locates the letters of the alphabet in the instruments and performers of a symphony orchestra; *Becca Backward, Becca Frontward: A Book of Concept Pairs* (1986), which works to illustrate opposites with the help of a young girl; and *Mouse Views: What the Class Pet Saw* (1993), which asks readers to identify larger objects from the limited vantage point of an escaped mouse. Additionally, McMillan's concepts often work at multiple levels, such as in *Counting Wildflowers*, which, in addition to being an exercise in counting, is also a primer in wildflower taxonomy; *Eating Fractions*, which functions as both an introduction to fractions and a recipe book; and *Puffins Climb, Penguins Rhyme* (1995), a book of children's verse which also highlights the differences between the puffins of Iceland and the penguins of Antarctica.

Awards

Three times McMillan has won the American Library Association's Notable Book Award—in 1986 for *Counting Wildflowers*, in 1990 for *One Sun: A Book of Terse Verse*, and in 1991 for *Eating Fractions*. *One Sun* also won the Outstanding Science Trade Book for Children prize in 1990, an award McMillan had captured once before, in 1986, for *Becca Backward, Becca Frontward*. That work also garnered offical praise in 1986 from the National Science Teachers Association.

AUTHOR'S COMMENTARY

Bruce McMillan

SOURCE: "Photographer or Photo-Illustrator: What's the Difference?," in *School Library Journal,* Vol. 37, No. 2, February, 1991, pp. 38-9.

I was talking on the phone with Dianne Hess, my editor at Scholastic Books. We were discussing our book in production at that time, ***Mary Had a Little Lamb.*** "When you explain it, I don't have a question with you using photo-illustrator instead of photographer on the cover. But Jean does. It's so clear when you explain it, why don't you talk to her." So I did. Jean Feiwel, editor-in-chief of Scholastic Books, posed the key question, "Why not just say photographer?" Without missing a beat, I replied, "I'm glad you asked."

What I do is so similar to what other children's illustrators do that if I had the option of mixing with a group of photographers or a group of illustrators, I'd head for the latter. I have more in common with them. I make books. My illustrating medium happens to be the photograph. We approach books in the same way. We are illustrators. We bring something to light. Is there truly a difference in referring to a book using photographs as being photographed or photo-illustrated? Indeed, there is. For a photo-illustrator, the book is the finished work of art.

All books that use photographs, however, are not photo-illustrated; some are photographed. I have done both. I was well into my children's-book career before I realized the difference, and began using the term photo-illustrator. The difference starts with the artist's approach to the work. A photographed book is a collection of individual creations. It's similar to stepping into a museum's photographic exhibit. Each photograph stands on its own. The statement that the artist intended is contained within the individual image. When you visit the exhibit, although there's an entrance, you may initiate your viewing from almost anywhere. Wherever you start, you can take in the entire exhibit and experience the full impact. It's a collection of individual images. The exhibit could be the work of one photographer or the work of many. Either way, each photograph is the artistic statement; each is the finished work of art. A photographer may walk into an art director's office, leave a pile of photos featuring a theme, and then wait to see what the art director, or the author, does with them. That's not what a photo-illustrator does.

A photo-illustrated book is also a collection of individual photographs, but there the similarity ends. When I'm photo-illustrating a book, I look beyond each individual image. Of course, I'm working to make sure that what is happening in the photograph stands on its own. But I'm looking beyond that. When I look through the viewfinder of one of my Nikons, I visualize the entire book. I see what's happening in the preceding and succeeding pages. I see how this fits into the whole. The finished work is not the individual image, but the entire book. It's one person's vision.

Is my wordless picture book, ***Dry or Wet?***, photographed or photo-illustrated? Although each photo can stand on its own, the images couldn't be placed randomly in the book. They were carefully planned to interplay with one another. There are seven children, and each child introduces readers to a new friend, the next child in the book. It's a subtle sequencing but the photos become a narrative—a story. It's more work, planning how each photo relates to the rest of the book, and requires much more previsualization. It makes this more than a collection of pictures that show dry or wet.

The same planning went into my books of "terse verse," ***One Sun*** and the forthcoming ***Play Day***. *One Sun* chronicled a child's day at the beach. Each two-word rhyming couplet was written and sequenced with the photos in mind. If I'd approached it as a photo-journalist, I'd have taken a pleasing picture for the title page of a boy at the beach, just as I found him, and it would have been fine. But as a photo-illustrator I previsualized and planned each page long before I started taking pictures. The book took shape when I began shooting. In this photo-illustrated book, the photos are all interrelated and provide a continuing look at the whole—the book—not just individual images.

When I photographed ***The Weather Sky*** I was taking individual photographs of the sky over the period of a year. It began as an unconnected series of cloud photographs. I didn't visualize quite how they would become a book but I had a list of cloud types I wanted to capture. I wasn't concerned with the interplay between the images. I always had my oldest Nikon loaded, ready to shoot the sky from my yard. I looked for dramatic sky and clouds—no sunsets or sunrises, and no horizons. I concentrated on the composition of the photo, and recording the cloud formations. Only one aspect of the book required any interplay, and it was minor. To show the passage of time, I photographed a maple tree against the sky to indicate the four seasons. Here, I had to relate the clouds in the sky to the clouds on the previous page. But, overall, it is a collection of individual images.

Is my rendition of *Mary Had a Little Lamb* photographed or photo-illustrated? I see it as photo-illustrated. Work from this book was included in The Original Art Show at The Society of Illustrators Museum of American Illustration. Here I had to visualize each photo as a part of the story, and also how it related to the whole. By illustrating the story, interpreting it as I saw it, I was bringing it to light. Could I let serendipity take place? Of course. After all, I had a lamb running around. While I was chasing the lamb and taking the photo, I had in mind the framework of the book. Did I press the shutter when the lamb was amusingly walking, right to left, and facing toward the left side of the frame? No. Did I press the shutter when he was against an unrelated background, even though it was a beautiful picture? No. I patiently waited until he was going in the other direction, left to right, the same way we read our language and turn the pages in our books. I waited until he was in front of the matching background found on the previous page. Only then did it fit into my design for the book. Will unexpected things happen that fit into the book when shooting, even if the book is so thought out? Sure they will. As Louis Pasteur noted, "Chance favors the prepared mind." I was prepared for my lamb's antics.

Is a book photographed or photo-illustrated? It all depends on the artist's approach. Is it a thematic approach of similar but unrelated images, which makes it a book of photographs, or is it a total-book approach, which makes it a book of photo-illustrations? When shooting the photographs was there a sense of where the image fit into the book? Was thought being given to whether it would be a left-page photo or a right-page photo? What about leaving out-of-focus space for the title text?

As an illustrator, I'm designing a page when I'm shooting the picture for that page. It's much more work than taking a single image for the pure joy of it. But, to use an oxymoron, it's enjoyable work. The artistic satisfaction from doing this—the inner delight of aesthetic ecstasy—is the reason I create books. When I photo-illustrate a book, the artistic satisfaction comes in two stages. First, when the photos are viewed individually, and then again when the work is seen as a whole.

A photo-illustrated book is usually the work of one person. It's their vision. This isn't always the case with a photographed book. Many times a writer will illustrate a book by selecting photos from the files of a stock photo agency, a government agency, or a major business such as a drug company with a file of germ photos. The photograph may have been made simply for record purposes, and no artistic statement was intended. Or perhaps it was taken as an artistic statement. Whatever the purpose of the photo, when it was made, there was no thought about how it would fit into a book. Can you imagine a collection of illustrator's works, artists who use watercolor or colored pencil or oil or whatever, put together to tell a story? Not likely. It is the vision of one artist that makes the book work, and the same holds true for the photo-illustrated book.

My math concept books, *One Two, One Pair!* and *Eating Fractions,* are photo-illustrated. There is a wordless, visual narrative that makes each book a story. The surprises at the conclusions don't come from the verbal elements in the books; those elements relate to the math concepts. It's the visual components that tell the story. There is a beginning, a middle, and my traditional happy ending. The books have been photographically sketched. Many photos were taken that will not appear in the book. They were taken as sketches, much like an illustrator who draws, to see what works and what doesn't. This is what I do as a photo-illustrator because, for me, the whole is greater than the sum of its parts. The book is greater than the sum of its photographs.

Bruce McMillan

SOURCE: "Playing with Math," in *CBC Features,* Vol. 46, No. 2, Summer-Fall, 1993, pp. 2-3.

When I was in school, math was a tool—a tool to be enjoyed as I learned how to use it. I enjoyed the logic of mathematics. It made so much sense. But it didn't seem like the kind of thing one would chat about with others, so I didn't. I still don't chat about math. But I've made math a part of my work. Of the thirty children's books I've written and photo-illustrated, five are math-related.

What I try to bring to my math-related concept books is what appealed to me during my early experiences with math—a fun time with logic. For example, I once thought about doing a book introducing the concept of the simplest number set of all—the pair. The story line of this book, *One, Two, One Pair!,* is the anticipation and joy of going ice skating. As with most of my concept books, I decided on a visual narrative approach. Early in the story I provide a subtle clue to the surprise ending. What appears to be one person putting on a pair of socks, mittens, skates, laces, and so on is actually a pair of people—twins.

Before photographing this book, I contacted a respected teacher from the largest school district in Maine and asked for a list of their K-6 teaching objectives for math. I was interested in which math skills students were expected to know at each grade level. Since my books are often used as teaching tools, in effect I'm a teacher as well as an author.

The list of math objectives stimulated a new book idea: cooking fractions. I like to cook. I first thought of doing this book for grade levels 3–6, based on the age levels in the list of objectives. I planned to show additive fractional units as children cooked something sumptuous and then subtractive fractional units as they ate it. However, I couldn't sell the idea to a publisher. They decided that this age group, grades 3–6, was too old for a picture book. So, I simplified my idea and refocused it for grades K–3. The result, *Eating Fractions,* is about a meal. Two children divide and share what they eat as fractional units. Each fractional unit is displayed on the left page in a photograph, graphic, and text, while the visual story line appears on the facing right page. The story progresses from halves to thirds to fourths. Then, to reinforce learning this concept, the story continues and repeats the progression of halves, thirds, and fourths, followed by a visual surprise—plus recipes—at the end.

Obviously, the list of teaching objectives was informative in pointing out what teachers are teaching. But it also showed me that the corresponding age levels aren't written in stone. When autographing this book at schools, bookstores, and libraries, I've noticed that the readers I'm autographing for range from kindergarteners to fifth-graders. My approach served as an introduction to fractions for younger students and at the same time reinforced the concept for older readers.

While I made *Eating Fractions* for children to enjoy as a story, as well as to help them learn a new concept, the overwhelming positive response from teachers has been gratifying. Thanks to them, it has become one of my biggest-selling books. I thought it would do well, but not quite this well. Teachers have told me one of the reasons why. Repeatedly, I heard, "There aren't any quality books about fractions. And we all teach fractions." *Eating Fractions* filled a void.

Teachers have also told me how *Eating Fractions* has led to hands-on learning. That's why I included the recipes. I'm a hands-on learner, and when I was planning this book I could foresee children dividing food, looking forward to eating it, and actually learning along the way.

There was another reason besides math for doing *One, Two, One Pair!* and *Eating Fractions.* I'd just completed my own twelve-year hands-on project—my house. Though I recently traveled far away to photograph a forthcoming book, *Penguins At Home: Gentoos Of Antarctica,* I didn't have to go far at all to photograph the math concept books—my newly finished home was the perfect setting for both.

Geometry is a subject that lends itself to a visual approach. I selected the "vehicle" to tell this story. Recalling my childhood field trips to a fire station in Bangor, Maine, I remembered the thrill of stepping out into a void, grabbing hold of the fire pole, and sliding down to the floor below where the fire engines were parked and ready to go. So began *Fire Engine Shapes.* It takes a graphic look at the geometric shapes found on parts of a fire engine, but I also included a game because I like to play. The little girl exploring the fire engine can be found in every photo, but it takes careful observation to do so. I thought the idea of looking for shapes while looking for the little girl would engage the minds of young readers. Had I foreseen how popular this phenomenon would become—looking for a person hidden in the illustration of a book—I might have titled this book *Where's Stephanie?* Waldo had not yet made his debut.

When I'm out speaking at schools I always like to bring along some surprises and props. I wish that my tricycle, the "star" of *The Remarkable Riderless Runaway Tricycle,* could collect frequent-flyer miles, as it often accompanies me on trips. On a few special occasions I've brought along a very large prop. In some of Maine's elementary schools, I've introduced students to "My 'star' . . . waiting outside by the playground . . . too big to come inside." When we go outside we find Engine 5, the very same one photographed in *Fire Engine Shapes.* It's a treat to see a whole school, class by class, walking around the actual fire engine, and picking out the geometric shapes.

The first numbers that children often utilize are related to time. When I began work on *Time To . . .* I had to consider a variety of clocks. I settled on a traditional-looking clock face, but there was a dilemma. A few years ago this wouldn't have applied but now it does: digital clock faces. So, in addition to using the traditional clock face, I also included the time in digital format on the same page.

In *Time To . . .* the progression of a child's day is seen in the photo on the right page, and the photo on the left page features a clock on the young boy's wall. What readers may not be aware of is that, although it appears the clock wall photos were taken in the boy's room, they weren't. I used extra wallpaper on a propped-up sheet of wallboard to make a false wall set and placed it in my new living room, twenty miles away. This way I could control the lighting in order to show the progression of time throughout the day.

I teach a children's picture book course, open to the public, at the University of Southern Maine and the University of New Hampshire. *Time To . . .* provided me with an example to use in my children's book classes of how two artists, working independently and having never met nor exchanged correspondence, can approach a theme and concept in a similar manner. It's fortunate that my book, *Time To . . . ,* and Mordicai Gerstein's book, *A Sun's Day*, were published at about the same time because it's uncanny how similar they are. The identical details in each book both amuse and amaze me.

My college degree is in biology and so when I began work on my first math concept book, *Counting Wildflowers,* it was also a taxonomy lesson. My editor and I agreed that children would be interested in wildflowers rather than garden flowers. It was a search for wildflowers which blossom at various times throughout the season. Every species of flower has its own biological clock. That's why I couldn't photograph dandelions—they had already blossomed and gone to seed by the time I began shooting.

Counting Wildflowers concludes with a photo of maiden pinks. After counting from one to twenty wildflowers, the reader finds a photograph filled with a profusion of delicate pink blossoms. What the reader doesn't know is that the photo was taken of flowers growing on very fertile ground—my septic field. Once again, I was photographing a math concept at home.

The profusion of flowers in that particular photo inspired a comment from a teacher which led me to a concept that may be what I focus on in my next math-related book. When I spoke at last year's annual Math Their Way Conference I floated this idea by some of the teachers. They all said, "That's great, we need a book on that." The topic? You'll just have to wait to find out. But I can tell you one thing. Though it's a math concept book, unlike four of my previous math concept books, it probably won't be photographed at my home—but you never know.

TITLE COMMENTARY

📖 *FINESTKIND O'DAY: LOBSTERING IN MAINE* (1977)

Kirkus Reviews

SOURCE: A review of *Finestkind O'Day: Lobstering in Maine,* in *Kirkus Reviews,* Vol. XLV, No. 13, July 1, 1977, p. 671.

McMillan's photos and text offer readers a chance to share the experience of lobstering in Maine with Brett, who doesn't look a day over ten but rows by himself past Stone Island all the way to Port Clyde, there to board Allison Welson's lobsterboat for his first tour as sternman. All morning Brett helps Allison haul in his traps, and each time they both guess how many lobsters will be coming up; through it all Allison finds time to explain about sorting out keepers, pegging the crusher claws, and throwing back "berried" females. Youngsters who don't know Allison as well as Brett does might find his manner a shade condescending, but he is an affable teacher and Brett, who steers the boat home, will be envied his opportunity and admired for proving up to it.

Publishers Weekly

SOURCE: A review of *Finestkind O'Day: Lobstering in Maine,* in *Publishers Weekly,* Vol. 212, No. 5, August 1, 1977, p. 115.

This is the finest kind of photo-journalism for boys and girls who like action-filled days of outdoor adventure and who don't mind learning, at the same time, the workings of the fishing trade. Nine-year-old Brett McMillan rows his dory past Stone Island at dawn, to join his friend, Allison Wilson. For his birthday, Brett's parents had given him his own lobster license. Today would be his first day as sternman on Wilson's boat. The friends spend the morning lobstering and trawling for halibut. Brett's father, the Maine photographer and author, records all the fun and hard work in artful black-and-white pictures and a clear, lively text. The story ends with Brett bringing home a surprise to his faithful dog, Tammy, a present to make up for leaving his pet lonely at home.

Hayden Atwood

SOURCE: A review of *Finestkind O'Day: Lobstering in Maine,* in *School Library Journal,* Vol. 24, No. 2, October, 1977, p. 106.

Text and photographs follow Brett, the author's son, as he boards the *Ruth M.* with Allison Wilson, a veteran lobsterman. The two spend the day along the Maine coast pulling and baiting traps, pegging lobsters, and fishing for halibut. Much basic information about lobsters and lobstering is imparted along the way, although the occupation tends to be glamorized here. Still, this is a perfect companion to the Carricks' *The Blue Lobster,* which details the life cycle of a lobster.

Barbara Elleman

SOURCE: A review of *Finestkind O'Day: Lobstering in Maine,* in *Booklist,* Vol. 74, No. 4, October 15, 1977, p. 377.

Sharp black-and-white photographs capture the flavor of young Brett's day as sternman (lobsterman's helper) aboard a lobsterboat, the *Ruth M.,* off the coast of Maine. With his friend Allison Wilson, Brett sets out in the early hours to check the lobster pots, where each creature is carefully measured for size and sex (females and those under 3 3/16 inches are thrown back). He feeds the sea gulls, finds a hermit crab to take home, and catches some halibut on the way to shore. Brett's day ends with a trip into the village, a long row back to his island home, and the happy sight of his dog patiently waiting his return. McMillan, whose son is the model for the photographs, keeps his text brief and to the point. Some of the photographs are too dark to see the detail clearly, but the excitement of the day is evident.

📖 *THE ALPHABET SYMPHONY: AN ABC BOOK* (1977)

George A. Woods

SOURCE: A review of *The Alphabet Symphony: An ABC*

Book, in *The New York Times Book Review,* October 23, 1977, p. 32.

There's the sound of music in *The Alphabet Symphony* but for all practical purposes it's a dim and distant tune. Bruce McMillan has focused his camera on the musicians and instruments of the Portland, Me. Symphony Orchestra and therein, supposedly, lies the alphabet. W is the four angled sticks that strike the timpani; Y is the fastening for the bongos; X is crossed flutes. All of this is quite artful and clever, the photography excellent. It is a faultless exercise in playing the scale but neither a musician—nor an acceptable alphabet—does it make. The instructional value is nil. The publisher has obviously anticipated this cavil by pointing out the book's mind-stretching potential with "wherever you are—wherever you go—let your imagination see!" Maestro, no encore please.

Barbara S. Worth

SOURCE: A review of *The Alphabet Symphony: An ABC Book,* in *Children's Book Review Service,* Vol. 6, No. 3, November, 1977, p. 23.

The sharp, clear, black-and-white photographs of the Portland Symphony Orchestra form the body of this text without words. Each photograph depicts a musical instrument and each musical instrument encompasses a letter of the alphabet. Below each photograph the letter configuration is reiterated in white on neutral background colors of brown, tan, gray, or taupe. On the whole, this is a very beautiful, sophisticated, and artistic book.

Gemma DeVinney

SOURCE: A review of *The Alphabet Symphony: An ABC Book,* in *School Library Journal,* Vol. 24, No. 3, November, 1977, p. 50.

This alphabet concept book uses the camera's eye to teach children the shapes of the letters of the alphabet. The unifying theme is a symphony orchestra. The letter "I" is depicted as a vertically held conductor's baton, for example, and the letter "X" is crisscrossing flutes. The book is an impressive invitation to visual imagining, but it is so similar to Barry Miller's *Alphabet World,* in which letters are paralleled in shape by familiar objects, that it would be an unnecessary duplication in a collection already using the Miller book.

Denise M. Wilms

SOURCE: A review of *The Alphabet Symphony: An ABC Book,* in *Booklist,* Vol. 74, No. 5, November 1, 1977, p. 479.

Though billed as an alphabet book, this is more an exercise in the recognition of shape, form, and symmetry. McMillan's close-up shots of musical instruments, tools,

or musicians show how some selected portions of them are suggestive of alphabet letters: the curved indenture of a string bass makes a C; the shadowy silhouette of a musician at his cello looks distinctly like an R; the top of a tuning fork against the backdrop of a drumhead represents the letter U. Used as a visual game this can generate fun as well as innovative sight training. But don't expect to use it as a conventional alphabet book. The instruments don't start with the associated letter; moreover, the contrivances sometimes employed to achieve the alphabet shape (three fingers depressing keys gets you an M) seem to stretch for effect. Instruments are labeled in an appended spread, necessitating flipping back and forth to answer questions or see just what the whole picture really is.

Ethel L. Heins

SOURCE: A review of *The Alphabet Symphony: An ABC Book,* in *The Horn Book Magazine,* Vol. LIII, No. 6, December, 1977, p. 656.

ABC books offer limitless possibilities for variations on a theme. A photographer has painstakingly selected—and shot from unusual angles—specific details of orchestral accouterments which parallel in shape the capital letters of the alphabet. For example, *S* is matched with the resonance hole of a cello, *N* to the configuration of three violin bows in action, and *U* to a tuning fork. Confusion cannot occur since there is no suggestion that the name of the instrument or object corresponds to the letter illustrated; only in two summary pages at the end of the book are the items identified in miniature reproductions of the pictures. Decidedly not for young children who are unacquainted with their ABCs, the book is rather for readers mature enough to appreciate visual analogies. While the photographer cannot equal Tana Hoban in imagination or ingenuity, his work does add to a growing collection of books which present a kind of basic training in observation.

THE REMARKABLE RIDERLESS RUNAWAY TRICYCLE (1978)

Publishers Weekly

SOURCE: A review of *The Remarkable Riderless Runaway Tricycle,* in *Publishers Weekly,* Vol. 213, No. 8, February 20, 1978, p. 127.

Photographer McMillan has made the most ingenious and fun-filled adventure out of this combination of imagination and solid reality. You wonder how he created the dazzling pictures of Jason's tricycle, but you don't have to know to enjoy the effects. Jason mopes on his doorstep after his beloved vehicle is sent to the town dump by his parents, who mistakenly judge it to be worn out. At the dump, the tricycle confounds the trash man by flying from the bulldozer and careening down the road. The following pages present hilarious scenes featuring Kennebunkport, Maine, residents who watch the tricycle tear past them to freedom and right back home to grateful Jason. A whiz of a reading adventure, the book is one for adults as well as kids to marvel over.

Craighton Hippenhammer

SOURCE: A review of *The Remarkable Riderless Runaway Tricycle,* in *School Library Journal,* Vol. 24, No. 9, May, 1978, p. 58.

Tragedy of tragedies. A perfectly good tricycle is thrown away and lands in the Kennebunkport Dump. But wait— it escapes the clutches of bulldozer, avoids a smelly grave and careens down the road past surprised cow and screeching train to fall off the end of a pier. The posed black-and-white photographs show that the tricycle's trip is not yet over as it rolls on making a nuisance of itself to an artist, a boat painter, and a cat. Eventually, it ends up back in the lonely arms of Jason, the young son of the wretched parents who perpetrated this foul deed. Some kids might enjoy this illogical escapade, but the ground rules for creating temporary suspension of disbelief in a fantasy world are disregarded here.

Kirkus Reviews

SOURCE: A review of *The Remarkable Riderless Runaway Tricycle,* in *Kirkus Reviews,* Vol. XLVI, No. 10, May 15, 1978, p. 545.

McMillan's full-page black-and-white photos give a documentary look to what is really a couldn't-happen fabrication about Jason's tricycle. Discarded by Jason's parents and taken to the dump, the tricycle falls from the bulldozer's bucket and goes rolling off—past a cow, across the trolley tracks, off a pier into a lobster boat, past the shops in town, and finally (after more adventures) right up to the stoop where Jason sits missing his trike. Set in Kennebunkport, Maine, whose residents posed for the photos, this makes simpletons of all the grownups involved—from "dump man" Ernest who chases the tricycle yelling "Stop! Stop! You're my trash!" through fireman Bob who squirts the tricycle with his hose to various head-scratching ("Well I'll be!") and shrieking, package-spilling others. Their overplaying, along with all the local landmarks, gives this the air of a well-staged amateur production—great fun for those who know the cast and setting, perhaps a diverting curiosity for others. (McMillan, though, is no amateur photographer.)

Charlotte W. Draper

SOURCE: A review of *The Remarkable Riderless Runaway Tricycle,* in *The Horn Book Magazine,* Vol. LIV, No. 3, June, 1978, p. 266.

Jason feels sad that his parents have consigned his tricycle to the town dump. The tricycle, however, with an insou-

ciance and willfulness reminiscent of the red balloon in the famous film, does not submit to the edict. About to be plowed under by a bulldozer, the tricycle escapes and finds its way home to Jason, passing on its way a ruminating cow, a workman on a lobster boat, a curious black cat, a trolley brakeman, and other sundry spectators. Each black-and-white photograph freezes a moment in the hectic journey of the child's velocipede—deftly balancing the concepts of realism and fantasy, constraint and freedom.

Ruth M. Stein

SOURCE: A review of *The Remarkable Riderless Runaway Tricycle,* in *Language Arts,* Vol. 55, No. 7, October, 1978, pp. 860-61.

The author uses his own black/white full-page photos to illustrate his fantasy of the tricycle that manages its own salvation after being dumped. The story seems patterned after "The Gingerbread Man," with a happier ending. While the minimal text contains conversation and a plot of sorts, its main purpose serves to connect the photographs. Though realistic illustrations can help identification with the young hero, they may prevent acceptance of the story's more imaginative aspects.

APPLES, HOW THEY GROW (1979)

Barbara Elleman

SOURCE: A review of *Apples, How They Grow,* in *Booklist,* Vol. 75, No. 13, March 1, 1979, pp. 1093-94.

From winter-frosted apple boughs to summer-ripe juicy fruit ready for picking, the development of the apple is carefully visualized and explained through appropriate, well-captioned black-and-white photographs. With a knowledgeable eye McMillan trains his camera on the forming buds, emerging petals, pollinating bees, and slow-swelling fuzziness that becomes the apple, giving these and other intermediate steps in the growing process full-page treatment. Juxtaposed are small photographs offering views of the entire tree, as well as semidistant shots that help put the close-ups in proper perspective, all supplemented with a concise, explanatory text. Despite the lack of color, strikingly used in [Millicent E.] Selsam's *The Apple and Other Fruits,* and the inclusion of some photographs too small to be distinctive, this is a well-planned ecology lesson on one of our most common fruits. Junior high and middle grade students who use [Elizabeth S.] Helfman's *Apples, Apples, Apples,* [Bernice Kohn] Hunt's *Apples: A Bushel of Fun and Facts,* or [Alvin and Virginia] Silversteins' *Apples: All about Them* will find this a useful supplement.

Kirkus Reviews

SOURCE: A review of *Apples, How They Grow,* in *Kirkus Reviews,* Vol. XLVII, No. 8, April 15, 1979, p. 454.

How do you read this? You can take a first trip through the book following only the large-print, one-sentence captions and the full-page photos that show the fruit's development from bursting bud to leafy cluster to blossom to swelling ovary and finally a juicy red apple. Or you can try to take in as well the series of three frames, each with a longer, small-print caption, that elaborates on each stage. McMillan's format is indeed distracting, and his dry, curt text will elude the designated three-to-eight-year-old readership: terms like "fruiting spurs" aren't explained; pollen "adheres"; at one stage "the complex sugars, or carbohydrates, break down into simple sugars, transforming the hard, tart apples. . ."; and the leaf's manufacture of food is condensed into three complex sentences. But his smashing close-up photos tell a story worth following.

Steve Matthews

SOURCE: A review of *Apples, How They Grow,* in *School Library Journal,* Vol. 25, No. 9, May, 1979, p. 54.

The growth of the apple has been chronicled in the superb *The Apple and Other Fruits* by Selsam and Wexler. Thus, *Apples* . . . is a second choice from the outset. Photographs, while aesthetically pleasing, lack clarity, and parts are obscured by a vague washed-out fuzziness. The large-print text would have been adequate but the author also includes smaller pictures and a caption-sized italic text supplying more details; an integration or choice between the two would have been less confusing and more successful.

Mary M. Burns

SOURCE: A review of *Apples, How They Grow,* in *The Horn Book Magazine,* Vol. LV, No. 4, August, 1979, p. 437.

A thoughtfully produced, well-designed visual documentary, the book traces the development of apples from the appearance of fruiting spurs in winter to the ripe apples in fall. Combining close-up photography with distance shots, the author-photographer has achieved variety without sacrificing specificity. For each step in the apple's development, he provides a microcosmic as well as a macrocosmic view, proceeding from a single detail to that detail seen in relation to the whole. In one sequence, for example, an individual blossom is seen as part of a cluster, then as part of the bough, finally becoming indistinct as part of the massed blossoms on a single tree. The accompanying text is really two texts in one: A straightforward declarative sentence in large type provides sufficient information for the beginning reader, and more sophisticated information is printed in captions for the small photographs. An artistic statement as well as a visual experience, the book reinforces the concepts of photography as an art form and of the photographer as illustrator.

Virginia A. Tashjian and Herbert J. Stoltz

SOURCE: A review of *Apples, How They Grow,* in *Appraisal: Children's Science Books,* Vol. 13, No. 3, Fall, 1980, p. 48.

Librarian: This fascinating photographic essay of how apples grow can be read on two levels: first by younger children (ages 5-8) who will find the large-print, blown up photographs and short captions interesting; second, by the 8-12 year olds who can read the shorter print and smaller photographic frames which go into more detailed explanation of the scientific truths behind the growth of apples. Some of the science is difficult and pre-supposes a knowledge of biological basics—but the photographs are so beautiful that it will "fly"!

Specialist: By using excellent black-and-white photographs the author describes how apples grow from dormant buds to ripe fruits. Young children can follow the apples development by looking at the pictures on the right-hand pages. Older children will be able to read the detailed descriptions and interpret the additional photographs on the left-hand page. This scientifically accurate book has a glossary.

MAKING SNEAKERS (1980)

Zena Sutherland

SOURCE: A review of *Making Sneakers,* in *Bulletin of the Center for Children's Books,* Vol. 33, No. 10, June, 1980, pp. 195-96.

With two photographs on each page, plus a few lines of print, the text follows the steps in the manufacturing of sneakers; the separate pieces are molded, cut, stamped, glued, pressed, sewn, etc. Result: a pair of sneakers. Not unlike other books about manufacturing, and not very stimulating information, particularly because the photographs do not always show (nor do the captions explain) what part of the sneaker is being handled.

Kirkus Reviews

SOURCE: A review of *Making Sneakers,* in *Kirkus Reviews,* Vol. XLVIII, No. 12, June 15, 1980, pp. 781-82.

Exactly, mechanically that: 26 pages of dry, unilluminating, and certainly uninspiring description of the manufacturing process which is illustrated concurrently in 54 identical-size, side-by-side photos (a band of photos, that is, stretching across the lower half of the wide pages). The text begins, bluntly: "First, sheets of rubber and chemicals are heated and mixed between two huge rollers"; it provides no amplification and very little explanation (how, for example, does one "mix" sheets); it makes no observations of a general nature—never allows for a reflective pause—and demonstrates nothing, indeed, beyond the many steps involved in making a pair of sneakers (on the assumption, perhaps, that that's enough of a lesson). The photos are similarly lacking in variety: all but one or two are close-ups of *parts* of machinery, parts of sneakers, hands holding parts of sneakers or inserting them in the machinery. We never see the factory or the people. And in its monotomy the book, counterproductively, actually makes the process dull.

Marilyn Payne Phillips

SOURCE: A review of *Making Sneakers,* in *School Library Journal,* Vol. 27, No. 1, September, 1980, p. 61.

The creation of a pair of joggers from rubber sheets and fabric rolls to the boxed end product is chronicled with 54 three-by-four-and-a-half inch black-and-white captioned photographs. Difficult vocabulary, the absence of a glossary to define such words as "bevel" and awkward sentence structure: "With a die (a metal pattern that is sharp as a knife), the cutter trims the sole using a machine that pushes the die down," make this book impossible reading for the intended audience. The visually unattractive and monotonous format is bottom heavy; only cropped, impersonal closeups are used in the lower half of each page with a scanty descriptive paragraph in the top half.

PUNOGRAPHY TOO (1980)

The New York Times Book Review

SOURCE: A review of *Punography Too,* in *The New York Times Book Review,* November 9, 1980, p. 41.

Two years ago, a writer/photographer from Down East with a weakness for puns combined his two occupational specialties to produce a paperback called *Punography.* A sufficient number of fanciers of wit's lowest form bought it to encourage him to commit this second offense—a collection of three dozen sequences of photographs certain to evoke groans from any well-bred viewer.

Cynthia L. Beatty

SOURCE: A review of *Punography Too,* in *Voice of Youth Advocates,* Vol. 4, No. 1, April, 1981, p. 45.

The title of McMillan's second book of visual puns is also a pun. It is a delightful collection of excellent b/w photographs which illustrate common expressions and give each a new meaning. The cover photos introduce the reader to the format of the book which encourages the reader to try to determine the expression pictured and thus makes the book a challenging brain teaser. Even the acknowledgments at the end are not without their own humor. The expressions and cliches are so common that most middle school students will be fa-

miliar with some of them, and junior high through adult will have heard almost all. It's a fun book to have around.

PUNIDDLES (with son, Brett McMillan, 1982)

Ilene Cooper

SOURCE: A review of *Puniddles,* in *Booklist,* Vol. 78, No. 15, April 1, 1982, p. 1020.

Another variation on the riddle concept, this time a visual one. Puniddles are pairs of photographs which together make a word. A fire burning in a fireplace and a picture of saltines? Firecrackers, of course. Most of the answers are supersimple, but the book should appeal to primary-graders and it could be used for group activity in a story hour. The black-and-white photos are clear and well composed, leaving little room for questions about what the puniddler had in mind.

Zena Sutherland

SOURCE: A review of *Puniddles,* in *Bulletin of the Center for Children's Books,* Vol. 35, No. 11, July-August, 1982, pp. 211-12.

Each page of this book carries a pair of black and white photographs; the object is to guess the word that they make together, and the answer is printed, upside-down, at the foot of the page. A wristwatch and a dog: watch-dog; a bee and a gull: beagle; a collie and a flower: cauliflower. There's some fun to this, but the weakness is quickly obvious, since there could be more than one answer to a picture—"cauliflower," for example, depends on knowing the breed of dog, while the dog picture for "watch-dog" does not.

HERE A CHICK, THERE A CHICK (1983)

Publishers Weekly

SOURCE: A review of *Here a Chick, There a Chick,* in *Publishers Weekly,* Vol. 223, No. 10, March 11, 1983, p. 86.

Small, newly hatched chicks demonstrate the meanings of simple words and their opposites, in this photo-concept book. A gawky chick is seen emerging from its shell to explain inside/outside, a fluffy one waddles up and down a red board, another heads round and round following a circular line of chick feed. Other concepts shown include high/low, in/out, stand/sit, asleep/awake, straight/crooked. Unfortunately, McMillan's attempt at here/there is not as successful as the others, since "here" and "there" are concepts dependent on the location of the speaker, rendered a bit confusingly here. The photos are striking and pages of chicks hopping about on a lush grass background should attract youngsters' eyes. Most endearing are juxtaposed pictures of a lonesome wee one ("alone") and a cozy group of fuzzy brothers and sisters ("together").

Pamela Warren Stebbins

SOURCE: A review of *Here a Chick, There a Chick,* in *School Library Journal,* Vol. 29, No. 9, May, 1983, p. 64.

This book teaches the concept of opposites using beautiful color photographs of lovable fluffy little chicks and it succeeds. Beginning with *begin,* an egg and a bag of feed is shown. The following two-page spreads introduce a word and its opposite with a chick or chicks demonstrating their meanings. Trails of feed are used to lead the chicks in different directions, *here* and *there,* and onto red boards to go *up* and *down.* Only *round* and *around* are questionable opposites. The yellow chicks and trails of light colored feed contrast well with the lush green grass on which they are photographed. The text is easily read and is an attractive part of the page. Each word, in large heavy black print, appears in a light yellow border. The book ends with *end* as the chicks walk away from us.

Ilene Cooper

SOURCE: A review of *Here a Chick, There a Chick,* in *Booklist,* Vol. 79, No. 18, May 15, 1983, p. 1220.

A baby chick comes out of his shell to show readers the meanings of words and their opposites. The handsome color photographs start on the title page with the word *Begin* in the right-hand corner. This is important because it shows the egg and a feed bag trickling grain on a wide expanse of lawn; if readers don't see the feed coming out of the bag, they'll probably be puzzled over the grain rows going in different directions on succeeding pages. The cracked egg demonstrates *Inside.* The emerging chick is *Outside. Asleep* and *Awake, Stand* and *Sit* are equally self-evident. A little harder to grasp is *Here* with a chick following a line of feed and *There,* the facing page showing him going in the opposite direction. Youngest readers will like the fluffy little chicks and their antics, which turn out to be a good learning device.

Zena Sutherland

SOURCE: A review of *Here a Chick, There a Chick,* in *Bulletin of the Center for Children's Books,* Vol. 37, No. 1, September, 1983, p. 12.

Color photographs on facing pages are used to present contrasting concepts (stand/sit, asleep/awake, straight/crooked, etc) and the characters are fluffy, appealing chicks. The pictures begin with a cracking egg (inside) and a bedraggled chick emerging (outside) and are usually good illustrations of the concepts of opposites, save for a few double-

page spreads like the one for here/there, where the chick is facing one way and looking at the eggshell, and then is moving away from it and facing the other way, or round/around, in which the chick appears to be doing exactly the same thing in both pictures, walking on a circular path of spilled seed. Nevertheless, useful—and certainly engaging.

M. Hobbs

SOURCE: A review of *Here a Chick, There a Chick,* in *The Junior Bookshelf,* Vol. 49, No. 3, June, 1985, p. 123.

Bruce McMillan's colour photography in **Here a Chick, There a Chick** shows a series of beautiful close-ups of a young chick against vivid green grass, with touches of red and beige as he explores wooden laths and trails of seed (both of which convey little to the young mind, but the colours are attractive). Beneath, in large black print against a yellow background, single words of direction and place are introduced. The paper, including the covers, is impractically flimsy for the early age envisaged, however, and the academic presentation to the adult buyer seems unnecessarily ponderous for such a slight work.

GHOST DOLL (1983)

Kirkus Reviews

SOURCE: A review of *Ghost Doll,* in *Kirkus Reviews,* Vol. LI, No. 17, September 1, 1983, p. J152.

Like **The Remarkable Riderless Runaway Tricycle,** this is a revival of the photographic fictions of 50 and more years ago—with photo-trickery conjuring up a "ghost doll" for plucky little Chrissy to find in the "haunted" house on the hill. The floating doll beckons her through imposing, near-empty rooms and up the (dramatic, darkening) circular staircase to the top of the house, meanwhile telling its doleful, antique tale of abandonment and loneliness. "I could be a doll again—your doll, if you really want me." But Chrissy must demonstrate her bravery by reaching out and touching the doll. Then the doll floats into a box and fades, the lid flies on, the box wafts itself out onto the grass, and Chrissy opens it to find— a real doll, "a doll that would never be lonely again." Sheer mush in sharp-edged, documentary guise (shot in a historic mansion in Kennebunkport, Maine, etc.)— though not as coy as *The Lonely Doll* and most other animal or toy photo-stories.

Denise M. Wilms

SOURCE: A review of *Ghost Doll,* in *Booklist,* Vol. 80, No. 2, September 15, 1983, p. 172.

Photographs, rather than drawings, illustrate this picture-book ghost story that will spark some shivers thanks to its realistic look. The story is about a young girl named Chrissy, who encounters a ghost doll when she explores the old house on the hill. The doll leads her on a trip to the top belfry, where it demands Chrissy touch it to prove she's brave: "I'll be your doll if you show me you're brave." The doll's previous owner had abandoned it, and the doll doesn't want to be bereft again. Chrissy obliges and the doll becomes real—for Chrissy to hug and keep forever. McMillan's pictures are effective in creating a sense of eeriness; it's a good thing the story is a light one with a happy ending. An interesting departure from the usual picture-book approach.

Leslie Chamberlin

SOURCE: A review of *Ghost Doll,* in *School Library Journal,* Vol. 30, No. 5, January, 1984, p. 66.

Like Dare Wright's classic, *The Lonely Doll,* **Ghost Doll** is a photo essay in black and white. The difference lies in the sweetness level. This is about Chrissy, who is lured into the upper reaches of a desolate mansion by an eerie floating plastic doll which becomes hers once she demonstrates bravery. The picture book format appears suitable for very young preschoolers, but parents would be hard pressed to explain the content to that audience. Why is this solitary young girl allowed to explore a vacant house? Do children of that age really need the concept of ghosts presented as flying underpants-clad dollies? As with his **Remarkable Riderless Runaway Tricycle** McMillan deserves credit for originality and execution of theme. The young actress displays generally credible expressions and the special camera effects are artful. It is unfortunate that the text is aimed at children too young for the story.

Zena Sutherland

SOURCE: A review of *Ghost Doll,* in *Bulletin of the Center for Children's Books,* Vol. 37, No. 6, February, 1984, p. 113.

Peering through the window of a deserted house, Chrissy thinks she sees a form that looks like a baby doll, bald and diapered. She goes in the house and follows where the doll's voice leads, learning that the doll is a ghost. Always drifting away from Chrissy, the doll says, "I'll be your doll if you show me you're brave," and when Chrissy is brave enough to reach out to touch the shadowy figure, the doll hurtles downstairs and into a box and out of the house. When Chrissy opens the box on the lawn, there is a real baby doll for her to love. The photographs have excellent shots of a handsome interior, but they are so contrived as an accompaniment to a slight and not very persuasive plot that the book seems, in toto, an insubstantial trifle.

Kathleen R. Roedder

SOURCE: A review of *Ghost Doll,* in *Childhood Education,* Vol. 60, No. 4, March-April, 1984, p. 288.

Chrissy responds to a call from inside the empty house. She sees a vague shape of a baby doll that seems to want her to follow it up to the top of the house. As a reward for her courage, the doll becomes real enough to cuddle. The story is beautifully told in eerie photographs and brief text. Delightful little girl and doll. A well-conceived, scary story for the young.

KITTEN CAN . . . (1984)

Ann A. Flowers

SOURCE: A review of *Kitten Can . . . ,* in *The Horn Book Magazine,* Vol. LX, No. 5, September-October, 1984, p. 583.

In the same winning vein as **Here a Chick, There a Chick,** which used baby chicks to illustrate opposites, the author-photographer features a fetching kitten to demonstrate the meaning of verbs. The sprightly, bright-eyed little cat goes through a series of small occupations, starting with "STARE," passing through such typical kitten activities as squeezing through a door, sniffing, stalking, climbing, eating—and ending with "REST." The winsome photographs show each activity quite clearly, although a few might suggest a different interpretation in a child's mind: "CRAWL" looks more like walking, and "DIG" looks much like playing. To illustrate a verb clearly seems to be far more difficult than to illustrate a noun. But the excellent colored photographs and the engaging calico kitten make an irresistible sequence.

Margaret L. Chatham

SOURCE: A review of *Kitten Can . . . ,* in *School Library Journal,* Vol. 31, No. 4, December, 1984, p. 73.

"Kitten can STARE, SQUEEZE, STRETCH, and SCRATCH," and do 20 other activities, ending with "curl up to REST." Each verb has its own full-page, full-color photo of a calico kitten showing how it's done. The photos capture the joy of observing a real kitten in action. *Kitten Can . . .* can be used as a springboard for creative motion or animal observation or just to add meaning to new words, making it a worthy companion to McMillan's **Here a Chick, There a Chick.**

Margery Fisher

SOURCE: A review of *Kitten Can . . . ,* in *Growing Point,* Vol. 25, No. 3, September, 1986, p. 4683.

Knowledge leads to respect and this simple sequence of photographs brilliantly shows the physical postures and capabilities of a kitten in a way that should help young children to appreciate the muscular control, mood and swift reactions of an animal they will also be happily treating as an individual companion. The calico kitten which illustrates a series of verbs (which, incidentally, gave the first impetus to the book) is supremely photogenic and the author, as photographer, has caught precisely the movements he wished to illustrate to give a thorough picture of this familiar domestic pet.

📖 COUNTING WILDFLOWERS (1986)

Zena Sutherland

SOURCE: A review of *Counting Wildflowers,* in *Bulletin of the Center for Children's Books,* Vol. 39, No. 8, April, 1986, pp. 152-53.

This is a counting book of many uses: (a) it's beautiful to look at (b) there is no mistaking the number of objects in each strikingly composed picture (c) the color-coded circles running between the clear black numerals and the written numbers add color identification possibilities (d) the close-up color photographs are clear and scientifically labelled to serve as a guide to garden/sidewalk variety flowers. Add to this a humorous surprise on the final photo spread, with three chicory flowers captioned "How many?" facing a mass of maiden pinks captioned "Too many to count" (a dare if ever there was one). Afterward comes a listing of the wildflowers' scientific names, their blooming periods, and places to look for them. A bargain for creative learning experiences.

Darian Scott

SOURCE: A review of *Counting Wildflowers,* in *The Christian Science Monitor,* June 6, 1986, p. B3.

This beautiful "photographic concept" book will easily foster in young children a love of what's free and beautiful in nature. Each page reveals an exquisitely presented wildflower in its natural habitat (whether thicket, field, backyard, or vacant lot), and the photography gives the feeling that the flowers could be instantly grasped and pleasurably held under one's nose!

At the bottom of each page, the number of flowers to be counted is represented by a matching number of shaded-in circles that are the same color as the flower being counted. Counting from one to 20 through the pages is a nature experience that brings the best outdoor botanical blooms indoors.

Denise M. Wilms

SOURCE: A review of *Counting Wildflowers,* in *Booklist,* Vol. 82, No. 20, June 15, 1986, p. 1542.

Crystal-clear color photographs of common American wildflowers are the mainstay of this counting book that also works as a handy field guide. The numbers run from 1 to 20, and below each picture is a line of circles that visually reinforces the sense of quantity. The numbers are spelled out as well. Names for each flower appear discreetly at the top corner of each page and an appended list provides scientific names, common locations, and time of blooming. An attractive, effective counting book for city children and a nice introduction for those who live in suburban or rural settings where many of these flowers are common.

Catherine Wood

SOURCE: A review of *Counting Wildflowers,* in *School Library Journal,* Vol. 32, No. 10, August, 1986, p. 85.

This carefully planned and executed counting concept book is rich in content, easily making it a book that can be returned to again and again. Number concepts 1 through 20 are presented in full-color, high-quality photographs of common field and woodland wildflowers. Each page is dominated by the photograph, in which clearly delineated blossoms are set against rich green backgrounds. Beneath the photograph appears the Arabic numeral; 10 or 20 discs, with a corresponding number of them filled in with the flower's color; and the number word written in capital letters. The photographs are captioned to identify the plant by its common name; a listing of the wildflowers' scientific names and natural locations appears at the end of the book, as does an explanatory note about the photography. Offering pleasure and clarity, this is a book that will be enjoyed by children and can be used in a number of ways by creative educators.

Margaret A. Bush

SOURCE: A review of *Counting Wildflowers,* in *The Horn Book Magazine,* Vol. LXII, No. 5, September-October, 1986, p. 610.

Dazzling photographs of twenty-three wildflowers are the major feature of this deftly constructed, multipurpose concept book. On the simplest level this is a counting book—one water lily is followed by two deep purple spiderworts, three forget-me-nots, and, finally, twenty common tansy blossoms. The book is also a simple identification guide, with the popular name of each variety appearing just above the photograph; all the flowers are listed again at the end along with the scientific name, months of blooming, and type of terrain where found. The counting device is sensibly and cleverly reinforced in a bold line of elements below each large picture; these consist of the numeral, a line of colored circles, and the number in word form. The pattern of circles teaches not only counting and color recognition but the rudiments of mathematical sets as well. While the set pattern of each page may appear stiffly repetitive to the adult eye, the repetition and use of symbols will serve the youngest viewers very well. This author-photographer has utilized compound concepts in earlier books, such as *Apples,* and *Here a Chick, There a Chick,* but the new book excels in clarity of design and striking presentation of an appealing subject. The beautifully composed pictures are satisfying and intriguing and should stimulate readers of all ages to renewed enjoyment and observation of wildflowers.

From Counting Wildflowers, *written and photographed by Bruce McMillan.*

Daphne Ann Hamilton and Susan D. Chapnick

SOURCE: A review of *Counting Wildflowers,* in *Appraisal: Science Books for Young People,* Vol. 20, No. 1, Winter, 1987, pp. 44-5.

Librarian: Whether you need a new counting book or simply enjoy beautiful color photographs of flowers, this book should be high on your list. Mr. McMillan has produced another concept book to rank with his delightful ***Here a Chick, There a Chick,*** and ***Kitten Can . . .*** If this book lacks the humor and action involved in the animals antics in the previous two titles, young children should be just as enthralled with the vivid colors and varying shapes of the flowers so outstandingly photographed by the author. Unlike many counting books, this one goes up twenty, and the pictures are captioned with a large numeral and corresponding number word in bold type; a clever additional device is the series of colored circles (ten for numbers up through ten, and twenty for numbers from eleven to twenty) with the appropriate number of circles picked out in the color of the flower in the accompanying photograph, and the remaining circles filled with a contrasting dark green. Above, the pictures are unobtrusively labeled with each flower's name, and a list at the back also contains the scientific name, and when and where to find it.

Though perhaps more of a picture book than a science book, the beauty and imagination of this title make it an outstanding addition to any collection.

Specialist: **Counting Wildflowers** has beautiful color photographs of flowers, from one perfect waterlily to a cluster of twenty yellow tansys. The pictures are clear and vivid, and can help children learn colors as well as counting. There are also rows of dots to count below each photograph, corresponding in color and number to the flowers depicted. Though a child may not sit through an entire book of counting flowers (maybe a count to ten would have been better for short attention spans), the adult reader can use the photographs, a few at a time, to make a game of "how many do you see here?" with the young reader. As a bonus for adults, and children interested in nature, the appendix at the end of the book contains interesting, accurate information about the flowers photographed.

BECCA BACKWARD, BECCA FRONTWARD: A BOOK OF CONCEPT PAIRS (1986)

Dorothy Solomon

SOURCE: A review of *Becca Backward, Becca Frontward: A Book of Concept Pairs,* in *Children's Book Review Service,* Vol. 15, No. 1, September, 1986, p. 4.

Facing pages use one or two word captions and full-color photographs to illustrate pairs of words, mostly opposites. The photographs feature four-year-old Becca doing typical children's activities. The pictures are very good, both in their appeal and photographic quality, as well as in their ability to illustrate the concepts clearly. A book where learning is fun.

Ellen Mandel

SOURCE: A review of *Becca Backward, Becca Frontward: A Book of Concept Pairs,* in *Booklist,* Vol. 83, No. 1, September 1, 1986, p. 65.

Exquisite color photographs take full advantage of scenic environments, utmost simplicity, and photogenic, blond-haired, young Becca to define basic concepts cleverly and effectively. Adding the last drops to a brimming glass of milk, then tilting the glass to catch any lingering sips, Becca is seen in juxtaposed full-page portrayals depicting "full" and "empty." Making her way from the back to the front of a grassy field, she demonstrates "far" and "near" on another spread. Six cartons of red raspberries face five similarly aligned containers of red raspberries and one box of black raspberries to distinguish between "same" and "different," while a turn of the page finds a box full of berries—"many"—followed by a nearly empty container, "few"; a final flip of the page shows a grinning, smudgy-faced Becca holding the empty carton above the large-print capital and lowercase letters, attractively used throughout the text, spelling "none." Capturing an unselfconscious youngster in uncluttered compositions glowing with natural and adeptly utilized artificial light, this is an exceptionally personable primer.

Constance A. Mellon

SOURCE: A review of *Becca Backward, Becca Frontward: A Book of Concept Pairs,* in *School Library Journal,* Vol. 33, No. 2, October, 1986, p. 164.

A dozen pairs of opposites illustrated with color photographs of a young girl. This is a well-designed book, with large, clear photographs to illustrate each of the pairs printed on facing pages and with the concept word printed in bold letters below each photograph. Becca is charming, the photographs are beautiful, and, in most instances, the concepts are very clear. Some explanation might be necessary in using this book with very literal young children—particularly in the presentation of the first two pairs. *Bottom* shows that part of Becca in shorts while *top* depicts her from bangs to waist pulling on a shirt. These are subtle rather than common uses of these two terms. *Above* catches Becca in midair over her bed while *below* shows her beneath the bed; *over* and *under* might be better understood by young children. With such cautions in mind, however, this should be a welcome addition to the world of concept books, providing useful contrast to such comparison books as Hoban's *Over, Under & Through & Other Spatial Concepts* and Peter Spier's *Fast-Slow High-Low.*

Publishers Weekly

SOURCE: A review of *Becca Backward, Becca Frontward: A Book of Concept Pairs,* in *Publishers Weekly,* Vol. 230, No. 18, October 31, 1986, p. 63.

This concept book is designed to teach children about opposites. Facing pages offer full-color photographs of a lovely little girl named Becca, demonstrating concepts like "Above," "Below," "Backward" and "Frontward." For instance, in "Above," Becca is shown jumping on a bed, while in "Below" she plays beneath it. It's quite a pretty picture book, with a simple storyline (Becca dresses and goes off to play, finally consuming all the berries in a berry box), with much appeal to preschoolers or those just beginning to learn about opposites.

Betsy Hearne

SOURCE: A review of *Becca Backward, Becca Frontward: A Book of Concept Pairs,* in *Bulletin of the Center for Children's Books,* Vol. 40, No. 4, December, 1986, p. 71.

The author of a previous photographed concept book, *Counting Wild Flowers,* McMillan here spotlights an attractive youngster in many natural poses illustrating opposites. "Bottom" is Becca's rear view in blue shorts, "Top" is Becca pulling on a red shirt; "Above" is Becca jumping on a bed; "Below" is Becca crawling under it. All of the white-framed compositions are simple, clear, appealing, and color-coordinated, with possibilities for small-group participation. After an adult reads "Full," as Becca pours milk to the top of her glass, it will be easy for listeners to guess "Empty" when she drains it on the next page.

Mary Margaret Pitts and Susan D. Chapnick

SOURCE: A review of *Becca Backward, Becca Forward,* in *Appraisal: Science Books for Young People,* Vol. 20, No. 3, Summer, 1987, p. 59.

Librarian: Similar in format to the author's earlier concept books, *Here a Chick, There a Chick* and *Kitten Care: A Concept Book,* color photographs show four year old Becca demonstrating a series of simple, opposite concepts. Familiar items and activities (whole/half or far/near) clearly convey concept pairs to very young readers.

Specialist: As with McMillan's other books, the photographs used to depict difficult concepts are sharp, to the point, interesting in composition and very colorful. Though I would not categorize this as a science book, the concepts it aims to present are depicted well. With the help of a lively four year old girl, Becca, and one word captions in bold letters, these photographs hold a reader's attention as well as make a specific point. Concept pairs such as above/below, full/empty, backward/frontward are successfully illustrated with interest and some humor.

The closing paragraph, "none," shows Becca with a smiling blueberry covered mouth and an empty blueberry box. These warm, clear images are very well done.

STEP BY STEP: ALL BY MYSELF (1987)

Kirkus Reviews

SOURCE: A review of *Step by Step: All by Myself*, in *Kirkus Reviews*, Vol. LV, No. 13, July 1, 1987, p. 995.

A series of color photographs of a baby aged four to fourteen months details the activities that lead to learning to walk.

Captioned "sleeping," "kicking," "rolling over," "kneeling and holding on," "tossing," "walking," "running," etc., 22 portraits show a thriving child as he develops. The diversity and freedom that foster learning are suggested by including wading in a gentle surf and climbing up and down a rough boulder; curiosity satisfied is represented by looking in, which necessitates standing on tiptoe; the joy of standing alone is expressed by clapping. Clear, well-composed and well-chosen photographs make this a highly satisfactory concept book for the very young.

Anna Biagioni Hart

SOURCE: A review of *Step by Step: All by Myself*, in *School Library Journal*, Vol. 34, No. 1, September, 1987, p. 167.

A child's attempt to walk and move independently from infancy to toddler stage proceeds in a stop-motion sequence from "sleeping" and "pushing up" with a comfortable home setting in the background to "clapping" and "climbing down" in what appears to be a backyard setting to "running home" on a sandy beach. Each full-color photograph of the little boy, one to a page, is tagged with a few words of explanation. Families with one and two year olds will enjoy looking at these familiar moments, unposed and natural. This book works not so much of itself, but because of the response it will call from children looking at it and the opportunity for discussion

that may follow. Confidently walking toddlers will enjoy looking back to when they themselves were Evan's size.

Denise M. Wilms

SOURCE: A review of *Step by Step: All by Myself*, in *Booklist*, Vol. 84, No. 1, September 1, 1987, pp. 67-8.

Babies and young toddlers like looking at each other, so chances are they'll be charmed by the sight of the little boy who works his way through these pages. McMillan's full-color, appealing photographs feature Evan at four months and follow him until he is fourteen months and an adept walker. The pictures are clear, page-filling shots of Evan at various stages; large-type words describing his progress (*sitting, stepping away, looking in*) are placed beneath the pictures. A likely choice for sharing with the youngest book viewers.

Zena Sutherland

SOURCE: A review of *Step by Step: All by Myself*, in *Bulletin of the Center for Children's Books*, Vol. 41, No. 3, November, 1987, p. 51.

The author-photographer took pictures of a baby boy over a period of ten months, beginning with Evan, four months old, sprawled in sleep. This is a story of motor control as Evan goes from sitting and crawling to standing, walking, climbing, running. The color photographs are of good quality, and it never hurts a book to have a subject so visually appealing. The text, in very large, bold type against spacious white margins, is abbreviated: "looking out" or "climbing up" or "wading." Not unusual, but unusually well done.

Margaret A. Bush

SOURCE: A review of *Step by Step: All by Myself*, in *The Horn Book Magazine*, Vol. LXIII, No. 6, November-December, 1987, p. 727.

"Sleeping . . . waking . . . kicking . . . pushing up . . . rolling over . . . sitting . . . stepping away . . . climbing up . . . running home." McMillan's album follows a little boy's increasing range of motion from very young infancy to early childhood. Full-page photographs in color, captioned only with the appropriate verbs or verbal phrases, convey a child's enjoyment and energy as he explores his environment in ever more active ways while growing through stages of babyhood and becoming a confident toddler. Beguiling in its simplicity and appeal, the book is intriguing in its multiplicity. The inherent charm of babies—especially for other babies, young children, and adults—ensures a wide range of pleased viewers. The book is also a lovely example of simple biography and a satisfying demonstration of the concepts of growth and the learning of locomotion.

DRY OR WET? (1988)

Kirkus Reviews

SOURCE: A review of *Dry or Wet?*, in *Kirkus Reviews*, Vol. LVI, No. 1, January 1, 1988, p. 57.

From the producer of five other concept books illustrated with photographs, notably **Step by Step,** an attractive vehicle for discussion and language development that is more complex than it first appears.

The first paired pictures seem almost too easy: of course it's the splashing child who's wet. But the clues grow subtler: the girl who holds the hose wears a clinging, dripping T-shirt, while the boy fending off water with an umbrella is still dry. Even in a bathtub, one may be dry; on the other hand, water may be concealed under bubbles. And why is the bathroom mirror sometimes wet? The full-color photos have an interesting range of settings; they should prompt plenty of good questions. A final page suggests the wealth of language related to the subject and credits the children who appear (three races, two sexes, several ages) by name.

Publishers Weekly

SOURCE: A review of *Dry or Wet?*, in *Publishers Weekly,* Vol. 233, No. 2, January 15, 1988, p. 93.

On each spread, facing full-color photographs illustrate the opposing concepts of wet and dry. Children frolic in the surf, then snuggle together in a towel; a child is splashed in the face by a hose, while another holds it safely with the water turned off; a flowerbed is pictured both dry and being watered down. As with his other books (**Here a Chick, There a Chick; Becca Backward, Becca Frontward**), McMillan's photographs are expressive and appealing, and there is a nice humor in several of the pairings. However, the book as a whole is less engaging and ultimately less successful than his previous works, for the concept here is a limited one, easily grasped in its first presentation; one quickly begins to crave new discoveries rather than repeated examples of the same. An afterword suggests that the photographs can be used to introduce other words and expressions—"splash," "spray," "high and dry," and so on—but for these lessons children would need to rely entirely on the prompting of imaginative adults.

Denise M. Wilms

SOURCE: A review of *Dry or Wet?*, in *Booklist,* Vol. 84, No. 13, March, 1, 1988, p. 1183.

Inviting color photographs show children in a variety of wet and dry modes, and the viewer is invited to talk about which is wet and which is dry. The activities, swimming, running under a sprinkler, or getting doused with a hose, are all ones that delight children, and the clarity of the pictures is remarkable. McMillan thoughtfully uses blacks and Asians as well as white children.

He also includes an author's note suggesting ways in which the book can expand vocabulary skills. Plenty of fun shines through the pages, making this an inviting, good-humored book to share with younger children.

Roger Sutton

SOURCE: A review of *Dry or Wet?,* in *Bulletin of the Center for Children's Books,* Vol. 41, No. 8, April, 1988, p. 162.

Concept picture books don't come much simpler than this one—facing before/after photographs illustrating "dry" and "wet"—but as is usual for him, McMillan (**Here a Chick, There a Chick; Counting Wildflowers**) demonstrates the concept with clarity, humor, and occasional wit. There's an exuberant splash into the swimming pool, the gleeful hosing down of an (extremely patient) dalmatian, a red umbrella raised in defense against the onslaught of the garden spray. Children are pictured in all the photographs; whether in the bathroom with the Anno/Escher-like wallpaper or in the gloriously summery backyard, everybody looks to be having a terrific time.

Jennifer Smith

SOURCE: A review of *Dry or Wet?,* in *School Library Journal,* Vol. 35, No. 8, May, 1988, p. 86.

Through stunning color photographs that capture the emotions and expressions of children, McMillan gives the stimuli needed for a discussion of *wet* and *dry.* Poses are completely natural, yet each photograph of children or a child playing with or in water is a portrait. This wordless book encourages children to go beyond identifying what is wet or dry in the pictures. With the guidance of an adult, they can learn new vocabulary as other wet and dry words (e.g., *splash, shower, wilted, withered*) are suggested to describe the action in the photographs. While children will certainly enjoy looking at this book on their own, it is its many uses for adult and child interaction that make it particularly effective and special.

FIRE ENGINE SHAPES (1988)

Kirkus Reviews

SOURCE: A review of *Fire Engine Shapes*, in *Kirkus Reviews*, Vol. LVI, No. 12, June 15, 1988, p. 900.

In the wordless **Fire Engine Shapes,** the "reader" explores a gleaming red fire engine to find seven geometric forms, including hexagon and oval; on a last page McMillan defines them and suggest 50 places where they might be found in the photos. Even more intriguing is the fire engine itself, and the puzzle of identifying the close-up shots with the help of the jacket portrait plus some subtler clues. Four-year-old Stephanie Tamaki adds interest to the photos.

Denise M. Wilms

SOURCE: A review of *Fire Engine Shapes,* in *Booklist,* Vol. 85, No. 1, September 1, 1988, p. 82.

Capitalizing on the certain attraction of fire engines, McMillan fashions a concept book about shapes by zeroing in on the forms that make up the construction of a fire engine. For example, rectangles are seen in the window outlines and a metal plate; triangles are formed by hinges and by a step; circles show up in lights and recessed door handles. The pictures are full-color close-ups á la Tana Hoban, and a four-year-old girl dressed in yellow overalls injects a dose of liveliness into the otherwise still photos. A note at the end depicts the shapes and the pages where they are found. An effective display that will prove a pleasant way for preschoolers to sharpen their visual discrimination skills.

Patricia Dooley

SOURCE: A review of *Fire Engine Shapes,* in *School Library Journal,* Vol. 35, No. 2, October, 1988, p. 125.

In this wordless celebration of the color, chrome, and contours of an Emergency One, super-sharp close-ups focus on the standard "big four" shapes—plus diamond, oval, and hexagon (all precisely described and "indexed" on the final page). Only one engine is featured, so this isn't the equivalent of a trip to the firehouse, but McMillan supplies a note on the truck's vital statistics, and on his photographic methods. Young viewers will also enjoy searching for the lively four year old Oriental girl who appears—but sometimes very marginally—in most shots. (And some adults will spot the homage to Demuth's famous painting of another Engine 5.) Like McMillan's earlier books and Tana Hoban's books, these photos help children to see the geometry of their surroundings with fresh eyes.

GROWING COLORS (1988)

Publishers Weekly

SOURCE: A review of *Growing Colors,* in *Publishers Weekly,* Vol. 233, No. 25, June 24, 1988, p. 110.

McMillan has created a feast of a colors book using fruits and vegetables of every hue. Each double-page spread has a small photograph of the whole plant and a large close-up of the fruit or vegetable. The colors are announced in bold type tinted in the appropriate shade. In the selection of vegetables, McMillan moves beyond ordinary supermarket produce, showing purple beans and brown peppers. At the end of the book, there is a picture glossary of all the colors and plants used. And in a final note, McMillan discusses his plant choices, their sources and his photographic techniques (such as misting the vegetables and fruits to enhance their natural colors). Such a brilliant presentation of colors will be an eyeful for any small child; older readers (and adults) will appreciate the composition and clarity of every photo, which sets off each piece of produce like a jewel.

Ronald Jobe

SOURCE: A review of *Growing Colors,* in *School Library Journal,* Vol. 35, No. 1, September, 1988, pp. 169-70.

A vibrant introduction to the beauty of colors in nature. Fourteen vegetables and fruits are dramatically visualized with full-page photographs, accompanied by a color word, as well as a glimpse of how the vegetables grow. Most effective are the shots of carrots and onions growing—their root tops showing just above the dark moist earth, green pods bursting with succulent peas, ravishing blueberries, a proud husk of golden corn, and melt-in-your-mouth blackberries. The intensity and vibrance of color is breathtaking. This is a spotless book—even the onions and potatoes pulled directly from the dirt are ultra-clean. Exceptional clarity and artistic composition of the dew-tipped photographs makes each suitable for framing. Cleverly complementing the traditional red rasberries and orange carrots are unusual variants portraying brown peppers and purple beans. However, while the close-up view of the vegetables and fruits is exciting visually, the lack of consideration for congruity of size is in sharp contrast to the stark simplicity of the book's concept. The pair of cantaloupes appear diminished in stature, yet the bright orange apricots are so large that they appear to be oranges. Also, the use of only upper-case letters will make the text difficult for young children to read. A final listing of the colors and the names of the fruits and vegetables is a valuable resources. A delicious book for a wide range of ages.

Betsy Hearne

SOURCE: A review of *Growing Colors,* in *Bulletin of the Center for Children's Books,* Vol. 42, No. 2, October, 1988, p. 48.

A luscious-looking book that will help children identify colors and possibly even develop a taste for vitamins in their natural state. Fruits and vegetables appear dewy fresh in the color photographs that fill the recto; a facing page features a smaller illustration of the plant above the word for the color. The word is in huge print matching the color named, and it's up to the child to say what food is pictured—raspberries, peas, corn, cantaloupe, etc. A balance of common and unusual items is considered, and several colors appear twice to enhance the guessing game. A concluding double spread gives (and shows) the answers for children learning to read on their own. Consistently well designed, with a background note on the picture-taking, this is notably a treat for kids and an example of photography as an art form in picture books.

Mary Lou Burket

SOURCE: "Growing Things," in *The Five Owls,* Vol. III, No. 4, March-April, 1989, pp. 63-4.

Bruce McMillan takes the camera into the garden in *Growing Colors.* Here, each two-page spread contains a large, close-up shot of a fruit or vegetable representing one of ten basic colors. There are some surprises: sweet peppers, for instance, are brown instead of green and beans are purple. On the companion page, a smaller photograph shows the fruit or vegetable as it grows—underground, on a shrub, tree, or vine.

While this is a simple book, it has the effect of making ordinary edibles seem vibrant. It is also handsomely designed. More importantly, perhaps, it shows that produce comes from plants—particular plants—and not from cartons and plastic wrappers.

SUPER, SUPER, SUPERWORDS (1989)

Roger Sutton

SOURCE: A review of *Super, Super, Superwords,* in *Bulletin of the Center for Children's Books,* Vol. 42, No. 7, March, 1989, p. 177.

This first lesson in comparatives and superlatives is disarmingly inculcated through photographs of a busy kindergarten. A stack of books in the library becomes *heavy, heavier,* and *heaviest* as a girl piles more and more into the arms of a friend. One girl's blouse is yellow, a boy's turtleneck is yellower, another girl's sweatshirt is yellowest. (*Yellower? Yellowest??*) Each trio of words is accompanied by a double-page spread of three cheerful photographs of kids at play. Probably most envied will be the child who was allowed to sharpen her pencil down to a stub to illustrate short, shorter, shortest. Page layout is consistent (small, bigger, biggest, photographs running from left to right) which may reinforce the concept but gives the book a static design. Because the words are confined to -er and -est comparatives (a limitation the afterword acknowledges) be prepared for a rash of good, gooder, goodest, but for what it does, this is one of the bestest language concept books around.

Leda Schubert

SOURCE: A review of *Super, Super, Superwords,* in *School Library Journal,* Vol. 35, No. 8, April, 1989, p. 86.

Happy, active children in a racially-mixed kindergarten class are used to illustrate degrees of comparison (positive, comparative, and superlative) in this visual grammar lesson. The excellent photos, three per set, move from small to large across double-page spreads, paralleling the comparisons. The three words per concept intensify from gray to dark black print and increase in size at the same time. For example, for *heavy,* a girl piles books into a boy's open arms, adding books till the pile is *heavier,* then *heaviest;* for *close* two smiling students move from sitting together to sharing a shy, *closest* hug. Familiar kindergarten activities include reading, measuring, and building; comparisons include full, high, small, short, few, and long. The kids are delightful, particularly one little girl who stars on every page and whose bright yellow sweatshirt echoes the inviting endpapers. The photographs have clear composition, crisp colors, and strong light. There will be lots to discuss with young readers curious about the activities depicted and the words chosen. A deceptively simple book, masterfully executed.

Kirkus Reviews

SOURCE: A review of *Super, Super, Superwords,* in *Kirkus Reviews,* Vol. LVII, No. 8, April 15, 1989, p. 627.

Another collection of appealing, beautifully composed photos from the author-photographer of *Dry or Wet?* and *Growing Colors,* etc. Here, the subject is adjectives' three degrees of comparison; the actors are members of a kindergarten class as they go through a day's activities. Each broad double-spread has three photos in graduated sizes illustrating the words: "heavy," "heavier," "heaviest" in the library, where a stack of books grows in the arms of a delighted boy; feeding a pencil to a sharpener to make it "shorter"; ending the day with the "loudest" shout. Meanwhile, a yellow-shirted girl provides unity by appearing in almost every photo; she and her classmates are credited by name in a final note, which also points out that irregular forms are not included and discloses photographic techniques used. A charming concept book, up to McMillan's usual high standard.

Ellen Mandel

SOURCE: A review of *Super, Super, Superwords,* in *Booklist,* Vol. 85, No. 17, May 1, 1989, p. 1551.

These crystalline photographs composed with an eye for color, action, and humor immediately put readers in mind of McMillan's *Becca Backward, Becca Frontward.* The camera focuses on children, particularly on one appealing girl who helps demonstrate degrees of comparison between adjectives. Each double-page spread features three photos of graduated size: the positive form of the adjective (e.g., long) is pictured at the upper left in the smallest picture. Next, the comparative form (longer) is expressed, followed at the far right in the largest picture by the superlative form (longest). Thirteen adjectives capture McMillan's flair for explaining concepts through pictures and, as a bonus, help illustrate the typical school activities of energetic kindergartners. Though precisely planned and meticulously executed, the photos convey an air of spontaneity—readers can almost feel a tickle under the arm and the growing weight of books laughingly piled on "heavy," "heavier," "heaviest."

Publishers Weekly

SOURCE: A review of *Super, Super, Superwords*, in *Publishers Weekly*, Vol. 235, No. 19, May 12, 1989, p. 290.

With a lively group of kindergartners, McMillan introduces the concept of comparison, with examples like yellow, yellower and yellowest or close, closer and closest. The children build a tower of blocks to demonstrate the various degrees of tallness. A single shouting girl is joined by her yelling friends to exhibit "loud, louder and loudest." McMillan's photographs present the world of kindergarten clearly and realistically, capturing moments that are funny, interesting or universal. At the end, the author offers details about his subjects and techniques, rounding out this superlative book about comparatives.

Miriam Martinez and Marcia F. Nash

SOURCE: A review of *Super, Super, Superwords*, in *Language Arts*, Vol. 67, No. 5, September, 1990, pp. 508-09.

This book combines a "visual grammar lesson" with a record of a kindergartener's day at school. As one child and her friends engage in such activities as reading, block play, and paper cutting, the text and photographs introduce the concept of comparative adjectives. Words and photographs combine on each two-page spread to illustrate three degrees of comparison for one adjective—as the child and a friend collect books in the library, the stack grows from heavy to heavier to heaviest. McMillan uses every possible visual element, from print size and boldness to photograph size and placement, to reinforce this language concept.

TIME TO . . . (1989)

Kirkus Reviews

SOURCE: A review of *Time to . . .*, in *Kirkus Reviews*, Vol. LVII, No. 13, July 1, 1989, p. 993.

From seven in the morning till nine at night, a kindergarten boy is shown each hour on the hour. On each left-hand page, the same wall clock shows the time (also given in digital and verbal form), together with some clues about the day's progress—a yellow sweater hangs on a book when the boy is home; the painting done at school appears beside the clock after he has returned in the afternoon. Right-hand pages show predictable activities, including a visit to the library. McMillan's photos are as attractive and well-composed as we have come to expect from this meticulous craftsman, though the children here seem a little more posed and self-conscious than usual. An excellent concept book.

Lori A. Janick

SOURCE: A review of *Time to . . .*, in *School Library Journal*, Vol. 35, No. 13, September, 1989, p. 241.

In this simple approach to a complex subject, children are introduced to the concept of telling time. Boldly colored photos follow a little boy's daily activities as each double-page spread advances the clock by one hour. On the left, readers are shown a large clock in the boy's room. The lower left corner of the page shows a digital display as well. This not only familiarizes children with different kinds of clocks, but also introduces the concept of A.M. and P.M. On the right-hand photo, they see the boy engaged in a different activity for each hour. These photos have a joyous, spontaneous look, just right for drawing youngsters into the book. While the concept of quarter and half hours is only mentioned at the end of the book, the two photos on the last page can be used as a transition into individual instruction. The appealing and effective layout, combined with McMillan's photographic expertise, make this a welcome addition to all libraries serving young children.

Phillis Wilson

SOURCE: A review of *Time to . . .*, in *Booklist*, Vol. 86, No. 2, September 15, 1989, p. 187.

McMillan has won just recognition for camera artistry in his books about counting, colors, and shapes, and his recent foray into adjectives, *Super, Super, Superwords,* is nothing less than a super success. Here, his infectious enthusiasm, coupled with a painstaking eye for craft, focuses on an introduction to time. Two aspects are taught: through an engaging child's sequenced activities (waking up, eating, going to school, etc.), the passage of time is demonstrated, and the hour-by-hour changes on a clock face, and the accompanying digital display at page bottom, show how time is measured. Typical school activities are featured; keen eyes will catch the subtle touches, such as the picture a child paints at 10:00 a.m. that appears on his bedroom wall in the 4:00 p.m. shot. The vigor and clarity of the overall presentation, and the naturalness of the children and the setting, add up to a "timely" purchase for librarians.

Publishers Weekly

SOURCE: A review of *Time to . . .*, in *Publishers Weekly*, Vol. 236, No. 13, September 29, 1989, p. 66.

Remember that buoyant feeling of triumph when you first grasped the concept of time? Photographer McMillan obviously does, and his new book is designed to give a boost to any child still puzzling over it. In each pair of bright full-color photos, a clock on the left-hand page shows the hour with, on the right, a corresponding activity from a child's daily routine (breakfast, school, brushing teeth, etc.). A digital display (on the bottom left corner of the left-hand page) introduces the idea of a.m. and p.m. as well. McMillan's carefully planned layouts and fresh, appealing images are a model of clarity, but it's his attention to detail (matching the gradual changes in shading and accessories on the left-hand pages to the shifting movement of the sun) that makes this such a splendid book. Interesting background on the photographer's materials and methods is included at the end.

Susan Hepler

SOURCE: A review of *Time to . . . ,* in *Language Arts,* Vol. 67, No. 1, January, 1990, pp. 79-80.

An hour-by-hour account of a boy's day (he's in school for a half day) from 7 AM to bedtime at 9 PM is cleverly chronicled in pristinely clean photographs. Each left-hand page displays a clock face mounted alongside a coathook and a shelf whose items change as the day progresses. For instance, the bear the boy sleeps with is placed back on the shelf in the morning but comes off again at bedtime and his school sweater is gone by 9 AM but is rehung after the dinner hour. Children learning to tell time get an extra boost from this left-hand page, too, as a digital rendering of the clock also appears. "Seven o'clock in the morning / Time to . . . Wake Up" is spread across the double-page spread.

On each right-hand page, we see in freeze-framed action what the boy is doing at a particular hour: going to school; eating lunch; buying apples at the store; swinging, or falling asleep. Most children learn to tell time from a clock face about the time they are learning to read. This book's design and format work well for teaching children to tell time. But it is also the perfect model for children to use to create their own "Time to . . . " books. In an interesting afterword to the adult reader, McMillan explains how he controlled and planned the photographs for this book.

Mary Lou Burket

SOURCE: A review of *Time to . . . ,* in *The Five Owls,* Vol. III, No. 3, January-February, 1990, p. 39.

Critics have a tendency to value picture books more as they become more elaborate. These days, we expect to be dazzled by subtleties of meaning as well as by sheer ornamentation in picture-book art.

Bruce McMillan's concept books, however, make a point of being limited. They might be easy to overlook if they weren't so functional, their orderly designs supported by highly controlled, full-color photographs. This new book is consistent with the pattern set by *Dry or Wet?* and *Counting Wildflowers.* Its purpose is to illustrate the fact that time passes and can be marked in hourly segments. On the left of every page spread is a clock and on the right is a boy engaged in something appropriate for the hour: breakfast at eight, school at nine, and so on. Time is represented three ways, by the face of the clock, by the words of the text, and by a digital display in a lower corner. But time is *expressed* by the boy's actions.

This would be an especially helpful book for kindergartners or younger children adjusting to new, more structured daily schedules. It doesn't teach how to tell time per se, but it suggests that time has pleasant associations and that there is comfort in knowing what comes next.

📖 *EVERYTHING GROWS* (written by Raffi, 1989)

Denise Wilms

SOURCE: A review of *Everything Grows,* in *Booklist,* Vol. 86, No. 3, October 1, 1989, p. 354.

The title song from Raffi's album, *Everything Grows,* is put into book form, backed by engaging photographs of kids, pets, and assorted other growing things. The pictures are lively and inviting, and the repetitive text has an appealing rhythm. This may lend itself well to children just beginning to read, especially if teachers introduce the song in a music lesson. Preschoolers, too, will respond to the book's strong visual appeal. This is simple, fun, and useful. Melody line and verses appended.

Liza Bliss

SOURCE: A review of *Everything Grows,* in *School Library Journal,* Vol. 36, No. 2, February, 1990, p. 84.

This book uses full-color photos to illustrate the lyrics of one of Raffi's loveliest songs: "A blade of grass, fingers and toes, / Hair on my head, / A red, red, rose. / Everything grows, anyone knows . . ." Unfortunately, the photos have a contrived look; that they show child-oriented objects (puppies, corn on the cob, dandelion fluff) and faces from several races compensates only a little. Like the song's lyrics, they are simple, direct, and warm; but they are shallow and belie the deeper meaning of the words. Lyrics and the song's melody line (transcribed with three sharps—very difficult for beginning musicians to play), with simple guitar chords, appear on the final page. This effort does not stand on its own as a picture book, nor does it do justice to the song it represents.

📖 *ONE SUN: A BOOK OF TERSE VERSE* (1990)

Kirkus Reviews

SOURCE: A review of *One Sun: A Book of Terse Verse,* in *Kirkus Reviews,* Vol. LVIII, No. 6, March 15, 1990, p. 427.

A day at the beach is celebrated in 14 descriptive, rhymed pairs of words accompanied by beautifully composed color photos of four assorted small children and close-ups of things they do and see. A "Wet pet" emerging from the surf or "Lone stone" poised at its edge; a "Scoop group" (two kids with trowels) or "Tan man" (lifeguard) who shares his "Neat seat" with a young admirer—each provides a glimpse of cheerful activity. A fine concept book that should inspire children to make up their own "terse verse."

Publishers Weekly

SOURCE: A review of *One Sun: A Book of Terse Verse*, in *Publishers Weekly*, Vol. 237, No. 15, April 13, 1990, p. 62.

If one picture is worth a thousand words, can two words make a poem? Yes, according to McMillan, whose new offering teams photographs of youngsters cavorting at the seashore with what he calls "terse verse"—two rhyming monosyllabic words, such as "wet pet," "whale pail" and "sand hand." Designed to introduce children to the concept of rhyme, the book's appealingly simple design belies McMillan's customary careful attention to detail—including a balanced racial mix of young models. Although the concept would seem a bit thin for an entire picture book, the skilled writer/photographer pulls it off with élan: neat feat.

Betsy Hearne

SOURCE: A review of *One Sun: A Book of Terse Verse*, in *Bulletin of the Center for Children's Books*, Vol. 43, No. 9, May, 1990, p. 222.

Warning: this book may be contagious and should be considered, at the very least, catching. Well, catchy, anyway. Each of fourteen rhyming phrases faces a full-page color photo of an engaging boy playing at the beach. The front cover starts the game (One Sun) and the back cover (Blue View) extends it. Between them comes a parade: *Sand Hand, Lone Stone, Snail Trail, Six Sticks, Small Ball, Wet Pet, Tan Man, Neat Seat, Stuck Truck, Whale Pail, Scoop Group, Round Mound, Pink Drink,* and *White Kite,* all so naturally pictured that there's not a trace of cuteness in any of the scenes of play among children who are Asian, black, and white. They all look suitably wet and sandy to offset the glamorous unlittered glitter of the ocean front. One page not only leads you speeding to another, but anyone listening will keep going after the book is over. Fun won!

Denise Wilms

SOURCE: A review of *One Sun: A Book of Terse Verse*, in *Booklist*, Vol. 86, No. 18, May 15, 1990, p. 1803.

McMillan defines terse verse as "two monosyllabic words that sound alike," ingeniously using them to celebrate a day at the beach. His crisp color photographs graphically record a young boy's pleasures, while his terse-verse text gleefully labels the pictures: "sand hand" for a child's sand-coated hand; "wet pet" for a dripping dog; "neat seat" for a lifeguard's perch. In addition, McMillan supplies an afterword about getting children to work out their own terse-verse combinations. Language art teachers should find this fun book a boon when introducing poetry.

Judith Gloyer

SOURCE: A review of *One Sun: A Book of Terse Verse*, in *School Library Journal*, Vol. 36, No. 7, July, 1990, p. 73.

McMillan offers a rhyming game set against the background of a sparkling summer day at the beach as an Asian preschooler is featured interacting with boys and girls of different races. He explains his terse verse—two monosyllabic words that sound alike but are not necessarily spelled alike—in a note on the last page, offering it as an introduction to rhyme. Only a few of his combinations lack similar spelling patterns ("one/sun"); others include "tan/man," "sand/hand," and "snail/trail." Contrived poetics aside, the book is attractively designed with the words in extra large white type on the verso, outlined with a strong black line against a sandy gray background. The right-hand pages are vivid, clear, full-color photos dominated by rich blues and sparkling sunlight. There is a strong textural element; readers can practically feel the sand in their shoes. Teachers may enjoy trying out the rhyming game concepts with their students, while everyone else will simply enjoy the pleasure of a perfect sunny day at the seaside.

MARY HAD A LITTLE LAMB (written by Sarah Josepha Hale, 1990)

Jane Marino

SOURCE: A review of *Mary Had a Little Lamb*, in *School Library Journal*, Vol. 36, No. 8, August, 1990, p. 142.

It is difficult to set a classic piece of poetry in the historical context in which it belongs and at the same time enable it to evolve and stay alive and fresh. But that is just what McMillan has so artfully done in this picture-book version of the poem. In an inventive blend of layout and design, he meshes the old and new together. The delicate endpapers and old-fashioned edgings to the photographs all serve as the proper background for the black, bespectacled young girl who is the model for Mary and the real coup of the book. This is a Mary who goes to school in an old-fashioned building, but with a male teacher. With her bright smile and yellow overalls, she is sure to connect with children meeting Mary for the first time. Mary has been portrayed elsewhere, such as in the picture-book version by Tomie dePaola as a lovely old-fashioned figure complete with pinafore and ringlets. McMillan has proven that this is no longer a universal portrayal. The fine design and excellent color scheme as well as the afterword, original poem, and explanations about the book make this a wonderfully crafted book that no library should miss.

Hazel Rochman

SOURCE: A review of *Mary Had a Little Lamb,* in *Booklist,* Vol. 87, No. 4, October 15, 1990, p. 446.

A favorite nursery rhyme comes back to its New England roots in a contemporary photo-illustrated version. McMillan's large, bright color pictures catch the mischief, the warmth, and the appeal of the pet story in the rhyming verse. This "Mary" is a black first-grader from Kennebunk, Maine, who wears eyeglasses and bright yellow overalls. She grooms, feeds, and romps with her lamb, and when "he follows her to school one day," the class erupts in delight, especially when he nuzzles the teacher's trouser legs. In contrast to the action are the gentle, playful scenes of child and animal nose to nose or in a cuddly embrace. McMillan adds a note at the end about the nineteenth-century author Hale, with the text of her original verses and a lesson from an 1857 McGuffey's reader.

📖 *ONE, TWO, ONE PAIR!* (1991)

Deborah Abbott

SOURCE: A review of *One Two, One Pair!,* in *Booklist,* Vol. 87, No. 10, January 15, 1991, p. 1061.

McMillan aims his camera and shoots sharp color images to explore the concept of pairs. The same line of text appears on each double-page spread: "One, Two, One Pair." He uses small, separate photos of each element of a pair on the left-hand side. On the right is a large photo of the pair together. The story line follows the step-by-step process of preparing to go ice skating. The photos show two hands (washing), two faucet handles, two eyes, two feet, two socks, two boots, two jacket sleeves, two earmuffs, two ice skates, and the climax—one pair of twins! The final shots of two cups of hot chocolate with whipped cream make a warm, tasty finale for this clever, smoothly flowing volume. Although [Tana] Hoban's photo concept books (for example, *Exactly the Opposite*) garner much attention, McMillan has also contributed sparkling visual feasts tied to a theme, including *Growing Colors.* Small children will delight in his latest effort, and it will be fun to see if they anticipate the twin connection.

Publishers Weekly

SOURCE: A review of *One, Two, One Pair!,* in *Publishers Weekly,* Vol. 238, No. 3, January 18, 1991, p. 57.

Just when it seems that there could not possibly be a new interpretation of the photo concept book, veteran McMillan (*Counting Wildflowers; Mary Had a Little Lamb*) offers a winner. Preparations for an ice-skating outing are the focus of this involving book, which explores "the basic math concept of number sets." "One," "Two," "A Pair!" are presented whimsically in vivid, colorful photographs, through a cheery succession of spreads that show, for example, one left hand, one right hand, then—on the facing page—a pair of hands washing. Eager page-turners will see bright red socks, yellow mittens, white ice skates with blue laces and more. The final pages contain a surprise: the engaging child model is actually two—a pair of twins who enjoy matching cups of hot cocoa topped with whipped cream. Like their snack, this book is satisfying and delicious.

Roger Sutton

SOURCE: A review of *One, Two, One Pair,* in *Bulletin of the Center for Children's Books,* Vol. 44, No. 6, February, 1991, p. 150.

McMillan's text for each double-page triptych is always the same: "One, two, one pair." The snappy, full-color photos show, in turn, the two parts of a pair (hands, faucets, feet) and the two together. All the objects pictured will be familiar to most young children, and there's a loose narrative sequence, showing a child washing up, getting dressed, and going out to skate on a frozen pond, where—surprise!—we see that there are actually two children, twins. A title page photo of one of them looking in a mirror is a sly twist; the girls sharing cups of cocoa makes a satisfying end. The spacious page design offers a lesson all its own, with the pictures of the two halves smaller than the facing photo of the whole. Clear and simple as can be, and a welcome spur for other-sock/mitten/shoe-hunting.

Louise L. Sherman

SOURCE: A review of *One, Two, One Pair!,* in *School Library Journal,* Vol. 37, No. 2, February, 1991, pp. 72-3.

A very focused concept book in which clear and captivating color photographs show the two parts of a pair on one side of each two-page spread, with the words "one" and "two" under them, and on the other side, the two together as "one pair." As the pictures progress, children will realize that the illustrations are showing preparations for going ice skating. However, only at the end will they realize that the child pictured is actually two children—a pair of twins. While text is limited to the words of the title, the book will give young readers much to talk about and describe in these pictures. Colors, clothing, and actions are clearly illustrated in the photographs. Equally good for preschoolers and children with special language needs, this concept book, while not as verbally clever as McMillan's *One Sun,* will be welcome in most collections.

📖 *THE WEATHER SKY* (1991)

Roger Sutton

SOURCE: A review of *The Weather Sky,* in *Bulletin of the Center for Children's Books,* Vol. 44, No. 8, April, 1991, p. 200.

After a general discussion of air masses and fronts, Mc-Millan devotes most of his book to clouds: the different kinds, the difference that altitude makes, different clouds in different seasons. The material is well-organized, both chronologically (proceeding from winter through spring) and visually, with each page devoted to a color photo of a cloud; a drawing of what the cloud looks like from the side, top to bottom; a diagram of the kind of front that would create such a cloud; and a clear, brief paragraph explaining and amplifying on the illustrations. This is a good guide to weather prediction through skywatching, although kids will wonder about the lack of information on thunderstorms, tornadoes, and hurricanes. On the other hand, what McMillan does include encourages readers to find the exciting in the everyday. A glossary and an index are appended.

Carolyn Phelan

SOURCE: A review of *The Weather Sky,* in *Booklist,* Vol. 87, No. 16, April 15, 1991, pp. 1638, 1640.

While its shape, size, and jacket suggest a picture book, this is actually one of the more challenging children's books on clouds and weather: challenging in the best sense, because readers willing and able to follow McMillan's explanation will come away with a fuller understanding of the subject. Students simply looking for pictures of the various types of cloud formations will find good, full-color photographs, clearly labeled, but they may miss the opportunity to put those facts into a broader and more practical context. On the other hand, taking advantage of what's offered here takes a fair amount of motivation and concentration. Beginning with cogent explanations of weather maps, air masses, highs, lows, fronts, and clouds, McMillan moves into the main part of the book, which follows the weather through the seasons. The first page of this section shows a humid summer day, followed on the next page by an approaching storm. Each page contains a large photo of the sky, a local-area weather map, and a vertical chart showing the height of the clouds (if any), as well as a paragraph of text setting the scene and explaining what's hapening. A fresh look at an age-old subject.

Margaret M. Hagel

SOURCE: A review of *The Weather Sky,* in *School Library Journal,* Vol. 37, No. 5, May, 1991, p. 104.

Avid weather watchers will enjoy this discussion of the different cloud types, the weather patterns with which they are associated, and the climactic conditions they bring. After an explanation of air masses and the various kinds of fronts, McMillan devotes the remainder of the book to pictures of the clouds produced by different combinations of air masses throughout the year. The well-chosen black-and-white illustrations and color photographs, which mostly feature cloud formations and an occasional tree, are as important in conveying the information as the text. They add enormously to the book's attractiveness. There is far more information and detail presented than in [Tomie] de Paola's *The Cloud Book,* which is for younger readers. A clear and coherent introduction to meteorology that will certainly encourage readers to do some forecasting of their own.

Kirkus Reviews

SOURCE: A review of *The Weather Sky,* in *Kirkus Reviews,* Vol. LIX, No. 9, May 1, 1991, p. 607.

The effects of the simplest weather fronts and the clouds associated with them throughout the year. Warm and cold fronts are shown using the symbols made familiar by TV meteorologists; a handy cloud-classification chart shows the shape and height of common clouds. Each page includes a carefully selected photo of the sky and cloud cover, a vertical cross-section drawing of the clouds with their height in both feet and miles, and a line drawing showing the fronts. The photos were taken in an area of Maine called "thunderstorm alley."

Maxine Kamin

SOURCE: A review of *The Weather Sky,* in *Children's Book Review Service,* Vol. 19, No. 11, June, 1991, p. 131.

Bruce McMillan photographed weather patterns over the course of a year in a part of Maine known as "Thunderstorm Alley". After a brief explanation of air masses, fronts and weather maps, the full-color photographs are accompanied by a description of the sky and a diagram of it depicted on a weather map. Though more technical than most weather forcasting books for children, a simple explanation of "Why is the sky blue?" is provided. Students of photography might find the explanation of the methods used helpful.

Carmen Oyenque

SOURCE: A review of *The Weather Sky,* in *Voice of Youth Advocates,* Vol. 14, No. 5, December, 1991, p. 338.

McMillan, who lives in Shapleigh, Maine, an area the National Weather Service refers to as "thunderstorm alley," has created a book illustrated with photographs taken at the same location throughout the year to illustrate the various weather patterns in each of the seasons. The book is arranged in sequence of the author's memory of Princess Summerfall Winterspring. Each page contains a color photo, a weather map, and illustrations of the clouds. The text is succinct. Terms used are defined within the text, in the margin of the page, and in a glossary at the end of the book. This interesting book is one that will be read again and used as a reference by those who are curious about changing weather and cloud patterns.

EATING FRACTIONS (1991)

Carolyn Phelan

SOURCE: A review of *Eating Fractions,* in *Booklist,* Vol. 87, No. 22, August, 1991, p. 2151.

Clear full-color photographs that illustrate concepts are McMillan's hallmark, but how many illustrators can match his claim to have "cooked, written, drafted, and photo-illustrated" a book? Challenging beginners to tackle fractions at the most basic level, he shows two children (Erin, who's white, and Melvin, who's black) dividing food into halves, thirds, and fourths, eating the pieces, and generally whooping it up in the kitchen. The infectious grins of the two kids, photographed eating the fractions (of banana, cloverleaf rolls, strawberry pie, and so forth), make this foray into mathematics an unexpectedly playful experience, climaxing when the kids surreptitiously feed a fourth of the pie to Lilly the dog, who's under the table. The book ends with hints on teaching fractional quantities while cooking and with recipes for the rolls, pizza, pear salad, and pie. A welcome addition to the math shelf.

Kirkus Reviews

SOURCE: A review of *Eating Fractions,* in *Kirkus Reviews,* Vol. LIX, No. 15, August 1, 1991, p. 1020.

Two winsome boys (one black, one white) share some yummy-looking food: a halved banana, a roll that breaks into thirds and thus can't be shared evenly, a quartered pizza. Each fraction is repeated; recipes are included ("Wiggle pear salad" and strawberry pie round out a vegetarian meal). McMillan includes notes on techniques and materials that contributed to his beautiful, appealing photos and on the boys who posed. Another excellent multidimensional concept book from a creative bookmaker.

Zena Sutherland

SOURCE: A review of *Eating Fractions,* in *Bulletin of the Center for Children's Books,* Vol. 45, No. 1, September, 1991, p. 16.

Clear, sharp color photographs show two children enjoying a banana, salad, pizza, and two kinds of baked goods. Each time the food is shown whole, and then it's cut into either halves, thirds, or quarters, then each fractional concept is repeated. The pictures show the children enjoying the food, and slipping some of it to an appreciative dog. Four recipes

are included, meant for adults but pointing out what processes can be contributed by children. The repetition of the concept is an aid to learning and the limitation of the text to just a few fractions is appropriate for young children.

Louise L. Sherman

SOURCE: A review of *Eating Fractions,* in *School Library Journal,* Vol. 37, No. 9, September, 1991, p. 248.

A mouth-watering introduction to fractions is served up by McMillan in this concept book. Full-color photos show one freckle-faced and one dark-skinned child preparing and eating an assortment of foods, each of which is pictured as a whole and then in either halves, thirds, or fourths. The progression from larger to smaller fractions is shown twice with different foods to reinforce the concept. The words for the fractions are given in very large print under the corresponding pictures along with their mathematical symbols. The foods—bananas, sweet rolls, pizza, corn, pear salad, and strawberry pie—look so appetizing that young readers will be eager to try the recipes given at the end of the book. None are difficult, and none use packaged foods or excessive sugar. The excellent photographs owe their appeal not only to their bright colors, clear focus, and good framing, but also to their winsome subjects, two infectiously happy children and a strawberry-pie eating shaggy dog. Ideal for food units in primary classrooms, this should see steady use in both school and public libraries.

Publishers Weekly

SOURCE: A review of *Eating Fractions,* in *Publishers Weekly,* Vol. 238, No. 44, October 4, 1991, p. 87.

Self-described "photo-illustrator" McMillan (*Mary Had a Little Lamb; One Two, One Pair!*) continues to focus his talents on the concept picture book—and once again brings his fresh perspective to this sometimes didactic genre. In this ingenious combination of fractions and food a perky pair of budding mathematicians, boy and girl, divide a series of foods into halves, thirds and quarters. After each division they (sometimes with help from a hungry dog) delightedly devour the *whole* thing. These kids, though obviously posed for the photos, seem to be really enjoying themselves; their pleasure and zest is contagious in the bright, almost shadowless images. Math was never so much fun or so wholesomely delicious. Recipes and suggestions for how children can use their new math skills to measure ingredients and prepare these kid-tested treats are included.

PLAY DAY: A BOOK OF TERSE VERSE (1991)

Kirkus Reviews

SOURCE: A review of *Play Day: A Book of Terse Verse,* in *Kirkus Reviews,* Vol. LIX, No. 18, September 15, 1991, p. 1231.

From Nights of the Puffling*s, illustrated by Bruce McMillan.*

A companion to **One Sun,** with slightly less inspired monosyllabic pairings involving toddlers and their interests ("brown crown," "fun run," "shirt dirt," etc.). As usual with this "photo-illustrator," the color photos are crisp and cleanly composed, the multiracial tots appealing, the educational content multifaceted, and the explanatory notes both exemplary and amusing ("This *'shot plot'* of energetic two-year-olds was no *'click trick.'* But, we ended up with a *'snap wrap'* in a *'smile style'*").

Nancy Menaldi Scanlan

SOURCE: A review of *Play Day: A Book of Terse Verse,* in *School Library Journal,* Vol. 37, No. 10, October, 1991, pp. 100-01.

Bright, full-color photographs of energetic multiethnic two-year-olds romping outdoors are the highlight of this **Play Day.** "Terse verse"—two monosyllabic rhyming words in bold yellow letters—accompany each double-page spread, describing the object or activity featured in the photo. While some of the rhymes are obvious, such as "green bean," and some—"toe

bow"—are very much in keeping with a toddler's broad sense of humor, others seem forced. Consider: a glass stuffed with bits of grass and labeled "grass glass," or "goat boat" to describe a plush stuffed toy atop a wooden boat in a pond. In one case, the same red toy initially referred to as part of a "bear pair" later becomes part of a "cub tub," which is potentially confusing to those learning to identify objects. While some of the samples work better than others, a "fine rhyme" or two are sure to emerge from those who share this book aloud.

Publishers Weekly

SOURCE: A review of *Play Day: A Book of Terse Verse,* in *Publishers Weekly,* Vol. 238, No. 47, October 25, 1991, p. 67.

A welcome companion to **One Sun,** this book, too, is a "neat treat"—a delightful collection of "terse verse" (a *very* short rhyme consisting of two one-syllable words) accompanied by equally engaging color photos. Accomplished author/photo-illustrator McMillan comes up with 14 word pairs and has selected a quartet of huggable two-year-olds to act out each of the verse concepts while clearly—and messily—enjoying themselves completely. The concepts include word pairs such as "fun run" "shirt dirt" and "blue shoe," all boldly photographed within a lush green scene—a summer lawn. As with most of the McMillan canon, the ideas can be extended well beyond the book's covers and the imagination is piqued by the arresting mix of visual and verbal imagery explored here.

Betsy Hearne

SOURCE: A review of *Play Day: A Book of Terse Verse,* in *Bulletin of the Center for Children's Books,* Vol. 49, No. 6, February, 1992, pp. 163-64.

As he did in this book's companion volume, **One Sun,** McMillan here photographs children (of various ethnic origins) engaged in activities described in rhyme on the facing page. "Fat bat" shows a small hand reaching for one of those oversize bats that toddlers wield so enthusiastically toward a plastic ball. "Shirt dirt" needs no explanation! While the last volume had a seaside theme, this one is squarely set in a grassy backyard, which lends vivid green backdrops for the color photography. Although one or two shots are just a touch cutesy ("goat boat" shows an expensive-looking stuffed toy floating atop a handcrafted raft), others reflect the children's natural enthusiasm ("fun run") or intense involvement ("feet seat). The pictures that show body parts and objects lack the emotional punch of facial expression but will serve admirably for identification games. The book as a whole seems a bit younger in its target audience than the previous one, though it generates the same creative possibilities for read-aloud chanting and word play.

📖 *THE BABY ZOO* (1992)

Kirkus Reviews

SOURCE: A review of *The Baby Zoo,* in *Kirkus Reviews,* Vol. LX, No. 1, January 1, 1992, p. 54.

Appealing color photos of 17 rare and unusual zoo babies are presented here, including the European mouflon, Bawean deer, and fishing cat as well as the more familiar giraffe and zebra. For each, the author gives the scientific name, a map indicating range, brief facts (plus endangered status), and the correct name for the baby; kit, pup, fawn, kid, joey, etc. Guides also provide the names for many other animal babies, the names for adult males and females, and the collective noun for each animal. Young children will enjoy the outstanding photos; older ones will also be intrigued by the brief facts.

Margaret A. Bush

SOURCE: A review of *The Baby Zoo,* in *The Horn Book Magazine,* Vol. LXVIII, No. 2, March-April, 1992, p. 217.

Striking full-page photographs of sixteen baby animals are the heart of this informative survey of species living in zoos. In a concluding note Bruce McMillan describes his work in photographing the animals; the beautifully composed pictures, defining the young animals against a soft-focus background, bespeak his patience and skill. A catalogue arrangement is used effectively. The common name of each animal—*spectacled bear, fishing cat, bactrian camel*—appears at the top of the page with pronunciation indicated as needed; the term designating the particular baby—*cub, kitten, calf*—dominates the page with shaded letters in formal typeface set in a stylized frame. A paragraph of miscellaneous information includes the scientific name and discusses physical characteristics, behavior, and natural habitats. A tiny map indicating native range is also provided for each animal. Several concluding pieces augment the album presentation, including a chart listing names used for young animals of various species and a short essay discussing the roles of contemporary zoos in educating humans and conserving animals. The inviting portraits and thoughtful development of information provide an appealing introduction to the animals and a versatile volume for libraries and classrooms.

Ellen Fader

SOURCE: A review of *The Baby Zoo,* in *School Library Journal,* Vol. 38, No. 5, May, 1992, p. 106.

This survey of 16 baby animals found in two American zoos boasts exceptionally well-composed full-color photographs opposite paragraphs of text that describe each animal's habitat, eating habits, and growth patterns. A map accompanies each entry, as well as a pronunciation guide for such species as Bactrian camel, New South Wales wallaroo, and Bawean deer. McMillan also indicates whether each species is threatened, endangered, or survives only in captivity. The usefulness of the book is further enhanced by a chart that lists most of the common names for animal young and a clearly reasoned discussion of the mission of modern zoos. The book will appeal to a wide range of ages: younger children will enjoy the eye-catching photos and the very large labels; older readers will appreciate the many details included. One spelling error—a joey "peaks out from its mother's pouch"—mars an otherwise excellent and novel presentation.

M. Jean Greenlaw

SOURCE: A review of *The Baby Zoo,* in *The New Advocate,* Vol. 6, No. 3, Summer, 1993, p. 220.

Information about baby zoo animals is introduced through double page spreads with text on the left and a color photo on the right. The text includes the name of the species, the name for that species' baby, a map of the habitat, and a brief paragraph on the habits and habitats. A chart at the end of the book provides additional species and the name of their young; there is an essay about zoos, and a graph gives further information on the names of adults and the appropriate collective noun. Though the information is necessarily limited by the format, the book can provide a springboard for further research.

Yvonne Siu-Runyan

SOURCE: A review of *The Baby Zoo,* in *Language Arts,* Vol. 70, No. 6, October, 1993, p. 491.

The incredible photo-illustrations combined with interesting text make this book a must for all school libraries. In this book, children are introduced to many baby animals and learn their baby names. For each baby animal, there is information about the region of the world in which they live, their habits, and their habitats. Especially interesting is the informational chart at the end of the book that gives specifics about the species name, the baby name, the adult female name, the adult male name, and the collective noun name.

📖 *BEACH BALL—LEFT, RIGHT* (1992)

Roger Sutton

SOURCE: A review of *Beach Ball—Left, Right,* in *Bulletin of the Center for Children's Books,* Vol. 45, No. 7, March, 1992, pp. 186-87.

A beach ball takes one big bounce—off the beach, up in the air, past some truly amazed people and animals, and finally back into the arms of its bouncer. No, not much of a story, but the real goal here is to illustrate the difference between left and right, a distinction far more perplexing than the laws of gravity. Each double page spread is centered by a big color photo straddling the gutter; each of the pages is labelled "left" or "right"; the beach ball is always on one side or the other. It's a bit repetitive, but reinforcing as well. As McMillan notes in a brief afterword, "in addition to determining which side of the photo the beach ball is on, children will learn that their left hand is holding the left page of the book, and their right hand is holding the right page of the book." That is, if the child is holding the book right-side up . . . but that's another story.

Kirkus Reviews

SOURCE: A review of *Beach Ball—Left, Right,* in *Kirkus Reviews,* Vol. LX, No. 7, April 1, 1992, p. 468.

A huge plastic ball appears on one side of each appealing double-spread photo here, with the added interest of a child (playing at the shore); an artist; a dog; a fire truck; or simply the foaming surf. Broad white margins on either side accommodate the reader's two hands—vividly labelled, as they hold the book, by the words "left" and "right," printed in the ball's rainbow colors. Every aspect of this basic concept book is worked out with McMillan's usual extraordinary care: many things in addition to the ball can be described as being at left or right; artfully, he controls his limited color scheme and contrives beautifully composed scenes that are virtually devoid of extraneous details.

In all: a delightful means of reinforcing an essential concept.

Deborah Abbott

SOURCE: A review of *Beach Ball—Left, Right,* in *Booklist,* Vol. 88, No. 18, May 15, 1992, p. 1684.

A very large beach ball is the star of McMillan's simple book about the concept of left and right. A single color photo showing a colorful Maine seascape or landscape covers the middle of each double-page spread, while wide, white side margins are labeled appropriately "left" or "right." Readers follow the path of the ball as it bounces from one side of the double-page spread to the other. An end note offers suggestions on how to use the book; however, the difficult concept may still not be fully understood by children. Still, this is a starting point, and other sources can be used for reinforcement.

Mary Lou Budd

SOURCE: A review of *Beach Ball—Left, Right,* in *School Library Journal,* Vol. 38, No. 6, June, 1992, p. 110.

Sunny, full-color photographs capture the splash of primary colors as an enormous beach ball bounds back and forth forming the focal point of this concept book. The ball sails across double-paged backdrops of curling sea surf, meadows, treetops, and fields of wildflowers. Its placement on alternating pages is designed to teach the elusive distinction between left and right. However, while the photos are eye-catching, some may confound young readers. Several spreads have split action—the ball is on one page, characters on the opposite—which diverts readers attention away from, rather than toward, the ball. Therefore, individual presentation is advised, with adult guidance. The words "left" and "right" are printed in large, lower-case letters in primary colors and positioned on the bottom of each appropriate page. Wide margins provide a clean outline for the distinctive photographs, which show representation of gender, age, and ethnic diversity. The very cheerfulness of this photo essay will make youngsters wish for their own ball to toss in the air on a balmy day at the beach or while walking in a grassy meadow.

GOING ON A WHALE WATCH (1992)

Kirkus Reviews

SOURCE: A review of *Going on a Whale Watch,* in *Kirkus Reviews,* Vol. LX, No. 14, July 15, 1992, p. 922.

Another brilliantly planned book from the creator of *Eating Fractions* and dozens of other excellent books utilizing his fine color photos. Every choice McMillan makes here is informed by intelligence and an awareness of his audience. Lucid photos of whales are paired with smaller drawings depicting the same scenes, clarifying and extending the photo images to what's going on underwater. Brief captions provide the correct words for what can be seen ("Paired blowholes"; "Humpback spout"; "Tail-lobbing splash"; "Footprint"; "Spinning breach"); each photo is also labeled with common and Latin names. The journey is traced on a real nautical map; shots of sea and cetaceans are varied with appealing photos of a couple of kids watching them. Notes on the four species observed and a three-page "visual glossary" nicely extend the information. A book that should find many uses with readers of all ages; it should also be a prerequisite for reading *Moby Dick.*

Carolyn Phelan

SOURCE: A review of *Going on a Whale Watch,* in *Booklist,* Vol. 89, No. 4, October 15, 1992, p. 435.

McMillan takes his camera out to sea, bringing his readers along on a whale watch boat to watch the whales and to watch two children as *they* watch the whales. While clear, full-color photographs document whale anatomy and behavior as seen above the water's surface, smaller diagrams show what is happening underwater at the same time. Two-word captions, such as "Humpback spout" and "paired blow holes," appear in large type below photos on facing pages forming a single concept on each spread.

Longer notes, illustrated with small photos, are appended. Few children have the opportunity to watch whales in the wild, but many will wish they could, after seeing the pictures here. An excellent choice for young children curious about whales.

Barbara Marinak

SOURCE: A review of *Going on a Whale Watch*, in *The Horn Book Guide to Children's and Young Adult Books*, Vol. IV, No. 1, Spring, 1993, p. 115.

By combining carefully selected words, skillful diagrams, and beautiful color photographs, McMillan offers the next best thing to a real whale watch. Humpback and fin whales lunge, breech, and do headstands in this photo-essay. Each photograph is accompanied by a short, descriptive phrase and a unique diagram that depicts what observers will never see—the whale's position under the surface. And for those who crave more detail, an excellent visual glossary concludes the book.

Valerie Lennox

SOURCE: A review of *Going on a Whale Watch*, in *School Library Journal*, Vol. 39, No. 4, April, 1993, p. 112.

McMillan takes readers on an excursion off the coast of Maine to look at whales. Through dramatic full-color photographs and a spare text, such behavior as a "Tail breach," "Headstand," and "Flipper wave" are shown and described. The excitement of the expedition is communicated through shots of the mammoth mammals intermingled with those of two children on the boat as they imitate the whales or react to the surrounding sights. The photos cover the upper two-thirds of each page while the large-type text appears against the remaining white page. Since all that is visible in each shot is the part of the whale, a small illustration showing a side view of the entire animal under water is inset. The full-color photographs are bright, intense, and absolutely sparkling. The children appear windblown, exuberant, and natural. This is first-rate nonfiction for preschoolers. At the same time, older children will enjoy the attractive introduction and the challenge of picturing the entire whale. A visual glossary concludes the book.

Tina Burke

SOURCE: A review of *Going on a Whale Watch*, in *Childhood Education*, Vol. 69, No. 4, Summer, 1993, p. 247.

A whale's dark body gleams in the water spray. Photos of minke, humpback and fin whales as well as dolphins are clearly captioned. Beneath each photo, a diagram shows the clues that tell watchers where to look for whales. Large black print and expressive photos of whales and students make this a possible read-aloud. The detailed diagrams and the glossary's whale facts, however, will invite close scrutiny by future marine scientists.

MOUSE VIEWS: WHAT THE CLASS PET SAW (1993)

Carolyn Phelan

SOURCE: A review of *Mouse Views: What the Class Pet Saw*, in *Booklist*, Vol. 89, No. 14, March 15, 1993, p. 1321.

McMillan uses photography to show kids familiar classroom sights from a mouse's point of view. When the class pet escapes, he explores the school on his own. Each right-hand page shows part of an object or set of objects highly enlarged, close up, and often at an odd angle. Below, a row of question marks invites viewers to guess what they're seeing. The answers include paintbrushes, computer keys, stacks of paper, pencil erasers, and blocks. On the following page, another full-color photograph shows the mouse playing around the object(s), now identifiable in a long-range shot. Children will see this brightly illustrated puzzle book, with its combination of story and game, as pure fun. Teachers will appreciate the chance to hone their students' observational skills and also to introduce mapping through the map at the book's conclusion, "Where the Class Pet Went," which shows a school floor plan with the mouse's journey clearly marked. Multiple uses, multiple audiences, multiple copies indicated.

Kirkus Reviews

SOURCE: A review of *Mouse Views: What the Class Pet Saw*, in *Kirkus Reviews*, Vol. LXI, No. 6, March 15, 1993, p. 375.

"Chase," a brown mouse, explores Maine's Margaret Chase Smith School while McMillan snaps a dozen familiar objects and places from the pet's closeup point of view; then, overleaf, he backs off to show the appealing little creature investigating the same, now-captioned, setting. The guessing game that results—it's not always easy to identify objects like a worn end of chalk, a stack of trays, or piano keys in closeup—is just one of several features here. The mouse tours the whole school (classrooms, gym, library, etc.), implicitly outlining a day's activities; there's also an outside photo of the school and a "map": a floorplan with the mouse's route. In addition, McMillan's vibrant, beautifully composed color photos are an inspiring demonstration of the intriguing patterns that can be found in everyday things.

Roger Sutton

SOURCE: A review of *Mouse Views: What the Class Pet Saw*, in *Bulletin of the Center for Children's Books*, Vol. 46, No. 8, April, 1993, p. 258.

The classroom mouse is loose, and photographer McMillan takes us along on its peregrinations through the school, challenging readers to identify the close-up photos of the objects the mouse finds in its travels. Dusty pink circles are revealed to be pencil erasers, another page turn identifies some silvery sticks as scissors; a pile of red plastic ridges turns out to be a stack of lunch trays in the cafeteria. This isn't a new idea (see Peter Ziebel's *Look Closer!*), but the photos are bright and tidy, preschoolers and kindergartners will enjoy the school supplies, and the mouse is a cute narrative guide. As usual, McMillan provides scrupulous technical notes, although his appended suggestion that the book could be used to enhance map-reading skills doesn't seem entirely to the point.

Myra R. Oleynik

SOURCE: A review of *Mouse Views: What the Class Pet Saw,* in *School Library Journal,* Vol. 39, No. 4, April, 1993, p. 100.

Distinguished full-color photographs and bold, simple text take beginning readers and a class pet on a mysterious journey over rulers, erasers, piano keys, and other common sites of a typical elementary school. *Mouse Views* is similar in concept to the popular "Look Again" books by Tana Hoban in showing that things are not always as they appear. However, without using a cutaway window, McMillan is able to trick and amuse readers by focusing his camera on the interesting colors, shapes, and familiar patterns that young children will delight in discovering as they turn each page to follow the mouse's meanderings. Sharp full-page photographs with accompanying lively narrative make this an excellent read-aloud, while independent readers will also enjoy predicting the mouse's destination and then turning each page to reveal his actual location from a slightly different angle. A map at the end of the book traces the mouse's jaunt through the school.

📖 *A BEACH FOR THE BIRDS* (1993)

Diane Nunn

SOURCE: A review of *A Beach for the Birds,* in *School Library Journal,* Vol. 39, No. 4, April, 1993, p. 137.

While the title suggests that many shore birds will be discussed, this book is basically about the endangered Eastern Least Tern. Approaching an older audience than in most of his previous books, McMillan focuses on a particular colony of the birds that nest on the Maine coast. He successfully describes and documents in the numerous photos their behavior and physical characteristics, such as the distinguishing black tip on the bill that appears during the summer. Clear explanations of courting and mating are presented, as well as interesting tidbits as to why the tern can drink salt water and easily walk on the sand. Full-color photographs of children fishing and splashing in the water and strolling along the beach parallel those of the Least Terns engaging in similar activities. Such juxtapositioning works better in books for younger readers. The text here is strong enough to stand alone; the glimpses of human activity distract readers' attention rather than enhancing the information. *A Beach for the Birds*

nonetheless encourages a closer look at shore birds and emphasizes the importance of protecting their habitats.

Kay Weisman

SOURCE: A review of *A Beach for the Birds,* in *Booklist,* Vol. 89, No. 15, April 1, 1993, p. 1426.

McMillan turns his considerable talents (both photographic and journalistic) to the least terns, an endangered sea swallow that summers along the North Atlantic coast. He offers much information about the life cycle, habitat, food requirements, predators, and specific behaviors of these birds. Throughout, he parallels the activities of the terns on their beach with those of the humans who summer on the opposite shore, noting similarities. McMillan's photography is superb, as always, and it makes this presentation more than just another endangered-animal book. Amazing shots of birds diving for prey and creating scrapes in the sand for soon-to-be-laid eggs, as well as close-ups of young hatchlings, make this a worthy purchase. Good-quality paper and the surf and sand photos on the endpapers further add to the elegance of the layout. Appended with least tern facts, glossary, and bibliography, this will be welcomed by report writers and browsers alike.

Kirkus Reviews

SOURCE: A review of *A Beach for the Birds,* in *Kirkus Reviews,* Vol. LXI, No. 7, April 1, 1993, p. 460.

In Kennebunk, Maine, endangered least terns find sanctuary on a beach where they can nest undisturbed by nearby vacationers. Since terns must keep their eggs *cool* by shielding them on hot days, privacy is essential to their survival. McMillan, best known for his award-winning concept books, includes dozens of such fascinating facts as he describes the characteristics and behavior of this graceful sea bird, skillfully relating them to his audience (with unobtrusive comparisons to children playing on the adjacent beach) and providing beautifully composed color photos—as many as four, harmoniously deployed, on each spread—for an evocative visual complement to the informative text. Specific, admirably detailed, lucid, well organized, inspiring: natural history at its best. A handy page of "Least Tern Facts" sums up statistics, range, etc.; glossary; bibliography; index.

Betsy Hearne

SOURCE: A review of *A Beach for the Birds,* in *Bulletin of the Center for Children's Books,* Vol. 46, No. 10, June, 1993, p. 322.

McMillan's full-color photodocumentary of the endangered Least Tern describes the bird's physical characteristics, its beach habitat along the Little River on the Maine coast, mating and reproduction cycles, and migration.

The Least Tern presents an interesting example of adaptation to a salt water environment, since it derives its water from the fish it eats and from actually imbibing salt water, with a special gland to collect excess salt and secrete it in concentrated droplets from nose holes on the upper bill. The text is clear and full of information, though it seems to jump around a bit when the author abruptly introduces comparisons between children's behavior and birds' behavior. The brilliant action shots are enough to lure kids into a nature watch of their own, however, and further facts are listed for reference at the book's end, along with a glossary and index.

PENGUINS AT HOME: GENTOOS OF ANTARCTICA (1993)

Kirkus Reviews

SOURCE: A review of *Penguins at Home: Gentoos of Antarctica,* in *Kirkus Reviews,* Vol. LXI, No. 15, August 1, 1993, p. 1005.

A close look at the Southern Gentoos, largest of the penguins on the Antarctic peninsula. Each page gives a color photo, a one-word heading, and a brief text detailing some aspect of the penguins' life—from arrival at the nesting area in the summer, when the temperature is a "scorchingly hot" 45 degrees, till the maturing chicks join their parents in the icy waters off the bottom of the world. Good scientific detail: the author describes how penguins flap their flippers to reduce overheating, how the glacial cliffs "look like they've been sprayed with pink paint" due to microscopic pink algae growing on penguin droppings, and how countershading keeps the penguins safe from predators. Crisp, appealing photos help tell the story.

Roger Sutton

SOURCE: A review of *Penguins at Home: Gentoos of Antarctica,* in *Bulletin of the Center for Children's Books,* Vol. 47, No. 1, September, 1993, p. 17.

Last seen wandering about the school with a class' pet mouse (*Mouse Views*), McMillan now goes down under, *way* down, to the shores of Antarctica where he observes the breeding and feeding behavior of the Gentoo penguin. At two and one-half feet tall, the Gentoos are the largest of the three brush-tail penguin species that inhabit the Antarctic peninsula (the largest penguin species, the Emperor, lives in more remote areas of the continent) and McMillan's photo-essay follows them from their summer (November) breeding season through egg incubation and chick-feeding to their annual molt and return to the sea for the winter. The color photos are clear and close-up, sharply observant of behaviors such as nest-building with rocks and the grooming that keeps feathers waterproof. Each page contains a photo and one paragraph about a particular characteristic of anatomy or behavior, and while the book is somewhat statically designed, it's easy to follow. Appended material includes a map, a bibliography (with only one children's book), and an index.

Elizabeth Bush

SOURCE: A review of *Penguins at Home: Gentoos of Antarctica,* in *Booklist,* Vol. 90, No. 6, November 15, 1993, pp. 620-21.

This attractive photo-essay has been designed with admirable care and intelligence. Each page is devoted to a discrete aspect of Gentoo physiology or behavior and then organized to follow the mating cycle of the colony. A word or brief phrase is printed in boldface type at the upper outside corner of each page, interpreting the central photo for browsers and introducing the theme of the text for more serious readers. Although McMillan's uniform half-page photos do capture engaging characteristics of this species, "cute" close-ups do not dominate. More often the penguins are photographed as comparatively small figures within the barren Antarctic landscape, a visual approach that aids in understanding their behavior. Even the endpaper and credit background photos have been selected to display the bleak and majestic ice cliffs of the Gentoos' habitat. The study includes a short essay comparing the Gentoo with Chinstrap and Adélie Brush-tails; a map of Antarctica, which notes the various species' breeding areas; and a short bibliography. The location of each photo site is clearly documented, and sources of verification of penguin facts are credited.

Lisa Wu Stowe

SOURCE: A review of *Penguins at Home: Gentoos of Antarctica,* in *School Library Journal,* Vol. 39, No. 12, December, 1993, pp. 128-29.

Once again, McMillan successfully draws readers into the world of the creatures he studies. This time he explores the Southern Gentoos of the Antarctic Peninsula. He combines brief one- to two-word headings like he utilized in *Going on a Whale Watch* and detailed descriptions like those he employed in *A Beach for the Birds* with his trademark, high-quality photographs. The full-color shots are beautiful, but not glamorized or sensationalized. While Gentoos are examined within the context of the Brush-tail penguins to which they belong, this is essentially a book about the single species. A helpful synopsis of Brush-tail traits is appended. Information about physical characteristics, feeding, locomotion, and breeding practices are well covered. Parents are said to "protect their chicks with 'umbrellas'—their own warm, waterproof bodies." Hungry chicks peck at the doors of "their baby food 'cabinets'—their parents' bills." Later, "'they put on their new 'snowsuits'—grow their new waterproof feathers." While these cute terms minimize the wonder of nature and detract from the book's scientific credibility, it is still a highly accurate account.

Aside from this minor flaw, this wonderful look at *Penguins at Home* will have wide appeal.

Beatrice L. Burch

SOURCE: A review of *Penguins at Home: Gentoos of Antarctica,* in *Science Books & Films,* Vol. 30, No. 3, April, 1994, p. 82.

Beautiful and unusually large close-up photographs, plus details of the habits of the gentle Gentoo penguins, form this outstanding slim juvenile book that will be enjoyed repeatedly by a general audience, and not only children. It is seldom that the scenic Antarctic peninsula and its specialized bird species are portrayed so clearly and inexpensively. On each page, written under a general caption, a large photo and well-chosen topic emphasizes characteristics of endearing bird species that are abundant in the Antarctic. Because the photographs are presented with great clarity, it seems as though the viewer is seeing actual birds in the Antarctic spring. Topics include rookeries and breeding, predators, feeding of the young by adults, problems of body heat control, calling, and moulting behavior. A summary follows on other brush-tailed species, with a somewhat unexpected comment on the current increase in penguins' numbers. Included, too, is a page with a map of Antarctica and penguin breeding sites that is superimposed over a fine close-up photograph of one of many immense icebergs floating in exquisite Gerlache Straits in the Antarctic spring. All in all, this is an outstanding book that is sure to be reread many times. Readers would also do well to look for the other 30 books by this author-photographer.

SENSE SUSPENSE: A GUESSING GAME FOR THE FIVE SENSES (1994)

Roger Sutton

SOURCE: A review of *Sense Suspense: A Guessing Game for the Five Senses,* in *Bulletin of the Center for Children's Books,* Vol. 48, No. 4, December, 1994, pp. 137-38.

A Puerto Rican setting (Culebra Island) provides McMillan with a tropical accent for the familiar game of photographic synecdoche: look at a close-up photo at an unfamiliar pattern or shape; turn the page to see the object revealed in its entirety. Here the game is spiced up with sensory multiple choice—along with guessing the object, kids are supposed to figure out which of the five senses the object stimulates. Thus a deep-pink curve turns into a flower to be smelled; coarse white threads are revealed to be a baby goat being touched by some island children. As McMillan acknowledges in a "Using this book" paragraph, there are no wrong answers, but since a stubborn kid could build an argument for almost any of the senses matching any of the pictures, the page-turning can be a bit of a letdown: that colorful parrot is sitting on someone's hand; are we looking at it, touching it, or hearing it? The last is the preferred answer,

but hearing is probably the most difficult of the senses to pin down in a photograph. Hana Machotka's *Outstanding Outsides* and Margaret Miller's *My Five Senses* are just two of many picture books to take on either of the concepts McMillan covers here; while the book is an attractive offering (with English and Spanish texts), it's probably an optional purchase for most collections.

Christina Dorr

SOURCE: A review of *Sense Suspense: A Guessing Game for the Five Senses,* in *School Library Journal,* Vol. 40, No. 12, December, 1994, p. 100.

An exquisite treat. What Aliki has presented in text and sketches in *My Five Senses*, McMillan has made into a game through his brilliant full-color photographs. Set on the Caribbean island Culebra, **Sense Suspense** features two young islanders using their senses to explore a variety of foods, plants, animals, shells, and musical instruments. Like Tana Hoban's *Look! Look! Look!* and *Take Another Look*, McMillan focuses first on a small part, and then changes perspective to include the whole object. Children are supposed to first guess what it is, and then identify which sense reacts most powerfully. The instructions for using the book appear at the end, and readers are assured that there are no incorrect answers. Several words and phrases appear in both English and Spanish, but the directions and information on Culebra are in English only. A sound, satisfying choice.

Mary Harris Veeder

SOURCE: A review of *Sense Suspense: A Guessing Game for the Five Senses,* in *Booklist,* Vol. 91, No. 7, December 1, 1994, p. 675.

Using photographs taken on the Caribbean island of Culebra, McMillan creates what he calls a "concept game." Children are invited to guess what object a close-up picture represents and then to turn the page to find the answer. For example, brightly colored swirls turn out to be part of a lollipop enjoyed by a little boy. Logos for the five senses appear on the double-page spreads, challenging children to determine which senses are likely to be used in relation to the pictured object. Possible answers, in both English and Spanish (with transliteration), are presented on a concluding double-page spread, and the words on back of the jacket are in Spanish. Also included are a thumbnail portrait of the island and a description of how best to use the game. Because some of the close-ups are fairly difficult to guess (a steel drum, a conch shell), this may be most successful as a portrait of Culebran (and Caribbean) life.

Evelyn Vanek

SOURCE: A review of *Sense Suspense: A Guessing Game for the Five Senses,* in *Journal of Youth Services in Libraries,* Vol. 8, No. 3, Spring, 1995, pp. 294-95.

This book is almost impossible to describe since it includes so many concepts and can be used in so many different ways. A very close-up photograph leads to a picture of the whole object on the following page, but rather than just guessing the object, children are asked which senses they would use to learn about the object. Spanish words are given for the different senses, and at the end of the book Spanish words are given for each of the objects pictured. There is even a map of the island where the photographs were taken, and a section called "Using this book" that gives some helpful information.

Children can't help but respond to the colorful photographs in this book, and the various ways of exploring the information can lead to discussions of the senses, the Spanish language, other countries, and the objects pictured.

PUFFINS CLIMB, PENGUINS RHYME (1995)

Publishers Weekly

SOURCE: A review of *Puffins Climb, Penguins Rhyme,* in *Publishers Weekly,* Vol. 242, No. 5, January 30, 1995, p. 99.

Master photo-essayist McMillan finds fetching fun in a few feathered friends as he pairs likenesses of two avian species with rhyming, two-word captions. Inhabiting literally opposite ends of the earth, puffins (from the North Polar region) and penguins (native to Antarctica) share an endearing gawkiness, and McMillan's unadorned, crystalline photographs capture surprising humor and personality in the simplest of situations. Spreads alternate between the two varieties, presenting both single subjects and groups in representative activities—"Puffins walk. Puffins squawk. Penguins brawl. Penguins call." The black-and-white birds' orange-toned beaks and feet lend intense splashes of color to the stark backgrounds—gray sea and rocks, clear blue skies, green grass. Though technically not of a feather, these birds flock together to provide an inviting nature study.

Mary Harris Veeder

SOURCE: A review of *Puffins Climb, Penguins Rhyme,* in *Booklist,* Vol. 91, No. 15, April 1, 1995, p. 1421.

Antarctic penguins and Icelandic puffins are pictured in photographs on alternating double-page spreads, with simple, rhyming text in very large black letters set below each picture. "Penguins glare. Penguins share. Puffins hide. Puffins glide." Unlike McMillan's *Night of the Pufflings,* which actually contains some of the same pictures that appear here, this book has no narrative. But the combination of clear rhymes and bright pictures will work well with groups and make the book good preparation for a field trip to the zoo, where puffins and penguins often appear together.

Dot Minzer

SOURCE: A review of *Puffins Climb, Penguins Rhyme,* in *School Library Journal,* Vol. 41, No. 5, May, 1995, pp. 100-01.

Through extraordinary photography, McMillan compares and contrasts the habits and habitats of the puffins of Iceland and the penguins of Antarctica. Each page of this stunning book holds oversized, full-color close-ups that exhibit, among other things, the birds flying, standing, grooming themselves, greeting one another, eating, and caring for their young. Large, oversized black type runs along the bottom of each page proclaiming, in minimalist verse, things like "Puffins land" and "Puffins stand," "Penguins nest" and "penguins rest." While books on puffins and penguins abound, the pairing of the two species here makes for a winner. An excellent introduction to the worlds of these two birds and to a discussion of their environments.

Frank M. Truesdale

SOURCE: A review of *Puffins Climb, Penguins Rhyme,* in *Science Books & Films,* Vol. 31, No. 8, November, 1995, p. 242.

This picture book takes an up-close look at two of humankind's favorite birds: penguins and puffins. Parents and teachers, like most of us, are drawn to animals that remind us of cuddly human babies; such animals become the subject of endless numbers of T-shirts, posters, stuffed toys, and picture books. However, few such picture books for children are as well done as this one. The author-photographer has no misconceptions about the biology of these two birds, which lay persons may emotionally group together, but which are in fact, geographically and phylogenetically, worlds apart. The final two pages of the book are concise accounts of the two species featured: Atlantic puffins and southern Gentoo penguins. Ecological, morphological, and behavioral characteristics of both are juxtaposed to offer teachers endless possibilities for discussion, after their young charges have perused the pictures and verse. The author had a twofold plan for his book: to introduce children to the behavior of two "amusing birds that live in remote places" and to present two-word minimalist poetry that consists of a repeating noun—either "puffins" or "penguins"—and a one-syllable verb, matched with photos that provide visual clues for perhaps unfamiliar verbs. Such a design has produced what should be a unique learning experience for young and old. And who knows, in addition to going to see penguins at the zoo, we might now be encouraged to visit Maine, where we may actually see some of the 150 pairs of Atlantic puffins that summer on the offshore islands.

The Reading Teacher

SOURCE: A review of *Puffins Climb, Penguins Rhyme,*

in *The Reading Teacher,* Vol. 49, No. 8, May, 1996, p. 652.

Celebrating the Icelandic Atlantic puffins at the top of the world and Antarctica's southern gentoo penguins at the bottom, Bruce McMillan's *Puffins Climb, Penguins Rhyme* will delight readers of all ages. McMillan's close-up color photographs provide a jubilant match for his playful minimalist verb verse, two-word rhymes with a one-syllable verb. Each double page alternates puffins and penguins and provides poetry with plenty of pleasing phrases—"Puffins hear. Puffins peer. . . . Penguins brawl. Penguins call." At the end are fascinating comparisons between the two birds. Finally, an author's note gives insight to the photographs and his choice of verb verse and challenges readers to create their own.

📖 *NIGHTS OF THE PUFFLINGS* (1995)

Susan Dove Lempke

SOURCE: A review of *Nights of the Pufflings,* in *Bulletin of the Center for Children's Books,* Vol. 48, No. 7, March, 1995, pp. 225-26.

On a small island 200 miles south of the Arctic Circle, Icelandic children play an important role in helping young puffins, or pufflings, survive their entry into the world. In *Nights of the Pufflings,* Bruce McMillan keeps his focus on the puffins, but gives us the human perspective through a little girl, Halla, and her friend Arnar Ingi as they watch the puffins and "wait and dream of the nights of the pufflings yet to come." Beginning in April, the puffins land on Heimaey and other nearby uninhabited islands to mate and to hatch their eggs, one per pair. They prepare their underground burrows, the same ones each year, and then tend the chicks through the summer. The children never see the chicks, which remain hidden beyond human reach in the burrows, but they watch the parents bringing back fish as often as ten times a day.

Finally, in August, the pufflings emerge to fly to the sea for the winter, and Halla and the other children of Heimaey begin their nighttime adventure of finding the babies who may have become confused by the village lights, and who have landed in the streets, where they may be hurt by cats, dogs, or cars. For two weeks the children "rescue thousands of pufflings" at night. They sleep late the next day, then head down to the beach with their cardboard boxes of pufflings, launching the babies out over the sea to safety.

Any book about puffins, with their colorful faces and generally comical appearance, is likely to have a certain charm. Not many photographers, however, have the technical and artistic skills of McMillan at his finest. Though he cannot show the newborn puffins, he makes up for it with shots of the adults with beaks clamped tightly on the catch of day, and he perfectly captures a puffin swooping in for a landing. The island scenery gives him crisp hues in the sky, grassy cliffs, snowy mountains, and sparkling

seas. The Icelandic gene pool provides platinum blond, pink-cheeked, blue-eyed schoolchildren (no adults are shown), wearing their thick multicolored sweaters on August nights. Even the nighttime pictures are vivid and dramatic, and they give us our first close-up shots of the pufflings.

For a photographer, McMillan can sure write a picturebook text, gaining our interest in the puffins with tidbits about their lives while foreshadowing the mysterious "nights of the pufflings" still to come. He works in a few Icelandic words with their pronunciations (Halla, for instance, is pronounced HATTL-lah), and carefully avoids any pitfalls of anthropomorphizing the birds or making the kids into cutie-pies or superchildren. McMillan doesn't burden the text with too much information, but he fills in, on the verso of the title page, when, where, and how the pictures were taken, and he concludes with a page of puffin facts and a brief bibliography of (mostly) adult books.

With the keen awareness most schoolchildren have these days of the deteriorating condition of the earth, *Nights of the Pufflings* has a uniquely satisfying twist for its grade school audience: because of the manmade lights, the puffins are put into danger, but the village children take responsibility for undoing the damage. No environmental preaching is done—the story simply speaks for itself. The fact that the island children have a fabulous time doing their job gives the book a special thrill.

Patricia Manning

SOURCE: A review of *Nights of the Pufflings,* in *School Library Journal,* Vol. 41, No. 3, March, 1995, p. 198.

An extremely handsome photo essay that shows a breeding season in a colony of North Atlantic puffins on Heimaey, largest of the Westmann Islands off the southwest coast of Iceland. McMillan hangs his informative text on the framework of young Halla and her friends, who await the first flight of the pufflings with eager joy. Many of these fledglings fail to reach the sea on this maiden flight, landing in Halla's village below the cliffs. Here the children wait, armed with cardboard boxes and flashlights, racing to rescue the pufflings before they become prey for cats or dogs, or run over by passing vehicles. Staying up all night, sleeping late into the morning, the children spend two unusual weeks rescuing thousands of baby birds and releasing them to the sea. McMillan's crisp full-color photos record courting and nesting behavior of the puffins and the activities of the children waiting for and performing their rescues. A fine book to foster empathy in young people as well as to inform them, and to show them that children can make a difference in the world.

Mary Harris Veeder

SOURCE: A review of *Nights of the Pufflings,* in *Booklist,* Vol. 91, No. 14, March 15, 1995, pp. 1331-32.

McMillan makes each bird, person, or place he photographs look special. In this book, he takes us to an island off the coast of Iceland, where Icelandic children and puffins alike seem alert and magical. On nights when the youngest puffins, called pufflings, take their first flight, the children organize to rescue the birds who don't make it to the sea. Readers will love the local custom as well as the fact that there's not a single adult shown organizing the lifesaving effort. The quality of light and the combination of crisp close-ups and beautiful landscapes that McMillan uses make every shot in the book seem to capture a perfect day.

Maeve Visser Knoth

SOURCE: A review of *Nights of the Pufflings,* in *The Horn Book Magazine,* Vol. LXXI, No. 4, July-August, 1995, p. 480.

Each spring, on a tiny island off the coast of Iceland, millions of puffins arrive to lay their eggs and raise their chicks. Halla and her friends watch for the puffins' return and wait for the summer and the "nights of the pufflings." The Icelandic children watch the puffins as they spend the summer feeding and protecting the young chicks, which remain hidden in underground nests. In August, when the baldusbrá flower is in full bloom, the children go out at night with cardboard boxes and flashlights to help the young pufflings make it safely to the ocean, where they will spend the winter. Each night for two weeks pufflings leave their borrows for the first time to make their first flights. Many land safely in the sea, while others set off in the wrong direction and land in the village. The children rescue the pufflings, who cannot take off from the flat ground and are likely to be run over by cars or caught by cats and dogs, and release them on the beach. The story of Halla, her friends, and their puffling rescue is a delightful and unusual one in which children make a real difference in their natural environment. Young readers have a natural affinity for the young of other species, and this fascinating story, combined with gorgeous color photographs, a simple, clear text, and handsome book design, makes an appealing package. McMillan includes the pronunciation of unfamiliar Icelandic names and words within the text and follows his story with an afterword about the North Atlantic puffins.

Arlene P. Bernstein and Robert A. Newton

SOURCE: A review of *Nights of the Pufflings,* in *Appraisal: Science Books for Young People,* Vol. 28, No. 4, Autumn, 1995, pp. 32-3.

Librarian: **Night of the Pufflings** is a well-done photo-essay of a not too well known occurrence in the world of birds: the migration of mature puffins from Newfoundland to the island of Heimaey off the coast of Iceland, where they nest, mate, lay eggs, and raise their chicks

to pufflings. The book follows a young girl named Halla and her friends as they await the puffins, observe their mating rituals, watch the puffin parents gather food for their chicks, and then rescue any stranded pufflings and set them free over the ocean.

The close-up photographs are superb. Pronunciations of Icelandic names and words are included in the text; the final page is devoted to information on puffins and pufflings; and a brief bibliography is included. In all, a very fine addition to any collection!

Specialist: This is a truly excellent book about Puffins and their young, called pufflings. The author, Bruce McMillan, provides us with a wonderful photographic essay of Puffins, the "clowns of the sea." He tells us of the return of the puffins to their breeding grounds, Heimaey Island, off the coast of Iceland. Here the puffins nest, lay eggs and raise their chicks to pufflings. This is also the story of an interesting tradition in which the children of Heimaey Island stay up through the night during the time of the pufflings first flights. Their part in the rescue and release of young pufflings who don't quite make it to the sea will be of interest to all. The author has thoughtfully provided as an appendix, further more detailed information on puffins and pufflings which the reader may care to relate to young children.

SUMMER ICE: LIFE ALONG THE ANTARCTIC PENINSULA (1995)

Melissa Hudak

SOURCE: A review of *Summer Ice: Life along the Antarctic Peninsula,* in *School Library Journal,* Vol. 41, No. 9, September, 1995, p. 212.

McMillan's fascinating offering documents the majestic beauty of the Antarctic and its variety of life forms. He includes informative sections on land plants, seals, whales, and penguins. The material on penguins is a special delight, discussing the order Sphenisciformes in general as well as individual species such as the chinstrap and Adélie. Even more interesting, however, are the facts given on such creatures as the krill, a tiny, shrimplike animal that is a vital part of the area's food chain. As is usual in McMillan's books, the full-color photography is brilliant in its beauty and attention to detail. However, the text is lively and knowledgeable, and could stand alone and still catch readers' interest. Few available titles on the topic for this age group provide such interesting glimpses of the region's wildlife. A wonderful find for report writers and browsers alike.

Carolyn Phelan

SOURCE: A review of *Summer Ice: Life Along the Antarctic Peninsula,* in *Booklist,* Vol. 92, No. 5, November 1, 1995, p. 468.

This photo-essay introduces readers to the animals and plants of the Antarctic Peninsula, the spur of land that stretches across the Antarctic Circle toward South America. After showing the landforms and glacial iceforms there, McMillan turns to the unexpected wealth of summer wildlife: algae and moss, plankton and krill, humpback whales and orcas, skuas and shags, seals and (of course) penguins. While the exceptionally clear, full-color photos are the highlight of the book, the text is informative not just in describing individual species, but also in showing how they relate to each other. A handsome introduction to the wildlife of the Antarctic Peninsula.

GRANDFATHER'S TROLLEY (1995)

Hazel Rochman

SOURCE: A review of *Grandfather's Trolley*, in *Booklist*, Vol. 92, No. 4, October 15, 1995, p. 412.

From *Eating Fractions* (1991) to *Going on a Whale Watch* (1992), McMillan's photo-essays have brought wit and beauty to informational books. Here he uses specially posed photographs to tell a simple historical fiction story about a small girl who rides the trolley car that her loving grandfather drives through the woods and then back again. The illustrations use the technique of the trolley era—black-and-white photos hand-tinted with oils—and the happiness between grandparent and child is movingly portrayed, especially when Grandfather allows her to help him drive the trolley home. However, it's not easy to make out the technical details in the impressionistic pictures, which may be more appealing to nostalgic adults than to children. The notes and background information are a fascinating part of the story. McMillan's grandfather worked as a trolley car motorman at the turn of the century. The trolley in the photographs is in a Maine museum, where visitors can still ride it.

Roger Sutton

SOURCE: A review of *Grandfather's Trolley*, in *Bulletin of the Center for Children's Books*, Vol. 49, No. 4, December, 1995, p. 133.

"I remember . . . "—not two words you generally want to start a picture book with, for they too often presage a nostalgic story more concerned with recollecting childhood than recreating it. In this picture book, illustrated with black-and-white photographs hand-tinted à la Ken Robbins, the narrator remembers when she was "a little girl," and would go help her grandfather run the trolley. Not much happens: they go down the track (*"Clackety-clackety, clackety clack"*), they stop at the end of the line and the girl goes for a little walk, she brings the power controls from one end of the train to the other, they go back. Although the most interesting moment, when the girl helps Grandfather with the controls, needs elucidation, this is sweet, faintly exotic in an old-timey way,

and certainly easy to follow—but there's no story. The photos are sweet as well, fuzzy at the edges and brightened with such touches as the girl's yellow hair ribbon blown in the breeze while Grandfather's white whiskers stream like a puff of smoke. A note explains that the trolley pictured is now housed at the Seashore Trolley Museum in Maine, where kids can take it for a ride.

Virginia Opocensky

SOURCE: A review of *Grandfather's Trolley*, in *School Library Journal*, Vol. 41, No. 12, December, 1995, p. 86.

Children don't need to understand the masterful photographic techniques to appreciate this bit of nostalgia set in the early 1900s. Grandfather, a trolley motorman, always saves a seat in the last row for his granddaughter, who then rides to the end of the line. On the return trip, she sits up front next to him. That's the story line but, combined with the artwork, there is much, much more. Clearly evident are the love between the girl and the elderly man; the sights, sounds, and motion of the trolley; the summer breeze that blows the little girl's hair and makes her eyes squint; and the sheer delight of the day. McMillan took the photographs in black and white, brown-toned them, and hand tinted them with oil paints, replicating photographic methods used during the heyday of trolleys. As always, his work is superbly executed. For anyone who has ever ridden a trolley as a child, this is irresistible. For those too young to have had the pleasure, it is evocative of life at a slower pace.

Renee Queen

SOURCE: A review of *Grandfather's Trolley*, in *Children's Book Review Service*, Vol. 24, No. 5, January, 1996, p. 51.

The author dedicated this book to his grandfather who drove a trolley car for many years. Neither children nor their parents have a good concept of what a "trolley" is, but this book, through a combination of photography and color tinting, enlightens readers. More important, however, is the tender relationship between the little girl and her grandfather as she rides the rails with him as his "number one helper." Lots of joy and love presented in a straight forward manner.

Peter D. Sieruta

SOURCE: A review of *Grandfather's Trolley*, in *The Horn Book Guide to Children's and Young Adult Books*, Vol. VII, No. 1, Spring, 1996, p. 38.

A young girl reminisces about riding the trolley on which her grandfather was the motorman. After traveling as a passenger, the narrator assists Grandfather at the controls. Hand-tinted photographs express the hazy, nostalgic appeal of the gentle text. An author's note explains that the trolley depicted is a restored vehicle from the Seashore Trolley Museum near Kennebunkport, Maine.

Additional coverage of McMillan's life and career is contained in the following sources published by Gale Research: *Contemporary Authors New Revision Series*, Vols. 13, 35; *Major Authors and Illustrators for Children and Young Adults; Something about the Author*, Vols. 22, 70.

Lane Smith

1959-

American illustrator and author of children's books.

Major works include *Halloween ABC* (1987; written by Eve Merriam), *The Big Pets* (1990), *Glasses—Who Needs 'Em?* (1991), *The Stinky Cheese Man: And Other Fairly Stupid Tales* (1992; written by Jon Scieszka), *The Happy Hocky Family!* (1993), *Disney's James and the Giant Peach* (1996; adapted by Karey Kirkpatrick).

INTRODUCTION

A popular and critically acclaimed children's illustrator known for his bold, unconventional style, Lane Smith has produced award-winning solo works and well-received collaborative books, particularly with author Jon Scieszka. The appeal of his drawings, which offer a range of views from childlike humor to sophisticated parody and feature dark, atmospheric effects as well as exaggerated characterizations, has attracted the attention of children and adults alike. Making his debut with the spooky imagery of *Halloween ABC* in the late 1980s, Smith later successfully added his irreverent humor and unique artistic sense to the wacky prose of Jon Scieszka in such works as *The True Story of the Three Little Pigs* (1989) and *The Stinky Cheese Man: And Other Fairly Stupid Tales*. Additionally, Smith's individual projects, including the dreamlike *The Big Pets* and inventive *Glasses—Who Needs 'Em?*, have brought him widespread attention and praise. Dilys Evans, commenting in the *Horn Book Magazine* on the affinity of Smith's nontraditional artistic approach with the perceptions of young people, wrote, "Lane Smith creates pictures that encourage children to find things, ask questions, and often answer back. His world is familiar territory; their imaginations plug right into this new-age outlet. Full of signs and symbols, visual jokes, and hidden messages, his art never stops trying to make contact."

Biographical Information

Smith was born on August 25, 1959, in Tulsa, Oklahoma, but spent his childhood in Corona, California. In his youth he occasionally traveled back to Oklahoma with his family along the famed Route 66, a highway once populated by curious-looking roadside attractions to which Smith in part later attributed his "bizarre sense of design." After high school, Smith enrolled in the California Art Center College of Design, studying illustration while cultivating an appreciation for Pop Art and the European design aesthetic. In addition, he studied the work of those who would become his artistic influences, from N. C. Wyeth and Arthur Rackham to animator Tex Avery. Smith graduated in 1983 and one year later opted to

pursue his career as a freelance magazine illustrator in New York City, where his drawings made the pages of such periodicals as *Time, Rolling Stone,* and *Esquire.* Soon Smith broadened from drawing to oil painting and expanded his interests into children's literature. He undertook a series of paintings on the theme of Halloween, with each representing a letter of the alphabet, and submitted these works to Macmillan Publishing. The company coupled his talents with those of poet Eve Merriam to produce his premier children's book, *Halloween ABC,* published in 1987. Though reviews of the work were positive, Smith's notoriety soared following the publication of his first collaborative effort with writer Jon Scieszka, *The True Story of the Three Little Pigs.* More works from this team followed, including 1992's *The Stinky Cheese Man: And Other Fairly Stupid Tales* and a humorous series of "Time Warp" books for middle-schoolers. Meanwhile Smith authored and illustrated several well-received books on his own. Still based in New York City, Smith has largely continued in his joint efforts with author Jon Scieszka and has pursued other illustrating projects, such as *Disney's James and the Giant Peach,* published in 1996.

Major Works

Smith's works may be divided into two categories, those he wrote and illustrated himself, and those he illustrated for other authiors, many of which feature his award-winning paintings and drawings. Among his self-illustrated productions is the entirely wordless *Flying Jake* (1989). Faced with the disappearance of his bird, young Jake begins the search for his missing pet and soon discovers that he can fly. Called eccentric, bizarre, and at times confusing by critics, *Flying Jake* nevertheless won approval for Smith's abstract illustration and for its pure inventiveness. In *The Big Pets* Smith creates a magical dream world in which small girls and boys possess enormous cats, dogs, hamsters, and other pets. Reviewers of the work called it enticing and imaginative, and praised its murky, fanciful illustrations. *Glasses—Who Needs 'Em?* gives us a young boy who fears that wearing his glasses will make him look like a dork. Smith proves him wrong by depicting all sorts of creatures—giraffes, rabbits, even dinosaurs—clad in spectacles. Wendy Wasserstein, writing for the New York Times Book Review, lauded, "*Glasses—Who Needs 'Em?* is one of those perfect children's books . . . it's a breezy read toward an enlightened end and all the way there incredibly beautiful to look at." With *The Happy Hocky Family!*, Smith simultaneously parodies and pays homage to the "Dick and Jane" reading primers of the 1950s. Featuring smiling stick-figure characters engaged in everyday activities, this spoof offers simple, humorous observations, such as, "I have a balloon. Do you have a balloon? . . . POP! I have a string. Do you have a string?"

Among Smith's most notable work as a children's illustrator are his many books with Jon Scieszka. *The True Story of the Three Little Pigs,* the first of these, presents this tale from the perspective of the wolf, who claims no malice in blowing down the pigs' houses, blaming his actions instead on a severe cold. Smith's paintings reiterate this view by portraying the wolf in glasses and a bow tie as a "sympathetic victim of circumstance," in the illustrator's words. *The Stinky Cheese Man: And Other Fairly Stupid Tales* continues in the same unconventional vein. No one bothers to chase after the book's title character, for example, a smelly cousin to the Gingerbread Man of fairy-tale lore. Other stories in the volume include those of "The Princess and the Bowling Ball," "Cinderumpelstiltskin," and "Chicken Licken"—who prophesies the falling of the book's table of contents. All of these are accompanied by Smith's offbeat, quirky illustrations. Other Scieszka/Smith books include the ongoing "Time Warp Trio" series, amusing stories for middle-graders about three young time travelers—beginning with *Knights of the Kitchen Table* in 1991—which feature Smith's pen-and-ink drawings. Aside from his partnership with Scieszka, Smith also combined his talents with those of poet Eve Merriam in his early alphabet book, *Halloween ABC.* On it he remarked in *Children's Book Illustration and Design,* "I think the book turned out elegant and bold but still very spooky. I was tired of all the cute Halloween books. Halloween should be scary and fun." Another of Smith's collaborative efforts is a shortened version of Roald Dahl's

classic entitled *Disney's James and the Giant Peach.* The work showcases Smith's dark artistic vision, as does Disney's motion picture version of the tale.

Awards

For his innovative illustrations, Smith has received a variety of awards, including the noteworthy citations listed below. *Halloween ABC* was honored as a *New York Times* Best Illustrated Book in 1987. *The Big Pets* earned Smith the prestigious Golden Apple Award from the Bratislava International Bienniale of Illustrations and first place at the New York Book Show in 1991. *Glasses—Who Needs 'Em?* received the Parents' Choice Award for Illustration in 1991. For the Caldecott Honor Book *The Stinky Cheese Man: And Other Fairly Stupid Tales,* Smith received the 1992 *New York Times* Best Illustrated citation, along with many more honors.

AUTHOR'S COMMENTARY

Lane Smith

SOURCE: "The Artist at Work," in *The Horn Book Magazine,* Vol. LXIX, No. 1, January-February, 1993, pp. 64-70.

I've always loved the more macabre side of things, probably because I had such a well-adjusted childhood. Halloween was my favorite time of year, and it's still my favorite theme. I must have been the only kid in elementary school who collected tapes of old-time radio shows like "The Shadow." I loved that whole theater of the mind. I came from a white-bread, middle-American background. I wasn't exposed to real culture until college. In my senior year everything came together, and all my pop-culture influences somehow started to fit into a historical context. I discovered Pop Art and the European aesthetic, and then something came together with all the things I was attracted to as a child. At the school I went to they taught slick advertising art, but I didn't like any of that. I found myself looking back at illustrators from Europe and from the 1940s and '50s, and those influences started coming out in my work. My instructors said, "When you get out of school, you're never going to find work in America." I was getting worried, but then the punk/new-wave movement came, and my work seemed to fit acceptably into that category.

I got my art training at the California Art Center, College of Design. I still do a lot of magazine editorial work, and that was what I studied at Art Center. At the time, they didn't have any children's book programs. I don't consider myself a children's book illustrator, just an all-around illustrator. I still do probably ten magazine pieces a month, and I do a lot of animation, but that's really just for myself. I think because of the success of ***The True Story of the***

Three Little Pigs!, people think of me as a children's book illustrator. I used to get all these magazine assignments on murder and rape and the economy, and now I get assigned topics such as childhood toys and children's phobias. So I think even the magazine people are thinking of me as a children's book illustrator. That's fine, because as you can see in *The Stinky Cheese Man and Other Fairly Stupid Tales,* I don't try at all to tone down what I do for children.

I moved to New York in 1984, and I was trying to learn how to paint. Before that, I had done mainly drawings. Every night I would do a different painting of the alphabet, with a Halloween theme. I did something like thirty paintings—an excess of the alphabet! So I took the paintings to Macmillan, and they got Eve Merriam to write poems around them—which I was thrilled about. We combined the poems with the art, and I changed some of the artwork to fit some new poems she had written. I had V for "Vampire," and she came up with "Viper," which I liked a lot, because I could use the *V* for the viper's open mouth. So *Halloween ABC* was published, and I was really pleased with it. But it was immediately banned everywhere. It was labeled *satanic.* It was actually good in a way, because it stirred a debate, and people would come to my defense in editorials. Ultimately, though, I think it hurt the book. If you're an adult writer like Salman Rushdie and you do that controversial book, it stirs up interest, and everybody buys the book. If you're a children's book person, they stay away. There *is* a definite dark side to my work. But there are certainly antecedents for it: N. C. Wyeth was really dark, as was Arthur Rackham.

I first met Jon Scieszka, my collaborator on *The Three Little Pigs* and *The Stinky Cheese Man,* through my friend Molly Leach, who is a designer and art director; she worked with Jon's wife, Jeri. Jon was a teacher, and he used to give his classes assignments in re-writing classic fairy tales. He was writing all the time, sending out his work to publishers, and getting rejected. So the two of us got together. He liked the books that I did, liked the dark side of them. We made up a book dummy; I did one painting; and we took it around. We were rejected by everybody. Finally Viking saw it, and they really liked it. Of course, I figured the same thing would happen to *The Three Little Pigs* that happened to all my previous books: it would be published, and then it would be attacked. I tried to be really careful in my depiction of the pigs—since the wolf actually kills and eats them—so you never really see them. I deliberately tried to make them appear as food. I think Jon thought of the wolf as a con artist trying to talk his way out of a situation. But I really believed the wolf, so I portrayed him with glasses and a little bow tie and tried to make him a sympathetic victim of circumstance.

The book came out to an amazing reception. It sold out in the first few weeks, and teachers and librarians embraced it because they loved the different point of view on the fairy tale. We just liked it because it was funny. Jon is a huge fairy-tale fan, a scholar. I like fairy tales, but that aspect of the book didn't appeal to me as much as the human-nature side.

The details are always what the children pick up on. Their favorite page is the painting of the cheeseburger that has a little mouse tail and rabbit ears sticking out of it. They love that. It's definitely gross, elementary-school humor, but they love it. Kids will pick things up on second and third readings. We'll be signing books at an autograph session, and they will say, "Do you know what my favorite page is? It's the one where the sticks fall as a table setting after the wolf sneezes the house down." And the child's mother will say, "I didn't notice that."

Jon and I like to put that kind of humorous detail in to amuse ourselves, but we know the children will pick up on it, too. It's visually interesting, and it's funny. I think adults can appreciate the book as a rather strange collage piece. But for children, the book becomes a puzzle, and they spend hours in front of it.

I'm really thankful for the success of *The Three Little Pigs,* because I'm no longer perceived as this evil, demonic person. People come up and embrace me and tell me how much they love the book. They seem to excuse the darkness of it, which the children excused all along. Children don't want something bland and sappy.

What appealed to me about *The Stinky Cheese Man* was not so much that it was another fairy tale but the fact that we were playing with all the conventions and really turning them upside-down—taking the classics and deconstructing them. Jon and I had been reading these stories in classrooms for years. Jon would pull them out and say, "Here are some stories that I wrote, and I thought they were great, but now I realize they are just kind of stupid." And they would get such a huge reaction from the children, **"The Stinky Cheese Man"** in particular. The children would just roll in the aisles. And then for the rest of the day you couldn't say anything else. You would be talking about some other book, and they would raise their hand and say, "How about 'The Stinky Car'?" Or they would come up after class and say, "How about 'The Stinky Cat'?" Because you know you are not supposed to talk about things being stinky. So we approached the publisher about doing the stories as a book. We wanted to really play with the conventions of a book, so we added transitional characters. We threw some stories out, and we worked together, going back and forth many times. It was a totally collaborative effort. When we got the go-ahead from Viking, we put the whole book together in a couple of months. And it's twice as big as the average picture book. It's fifty-six pages, as we so blatantly announce!

Jon and I both have all the same influences—"Monty Python," *Mad* magazine, comic books—so we were completely on the same wavelength. When I was young, I loved books, but I also read comic books, and I think a lot of people still have a resentment against comics and think that they are not real reading. But I would read Classics Illustrated, and they encouraged me to go read Jules Verne. And then I think my palette, my sensibilities, and my composition were greatly influenced by films I saw as a child, especially the old Disney films like *Snow White* and *The Jungle Book.*

Some of my work in *The Stinky Cheese Man*—the ugly duckling sequence in particular—is directly influenced by Tex Avery. He was an animation director from the forties—the one who always had his cartoon characters' eyeballs popping right out of their heads. All his work was very exaggerated. It was the antithesis of the cute Disney style. I paid tribute to Avery in *The True Story of the Three Little Pigs!*—the brand name of the sugar is called "Tex Sugar." Jon and I are both big fans of his. If I were reviewing *The Stinky Cheese Man,* I might compare it to the work of Tex Avery and also Buster Keaton and Robert Benchley.

The Stinky Cheese Man is a parody, but it's a parody for children. It's not parody for adults in the guise of a children's book, going over the children's heads just as an excuse to do a really sophisticated book. *The Stinky Cheese Man* is the book that I am the most pleased with from beginning to end. The stories work on their own; it works as a whole; and its transitional elements give it a filmlike quality. It has running gags. It's completely resolved at the end. And it's really fun.

I think pacing and timing are very important in picture books, but so is content. For instance, in *The Three Little Pigs,* we say that "the real story is about a sneeze and a cup of sugar." We wanted to stop for a minute in the progression of the book and actually say, "This is the real story!" So we have a whole page that just says that, with the letters all made from various elements in the story—straw, bricks, a pig's snout for the letter *O.* Then the tension starts to build, and you go in tighter with the nose starting to itch, and then you get the double-page sneeze. And it really explodes, literally and visually. That sort of approach comes second nature to me now, but the way I think visually is clearly influenced by the animation I saw as a child.

I love the fact that with children's books, you can turn the page and have a joke. That's another reason why *The Stinky Cheese Man* became fifty-six pages. We wanted room for timing. We wanted a blank page just so we could say, "This page is blank." The ugly duck story could have been told in just one illustration, but it's more fun to turn the page, and the comedic timing is better. You could flip those pages quickly, and it's almost like animation.

All my work, whether in magazines or animation, definitely reflects my childhood influences, and the themes that I draw upon are related to childhood. In the children's books I am particularly aware of this. In *The Stinky Cheese Man,* for example, the table of contents falls and squashes everybody, but I never show blood. *The Three Little Pigs* could have been a field day for some budding cartoonist; there's the potential for a lot of violence. But even in *The Stinky Cheese Man* I keep it funny; I don't emphasize the gory aspects. On the last page, where the giant eats the red hen, I didn't even, at first, have her bonnet in the picture. The publisher asked me to make everything a little more clear. I thought it was already pretty gruesome; you see the giant picking his teeth with one of her feathers. Actually, I repainted one of the

giant's eyes because I had both eyes looking kind of demonic, and it really scared me. So I edited it myself. Now it's a fairly friendly eye.

I put about ten times the amount of detail in the art of *The Stinky Cheese Man* as I did in *The Three Little Pigs,* and I am glad that I made that effort. We're not being preachy, but we want to educate children visually and expose them to fairy tales. The best thing about *The Three Little Pigs* was that the children who read it all went back and started rereading classic fairy tales.

I work in oil on illustration board. My work is always being described as watercolor or airbrush, or egg tempera, but definitely everything I do is oil paint on board. I get texture from a variety of means. Usually it involves some sort of acrylic paints or sprays to cause a reaction. We joked in *The Stinky Cheese Man* that the illustrations were done in oil and vinegar; actually, it is an apt description, because I'm constantly getting things to bead up and play off each other. Sometimes, if the painting gets really thick, I'll sand down areas to another layer. I've always been attracted to texture. I think that's why I don't have that many imitators. It's not that they can't draw the way I do; they can't get the texture they want. I do collage because it is a natural extension of my work with texture—being able to get more variety in the art. Children love it, too; they love the fact that they can take a piece of gum or a stick and put it in their drawings.

I've never really wanted to do fine arts or sculpture. I just love the print medium. I always thought it would be kind of depressing to work for months on a painting and then just have it hang in somebody's house. I've sold some of the paintings from the books through children's art galleries, but I've decided not to do much of that, because I miss them too much. But I have a wonderful existence—I've been able to create the children's books that come naturally to me.

Jon Scieszka and Lane Smith with Stephanie Zvirin

SOURCE: "The *Booklist* Interview," in *Booklist,* Vol. 89, No. 1, September 1, 1992, p. 57.

[The following excerpt is from an interview by Stephanie Zvirin.]

When A. Wolf burst on the children's book scene in 1989 with his revisionist "autobiography." *The True Story of the 3 Little Pigs* (by A. Wolf), he shared credit with Jon Scieszka and Lane Smith. Though Mr. Wolf is now cooling his paws in jail, Scieszka and Smith are still turning fairy tales upside down with a quirky humor that occasionally carries over into real life conversations. In a chat with *Booklist,* they talk about their work, their experiences with kids, and their latest book, *The Stinky Cheese Man,* reviewed on the opposite page.

BKL: *Lane, how did you get into the children's book business?*

SMITH: Well, I always thought I would do children's books sometime, but I wasn't sure when. When I came to New York in 1984, I had a portfolio of illustrations I took to various magazines. I worked on the magazine stuff for a couple of years, but at night I would do paintings. I got out of art school not really knowing how to paint, so every night I would do a Halloween picture. I figured I might as well have a theme. I wasn't really thinking of a children's book at the time, but after a couple of months, the work started to look like one. I took it to Macmillan, and they agreed: it became my first book, **Halloween ABC,** and I've lived happily ever since. Then I did another book for them, and that's when I met Jon. . . .

BKL: **Pigs** and **The Stinky Cheese Man** *are both based on "messed up" fairy tales, but the books are really very different. For one thing, there's not as clear a separation between text and art in* **The Stinky Cheese Man** *as there is in* **Pigs**.

SCIESZKA: Though there was a core collection of stories, **The Stinky Cheese Man** was really a collaboration. I don't think there's any way to pick apart who did what. When Lane and I went out to visit schools after **The Three Little Pigs** was published, I started reading the stories as fairy tales that *didn't* work. Lane would illustrate them as I spoke. Kids would really crack up.

SMITH: We weren't expecting to have second and third graders rolling in the aisles. Then we started thinking seriously about assembling the bits into a cohesive form.

SCIESZKA: We definitely refined all the language during those visits, and we eventually chose the Stinky Cheese Man as the title character because his story was the one that always had the kids chanting along.

BKL: *Who was responsible for the different type sizes, the upside-down pages, things like that? Was that you, Lane?*

SMITH: Well, I think it was both of us, and also Molly Leach, who was the book designer. She helped us with construction. It was Molly's idea to have type fill the entire page, whether there were 20 words on the page or 2. That was a nice, sophisticated design approach, but it also helped add punch to some of the lines. We were all aware that the book relied a lot on rhythm.

BKL: *Isn't some of this book pretty sophisticated for children? There's a joke about* ISBN *numbers, and you picture yourselves as Washington and Lincoln on the jacket flap. Will young children get the jokes?*

SMITH: Oh, sure. And things that they don't get, they'll ask about—like when Jon brings in Black Beard in his Time Warp Trio books. If kids haven't heard of Black Beard, they may decide to look him up. Plus, it's always nice to sharpen kids' observation skills. Kids have probably seen hundreds of books with endpapers at the end and never given it a second thought. But if you put an endpaper in the middle—or if the "Table of Contents" falls on someone . . .

BKL: [*Will you*] *do more stories to, as you say, "goof on"?*

SCIESZKA: I suppose I will do something different inevitably, but I keep coming back to the books I really like to read—classics like *Don Quixote,* where Sancho tells weird stories that go nowhere, or *Tristram Shandy.* I think that's really funny stuff. I think we've reached our fairy tale finale, though.

BKL: *Lane, what about you?*

SMITH: Well, there are so many serious books out there and lots of people who do them really well. But there aren't many people who do really goofy work. It's so refreshing to see kids who really respond to funny stuff, and if that gets them to read. . . .

GENERAL COMMENTARY

Dilys Evans

SOURCE: "An Extraordinary Vision: Picture Books of the Nineties," in *The Horn Book Magazine,* Vol. LXVIII, No. 6, November-December, 1992, pp. 759-63.

Lane Smith stands out as a new visual voice for children of this decade. Drawing was always a favorite activity in school. In junior high he had a passion for superheroes and thought for a while that he would be a cartoon artist. He was mesmerized by the intense, richly hued dark color of old films like *The Jungle Book* and *Snow White;* the unusually dark-toned full-color palette of his picture books reflects this early influence. Intensely creative and a natural humorist, he has truly found his home in children's books.

His first book was **Halloween ABC,** with a text by Eve Merriam; his second, **Flying Jake,** was an homage to comic books. Soon after the publication of the second book, Smith met Jon Scieszka at a party and made an immediate connection. Scieszka was quick to react to Smith's droll visual humor. Their first collaboration, **The True Story of the Three Little Pigs!,** was an immediate success. Working together, both author and illustrator began to think of the total book in a specifically visual way, so that the design and format of each book would remain constant. The look became a part of the overall expression, and white space as well as carefully integrated type was used throughout.

Published in 1991, Smith's **The Big Pets** tells a simple story. "The girl was small and the cat was big. And on certain nights, she rode on his back to the place where the milk pool was." A magical nighttime story, the text is simple and direct, while the pictures create a fantasy dream world that is warm and cozy as well as richly beautiful. The color in the book is dark and jewel-like, as the fresh white space of each page frames the art and brings out the color. The pictures seem almost to glow.

To create this color, Lane Smith uses a complex process: "My medium is a combination of oil paint and acrylic sprays. I work in transparent glazes, which not only dries the paint, but also causes a reaction, since acrylic is a water-based paint. Technically, you shouldn't combine the two, because it wasn't made for that purpose. I stumbled onto the process maybe ten years ago, and that's how I get all these strange textures, the way the paint beads up. I may put on as many as fifteen really thin coats before I actually go in and model things and add darks and lights. I work in yellow, red, and blue and keep building them up until it becomes this rich monochromatic ground. But if you look carefully, or with a magnifying glass, you'll see all the impressionistic dots of color coming through. Then I'll go in with lights and darks, and if it still doesn't look right, I'll go in with collage elements, torn paper. It's a process of exploration."

Lane Smith creates pictures that encourage children to find things, ask questions, and often answer back. His world is familiar territory; their imaginations plug right into this new-age outlet. Full of signs and symbols, visual jokes, and hidden messages, his art never stops trying to make contact.

Marisa Bulzone

SOURCE: "Children's Book Illustration: Is This the New Golden Age?," in *Communication Arts*, Vol. 34, No. 8, January-February, 1993, pp. 94-107.

At the opposite end of the spectrum from [Gary] Kelley stands Lane Smith, a surprising new superstar of the children's book publishing world—surprising not only because of his decidedly nontraditional illustration but also because of his phenomenal success in the field. The first of Smith's collaborations with writer Jon Scieszka, *The True Story of the Three Little Pigs,* has sold over 550,000 copies in two years. The follow-up title *The Stinky Cheese Man and Other Fairly Stupid Tales,* sold out a 100,000 copy first print run—before the book even hit the shelves.

Well known for his work in magazines such as *Rolling Stone, Atlantic Monthly, Time, Newsweek, Mother Jones* and *The Progressive,* Smith has also achieved critical success for the books of which he is the sole author/ illustrator. In addition to the aforementioned titles, Smith has published *Halloween ABC, Flying Jake, Glasses— Who Needs 'em?,* and *The Big Pets.* He and Scieszka have also produced a series of illustrated novels based on the adventures of "The Time-Warp Trio," that are directed to seven-to nine-year-old boys. Both his first and third books, *Halloween ABC* and *Glasses—Who Needs 'em?,* appeared on the prestigious *New York Times* Ten Best Illustrated Children's Books of the Year list.

Smith's interest in illustrating children's books goes back to his days at Art Center College of Design, but his suc- cess in the field is characterized by persistence and what he terms "a natural progression" based on experience. Despite critical acclaim, *Halloween ABC* and *Flying Jake* were not well received in the marketplace. Disillusioned but not discouraged, Smith continued to develop dummies for children's titles and also met and began to collaborate with Scieszka. Smith recalls telling the writer at the time: "Don't expect anything to come of this."

A dummy for the book that would eventually become *Glasses—Who Needs 'em?* made the rounds of a number of publishers before Smith met with Regina Hayes, president and publisher of Viking Books for Children. Although *Glasses* was rejected outright, Smith pulled out his work for *The True Story of the Three Little Pigs* just as he was about to leave.

Recalling that first meeting, Hayes says, "Beyond the illustration, it becomes a question of what is needed to make a book endure. I was knocked out by Lane's illustration, but when he showed me *Glasses,* which I think he had envisioned as a small gift book, I didn't feel children would respond to it. Then, as he was leaving, he pulled out *The True Story of the Three Little Pigs* almost as an afterthought. We accepted it immediately.

"Jon and Lane then went out on the road, visiting schools and bookstores, and the book really began to take off. I think it was a real revelation for Lane being in the classroom, talking to kids and seeing what they responded to and found funny. After that he went back to *Glasses* and gave the pictures a context. I think he saw that children don't have the frame of reference of having read many books; they really need a plot line to carry them along."

Smith concurs that his attitudes have grown, saying: "When I came up with *Glasses* I thought, 'Wouldn't it be funny if I did a book and the only thing the people in the drawings had in common was that they all wore glasses?' To me, this was a real laugh riot, but everyone rejected it; they just said 'what the hell is this?' So I let it sit for a while and when I came back to it I thought, 'well . . . maybe that wasn't so funny; maybe I'll actually do a story.' And I think this shows how my thinking has changed a bit too, meeting real kids and being around Jon. I added the kid and the doctor and made it into this confrontational thing with the doctor pointing out all the different faces. Now it works as a kid's book and it's still kind of my original story—it's still kind of funky."

Echoing Kelley's attitude, this integrity of style is important to Smith. He says: "I imagine that if there was a forum for adult books with pictures, I might be doing that instead, but fortunately I haven't had to compromise my work. When I started, I just assumed I would do what I do and not have to tone it down and I wouldn't sell any copies—and that's kind of how it went for the first two books. Somehow there was this weird little fluke with the *Three Little Pigs* book and I got accepted for what I do. I think it's really neat that I can do these books and they still look like my editorial work."

Smith does see subtle effects on his illustration that can be directly traced to his work in this medium: "I'm more confident now that I can paint whatever I write. When I did my first book, I was just learning how to paint, so I tended to keep everything simple; a single figure in an environment. I don't avoid having a lot of elements now."

More surprising to the illustrator is the impact that success in children's books is having on the kind of commercial assignments he gets. He relates: "My work was always dark and stylized and I used to get all the hard-edged jobs—the bleak economy, abortion rights, murder. Now I get calls from like, *Child* magazine, and they ask, 'Can you do an article on the first day of school?' Or *Parents* magazine calls and wants me to do something on new playground accessories. I know they're calling me because of the books, but my tendencies are still sort of dark and I still try to put a little edge on things. So if it's an article on playground toys, my first tendency is to have the slide breaking and the kid falling on the ground—and that can be a problem."

Smith's view of the children's book industry is optimistic, yet tempered by realism. Like others, he cites the often stifling power still held by librarians and their large market share, coupled with their stubborn resistance to all but a few wordless books. He also says that for every 500 copies of *The Three Little Pigs* he autographs at a book signing, there will be one copy of *Flying Jake* or *The Big Pets.* "It's kind of a fluke that they let me in this business—90 percent of the books out there are still those cute ones. I think I've been somewhat vindicated because my books are starting to sell, but there's still an attitude that these books don't sell and you have to get past that with booksellers. I mean, you see kids who are riding around with these skateboards covered with funky graphics and then their moms are making them read 'rub the bunny' books. I have my fingers crossed because the more innovative things that are out there, the easier it makes my job. I just know that I wouldn't do books unless I could try to do something that I haven't seen before or that I could be proud of."

The success of the Smith/Scieszka collaboration has not taken place without comment and small controversy in the industry. In every aspect, from the text to the illustration to the type design to the sales figures, these books are decidedly nontraditional—and definitely not cute. Shannon Maughan, associate children's book editor for *Publishers Weekly,* the widely read trade magazine of the book industry, cuts right to the heart of the issue in stating: "Editors and publishers are always looking for something fresh, but there's a bottom line in this business as well. Success runs on a book-by-book basis with the more sophisticated titles—and if it's too sophisticated, it will fail." Regina Hayes agrees in principle and in reference to *The True Story of the Three Little Pigs,* states: "Let me say flat out that in 25 years of publishing I have never seen a book sell like this one, or half, or even a quarter. Everyone says now that we were so brave [in publishing this book], but we truly never thought it was a risk, and

From The True Story of the Three Little Pigs, *written by Jon Scieszka. Illustrated by Lane Smith.*

the proof is that when we saw the art we just knew we had to have a poster for the book. Marketing money is as scarce as hen's teeth in publishing and usually you only do that for the books you know will be important."

TITLE COMMENTARY

📖 *HALLOWEEN ABC* **(written by Eve Merriam, 1987)**

Kirkus Reviews

SOURCE: A review of *Halloween ABC,* in *Kirkus Reviews,* Vol. LV, No. 15, August 1, 1987, p. 1160.

Twenty-six inspired, eerie poems, in a picture book illustrated in a fine, spooky style by a newcomer to children's books.

Ranging from the obvious Jack-o'-lantern and Ghost to the nicely gruesome Pet " . . . that's not the least bit vicious, / yet finds the neighbors quite nutritious," [Eve] Merriam's verse delights with its neat rhymes ("Demon: ' . . . put your hate in, / Satan; pass the pitchfork, please, / Mephistopheles . . . '"), sly humor, and bits of philosophy (" . . . the mask that no one detects: / your face that the mirror reflects"), while using language more felicitously than Prelutsky in his robustly comic *Nightmares.* Lane's oil-on-board paintings, in smoky, dark, earth tones, reflect and extend the text: a haunted house sways sinuously in the wind, its facade glowering like a jack-o'-lantern, the smoke from its chimney reiterating the letter H; the hand that holds the "Delicious, malicious" apple sports talons that repeat the image of flames from which it rises. Elegant in design, precise in image, this is a sophisticated style that should be popular for its subject, with appeal for any age that enjoys the macabre side of Halloween.

Carolyn Phelan

SOURCE: A review of *Halloween ABC,* in *Booklist,* Vol. 84, No. 4, October 15, 1987, p. 398.

An alphabet book that does *not* belong on the picture-book shelves, this is the poet's view of the holiday that is, paradoxically, our most frightening and most child-centered. [Eve] Merriam wastes no space on trick-or-treat frivolities, but goes straight to the heart of darkness . . . Next to the poem on each page is one of Smith's full-color, richly atmospheric paintings. Deep, mottled earth tones form a background for the lively, yet sinister, images. While the illustrations are more sophisticated than in most picture books, they are definitely accessible to young people. Older children will enjoy the book despite the picture-book format. A ticket to Halloween shivers, if not nightmares.

Kay E. Vandergrift

SOURCE: A review of *Halloween ABC,* in *School Library Journal,* Vol. 34, No. 3, November, 1987, p. 100.

These 26 Halloween poems, one for each letter of the alphabet, are, like most of [Eve] Merriam's work, imaginative, inventive, and playful. Her unusual rhythms, rhythmic schemes, and twists of word or image are often humorous as well as seasonally spooky. For instance, the letter "P" is represented by "a pet that's not the least bit vicious, / yet finds the neighbors quite nutritious." Smith's dark oil paintings on ecru pages match both the mood and the wit of the poems. They are appropriately primitive in style, clever, gently frightening, and often truly funny. The capital letters on each page are integrated into the pictures, made of sticks or bones or bat wings or an animal's tail.

📖 *FLYING JAKE* (1989)

Publishers Weekly

SOURCE: A review of *Flying Jake,* in *Publishers Weekly,* Vol. 233, No. 6, February 12, 1988, p. 83.

In one moment, Jake is leaping after his pet bird, which has escaped from its cage. In the next, he is flying! Jake soars and dips through the sky, discovering just what it's like to be a bird. After splashing in the birdbath, roost-

ing—briefly—in a hornet-infested tree, perching in a nest and playing his harmonica for the surrounding birds, Jake accompanies his pet up into the clouds. There he dances and frolics with an array of fun-loving, fantastical fowl until, weary at last, he flies back to his own house and bed. It requires close attention to follow some sequences in this wordless picture book, but the effort is amply repaid. Lane's illustrations are jaunty, fanciful and energetic. They convey the unbounded freedom and exhilaration of flight and render with great humor the reactions of those below, from Jake's astonished neighbors to his staid, oblivious parents and finally to his cat, who cheers him on. A somewhat eccentric, thoroughly delightful adventure.

Signe Wilkinson

SOURCE: A review of *Flying Jake,* in *The New York Times Book Review,* June 12, 1988, p. 34.

When his bird escapes its cage and vanishes out the window, Jake takes off in hot pursuit with the reader close behind. Past Jake's preoccupied parents, over rooftops, into a bird's nest, through the clouds to a divinely quirky, bird-filled heaven we all fly, finally returning to Jake's room and an understanding that the birds, like imaginations, are meant to fly free.

Lane Smith tells his tale of *Flying Jake* without words, relying on his winsome drawings to work as a storyboard for readers and nonreaders. Some parents may be put off by Mr. Smith's punky style and his use of a palette that features the blacks and browned-down blues more commonly found in SoHo fashion statements than in children's literature. They shouldn't be. There are some hard-to-decipher scenes that don't make this an easy book to look at, but children will respond to Jake's peculiar charms, especially once they see that Mr. Smith's sometimes menacing figures are telling a loving tale.

Mr. Smith arranges his drawings like movements in a symphony. Through clever sizing and placement on the page, he achieves a rhythm that underscores the action and almost makes up for the lack of text.

Almost, but not quite. Looking at a picture book with a child is a different proposition from reading one together. It's like watching a movie with the sound turned off—even if the story line is clear, it can leave the viewer feeling oddly deaf. Gone are Jake's voice, the sound of wings flapping and the chatter of communing birds. Instead of a writer's well-crafted cadences, the parent ends up breaking the silence with such mellifluous prose as, "What's Jake doing here? No. I don't think he's being eaten by alligators. Those are birdie beaks, not reptile jaws, and look! He's smiling. I think. . . . "

The wordless story, in this case, is obviously an artist-driven genre, and in the hands of an intriguing stylist like Mr. Smith it turns out to be a technical success. But the limits of the approach make the book more a showcase of late 1980's graphic style than a cozy bedtime partner.

Still, *Flying Jake* isn't for illustration aficionados alone. Mr. Smith's style offers a minor-key look at the world that is a welcome relief from the vast oversupply of C major art and morality found in many books for young children. He has created a rich picture poem that gives readers of any age a certain feeling about flight among the birds. While greatly enjoying the ride, this reader thought: turn up the sound.

Carol McMichael

SOURCE: A review of *Flying Jake,* in *School Library Journal,* Vol. 35, No. 9, June-July, 1988, pp. 94-5.

This wordless picture book is sure to be more than most children can comprehend. Jake, a small boy, allows his bird to escape from its cage, and as Jake reaches out to catch it, he too can suddenly fly. The illustrations, done in muted chalk tones of yellow, brown, and mauve, exhibit the chaos and happiness that Jake causes when he is as free as a bird. Illustrations are abstract, with squared off heads and strangely lined backgrounds. Many appear in panels, with as many as 14 separate pictures in a double-page spread. Action is not always clear. Children may pick this book up, but they will quickly put it down because of the busy, confusing story and bizarre illustrations.

THE TRUE STORY OF THE THREE LITTLE PIGS (written by Jon Scieszka, 1989)

Publishers Weekly

SOURCE: A review of *The True Story of the Three Little Pigs,* in *Publishers Weekly,* Vol. 236, No. 4, July 28, 1989, p. 218.

In this gaily newfangled version of a classic tale, [Jon] Scieszka and Smith argue in favor of the villain, transforming the story of the three little pigs into a playfully suspicious, rather arch account of innocence beleaguered. Quoth the wolf: "I don't know how this whole Big Bad Wolf thing got started, but it's all wrong." According to his first-person testimony, the wolf went visiting the pigs in search of a neighborly cup of sugar; he implies that had the first two happened to build more durable homes and the third kept a civil tongue in his head, the wolf's helpless sneezes wouldn't have toppled them. As for his casual consumption of the pigs, the wolf defends it breezily ("It seemed like a shame to leave a perfectly good ham dinner lying there in the straw") and claims cops and reporters "framed" him. Smith's highly imaginative watercolors eschew realism, further updating the tale, though some may find their urbane stylization and intentionally static quality mystifyingly adult. Designed with uncommon flair, this alternative fable is both fetching and glib.

John Peters

SOURCE: A review of *The True Story of the Three Little Pigs,* in *School Library Journal,* Vol. 35, No. 14, October, 1989, p. 108.

Victim for centuries of a bad press, Alexander ("You can call me Al") T. Wolf steps forward at last to give his side of the story. Trying to borrow a cup of sugar to make a cake for his dear old Granny, Al calls on his neighbors—and can he help it if two of them built such shoddy houses? A couple of sneezes, a couple of dead pigs amidst the wreckage and, well, it would be shame to let those ham dinners spoil, wouldn't it? And when the pig in the brick house makes a nasty comment about Granny, isn't it only natural to get a little steamed? It's those reporters from the *Daily Pig* that made Al out to be Big and Bad, that caused him to be arrested and sent to the (wait for it) Pig Pen. "I was framed," he concludes mournfully. Smith's dark tones and sometimes shadowy, indistinct shapes recall the distinctive illustrations he did for [Eve] Merriam's **Halloween ABC**; the bespectacled wolf moves with a rather sinister bonelessness, and his juicy sneezes tear like thunderbolts through a dim, grainy world. It's the type of book that older kids (and adults) will find very funny.

Marcus Crouch

SOURCE: A review of *The True Story of the Three Little Pigs,* in *The Junior Bookshelf,* Vol. 54, No. 3, June, 1990, pp. 128-29.

This is as told by an interested party, the wolf himself, not 'big bad' but just a neighbour with a cooking problem and a cold in the nose. He never meant to huff and puff, but those sneezes were devastating—and who could blame him for not leaving the piggy corpses to spoil. A Wolf tells his sad story from prison where he is being guarded by a most unsympathetic pig-screw. The words are beautifully put together, the pictures—by Lane Smith—highly selective, very dramatic. Here is an artist who has got right to the heart of his subject . . . . Scieszka and Smith have started from scratch and made their book by pure creativity.

THE BIG PETS (1990)

Publishers Weekly

SOURCE: A review of *The Big Pets,* in *Publishers Weekly,* Vol. 237, No. 51, December 21, 1990, p. 55.

"The girl was small and the cat was big," begins a bizarre nighttime journey during which small children and their giant pets frolic somewhere in the dreamy heavens. The girl and her oversize cat are joined at the Milk-Pool by other happy felines, who lap milk as the children swim. Dog fanciers flock to the Bone Gardens, where friends and pets dig for fossils; Hamster Holes are the favorite haunt of hamsters and their owners, who take turns popping in and out of the ground. Told in a simple, straightforward style, this fantastic story is enhanced with dark, jewel-like paintings that exhibit an almost phosphorescent glow. Smith's (**The True Story of the Three Little Pigs** [by Jon Scieszka]) sophisticated illustrative technique has mellowed handsomely. His use of collage has been minimized, and his attention to content and dimension have resulted in enticing illustrations that provide the perfect landscape for this nocturnal romp.

Leone McDermott

SOURCE: A review of *The Big Pets*, in *Booklist*, Vol. 87, No. 11, February 1, 1991, p. 1132.

Probably every pet owner has at some time longed to enter a pet's world—children have been known to go so far as to declare themselves cats and dogs. That longing is the inspiration for Smith's quirkily imaginative picture book. "The girl was small and the cat was big. And on certain nights she rode on his back to the place where the Milk-Pool was." A little black-haired girl in a nightshirt and her gigantic tawny pet visit dreamlike landscapes that would gladden the heart of any feline. In addition to the Milk-Pool, where the girl swims while the cat drinks, there is a Scratching Forest of enormous trees and a field of enticing Stringy Vines. Along the way, the two meet other happy pairs galloping through Hamster Holes and digging in the Bone Gardens. With just a few lines of text per page, the book is dominated by Smith's fanciful illustrations in dark, smoky tones and shimmering pastels. These share the stylized, exaggerated quality of his work in *The True Story of the Three Little Pigs* [by Jon Scieszka] and also possess a mysterious haziness that enhances the nighttime atmosphere. One especially ebullient picture shows the girl and cat sliding down the Milky Way—drawn as a spiral of spilled milk surrounded by planets that dangle from strings like so many cat toys. Pet owners of all ages will enjoy Smith's playful and sweetly oddball visions of animal-human friendship.

Andy Sawyer

SOURCE: A review of *The Big Pets*, in *The School Librarian*, Vol. 41, No. 2, May, 1993, p. 58.

This solo effort by Lane Smith may, at first sight, lack the triumphant originality of his work with Jon Scieszka (*The true story of the three little pigs* and *The stinky cheeseman*). A simple journey through a dream realm where children are small and their pets are big, the text is merely descriptive of his tumbling, darkly whimsical illustrations, which straddle the borders of surrealism and naivety. Nevertheless, there's a beautiful poignancy in the way he leads up to the picture of one little boy sitting alone with his pet cricket while the other children romp with cats, dogs, hamsters, and even snakes. The simplicity of the text and the comforting ending might suggest that this is a picture book for very young children and indeed (as with Maurice Sendak's similar *In the night kitchen*) young children who are not yet conditioned into thinking that realistic art is the only art will be a very good audience. Certainly it has a charm of its own

and children will readily respond to its beautiful evocation of the love of pets. As also with Sendak, however, it will be a shame if older children are not introduced to books like this, especially in the context of their own art work.

KNIGHTS OF THE KITCHEN TABLE and THE NOT-SO-JOLLY ROGER (written by Jon Scieszka, 1991)

Roger Sutton

SOURCE: A review of *Knights of the Kitchen Table* and *The Not-So-Jolly Roger*, in *Bulletin of the Center for Children's Books*, Vol. 44, No. 11, July-August, 1991, p. 274.

The "Time Warp Trio" consists of three friends, one of whom has received a wish-granting magic book as a birthday present from an uncle. The book sends them back in time to Camelot (*Knights*) and a desert island (*Roger*). The device is tired, the puns are weak, and the tone is too knowing. The jokes are dumb, mostly based upon the boys' anachronistic attitudes and slang: "Your mother was a sardine can," says Fred to the armored Black Knight. There are lots of sound effects, lots of explosions, and lots of disgusting emissions ("Ten brave knights fell like bowling pins, victims of gas warfare"); while it all adds up to standard fourth-grade chucklebait, the three boys are indistinguishable and the plots predictable. Smith's pen sketches have more personality than the text, but their new-wave weirdness only underlines the staleness of the stories. [Jon] Scieszka's picture-book texts have proven him capable of tight, funny prose: books for newly independent readers deserve no less.

Trev Jones

SOURCE: A review of *Knights of the Kitchen Table* and *The Not-So-Jolly Roger*, in *School Library Journal*, Vol. 37, No. 8, August, 1991, p. 169.

A book from his magician uncle transports Joe and his friends, Fred and Sam, back in time to swashbuckling adventures fraught with dangers at every turn. In the first story, quick thinking and daring-do save them from a fire-breathing dragon and a foul-smelling giant; in the second, an encounter with the dreaded Blackbeard almost causes their demise. Tongue-in-cheek humor, laced with understatement and word play, makes for laugh-out-loud reading, as verbal insults are hurled, and the boys outwit their foes. Villains and heroes clash, as do modern and archaic language and dress, causing misunderstandings and mayhem. Short, easy-to-read sentences and lots of zany dialogue perfectly suit the breathless pace. Smith brings new dimension to black-and-white drawings, as looming villains tower over the trio, brandishing swords or lances, and the boys escape their captors. A true melding of word and pictures, and jolly good fun.

Elizabeth-Ann Sachs

SOURCE: A review of *Knights of the Kitchen Table* and *The Not-So-Jolly Roger*, in *The New York Times Book Review*, October 6, 1991, p. 23.

The black and white illustrations for both books, done by Lane Smith, are wonderfully menacing and appropriately silly, in keeping with Mr. Scieszka's style of writing. Mr. Scieszka and Mr. Smith are a great team; their wildly popular first collaboration, ***The True Story of the Three Little Pigs,*** was a witty, innovative book, and I happily look forward to more of their collaborations.

R. Baines

SOURCE: A review of *The Not-So-Jolly Roger,* in *The Junior Bookshelf,* Vol. 56, No. 5, October, 1992, pp. 200-01.

Uncle Joe, the magician, has given Joe "The Book" as a birthday present. Linked, either on purpose or accidentally, with certain words, The Book has the power to transport those near it to a different place, in a different time. This is how Joe and his friends Sam and Fred come to be atop three swaying coconut palms on a desert island, whilst a huge wooden ship flying the Jolly Roger sails towards them. It is necessary for the boys to retrieve The Book to return them to the twentieth century, a quest which involves forming a dangerous and volatile liaison with Blackbeard the Pirate and his men.

Jon Scieszka's brief story is elegantly printed and the book is enhanced by a glossy loose cover. The three boys' adventure is fast-moving and lively, and Lane Smith's dark and distinctive drawings—especially the portraits of Blackbeard himself—are a delight.

📖 *GLASSES—WHO NEEDS 'EM?* (1991)

Christine A. Moesch

SOURCE: A review of *Glasses—Who Needs 'Em?,* in *School Library Journal,* Vol. 37, No. 10, October, 1991, p. 105.

When a young patient states, "I'm worried about looking like a dork," the optometrist lists others who wear spectacles—"monster-movie" stuntpeople, famous inventors, entire planets. Just when he decides the doctor is crazy, the boy looks through the glasses and sees what he's been missing (almost everyone and everything in the world wearing glasses). Smith's illustrations are as offbeat as his work in [Jon] Scieszka's ***The True Story of the Three Little Pigs.*** His text is just as wacky, and reflects a young boy's resistance not only to the idea of wearing glasses, but also to the optometrist's efforts to fit him. The page layout features different colors and typefaces at every turn. Unfortunately, it's sometimes difficult to read the print on a dark page.

Wendy Wasserstein

SOURCE: "One Spectacle After Another," in *The New York Times Book Review,* November 10, 1991, p. 54.

Mr. Smith's illustrations are consistently witty and whimsical, but never sentimental or soppy. Mom, who wears glasses, looks as if she knows a great deal about Turgenev, and little sister, whose tongue and tonsil are concurrently protruding, "wears green rubber bands in her hair and T-shirts with unicorns on 'em." This bespectacled mother-and-daughter team has been spotted at book fairs and yogurt stands nationwide.

But Mr. Smith's imagination and illustrations really begin to fly when he leaves behind the world of humanoid eyeglass wearers and moves into the spectator fashions of cats, dogs, snowmen and robots. Frankly, I can't decide if I want to marry the planet that wears glasses or the little green man with four arms and two sets of frames to match. I know I am in love with both of them.

Furthermore, from Mr. Lane's point of view, there is quite suitable eye gear for fish, oil paintings, possums and potatoes as well. In fact, the only animal, vegetable or mineral that seems not to require a bit of perception correction is a carrot. When the impressionable young patient exclaims to the never-tiring doctor, "Well, if you're going to insist on rabbits wearing glasses, maybe we should give some specs to their carrots too!" the doctor offhandedly answers: "Don't be ridiculous. *Carrots* don't *need* glasses."

Glasses: Who Needs 'Em? is one of those perfect children's books—or for that matter, grown-up books; it's a breezy read toward an enlightened end and all the way there incredibly beautiful to look at. I was not surprised to read in the author's biographical note that Lane Smith belongs to the four-eye fraternity. I want details about not only his frames but his lens prescription as well. His is truly a fanciful and liberating way to view the world. Perhaps eye-wear emporiums would be well advised to consult with Mr. Smith and develop new potato and Hong-Kong-Flu bug bifocals. For my money, I pity the poor carrot who will never see the world through tortoise or wire-rim Giorgio Armani frames.

Lolly Robinson

SOURCE: A review of *Glasses—Who Needs 'Em?,* in *The Horn Book Magazine,* Vol. LXVII, No. 6, November-December, 1991, pp. 731-32.

Lane Smith is at it again, bringing his fresh perspective and playfully distinctive art to the problem of a reluctant child's first pair of glasses. The text, an argument between a boy and his doctor, is set in contrasting colors, depending on who is speaking. When the usual arguments—"'your mom wears glasses . . . your dad wears glasses . . . your sister wears glasses'"—don't win the boy over, the doctor suggests more and more outlandish creatures who wear glasses: "Giant dinosaurs wear glasses . . . and little worms . . . and tall giraffes . . . and short fuzzy bunnies.'" The boy, disgusted by the juvenile humor, is about to leave when the doctor sneaks a pair of glasses in front of his eyes and a two-page spread reveals what he has been missing: all those creatures really do wear glasses! Lane Smith's art is perfectly suited to this story, with his soft-edged, out-of-focus areas of deep color rubbed into a textured background and punctuated with white dots for teeth, black dots for eyes, and thin brush lines for glasses. As in *The True Story of the Three Little Pigs* [by Jon Scieszka], Smith uses collage when appropriate and provides fascinating endpapers with a combination of old advertisements and original art. Even the bar code on the back cover has been incorporated into a pair of spectacles!

Trevor Dickinson

SOURCE: A review of *Glasses—Who Needs 'Em?*, in *Books for Keeps*, No. 74, May, 1992, p. 29.

Glasses—Who Needs 'Em? is an intriguing and very clever oddity which may not be universally popular—but I love it! The endpapers comprise reprints of old adverts for spectacles. The text, in different colours and, like a sight test, of different sizes, explores a mad optician's attempts to persuade his young client that glasses are fine. With bizarre, striking illustrations, the book will have devotees across the age-range.

THE GOOD, THE BAD, AND THE GOOFY (written by Jon Scieszka, 1992)

Publishers Weekly

SOURCE: A review of *The Good, the Bad, and the Goofy*, in *Publishers Weekly*, Vol. 239, No. 22, May 11, 1992, p. 72.

The third field trip of the Time Warp Trio lands them in the heart of the Old West. Far from enjoying the pulsating adventure of TV westerns, however, Fred, Sam and Joe suffer the dust-choked, mosquito-infested monotony of a cattle drive—until the Indians show up. Once again the threesome utilizes a bit of 20th-century cunning to save their hides and outwit their opponents. [Jon] Scieszka's zany sarcasm sets a lively pace and offers up subtle parodies of popular western stereotypes. (This time, the Indians get to be the good guys.) Despite some clever wordplay, the story lacks the inventiveness and high-pitched excitement of the trio's previous adventures. Nonetheless, these collaborators' fans will no doubt gobble up this latest time-travel installment as they eagerly await the next one. Smith's black-and-white illustrations possess his characteristic brio—a double-page spread of a cattle stampede is particularly flashy.

Gale W. Sherman

SOURCE: A review of *The Good, the Bad, and the Goofy*, in *School Library Journal*, Vol. 38, No. 7, July, 1992, p. 64.

This third book in the series moves at the same breakneck pace set in *Knights of the Kitchen Table* and *The Not-So-Jolly Roger*. The title of the new book brings back memories of the classic "Spaghetti Western," *The Good, the Bad, and the Ugly*. There are similarities beyond the titles. [Jon] Scieszka's book also includes an ample dose of humor, a lively pace, and on-target dialogue. A spell, accidentally cast, transports Joe, Fred, and Sam back to the Chisholm Trail of 1868. They narrowly escape two stampedes, a flash flood, being scalped by Cheyenne braves, and a charge of the Seventh Cavalry lead by Lieutenant (soon to be General) Custer. Sam's knowledge, "'Magic . . . picked up in a book,'" and a Time Freezer spell save the day and return the trio to the present. Smith's typically zany pencil and charcoal drawings heighten the drama and enhance the wacky mood of the story. It seems that while Joe's magic book remains in the possession of the Time Warp Trio, wild adventures are bound to reoccur and please readers. Great fun!

THE STINKY CHEESE MAN: AND OTHER FAIRLY STUPID TALES (written by Jon Scieszka, 1992)

Publishers Weekly

SOURCE: A review of *The Stinky Cheese Man: And Other Fairly Stupid Tales*, in *Publishers Weekly*, Vol. 239, No. 42, September 28, 1992, pp. 79-80.

Grade-school irreverence abounds in this compendium of (extremely brief) fractured fairy tales, which might well be subtitled "All Things Gross and Giddy." With a relentless application of the sarcasm that tickled readers of *The True Story of the Three Little Pigs*, [Jon] Scieszka and Smith skewer a host of juvenile favorites: Little Red Running Shorts beats the wolf to grandmother's house; the Really Ugly Duckling matures into a Really Ugly Duck; Cinderumpelstiltskin is "a girl who really blew it." Text and art work together for maximum comic impact—varying styles and sizes of type add to the illustrations' chaos, as when Chicken Licken discovers that the Table of Contents, and not the sky, is falling. Smith's art, in fact, expands upon his previous waggery to include increased interplay between characters, and even more of his intricate detail work. The collaborators' hijinks are evident in every aspect of the book, from endpapers to copyright notice. However, the zaniness and deadpan delivery that have distinguished their previous work may strike some as overdone here. This book's tone is often frenzied; its rather specialized humor, delivered with the rapid-fire pacing of a string of one-liners, at times seems almost mean-spirited.

Roger Sutton

SOURCE: A review of *The Stinky Cheese Man: And Other Fairly Stupid Tales*, in *Bulletin of the Center for Children's Books*, Vol. 46, No. 2, October, 1992, p. 34.

From The Big Pets, *written and illustrated by Lane Smith.*

The jokes here don't stop with the stories. The introduction, for example, *zens* introductions: "If you read this last sentence, it won't tell you anything." Similarly, the upside-down dedication page urges readers on to better things: "Whoever looks at that dedication stuff anyhow? If you really want to read it—you can always stand on your head." An endpaper, courtesy of narrator Jack, shows up in the middle of the stories: "Shhhhh. I moved the endpaper up here so the Giant would think the book is over." The Little Red Hen, who has nagged her way through the entire volume, turns up on the back cover to kvetch about the ISBN. Such bibliometricks—meta-tricks?—are entirely at home in this jigsawed tale-type storyworld, which is as dark, the pictures tell us, as the Grimms'. Bertolt Brecht and Edvard Munch lurk just beyond these illustrations, which present a sinister fairy-land cabaret. "Rendered in oil and vinegar," the pictures are funny but spooky: the smell lines wafting from the Stinky Cheese Man reek of something stranger than cheese; the giant's face as he eats the bread (and the little red hen who made it) leers like a fallen man-in-the-moon. The effect, though, isn't scary, because the book is too funny and, besides, it keeps reminding us that it's a book. The book also keeps reminding readers that they're reading, a tap on the shoulder that feels less like a monitory nudge than it does a congratulatory slap on the back.

Mary M. Burns

SOURCE: A review of *The Stinky Cheese Man and Other Fairly Stupid Tales,* in *The Horn Book Magazine,* Vol. LXVIII, No. 6, November, 1992, p. 720.

[Jon] Scieszka and Smith have done it again! Blend *Saturday Night Live* with *Monty Python,* add a dash of *Mad* magazine with maybe a touch of "Fractured Fairy Tales" from the old *Rocky and Bullwinkle* show, and you have an eclectic, frenetic mix of text and pictures with a kinetic display of typefaces, rivaling the fireworks extravaganza on the Fourth of July. Even the page arrangement is unconventional, so that the entire book is a spoof on the art of book design, the art of the fairy tale, and whatever other art one might wish to parody. The individual tales are part of a zany whole in which the Little Red Hen, a kvetch if ever there was one, reappears periodically to complain about the dog, cat, and mouse who refused to help her plant her wheat. She and Jack (of beanstalk country) serve as a kind of running commentary on this theater-of-the-absurd in picture-book format. The concluding spread suggests that the annoying fowl gets her comeuppance—and not one she expected. . . .

The farcical tone of the whole may carry this concoction to the attention of primary schoolers, but it will enjoy its real success among middle-school through senior-citizen audiences. Another masterpiece from the team that created *The True Story of the Three Little Pigs!*

Signe Wilkinson

SOURCE: "No Princes, No White Horses, No Happy Endings," in *The New York Times Book Review,* November 8, 1992, p. 29.

After their clever parody, *The True Story of the 3 Little Pigs,* written from the innocent wolf's point of view, Jon Scieszka and his illustrator sidekick, Lane Smith, have decided fracturing a fairy tale isn't enough. In *The Stinky Cheese Man: And Other Fairly Stupid Tales* the dynamic duo and their indispensable designer, Molly Leach, have blown up the very idea of an illustrated fairy-tale book. In the explosion, type, table of contents, International Standard Book Number and narrative order itself have landed in self-conscious disorder all over the pages of this beautifully put together book for adults and hip mid-size children.

The Stinky Cheese Man exuberantly eviscerates the recent yuppie publishing conventions that have produced lovely staid book after lovely staid book from accomplished illustrators who keep the ink and royalty checks flowing by redrawing every classic tale we adults remember from our increasingly distant childhoods. When the Western European favorites run dry, these same publishers dig for legends from any remote ethnic tribe some other illustrator hasn't plundered first. Mr. Scieszka and Mr. Smith couldn't care less about reassuring stories from anyone's sacred traditions.

While the front cover of *The Stinky Cheese Man* looks like gentle good fun, the back cover and inside flaps quickly suggest the anarchy that awaits inside. The little reddish hen on the back makes fun of the ISBN, and one blurb from the flap brags that there are 75 percent more pages than "those old 32-page 'Brand-X' books." The title page reads "Title Page" in blaring 2 5/8-inch-tall generic black type. The first story gets started on the endpaper, immediately bogging down when Jack, the self-described narrator, complains that a story can't start on the endpaper. All very post-modern. . . .

The stories that follow take stock characters of the princess and talking-animal variety, set up familiar situations and play them out without the fairies. Thus the deep, dark woods of Grimm have been cleared out, removing all mysterious shadows where life-altering transformations of a magical nature might take place. The ugly duckling grows up to be an ugly duck. It takes a bowling ball instead of a pea to jar a princess's sensibilities. The frog prince isn't a prince and just leaves a slimy residue on the gullible princess's lips. That tiresome scold, the little red hen, gets eaten by the "Jack in the Beanstalk" giant.

The good news is that no handsome princes on white horses come to the rescue of defenseless damsels. The bad news is that *no one* comes to *anyone's* rescue. Like most of the other characters here (save cagey Jack of beanstalk fame), Cinderella ends up worse off than before the ball and its promise of a shining castle on the hill. This Cinderella isn't pretty, but she's as good a metaphor as any for the selfish 80's.

If Cinderella is not pretty, then neither are Lane Smith's illustrations. They are rich, layered and ugly distortions of the familiar characters we are used to seeing in more cheerful Disneyesque hues. Grotesque figures sort of float out of dark, amorphous backgrounds and co-exist with bits of type and collage images of "real" animals clipped from other, more anatomically correct texts. While not conventionally beautiful, they do what all good art must—create an alternate and believable universe. That last trick isn't easy, because the type and layout are always bursting their bounds, confronting rather than comforting the illustrations.

The type itself becomes both part of the stories and part of the artwork. It bends, it slides, it gets larger, it shrinks. When Jack tries to slip out of the giant's grip, he does so by starting a story that will never end so that the giant won't have the opportunity to eat him up. The typography complies and starts compressing, running right off the bottom of the page, giving the visual feeling that it will go on forever.

Kids, who rejoice in anything stinky, will no doubt enjoy the blithe, mean-spirited anarchy of these wildly spinning stories. It will take an older reader to catch or care about all the references to misappropriated book parts, such as the sent-up author bios and table of contents. For those who are studying fairy tales at the college level, *The Stinky Cheese Man* would be the perfect key to the genre, but

no one would mistake it for the old-fashioned originals. Collectors of illustrated children's books won't want to miss it.

THE HAPPY HOCKY FAMILY! (1993)

Publishers Weekly

SOURCE: A review of *The Happy Hockey Family!*, in *Publishers Weekly*, Vol. 240, No. 29, July 19, 1993, p. 250.

Step aside, Dick and Jane, or the very hilarious Happy Hocky Family might just run you over. Deftly parodying the repetitious, simplistic sentence structure of basal readers with lots! of exclamation points, Smith adds his signature prankishness to a series of banal family escapades: "I have a balloon. Do you have a balloon? I have a balloon. My balloon is red. If you had a balloon, what color would it be? My balloon is red. POP! I have a string. Do you have a string? I have a string." In keeping with the campy tone, the artwork has a stylishly retrograde appeal, featuring smiley-faced stick figures block-printed in primary colors onto beige construction paper-quality pages. Unlike the frenzied intersection of word, image and design that distinguishes the artist's previous works (including *The Big Pets* and, with author Jon Scieszka, *The Stinky Cheese Man and Other Fairly Stupid Tales*), the comic impact of this book derives from Smith's deliberate pacing. Each punchline is delivered with a master comedian's timing. Go, Smith, go. All ages.

Steven Engelfried

SOURCE: A review of *The Happy Hocky Family!*, in *School Library Journal*, Vol. 39, No. 9, September, 1993, p. 220.

If you combined "Dick and Jane" with the Addams Family, you might end up with a family like the one in Smith's wickedly funny new book. Using the format of old-fashioned primers, the author introduces the Hocky family. Through 17 very short "stories," he parodies the style of basal readers, but adds hilarious tongue-in-cheek humor: "I have a balloon. Do you have a balloon? I have a balloon . . . my balloon is red. POP! I have a string. Do you have a string? . . . " Smith's child-like pictures enhance the satire perfectly. With its simple shapes and dull primary colors set on plain brown paper, the book has the look of a 1950s reader. One page shows the six Hockys visiting the zoo. Newton the dog likes the crocodiles best. The facing page shows just five Hockys, and a leash trailing into a crocodile's jaws where Newton used to be. While poking fun at the genre, *The Happy Hocky Family* is actually an excellent choice for early readers. Short sentences, repetition, and generally simple vocabulary make it accessible to lower grade children, who will love the jokes (as will older children and many adults). A unique and inventive idea, wonderfully executed.

Edward Koren

SOURCE: "Dick and Jane Had It Easy," in *The New York Times Book Review,* November 14, 1993, p. 44.

Lane Smith's new book *The Happy Hocky Family!* is a playful, wonderfully subversive discourse on the idea of family in the 90's, as well as a winningly inventive word book for the less sociologically inclined preschooler. Mr. Smith's traditional, patriarchal family, by its very survival, plays on the radical alteration of the American family over the last four decades. The cultural definitions of family absorbed by an earlier generation of "Dick and Jane" readers (as well as the early television versions of functional families like those portrayed on *Leave It to Beaver* and *Father Knows Best*) provide Mr. Smith with a stereotyped backdrop for his own fictional family. Mr. Hocky in a fedora, pipe and tie, Mrs. Hocky in a housedress and the three well-spaced kids, Henry, Holly and Baby, are joined by Newton the dog, a stand-in for Spot.

What Mr. Smith has done here is quite deft and winning. He has used this earlier genre as a basis for an affectionate spoof, and he has also provided (in a beginners' book with a lot of accessible words) a fresh and sympathetic way for children to deal with such subjects as disappointment, accidents, mistakes and deceptions—and even happiness. The book is composed of 17 episodes, each one the kind of innocent event that often, in children's stories, can make for banal resolutions. But the young denizens of the Happy Hocky family exist in a world of simple words and events with complex results for kids, a much more sophisticated version of the cautionary primers with the themes of endurance, acceptance and improvisation.

In the first episode, for example, Baby Hocky's delight in the red balloon she (or he?) holds is shattered by an impressive full-page POP! as the balloon explodes in red shards. Sadness gives way to the pleasure of discovering that if you cannot have the balloon itself, then you can console yourself with the string that once held it: invention triumphant over adversity (can-do-ism over depression?).

The second episode concerns Holly's efforts to get her boat to float. This vessel—an anthropomorphized mix of "Little Toot" and "The Little Engine That Could"—reacts to Holly's fervent encouragement: "You're right. . . . I CAN do it. . . . I CAN DO IT!" and floats out of sight, never to return. Mr. Smith's solution for a melancholy Holly is her determination to get a new boat.

In this book, things do not turn out the way kids want or expect, and human frailty is simply part of life. Adjustments must be made to disappointment. Henry's birthday wish list is only partly fulfilled; the children's chores end with small accidents of inattention. And in one of the most winning sequences, Holly's sense of responsibility toward her ant colony results in the ants being turned loose in the household's spanking new 1950's kitchen. The kitchen, the pride and delight of Mr. and Mrs. Hocky, is a delight to us, too—its rounded, modern appliances, bowls, salt and pepper shakers remind us of the mythic time of happy family life, when Mom always had brownies on the table and milk in the fridge. Other episodes tell of visits from Grandma Hocky (complete with her overwhelming perfume) and Cousin Stinky, and how the Hocky kids subvert them both.

Readers expecting illustrations as luminous and ambitious as those in Mr. Smith's other books, like *The Big Pets* or *The True Story of the Three Little Pigs,* will find something entirely different here. Mr. Smith has adapted the reductive, spare illustrative style of the beginner books of the 1950's to his signature playfulness and sly wit (he has even altered his publisher's Viking ship logo). The members of the Hocky family are represented as modified stick figures on unelaborated pages, beautifully designed and paced. The colors are mostly primary, the outlined heads a sophisticated accumulation of dots for eyes, triangles for noses and lines for smiling mouths. Their clothes are textured collages of stripes, checks and polka dots, while their arms, legs and finely wrought hands are like those of insects. Mr. Smith's draftsmanship, wonderfully expressive, still manages to create a family that is general and unspecific, one that could be of any racial or ethnic group. So who wouldn't be happy to drop in on the Hocky family and visit awhile in their snug book-home?

Quill and Quire

SOURCE: A review of *The Happy Hocky Family!,* in *Quill and Quire,* Vol. 60, No. 2, February, 1994, p. 40.

Readers know that Lane Smith (illustrator of *The Stinky Cheese Man* and *The True Story of the Three Little Pigs* [both by Jon Scieszka]) delights in the original and the unexpected. As author, he also enjoys the slightly outrageous. Using the style of a primary reader—very simple vocabulary and sentence structure with much repetition—he satirizes both the style of readers and the content of contemporary "message" picture books. The miniature stories in *The Happy Hocky Family* all possess irony and a real edge, as Smith cocks a snook at the countless picture books designed to dispel fears, provide models for behaviour, or reproduce the routine activities of a child's day. Tired of the monster under the bed that shrinks when the protagonist applies positive thinking? Read **"Henry's Bedtime Story,"** in which he tells his little sister about the scary monster who steals little children at night. It's no good to lock the door; he comes in through the window. Had enough of characters who always share, never touch what belongs to others, and confess their misdeeds? Henry makes paper airplanes out of his sister's homework and goes outside to play when she can't find it. And that's just a sampling from this alternative picture book. Bold and simple illustrations in primary colours feature a family of stick figures with stereotyped features. For adults and sophisticated children.

Maurice Saxby

SOURCE: A review of *The Happy Hocky Family!,* in *Magpies,* Vol. 9, No. 3, July, 1994, p. 26.

Were the text to be separated from Lane Smith's drawings and Molly Leach's design one would be tempted to say that this is great stuff for the beginning reader's word attack skills. And it is. One could use a "look and say" approach (there is plenty of controlled repetition); vocabulary is built up gradually and in context; some words can easily be sounded out phonetically; others like re-spons-ib-il-ity can be structurally analysed or syllabified. The text is an answer to a Year 1 teacher's dream—or that of an enthusiastic parent of preschoolers. It is a "reader" and a concept book par excellence. But it is far, far more than that. It is really about the everyday doings of the expansive Hocky family—pictured in blocked, geometrical stick-like figures—and extremely witty and funny. This is the stuff of warm, fulfilling family life (very old-fashioned): an environment that arouses curiosity, stimulates learning and promotes literacy and a love of books. My copy is ear-marked for the next child to be born into the Saxby clan: a superb "birthing" present.

📖 *YOUR MOTHER WAS A NEANDERTHAL* (written by Jon Scieszka, 1993)

Janice Del Negro

SOURCE: A review of *Your Mother Was a Neanderthal: The Time Warp Trio,* in *Booklist,* Vol. 90, No. 3, October 1, 1993, p. 346.

Sam, Joe, and Fred, the Time Warp Trio who made their first appearances in *Knights of the Kitchen Table* and the *Not So Jolly Roger,* travel back to the Stone Age and are immediately in trouble. First of all, they don't have "The Book" that enables them to travel in time, and second of all, they're naked. Sam, with a large leaf and a piece of vine, invents clothes—just in time for them to be discovered by "cavegirls." Sam, Joe, and Fred escape (they think) the hostile women, take refuge with men hiding from a saber-toothed tiger, flee a woolly mammoth, and save the day with some simple physics involving a fulcrum and a lever. Scieszka's text is funny and fast, always clever and never cute (OK, naming the cavegirls Nat-Li, Lin-Say, and Jos-Feen is cute, but that's the only part), and Smith's pen-and-ink drawings add a rollicking, somewhat riotous air to the proceedings. This is the kind of book that kids tell one another to read—a surefire hit to the funny bone, whether read alone or aloud.

📖 *MATH CURSE* (written by Jon Scieszka, 1995)

Lucinda Snyder Whitehurst

SOURCE: A review of *Math Curse,* in *School Library Journal,* Vol. 41, No. 9, September, 1995, p. 215.

From the inventive minds of Scieszka and Smith comes an unusual take on the subject of mathematics. More for the "Time Warp Trio" audience than for *Stinky Cheese Man* devotees, *Math Curse* opens with the ominously simple statement, "You know, you can think of almost everything as a math problem." From that point on, the young narrator is overwhelmed with daily math. Getting dressed, eating breakfast, getting to school—everything involves addition, subtraction, measurement, probability, etc. Questions are boxed and numbered within the narrative, just as they might appear in a textbook. The questions, however, are not always typical workbook queries. For example, "I take the milk out for my cereal and wonder: 1. How many quarts in a gallon? 2. How many pints in a quart? 3. How many inches in a foot? 4. How many feet in a yard? 5. How many yards in a neighborhood? How many inches in a pint? How many feet in my shoes?" Some of the humor may have to be explained to readers. Kids will be able to figure out most of the problems on their own, depending on their grasp of fractions. Smith's illustrations are wild and rollicking. Combining drawings with collage, he creates a multi-textured school scene that reflects the narrator's confusion. Numbers are everywhere, but so are whimsical touches such as the individual expressions on the 24 cherries that adorn the class's cupcakes. This title can certainly be used as light-hearted relief in math class, but the story will be heartily enjoyed simply for its zany humor and nonstop sense of fun.

Deborah Stevenson

SOURCE: A review of *Math Curse,* in *Bulletin of the Center for Children's Books,* Vol. 49, No. 2, October, 1995, pp. 68-9.

Having satisfactorily warped the course of folklore in *The Stinky Cheese Man,* [Jon] Scieszka and Smith now take on a more challenging and humor-resistant subject: math. The result is a story problem gone exponentially berserk. A mopheaded Smithbeing (labeled a girl on the jacket flap but pretty androgynous) finds her world incalculably altered when her math teacher tells her how math can apply to everything in life: "Mrs. Fibonacci has obviously put a Math Curse on me. Everything I look at or think about has become a math problem." Then follows, as the narrator tries to make it through her day with the sea of numbers pursuing her, a sequence of genuine and bizarre math problems ("Estimate how many M&Ms it would take to measure the length of the Mississippi River"), classic logic puzzles (Mom and Dad do a duet version of "All Cretans are liars"), sly allusions (Mrs. Fibonacci appropriately enough counts in a Fibonacci series), and really smart dumb jokes (a long problem involving the number of kids getting on and off the school bus finishes up with "True or False: What is the bus driver's name?") culminating in a goofy pun (the narrator breaks out of her math prison by using two halves of chalk to make a (w)hole). This isn't coating math with fun to make it palatable, it's genuine math as genuine fun; kids who count Scieszka and Smith as a favorite team will relish the book for its own sake, while teachers searching for a way to link the pleasures of game-playing with the skills of math might use this to invigorate a class. Finishing touches include a panoply of math and measures charts on the endpapers, a Venn diagram of author and illustrator credits, and a binary-mode price; answers to the problems posed within the text are, I swear to Euclid, printed upside-down on the book's back cover along with the inverted bar code.

Joanne Schott

SOURCE: "Diversity in Unity," in *Quill and Quire,* Vol. 61, No. 10, October, 1995, p. 47.

When Mrs. Fibonacci tells her class they can think of almost everything as a math problem, one girl becomes doomed to do exactly that. Getting dressed turns into categorizing, counting, and totalling shirts. With breakfast comes measurement. How many pints in a quart? Inches in a foot? Inches in a pint? Tempted to explain about different systems of measurement for length and volume? Try again—there has to be an answer to every question and this answer is "none."

When it's time for the real math class, the subject is simple, just counting. On the planet Tetra, where hands bear only two fingers, counting starts with 1, 2, 3, 10. What are the next five numbers? A text made up mostly of questions and answers is fun to read when [Jon] Scieszka applies his inventiveness. Even the book's dedication gets turned into an unusual but solvable math problem. The curse falls on the reader, too, as trying the problems becomes compulsive. Along the way the author lets us in on the secret that math itself can be a form of play. There's all kinds of play in the illustrations too. Geometric patterns, collages with clever use of mathematical themes, a touch of the surreal, and arresting graphic design combine to make the illustrations equal partner to the text.

Maria B. Salvadore

SOURCE: A review of *Math Curse,* in *The Horn Book Magazine,* Vol. LXXI, No. 6, November-December, 1995, p. 738.

Math. It's a curse. Particularly when one day your teacher, Mrs. Fibonacci, suggests that almost everything can be thought of as a math problem. And it is. Getting up, getting dressed, getting breakfast—it's all a problem, a math problem. Entering class with twenty-four kids ("I just know someone is going to bring in some cupcakes to share"), each subject studied, having lunch—all involve math problems: addition, subtraction, division, fractions, algebra, counting systems, augh! Just when you figure out a way to break the math curse, Mr. Newton, your science teacher, says, "You know, you can think of almost everything as a science experiment." Readers will empathize, recognizing the narrator's plight as they calculate, contemplate, and chortle through this rollicking

book by the duo [Jon Scieszka and Lane Smith] who created *The True Story of the Three Little Pigs* and who fractured folktales in *The Stinky Cheese Man.* From cover to copyright to flap information (with everything in between), textured, modern, abstract art and text in varied typefaces are completely integrated to create a sophisticated, humorous look at a subject that often creates the high level of anxiety so well portrayed here. A tour de force created by the convergence of two brilliant, slightly zany, and innovative talents.

📖 *DISNEY'S JAMES AND THE GIANT PEACH*
     (adapted from the film by Karey Kirk-
     patrick, Jonathan Roberts, and Steve Bloom,
     1996)

Ilene Cooper

SOURCE: A review of *Disney's James and the Giant Peach,* in *Booklist,* Vol. 92, No. 17, May 1, 1996, p. 1511.

If you haven't heard the news by now, you soon will. Disney's latest production is an animated version of *James and the Giant Peach,* with illustrations by Lane Smith. . . .

Now, with a text by screenwriter [Karey] Kirkpatrick, Disney is offering a picture-book version of the movie that has condensed and changed the story, and in the process, flattened it considerably. The book may be all right for the preschool set who have seen the film and want to enjoy the full-color artwork again, but there is no substitute for the original. To that end, Knopf has reissued *James* with new pen-and-ink artwork by Smith. The art in both books is pure Smith, lots of geometric shapings and Stinky Cheese Man-style faces. Kids new to the story or fresh from the movie won't mind a bit, but the contemporary artwork may cause a sigh among older readers who are fans of Nancy Burkert's delicate and detailed illustrations.

Deborah Stevenson

SOURCE: A review of *Disney's James and the Giant Peach,* in *Bulletin of the Center for Children's Books,* Vol. 49, No. 10, June, 1996, p. 331.

Yes, not only is there the book *about* the movie, there's the book *of* the movie. Disney's novelization whips through the happenings at a brisk clip, following James' modified adventures as he and his insect friends travel to New York in the giant peach while he attempts to shake off his fears of the horrible aunts (who, in this version, pursue him). The stripped-down account allows for little characterization, and it emphasizes the programmatic sappiness of the movie's empower-yourself theme (nor does it include any of [Roald] Dahl's original poems). The book is really a showcase for Lane Smith's darkly peachy art (Smith has also illustrated the new edition of Dahl's original text, as well as working on the movie), which retains the sharp Dahlian edge that the story here lacks. The illustrations evoke the monstrous opponents and forlorn little James particularly well, although one often longs for a wider view (a stunning exception is an initially perplexing aerial view of the peach soaring over the Arctic ice). If the movie's hot, this book will get a lot of wear; even if it's not, **Stinky Cheese** fans won't want to miss one of their heroes in artistic action.

TUT, TUT **(written by Jon Scieszka, 1996)**

Reading Time

SOURCE: A review of *Tut Tut,* in *Reading Time,* Vol. 41, No. 2, May, 1997, p. 40.

Joe, Sam and Fred have finished their Ancient Egypt project early, and then Joe's little sister (and her cat) fiddle with their magical time travel book and they all end up in Ancient Egypt and risk being turned into mummies if they can't get their act together pretty quickly. The type of fast-faced, tongue in cheek humour that really appeals to kids in grades 5-8, with lots of humour and inventive twists and turns, not to mention fierce crocodiles and secret rooms in ancient tombs. Sure to be a great success as it is based around two really popular topics—Ancient Egypt and time travel, with humour and adventure as well. The cartoon-style black and white illustrations also add to the book's reviews appeal. Keep an eye out for the rest of the Time Warp trio series.

Additional coverage of Smith's life and career is contained in the following sources published by Gale Research: *Authors and Artists for Young Adults,* Vol. 21; *Contemporary Authors,* Vol. 143; *Something about the Author,* Vol. 76.

CUMULATIVE INDEXES

How to Use This Index

The main reference

> Baum, L(yman) Frank 1856–
> 1919 15

list all author entries in this and previous volumes of *Children's Literature Review:*

The cross-references

> See also CA 103; 108; DLB 22; JRDA
> MAICYA; MTCW; SATA 18; TCLC 7

list all author entries in the following Gale biographical and literary sources:

AAYA = *Authors & Artists for Young Adults*
AITN = *Authors in the News*
BLC = *Black Literature Criticism*
BW = *Black Writers*
CA = *Contemporary Authors*
CAAS = *Contemporary Authors Autobiography Series*
CABS = *Contemporary Authors Bibliographical Series*
CANR = *Contemporary Authors New Revision Series*
CAP = *Contemporary Authors Permanent Series*
CDALB = *Concise Dictionary of American Literary Biography*
CDBLB = *Concise Dictionary of British Literary Biography*
CLC = *Contemporary Literary Criticism*
CMLC = *Classical and Medieval Literature Criticism*
DAB = *DISCovering Authors: British*
DAC = *DISCovering Authors: Canadian*
DAM = *DISCovering Authors: Modules*
    DRAM: *Dramatists Module;* *MST*: *Most-Studied Authors Module;*
    MULT: *Multicultural Authors Module;* *NOV*: *Novelists Module;*
    POET: *Poets Module;* *POP*: *Popular Fiction and Genre Authors Module*
DC = *Drama Criticism*
DLB = *Dictionary of Literary Biography*
DLBD = *Dictionary of Literary Biography Documentary Series*
DLBY = *Dictionary of Literary Biography Yearbook*
HLC = *Hispanic Literature Criticism*
HW = *Hispanic Writers*
JRDA = *Junior DISCovering Authors*
LC = *Literature Criticism from 1400 to 1800*
MAICYA = *Major Authors and Illustrators for Children and Young Adults*
MTCW = *Major 20th-Century Writers*
NCLC = *Nineteenth-Century Literature Criticism*
NNAL = *Native North American Literature*
PC = *Poetry Criticism*
SAAS = *Something about the Author Autobiography Series*
SATA = *Something about the Author*
SSC = *Short Story Criticism*
TCLC = *Twentieth-Century Literary Criticism*
WLC = *World Literature Criticism, 1500 to the Present*
YABC = *Yesterday's Authors of Books for Children*

CUMULATIVE INDEX TO AUTHORS

Author Index

Author Index

CUMULATIVE INDEX TO NATIONALITIES

CUMULATIVE INDEX TO TITLES

Title Index

Title Index

Title Index

Title Index

Title Index

Title Index

Title Index

Title Index

ISBN 0-7876-1141-7

90000

9 780787 611415